D0845143

Siege Train

The Edward Manigault Diary

Post-Courier Photo by William A. Jordan

Siege Train

The Journal of a Confederate Artilleryman in the Defense of Charleston

edited by
Warren Ripley

Published for the
CHARLESTON LIBRARY SOCIETY
by the
UNIVERSITY OF SOUTH CAROLINA PRESS

Published in Columbia, South Carolina, by the
University of South Carolina Press

First Edition

Manufactured in the United States of America

Library of Congress Cataloging-in-Publication Data

Manigault, Edward, 1817-1874
  Siege train.

  Bibliography: p.
  Includes index.
  1. Manigault, Edward, 1817-1874—Diaries.
2. Charleston (S.C.)—History—Siege, 1863—Personal
narratives.   3. Soldiers—South Carolina—Charleston—
Diaries.   I. Ripley, Warren, 1921-   . II. Charleston
Library Society (S.C.)   III. Title.
E475.62.M36   1986   973.7′ 35   86-7021
ISBN 0-87249-491-8

Contents

Photographs

Maps

Line Illustrations

Introduction

On 10 July 1863, Federal troops on Folly Island, near Charleston, S.C., jumped across a narrow salt-water inlet in an impressive assault to capture the south end of Morris Island.

That same day on nearby James Island, Confederate Maj. Edward Manigault began a diary which is today one of the most unusual documents to survive the war.

It encompasses 13 months of combat. There are minor gaps, but overall it is a day-by-day, sometimes hour-by-hour, account of life at the front during the Civil War.

The manuscript is penned on both sides of light-blue, lined paper 7¾ x 12¼ inches, bound between cardboard covers. It is primarily an official journal — officers had been ordered to keep diaries *(see Appendix 2, p. 253)*. However, Manigault did not receive the order until "some time in August" as he remarked under the date of 14 July. Consequently, entries for July and part of August were written from memory aided, no doubt, by unit records and, probably, personal notes. Evidence of this is found in several instances where Manigault, with no break in the writing, mentions events he could not have known at the entry date. For instance, on 11 July he mentions Battery Ryan, a work on James Island named, like most Confederate fortifications in the area, for an officer killed in action. However, William H. Ryan was not killed until a week later, 18 July.

A number of daily entries are recorded in the Official Records *(see Appendix 2, p. 256-265)*. Many are quoted verbatim. A few reflect deletion of administrative details and items of little interest to higher headquarters but which could be vital to an intelligent officer interested in protecting himself against possible future criticism of his actions. These include such tidbits as the time an over-jubilant soldier of a neighboring unit took a shot at a crane — as all large wading birds often were called in those days — wandering through the camp. He missed the bird, but killed a horse belonging to Manigault's outfit, much to the disgust of the major. He had to investigate and fill out the resulting paperwork.

On the other hand, diary entries which found their way into the Official Records often have additional details such as terrain features. These would have been well-known to Manigault and are omitted in the diary. However, he included them in his reports to higher headquarters because they would have been of value to superiors who were unfamiliar with the local scene.

Although the diary is official, there are numerous personal touches. The farmer and outdoorsman in him comes to the fore, for instance, when he mentions hearing rice birds (bobolink) flying over, a harbinger of fall.

He even inserts amusing anecdotes in descriptions of infantry fighting. When his horse was shot from under him during a spirited engagement, he records his momentary uncertainty about whether to save the saddle — a valuable piece of personal property — or save his skin. Common sense dictated the latter. Some days later the horse recovered and wandered home — still carrying the saddle. Such personal remarks enliven official reports and enable an officer, who was utterly fearless yet inherently modest, to describe his own courageous actions without apparent braggadocio.

Civil War scholars will find some of his administrative details available in no other source. He describes, for instance, the procedures of artillery practice in the field against a target constructed by his men. Normally, such practice was conducted against the enemy, a far less scientific form of training. He also gives numerous tables recording the results of combat firing and statistics such as weights of projectiles, charges, ranges and elevations. He also describes how certain types of artillery projectiles, until now merely names to modern historians, actually worked, or failed to work, against an enemy.

Manigault's batteries participated in several significant events well-known to Civil War students. His guns took the so-called "Swamp Angel" under fire in an attempt to prevent the huge cannon from shelling the city of Charleston. The Confederate efforts were not successful, but the major's journal adds considerable information to the story of this phase of the war at Charleston. In addition, he fired on Morris Island during the bitter campaign to capture Battery Wagner. His guns participated in the unsuccessful attempt to capture the U.S. gunboat *Marblehead* in the Stono River.

More important, the journal provides a vivid picture of day-to-day operations, as well as the trials of a competent, but uncelebrated, battalion commander trying to accomplish his job under the stress of combat. The diary is sometimes repetitious, but it compensates by providing a wealth of information for researchers and, surprisingly, the detail detracts very little from the journal's entertainment value for the casual reader.

Manigault, an intelligent observer and an accomplished artist, enlivened the journal with several maps and occasional sketches of objects difficult to describe in words. His language, while articulate, abounds with the peculiar capitalization common to the day. There also are scattered spelling errors, probably due more to haste and stress than to lack of knowledge. These have been faithfully transcribed in an effort to retain the flavor and authenticity of the original manuscript. Punctuation, often lacking, has been added or changed as necessary in the interest of clarity. In addition, the daily diary dates, which vary in style, have been standardized for sake of convenience.

The handwriting is neat but varies in size, becoming more condensed in the latter half of the journal as though Manigault began to feel concerned about conserving paper. The volume ends on 31 Aug. 1864 with an inspection of batteries and troops along the Stono River. This required several pages and Manigault was forced to utilize the inside of front and rear covers in order to squeeze it in.

However, although the end of the month offered a convenient conclusion to the book, there is no reason to believe that Manigault suddenly stopped keeping a diary. In fact, it is probable that the journal was continued and a second volume, unfortunately missing, was brought to an untimely end when Manigault was wounded and captured 10 Feb. 1865.

If this was the case, the existing manuscript probably was deposited for safekeeping with some member of his family in town while Volume 2 remained at his unit headquarters and disappeared after his capture. Volume 1, unpublished and unread, was preserved with other family papers and currently is owned by the major's great-great nephew, Peter Manigault of Charleston.

Edward Manigault — the name is pronounced "Man-i-go" — was of French Huguenot extraction. His ancestors arrived at Charleston in 1687 and immediately assumed economic and social leadership in the colony. His great-grandfather, Gabriel Manigault (1704-1781), colonial rice planter and businessman, was considered one of the wealthiest men in the colonies. He also was an ardent patriot during the Revolution. When Charleston was threatened by British attack in 1779, the 75-year-old patriarch and his 15-year-old grandson took their places in the lines for defense of the city.

The grandson, Joseph (1763-1843), was Edward's father. Joseph married twice, first to Maria Henrietta Middleton (1772-1791), daughter of Arthur Middleton, signer of the Declaration of Independence. She was 16 at the time of her marriage and died without issue. Joseph then married Charlotte Drayton (1781-1855). She was a daughter of Dr. Charles Drayton (1743-1820) and niece of the Revolutionary War leader, William Henry Drayton.

Joseph and Charlotte had eight children of whom the two youngest, Edward and Arthur Middleton Manigault (1824-1886) became the best known. Arthur served in the heavy fighting around Churubusco and Chapultepec during the War with Mexico and became a brigadier general in the Confederate Army. His journals describing both wars were published by the University of South Carolina Press in 1983 under the title, "A Carolinian Goes to War."

Edward never married and much of his life is a mystery. Despite extensive search, no portrait or photograph of him has been found. With the exception of the Civil War era — documented by the journal, military personnel records and a bit in the Official Records — little is known of his life. Such information as has been found on his civilian career and previous military service has been pieced together from scattered and intermittent correspondence plus a few other records that have survived.

Based on this admittedly sketchy information, we know that Edward was born at Charleston 8 Mar. 1817 and grew up in the magnificent Joseph Manigault house, built by his father in 1803 from plans drawn by his uncle, Gabriel Manigault (1758-1809), noted architect of the day.

The Joseph Manigault House today. Gate, or summer, house at left.

In later years, Edward surveyed the property and his sketch accompanied the deed when the house was sold by the Manigault family in 1852.

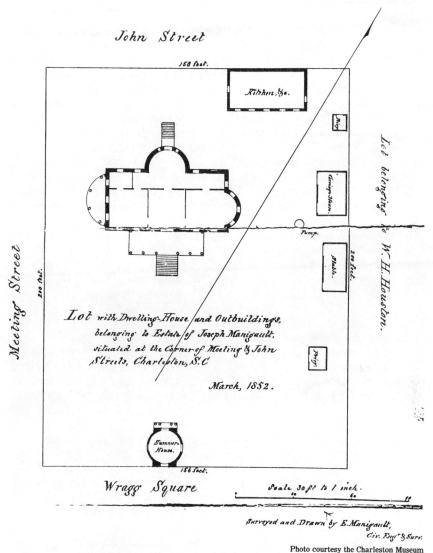

Edward Manigault's survey of the Joseph Manigault House and lot.

The building was acquired by the Charleston Museum in 1933 and is open to the public as one of Charleston's several house museums.

He was educated at the South Carolina College at Columbia, S.C., forerunner of the University of South Carolina. School records relate that he was a member of the Clariosophic Society, a student literary and debating group, and graduated in 1835 with the A.B. Degree, indicating a firm foundation in the classics. However, he presumably also was well-grounded in mathematics to support his later civilian occupation of civil engineer.[1]

No record has been found of Edward's career immediately following graduation. However, the War with Mexico brought him into military service as a captain in the 12th Infantry Regiment, one of several such units raised by the United States for service during the war. His commission was dated 8 Mar. 1847 and the rank seems surprisingly high for a man who apparently had little or no formal military training, except, possibly, a stint in the local militia. Many West Pointers, including Braxton Bragg, George Gordon Meade and P.G.T. Beauregard, began the war as lieutenants. Consequently, one would suspect that Manigault's appointment resulted from extensive civilian experience in a field of value to the military, such as engineering, or, in keeping with customs of the day, perhaps a bit of political assistance.

Official correspondence[2] states that he was sent on recruiting duty to Spartanburg, S.C., where on June 3rd. he reported having recruited 20 men and requested funds to send them to Fort Moultrie near Charleston. A week later, he asked permission to retain the recruits at Spartanburg in the hope that they would attract others. In fact, he predicted that the number would double within two or three weeks and then the march to Charleston might be even more productive. However, he admitted that board and lodging would cost the government 40 cents a day per man which would be higher than if he sent them to Moultrie immediately. He also mentioned spending $72 for employment of a drummer and fifer to be used in recruiting.

Whether Manigault attained his goal of 40 recruits is not disclosed in surviving correspondence. However he did return to Charleston where, on 16 July 1847, he was promoted to major and transferred to the staff of the 13th U.S. Infantry Regiment. He was ordered to New York, sailing on 5 Aug. and arriving on the 10th, to recruit for both the 12th and 13th Regiments in that state and Pennsylvania.

Following some two months of this duty, Manigault returned to Charleston with a number of recruits aboard the ship *Orphan* en route to Vera Cruz, Mexico. Additional troops were loaded at Charleston and when the *Orphan* sailed, 19 Oct. 1847, she had aboard 183 men and officers of the 12th Regiment, under command of Maj. Maxcy Gregg (later a brigadier general in the Confederate Army) and 81 of the 13th commanded by Manigault.

By the time they arrived at Vera Cruz, the fighting was over. This led to a general exodus from Mexico of all high-ranking officers who could manage to be relieved, and newcomers, such as Manigault, inherited occupation duties. No contemporary correspondence regarding his

[1] *Alumni records, University of South Carolina, Columbia, S.C.*

[2] *Mexican War records, the National Archives, Washington, D.C. Microcopy M567, primarily rolls 351 and 352.*

service during this period has been found. However, in an 1863 letter recalling his Mexican War service,[1] Manigault stated that, as a major, he commanded the 13th Regiment for seven months until it was disbanded at Mobile, Ala., 18 July 1848. He arrived in Charleston on the 25th.[2]

Manigault's career during the next few years is difficult to follow. Later correspondence makes only one mention of this period. In a letter to South Carolina Gov. William H. Gist, dated 19 Nov. 1860,[3] Manigault stated that he served as a lieutenant of ordnance in 1851-52. This would indicate that he agreed to reduction in rank to remain in service following the Mexican War. If so, he remained only until 1854 when he accepted the position of assistant engineer with the Columbia (S.C.) and Savannah (Ga.) Railroad, then under construction. The following year he was promoted to chief engineer of the railroad and in 1860 was appointed general superintendent. He tendered his resignation near the end of that year and began his Civil War service.

The letter to Gov. Gist, in which Manigault mentioned his ordnance experience, had a far-reaching effect on his Civil War career. In it, he offered his services to the state of South Carolina in any capacity consistent with his engineer training. However, he also described in specific detail the deplorable condition of certain artillery carriages in storage at Charleston and offered to superintend their repair. The offer apparently appealed to the governor and led to Manigault's appointment as Chief of Ordnance for the state with the rank of colonel, a service that no doubt influenced his later selection for the artillery.

After about a year, Manigault became dissatisfied with the ordnance post and resigned. Apparently, he believed that Confederate ordnance men were taking credit for many operations in the Charleston area performed by his South Carolina department. Moreover, he and his brother, Gabriel Manigault (1809-1888), who was serving on the state Board of Ordnance, felt that the general public confused the work of the state board with other military measures for defense of the state. These measures, the brothers believed, were, as Gabriel put it: "...under the control of military and engineering incapacity...."[4]

Edward resigned effective 1 Oct. 1861. However, during the preceding month, while he was winding up his affairs as Chief of Ordnance, a petition was circulated urging him to organize and lead a battalion for defense of the area between Charleston and the South Santee River, some 50 miles to the north. In a letter dated 18 Sept. 1861, amplified by another two days later, to South Carolina Rep. William Porcher Miles in Congress at Richmond,[5] Manigault stated that the petitioners

[1] See letter, Appendix 2, p. 253.

[2] Diary of Charlotte Drayton Manigault.

[3] See letter, Appendix 2, p. 251-252.

[4] See letter from Gabriel Manigault, 21 Sept. 1861, Appendix 2, p. 252.

[5] These letters are in the William Porcher Miles papers (No. 508), Southern Historical Collection, University of North Carolina Library, Chapel Hill, N.C.

were disillusioned with militia units assigned to the area and wanted the battalion for protection. He asked Miles' assistance in placing the request before President Jefferson Davis.

The petition was successful and on 31 Oct. 1861 Manigault was appointed a major, although generally called colonel in deference to his former rank. He assumed command of the 6th Infantry Battalion, generally known as Manigault's Battalion, South Carolina Volunteers, 22 Dec. 1861 at McClellanville, a village about 45 miles north of Charleston. This was a mixed unit of infantry, artillery and cavalry raised for local defense by special permission of the War Department. It served until May 1862 when it was broken up due to enactment of the Conscription Act which provided for enrollment of men for three years or duration of the war.

Manigault was now out of a job. No record has been found of his service during the next few months. However, it is unlikely that a man of his abilities and restless energy could have remained unemployed amid the wartime activity and excitement in Charleston.

We do know that he saw action 7 April 1863 at Fort Sumter while serving as a volunteer on the staff of Brig. Gen. Roswell S. Ripley, commander of the First Military District at Charleston.[1] This was the celebrated "Ironclad Attack" which pitted armored warships against the defenses of Charleston, primarily Fort Sumter. The attack, which if conducted differently might have resulted in the fall of Charleston and probable shortening of the war, failed dismally. It also set the stage for later developments to which Manigault's journal is directly related.

The following month, 18 May 1863 to be specific, Manigault wrote to the Secretary of War[2] requesting command of an artillery unit known as the South Carolina Siege Train, an unusual military organization even in those days.

Artillery of the Civil War era was divided into three broad categories. Field artillery was composed of light, maneuverable weapons expected to accompany troops in the field. Seacoast artillery consisted of heavy pieces mounted in fortifications, mainly along the coast. Siege and garrison artillery fell in between. The weapons were too heavy to be readily maneuverable, but sufficiently light to be brought to the front in a static situation.

The combined term, "siege and garrison," normally was abbreviated to "siege" if the pieces were operating in the field or "garrison" if mounted in small fortifications. Operationally, siege pieces often were combined into a "train." This was a somewhat nebulous organization consisting of varying numbers of cannon proportioned according to type and caliber. However, conformity to theoretical equipment tables seldom occurred in the weapons-starved Confederacy and Manigault's

---

[1] *O.R. XIV, pp. 260, 266.*

[2] *See letter from Manigault to James A. Seddon, Secretary of War, Appendix 2, p. 253.*

siege train was no exception. Moreover, as the diary shows, his men spent more time manning seacoast weapons or serving as infantry than in their designated role.

Manigault was appointed a major in the Confederate Army 23 May 1863 and assumed command of the Siege Train on the 22nd. of the following month. The unit was located in Charleston at the time, but moved to nearby James Island 10 July in connection with the Federal attack on Morris Island.

The story of Charleston's role in the Civil War is available in many published sources and is too lengthy for repetition here. However, a brief synopsis of events leading up to the Morris Island campaign is necessary for a clear understanding of the part played by Manigault during the succeeding months.

Fort Sumter surrendered to Confederate forces 14 April 1861 and South Carolina was free of Northern troops until November. In that month, the Federal Navy shot its way into Port Royal Harbor, some 60 miles down the coast from Charleston. The ships destroyed two small forts guarding the entrance and Union troops occupied Hilton Head Island on the southern shore. This provided a secure foothold which rapidly escalated into a major base to support a naval blockade of the coast and later Army operations.

The Port Royal engagement, 7 Nov. 1861, convinced Confederate military men that defense of barrier islands along the South Carolina seaboard was impractical. The powerful U.S. fleet could overwhelm isolated garrisons virtually at will. Consquently, the Southerners abandoned most of the islands and built defenses farther inland along various narrow creeks and rivers where attacking warships would be channelized within range of the Southern guns and be unable to maneuver and bring their heavy broadside batteries to bear.

Unfortunately, the Confederates overreacted and abandoned the mouth of the Stono River, only 10 miles south of Charleston, which should have been defended. The Yankees promptly moved into the gap. Warships anchored in Stono Inlet, and, under protection of their guns, troops landed 2 June 1862 on the southern tip of James Island and set up camp. It was not a happy situation, however. Mosquitoes were bad, and Confederate artillerymen made life uncertain by long-range fire from a small earthwork, later named Fort Lamar, at the pre-Civil War community of Secessionville. The Yankees could do little about the mosquitoes, but the fort was an enticing target. They attacked it 16 June 1862.

Although badly outnumbered, the Confederates defended the fort tenaciously. The attack was beaten off with heavy Federal loss — 700 admitted by Northern officers and higher totals claimed by the Confederates. Moreover, just as the Southerners had discovered the power of the U.S. Navy at Port Royal, Fort Lamar taught the Yankees a valuable lesson — don't tangle with the Confederate Army beyond protective range of the warships' guns. These two principles were to color military thinking in the Charleston area for the remainder of the war.

A short time after the Battle of Secessionville, as the engagement is called, the Federals broke camp and reboarded their transports leaving control of Stono Inlet to the warships whose guns turned the lower part of James Island into a no man's land, peopled intermittently by patrols of one side or the other.

A few months later, while the Federal Army still was licking its wounds, the Navy tried its hand against Charleston. The Confederates, well-aware of their weaknesses, feared the ironclad warships would run past Fort Sumter and bring the virtually helpless city under their guns. However, the ranking Navy officer, Rear Adm. Samuel F. DuPont, chose instead to hurl his ironclads against the fort. This, the Ironclad Attack of 7 April 1863 which Manigault witnessed from inside the fort, proved no more successful, although not so bloody as Secessionville. DuPont lost only one man killed and 22 wounded. His ships were badly mauled, however, and one sank the next day. These two failures brought a more determined attempt to take the city — this time a sustained campaign combining both Army and Navy.

Military men of the day recognized six possible approaches to Charleston.

First, and most direct, was purely naval — bypass, or subdue, the forts guarding the entrance, sail into the harbor and demand surrender of the city or destroy it. Battering down Fort Sumter had been tried 7 April 1863 and proved a failure. No attempt was made to bypass the forts.

Second — land well to the south, march northeast and take Charleston from the rear. This route was successfully used by the British in 1780. However, it involved operations well away from supporting naval gunfire and would take far more troops than the North had on hand.

Third — land on James Island and fight across it to the harbor. This would bring the city within easy artillery range. It also could prevent supply of Fort Sumter causing evacuation or surrender of that bastion and thus removing a major impediment to the fleet entering the harbor. This approach, because the South had insufficient forces to adequately man the James Island defenses, was the most threatening from the Confederate point of view. However, having been defeated at Secessionville, the Federals never seriously attempted this route which would have taken them beyond range of supporting naval gunfire.

Fourth — land troops on the coast north of the city, then, using various creeks, approach Charleston from the flank or rear. Most of these streams were too shallow to be navigated by the ships, and the Confederates would have had little difficulty handling an attack by small boats.

Fifth — land troops on the barrier islands immediately to the northeast of the harbor entrance, Sullivan's Island and the Isle of Palms. A landing on the latter, in those days known as Long Island, wouldn't be much better than coming ashore farther north. Sullivan's Island was closer to the city, but would involve an amphibious assault from the open sea on a beach exposed to the fire of strong fortifications. Then, assuming success, the invaders would have to cross several easily defended creeks and, finally, the Cooper River, an imposing tidal stream. The crossings would be beyond range of supporting naval gunfire.

Sixth — invade Morris Island (immediately southwest of the harbor entrance) from Folly Island, which was held by Northern troops. Morris was defended by batteries at the south end near Folly, by Battery Wagner nearer the center and by Battery Gregg at the north end adjoining the harbor. On the surface, this appeared to be a risky undertaking. However, the Morris Island approach offered several advantages. The distance across Light House Inlet, separating Morris and Folly, is less than half a mile over calm waters. Best of all, the fleet could enfilade all the Confederate batteries during any attack. Theoretically, after taking Morris Island, Fort Sumter would be untenable or could be battered into submission by heavy land artillery. The fleet could then fight its way past the Sullivan's Island forts into the harbor. So much for theory. In practice, it didn't work out that way.

During the weeks preceding the jumpoff, the North built batteries on the northern end of Folly — actually called Little Folly in those days when a stream, now filled in, divided the island. The work was accomplished in secret and although the Confederates later claimed they knew all about it, when 47 artillery pieces opened on the batteries at the southern end of Morris at daylight July 10th, it was more than a surprise. It was a definite shock. Under cover of the bombardment, small boats carrying the first wave of Federal infantry swept across the inlet, landed the troops and went back for more. The defenders suddenly discovered they could not depress their cannon sufficiently to hit the boats or men on the beaches and, although they fought bravely as infantry, the batteries were soon overrun. The attack rolled forward, over the sands of Morris in scorching July weather, until it finally bogged down from sheer exhaustion under the guns of Battery Wagner.

The next morning, an assault was launched against Wagner which made little impression on the fort. The attackers withdrew and regrouped. A week later, 18 July, they tried again. This was a major assault supported by the fleet which shelled Wagner most of the day. Isolated units fought their way into the bastion, but after vicious fighting by both sides, much of it hand-to-hand in the dark, the attack was hurled back with extremely heavy Northern casualties. This led to a slow, grinding approach to Battery Wagner and some of the bitterest fighting of the war. Eventually, during the night of 6-7 Sept., Morris Island was quietly evacuated. At dawn, the Yankees stood on the northern tip of the island, within sight of, but still a long distance from, the city they coveted. Fort Sumter, theory to the contrary, not only survived, but continued to stand through some of the most intensive bombardment of the war. It also confirmed the Southern viewpoint that the Morris Island approach offered relatively little danger to Charleston.

Manigault's Siege Train was sent to James Island initially to help defend that island against a Federal diversion made in conjunction with the 10 July Morris Island assault. The James Island attack was purely secondary and designed to prevent reinforcement of Morris Island during the main assault. The Siege Train saw no action at this time and the Federal troops soon were recalled.

The major's subsequent career, until 31 Aug. 1864, is fully documented in the journal. The months following, however, are a complete blank — until 10 Feb. 1865. On that date, Manigault commanded a small infantry force which stubbornly defended a line of rifle pits for four hours against vastly superior numbers in the Battle of Grimball's Causeway, generally considered to be the final engagement of the war in the Charleston area.

The Confederates were spread extremely thin — 308 men to defend a mile-long line. The number was further diminished by the necessity of stationing guards at Rivers Causeway on the Confederate left and retaining a small reserve. Consequently, Manigault had only 161 men to defend Grimball's Causeway which came under attack. Elements of five Northern regiments, estimated at more than 1,200 men, were involved although, apparently, not all were committed.

Manigault said his casualties totaled 25 compared to 88 for the enemy. Other authorities push both totals slightly higher.

During the subsequent Confederate retreat, Manigault was wounded. Believing death imminent, the major ordered his men to leave him. He later was reported by the Confederates as killed in action and is so listed in the Official Records.[1] However, the wound was not mortal. He was captured, but far from conquered. A Federal officer, writing years after the war, stated that after Manigault was carried to a Union aid station, where a Minie ball was removed from his hip, the major spent the remainder of the evening verbally — and stubbornly — refighting the battle with the Yankee surgeon who patched up his wound.[2]

Fortunately, the major left a detailed description of the engagement. This narrative *(see Appendix 1, pp. 243-248)* was penned 9 Feb. 1866, almost exactly a year after the battle and while he was still on crutches from his wound. Although not written for publication, it was printed in a local newpaper in 1902, many years after his death.

Manigault's abrupt departure from active Confederate service terminated plans of higher authority to combine the Siege Train with other units into a regiment which Manigault, to be promoted to colonel, was to command.[3]

---

[1] *See Appendix 1, p. 250.*

[2] *Ibid, p. 249.*

[3] *Letter in Manigault's personnel records, dated 12 Jan. 1865, from Lt. Gen. William J. Hardee, commander, Dept. of S.C., Ga. and Fla., to Gen. Samuel Cooper, Adjutant and Inspector General, at Richmond, Va.*
Gen. P.G.T. Beauregard, in a letter to Hardee dated 29 Dec. 1864, also had recommended promotion of Manigault. [OR LIII, p. 386]

Taken first to Folly Island, the major was transferred to Hilton Head Island and then to the U.S. General Hospital for Prisoners of War at Beaufort, S.C. He was discharged from the hospital 9 May 1865 and returned to Hilton Head where he signed a parole on the 10th. The following day, Manigault left Hilton Head Island for Charleston, once again a free man.

I, *Edward Manigault*, do solemnly swear, in the presence of Almighty God, that I will not, by word, act, sign, letter or message, give aid or comfort to any person or persons, hostile to the United States, and do give my parole of honor that I will not take up arms against, nor serve as military police or constabulary force in any fort, garrison or field work, nor as guard of prisoners, depots or stores, nor to discharge any duty usually performed by soldiers, until released from this obligation.

Subscribed and sworn to before me,)
at Hilton Head, S. C., this..*10*..
day of..*May*......1865.)

Edward Manigault

B. W. Thompson
MAJOR & PROVOST MARSHAL GENERAL.

Parole signed by Edward Manigault 10 May 1865.

No mention has been found of Manigault's postwar activities until notices of his death in 1874. Logically, he would have resumed his engineering career at Charleston. However, since employment for engineers in the prostrate South after the war was virtually nonexistent, he may have turned to farming. The place of his death near North Santee River, where the Manigault family held extensive land holdings, seems to substantiate this. The circumstances, reported in two tantalizingly brief notices in a Charleston newspaper, "The News and Courier," are as follows:

> [*7 Oct. 1874*] "FATAL ACCIDENT: Maj. Edward Manigault was thrown from his sulky near Georgetown on Friday last [*2 Oct. 1874*] and so badly injured that he died almost instantly. Mr. Manigault was a brother of Gen. A.M. Manigault and during the Confederate war served as a major of ordnance. He was fifty-eight years old at the time of his death. He was a devoted son of the South and a gentleman much respected in every relation of life."

> [*12 Oct. 1874*] "MANIGAULT — Died on North Santee, on the evening of the 2d. of October 1874, Major Edward Manigault, in the fifty-eighth year of his age."

His body was returned to Charleston and buried there in the family vault in the Huguenot Church cemetery.

W.R. — 1986

xiii

Acknowledgments

Few manuscripts have been edited entirely by a single person. This was no exception. Many individuals and organizations have contributed their time and knowledge, and to them I offer my sincere thanks.

Primarily, I am indebted to the late Edward Manigault, great-nephew and namesake of the Major. He suggested publication of the Diary and allowed me to edit it. Without his interest, a major Civil War document might have remained buried amid other family papers. To him, and to his son, Peter Manigault, current owner of the Diary who has permitted the work to continue, I am deeply grateful.

My appreciation also is extended to Arthur Manigault Wilcox whose knowledge of the Civil War, and especially naval history, has proved invaluable in answering the numerous questions that inevitably arise in a work of this sort.

In addition, I wish to express my gratitude to Edwin M. Olmstead of Mt. Holly Springs, Pa.; Dr. Richard J. Sommers of the U.S. Army Military History Institute, Carlisle Barracks, Pa.; and Thomas Connelly of the University of South Carolina faculty. They were selected by the University of South Carolina Press to read the finished manuscript, and their comments and suggestions have been extremely beneficial.

Finally, my sincere thanks to all who have assisted me in numerous ways, large and small. They include — and I apologize in advance to anyone inadvertently overlooked — William D. Chamberlain, Richard L. Schreadley, Thomas W. Nielson and Michael M. Gildea, all members of the Post-Courier editorial staff, who always were within easy reach for comment or question. To William L. Guerry, staff artist, for numerous drawings; Robert A. Nettles, Thomas K. Spain, and William A. Jordan of the newspapers' Photography Department; James Edwin Stokes Jr., Ervin Theodore Sanders and June Elizabeth Rabon of the Photocomp Department; and Dennis W. Anderson of the Camera Department. To Frankie H. Webb, curator of the Charleston Museum's Joseph Manigault and other historic houses; David R. Ruth and Charles D. Wyatt of Fort Sumter National Monument; Librarian Catherine E. Sadler, and assistants Patricia G. Bennett, Janice L. Grimes and Dedree P. Syracuse, all of the Charleston Library Society; Joel Alvis,

Presbyterian Historical Foundation, Montreat, N.C.; and the Rev. Ronald Botsford, First Presbyterian Church, Highlands, N.C.

Also: William W. Humphreys, Winnie C. Hay, Charlotte H. and E. Gordon Hay, Charles Relyea, and S.C. Sen. Arthur Ravenel Jr., all of Charleston; Allen Stokes, librarian of the South Caroliniana Library, Columbia, S.C.; John Heiting, associate director, McKissick Museum, University of South Carolina, Columbia, S.C.; William E. Lind, the National Archives, Washington, D.C.; Lyndon Hart, State Library, Commonwealth of Virginia, Richmond; Earle Jackson, University of South Carolina Press, and to the staffs of the South Carolina Archives in Columbia and the South Carolina Historical Society at Charleston.

W.R.

Abbreviations used by Maj. Manigault

&c.	Et cetera
a.a.a.g.	Acting Assistant Adjutant General
A.A.A. Genl.	Acting Assistant Adjutant General
Abs.	Absent
Accd.	Accounted
Acct.	Account
Actg.	Acting
A.D.C.	Aide-de-camp
A.I. Genl.	Acting Inspector General (or Assistant Inspector General)
A. & I. General	Adjutant and Inspector General
Am.	Ammunition
Amb.	Ambulance
Amm.	Ammunition
App.	Appearance
A.Q.M.	Assistant Quartermaster (or Acting Quartermaster)
Arty.	Artillery
Bar.	Barrel
Batt.	Battalion
Brig. Genl.	Brigadier General
Cal.	Caliber (calibre as Manigault spelled it)
Cart.	Cartridge
Cav.	Cavalry
C.H.	Courthouse
Ck.	Creek
Co.	Company
Col.	Colonel
Col.	Columbiad
Col^d.	Columbiad
Com.	Commissary
Com.	Commissioned (officer)
Comd.	Commander
Comdg.	Commanding
Comp.	Company
Coms'y.	Commissary
Com'y. (or Comy.)	Commissary
Con.	Conical (conical shot or shell)

xvii

Corp.	Corporal
Corp^l.	Corporal
C&S RR	Charleston and Savannah Railroad
Cwt.	Hundredweight. Artillery pieces generally were stamped with the weight, either in conventional form or using the British hundredweight of 112 pounds, quarters of 28 and the individual pounds. Typical markings on a 32-pounder might be: 27-2-11. This translates to 27 x 112 = 3,024, plus 2 x 28 = 56, plus 11 = 3,091 pounds.
Dept.	Department
Detach^t.	Detachment
Do.	Ditto (the same as)
Engr.	Engineer
F.O.D.	Field Officer of the Day
F. Off. of Day	Field Officer of the Day
h.	hour (as in 9h. or 9 o'clock)
Hd.	Head (as in headquarters or head of a stream or causeway)
Hd. Qrs.	Headquarters
How.	Howitzer
How^t.	Howitzer
Inf.	Infantry
Infty.	Infantry
Insp. Genl.	Inspector General
Inst.	Instant (as in dates, the 9th instant)
Jas. Isld.	James Island
Lt.	Lieutenant
Lt.	Light (Light House Inlet or Light Artillery)
m.	Minute (as in 9h. 10m.)
Mag.	Magazine
Med.	Medical
Mil.	Military
Mil. Dist.	Military District
Min.	Minute
N.C.	Noncommissioned (officer)
N.C.O.	Noncommissioned Officer
N. Com.	Noncommisioned (officer)
Non. Com.	Noncommissioned (officer)
Off.	Officer
Ord.	Ordnance
Ord. Off.	Ordnance Officer
P.B.L.A.	Palmetto Battalion Light Artillery
Perc.	Percussion (percussion fuse)
Pndr.	Pounder (32-pounder rifle)
Pr.	Pounder (32-pounder rifle)
Pres^t.	Present
Priv.	Private
Qr. M.	Quartermaster
Reg.	Regiment
Reg^t. or Regt.	Regiment
S.	Siege (South Carolina Siege Train)
S.C.	Sea Coast (sea-coast howitzer)
S.C.	South Carolina
S.C.C.	South Carolina Cavalry

S.C.V.	South Carolina Volunteers
Sergt. or Sergt.	Sergeant
So. Ca.	South Carolina
Sta.	Stationed
Surg.	Surgeon
Virg.	Virginia
X Roads	Crossroads

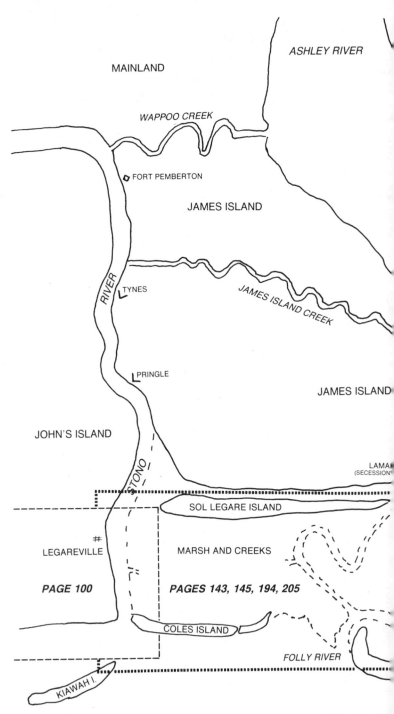

ASHLEY RIVER

MAINLAND

WAPPOO CREEK

▯ FORT PEMBERTON

JAMES ISLAND

RIVER

⌐TYNES

JAMES ISLAND CREEK

⌐PRINGLE

JAMES ISLAND

JOHN'S ISLAND

STONO

LAMA▮
(SECESSION▮

SOL LEGARE ISLAND

⌗
LEGAREVILLE

MARSH AND CREEKS

PAGE 100

PAGES 143, 145, 194, 205

COLES ISLAND

FOLLY RIVER

KIAWAH I.

Map adapted from one of the foldout charts in rear of the book.

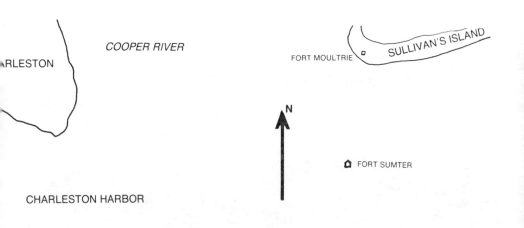

COOPER RIVER

CHARLESTON

FORT MOULTRIE

SULLIVAN'S ISLAND

N

FORT SUMTER

CHARLESTON HARBOR

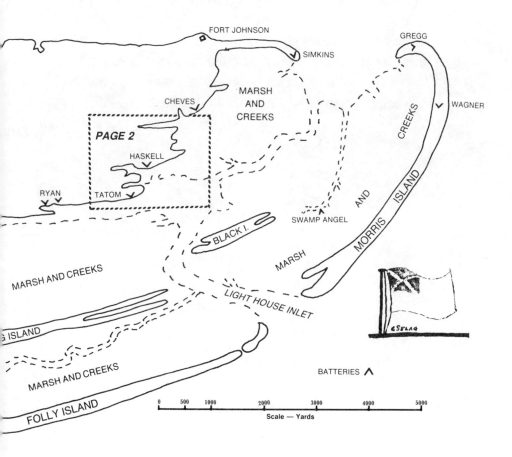

FORT JOHNSON

GREGG

SIMKINS

MARSH
AND
CREEKS

CHEVES

WAGNER

PAGE 2

CREEKS

HASKELL

RYAN

TATOM

MORRIS ISLAND

AND

BLACK I.

SWAMP ANGEL

MARSH

MARSH AND CREEKS

LIGHT HOUSE INLET

ISLAND

BATTERIES ∧

MARSH AND CREEKS

C S FLAG

FOLLY ISLAND

0   500   1000   2000   3000   4000   5000
Scale — Yards

Large-scale drawings of designated areas will be found on the pages indicated.

xxi

Explanatory notes to the text are listed numerically following each Journal entry.

Brief biographies of individuals and information on units mentioned by Maj. Manigault are discussed in Appendix 3. Page numbers in the general index marked by an asterisk refer to the Appendix 3 listings.

The Diary

of

Edward Manigault, Major, C.S.A.

Friday, 10 July 1863.

At 5h. 5m. A.M. the Yankee Batteries on Little Folly Island opened upon Southern End of Morris Island. The fire was very heavy (said to be from 44 pieces in Battery) and in a few hours the Enemy landed and took possession of the Southern half of the Island.[1]

The Siege Train, S.C.V.[2] received orders to move over to McLeod's [*House*] on James Island and there await further orders. At 9 A.M. the Train moved over the Ashley Bridge and reported at 10 o'clock at McLeod's. Col. Gonzales did not arrive at that point for an hour or so after when Major Manigault, in Command of the Train, reported to him in person.

About 11½ A.M. or 12 M. Col. Simonton, Comdg. the Island, ordered the train to a field near Holmes' house on James Island Creek, near the New Bridge over that stream. Co. "A" was disposed on the Field in rear of Holmes' House resting on the Cross Road leading to New Town Cut, and Co. "B" was put in position near New Bridge over James Island Creek. The 32nd Georgia Infantry, Col. Harrison, and one Battalion of 11th S.C.V. [*infantry*] had just arrived at the latter point before Co. "B". The 32nd Georgia moved on a couple of miles further in the afternoon. The Battalion of 11th S.C. remained at the Bridge 'till 8 o'clock Saturday evening. (Note that Co. "C" of Siege Train had been detached for one or two weeks before and was stationed in separate sections near the "Artillery Cross Roads.")

Major Manigault, by order of Col. Simonton, got a Corporal and 6 men from Lt. Col. Izard of 11th S.C.V. and established a Picket about ⅓ mile in front of the Bridge.

---

[1] *See Introduction, page xi. The Federals stated 32 guns and 15 mortars were used.* [OR XXVIII (1) p. 349]

[2] *South Carolina Volunteers. See pp. xv-xvii for other abbreviations used by Maj. Manigault.*

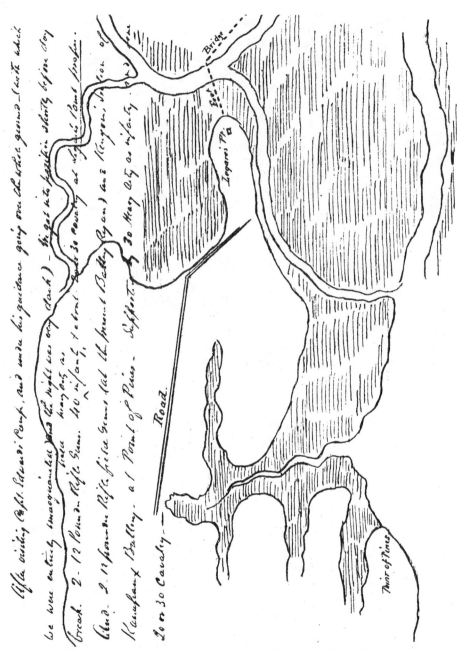

This drawing of a small portion of James Island (see map of area, page xviii) was included by Maj. Manigault in the Diary entry of 11 July 1863. Point of Pines was the future site of Battery Tatom and Legare's Point of Battery Haskell.

Saturday, 11 July 1863.

Companies remained in same positions. Major Manigault had vistas cut through the woods which lined the Creek and put all four Howitzers in position for commanding the Creek. He then rode & examined the lines of Pickets in his front so as to judge of what notice would probably be given to the Siege Train before the enemy could be upon it. Returned from Reconnaissance about 3 p.m. During ride met Genl. Hagood at Dills' Landing on Stono.

At dark the Yankee Gunboats commenced shelling woods near Grimball's & Legare's. Reported that the enemy was advancing (official). Shortly after dark the Battalion of 11th S.C.V. under Lieut Col. Izard moved on by order from Hd. Qrs. toward Secessionville. Shortly after Major Manigault was ordered to move Co. "A" Siege Train towards Legare's Point and himself ordered to Genl. Hagood's Hd. Qrs. for further instructions. Ordered to occupy as soon as possible Legare's Point with Battery of Co. "A" aided by Section of Kanapaux Light Battery and supported by Cavalry of Capt. Edwards' Command, Batt.[1] of 5th Reg. S.C. Cavalry encamped at Legare's[2] (Point of Pines) and Detachment of about 70 of Frederick's Reg. 2nd S.C. Arty.

After visiting Capt. Edward's Camp and under his guidance going over the whole ground (with which we were entirely unacquainted and the night very dark) we got into position shortly before daybreak. 2 12 Pounder Rifle Field Guns, 40 heavy arty as infantry & about 20 or 30 cavalry at Legare's Point proper. And 2 12 pounder Rifle field Guns (at the present Battery Ryan) and Kenyon's Section of Kanapaux Battery at Point of Pines, Supported by 30 Heavy Arty as infantry and from 20 to 30 Cavalry.[3]

[1] Manigault's use of the word "Battalion" is puzzling. Edwards, a captain, normally would have commanded a company. It is possible that in this case Edwards was commanding two or more companies with the unofficial designation of battalion. However, it is more likely that Manigault was trying to identify the men as belonging to Edwards' former unit (the 14th Battalion) which had been combined with others to form the 5th Regiment. [See entry in Appendix 3 for Edwards and the units]

[2] Manigault uses the name "Legare's" to refer to both Point of Pines and Legare's Point. The latter (Battery Haskell) was his headquarters. Battery Tatom (Point of Pines), and nearby Battery Ryan and Redoubt No. 1 also were under his command.

[3] This paragraph is written over part of the sketch reproduced on page 2. As mentioned in the Introduction, page i, July entries were penned in August. Manigault, on 11 July, could not have known the name of Battery Ryan which was designated to honor Capt. William H. Ryan who was killed 18 July at Battery Wagner. Battery Ryan was officially named on 21 August. However, it may have been known by that name for a short time prior to publication of the official order.

[Sunday, 12 July 1863, omitted in diary.]

Monday, 13 July 1863.

Col. Kemper came to Legare's Point about Midday and by his

instructions we fired several shells from 12 Pounder Bronze Rifles over to Black Island.

Tuesday, 14 July 1863.

At Dark on 14th, Capt. Gregorie, Engineers, with large fatigue party of 61st Georgia — 200 men — commenced a breastwork & Batteries for 2 guns at Legare's Point. (The orders to Keep diary were never received by Comdr. of Siege Train until some time in Augt.)

Wednesday, 15 July 1863.

One 24 Pounder delivered at Battery Haskell[1] (5.82 Cal. Rifled). In afternoon fired over Black Island at Gunboats near Lt. [Light] House Inlet. So did Lt. Chapman from his position (Battery Ryan). The enemy replied to Chapman and he at the second or third shots got two shell jammed in his guns. Just at this time received orders for Rifle Battery Co. "A" to be at "Artillery Cross Road" at 12 o'clock at Night. The sections got off after great delay. Fatigue party of 8th N.C. working at Legare's Point (200 men in three Reliefs).

[1] Named in orders of 21 Aug. 1863 for Capt. C.T. Haskell Jr. who was killed during the fighting on Morris Island 10 July 1863.

Thursday, 16 July 1863.

Skirmish at Stono [River]. Gunboat "Pawnee" attacked at Grimball's by our artillery.[1]

[1] The Confederate attack on the Pawnee was part of a larger operation against Federal troops on James Island. The Yankees had invaded the island as a diversion to prevent Confederate reinforcement of Morris Island during the Federal assault 10 July 1863. The Confederates attacked about dawn 16 July with the limited objectives of driving in the enemy pickets and, by a flank movement, cutting off part of the Yankee encampment. The assault sent the pickets scampering back to their main line. However, most of the Federals moved quickly and escaped capture by the flanking maneuver. The Pawnee, anchored in Stono River, initially was unable to bring her guns to bear on the field artillery firing at her. She sustained minor damage from hits before slipping her cable and falling downstream. The vessel, joined by several others, then laid down gunfire in support of the Federal infantry. The Confederates, having attained one of their objectives and partially accomplished the other, were now under heavy fire. They broke off the attack and withdrew with a loss of three killed and 15 wounded or missing. The Yankees reported 14 dead and 32 wounded or missing. That night, the Federals evacuated James Island. The southwestern tip then became a no man's land occupied by Confederate pickets, but controlled by the guns of the Yankee fleet anchored near the mouth of the river. [OR XXVIII (1) pp. 372, 581-591]

Friday, 17 July 1863.
Lieut. Mellichamp sick.

Saturday, 18 July 1863.

A tremendous Bombardment of Battery Wagner and Assault at Nightfall.[1] The Yankees repulsed with great loss. Gen. Taliaferro in Command of Wagner. I laid out Rifle Pits on Cremailliere at Point of Pines. The Infantry Supposed Set to work on it.

[1] *This attack (see Introduction, p. xi) resulted in more than 1,500 Federal casualties compared to some 200 for the Confederates. Numerous reports of the engagement will be found in OR XXVIII (1) and in OR LIII (Supplement) pp. 5-15.*

Sunday, 19 July 1863.

A day of perfect quiet. Burying the dead.[1]

[1] *Manigault obviously is referring to burial by others of the dead on Morris Island from the previous night's assault on Battery Wagner.*

[Monday-Tuesday, 20-21 July 1863, omitted in diary.]

Wednesday, 22 July 1863.

Received one 4 inch Blakely Gun at Legare's Point.[1]

[1] *Blakely rifles, in various calibers, were excellent artillery pieces imported from England.*

Thursday, 23 July 1863.

Received one 4.62 in. Rifle Gun at Legare's Point (No. 1).[1]

[1] *This gun probably was a 12-pounder smoothbore that had been rifled by the Confederates.*

Friday, 24 July 1863.

A tremendous Bombardment of Wagner by the Iron Clads until interrupted about 9 A.M. by Flag of Truce Boat to exchange wounded prisoners.

This was the severest & most damaging Bombardment experienced by Wagner — in 4½ or 5 hours near 9,000 [*(2,500), apparently a later correction, is written outside of the paragraph.*] shot & shell were thrown at & into Wagner. This is Estimate by Genl. Taliaferro. The discharges really did not appear to average more than 28 seconds apart. One Magazine was completely uncovered. If it had not been for the Flag of Truce, it would have been necessary to evacuate or surrender Battery Wagner.[1]

[1] *Arrangements for the flag of truce had been made several days previously. The exchange of wounded prisoners, 104 Federals for 45 Confederates, forced a halt in the*

firing and it was not resumed. *Despite the heavy bombardment by some 10 warships and land batteries, Confederate engineers pronounced the fort still serviceable. It held until the night of 6-7 Sept. 1863. [Johnson, Defense of Charleston Harbor, Appendix, p. viii; OR XXVIII (1) pp. 78-79, 380-381]*

[Saturday, 25 July 1863, omitted in diary.]

Sunday, 26 July 1863.

Col. Gonzales arrived at Legare's Point at 5 A.M. or 4:30 A.M. After breakfast examined the Batteries of which I pointed out defects. He disapproved of them and I prepared an unfavorable Report.[1] Captains Beauregard & Proctor dined with us.

[1] *Manigault criticized the layout of the position due to its lack of protection for the guns and cannoneers and its restricted field of fire. The full text of the report and the answer of the engineers, from OR XXVIII (1) pp. 552-554, is reproduced in Appendix 2, pp 253-255.*

Monday, 27 July 1863.

Sent my Report of defective character of Batteries to Col. Simonton to forward to proper authority. About 12 or 1 o'clock Col. Simonton, Col. Harris and Col. Romain [*Roman*] visited Battery Haskell and Col. Harris gave instructions to Lieut. Stiles to put 5 or 6 long Range guns in Embrazure looking toward Morris Island from Graham's Hd. Qrs.[1] to Battery Wagner inclusive. Received a 30 pounder Parrott Gun[2] at Legare's Point.

[1] *Col. Robert F. Graham, commander of the 21st S.C. Infantry, was in command of Confederate troops on Morris Island during the Federal attack of 10 July 1863. The site of his headquarters, referred to elsewhere in Manigault's journal as a house, has not been identified. However, it probably was the old lighthouse building near the south end of the Island referred to in Northern reports as the Beacon House.*

[2] *The Parrott, a standard Federal weapon, was the development of Robert Parker Parrott, proprietor of the West Point (N.Y.) Foundry. It was produced in a wide range of calibers from three to 10-inch bore diameter and fired projectiles weighing from roughly 10 pounds to 300. It consisted of a rifled, cast-iron barrel reinforced at the breech by a wide, wrought-iron band. Manigault's 30-pounder (bore 4.2 inches) probably was a Confederate reproduction although it could have been a captured Federal weapon. [Ripley, Artillery and Ammunition of the Civil War, pp. 109-126, 370-371]*

[Tuesday, 28 July 1863, omitted in diary.]

Wednesday or Thursday, 29 or 30 July 1863.

Genl. Beauregard, Gov. Bonham & Col. Harris visited Battery Haskell and both Genl. Beauregard & Col. Harris gave particular instructions to Capt. Ramsay about the construction of [*the*] Battery.

Thursday, 30 July 1863.

Sergeant Major [*Augustus T. Gaillard*] went off to hospital (Country Fever). [*Apparently appended later:*] Rather Typhoid Fever.

[Friday-Thursday, 31 July-6 August 1863, omitted in diary.]

Friday, 7 Aug. 1863.

Early in the forenoon the Engineer Hands without any notice given to the Commanding Officer, [*Manigault*] removed the 8 in. Sea Coast Howitzer from Platform No. 2, South Face of Battery Haskell and commenced alterations in the Parapet & Platform. As the Battery has been regarded as approximately ready for several days, and as the changes as marked out did not appear to be essential, the Commanding Officer immediately protested against any such sweeping changes (for the other platforms & parapets were marked out to be altered in a similar manner) being made at that late stage of operations, urging that any advantage from change of form would scarcely be equivalent to the delay which would occur at a time when it was so immediately important to open fire upon Morris Island. This protest was forwarded to the Hd. Qrs. of the Brig. Genl. Comdg. [*W.B. Taliaferro*] and finally returned on the ground that he had no right to interfere with the Engineers in the Construction of Military Works (Note that a copy of Protest was sent to Capt. Ramsay, Engr. in Command.)

The 8 in. S.C. [*Sea Coast*] Howitzer having been moved from its position by the Engineers and therefore unavailable at that point, orders were given by the Comdg. Off. to move it to Platform No. 11 but by some carelessness and want of Skill on the part of the Drivers of the Teams, the Gun was carried too near the edge of the Marsh and therefore it stuck in the mud and was not got into its proper position until Sunday, 9th inst.

At night, in consequence of orders received from Hd. Qrs. unusual vigilance & caution was exercised. Several of the Officers spent a large part or the whole of the night on the Ramparts and the Supporting force was largely increased.

Saturday, 8 Aug. 1863.

The Comdg. Officer of Artillery [*Manigault*] sick. The Engineers removed Smooth Bore 24 pndr. from Platform No. 4 without giving any notice.

[Sunday, 9 Aug. 1863, omitted in diary.]

Monday, 10 Aug. 1863.

Comdg. Off of Arty still sick. The 4 inch Blakely gun was moved from Platform No. 5 by the Engineers without giving any notice. This makes three guns moved out of position and for the time rendered useless

7

without consulting with, getting the consent of, or even giving notice to, the Comdg. Off. His sickness prevented any further action on his part.

Tuesday, 11 Aug. 1863.

A 10 pndr. Parrott Gun moved out of position by the Engineers without notice to Comdg. Officer. Artificer of Co. A., Siege Train and two Artificers of Capt. Johnson's Co. "C" Georgia Siege Train, busily engaged all afternoon in fitting Bolsters[1] to the defective Mortar Beds. Weather intensely hot, which made the labor difficult & exhausting.

Commanding Off. returned to out-door duty. He found only one 8 in. S.C. How. [*Sea Coast Howitzer*], one Rifled 24, & one 30 pndr. Parrott (not suited for repelling attack in boats) in position for use toward the South & So. East.

[1] *Technical terms are explained in the glossary.*

Wednesday, 12 Aug. 1863.

Artificers still at work completing Bolsters to Mortars. At work, however, only in the early morning and afternoon, in consequence of the intense heat.

At 7½ or 8 o'clock A.M. the Comdg. Officer of Arty. found the Engineer hands about to move the only three remaining guns to the South. As no Engineer was present, he called the Overseer, and asked under whose orders he was acting; he said that he was acting under the orders of the Engineer there stationed, but that he believed that the final order under which they were acting were written orders from Col. Harris. On being asked if he intended to move any of the Guns then in position, he said yes; that he was going to move all three. The Comdg. Officer of Arty (Major Manigault) then forbade him to touch one of the guns until the orders under which the Engineers were acting were brought to him, so that he could judge of the competency of the person giving the order, in such a matter as the moving the Guns of a Battery without the consent of the Comdg. Officer of said Battery, or of Artillery of Said Battery. He then placed a Sentinel over each Gun and ordered the Senior Lieut of Arty then present to prevent their being moved.

About 12 M. Gen. Beauregard visited Battery Haskell. The Comdg. Officer was not present, and therefore knows nothing personally of what took place. But Lieut. Evans, the Engineer on duty, says that he appeared surprised at the changes which had been made, and those which he was informed were still intended and said that they were not in accordance with his instructions. On being shown the order (which was sent by Telegraph) from Major Echols directly, but coming from Col. Harris, he said that his instructions had been misunderstood. He was told of Major Manigault's having prevented the Engineer hands from moving the Guns. What comment he made on it is not known. He then himself gave certain orders for the erection of Merlons on Batteries Nos. 9 & 11, entirely different from those which the Engineers had intended carrying out.

It must be noted that the Engineers, working under the order sent by Telegram dated Aug. 4, 1863, were proceeding to shut off every gun from Black Island and the Creeks & Marshes in that direction, and to confine every one of them to the same Field of Fire, to wit, Morris Island from Graham's Hd. Qrs. to Battery Wagner inclusive.

This was entirely different from the instructions given by Col. Harris to Lieut Stiles July 27 when he told him to consult with Major Manigault and select 6 positions for long range guns and direct them through embrazures to Morris Island from Graham's Hd. Qrs. to Cummings Point inclusive. (It must be noted that I had informed Col. Harris that including heavy & light, I had six Rifle pieces which could reach Morris Island.)

Also different from the instructions which Gen. Beauregard & Col. Harris had given to Captain Ramsay in presence of Major Manigault on 29th or 30th July when they visited the works together. These orders distinctly provided for 6 long range Guns to be put in Embrazures looking to Morris Island (including one, however, in Battery No 7 which could be trained either towards Morris Island or Black Island). The other guns would be left to bear upon the Creeks & Marshes, and upon Black Island, 'tho some of them would have merlons placed upon the Parapets, in such a way that they would be protected from a fire from either direction and yet by moving the Gun to the right or left, it might still be brought to bear in either direction. The result of these orders was, that for the Guns mounted on Siege Carriages, fire would be exclusively directed thro' Embrazures on Morris Island, and completely shut in from the fire of Black Island by Chambers closed on the South. Five would command Black Island, and the Creeks & Marshes between Battery Haskell & Black Island. While one Battery (No. 7) having a double platform and a very heavy merlon just about midway of the parapet in front, could fire with great advantage in either direction. This, while it devoted five Guns to Morris Island, and made them unavailable for any other direction, yet left 6 guns available for Black Island and for the defence of the work against any incursion or expedition of the enemy in Barges, &c. In their final plan the Engineers were departing entirely from these instructions, and were proceeding as fast as possible to render the Battery totally incapable of defending itself from any attack on the South by shutting off every gun which bore in that direction. (As it is now Aug. 15, only the guns in Nos. 7, 9, & 11 can bear towards the South. Nos. 1, 2, 3, 4, 5, 6, 8 & 10 are shut in closely and can only be fired towards Morris Island from Graham's Hq. Qrs. to Battery Wagner inclusive.) [*Parenthetical statement presumably was inserted later.*]

Received orders to send horses to the Charleston Arsenal for four 3½ in. Blakely guns with ammunition &c. Sent for Pass for Detach[t] [*detachment*] of Artillery Horses & Drivers.

Thursday, 13 Aug. 1863.

Sent Battery Horses of Co. "A" Siege Train to Arsenal in Charleston for the four 3½ in. Blakely Guns together with wagons for ammunition. The Lieutenant returned and reported that he could not bring out the Guns as the limbers of these Guns were arranged in the English fashion with Shafts instead of Poles and they could get no wheel Horse harness to suit.[1] The ammunition was brought down to Battery Ryan. These facts were reported immediately to the Chief of Artillery, Col. Gonzales.

Moved Smooth Bore 24 pndr. back into Chamber No. 4, enfilading a portion of the creek in front of Battery Haskell, but field of Fire confined (Morris Island from Graham's Hd. Qrs. to Battery Wagner).

[1] *American field weapons normally were drawn by a six-horse team — arranged in three pairs and termed, from the front, as lead, swing and wheel pair. The wheel horses were on either side of the pole of the limber (see glossary) which served for guidance in similar fashion to the tongue of a wagon. The limbers of these British-made Blakelys had shafts, which ran on either side of a single wheel horse. Consequently, the lieutenant's American harness could not be used. See entry of Friday, 25 Sept. 1863. [Ripley, pp. 193-196]*

Friday, 14 Aug. 1863.

Col. Gonzales & Capt. Ramsay visited Batteries Ryan & Haskell about 11 A.M. Major Manigault informed Col. Gonzales of the failure to bring out the 3½ in Blakely Guns and the cause of it. (He had not received the communication addressed him on the subject).

At about 3 P.M. copy of an order from Gen. Hagood came to Hd. Qrs. Legare's House directing Lieut. [*W.W.*] Legare, Ordnance Officer, to call on Major Manigault for horses to move from Battery Haskell to Battery Ryan 2 24 pndrs. Rifled, 1 30 pndr. Parrott & 1 10 pounder Parrott. The Horses were furnished as desired and every assistance rendered and the Guns all moved to Battery Ryan before dark.

Lt. Col. Yates paid a visit to the Battery about 2½ P.M.

Saturday, 15 Aug. 1863.

Lt. Brux at Point of Pines reported that a Yankee Sentinel was seen at the "Mud Fort"[1] nearest Black Island. Only one man appears to have been seen and he was armed with a musket, but several saw him after their attention was called to him. They did not see his gun, however.

Private Mordecai of Co. "A" Siege Train accidentally shot himself through the left hand with a pistol. No bone broken.

We received another 4.62 Rifle about this time which was first fired on the 20th in Gun Chamber No. 1 and burst on 22nd. This was the true No. 2 but bursting so soon it was lost sight of and the 4.62 Rifle received

Aug. 30 was called No. 2. [*This paragraph was inserted at an unspecified later date.*]

¹ This "Mud Fort" was built by the Federals in the marsh behind Morris Island not far from the east end of Black Island. Technically, it was named the Marsh Battery, but soon its single heavy cannon would be known to both sides as the "Swamp Angel." The gun lofted 150-pound shells approximately 8,000 yards, an incredibly long range in those days, into the city of Charleston. Firing began at 1:30 a.m. 22 Aug. 1863 and continued intermittently until the rifle burst at the 36th round about 1 a.m. 24 Aug.

Damage to Charleston was negligible, but firing on a city containing women and children opened an entirely new dimension to warfare in the Charleston area and resulted in acrimonious messages between the opposing commanders which, in the end, accomplished very little.

Construction of the Marsh Battery, however, was one of the most ingenious engineering achievements of the war. It was built on a substance known locally as "pluff" mud, a gooey composition that entraps anyone taking more than a few steps. The engineers, using the principle of counterbalance, devised a method of floating the platform and gun on the mud. They pushed plank pilings into the mud until they reached a solid sand bottom about 20 feet below. The pilings were arranged in the shape of a square box, open at top and bottom. Inside the box, on a bed of marsh grass, tarpaulins and well-rammed sand, was laid the platform of three layers of heavy planks. The platform was not connected to the box and merely floated inside. Surrounding the box, on another bedding of marsh, tarpaulins and sand, was laid a grillage of logs. Atop the logs were piled thousands of sandbags. The purpose of the bags was twofold. They formed a parapet for the battery and, more important, counterbalanced the weight of the platform and, mounted on it, an 8-inch Parrott rifle weighing approximately 16,500 pounds. If the platform and gun sank into the box, the pressure of displaced mud forced the grillage upward. The weight of more sandbags added to the parapet forced the grillage down and brought the platform back to its proper level. After more than a century, the grillage has disappeared. The platform and box of planks remain today, buried under two or three feet of sand (from the sandbags) and mud.

[Information on the Marsh Battery will be found in a number of contemporary sources, primarily Gillmore's Engineer and Artillery Operations Against the Defenses of Charleston Harbor, 1863; OR XXVIII (1 & 2) and XXXV (1 & 2); and Charleston newspapers, the Charleston Daily Courier and the Charleston Mercury during the period 24-26 Aug. and the Mercury of 7 Sept. See also, Ripley, pp. 118-122.]

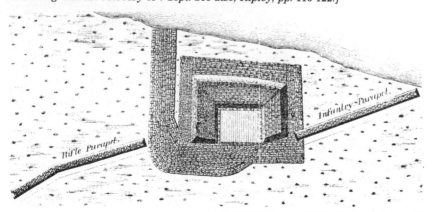

Gillmore, Engineer and Artillery Operations, facing p. 278

Marsh Battery platform surrounded by grillage holding sandbags.

[**Sunday, 16 Aug. 1863, omitted in diary.**]

Monday, 17 Aug. 1863.

The Yankees opened a heavy fire on Battery Wagner & Fort Sumter from early dawn. All their land Batteries, the *Ironsides*,[1] four Monitors[2] (two others near but not engaged) and several wooden Gunboats[3] took part in the Bombardment. Day very calm & water smooth. The wall of the Gorge of Sumter very badly damaged.[4]

In obedience to orders from Genl. Hagood, opened fire at 11 A.M. from the 8 in Columbiad[5] in Battery Haskell. According to instructions, directed the fire entirely on the heavy Rifle Batteries to South of the House on Morris Island known as Graham's Hd. Quarters. Fired 27 shots from this Columbiad in course of day. With 8 lb. cartridges, average elevation of 22° 30'. With 10 lb. cartridges, an average Elev. of 20°, The practice was not good and all the shells failed to burst except about three. Lieut. Lake, Co. "K" 2nd Regt. Artillery, with Detachments from that Regiment was in charge of the Columbiad.

At 4½ P.M. opened fire with 10 inch S.C. [*Sea Coast*] Mortar No. 1...direction the first Yankee Battery to left of Graham's Hd. Qrs. Charge 10 lbs. Powder. Shell went clear over Morris Island and fell in water beyond. Did not burst. Second Shot 10 lbs. went over island — did not burst — 3rd Shot 8 lbs., Shell fell on Morris Island — did not burst. 4th — 8 lbs. powder — went over island — did not burst. Ceased firing at 5:30 P.M.

The fuzes were old, and the priming much shrunk & cracked. We tried a fresh priming of Whiskey & Mealed powder but without effect.

[1] *The New Ironsides, a heavily-armored, bark-rigged, screw steamer 230 feet long and displacing 3,486 tons, was commissioned at Philadelphia in 1862. She was the most powerful warship in the Charleston area, mounting two 6.4-inch Parrott rifles, 14 11-inch Dahlgren smoothbores and several smaller weapons. [ONR Series 2, Vol. I, p. 159]*

[2] *Three types of monitors were used in the Federal blockade of Charleston. The first and second types were both single-turret vessels, advanced versions of the original Monitor which fought the Confederate Virginia in Hampton Roads in March 1862. They differed in armament, one type mounting a 15-inch Dahlgren smoothbore and an 8-inch Parrott rifle and the other two Dahlgren smoothbores, 15 and 11 inch. The third type was represented by a single vessel, the Keokuk. She had twin turrets with an 11-inch Dahlgren in each. She was lightly armored and sank following engagement with Fort Sumter 7 April 1863. [Dictionary of American Naval Fighting Ships, Navy Department, 1968, Vol. III, pp. 758-761; ONR Series 2, Vol. I (see names of individual ships)]*

[3] *Gunboats used in the blockade were a hodgepodge of wooden vessels mounting an armament just as varied. They generally handled the duties of intercepting blockade runners and engaged the major Confederate forts only at respectful ranges. [ibid]*

[4] *This was the beginning of the first major bombardment of Fort Sumter. It lasted until 2 Sept. and resulted in two Confederates killed and 50 wounded. An estimated 6,800 rounds were fired by the fleet and heavy batteries located on Morris Island. In all, the fort weathered three major and eight minor bombardments totaling some 43,000 projecties and resulting in more than 300 Confederate casualties. [Johnson, Gillmore, and OR XXXV (1 & 2) passim]*

Tuesday, 18 Aug. 1863.

Yankees at daybreak commenced heavy fire from their land batteries on Fort Sumter. At 6 A.M. opened fire with 8 in. Columbiad. At 6:30 A.M. opened fire with 30 pndr. Parrott. Only three shells from each gun burst in course of day. At 7 A.M. fired two Shots from 10 in. S.C. [*Sea Coast*] Mortar No. 1. At second shot the front transom was entirely split and the Bed became useless. Then fired two shots from Mortar No. 2. None of the Shell burst. Suspended mortar firing until we could get better fuzes.

A little before Midday, a heavy N.E. Wind commenced blowing which affected the accuracy of the fire. The *Ironsides* and the Monitors hauled off in consequence of the high wind.

Fired 34 Shot with 30 pndr. Parrott when calm with an elevation of about 13° and after the wind rose elevation of 14°. These appeared to be the proper elevations for the distance.

Fired 47 Shot with 8 inch Columbiad — 27 with 8 lb. Cartridges and elevation of 22° (average) — 20 with 10 lb. cartridges & Elev. of 20°.

Ceased firing about 6 P.M.

About 7:30 P.M. fired Mortar No. 2 at advanced Yankee Batteries simply to try the new Fuzes furnished us. 1 Shot.

Very little firing from any point (except perhaps Battery Cheves[1]) during the night which was dark & Stormy.

[1] *Named for Confederate Capt. Langdon Cheves who was killed when the Federals captured the south end of Morris Island 10 July 1863. [OR XXVIII (1) pp. 58, 370; OR XXVIII (2) p. 299]*

Wednesday, 19 Aug. 1863.

Opened fire at 5:30 A.M. with 8 in Columbiad & 30 pounder Parrott gun. Also, shortly after with 10 inch S.C. [*Sea Coast*] Mortar. At the 13th Round the 30 pndr. Parrott Gun burst. One man badly stunned, and one slightly so. No other damage done. This took place at 7:45 A.M. After four shots with mortar, suspended firing it until I could communicate with Capt. Mitchel at Battery Simkins,[1] and make arrangements for signalling to me the range of our mortar shells.[2]

The Fuzes, as before, proved very defective, very few of the Shells bursting.

At 11:30 A.M. commenced firing with the 4 inch Blakely Gun. The shells failed to reach Morris Island, and after nine shots we ceased firing.

At about 12 M. commenced firing 10 in. S.C. [*Sea Coast*] Mortar, Capt. Mitchel having sent one of the Signal Corps to signal to us whether our

Shells fell short, went over or proved correct.

Moved a Rifled 24 Pounder from Battery Ryan to Battery Haskell and put it in Battery.

Four 3½ inch Blakely Guns for Co. "A" S.C. Siege Train arrived about 12 o'clock last night from the Charleston Arsenal.[3]

Ceased firing at 6:45 P.M.

Mortar Platform for No. 2 unserviceable and needs being re-laid.

The 8 in. Columbiad fired 54 Shells.

The 30 pndr. Parrott 13 Shells.

The 4 in Blakely 9 Shells.

The 10 in Mortar 18 Shells. [*In the Diary, 28 is struck out and 18 inserted.*]

At 11:45 Received orders to fire upon advanced Yankee Batteries on Morris Island.

[1] *Located near Fort Johnson and previously called the Shell Point Battery, this fortification was named 21 Aug. 1863 in honor of Lt. Col. J.C. Simkins of the 1st S.C. (Regular) Infantry who was killed in the 18 July Federal attack on Battery Wagner.*

[2] *Remote observation of artillery fire was not a common practice during the Civil War.*

[3] *Manigault, on 25 Sept. 1863, explained that standard American 6-pounder limbers were used to deliver the guns while the British limbers were being altered to the American system. See also 13 Aug. 1863 and note.*

Thursday, 20 Aug. 1863.

12:30 A.M. Commenced firing with 8 inch Columbiad & 10 in. S.C. [*Sea Coast*] Mortar on advanced Yankee Batteries in obedience to orders just received.

Fired slowly, 10 Shells from Mortar (which generally appeared to burst tolerably well) and 14 shells from 8 in. Columbiad which did not burst. Ceased firing about half past four o'clock as the Mortar Platform was totally unserviceable, and the prepared ammunition for the Columbiad began to fall short. The enemy made no reply whatsoever until after daybreak when they commenced firing upon Sumter. As soon as it was light enough, set a strong party to work moving Mortar No. 1 (the Bed of which was disabled) from platform No. 1, which was sound, and shifting Mortar No. 2 to the sound platform. The work was heavy and occupied much time.

In pursuance to orders sent him at 12 o'clock last night, Capt. Webb at 4 A.M. sent Horses & Drivers to Grimball's place to man the Rifle 24 pndr. in case of necessity.

At 8 o'clock another Mortar Bed arrived from Lieut. Legare's and hands with Gin to mount it. It was accordingly mounted.

Got 24 Pounder Rifled Gun in position — also the 4.62 inch Gun. To obtain the requisite elevation for distant firing required much labor.

In the afternoon, the Engineers repaired Mortar Platform No. 2. The platform will bear one or two days slow firing.

Fired 20 Shots from 4.62 in. Rifle Siege Gun, twelve of which were directed to Morris Island and eight at the Mud Battery in the Marsh S.E. from Legare's Point. With 3 pnd. Charge of powder the 4.62 in. Rifle required about 20° Elevation to reach Morris Island and 10½ deg. to reach Mud Fort in Marsh.

Fired 6 Shots with 24 Pounder — three at Morris Island and three at Mud Fort. Elevation for Morris Island 15° with a 4 lb. charge of powder. 8° Elevation for Mud Fort.

In the afternoon Gen. Taliaferro & Col. Gonzales visited Battery Haskell.

Friday, 21 Aug. 1863.

Land batteries commenced firing on Sumter at an early hour. Battery Simkins & Battery Cheves replying. At about 8½ A.M. commenced firing with two 10 inch Mortars on advanced Yankee Batteries.

At the first Shot the Mortar Bed furnished yesterday commenced to crack & split at the Right Cheek. At the 11th Round the Mortar bed became totally unserviceable. Fire was continued with the remaining Mortar. Requisition immediately made on Lt. Legare, Ord. Officer, for another Mortar Bed.

At 12 M. the 4.62 in Gun from Redoubt No. 1 was moved to Battery Haskell and put in Battery on Platform No. 3 directed on the Battery building in the Marsh.¹ This is 4.62 in Rifle No. 1.

At 10 o'clock A.M. Lieut. Wilson with a Detachment of 40 men from Co. B Siege Train, Capt. [*S. Porcher*] Smith comdg., reported for duty at Legare's House.

At 10½ A.M. o'clock Capt. Smith reported with Teams to assist Capt. Webb in moving to Siege Battery on the Stono (below Dills).

About the same time Lieut. Charles E. Gregg of Co. "C" Siege Train brought an order for the two Bronze 12 pndr. Rifle Guns (Regulation Pattern) of the Palmetto Guard. The Guns were delivered to him.

About 4 o'clock P.M. Captain Webb marched with his Company for Battery on the Stono.

At 4½ o'clock another Mortar Bed arrived from Fort Johnson, but of the same pattern as the one broken today. The Material was of Pine. It will not be able to endure continued firing with the Maximum Charge of 10 lbs. of powder.

About 2 o'clock commenced firing Solid Shot from 8 in Columbiad at advanced Yankee Batteries. Used solid shot because we could not get prepared Shell.

At 6 P.M. Ordnance Wagon arrived with 12 Barrels Powder, 2 Columbiad chamber-sponges and fuze plugs for Columbiad Shell — 2 Worms.

At 4 P.M. Lieut. Wilson & 15 men of Co. B. ordered to Battery Wagner.

Fired 11 Shot with one Mortar, 32 with another and 5 with Columbiad.

Edward Manigault
Major &c.

¹ *This was the Marsh Battery (see Saturday, 15 Aug. 1863, note), or Mud Battery as Manigault called it previously.*

Saturday, 22 Aug. 1863.

Land Batteries firing on Fort Sumter from an early hour. Two Monitors & the Ironsides bombarding Battery Wagner for about two or three hours during the morning.

Commenced firing with one 10 inch S.C. [*Sea Coast*] Mortar about 6 o'clock upon the advanced Yankee Batteries on Morris Island. At the 10th Round the Mortar Bed gave way in consequence of the splitting of the Front Transom. Both Mortars are consequently useless. About 7 A.M. commenced firing on advanced Batteries with 8 in Columbiad (having received Fuze plugs last night).

At about 1200 M commenced firing 2 4 62/100 in [*normally called 4.62 inch*] Rifle Siege Guns, 1 Rifled 24 pndr. (5.82 in. Cal) and one 24 Pounder and the 8 in Columbiad on the Marsh Battery to S.E. of Legare's Point. Hit this Battery several times but do not know if any damage was inflicted. (Reported hit 15 or 17 times.) [*Parenthetical material apparently inserted later.*]

At 2:20 P.M. the 4.62 in Rifle Siege Gun on Platform No. 1 burst. The breech was blown out without any other damage being done. The Bands were neither broken nor thrown off and the rear one only somewhat loosened.

Manigault's sketch of broken gun

Ceased firing about 3½ o'clock for 1 hour. Opened and fired two or 3 shots and ceased as we had reason to suppose that there was a Flag of Truce Boat out.

> The 8 in Col. [*Columbiad*] 31 Shots (21 at Marsh Battery).
> The 4.62 Rifle, 7 Shots (Burst).
> The 24 Pndr. (5.82 Cal) 20 Shots.
> The 4.62 in. 12 Shots.
> The 24 pndr. Smooth, 9 Shots.
> The 20 pndr. Parrott 9 Shots. All premature Explosions.

It is said that we hit the Marsh Battery from 15 to 17 times. Do not suppose any damage was enflicted. It was omitted to be stated in the proper place that about 10 o'clock A.M. Capt. Johnson, Co. "C" Georgia Siege Train, commenced (by order) firing from his 20 pndr. Parrott Gun. Every Shell burst near the Muzzle of the Gun. (The inferiority of the iron from which the Shells are cast is supposed to be the Cause.) After firing 9 Shots he was directed to cease firing as the fragments of the Shells endangered the men at the Guns somewhat in advance of him.

At 1:15 P.M. A Board consisting of Major Manigault, Capt. Webb and Lieut. Hasell assembled at Legare's House in accordance with Special Order No. 10 from Hd. Qrs. Chief of Arty dated Aug. 21, 1863, and after invesigating the circumstances attending the bursting of 30 pndr. Parrott Gun on 19th Inst. reported to Hd. Qrs.

It is well to state here that between 1 A.M. and daylight this morning several Shells were thrown into the City of Charleston from one or more of the Yankee Batteries. It is supposed that these shells were thrown from the Battery in the Marsh to S.E. of Legare's Point.[1]

Edward Manigault
Major Comdg. Arty
Legare's Point

[1] *Manigault's supposition was correct. See 15 Aug. 1863, note*

Sunday, 23 Aug. 1863.

At 3 o'clock A.M. heavy firing heard in the direction of Fort Sumter. As there was a heavy fog, nothing could be seen but from the peculiar sound of the Shells, we concluded that two or more Monitors were firing at short range on Fort Sumter. The fire appeared to be returned from the Fort. The fire lasted heavily from half an hour to three quarters of an hour when it slacked off. The Monitors appear to have gone off before the Fog lifted. The Ironsides went out about 8 A.M. just after the Fog lifted.

At about 8 A.M. commenced firing from 8 in. Columbiad in Battery Haskell [*first at the Marsh Battery and afterward*][1] on heavy rifled Battery to south of Graham's Hd. Qrs. Could not fire sooner in consequence of Fog. Did not open fire with the other guns as no one was visible on the Battery in the Marsh. (Note, the first few shots with Columbiad at Marsh Battery).

Sent Capt. S.P. Smith to City on Special Ordnance Service to return tomorrow.

Lieut. Lake, Co. K, 2nd Artillery who has been in charge of the Columbiad and Mortars, was at 4 o'clock this Evening relieved by Lieut. Pitts of the same Regiment. This was by special request & arrangement of Lt. Col. Brown.

At 5 P.M. commenced firing the 8 in. S.C. Howitzer and 4 inch Blakely on the Marsh Battery to S.E. of Legare's Point so as to get the direction and range for Night firing, the other guns being already trained.

The Columbiad fired 22 Shots before Lt. Lake was relieved and 3 Shots after Lt. Pitts took charge. Lieut. Lake fired the Columbiad 200 times.

Closed here at 8 o'clock P.M.

Edward Manigault
Major &c.

At 3 o'clock P.M. got orders from Genl. Taliaferro to open fire on the Marsh Battery precisely at 10 p.m. with all the available guns.

At 10 o'clock had all the guns ready. Believing that my watch was not correct, not knowing what orders the commanders of the other Batteries had received, and not wishing to commence firing before the other batteries were ready, I waited until 15 min. past 10 o'clock and then commenced firing. The Batteries on the left (Battery Cheves & Shell Point Batteries) took it up immediately. The fire was kept up pretty sharply for about three quarters of an hour. As the Batteries on the left slackened their fire very much and as we had no orders as to the length of time during which the firing should be continued, I rode to Major Glover's Quarters and requested him to send a Dispatch to Genl. Taliaferro asking whether it was intended to keep up the fire all night. This dispatch was sent and the only reply stated that Genl. Ripley's orders were to keep up a brisk fire. We then recommenced firing steadily. About three quarters after Eleven, the Marsh Battery opened with a heavy Rifle Gun and commenced Shelling the City of Charleston. All the Batteries commenced heavily upon it, but did not prevent the enemy from Continuing their Shelling. They fired (19) Nineteen Shells in all, of which, however, three or four broke or burst prematurely near the Gun. There were some showers about this time. The Yankees fired their last shell about 1 o'clock Monday, 24th Aug.[2]

[1] Inserted material is from part of Manigault's report reproduced in OR XXVIII (1) p. 555. [See Appendix 2, pp. 257]

[2] See 15 Aug. 1863, note. The Federal gun exploded about 1 a.m. 24 Aug.

Monday, 24 Aug. 1863.

As near as I could judge by the Reliefs of the Infantry Guard, Judging, however, by the probable time necessary to fire 19 Shots from so heavy a gun, it was probably nearer two o'clock. Pretty heavy shower about this time. Shortly after this received orders from Genl. Taliaferro to withhold fire as the enemy was silent. Batteries Cheves and Simkins continued firing slowly.

A second dispatch arrived about 3 o'clock from Capt. Nance saying that the Marsh Battery was shelling the City and directing that as heavy a fire should be brought to bear upon it as was possible.

As this order was evidently given while the enemy was still shelling and as that reason no longer existed, I did not recommence fire.

It had been a mooted point on Friday night whether the Shell were thrown into the City from the Marsh Battery or from Morris Island. No doubt can longer be entertained on this score. Our Guns were all carefully trained upon the Marsh Battery before dark, and Slats nailed to guide the Trails and Wheels.[1] When the gun of the Marsh Battery was fired the flash was very nearly precisely in the prolongation of the axis of each of the guns. And as the Guns in South side of Battery Haskell are disposed on a curved line, and the two guns on the Flanks are 400 [*417 is penned above 400 in the Diary.*] yards apart, there can be no doubt but that they were directed to one point, and that point the "Marsh Battery."

Furthermore, the time occupied by the sound travelling to Battery Haskell (6 or 7 seconds) corresponded with the rate of motion of sound for the distance 1¼ to 1½ miles.

We could not judge very well of the accuracy of our own firing as most of our Shells failed to explode. Some of the fire from Battery Cheves was very good and some from Battery Simkins. Many of the Brooke Rifle Shell fuzes failed to ignite and hence we were unable to see their flight.

About Midday wrote a Report to Genl. Taliaferro showing the unprepared condition of our Batteries. Also gave list of our Guns and Cannoneers.

Major Glover went to the City about 5½ A.M. this morning and left Major Manigault in Command.

Before dark trained the Guns on the "Marsh Battery" preparatory to Night Firing.

The Enemy did not open from his Marsh Battery during the night and our Batteries did not fire.

Heavy Showers during the night.

Edward Manigault
Major Comdg. Arty
Legare's Point

[1] *Nailing slats on the platform to guide the wheels and trail was the normal method of preparing a gun to fire at night.*

Tuesday, 25 Aug. 1863.

During the night the enemy has thrown up another Battery in the Marsh about 400 yds. East of the East End of Black Island. This Battery is about the same distance from Battery Haskell as Black Island is, viz. 1¼ miles. (The conclusion I draw from the erection of the Battery is that the Enemy is about to attack this point and it would be folly to suppose that he will confine himself to building Batteries in the Marsh, and neglect the firm ground of Black Island, which is not more distant and possesses so many superior advantages. I have no doubt therefore that there either are, or soon will be, strong Batteries on Black Island.)[1]

Only the base of the Battery is as yet thrown up (probably to a height of 4 ft.) It is likely that the remainder of the height will be given by sand bags. There are only two platforms in Battery Haskell from which Guns can be brought to bear upon this New Battery.

In consequence of the heavy Rain of last night, five Platforms were under water this morning, and one or two of them could not be drained as they were below the level of the water in the Borrow Pits. The

Engineers have been called on by me (in pursuance of instructions from Genl. Beauregard) to take measures to drain the Borrow Pits but nothing has been done. On the Contrary a road has been Made which backs up an additional quantity of water.

A Considerable Engineer force employed in finishing Magazine at Battery Ryan (Central Battery). The Magazine, which is double, ie, two compartments, is however very small. [*and the water was dripping through it at 2 p.m. today*][2]

At 2 P.M. the 8 inch Navy Shell Gun (from Isaac P. Smith)[3] was mounted in S.E. Angle of Redoubt No. 1. It is mounted on Columbiad Carriage of Pine wood 1½ inches too wide between the Cheeks. The maximum Elevation possible is 10°. The Elevating Screw is out of order.

At 2 P.M. Capt. [*S. Porcher*] Smith, Co. "B" S.C. Siege Train, arrived at "Point of Pines" with one Section of his Battery in accordance with orders given him.

At about 4 P.M. Col. Gonzales visited Battery Haskell on a tour of inspection (Special, in consequence of unfavorable report as to the condition of the Platforms under my command.)

At 7 P.M. Received orders to fire on Morris Island with all available guns to South of Battery Wagner, as the enemy was reported advancing. Opened immediately from the 8 inch Columbiad, as soon as possible from the 4.62 inch Rifle & 24 pndr. Rifle. As these latter guns had their wheels mounted on Skids (to give elevation) and were trained upon the Marsh Battery, it took some time to give them the new direction. Thirty three (33) Shots were fired from the Columbiad, twenty two (22) from the 4.62 inch Rifle & (15) fifteen from the 24 Pounder Rifle (5.82 Cal). When the firing of Small arms ceased in front of Battery Wagner the fire of our Guns was slackened and finally ceased also. It did not appear to us that an actual assault was made on Battery Wagner, as our Pickets in front of the Fort were never driven in.

The enemy made many signals from Light House Inlet viz Rockets and Red, Blue, Green & White Lights during the fight in front of Battery Wagner.

Captain Smith's two Howitzers were got into position at Point of Pines and the artillerists remained at their guns until a late hour.

The Infantry Supports at Batteries Haskell & Ryan were strongly re-inforced about 8 O'clock by Major Glover.

At 1 A.M. Two Ordnance Wagons arrived from Fort Johnson with Blakely Shell (13 Boxes 6 each), 8 inch Grape, 4.62 Shell plugged up, Friction Tubes, Rammer & Staff, Sponge & Staff.

Several Showers of rain during night commencing at about 8½ P.M.

Edward Manigault
Major Comdg. Arty

[1] *Marsh Battery No. 2, as Manigault called it 26 August, apparently was intended as a dummy. Manigault was mistaken in his belief that Haskell would be attacked but correct in assuming that the Federals would fortify Black Island.*

²Bracketed material was omitted in the journal but appears in the copy of Manigault's report in OR XXVIII (1) p. 556. See Appendix 2, pg. 257.

³The Isaac P. Smith, one of the Federal gunboats, was a 171-foot, propeller steamer of 453 tons. She mounted a 30-pounder Parrott rifle as a pivot gun and eight 8-inch smoothbores in broadside. The smoothbores are listed in the Official Naval Records as Dahlgrens. However, Dahlgren made no claim to having designed an 8-inch which could have been used at this period, nor have surviving specimens been found. The guns, presumably, were 8-inch Navy shellguns as mentioned by Manigault on p. 190.

The Smith, on routine scouting duty, was accustomed to prowl farther up the Stono River than was prudent, and the Confederates set a trap for her. Under cover of darkness, they built gun platforms on both sides of the river. Then, with platforms ready and the guns carefully concealed, they waited for the Smith. On Jan. 30, 1863, she started upriver. The Confederates let her pass, then rolled the guns onto the platforms. When the vessel started downstream, the batteries opened.

The Smith made a run for it, but hemmed in by the narrow stream, she was unable to maneuver and bring her broadside batteries to bear except for the few moments when she was almost directly opposite one or another of the Confederate batteries. She got part of the way to freedom, then a shot hit her boiler. With pressure dropping, she was forced to anchor and surrender.

The Confederates towed her upstream, beyond hope of rescue by other gunboats, and then examined their prize. In addition to her armament, which the Confederates badly needed, they had captured or killed the entire crew of some 117 officers and men. Rechristened the Stono, the vessel served as a guard boat in Charleston Harbor. She later was converted to a blockade runner, but grounded attempting to leave the harbor. Refloated, she apparently returned to guard duty and reportedly was burned at the evacuation of Charleston in Feb. 1865.

Although Manigault had not joined the Siege Train and was not present at the capture, a number of the unit's guns and personnel participated in the action. [OR XIV, pp. 199-204; ONR XIII, p. 563; ONR (Series II) I, (Ship Statistics); Charleston Daily Courier, 8 June 1863; Roman, The Military Operations of General Beauregard (Vol. 2), pp. 59-60; Burton, Siege of Charleston, 1861-1865, p. 123]

Wednesday, 26 Aug. 1863.

Captain Lee of the Engineers engaged in Opening the Embrazures of Battery Haskell, so as to give a [*Inserted above "give a" are the words, "extend the"*] field of Fire towards the South. This prevented any fire from our Guns for the greater part of the day. In the afternoon fired several Shots at the Battery No. 1 in the Marsh.

Nothing more has been done by the Enemy on the Marsh Battery No. 2. It is very possible that this Marsh Battery No. 2 may be only a Sham to attract our notice and draw our fire while the true batteries are on Black Island.

At 6:40 P.M. an attack was made upon the Rifle Pits in front of Battery Wagner.¹ All of the James Island Batteries opened a rapid fire upon the portion of Morris Island to South of the Battery. The 8 inch Columbiad, 24 Pndr. Rifle & 4.62 inch Rifle in Battery Haskell were used for this purpose. After some time as the musketry at Battery Wagner ceased, our fire was suspended. Later I received orders from Genl. Taliaferro to continue at intervals the fire as nearly as possible on the Rifle pits which were reported to be in possession of the enemy. This was done throughout the night from Two Guns (8 in. Columbiad & 4.62 Rifle) at intervals of 10 or 15 minutes.

The Detachment from the Siege Train (20 men) which has been doing duty at Battery Wagner was relieved at 1 A.M. tonight.

Night Stormy & rainy — wind at first from S.E. — then from N.E.

Edward Manigault

Major Comdg. Arty

Legare's Point

When the Rifle pits at Battery Wagner were attacked from 6:40 to 8 P.M., the Columbiad fired 20 shots — 4 shots from 24 pndr. Rifle — 5 shots from 4.62 in. Rifle.

The Columbiad also fired 5 Shots in afternoon at Marsh Battery No. 1. Also 9 at night on "Old Rifle Pits."

[1] *At dusk the 24th. Massachusetts Volunteers, supported by the 3rd. New Hampshire, made a quick dash on the Confederate rifle pits in front of Battery Wagner. The action was over within five minutes and the Federals captured approximately 70 men. Few escaped. The Confederates considered a counterattack, but decided against it in view of the superior strength of the enemy. [OR XXVIII (1) pp. 296, 498, 506; OR XXVIII (2) p. 66]*

Thursday, 27 Aug. 1863.

The enemy very busy in entrenching himself in the Sand Hill in front of Battery Wagner at a distance of 200 to 250 yds. The 8 in. Columbiad at Battery Haskell was brought to bear upon them and continued firing slowly until the ammunition was so nearly exhausted as to render it prudent to reserve what remained. (The difficulty is to procure 8 in. Shells.) The 24 pndr. Rifle and 4.62 in. Rifle were then brought to bear and continued firing slowly (with some interval from 3 to 4 P.M.) during the remainder of the day. Some very good shots were made with the 4.62 in. Rifle but the failure of the Shells to explode rendered the fire comparatively ineffective.

Battery Simkins was also firing slowly at the Same point. Battery Cheves did not fire.

At 8 P.M. received orders to be prepared for firing on Morris Island to South of Battery Wagner in case of further attack on that Post. The Guns were accordingly made ready but as no attack took place, we did not fire at all during the night.

Edward Manigault

Major Comdg. Arty

Legare's Point

Fired today from 8 inch Columbiad, [*The number "20" is overstruck "27."*]

From 24 pndr. Rifle 19 Shots.

From 4.62 in. Rifle 25 Shots.

Friday, 28 Aug. 1863.

Some object like a gun is visible this morning in Marsh Battery No. 2. It is impossible to decide, however, whether it is a real gun or not. The Battery has not been built higher than it was when first observed on morning of 25th inst.

About 11 A.M. Major Mallet of the Ordnance Department, came to Legare's Point to inspect the condition of the Fuzes and other Ordnance Stores. He remained witnessing the firing &c. for a couple of hours.

About 3 P.M. Col. Leay [Lay], Inspector Genl. of Artillery, visited Battery Haskell and remained until 4½ P.M.

Fired at the "Old Rifle Pits" in front of Battery Wagner.
With the 8 in Columbiad, [The number "10" is overstruck "5."]
With the 24 Pndr. Rifled 8 Shells.
With the 4.62 in. 18 Shells.
Heavy rain about 6 P.M.

Captain Lee's hands occupied in opening the Embrazures at Battery Haskell more to the Southwards.

Saturday, 29 Aug. 1863.

Continued firing steadily upon the advanced Yankee Works near the "Old Rifle Pits" in front of Battery Wagner. Did not use 8 in Col. as the scarcity of Ammunition warned us of the necessity of reserving some of it. After a good many shots found that the 24 pndr. Rifle could not be relied on at that distance with the new shell furnished us. The Shells made by J.M. Eason & Co.[1] according to a pattern which was furnished with the original Blakely Gun sent to this country (Prioleau Gun)[2] reached Morris Island, but they have all been expended and the other shells furnished cannot be relied on at all and have all fallen short. Consequently, fire was suspended from 24 pndr. Rifle. Continued firing throughout the day with the 4.62 in. Gun, very often striking in the midst of hills in which the enemy's working parties were, but as the Shells never exploded, little effect could have been produced.

Engaged in repairing Elevating Screw of the 8 in. Navy Shell Gun in Redoubt No. 1. Sent an urgent Requisition for Manoeuvering handspikes for Carriage of same.

About and after Midday there were noticed some heavy discharges from the Enemy's Guns down at Light House Inlet. Supposed to be practice at some of the Batteries erected there by the enemy. Not aware of any projectiles thrown from thence towards any of our works.

At 4½ P.M. Capt Smith experimented with some Shells from his 8 in. Siege Howitzer to ascertain his ability to shell Black Island. 1st Shell filled with Sand and plugged up fired with 3½ lbs. Cartridge fell a little short, 13½ deg. 2nd, filled and fuzed, 3½ lbs cart. Just reached the Edge of Island. Did not explode. 13½ deg.

3rd. Filled & fuzed, fell a little short. 3½ lbs. Elev. 13½° did not explode.

4th. 4 lbs. Cartridge, 13½° Elev. fell short, did not explode.

5. 4 lbs. Cartridge, 13½° Elev. fell short, did not explode.

6. 4 lb. Cartridge, fitting chamber well, 13½° Elev. fell in woods, did not explode.

7. 4 lb. Cartridge, fitting Chamber well, 13½° Elev. fell in woods, did not explode.

Ceased firing.

Genl. Taliaferro & Col. Harris visited Battery Haskell and Point of Pines about 4 to 6½ P.M. It was decided to Make certain Changes in the Works.

Ceased firing at Battery Haskell about Sunset.

Edward Manigault

Major Comdg. Arty &c.

Note. 13½ degrees was the greatest Elevation which could be got on the 8 inch Siege Howitzer standing on a level Platform. By means of mounting the Wheels on Skids greater Elevation may be got.

[1] *J.M. Eason & Bros, a Charleston foundry and machine shop, operated by J.M. and T.D. Eason. It produced ordnance materials for the Confederacy. [Ripley, pp. 74, 75, 362]*

[2] *This small weapon was the first rifled cannon used in combat in America. It was made in England and presented to the State of South Carolina by Charles K. Prioleau of Frazer & Co. in London. Mounted on Morris Island at the beginning of the war, it fired a 12-pound rifle projectile with unprecedented accuracy into the walls of Fort Sumter during the initial bombardment 12-13 Apr. 1861. Damage to the fort was slight, but the Federals, listening to its projectiles boring into the brick walls, knew they were hearing the sounds of the future. [Ripley, pp. 148, 149]*

Sunday, 30 Aug. 1863.

During the Morning fired 17 Shots from the 4.62 in. Rifle upon the hill 200 or 250 yds. in front of Wagner. The wind was high and blustering and interfered with the accuracy of the firing. Only four Shells were seen with certainty to fall in the midst of the Space occupied by the Working parties. None of the Shell exploded.

In consequence of the rain and the thickness of the atmosphere preventing a satisfactory sight of the fall of the shell at such a distance, firing was not resumed in the afternoon.

Up to 3 P.M. today the 4.62 Rifle has been fired 155 times and the vent is much enlarged and somewhat ragged on the outside. It is not known how often it may have been fired before it came to Battery Haskell. It was fired 7 times in Redoubt No. 1.

Up to same time the 24 pndr. Rifle has been fired 87 times at Battery Haskell. It is not known how often it may have been fired previously, but probably very often as this is one of the Guns used at the Battle of Secessionville [1] and was in the Battery which was there at that time.

About 10 or 11 o'clock at night heavy firing between Battery Wagner & the advanced Yankee Batteries with occasional shots from Battery Simkins.

About 3 or 4 o'clock in the morning some heavy firing apparently from the direction of Sullivan's Island. Daylight disclosed a Steamer aground on the Bar apparently in front of the Moultrie House.

This wrecked Steamer afterwards proved to be the [Confederate] Steamer Sumter which had conveyed troops to Battery Wagner, and was returning with the troops relieved (20th S.C.V., Keitt, and some others) when taking an unusual channel & showing no lights she was fired on & sunk by Fort Moultrie.

Late this afternoon Received at Battery Haskell one 4.62 in. Rifle Siege Gun. Weight 5,750 lbs. Marked B.F. (Bellona Foundry) J.L.A. [initials of Dr. Junius L. Archer, owner of the foundry] 1862 [date when the gun was made]. Band [reinforcing band over the breech] 19 in. long x 2 in. thick. Gun & Carriage look new. Siege Carriage.

[1] See Introduction, pp. ix, x.

Monday, 31 Aug. 1863.

J.H. Lopez, Artificer of Co. "A" Siege Train, was sent into City to endeavor to procure well-seasoned Oak for Mortar beds.

Lieut. Nesbit sick. This is particularly unfortunate as he was the only officer who was available for the special service of the Rifle Guns firing on Morris Island. [Application has been made to headquarters for a detail — of one, at least — of Capt. Webb's (Company A, Siege Train) lieutenants, but no notice has been taken of it.][1]

The Companies and Detachments at Legare's Point Inspected and Mustered about 12 M. today.

[In consequence of the high wind, Lieutenant Nesbit's sickness, and the occupation of other officers in inspection and muster and other duties usual on last day of month, there was no firing from Battery Haskell to-day. These latter reasons would not be sufficient, and would not be given if it were not that it is seriously doubted whether, at 2⅝ miles' range, and with a high wind blowing, we can effect anything with our shells, which do not explode.][1]

Ninety Eight (98) 8 inch Columbiad Shells received today. Also 200 Sabots for same.

At 2:30 P.M. four Monitors moved up and engaged Fort Moultrie, Battery Bee, Battery Beauregard & Battery Gregg, all at long range except Battery Gregg. After about 1½ hours they retired, one it is thought precipitately.

Generals Taliaferro and Hagood visited Battery Haskell about 5 P.M. Col. Roman, Col. Leay [Lay] & others.

The Engineers engaged today in strengthening the Parapet of "Battery Tatum"[2] (Point of Pines).

Edward Manigault
Major Comdg. Arty.

[1] *Manigault, apparently anticipating a reprimand from his criticism of superiors, omitted the bracketed items from his journal probably knowing that he would be requested, or ordered, to delete them anyway. However, he forwarded the unexpurgated version to headquarters. [See Official Records entry for 31 Aug. 1863 in Appendix 2, p 260. See also Diary entry of 6 Sept. 1863 and note 2]*

[2] *This earthwork was named in honor of Capt. W.T. Tatom who was killed 18 July 1863 while leading a counterattack to drive Federal troops out of Battery Wagner. Manigault's spelling of the name, in most cases erroneously as "Tatum," has been followed throughout the journal. [OR XXVIII (1) pp. 373, 535, 536]*

Tuesday, 1 Sept. 1863.

Very busy making up Monthly Return, Ordnance Returns, Weekly Returns Artillery, &c. Made Report to Chief of Artillery of Bursting of 4.62 in. Gun Aug. 22. Also Report of Capt. Smith's experiment in Shelling Black Island from Point of Pines. [*See Saturday, 29 August 1863.*]

At 12:30 P.M. Genls. Ripley & Taliaferro visited Battery Haskell.

Engineer hands at 1 P.M. commenced repair of Magazine at Battery Ryan. At same time they commenced more thorough drainage of the interior of Battery Haskell.

I visited Battery Cheves to see the 8 in Navy Shell guns of 55 cwt., one of which is promised to Battery Haskell under certain contingencies. Took the Measurement of Same. Rode to Fort Johnson and saw Col. Yates, who said we could have one of the Guns [*and*] a Columbiad pattern Carriage & Chassis provided there were two of the Carriages. As there was only one, of course we could not get it.

At 7 P.M. [*Numeral 6 overstruck with 7.*] the 2nd Battalion of 25 S.C. Regt. (Eutaw) was relieved by the 54th Georgia, Lt. Col. Rawls, Comdg. The Eutaw Battalion immediately marched to Fort Johnson to embark for Morris Island.

At 11 P.M. heavy Cannonade commenced between Fort Moultrie & Batteries Bee, Beauregard & Gregg, and the Yankee Iron Clads. This firing lasted nearly all night.

Edward Manigault
Major Comdg. Arty.

Col. Way, 54th Georgia, took Command of the Post shortly after Nightfall.

Wednesday, 2 Sept. 1863.

At early dawn, 4 Monitors were seen to go off from the Neighbourhood of Fort Sumter. Some persons assert that there were six of them but this is far from certain. Their fire appears to have been principally directed against Fort Sumter.

During the Morning, and again in the afternoon, we fired with 8 in. Columbiad on Marsh Battery No. 1 whenever any body was seen about it. Fired 9 Shots.

Genl. Beauregard, Genl. Taliaferro & Genl. Hagood visited Battery Haskell about 12½ P.M.

Sent the Wagon into town to carry the Wrought Iron Work of two Mortar Beds to the Charleston Arsenal to be used in the new Mortar Beds which are being Cast for Battery Haskell.[1]

Very quiet during the night, scarcely any firing at all except occasionally from Battery Wagner.

A 10 inch S.C. [*Sea Coast*] Mortar Bed[2] brought to Battery Haskell about 8 P.M.

Edward Manigault
Major &c.

[1] *Cast-iron beds were to be fabricated to replace the pine beds which were not satisfactory. Apparently seasoned oak could not be found. [See Monday, 31 Aug. 1863]*

[2] *Entry of Friday, 4 Sept. 1863 indicates that this was one of the old pine beds.*

Thursday, 3 Sept. 1863.

At about 10 A.M. sent Carriage & Limber of 30 pndr. Parrott which burst Augt. 19 to Central Ord. Depot in Charleston, together with the Chase portion of the Exploded Gun. Lt. Col. Waddy, Chief of Ordnance, had directed the Carriage & Limber only to be carried to the City, but in pursuance of a verbal order from Genl. Beauregard given yesterday, such portion of the Gun as could be got on the Carriage was sent also. Lt. Legare, Ord. Officer, furnished the Mules & Drivers.

Moved the 4 inch Blakely Gun from Platform No. 7 in Battery Haskell to Platform No. 9. Moved 4.62 in. Rifle received Augt. 30, to Platform No. 7 but accidentally it was dismounted while being shifted from the Travelling Bed to Trunnion bed.[1] As we had not blocks, Ropes, &c. sent immediately to Lieut. Legare, Ord. Officer, requesting that a Garrison Gin should be sent down with hands to mount the Gun. The Gin arrived at Battery Haskell at 7 P.M. but no Tackle with it.

The labour of shifting Guns in Battery Haskell is very great, as the Road of communication in rear of the Platforms is cut through by open drains between each two platforms, in order to drain the Borrow pits — hence heavy skids have to be moved from drain to drain to pass the Guns over.

In the forenoon fired 10 Shots from the 8 in. Columbiad at Marsh

Battery No 1 about which some persons were to be seen. Only one of the Shots struck the Battery, though several passed near it.

Lieut. Nesbit sent into Charleston on Surgeon's Certificate as he was much prostrated by sickness. Capt. [*S. Porcher*] Smith was allowed to go with him on 4 hours leave of absence in order to accompany him to Hospital. In consequence, however, of several hours delay at the Ashley River Bridge (which is being repaired) Capt. Smith did not return to Legare's Point until 8 P.M.

As a good many of the enemy were visible in the Hill to South of Battery Wagner about 5 P.M. commenced firing from 8 in. Columbiad and 4.62 in. Rifle No. 1. Fourteen Shots were fired from the 4.62 in. Rifle & Ten from the Columbiad. Only one of the Shells from each Gun burst, and in both cases they burst Short. Four (4) of the Shells from the 4.62 in. Gun fell in the midst of the Enemy, but as they did not burst, it is not likely that much, if any, damage was done. The practice with the 8 in. Columbiad was rather wild and none of its shells were certainly seen to fall in immediate contiguity of the Enemy.

At dark ceased firing as it was impossible to place any reliance on our shells by night.

At 5 P.M. Lieutenants Brux & Mellichamp of Co. "A" Siege Train, reported for duty at Battery Haskell.

At 5 P.M. the Enemy fired three Shots from the East end of Black Island towards Battery Haskell. The Shots, from the sound of the explosion, appeared to come from a Rifle piece of small caliber, say at utmost a 30 Pndr. Parrott. All the shell appear to have broken or burst prematurely, so that none reached Battery Haskell. After three Shots the Enemy ceased firing.

Edward Manigault
Major Comdg. Arty.

P.S. Battery Haskell did not reply to the enemy's fire from Black Island as it was not annoying and a reply not deemed worthwhile.

An Unusual quiet today — Very little firing on either side.

[1] *See Glossary, Carriages, Siege.*

Friday, 4 Sept. 1863.

One of the 10 inch S.C. [*Sea Coast*] Mortars remounted but on an old pine Mortar Bed which will not probably stand many shots. The 4.62 in. Rifle which was accidentally dismounted yesterday, was also remounted.

About 1 P.M., as the enemy was seen working very assiduously on a Battery or Breastwork in front of Battery Wagner, which Battery was on a line open to direct enfilading fire from Battery Haskell, we commenced firing on them with 4.62 in. Rifle No. 1. Fired 18 Shells of which two broke to pieces or burst prematurely, three burst Short, Three or four Shots were very good and made the workmen Scatter, but those shells did not burst and the men, who must be practised hands, returned immediately to their work without one moment's delay or loss of time. About 3 Ceased firing, to let the gun Cool, and allow the Men to get their dinner.

At 5 P.M. Commenced firing from same gun (which is by far the most accurate and reliable one we have) and fired 18 shells of which three burst short and three of them exceedingly near the working parties. Several Shells also, which did not burst, fell in close proximity to the working parties. We could not at the distance see if anyone was injured (though observing by the aid of two glasses); the workmen scattered whenever a shell went near them, but instantly returned to their work as soon as the danger was past.

At 6:15 P.M. The enemy's Reliefs moved up from the neighbourhood of Graham's Hd. Qrs. They appeared so numerous that they were supposed to be intended for an Assault and fire was opened from the 8 in. Columbiad on them. Six shells were thrown at them which however did not burst. It then became evident from the number of men returning from each Battery towards the South that the body of men first seen was simply the Relief. Total No. Shots we have fired from 4.62 in. No. 1 up to this time 223.

Ceased firing at Dark.

The Marsh Battery No. 1 of which the parapet to the North was considerably damaged by the explosion of the gun in the work, has been repaired. The Muzzle of the gun which showed over the parapet, no longer appears; it is probable from appearances that the damaged Gun will be replaced by a new one.[1]

Edward Manigault

Major Comdg. Arty.

Very little firing during the night, only a few occasional Shots from Battery Cheves.

Junior 1st Lieut. S.J. Wilson reported with 2nd Section of Battery of Co. "B" S.C. Siege Train for duty at Battery Ryan.

---

[1] *Manigault's supposition was partially correct. The 8-inch Parrott rifle of the Marsh Battery was replaced by two mortars which fired on Fort Sumter, not the city. They were replaced in August 1864 by a 30-pounder Parrott which also played against Fort Sumter. [OR XXXV (1) p. 235; ibid. (2) p. 43]*

1865 photograph of Marsh Battery with 30-pounder Parrott.

Saturday, 5 Sept. 1863.

The Ironsides and two or three Monitors bombarded Battery Wagner from early dawn. The land batteries aiding slightly. This was continued until about Midday. The bombardment was very heavy. Battery Wagner returned the fire slowly until about 10 A.M.

In the afternoon the Bombardment was Continued by the Heavy Rifle Batteries near Graham's Hd. Qrs. (the Ironclads having retired). The Bombardment of the afternoon was also very heavy.[1]

About 5½ P.M. received notice from Genl. Hagood that an attack on Cummin[g]s Point was probable. All the available guns were prepared for firing upon Morris Island in case of an assault.

Seven Shots were fired in afternoon from 4.62 Rifle No. 1. Some of the shots were good but only one Shell burst. (Total 230 Shots).

Six shots were fired from Smooth Bore 24 pndr. at Second Battery in front of Graham's Hd. Qrs. One of the Shots struck very near the Battery. 2½ Miles.

In preparing the 4.62 Rifle No. 2 for firing at Sunset a Gunners Gimlet was accidentally broken off in the vent, thus for a time spiking the piece.

After night a Monitor took up a position to N.E. of Battery Gregg occasionally firing and being fired on by Battery G. [*Gregg*]. The Yankee land Batteries shelled Wagner and the Sand Hills between Wagner & Gregg.

Edward Manigault
Major Comdg. Arty.

Capt. Mickler preparing for some scouting Expedition.

During the attack on Cummin[g]s Point,[2] the 4.62 in. No. 1 fired 11 times — 241 Shots. The 24 Pndr. Rifle fired 7 Shots (94 in all). 24 Pndr. Smooth, 13 Shots. 8 in. Col. 14 Shots.

[1] *This bombardment was particularly destructive to Battery Wagner. The Federal siege trenches were within a few yards of the fortification and almost continuous bombardment prevented the garrison from making necessary repairs. The commanding officer notified headquarters early 6 Sept.: "The parapet of salient is badly breached. The whole fort is much weakened. A repetition to-morrow of to-day's fire [aliuding to 5 Sept.] will make the work almost a ruin. The mortar fire is still very heavy and fatal, and no important work can be done. Is it desirable to sacrifice the garrison? To continue to hold it is to do so...." The casualties at Battery Wagner on 5 Sept. were 100 out of 900 in the garrison. [OR XXVIII (1) pp. 87-89]*

[2] *See 6 Sept. 1863, Note No. 1*

Sunday, 6 Sept. 1863.

At 1 o'clock A.M. precisely, being about one hour after moonrise, the Yankees attacked Cummin[g]s Point in Barges.[1] A heavy fire from the Boat Howitzers, and a sharp musketry fire opened the attack. Battery Gregg does not appear to have fired her heavy Guns at all.

The Yankee land batteries immediately commenced to shell heavily both Wagner and the portion of the island between Wagner and Gregg.

The James Island batteries immediately directed their fire on different portions of Morris Island.

One 8 in. Columbiad, one 24 Pounder Rifled, on 24 pndr. Smooth, one 4.62 inch Rifle at Battery Haskell directed their fire towards the Calcium light visible on one of the Mortar Batteries nearly a half mile South of Battery Wagner (from ⅓ to ½ mile.) One 10 inch Mortar fired towards a Battery still nearer Graham's Hd. Qrs. After 20 or 30 minutes, the attack on Cummin[g]s Point appears to have been repulsed. The fire on both sides gradually subsided. At 3½ A.M. dismissed the men from their guns. The 8 in. Columbiad was fired 14 times, the 10 in. Mortar 11 times, the 24 pndr. Rifled 7 Shots, 4.62 inch Rifle 7 Shots, the 24 pndr. Smooth Bore 13 Shots.

The enemy fired steadily after this and only occasional shots were fired from our Batteries.

At Day dawn the Monitors & Land batteries commenced heavy Bombardment on Battery Wagner.

I sent to Hd. Qrs. the following papers: (1) Weekly Return Ordnance at Battery Haskell (Waddy) [i.e., sent to Lt. Col. J.R. Waddy]. (2) Weekly Return do at Redoubt No. 1 (Waddy). (3) Return Small Arms, Accoutrements & Ammunition at Battery Haskell & Redoubt No. 1 (Cunningham). (4) Requisition for Mechanic to drill vent of 4.62 Gun No. 2. Also friction tubes, 1,000. ([1st Lt. W.W.] Legare & Cunningham). (5) Also Capt. Webb's Return Lt. [Light] Artillery to Col. Gonzales. (6) Also note to Capt. W.T. Taliaferro about an objectionable portion of My Diary at 31st ult.[2]

About 12 M. a Barbette Carriage & Chassis for a double-banded 24 Pndr. Rifle arrived at Battery Haskell. It would have been much better if the Carriage & Chassis were intended for being traversed on a full circle. If so, and the Gun were placed in the left platform of South Face of Battery Haskell, it could bear on all parts of Morris Island, and also on Black Island and the Creeks & Marshes clear round to Secessionville. With the present Carriage & Chassis, the Gun will be able to bear on only one of these islands and be useless for the other.

At 3½ P.M. a double-banded 24 pndr. was brought to Battery Haskell. Inner Band 31 in. long x 1⅝ in. thick; outer Band 25¾ in. x 1¾ in.

Also about dark 54 Solid Conical Shot 14½ in. long weighing 80 lbs. each and 15 inches long, which were said to be intended for the above described gun. The weight of these shot is entirely too great (= 3½ times Round Shot).

At 7 P.M. received notice that Morris Island would be evacuated to-night, with orders to have all available guns ready to Check the advance of the Yankees upon our retreating troops. The guns were accordingly prepared as directed, and the Detachments at their pieces — Until 12 O'clock nothing indicated an intention to evacuate.

Edward Manigault
Major Comdg. Arty.

Note. The 4.62 inch Rifle No. 1 has been fired by us 241 times up to 3½ A.M. Sept. 6, 1863.

P.S. It is said that Battery Wagner was evacuated about 11 O'clock.[3]

[1] *Gen. Beauregard, in his report of the attack on Cummings Point, differed slightly on the time. He said: "... About 1.30 o'clock the morning of the 6th, they [the enemy] were seen approaching in from fifteen to twenty barges by the passages leading from Vincent's and Schooner Creeks [Vincent's Creek no longer exists] that lie between James and Morris Islands. The garrison at Cummings Point [Battery Gregg] was on the alert and received them with a brisk fire of grape and musketry. The enemy was evidently greatly disconcerted, and, after discharging their boat howitzers, retired." [OR XXVIII (1) p. 88]*

[2] *The note to Capt. Taliaferro has not been found. However, see Diary entry of 31 Aug. 1863 for probable explanation.*

[3] *By 6 Sept. 1863, Federal siege lines were within a few yards of Battery Wagner and the Confederates realized that to remain longer would mean a needless sacrifice of the garrison. The evacuation was conducted smoothly under heavy enemy fire between 9 p.m. 6 Sept. and 1:30 a.m. of the 7th. The wounded were removed first. Then the garrisons of Wagner and Battery Gregg, located about half a mile away on the north end of Morris Island, marched to waiting boats. A small rear guard in each fort kept up a semblance of defence by firing from different locations along the parapets. The cannon were spiked insofar as the worn vents would allow. Fuses were laid to the magazine in each fort. Then, after all officers of the rear guards had observed that the fuses were burning, the forts were abandoned. However, either the fuses were defective, as Beauregard surmised in his report, or were cut by enemy fire. In any case, the magazines failed to explode and the forts were occupied within a few hours by the Federals. During the folllowing weeks, both fortifications were repaired, strengthened and renamed. Battery Wagner was called Fort Strong, in honor of Brig. Gen. George C. Strong, and Gregg became Fort Putnam, for Col. Haldimand S. Putnam. Both officers were killed in the 18 July 1863 assault on Battery Wagner. [OR XXVIII (1) pp. 16, 90-93, 104-107; OR 53, pp. 5-8, 94]*

Monday, 7 Sept. 1863.

About 2 A.M. or 2½ A.M. the Yankees appeared to have become aware that some unusual movement was going on for they ceased throwing Shell into Wagner, and commenced Shelling the ground between Wagner & Gregg tolerably vigorously.

At 3 A.M. three Rockets were thrown up in the direction of Shell Point, which was the signal previously decided on for opening fire upon the Sites of Batteries Wagner & Gregg (for it had been intended to blow them up). As the expected destruction of the Works had not taken place, and as Col. Yates, so much nearer the scene of operations, [*Yates was at Fort Johnson*] did not open fire, I for some minutes hesitated to fire. Under Gen. Taliaferro's direction (who spent the night from about 10 o'clock to 3½ o'clock in the Morning at Battery Haskell) I dispatched a Courier to Col. Yates to inquire if any change had been made in the Signals previously decided on. In the mean time commenced firing slowly upon Morris Island to South of Wagner, and gradually (as Col. Yates' reply did not arrive) upon Battery Wagner itself. Fired until daylight and then ceased.

2nd Battalion of the 25th S.C.V. from Battery Wagner arrived at their Camp at Legare's about day break. They have been on duty at Battery Wagner since Tuesday Night, Sept. 1, or rather some Companies of the Battalion went over that night, and the rest the next night.

Batteries Simkins & Cheves firing on Gregg & Wagner and the intervening space during the day. The enemy did not return the fire. Battery Haskell did not fire until about 5 P.M. and then only a few Shots.

The Engineer Hands engaged in constructing a Covered Way from the Mortar Battery on Right Flank of Battery Haskell to the Covered Way already constructed on North of Road to Point.

At 6:15 P.M. the Ironsides and five Monitors entered the Harbor and had an engagement with Fort Moultrie and Batteries Bee & Beauregard. This lasted from ¾ of an hour to 1 hour. The firing was at long Range. Shortly after 7 P.M. the Ironclads retired.

Genl. Hagood visited Battery Haskell at Night fall and gave directions for increased vigilance, &c. Afterwards he visited Battery Ryan.

The Shots fired from Battery Haskell on Morris Island from 3:15 A.M. till day-break were as follows: 10 in. Mortar 8 Shots. Columbiad 4. 24 Pounder Smooth 7 Shots. 24 pndr. Rifled 4. 4.62 in. 4. Total 27 Shots.

Edward Manigault

Major Comdg. Arty.

Total No. of Shots from 4.62 in. Rifle No. 1 up to day light Sept. 7, 245.

66 8 in. Col. [*columbiad*] Shell, Strapped & filled, 300 Friction tubes, received from Lieut. Legare at 5 P.M.

Frame work for Platform & Pintle Block for Barbette Carriage recd. about 5 P.M.

Tuesday, 8 Sept. 1863.

At 9 A.M. a heavy explosion occurred at Fort Moultrie. Many Shells were heard to explode one after another. Shortly after a heavy volume of Smoke was seen to issue from one of the Monitors lying at Cummin[*g*]s Point, which is supposed to have been aground since yesterday afternoon.[1]

About 10 A.M. three Monitors advanced toward Fort Moultrie in line of Battle, and the Ironsides took up position near Cummin[*g*]s Point while one or two other Monitors lay back near Morris Island S.E. of Battery Gregg. Fort Moultrie, Batteries Bee and Beauregard opened fire on them, and a cannonade commenced which lasted until after 1 P.M. One of the Monitors had her Smoke Stack knocked quite away. What other damage was inflicted upon the Monitors or Ironsides is not known. The Ironsides maintained a heavy fire from the Channel in line with Battery Gregg. Her distance from Fort Moultrie must have been at least 1,800 to 2,000 yds. One or two of the Monitors advanced pretty near Fort Moultrie which allowed one especially to come near her and then opened at once from many of her guns. The Monitor immediately moved off. All the iron Clads retired about 2 P.M. except the Monitor supposed to be aground at Cummin[g]s Point. Batteries Bee & Beauregard & Moultrie fired many Shot at her while in this position.

Captain Gregorie set the Engineer hands to work to make [a] Platform for the double-banded 24 pndr. Rifle Gun Chamber No. 1. Also heaped More earth upon the Gun Magazine. As Captn. Gregorie consulted me about the position & direction of fire of this Gun, I told him that its position was intended to be on Siege Platform No. 1 and the field of Fire from Battery Wagner round to Black Island & as far West as possible. I told him that it was intended to have Gun Chambers Nos. 2, 3, & 4 as they are, viz — Embrazured for Siege Guns with Field of fire from Wagner Southwards to include Marsh Battery No. 2. No. 5 Embrazured for Field guns to look up Creek towards Black Island. No 6 to remain for Field gun Embrazured Eastwards to sweep the Creek. No. 7 (double platform) to remain as it is to fire either way. No. 8 to be prepared for 8 in. Navy Gun Mounted on Columbiad Carriage, full circle. No. 9 Platform widened by order of Gen. Beauregard; no other change. No. 10 Platform raised and Embrazured for Black Island. No. 11 Left as it is (Genl. Beauregard). Supplementary Platforms for Field Guns between Nos. 9 & 10, and 10 & 11 I did not think it worth while altering. This will give 10 guns directed towards Morris Island from Wagner round to Marsh Battery No. 2 (one of them however is a field piece for Sweeping the Creek) and 7 guns for Black Island and Marshes West. It must not be supposed that there are seventeen guns, but Nos. 1, 7, 8, 9 & 11 fire either way, and therefore Count twice. The No. will be 12 when all the Chambers are filled, including the 8 in. Columbiad. Or thirteen if an additional gun is put on the Platform to extreme N. East extremity of Battery.

It was also agreed that the Traverses between Nos. 1 & 2, 2 & 3, 3 & 4, should be altered to a direction at Right Angles with face, so as to provide against an enfilading fire from Battery Gregg.

No Platforms as yet at Battery Tatum or Battery Ryan. Two 8 in. Siege Howitzers in position at Tatum and 1 12 pndr. Rifle Bronze Field gun — Two 8 in. Siege Howitzers at Battery Ryan — of which the Parapet is cut down about 9 inches or a foot by order of Genl. Hagood last night.

The Monitor which appeared to be aground at Cummin[g]s' Point got off at the top of the tide (about 4 P.M.)

Shots were fired from 4.62 in. Gun No. 2 at one of the Batteries to North of Graham's Hd. Qrs. This was partly for trial as the range of the Gun has not yet been satisfactorily determined. 5 Shells fired.

Edward Manigault
Major Comdg. Arty.

Several Houses on Sullivans Island were destroyed by fire today in the Neighbourhood of Fort Moultrie. Supposed to be set on fire by the

Shells from the Monitors. The conflagration still continued at Nightfall.

P.S. I have to complain of the character of the Rifle projectiles lately furnished me. As for instance, Solid Conical Shot for 4.62 in. Gun, weighing 40 lbs. = 3½ times the weight of Spherical projectiles of same calibre. Shell for 24 pndr. Rifle (5.82 in. Cal.) weighing 60 lbs. = 2½ times weight of solid spherical shot of same Calibre. Solid Conical Shot of 80 lbs weight = 3½ times weight of solid Spherical shot of Same diameter. And this last for a gun not originally intended as a Rifle, but simply converted by Rifling & Banding. Not only will the guns be enormously strained by these projectiles fired at high Elevations and soon burst, but also, with smaller charges than 10 lbs. & 5 lbs. of powder, respectively for the 5.82 in. & 4.62 in. Calibres, the Range will not be great. If great penetration were required at distances of from half a mile to 1 mile then these heavy solid shot might be suitable, but They are entirely unsuitable for a Range of 2½ miles, which is required for Morris Island (at least without increasing the Charge of Powder to an extent extremely dangerous with any guns we have.)

Fired 6 Shots with 4.62 in. Rifle No. 1 at Battery to Right of Battery Wagner. 1st Shot 15° 20 sec. Fuze, fell Short. 2nd Shot 15° 20 Sec., fell short. 3rd Shot 15½°, not seen. 4th Shot 15½° 20 Sec. Not Seen. 5th do 16½ deg. not seen. 6th 16 deg. not seen. [*Total*] 6 Shots.

[1] *The monitor Weehawken went aground while buoying the narrow channel off the north end of Morris Island. As the tide dropped, exposing her hull beneath the armored overhang, Fort Moultrie and other batteries opened a slow fire upon her. This brought the New Ironsides and five other monitors to her assistance, precipitating a hot engagement, primarily with Fort Moultrie. Although aground, the Weehawken got off several shots, one of which, a 15-inch shell, glanced off the muzzle of an 8-inch columbiad in Fort Moultrie and burst amid some shell boxes which were thought to be safely protected by a traverse. The resulting explosion killed 15 men and wounded another 12. After some five hours, the fleet broke off action and retired. With rising tide in the afternoon, the Weehawken, despite several hits on her hull, was refloated and retired to her anchorage. [OR XXVIII (1) pp. 712-723; ONR 14, pp. 549-551]*

Wednesday, 9 Sept. 1863.

At about 1:30 A.M. heavy firing heard in the direction of Fort Sumter. The principal firing of heavy guns appeared to be from Fort Moultrie and Battery Simkins. The report of Small Arms heard from the direction of Fort Sumter.[1] Battery Cheves also firing on Morris Island.

The Artillery officers at Batteries Haskell, Tatum, Ryan & Redoubt No. 1 immediately notified to hold their commands in readiness. Battery Haskell did not fire upon Morris Island, although every thing was in readiness to do so, as the nature of the attack made in the harbor was not understood.

After daylight two or three deserted barges seen between Fort Sumter and Cummin[g]s Point.

The Enemy perfectly quiet to day, and their Iron Clads made no attempt to enter the harbor. Batteries Simkins & Cheves firing slowly

& Steadily upon Morris Island.

About 3 P.M. the Enemy sent a Flag of truce on a small steamer. She was stopped by Fort Moultrie before entering the Harbor. It is thought here that we communicated with her by means of a small rowing boat or Barge.

[1] *Following evacuation of Morris Island, 7 Sept. 1863, Adm. John A. Dahlgren, commander of the blockading fleet, was convinced that Fort Sumter was now untenable, He assumed the Confederates had sense enough to know it and would have reduced the garrison accordingly. He launched a night attack of some 400 men in small boats against the mass of bricks and rubble into which the fort had been pounded by weeks of Federal bombardment. Unfortunately for Dahlgren's men, their admiral was mistaken. The fort had been systematically stripped of cannon and artillerymen. It now was manned by seasoned infantry who were thoroughly alert to the possibility of attack. When the first boats landed, the rubble blazed with small arms fire. Prearranged signals soon brought protective artillery fire from Fort Moultrie and other Confederate batteries against the base of Fort Sumter. The men who had landed huddled amid the rocks. Those still in the boats made a hasty retreat. The Confederates said they inflicted 21 casualties and captured 106 prisoners. Dahlgren admitted three dead and 114 captured. In addition, the Confederates picked up five boats and five stands of colors. Only 104 Southerners were engaged and they had a field day — not a single man was injured. [OR XXVIII (1), pp. 125, 126, 724-728; ONR 14, pp. 606-640]*

Thursday, 10 Sept. 1863.

At 1 A.M. our Picket Boat Stationed at the junction of Legare's Creek with Schooner Creek returned to Battery Haskell and reported that boats were advancing. The cannoneers immediately took post at their Guns (They had been sleeping in the Gun Chambers.) The infantry support took post in line behind the parapet. A re-inforcement of 100 infantry was sent immediately to Battery Haskell by Col. Way of 54th Georgia.

The Artillerists of Batteries Tatum, Ryan & Redoubt No. 1 were also in readiness at their Guns, and measures taken to throw in strong Infantry support at the first sign of danger.

The Enemy, however, did not show himself.

At 7:30 A.M. left Legare's for the City to attend a Meeting of a Board of Survey, ordered to report upon the quality and condition of the Fuzes furnished to troops in this Department, &c.

At 11 O'Clock the Board met at the Mills' House [1] and adjourned thence to the Arsenal [2] where they tried a great variety of Fuzes. They remained at the Arsenal until 3 P.M. when they adjourned.

I left the City about 6:10 P.M. and arrived at Legare's about 8:30 P.M.

Nothing worthy of note is said to have occurred at Batteries Haskell, Tatum, Ryan or Redoubt No. 1 during the day.

Capt. [*S. Porcher*] Smith tried several of his Spherical case over the water toward Black Island. He was Much pleased with the apparent effectiveness of his projectiles for firing upon an expedition in [*"The Field" is crossed out and the following inserted:*] boats or barges.

Lieutenants Brux and Mellichamp also tried the effect of Grape from their pieces. They were very much pleased with the Results.

Edward Manigault
Major Comdg. Arty.

24 Pndr. Smooth 1 discharge of Grape ¾° Depression.
4 in Blakely 1 discharge of Grape 1° Elevation.
Capt. Smith fired 9 Spherical Case.

1	2 Sec. Fuze	4° Elev.	Struck water. Ricochetted twice & burst.
2	do do	do	Burst 15 ft. in air.
3	3 Sec.	6°	Burst about 20 ft. in air app. 50 yds. in advance of 2 Sec. Shell.
4	3½ Sec.	6°	Burst about 10 ft. in air app. 50 yds. in advance of 2 Sec. Shell.
5	4 Sec.	7°	Burst about 10 ft. in air. Distance could not well be estimated.
6	4 Sec.	7°	Burst as before.
7	5 Sec.	9°	Burst 30 ft. high.
8	5 Sec.	8½°	Burst 20 ft. high.
9	5 Sec.	8°	Burst 10 ft. up.

[1] *The Mills House was an excellent hotel of the day. The building was demolished in 1968 and replaced by a modernized reproduction which operates today as a hotel under the same name.*

[2] *The U.S. Arsenal was taken over by South Carolina troops in 1860. Following the war, it became a boys' school. The site is occupied today by the Medical University of South Carolina.*

Friday, 11 Sept. 1863.

Nothing worthy of note during the Morning. Battery Simkins the only work on our side firing upon the Enemy. The Enemy not replying at all.

At 5:30 P.M. commenced to try the Ranges of the 8 in. Navy Gun at Redoubt No. 1.

1st Shot	8 lbs. Powder.	Shell.	5° Elev.	4 Sec. Fuze.	Burst high & Short at first Marsh.
2nd "	"	"	" 5° "	5 " "	Burst at proper height beyond Marsh.
3rd "	"	"	" 7° "	7 " "	Did not burst.
4th "	"	"	" 10° "	10 " "	Did not burst. Fell short of Black Island. Say ¼ or ⅓ mile.
5th "	"	"	" 10° "	10 " "	Burst Well and at Cor. Hgt. Fell Short Black [Island] ¼ to ⅓ mile.

As the Redoubt is open to the view of the vessels in Light House Inlet, the enemy of course witnessed this firing, and one of his Steamers opened upon the Redoubt with a Rifle Gun. Five Shells were fired at the Redoubt, one of which broke to pieces prematurely and the other four fell in the neighbourhood of the Redoubt. We had no means of replying to their fire not having any gun of Sufficient range (2½ to 2¾ miles).

Gun Chamber No. 1, Battery Haskell, was this afternoon finished and ready for Mounting the 24 Pndr. Banded Rifle. Traverses No. 2 & 3 (from Left) Completed as altered in new direction (at Right Angles with face of work). Gun Chamber No. 5, Another Embrazure for Field Piece, was opened to the South so as to Sweep the Creek in that direction. The Embrazure looking Eastwards was purposely left open.

Edward Manigault
Major Comdg. Arty.

Saturday, 12 Sept. 1863.

Attempted to Mount the double Banded Rifle 24 Pounder in Gun . Chamber No. 1 at Battery Haskell, but were unable to do so in consequence of the deranged condition of the Gin furnished us. Sent a request to Lieut Legare, Ord. Officer at Dill's Bluff to have the Gun Mounted. In the mean time Set the Artificer of Co. "A" S.C. Siege [Train] to work to repair the defects of the Gin.

Nothing further worthy of note occurred.

Edward Manigault
Major Comdg. Arty.

Sunday, 13 Sept. 1863.

The Garrison Gin adjusted, and double-banded 24 Pounder Mounted in Gun Chamber No. 1. The Carriage admits of about 17° Elevation. No Sights have been furnished.

Lt. Legare, Ord. Off., came to these Hd Qrs. and requested that I would have one of the 24 pounder unbanded Rifles hauled to the Charleston Arsenal to be banded in pursuance of order from Gen. Beauregard to that effect. He stated that it was almost impossible for him to do it. I agreed to have it hauled tomorrow as it was then too late to do so.

Sent to Hd. Qrs. "Weekly Reports" of Ordnance and Ammunition. Also requisition for Blank forms for said Returns. Also forwarded, but too late to be acted on to day, Requisition for Cartridges for Small Arms of Detachments of heavy Arty doing duty at Battery Haskell & Redoubt No. 1. Also Requisition for Ammunition for 8 in. Howitzers of Co. "B" Siege Train.

Edward Manigault
Major Comdg. Arty.

The 2nd Battalion of the 25th (Eutaw) S.C. Regt. was relieved from duty at this post and marched about 4½ P.M. to Hd. Qrs. of Regt. near Freer's house.

The 19th Georgia took their places as an Infantry support to the Batteries. Captain Mordecai, A.Q.M. [*Acting Quartermaster*] of the Battalion, was thrown out of his Wagon and had a Rib broken besides other injury.

Monday, 14 Sept. 1863.

Sent a Communication to Col. Gonzales about the 24 Pounder Rifle ordered to be sent to Charleston Arsenal 6 h. 5 m. A.M. (Note, This letter was written last night, but as Col. Way and his Adjutant were asleep, who I wished to forward it, I deferred sending it till this Morning.)

At 8 A.M. Captain [*S. Porcher*] Smith's Drivers & Mules went down to Battery Haskell for the 24 Pndr. Rifle to be carried to the Charleston Arsenal to be banded. The gun was put into travelling bed and started for the City.

At a quarter to 10 A.M. Courier brought a letter from Col. Gonzales suspending the order. As the gun was already on its way to the City, it was not stopped.

At 3½ P.M. a large Working party of the enemy Could plainly be seen at work on a Battery or Covered Way on Black Island (about the Center of Island where the woods are most open). At 4½ P.M. Commenced firing on this working party from 8 in S.C. [*Sea Coast*] Howitzer at Battery Haskell and from 8 in. Siege Howitzer at Battery Tatum. Fired 8 Shots with S.C. [*Sea Coast*] Howitzer and five Shots with Siege Howitzer.

8 in. S.C. [*Sea Coast*] Howitzer:

1st Shot	8 lb. Cartridge	10° Elev.	10 Sec. Fuze	Dist. 1¼ Miles	Premature Explosion. Shell broke to pieces.
2nd "	8 " "	10° "	10 "	" " "	" " "
3rd "	6 lb. Cartridge	10° "	10 "	" " "	Fell short & Exploded in Marsh.
4th "	6 " "	12° "	10 "	" " "	Exploded short & high.
5th "	6 " "	11° "	10 "	" " "	Fell short. Did not explode
6th "	6 " "	12° "	10 "	" " "	Exploded high & Short.
7th "	6 " "	12° "	14 "	" " "	Exploded in Woods on Black Island.
8th "	6 " "	12° "	14 "	" " "	Not positive whether it exploded in the Woods or beyond them.

Ceased firing at Dark.
8 in. Siege Howitzer:

1st Shot	4 lbs.	15° Elev.	12 Sec.	Appeared to fall on Island to Left [of] Working Party.
2nd "	"	"	"	Appeared to fall to Right of Working Party.
3rd "	"	"	"	Exploded in air Short & High.
4th "	"	"	13 "	Did not explode & did not see it.
5th "	"	"	12 "	Fell Short. Did not explode.
6th "	"	"	"	Did not see where it went.

The Working Party was Considerably annoyed by the Shelling and appeared to do but little work after the Shelling Commenced.

Edward Manigault

Major Comdg. Arty.

Capt. Mordecai, who [was] hurt with accident yesterday, went into City this afternoon to put himself in hands of a Surgeon.

Tuesday, 15 Sept. 1863.

Adjutant Gardner went into City on Ordnance and other business. As a few men could still be seen at work on Black Island, commenced firing on them with 8 in S.C. [Sea Coast] Howitzer. The Range of the Shells was good enough but very few of them exploded.

At 11:05 A.M. the Magazine at Battery Cheves blew up, killing 1 Lieutenant & four Men and wounding two others. The accident is supposed to have originated from the explosion of a Shell from which the Sergeant of the Magazine was extracting a fuze in order to substitute a longer one for it. The Magazine was completely destroyed. None of the Guns injured or dismounted.

At 5 P.M. commenced trying Range for Black Island of 10 in. S.C. [Sea Coast] Mortar. Fired 6 Shots. Distance 1⅜ to 1½ miles.

1st Shot	4 lbs. Powder.		16.7 Sec. [Fuse].		Shell burst high in air.
2nd "	4 "	"	20.9 "	"	Fell short & burst in Marsh.
3rd "	4½ "	"	20.9 "	"	Fell to Right & Short. Burst in Marsh.
4th "	5 "	"	20.9 "	"	As well as could be judged, tolerably well but [a] little Short.
5th "	5¼ "	"	21.66 "	"	To Right but apparently at proper distance.
6th "	5¼ "	"	22.02 "	"	Fell to Right, good Range & Height.

Fired with 8 in. S.C. [Sea Coast] Howitzer 10 shots in forenoon and

Seven in afternoon. Total 17 in all at the working party on Black Island. Not more than 6 or 7 Shells exploded. The Elevation of 11° gave the best ranges. Many of the shells fell in and around the work or Covered Way fired at, but as few of them exploded, but little damage could have been done. The enemy, however, threw bushes in front of the work in order to prevent our seeing if any men were there or not from which we judged that we were annoying them.

Fired also 4 Shell with the 4 in. Blakely Gun. The results were unsatisfactory. The projectiles flew very wildly. Elevations 13°, 14°, 15° & 16½°.

Edward Manigault
Major Comdg. Arty. &c.

Lt. Nesbit returned from Charleston this Morning from Sick furlough.

Wednesday, 16 Sept. 1863

Iron 10 in. S.C. [*Sea Coast*] Mortar bed delivered at Battery Haskell this morning.[1]

The following Ammunition delivered at Battery Haskell by Lieut. Legare — 7 boxes (173) 8 in. Naval Gun Cartridges, 8 lbs. [*each*].

24 8 in. Solid Shot.

35 8 in. Shell.

58 Boxes = 166 5.82 in. Rifle Shot, 45 lbs. wgt. Tennessee Cup. (first we have received of this kind.)[2]

4 Boxes = 16 4.62 in. Rifle Shot, 19 lbs. wgt. Tennessee Cup.

2 Boxes = 96 4 in. Blakely Shell, filled.

The Garrison Gin sent for by Capt. Hill, Ord. Off. Fort Johnson, to replace one which had been disabled by one of the enemy's Shells.

Much Rain during the day. No force visible on Black Island, though one or two individuals were seen there in the course of the day. No firing from Battery Haskell.

Genl. Hagood visited Battery Haskell at Night fall.

Lieut. Mellichamp Sick. Lieut. Nesbit, who reported for duty this Morning, occupied his place at the Battery.

Edward Manigault
Major Comdg. Arty. &c.

[1] *This was one of the new, iron mortar beds. See Diary entry, Wednesday, 2 Sept. 1863.*

[2] *The Tennessee cup, or sabot, also was known as a Mullane. It was designed to diminish the escape of gases and impart a rotary motion to a rifle projectile during firing, similar in effect, if not appearance, to the rotating band of later artillery projectiles. The device consisted of a shallow copper cup, up to about half-an-inch thick. It was attached to the base of a projectile by a heavy, centrally located screw and had three projecting studs which mated with holes cast in the base of the projectile. When the round was fired, the outer edges of the soft copper cup were squeezed into the rifling of the barrel. The studs prevented the cup from turning without rotating the projectile.*

Thursday, 17 Sept. 1863

An Equinoctial blow commenced during the night from the East & S.E. accompanied by heavy showers of rain.

Wind continued heavy all day. Heavy Showers of Rain. Had the ditches in the interior of Battery Haskell opened so as to drain off the water. All other Work suspended.

The Ironsides and four Monitors lay all day in the Channel off Morris Island nearly abreast of Graham's Hd. Qrs. They appeared to have very little Motion. The wooden vessels were rolling & pitching heavily.

About 10 P.M. the Sentinel at Col. Way's Hd. Qrs. reported small arms firing in the direction of Battery Ryan. This proved to be a false alarm.

Edward Manigault
Major Comdg. Arty.

Capt. Johnson, Co. "C" Ga. Siege Train, got permission to occupy Mellichamp's house with his Company. He went there about Midday.

Friday, 18 Sept. 1863

Fine clear day. At 9½ A.M. the working party of the enemy being seen on Black Island, commenced firing 8 in. S.C. [*Sea Coast*] Howitzer on them. Slowly & Steadily Fourteen Shells were fired of which only one burst. The Ranges of many of the shells was, however, very good. Elev. 11°, Fuze 14 Sec. for 10 Shots, 12 Seconds for 4 Shots.

At 11 A.M. commenced firing slowly & Steadily upon Black Island with 10 in. S.C. [*Sea Coast*] Mortar. Fired 19 shells of which four or five fell admirably on the Island and burst effectively, but owing to the excessive wetting of the last two days, the Mortar Fuzes generally did not prove as reliable as usual. Charge of powder 5¼ & 5⅜ lbs. Fuzes 21.3 Sec, 21.6 Sec, 22.02 Sec, 22.4 Sec, 22.8 Sec, 23.9 Sec. The irregularity of the burning of the Fuzes did not permit us to decide positively upon the proper length of Fuze.

At 1 O'Clock commenced firing 4.62 inch Rifle No. 2 with Solid Shot upon Black Island. Fired four Shots with excellent Range.

About 2½ P.M. Genl. Taliaferro came to Battery Haskell and remained for an hour and a half. By his direction we opened fire from the 8 inch Columbiad & 4.62 in. Rifle No. 1 upon Working parties in Battery Wagner who were plainly visible to us. The practice of the 8 inch columbiad was rather wild, but the Shell from the 4.62 Rifle always made the men constituting the working party leave their work and shelter themselves, tho' for some reason or other the Shells, with the usual elevations, passed over. The usual Elevation for firing upon any object in the immediate vicinity of Battery Wagner has been, with 4.62 in. Rifle No. 1, 13½°, but today 12° and even in one instance 11° appeared to be sufficient Elevation — Note, Clear atmosphere & Westerly wind.

At the 12th Shot and at 5 H. 10 M. P.M. the 8 inch Columbiad burst, Mortally wounding Private Wade Mills of Co. "K" 2nd Regt. S.C. Arty. and breaking the Right leg (about 6 in. above the Ancle) of Private Oliver Berry of the same Company & Regiment. Private Mills' Right thigh was completely severed about 6 inches below the hip, and his left leg broken about 5 inches above the ancle. He was terribly Mangled and died about 8 O'Clock. He was from Edgefield Dist[rict] S.C. and his family is said now to be in Graniteville [S.C.]. Private Berry was sent to the City in an ambulance after his leg was set. He also is from Edgefield.

The Columbiad was fired with 10 lbs. of powder, a solid Shot, and at an elevation of 19½ degrees when it burst. The Cartridge & Shot were reported as being "home." [i.e., both rammed firmly against the bottom of the barrel.] At the previous discharge, the Shell had burst about 20 or 30 feet in front of the Gun. From a point 2 ft. in front of the center of the Trunnions, the Chase remains perfect. The Body & Breech of the gun is separated into two equal portions, the plane of Fracture being vertical and directly through the vent & axis of the Bore. One of these pieces was thrown over a house 10 ft. high and fell to the Right at a distance of 75 ft. from the Chassis. The other half was thrown to the left crushing the leg of Private Mills against the Stump of a Cedar Tree and fell at a distance of 30 ft. from the Chassis. The Gun Carriage was destroyed; the Chassis uninjured.

This gun has been fired by us about 393 Times, with average elevation of 20°. The Charge usually 10 lbs. of Powder and a Columbiad Shell (50 lbs). But occasionally 8 lb. charges were used with an Encreased Elevation of about 2 degrees. Also some 8 in. Solid Shot have been fired. The Bore appeared to be as perfect as possible, with the exception of a very slight hollow or "lodgement" a little in front (5 in.) of the Chamber (1/32 in. deep, say) and a slight "score" in the Chase part of the Bore. The vent was somewhat enlarged and irregular but to no great extent.

I have been informed by a well instructed Ordnance Officer of great experience (Captain, now Genl. Boggs) that the Guns of 1855 & 1856 had generally proved not to be guns of much endurance.

The Marks upon the Gun were as follows:

Right Trunnion marked R.P.P. [stamped above] W.P.F. Left Trunnion, 1855. On Breech, 9206. On Muzzle [face], No. 80 [at top] B.H. [at bottom]. Near the Trunnion "Sight Mass," U.S.[1]

About 1 O'clock today Col. Charles C. Jones experimented upon the Ranges of Breech loading Cannon of about 3½ in. Cal., the invention of Dr. Foote.[2] The firing took place from Redoubt No. 1 and the Shells were directed towards the Enemy's shipping in Light House Inlet. The result of his Experiments is not known.

Edward Manigault
Major &c.

The Col[*umbiad*] fired 12 times — 393 Shots in all. 4.62 in. No. 1 fired 9 times — 254 Shots in all. 4.62 No. 2, 4 times — 9 Shots in all. 8 in. S.C. [*Sea Coast*] Howitzer, 14 Shots. The 10 in. S.C. [*Sea Coast*] Mortar, 19 Shots.

At 4 P.M. this afternoon, Sept. 18, Captain Webb reported at Battery Haskell with his Company "A" S.C. Siege Train — He having just been relieved from duty at the "Battery on Stono below Dills." [*Battery Leroy*] Seventeen of his men, however, are still at Battery Pringle. Detachment of Capt. Johnson's Co. hitherto at Battery on Stono reported at Section 2.

[1] *Typical markings on a cannon of that day. R.P.P., initials of Robert Parker Parrott, proprietor of the West Point Foundry (W.P.F.), West Point, N.Y. 1855 was the date the tube was manufactured; 9206, the weight in pounds; No. 80, the gun number; B.H., the initials of Benjamin Huger, the officer who inspected it for the Army; and U.S., denoting ownership by the United States. [Ripley, pp. 245, 246, 356-365]*

[2] *No information has been found on Dr. Foote or his weapon.*

Saturday, 19 Sept. 1863

As a party of Engineer hands were engaged in thickening our parapets at Battery Haskell &c. we did not fire early. But about 11 A.M. as a large number of Yankees could be seen in Battery Wagner, Commenced firing upon them with 4.62 in. Rifle No. 1. Fired 7 Shots with good effect when the rear Band of the piece showed symptoms of Starting from the one in front of it and the black, semi-liquid unctuous residuum from inflamed gunpowder oozed out from between the bands. Ceased firing from this gun, which must now be regarded as positively dangerous, and unfit for use. (Total Number of Shots fired from it by us — 261, at an average elevation of 13½ degrees, 4 lbs. of Powder, and Average Weight of projectile probably 27 or 28 lbs.) The Vent is very much enlarged and quite ragged.

At about 12 M. the second 10 in. S.C. [*Sea Coast*] Mortar Bed of Iron was delivered at Battery Haskell. (4.62 Rifle in Morning fired 8 Shots.) [*This would have been 4.62-Inch Rifle No. 2*].

At 4½ P.M. Commenced firing 4.62 Rifle No. 2 on Battery Wagner. Fired 6 Shots with average elevation 13½ degrees. Two of the Shells burst.

At the same time, Commenced firing on Black Island with 10 in. S.C. [*Sea Coast*] Mortar. Made two or three excellent Shots. (7 in all). Charge of powder 5¼ to 5⅜ lbs., length of fuze 6 in. — 22.8 Sec.

About same time Commenced firing double banded 24 pndr. Rifle (5.82 Cal.) in Chamber No. 1 on Battery Wagner. Fired only three Shots at 11° 30', 13°, 14° 30' all of which fell Short. Charge of powder 5 lbs. The vent of this gun is defective (not straight) and it is difficult to use the priming wire in consequence. The elevating Screw also gives trouble.

About 8 P.M. the Garrison Gin from Fort Johnson was delivered at Battery Haskell to be used in Mounting the Mortars on their new Beds.

Lieut [*William Stewart*] Simkins, acting Insp[ector] Genl. [*General*] for Genl. Hagood, visited the Post at Legare's Point about 12 M. and remained till 4 P.M.

Recapitulation:

4.62 Rifle No. 1 fired 7 Shots making total of 261.

4.62 Rifle No. 2 fired 14 Shots making total of 23.

5.82 Rifle, double banded, fired 3 Shots making total of 3.

10 in. Mortar fired 7 Shots.

Edward Manigault

Major, Comdg. Arty.

P.S. Lieut. Pitts' Detachment of Cos. "B" & "K" 2nd Regt. S.C.A. [*S.C. Artillery*] were relieved from duty at Battery Haskell and reported to Lt. Col. Brown at Secessionville.

Sunday, 20 Sept. 1863

Engineer Force opened Embrazure towards Black Island in Gun Chamber No. 10. Engaged also in thickening parapets, &c.

Detachments of Cos. "A" & "B" Siege Train engaged in mounting Mortars on their iron Beds.

In afternoon fired 2 shots and 6 Shells from 4.62 Rifle No. 2 on party of the Enemy visible on Black Island. The Shells were all thrown with precision but only two of them burst. The enemy's party either left the part of the island where they could be seen or concealed themselves. (Total No. Shots 4.62 in. No. 2, up to this time, 31.)

Batteries Simkins and Cheves firing somewhat today, but comparatively little.

Edward Manigault

Major, &c.

Elevation of the 4.62 Rifle for Black Island 8°. Shots 19 lbs. weight. Shells 25 lbs. The ranges of the shot slightly exceeded those of the Shell.[1]

[1] *Normally, shot would be heavier than shells, if of the same size. The unusual weight difference here indicates that the shells were somewhat longer.*

Monday, 21 Sept. 1863

Completed the mounting of both Mortars. About 12 M. commenced firing upon some men visible upon Black Island. Fired 12 Shots with

the 4.62 inch Rifle No. 2 but with very little precision as from differ-
ences in the quality of the powder, or in weight of the cartridges, it
today required 9½°, 10° and even 11° to attain the range which was
yesterday attained with 7¾° and 8° and this was the same kind of shell
which was used yesterday.

At 2 P.M. fired 2 shots from 24 Pnd. Banded Rifle at Battery Wagner
15° and 16½°. Both fell short.

In afternoon fired 6 Shots with 4 inch Blakely gun at Black Island.
The results very unsatisfactory. We can make nothing of this gun with
the projectiles furnished us.

Also, fired with 10 inch Mortar 5 Shells at Black Island; two or three
of them fell well. Also fired 2 Shots with 24 Pounder Rifle (double
banded) at Battery Wagner. Fell Short.

About dusk, Nine Torpedoes[1] were delivered at Battery Haskell with
their Mooring Weights. These were sent by Lieut. E.A. Ford of the
Engineers In Charge of same.

In the Morning, Capt. [*S. Porcher*] Smith fired 4 Shots from Battery
Tatum toward Black Island with his Howitzer. Two of these Shells
exploded. The ranges used were not uniform.

Edward Manigault
Major, &c.

Mortar No. 2:

1st. Shot	5⅜ lbs. powder.	Length of Fuze 6 in.	Went over, did not burst.
2	5⅜	5.9	Went over.
3	5¼	5.7	Good.
4	5¼	5.8	High.
5	5¼	5.9	Good.

8 in. Howitzer No. 2.

1st.	4 lbs.	17° [*Elevation*]	Struck in Marsh and burst.
2		19°	[*Struck*] on Island & burst.
3		19°	did not see.
4		18°	did not see.

4.62 Rifle No. 2, 12 Shots. Total 43.
Blakely, 6 Shots.
8 in. Howt. No. 2, 4 Shots.
10 in. Mortar No. 2, 5 Shots.

[1] *The Confederates used various types of torpedoes which would be called mines
today. Manigault probably referred to a barrel torpedo which, in its most basic form,
consisted of a watertight keg, holding gunpowder, to which had been affixed pointed
ends to provide buoyancy and streamlining against the current. Anchored in a channel
to float a few feet beneath the surface, the torpedo was intended to explode when a*

vessel struck one or more pressure igniters attached to the keg. Although far from reliable, torpedoes did sink a number of ships during the war and generated a healthy respect among seamen expected to operate in waters where they had been laid.

Typical barrel torpedo used in the Charleston area.

Tuesday, 22 Sept. 1863

In Forenoon fired from 4.62 in Rifle No. 2 five Shells over to Black Island at some of the enemy visible there. Four of the shell struck just where the men had been seen but no explosion took place.

Mortar No. 1 also fired 6 Shots on Black Island in the forenoon. None remarkably good.

At 11 A.M. commenced firing with 24 Pounder Banded Rifle at working parties in Battery Wagner. Fired five Shell. All fell short & none burst.

Lt. E.A. Ford and Lt. Elmore, assistants of Genl. Rains in Torpedo Service, came to Battery Haskell about 11 A.M. The Picket boat was furnished to them and they examined the Creeks in the neighbourhood of Batteries Haskell, Tatum & Ryan with a view to the selection of positions for their Torpedoes [*Delivered at Battery Haskell the previous evening*]. They left Battery Haskell about 1 P.M.

In the afternoon fired 24 Pounder double banded Rifle at Working parties in Battery Wagner. Elev. 17°. Charge 6 lbs. All fell short.

Table of Fire.

4.62 in. Rifle No. 2. 4 lbs. powder. 8° Elev. Dist 1¼ to 1⅜ miles. 5 Shots of which four good. Total Number of Shots up to this time 48.

Mortar No. 1

1st Shot	5⅜ lbs powder	5.8 in. length of Fuze	22.04 Sec.	Fell short & high.
2	5⅜	5.7		high.
3	5¼	6		[*No entry for result*]
4	5¼	5.7		not seen.
5	5⅛	5.8		over.
6	5⅛	5.9		high.

24 Pounder Double banded Rifle.

1st Shot	5 lbs powder	45 lb Shot	Tenn. Cup	Elev. 17°	fell short.	
2	5	40 lb Shell		17°	do	do
3	6	45 "		17°	do	do
4	6	40 "		17°	do	do
5	6	40 "		17°	do	do
6	6	45 lb Shot		17°	do	do

In Afternoon.

1	6	45 "		17°	do do
2	6	40 Shell		17°	do do
3	6	43 Eason's hollow Shot		17°	Think it went over.
4	6	40 Shell		17°	did not see.

4.62 Rifle No. 2, 5 Shots = 48 in all.
5.82, 9 Shots = 14 in all.
10 in. Mortar No. 1, 6 Shots.

Edward Manigault
Major, Comdg. Arty.

Engineer force completed Platform No. 10 in Battery Haskell, Raising & relaying.

Wednesday, 23 September 1863

Strong N.E. Wind & Cloudy. Fired 10 Shell with Mortar No. 2 over towards Black Island. Practice not very good. Two Shells did not burst at all.

Genl. Hagood visited Battery Haskell about Midday.

About 2½ P.M. sent three wagons to Fort Johnson to get lumber for laying the platforms of Battery Ryan.

At 4:45 P.M. tried whether We could reach Enemy's Vessels in Light House Inlet with our Mortars at Battery Haskell. All the shells, however, fell short. From point of view at Redoubt No. 1, none could be seen to fall clear (in appearance) of Black Island. A large boat full of men was seen to row off from Black Island.

The enemy opened fire from two Steamers on Secessionville and threw about 20 or 25 Shell, mostly percussion.

We fired four Shots with 4.62 No. 2 on Enemy's Camp on Morris Island to left (North) of Craig's Hill. At the first Shot the men streamed out from the tents in a way that showed that the Shot must have either passed over or reached them. The same result followed each of the other Shots.

Generals Taliaferro & Wise with Col. Page, visited Battery Haskell this evening.

Mortar No. 2. Morning. At Black Island 1⅜ miles distance.

1	5⅜ lbs. powder.	5.9 in. Fuze.	22.42 Sec.	over. did not burst.
2	5¼ "	5.8 "	22.04	High. burst.
3	5¼ "	5.9 "	22.42	Burst. higher.
4	5¼ "	6 "	22.80	Burst higher still.
5	5¼ "	6 "	22.80	Burst high.
6	5¼ "	6.1 "	23.18	Burst high, about same as last.
7	5¼ "	6.1 "	23.18	Went over Island.
8	5¼ "	6.2 "	23.56	Went a little over Island.
9	5¼ "	6.2 "	23.56	a little over, did not burst.
10	5¼ "	6 "	22.80	Very good.

Afternoon 4.45 P.M. at Enemy's vessels in Lgt. Ho. [*Light House*] Inlet.

1	10 lbs. powder.	7 in. Fuze.	26.6 Seconds.	Fell short of vessels. Burst well.
2	10	7.5	28.5	" " " "
3	10	7.5	28.5	could not see.
4	10	7.5	28.5	Fell short of vessels.
5	10	7.5	27.74	" " " "
6	10	7.5	28.5	" " " "

Total shots today with Mortar No. 2, 16 shots. Rear Transom a little split.

4.62 No. 2 [*fired*] At Yankee Camp near Craig's Hill 2½ miles.

1st Shot	4 lbs powder	19 lb Solid Shot	15° Elevation.	Apparently went near Yankee Camp.
2	do	25 lb Shell	16° "	20 Sec. Fuze. Burst high & Short.
3	do	25 lb Shell	16° "	[*No entry for results*]
4	do	25 lb Shell	16° "	[*No entry for results*]

Total No. of Shots with 4.62 No. 2, 52 Shots in all — up to this time.

Thursday, 24 September 1863

About 10 A.M. received orders from Genl. Hagood to open fire upon Marsh Battery No. 1 as the Enemy was reported by Major Blanding to be at work there. Accordingly opened fire on it with 24 Pounder banded Rifle, and 24 pounder Smoothbore. Fired 6 Shots with the former at an average Elevation of 9°. Supposed that it struck the right extremity of the Battery once. None of the other shots struck it. Fired 12 Shots with Smooth Bore 24. Average elevation 9°. Two Shots either went in, or immediately over the Battery.

From Battery Haskell only two or three men could be seen and they did not appear to be at work. Our fire was continued about two hours and then was stopped.

About 10 A.M. Major J.G. Barnwell, Inspector of Batteries, came to Battery Haskell and inspected the Guns, Batteries, magazines, &c. He then proceeded to Batteries Tatum & Ryan and Redoubt No.1 which he also inspected.[1]

In the afternoon, as large numbers of men were visible on Battery Wagner, opened fire with double banded 24 pndr. Rifle in Battery Haskell. Fired three Solid Shot with Tennessee Cups, weight 45 lbs. 17° Elevation. Charge powder 6 lbs. All three fell short. Fired then four hollow shot of Eason's Manufacture, with leaden Base or Sabots. The first, at 17°, evidently went over Wagner, making the Working party leave their work and shelter themselves. The second, fired at 15° Elev., also went over. The third, at 14°, appeared to pass over the Right Extremity of the Fort and struck the sand a little beyond. The fourth, at 13°, fell a little short. This is the only projectile with which this 24 Pounder Rifle appears to shoot reasonably well. With any other projectile, 6 lbs. of powder and 17° Elevation (the greatest we can get) this gun cannot reach the Island.

Sent Wagons to Fort Johnson to get more lumber for the Platforms of Battery Ryan and also afterwards for some Boards, from the buildings to be pulled down, to make shelters for the Men.[2]

24 pnd. Double Banded Rifle fired 13 shots today. Total 27 up to this time.

24 pnd. Smooth Bore [*fired*] 12 Shots. Total, [*Not entered*].

Edward Manigault
Major Comdg. Arty. &c.

[1] *See Appendix 2, p. 265-267, for report of Maj. Barnwell's inspection recorded in OR XXVIII (2) pp. 377-379.*

[2] *Manigault, in a note which has not been found, apparently had requested permission to salvage this lumber for his men. The following letter is in the collections of the Charleston (S.C) Library Society:*

Hd Qrs Advanced Forces
Sept 22, 1863

Maj. Edward Manigault:
> *Maj.*
> *In the absence of Col. Simonton, I take the liberty in reply to your note to say that as far as we are informed at these Hd Qurs no restrictions have been placed upon the removal of the boards alluded to and suppose they are free to all who may desire to use them. I have no official information on the subject but from what I have heard feel assured that you have as much right in the denoted houses as anyone else.*

Very Respectfully
Your Obdt. Svt.
G.H. Moffett
1st Lt. & Adjt.

Friday, 25 September 1863

Captn. Webb, Comdg. Co. "A" Siege Train, sent to Charleston Arsenal

1865 view of the Charleston Arsenal. Note cannon and limber at right.

for the limbers belonging to his Battery of 12 Pounder Blakely field guns (3½ in. Cal). These came out from England arranged to be used with Shafts instead of Poles. They have been left at the Arsenal for alteration since August 18th when the Guns came out with ordinary 6 pndr. limbers for temporary use.[1] The detail sent for the limbers returned with them in the Afternoon.

In the course of the Morning fired 13 Shells from Mortar No. 1 at Black Island. A party of the enemy was seen upon the Island though not apparently a working Party. It rather appeared to be a picket stationed there. Four shots were exceedingly good; three rather high; three others decidedly too high & three were not seen and did not burst.

Fired also 12 with the double banded 24 Pounder Rifle at Battery Wagner, large numbers of men being seen at work within it. Commenced at 9 A.M. Struck the top of the parapet once, and made three other good shots. Two were not seen. The others either fell to the Right or were short. In the afternoon (3½ P.M.) fired another shot which fell short.

Fired also 7 Shots from 4.62 No. 2 at Battery Wagner. None of the Shells burst and most fell short. Ceased firing about 2¼ P.M. Charge of powder 4 lbs. Wgt. of Shell 25 lbs. 15° to 17° Elev.

Just before dark a boat was seen moving very rapidly from Marsh Battery No. 1 towards Battery Wagner (the tide being very high). Fired three shots at her with 24 Pounder Smooth Bore. The first Shot fell behind her but very near. The other two shots were fired after it became too dark to see her distinctly. Estimated distance first Shot 1½ to 1⅝ miles. Second and third shots 1¾ to 2 miles.

Engineer force engaged today in sodding & completing Traverses and in raising Causeway at Battery Haskell above the level of Spring Tides.

Lieut. Ford's Men laid a row of floating Torpedoes at the Mouth of the Small Creek which runs past Battery Haskell and empties into Schooner Creek about 300 or 400 yds. below.

This necessitated an alteration in the position of one Picket boat at Night. Due notice was given to Col. Way, commanding the Post, and I myself accompanied the first picket and pointed out the position of the Torpedoes.

Tables of Fire.

Mortar No. 1 Fired on Black Island. Distance 1⅜ to 1½ Miles.

No. of Shot	Charge Powder	Length of Fuze		
1	5¼ Lbs.	5.9 in.	22.42 Sec.	High
2	5¼	6	22.8	Good
3	5¼	6	22.8	high
4	5¼	6	22.8	little high
5	5¼	6	.22.8	did not see
6	5⅜	6	22.8	good
7	5⅜	6	22.8	good
8	5⅜	6.1	23.2	a little high
9	5⅜	6.1	23.2	did not see
10	5⅜	6.1	23.2	a little high
11	5⅜	6.1	23.2	did not see
12	5⅜	6	22.8	good
13	5⅜	6	22.8	high

24 Pounder Banded Rifle. [*Fired*] At Battery Wagner, distant 2⅜ Miles.

1	6 lbs. powder.	14° Elev.	Eason's Hollow Shot, 43 lbs.					To the Right & Short
2	do	15°	"	"	"	"	"	not seen
3	do	14½°	"	"	"	"	"	Struck the Parapet
4	do	14½°	"	"	"	"	"	good
5	do	14½°	"	"	"	"	"	To the Right
6	do	14½°	"	"	"	"	"	good
7	do	14½°	"	"	"	"	"	Short
8	do	14¾°	"	"	"	"	"	Short
9	do	14¾°	"	"	"	"	"	good
10	do	14¾°	"	"	"	"	"	not seen
11	do	14½°	"	"	"	"	"	Short
12	do	17°	Shell weighing 40 lbs.					Short

Afternoon.

13	do	14½°	[*Eason's*] Hollow Shot	Short

Thirteen Shots to day. Total 40 Shots in all.

4.62 in. Rifle No. [*Not listed, but obviously No. 2*]. Point of Fire, Battery Wagner, 2⅜ miles.

7 Shots 14°, 15°, 16° & 17° Elevation. All but two fell short. The other two either not seen or supposed to go over.

Total No. of Shots with 4.62 No. 2, 59 up to this time.

About 4.30 or 5 P.M. a heavy explosion occurred in Battery Wagner, caused apparently by a Shell from Battery Simkins.

Edward Manigault
Major Comdg. Arty. &c.

¹ *See 13 Aug. 1863, note.*

Saturday, 26 September 1863

Capt. Webb, Co. "A" S.C. Siege Train, sent to the Charleston Arsenal the 6 pndr. Limbers which he has been using with his Blakely Guns in place of the Limbers proper to these guns. [*See Friday, 25 Sept. 1863*]

Fired 8 Shots with Banded 24 Pounder Rifle at Battery Wagner.

1st Shot	5½ lbs. powder.	14¾° Elev.	Eason's 43 lb. Hollow Shot			Struck Parapet.
2	"	"	"	"	"	"	To Right
3	"	"	"	ʰ	"	"	Did not see
4	"	"	"	"	"	"	fell Short
5	"	"	15°	"	"	"	Went over
6	"	"	14¾°	"	"	"	Good
7	"	"	14¾°	"	"	"	fell Short
8	"	"	14¾°	"	"	"	fell Short

Total No. Shots up to this time, 48.

Engineer force engaged in thickening the Earth on South Side of Gun Magazine at Battery Haskell.

Col. Gonzales visited Battery Haskell at dark and remained till 7½ P.M.

Edward Manigault
Major Comdg. &c.

Sunday, 27 September 1863

Had a careful policing of the different Camps.

Genl. Hagood visited Battery Haskell at 10 O'clock A.M.

In the afternoon fired three shots toward Black Island with one of the 3½ in. Blakely Guns of Co. "A" S.C. Siege Train.

1st Shot	8° Elev.	12 Sec. Fuze	Fell short of Black Island, did not burst.
2	"	10°	do	" " " "
3	"	12½°	do	" " " "

Unusually quiet. Battery Simkins firing slowly on Battery Wagner.

Edward Manigault
Major Comdg. Arty.

Monday, 28 September 1863

The Engineer force commenced this morning to raise the Frame Work for the Bomb Proof at Battery Haskell.

About Midday the Enemy's heavy Rifle Battery below Graham's Hd. Qrs. commenced firing upon Fort Sumter and continued to do so for several hours.[1]

About 4.30 P.M. as there were several persons seen in Marsh Battery No. 1, four Shots were fired at them from double banded 24 pndr. Rifle at Battery Haskell.

No. 1	6 Lbs powder	Con.* Shot wgt 45 lbs. Tenn. Cup.	8° Elev.	Good.
2	do	" " " "	do	To the Right.
3	do	Con.* Shell, Wgt 40 lbs.	do	Fell Short.
4	do	Con.* Shot 45 lbs, Tenn. Cup	8½ °	Passed over Wagner.

*[Conical]

Total No. of Shots up to this time, 52.
The enemy disappeared.

Edward Manigault
Major Comdg. Arty.

[1] *This was the start of the first minor bombardment of Fort Sumter. It lasted from 28 Sept. through 3 Oct. and cost the Confederates three casualties. The Federals expended a reported 570 rounds against the fort. (See Monday, 17 Aug. 1863, Note No. 4.)*

Tuesday, 29 September 1863

Engineeer force still engaged in raising frame of Bomb Proof. Col. Way of 54th Georgia went to Savannah on duty. The enemy's heavy Rifle Batteries still firing upon Sumter, but apparently not very successfully. Battery Simkins firing slowly upon Wagner.

At 12 M. fired 3 shots from 4.62 No. 2 on Black Island, several men being seen together there. 1st Shell gave a premature explosion, the other two did not explode. Elev. 8½ °, last Shot 10½ °. The party sheltered or concealed themselves. (62 Shots in all.)

At 5 P.M. fired two shots from 24 Pounder Smooth Bore upon Marsh Battery No. 1 as several Men and apparently a boat were seen there. Elev. 8°. Neither shot struck, but fell quite near, one to Right and the other to left.

Sergeant Major Gaillard returned from Sick furlough today.
Total No. of Shots fired from 4.62 No. 2 up to this time, 62.

Edward Manigault
Major Comdg. Arty.

Legare's Point, James Island.
Wednesday, 30 September 1863

Engineer force still engaged in Completing frame work of Bomb Proof at Battery Haskell and in completing some Traverses.

The enemy firing from their heavy Rifle Batteries below Graham's Hd. Qrs. on Fort Sumter, Battery Simkins & Fort Johnson. Most of the Shells thrown at Fort Johnson were of 6½ in. diameter, supposed to be 100 Pounder Parrott Shells.

In afternoon an Inspection of the Artillery forces on Section 2.

None of the Batteries of Section 2 fired at all today.

Edward Manigault
Major Comdg. Arty.

Legare's Point, James Island.
Thursday, 1 October 1863.

Work on the frame of Bomb Proof suspended in consequence of the want of Material. The Engineer wagons engaged in hauling timber for this purpose and Excavation heaping Earth near the Bomb Proof.

The enemy's fire encreasing on Fort Sumter, Fort Johnson & Battery Simkins. This fire is altogether from his heavy Rifle Batteries to South of Graham's Hd. Qrs. Our fire in return was slow and irregular.

At 2½ P.M. fired three shots on Black Island as a working party could be seen on the portion of the Island where the Woods and Marsh open. These shots were fired from 4.62 in. No. 2 in Battery Haskell.

lst Shot	4 lbs powder.	28 lb Shell	9° Elev.	10 second Fuze	Dist 1⅜ Mile. Passed over. Did not burst.
2 "	4 "	28 "	8½° "	10 " "	Passed over. No burst.
3 "	4 "	28 "	8° "	8 " "	Good. Did not burst.

Total No. Shot from 4.62 No [2] up to this time, 65.

The Enemy did not fire upon any Battery in Section 2, and there are no casualties to report.

Edward Manigault
Major Comdg. Arty.

Legare's Point, James Island.
Friday, 2 October 1863.

One portion of Engineer hands employed in cutting & hauling timber for Bomb Proof at Battery Haskell; others employed in heaping earth near to the frame leaving room for insertion of timber & planks. Great delay in consequence of want of Lumber.

The Enemy still firing on Fort Sumter & Fort Johnson, but not so vigorously as yesterday. Fort Moultrie and the batteries on Sullivan's Island (and also Cheves occasionally) firing on Batteries Gregg & Wagner upon which work is progressing tho rather slowly. The Palisades or stockades around these Batteries are progressing rapidly.

Some men seen upon Black Island, but as we had a considerable negro force engaged upon the Bomb proof at Battery Haskell, it was not deemed advisable to fire upon them lest the enemy's fire might be drawn upon that Battery.

Battery Haskell neither fired nor was fired upon. No casualties to report. Note that Black Island is being very rapidly cleared by the enemy. On one portion of Island, the woods scarcely serve as a screen at all. A great difference perceptible this Morning.

Edward Manigault
Major Comdg. Arty. &c.

Legare's Point, James Island.
Saturday, 3 October 1863.

Engineer Wagons still hauling in Lumber for Bomb proof. Hands engaged in lining sides of Bomb Proof with split & squared half logs and piling and ramming earth against it.

Enemy firing from Rifle Batteries below Graham's Hd. Qrs. on Fort Sumter, Fort Johnson, Batteries Simkins & Cheves. Fort Moultrie & Batteries on Sullivan's Island, [and] Battery Simkins firing on Gregg & Wagner. Battery Cheves firing on Wagner, and occasionally on the Rifle Batteries to south of Graham's Hd. Qrs. The Yankee practice at Battery Cheves at about 2 P.M. was excellent.

At 2 P.M. Commenced firing Mortar No. 2 on Wagner.

1st Shot	10 lbs Powder	7 in. Fuze	26.6 sec.	Shell fell to Right on Morris Island but a little Short. Did not burst.
2 "	10 "	6.9 in.	26.22	Burst very high and to left.
3 "	10 "	6.9	26.22	Did not see.
4 "	10 "	7	26.66	Burst very high & to left.

Cease firing at 3 P.M.

At 5 P.M. Resumed firing 10 in. Mortar No. 2. Fired 4 Shots at the Same point.

1st Shot	10 lbs Powder	7 in. Fuze	26.6 Sec.	Dis. 2⅜ Miles. Did not burst, nor was it seen.
2	10	7	" "	Burst high, say 1,000 feet in air.
3	10	7	" "	Fell a little short & to Right. Did not burst.
4	"	7	" "	Burst very high.

Genl. Taliaferro & Staff visited Battery Haskell about 1 P.M. No casualties to Report.

Edward Manigault
Major Comdg. Arty. &c.

Legare's Point, James Island.
Sunday, 4 October 1863.

Very little firing going on on either side. A day of unusual quiet. No casualties to report.

(Countersign "Clinch")

Edward Manigault
Major Comdg. Arty.

Legare's Point, James Island.
Monday, 5 October 1863.

Major Manigault went into City on 12 hours leave of absence. The 4.62 in. Rifle No. 1 was sent to the Charleston Arsenal for bouching[1] or condemnation as might be decided on by proper authority. Capt. [*S. Porcher*] Smith's (Co. "B") Mules & drivers carried the Gun in.

The work on Bomb Proof at Battery Haskell progressing well. No firing from that Battery.

Batteries Cheves & Simkins firing at Gregg & Wagner.

(The dismounted 32 Pounder with its Carriage & Chassis was Moved from Redoubt No. 1 to some point on the New Lines.) [*Parenthetical material apparently added at a later date*].

Edward Manigault
Major &c.

[1] *Powder gases from continued firing eroded the vent of a cast-iron cannon. Consequently, the vent was bouched (bushed) with a plug of a different metal, such as copper, through which a new vent was bored. [Ripley, p. 353]*

Legare's Point, James Island.
Tuesday, 6 October 1863.

Lieut. Legare, Ord. Off., delivered One 30 pounder Parrott (No Marks at all on this 30 Pndr. See Memorandum Pocket book.[1]) and one 24 Pounder Banded Rifle gun at Redoubt No. 1 and removed from thence to Battery Ryan One Unbanded 24 Pounder Rifle (This last was moved the day before.)

Batteries Simkins & Cheves firing upon Gregg & Wagner (slowly). The Enemy not firing at all in return.

About 4 P.M. commenced firing with 10 in. Mortar No. 2 at Battery Haskell upon Battery Wagner when a good many men were seen at work. The result of our fire shows that Battery Wagner is at the utmost limit of the range of our Mortars, as with the Maximum Charges of powder most of the Shells fell a little Short. The Mortar was tried at

43° Elevation as this result was shown on previous occasions at 45°.

1st Shot	10 lbs powder.	43° Elev.	7.2 in.	27.36 Sec.	A little Right but good.
2 do	do	do	do	do	Burst very high.
3 do	do	do	4.4	26,4	Did not burst. Fell Left. (Fuze 6 Sec. to 1 inch)
4 do	do	do	7.2	27.36	Fell to Left.
5 do	do	do	7.2	do	” ” Right
6 do	do	do	7.2	do	” ” Left

It must be understood that the Mortar Platform is very bad, hence neither range nor accuracy can be expected.

(Countersign "Ashley")

No Casualties to report.

Edward Manigault
Major &c.

¹ *Not found.*

Legare's Point, James Island.
Wednesday, 7 October 1863.

Capt. Smith and Lieut. Phillips went to Charleston on leave for the day. Sent in "Full Monthly Reports" of Heavy Artillery for Battery Haskell & Redoubt No. 1 in accordance with Genl. Orders No. 43, Hd. Qrs. 1st Mil. Dist. [*Military District*] dated Oct. 5, 1863. Sent this [*through*] regular Channel to Capt. C.C. Pinckney.

Very few of the enemy visible on any of their works during the Morning. More visible on Battery Wagner in afternoon. Batteries Simkins & Cheves firing. About 10 O'clock the Enemy fired several shot from Gadberry Hill at Battery Cheves, apparently none of these exploded so far as could be observed from Battery Haskell.

The top or roof of the Bomb proof was Covered with a layer of Sod to fill up the interstices between the timbers. The Earth on the sides was banked and packed pretty nearly up on a level with top of Frame work.

Col. Way returned from Savannah. Arrived at Legare's Point about 3 P.M.

No Casualties to Report.

(Countersign "Cooper")

Edward Manigault
Major Comdg. Arty.

Legare's Point, James Island.
Thursday, 8 October 1863.

Bomb proof at Battery Tatum [*Ryan is lined out and Tatum inserted*] commenced. That at Battery Haskell progressing.

About 1 P.M. Genl. Taliaferro, Col. Harris, and Captain Du Barry visited Battery Haskell for the purpose of inspecting the Battery, Guns & Mortars.

Capt. Du Barry was specially sent by Genl. Ripley to examine and Try the ranges of our Mortars. Fired two Shells from Mortar No. 2 at Battery Wagner.

1st Shot, 10 lbs powder (Chamber full) 45° Elev. Fuze 7.2 in. 27.36 Sec. Burst high in air and to Left.

2nd Shot, 10 lbs. 45°, 8 in [*Fuse*] 30.4 [*Seconds*]. To Right & little Short. Burst after falling.

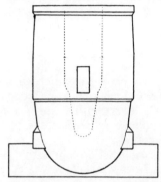

Sketch from the 1850 U.S. Ordnance Manual of the type 10-inch Sea Coast Mortar used by Maj. Manigault

Fort Moultrie, Battery Bee On Sullivan's Island, and Batteries Simkins & Cheves firing on Gregg & Wagner. The Yankees did not reply at all.

No casualties to report.

(Countersign "Mississippi")

Edward Manigault
Major Comdg. Arty.

Legare's Point, James Island.
Friday, 9 October 1863.

Adjutant Gardner went into City on leave for the day.

Sent in Requisition for Ordnance Stores for Battery Haskell and another for the 24 pndr. Rifle & 30 pndr. Parrott just sent to Redoubt No. 1 (thro. the regular Channel.)

Genl. Ripley reviewed the Brigades of Generals Colquitt & Hagood or rather only such portions of them as could with safety be withdrawn from the Lines. The Artillery serving on Section 2, for this reason, took no part in the Review.

The work on the Bomb Proofs progressing.

Our Batteries Simkins & Cheves kept up a steady fire upon Gregg & Wagner all night and this Morning. The Gadberry Hill Battery commenced firing on Fort Johnson about 2 O'clock in the afternoon and continued until dark.

In pursuance of Orders received, Capt. Webb sent one of his Caissons to the Charleston Arsenal to have the Girarday fuze [1] attached to the Shells of the 3½ inch Blakely Guns of his Battery.

Sent in application for platforms at Battery Ryan & Redoubt No. 1

No Casualties to report.

(Countersign "Johnston Island")

Edward Manigault
[*Rank, etc. omitted*]

[1] *This percussion fuse was the invention of Isadore P. Girardey of the Ordnance Dept. at Augusta, Ga. The device was substituted for the paper time fuse in a projectile, thus converting the shell into one that would burst on impact. [Field Artillery Projectiles of the American Civil War, by Thomas S. Dickey and Peter C. George]*

Legare's Point, James Island.
Saturday, 10 October 1863.

Capt. Webb went into Charleston to select 5 horses for which he had an order. Fort Moultrie, Batteries Simkins & Cheves firing on Gregg & Wagner. In the afternoon the Battery at Gadberry Hill firing pretty heavily on Fort Johnson. A Mortar was opened from Battery near Gadberry Hill for the first time this afternoon.

The Bomb Proof at Battery Haskell progressing. The foundation pit for that at Tatum [*Ryan is overstruck and Tatum inserted*] was completed yesterday and no work was going on upon it today.

Capt. Mordecai, Asst. Qr. Master, S.C. Siege Train, reported for duty today, though not quite recovered from the effects of his accident. [1]

No Casualties to report.

(Countersign Potomac)

Edward Manigault
Major, &c.

[1] *See Sunday, 13 Sept. 1863.*

Legare's [Point], James Island.
Sunday, 11 October 1863.

Fort Moultrie and Battery Simkins firing upon Gregg & Wagner. About 4 P.M. one or more Mortars from a Battery near Gadberry Hill opened upon Battery Simkins and continued firing until near dark.

The usual Sunday Inspections &c. at the different Batteries of Section 2.

No Casualties to Report.

(Countersign "Ringgold")

Edward Manigault
Major Comdg. Arty.

Legare's [Point], James Island.
Monday, 12 October 1863.

In pursuance of instructions from "Hd. Qrs. James Island" Captain Webb had the two 12 pounder Bronze Rifles, James Pattern,[1] hauled to the Charleston Central Ordnance Depot, Citadel Square, and delivered to Captain H.L. Ingraham, Comdg. Depot. These guns were sent into the City in order that they might be "rebored" or what is technically called "Bored Up" to 18 pounder.[2]

Fort Moultrie, Batteries Simkins & Cheves firing upon Gregg & Wagner. In the afternoon, Mortars from neighbourhood of Gadberry Hill firing upon Battery Simkins & Fort Johnson.

Bomb proof at Battery Haskell progressing.

Capt. S.P. Smith, Co. "B" Siege Train went to Charleston on Surgeon's certificate.

About 10 A.M. a banded 32 Pounder Rifle arrived at Legare's intended for Battery Haskell. As from the tenor of instructions from Head Quartrs 1st Military District, dated Oct. 7, it appears that Battery Haskell is henceforth "to be armed only for defensive purposes," and such long range guns as are intended for Batteries Tatum, or Ryan, and Redoubt No. 1 are to be "on Siege Carriages" I concluded that There was some Mistake and had the gun left just in front of the Head Quarters at Legare's [Point] and gave notice of the Same to Capt. Taliaferro, A.A.G. [Assistant Adjutant General] from whom the said instructions had been forwarded to me.

I carefully examined 27 cartridges for 30 pounder Parrott sent to Redoubt No. 1 a few days ago, and found them to be filled with Musket or Rifle powder (the grain was Small Musket grain). I immediately had them reboxed in order to send them back to Lieut. Legare by the first opportunity.

Col. Gonzales, Chief of Artillery, Came to Head Quarters Legare's [Point] about 1 P.M. and afterwards examined the Batteries & Guns, carefully, at Haskell, Tatum & Ryan. He did not go until 6 P.M.

No Casualties to Report.

(Countersign "Wagner")

> Edward Manigault
> Major Comdg. Arty.

The 19th Georgia were relieved this afternoon and its place supplied by the 18th S.C. which went on Guard same night.

[1] U.S. Gen. Charles Tillinghast James invented a rifle projectile and developed a method of rifling older cannon to fire it. [Ripley, pp. 18, 19, 169-170, 300, 301]

[2] The reboring would have changed the caliber from 4.62-inch to 5.3-inch.

Legare's [Point], James Island.
Tuesday, 13 October 1863.

Engineer force engaged in laying down a substantial platform for

Mortar No. 2.

The Bomb Proof at Battery Haskell progressing.

Nothing occurred worthy of note.

No Casualties to report.

(Countersign "Gregg")

Edward Manigault
Major Comdg. Arty.

Legare's [Point], James Island.
Wednesday, 14 October 1863.

Rained in the Morning, which prevented the moving of the Shanties according to orders received yesterday.[1] About 60 hands engaged on the Bomb Proof and 10 on Mortar Platform.

Fort Moultrie, Batteries Simkins & Cheves firing on Gregg & Wagner. The enemy did not reply.

No casualties to report.

(Countersign "Sumter")

Edward Manigault
Major Comdg. Arty.

[1] *See Diary 19 Oct. 1863.*

Legare's [Point], James Island.
Thursday, 15 October 1863.

Rain during the greater part of Morning. About 62 to 65 hands engaged on the Bomb Proof at Battery Haskell. Mortar Platform in Chamber No. 2 Completed To day.

Battery Cheves and Battery Simkins occasionally firing. The Enemy did not reply.

Nothing occurred worthy of note.

No Casualties to report.

(Countersign "Johnson").

(Captain Mitchel came to Legare's to make out a Report on Fuzes in conjunction with myself.)

Edward Manigault
Major Comdg. Arty.

Legare's [Point], James Island.
Friday, 16 October 1863.

Genl. Beauregard reviewed the Brigades of Genls. Hagood & Colquitt. The Artillery force of Section 2 not included in the Review.

The Batteries on both sides unusually quiet. No firing at all from the Enemy.

The Bomb Proof at Battery Haskell raised nearly to the required height. Additional Posts being introduced under the Cap pieces of frame as in places they showed signs of crushing under the weight.

Lieut. Nesbit went to City on leave for the day.

No Casualties to report.

(Countersign "Simkins")

Edward Manigault
Major Comdg. Arty.

Saturday, 17 October 1863.

Very little firing from any quarter today.

Laid down a platform for Howitzer No. 1 at Battery Ryan to day. The plank for this was picked up in the Marsh, being portion of the lumber intended for Foot Bridge from Legare's Point to Morris Island.[1] Laid down by Carpenters of Co. "B".

Engineer hands engaged in laying Platform for Mortar No. 1 at Battery Haskell.

Sent Box containing 27 Cartridges for 30 pndr. Parrott (3½ lbs Musket powder) back to Lieutenant Legare.[See Monday, 12 October 1863]

No Casualties to report.

(Countersign "Cheves").

Edward Manigault
Major Comdg. Arty.

[1] *The South Carolina marsh, with its attendant mud and small creeks, is virtually impassible to men on foot. Consequently, both sides bridged the marsh between dry-land areas. The bridges generally consisted of poles, or planks, shoved vertically through the mud to a firm bottom. Stringers were attached at the top and planks laid for a deck. Such bridges were crude in appearance but sufficiently sturdy to carry troops, a few at a time.*

Legare's [Point], James Island.
Sunday, 18 October 1863.

Fort Moultrie, Batteries Simkins & Cheves firing occasionally on Gregg & Wagner. The Enemy did not reply at all.

One of the Battery Horses of Co. "A" S.C. Siege Train, died from the effects of a wound inflicted with an axe by a Negro belonging to Ast. Surgeon Pope of 18th S.C.V. on Thursday last, the horse having broke loose and gone into that Camp. Board of Survey met and reported on the Case.

No Casualties to Report

(Countersign "Ryan")

Edward Manigault
Major Comdg. Arty.

Legare's [Point], James Island.
Monday, 19 October 1863.

Fort Moultrie, Batteries Simkins & Cheves firing on Gregg & Wagner.

The enemy did not reply.

Lieut. [*John B.W.*] Phillips, Actg. Ord. Off. sent to Hospital in City.

About 70 fresh Negro hands (from Chesterfield [*County, S.C.*]) engaged on Bomb Proof at Battery Haskell to day. Those previously employed were discharged Yesterday. No work going on on Mortar Platform No. 1, probably from want of flooring plank.

All of the Shanties occupied by the Detachments for the Guns at Battery Haskell were moved to day "100 yds. from any of the Batteries."[1] Three of them had been moved since Saturday.

No Casualties to report.

(Countersign "Gary")

Edward Manigault
Major Comdg. Arty.

Order No. 74 from Hd Qrs. Genl. Hagood dated 13th Oct. received this afternoon to relieve Lt. [*A.A. or J.B.*] Connor's Detachment 2nd S.C. Arty from Redoubt No. 1. Order immediately extended [*i.e., expanded by adding*] and Capt. [*George W.*] Johnson put in Command of Redoubt.

[1] *The order for this has not been found.*

Legare's [Point], James Island.
Tuesday, 20 October 1863.

About 100 Negroes engaged in finishing Bomb Proof at Battery Haskell and 35 engaged in thickening Breast Work between Gun Chamber No. 11 and Mortar Battery No. 2 and about 70 engaged in raising frame of Bomb Proof at Battery Tatum and digging out entrances to same.

Genl. Hagood visited Battery Haskell about 10½ A.M.

Lieut. Chapman went off on leave of absence for 7 days on important private business.

Fort Moultrie, Battery Beauregard, Simkins, Cheves all firing slowly & steadily on Batteries Gregg & Wagner. No reply from the enemy who, however, is progressing in his work on both the above named batteries, as well as two batteries between them commenced within two or three days. He is showing also a good deal of activity on one or two of the Batteries below Wagner, probably dismounting Guns.

For the first time in several weeks, the "Ironsides" moved from her anchorage opposite Graham's Hd. Qrs. and steamed up to a point opposite to Battery Wagner and then back to a point below her former Anchorage. The Yankee floating Derrick, or Derrick Steamer, was towed about 9½ or 10 o'clock by another Steamer up Folly River toward Stono.

About 7 P.M. received from the Inglis Light Arty (probably by order from Col. Gonzales) two 6 pndr. Iron Guns old Pattern. One of these guns will be put in Gun Chamber No. 6 at Battery Haskell. Some old harness was sent at the same time which I declined receiving. It was probably sent under the supposition that the two 6 pounders were to be used as field artillery whereas they are intended for flank defence in Battery Haskell and perhaps Battery Tatum.

At 8½ P.M. one of the best Battery Horses of Co. "A" Siege Train died very suddenly, apparently of Colic.

No Casualties to report.

(Countersign "Pringle")

Edward Manigault
Major, &c.

Legare's [Point], James Island.
Wednesday, 21 October 1863.

About 90 Negroes engaged in finishing the Bomb Proof at Battery Haskell, also 30 engaged in throwing up a merlon to left of Gun Chamber No. 11 which I cannot approve of. If this does give more protection for a fire from Morris Island (Say an enfilading fire from Battery Gregg) it also effectually cuts off the fire of the Gun in No. 11 from Enfilading or sweeping the creek & beach in front of Battery Haskell. And this fire is especially important if Battery Haskell is to be reduced to a "defensive work" and to have as I understand only 5 or 6 guns mounted.[1] There were also about 70 engaged putting up Bomb Proof at Battery Tatum.

Fort Moultrie & the Sullivan's Island Batteries, [and] Batteries Simkins & Cheves, firing upon Gregg and Wagner and the fortifications the Enemy is constructing between those two works. The enemy did not reply.

At 5 P.M. an 8 in Col^d. [*Columbiad*] from Battery Cheves was delivered at Battery Haskell, but no carriage is ready for it.[2]

No Casualties to report.

(Countersign "Bee")

[*Not signed*]

[1] *Special Order No. 216, Hq., Dept. of S.C., Ga. and Fla., dated 21 Oct. 1863, specified eight guns and two mortars in Battery Haskell. [See Appendix 2, pp. 267, 268; OR XXVIII (2) pp. 438, 439]*

[2] *The above order stipulated that an 8-inch columbiad was to be sent to Haskell from Battery Cheves.*

Legare's [Point], James Island.
Thursday, 22 October 1863.

Fort Moultrie, Battery Bee, Simkins & Cheves firing upon Gregg, Wagner and the batteries which are being constructed between those two works. The enemy is not replying.

About 11 A.M. Capt. Schooler and Lieut. Elmore came to Battery Haskell. Capt. Schooler was authorized to visit the Batteries and inspect their fuzes &c. and all officers were instructed by Genl. Jordan to facilitate his operations.

At Captn. S's request — fired 5 Shots at Battery Wagner from 10 in. S.C. [*Sea Coast*] Mortar No. 2.

1st Shot	10 lbs powder	7.4 in. Fuze	28.1 Sec. Charleston Made Fuze "July 1863."	Fell Right & Short. Did not burst.
2	" 10 "	7 in. "	26.6 do do do	Burst high & Right.
3	" 10 "	7 in. "	26.6 do do do	Fell little Short & little to Left; did not burst.
4	" 10 "	7 in. "	26.6 Augusta Fuze.	Burst very high and Much to Right.
5	" 10 "	7 in. "	26.6 Charleston, Sept. 1863 (Calhoun)	Burst high & Right. (This is the first of these fuzes used.)

Capt. S. left Battery Haskell about 2 P.M.

Bomb Proof at Battery Haskell completed about 11 A.M. About 65 hands engaged in modifying the Battery about Gun Chamber No. 11 of Battery Haskell. About 90 hands engaged in throwing up Bomb Proof at Battery Tatum. About 40 engaged in repairing Road & Bridge ¼ mile West of Legare's House where the Road makes an angle going up towards Fort Johnson.

At about 11 P.M. orders Came from Hd Qrs. to furnish horses and assist in Moving Guns to the New Lines tomorrow.[1]

No Casualties to report. (Countersign "Moultrie")

Adjutant [*John H. Gardner*] went into City on leave for the day.

Capt. [*S. Porcher*] Smith returned from Hospital about Midday.

Edward Manigault

Major Comdg. Arty.

[1] *The original defense line for James Island traced a roundabout route from Fort Pemberton, on the Stono River, to Fort Lamar at Secessionville (see map). It not only was extremely long, about five miles, but it gave up a large portion of James Island to the enemy. Moreover, its defensive system, consisting of an infantry line supported by small fortifications for artillery (redoubts and redans) was poorly designed for flat country. It placed the artillery behind the infantry thus endangering friendly troops when the guns were fired. The new line ran from Fort Lamar straight across to Battery Pringle, some four miles downriver from Pemberton. It was a much shorter line, left far less land for a lodgement by the enemy, and was strongly built to permit mutually supporting action by infantry and artilllery. [Roman (2) pp. 4, 5; OR XXVIII (2) pp. 264, 366, 408, 409]*

Friday, 23 October 1863.

Captn. [*S. Porcher*] Smith's horses off before day to new Bridge over James Island Creek to haul guns to the New Lines. Capt. [*George W.*] Johnson's also, very early for the same purpose. Capt. Webb's ready to report to Ordnance Sergeant Hitchcock for the same purpose.

Heavy showers from about 7 A.M. until 10 A.M.

Sent one 24 Pounder Smooth Bore (from Gun Chamber No. 4 Battery Haskell) to Redoubt No. 4 New Lines with Implements & ammunition.

Capt. Webb had five traces broken in hauling heavy Guns to New lines. There was no injury to Capt. Smith's Harness.

About 90 hands engaged at Bomb Proof of Battery Tatum and about 40 engaged in repairing road very necessary for movement of Light Artillery to Battery Tatum.

About 8 or 8.30 P.M. firing of Small arms heard in the direction of the harbor towards Fort Sumter. This firing was very much like picket firing in sound. The Cause was not known.[1]

No Casualties to report.

(Countersign "James")

Edward Manigault
Major

In Moving the heavy guns to the new lines yesterday the following was the amount of damage to harness according to Capt. Johnson's Report. 17 traces broke. 3 Saddle girths. 2 Haim [hame] Straps. 2 Trace Straps. 1 Saddle Strap. Capt. Johnson has no leather for repairs tho he has made two requisitions for it.

E.M.

[1] *Lt. Col. Stephen Elliott Jr., commanding at Fort Sumter and nearer the scene, reported 24 Oct. 1863: " ... About fifty discharges of small-arms from the beach near the Moultrie House [Sullivan's Island] were observed at 9 o'clock last night." Elliott apparently had no more idea of the cause than Manigault. [OR XXVIII (1) pp. 629, 630]*

Legare's [Point], James Island.
Saturday, 24 October 1863.

Rainy day. Cleared off about 4 o'clock in afternoon. Battery Simkins & Cheves firing upon Gregg & Wagner. No reply from the Enemy. About 5 O'clock in the afternoon some heavy firing apparently at Sea.[1]

Large number of negroes (150 to 200) engaged on Bomb Proof of Battery Tatum, and in thickening parapets to said work.

No Casualties to report.

(Countersign "Ramsay")

Edward Manigault
Major, &c.

Lt. Nesbit went off on 4 days furlough.

[1] *No explanation of the firing has been found. It also was heard by Lt. Col. Stephen Elliott Jr., commander of Fort Sumter. On 25 Oct. 1863 he reported: " ... At sunset yesterday, there was heavy firing from a blockader some 10 miles to the northward and eastward." [OR XXVIII (1) p. 630]*

Sunday, 25 October 1863.

Batteries Simkins & Cheves occasionally firing in earlier part of the day but it was altogether a very quiet day.

The Sodding on one Side of the North Entrance to Bomb Proof at Battery Haskell fell down last night partially closing the entrance. The high tides flow and ebb in Gun Chamber No. 5 at Battery Haskell.

Late in afternoon a considerable working party of the enemy seen at the End of the Causeway nearly in direction of Craig's Hill [*Morris Island*] where it abuts on the Creek, apparently embarking something. Could not tell exactly what they were doing.

No Casualties to report.

(Countersign "Glover")

Edward Manigault
Major, &c.

Legare's [Point], James Island.
Monday, 26 October 1863.

About 90 hands engaged on Bomb proof at Tatum and about 25 or 30 on the alteration in the Battery. About 70 hands engaged in altering the Battery at Ryan. A few also altering Gun Chamber No. 11 at Battery Haskell.

About 12.30 P.M. Battery Gregg commenced firing, and soon after Battery Wagner. The hours given to me were 12.25 for Gregg and 12.55 for Wagner. They fired upon Sumter & Johnson principally but occasionally at Fort Moultrie. Fort Moultrie & batteries on Sullivan's Island, Fort Johnson, Battery Simkins & Cheves replied. The firing continued until after dark.[1]

No Casualties to report.

(Countersign "Means")

Edward Manigault
Major, &c.

The 18th S.C.V. [*Manigault's Battalion*] relieved from duty at Hd. Qrs. Section 2, James Island.

[1] *This was the beginning of the Second Major Bombardment of Fort Sumter. It lasted from 26 Oct. to 6 Dec. 1863 and was designed to destroy a three-gun battery which the Confederates had erected on the right face of the fort. By the time the firing ended, between 18,000 and 19,000 rounds had been hurled at Sumter. Damage was extensive, but repairs were made at night despite heavy mortar fire. Confederate casualties numbered about 100, a third of them dead. The right flank of the fort, against which most of the fire was directed, was cut from a height of 40 feet to 20, but the rubble formed a solid base for the remaining wall. The main objective of the bombardment, destruction of the three-gun battery, failed. The guns remained serviceable. [OR XXVIII (1) pp. 630-642; Johnson, pp. 170-185, xiv, xv; Civil War at Charleston, pp. 75, 76]*

Tuesday, 27 October 1863.

The enemy opened fire about 6.45 A.M. and continued firing all day from Gregg, Wagner and the intermediate Battery. Fort Moultrie and the batteries on Sullivan's Island, and Simkins returned the fire.

The 8 in. Col^d. [*Columbiad*] delivered at Battery Haskell on 21st was Mounted to day in Left flank of Battery Haskell. The Gun has been drilled out for Bouching to the usual Size 11/16 inch but no bouche introduced. The Carriage, which was brought this Morning, has never been used, but from remaining a long time at Arsenal with Oiling &c. the excentrics were worked with great difficulty. Took off wheels and Cleaned and greased as far as was possible. Ordnance Sergeant Sullivan was sent down to put the Carriage in order. The Manoeuvering bars did not fit the axles.

A large negro force (probably near 200) working on Bomb Proof at Battery Tatum, and on both Sections of Battery Ryan.

About 5 P.M. Steamer lying in Light House Inlet commenced Shelling both Sections of Battery Ryan, probably induced to do so by seeing the number of hands at work. She threw about 4 Shells at right section of battery and about 9 at the Left Section. Of the latter, 3 fell very near together about 50 or 60 yds from the Magazine and three went over some distance. No damage done.

Two Shells which did not explode were dug up and were found to be 5 in. in diameter & 14 inches long. Percussion, weight about 40 lbs.[1]

Shell sketched by Manigault.

After Shelling Ryan for some time the Steamer commenced firing on Secessionville. Ceased at dark.

The firing from Gregg & Wagner continued slowly during the whole night.

No Casualties to report

(Countersign "Gadberry")

Edward Manigault
Major, &c.

Note, That during the last two days one or more Monitors have taken part in the firing on Sumter. On Monday for a Short time one of the Gunboats went up towards the upper end of Morris Island and fired some Shots: She did not remain long however.

Two Companies of Charleston Battalion (Abney's Companies) Came to Legare's [*Point*] on Picket or Support duty.

[1] *Manigault's description and drawing is of a typical U.S. Schenkle shell. It would have been fired by a 5.1-inch Dahlgren 50-pounder rifle, a type used by many of the Federal ships. Several of these projectiles have been found in recent years on James Island.*

Legare's [Point], James Island.
Wednesday, 28 October 1863.

The enemy to day fired principally at Sumter. Fort Moultrie & batteries on Sullivan's Island replying. Battery Simkins firing her Mortars principally. (Note. Batteries Gregg, Wagner, an intermediate battery and one Monitor firing to day.) [*Parenthetical note was inserted in the diary above the date*].

Col. Harris came to Battery Haskell about 12 P.M. and inspected the Work Carefully with a view to remodelling the Gun Chambers & Embrazures. He gave directions to Capt. Gregorie to carry out the plans he decided on, Viz:

1st. Mortar Chamber No. 1 in Mortar Battery No. 1 (West) to be converted into a Gun Chamber. West Embrazure commanding Creeks & Sound in front of "Tatum". South Embrazure to cross fire to South & S.E. with 8 in. S.C. [*Sea Coast*] Howitzer in Gun Chamber No. 11. (Carronade to be mounted here).

2. Platform in No. 11 extended and Embrazures arranged for clear field of fire S. & West also to enfilade Creek & beach Eastwards. (8 in. S.C. [*Sea Coast*] Howitzer here).

3. No. 10 South Embrazure as at present or opened more to West. East Embrazure so as to Sweep Creek & Beach Eastwards.

4. No. 8 arranged for two Embrazures, South and Eastwards. This he regards as an excellent Battery or Chamber.

5. No. 7 to be left as it is. Intended for a Rifle.

6. No. 5 to be arranged to fire both ways, the South Embrazure more opened to the West. This will be the Center Battery flanking or Enfilading the Half Arc either way unless Capt. Gregorie can attain this objective better from No. 4.

7. No. 1 to remain nearly as it is except perhaps that the top of parapet be shaved off so as to permit the 24 Pndr. double banded Rifle to be more depressed.

8. 8 in. Columbiad to be shut off from Wagner. To fire to S.W. and S.E. at Marsh Battery and N.E. to Left & Rear of Haskell.

9. Extreme N.E. Gun Chamber to be arranged for a 42 Pndr. Carronade probably on Siege Carriage. This will also be cut off from fire of Wagner.

10. Such Gun Chambers as have not been mentioned, May be modified if necessary so as not to Mask fire of those selected. But otherwise had better be retained as far as possible for future use in case We can get more guns.

These as near as I can recollect were the instructions given by Col. Harris which were partially given to Me as Capt. Gregorie did not arrive until We had passed No. 7 going Eastwards.

About 60 Negroes engaged on Bomb proof at Battery Tatum, 6 or 8 Thickening Parapet for Rifles in Center of Tatum, and about 40 on Gun Chamber to be placed at Salient of Cremailliere Line to West [*The word "Right" is inserted additionally above "West".*] of Battery proper of "Tatum". Also 60 or 70 at Battery Ryan (Left).

Lieutenants Chapman & Nesbit returned from furlough to day.

I should also state that Col. Harris directed the Gun Chambers to have the preference of guns as follows:

1st No. 11 8 in. S.C. Howitzer	2nd. East Flank 8 in. Cold. (iron)
3rd No. 1. Double banded 24 pndr.	4th. No. 5
5th. Mortar Chamber No. 1	6th. No. 10
7th. No. 8	8th. Extreme N.E. Chamber.

The Enemy fired slowly all night.
No Casualties to report.
(Countersign "Marshall")

Edward Manigault
Major Comdg. Arty.

Received to day 4.62 Rifle No. 1 which we used at Haskell and which was sent from thence to Charleston Arsenal Oct. 5th instant. Marks,

Right Trunnion [*Junius L. Archer, proprietor of Bellona Foundry, Richmond, Va.*]

On Left Trunnion [*Date of manufacture*] On Muzzle No. 3. [*Number of the gun*] It has been rebanded and Rebouched.

Legare's House, James Island.
Thursday, 29 October 1863.

Firing from Gregg, Wagner, the intermediate battery and one or more of the Monitors. The firing was principally at Fort Sumter & very heavy. Battery Simkins and the Brooke Gun Battery near Fort Johnson replying slowly. I did not see Fort Moultrie or the Sull. Isld. [*Sullivan's Island*] Batteries firing.

Large force of negroes as before working at Batteries Tatum & Ryan.

In the afternoon Seven other companies of the "Charleston Battalion" arrived at Legare's to take the place of the 18th S.C.V. for picket duty (and as support to the Batteries). This makes Nine Companies now here (Capt. Buist's, the Tenth, being in Christ Church Parish).

At 2 P.M. to day received at Battery Haskell one 24 Pounder Smooth Bore from Major Campbell on the "Western Lines." This gun is in a damaged condition, having the Knob of the Cascable knocked off and also a part of the Breech. The Carriage is also old & Rotten. The Right wheel (unlimbered) has the nave entirely decayed. The gun is intended to shoot Grape & Canister with light charges but it is scarcely fit for use. With the Gun came Ammunition & Implements.

The enemy fired slowly all night.
No Casualties to report
(Countersign "Smith")

Edward Manigault
Major &c.

Legare's House, James Island.
Friday, 30 October 1863.

A very heavy fire from the enemy on Fort Sumter before day and continued throughout the day. Batteries Gregg & Wagner and the intermediate Battery were firing. Battery Simkins & the Brooke Gun Battery firing slowly in reply.

About 10 O'Clock saw a floating Pile Driver belonging to the Enemy engaged in driving piles a little to the West of Black Island.

Opened fire upon her from Redoubt No. 1 with 8 inch Navy Shell Gun & 30 Pounder Parrott about 11.55 A.M.

8 in Navy Shell Gun

Shot	Powder	Elev.	Fuze	Distance	Result
1st Shot	8 lbs	12° Elev.	10 Sec. Navy Fuze	Dist. Estimated 1¾ miles.	Burst high & Short.
2 "	do	14°	15 " " "	do do	Fell left about correct dist. No Burst.
3 "	do	14°	15 " " "	do do	Burst high & Right
4 "	do	15°	15 " " "	Dist. Est. 2 Miles.	Fell Right, did not burst.
5 "	do	16°	15 " " "	do do	Burst high & Left.
6 "	do	15°	15 " " "	do do	Burst high.
7 "	do	do	18 " " "	do do	Good Line Shot. Very little Short. Selma Fuze.
8 "	do	do	17 " " "	do do	To left, did not burst. [Selma Fuze]

30 Pounder Parrott, at Pile Driver 1¾ to 2 miles distant.

Shot	Powder	Elev.	Fuze	Distance	Result
1st Shot	3½ lbs Powder	8° Elev.	8″ Fuze	Dist. 1¾ Miles.	Fell Right and nearly at proper distance.
2 "	" " " "	9° "	8″ "	" "	Good line Shot but burst too soon.
3 "	" " " "	10° "	11″ "	" "	Burst high & to Left.
4 "	" " " "	12° "	15″ "	" "	Fell a little left & Far enough. Did not burst.
5 "	" " " "	11° "	13″ "	" "	Good line but little Short. Very close apparently.
6 "	" " " "	12° "	13″ "	Dist. 2 Miles.	Fell to Right. Did not burst.
7 "	" " " "	11½° "	13″ "	" "	Burst a little high but apparently threw fragments around the Pile Driver.
8 "	" " " "	11½° "	13″ "	" "	McEvoy Igniter, little Short, excellent line. Did not burst.
9 "	" " " "	12° "	12″ "	" "	Fell Right . Not very good. Did not burst.
10 "	" " " "	12° "	11″ "	" "	McEvoy Igniter, premature Explosion.

The Pile Driver by this time had increased her distance so much that we gave over firing.

The Fuzes used with the 30 pndr. were new Richmond Fuzes 15 Sec to 1 inch.

Large force of negroes still engaged on Battery Tatum and Battery Ryan.

Lieut. Legare delivered to day at Battery Tatum three (3) 24 Pounder Austrian Howitzers (Bronze field) and one light Smooth Bore 32 on Siege Carriage. Also ammunition and Implements &c. As no platforms are ready of course no guns could be got in position.

At about half past 5 P.M. the enemy ceased firing and did not recommence for an hour or two, then firing slowly through the night (probably one gun in ten or fifteen Minutes). "Charleston Battalion" (27th S.C.V.) first time on Picket to Night (very late). Col. Way says he posted them himself.

No Casualties to Report.

Countersign "Pinckney"

Edward Manigault
Major &c.

Saturday, 31 October 1863.

Col. Way, 54th Ga. Vol., went to Savannah on Furlough. Maj. Abney in Command.

Artillery of Section 2, James Island, inspected & Mustered by Capt. J. Ward Hopkins of Sumter Guard, 27th S.C.V. (Late "Charleston Battalion"). The 54th Georgia by Capt. S.P. Smith. The 27th S.C.V. ("Charleston Battalion") by Captn. [J.C.] Edwards of 5th Regt. S.C. Cavalry.

The Enemy firing sharply from Gregg, Wagner and intermediate batteries from Early dawn, though from the peculiar State of the Atmosphere, the reports of the Guns could scarcely be heard from Hd. Qrs. at Legare's House. Towards Midday the fire Slackened. Precisely at 12 M. two Monitors moved up near the upper end of Morris Island, and the fire was resumed heavily both from themselves and the Shore Batteries, and continued till dark. Battery Gregg apparently directed the fire of one or more rifle guns on the S.W. Angle of Sumter with great precision and very destructive effect.[1] Battery Simkins and the Brooke Gun Battery fired occasionally on the Enemy.

A large negro force still engaged on Batteries Tatum & Ryan. The Flanking gun Chamber to Right of Tatum completed all to the platforms. The one Gun battery or Chamber on Point to East of Tatum commenced to day at 1 P.M.

Note that one of the Austrian 24 Pndr. Bronze howitzers brought to Battery Tatum on Friday 30th inst. was carried away the same day leaving only 2 behind.

Capt. Webb went with Drivers & horses to the Charleston Arsenal and brought away to Sect. 2 the Caisson containing Ammunition and 3½ in. Blakely Shell to which Girardey fuzes have been attached.

About 9.30 A.M. three Gunboats in Folly River commenced Shelling our Pickets about Mr. Solomon Legare's place. This Shelling lasted one or two hours.[2]

No Casualties to Report.

(Countersign "Marion")

Edward Manigault
Major &c.

Moved 4.62 in. "No. 1" rebanded and bouched into position at Battery Tatum.

8 in. Col^d. [*Columbiad*] in Gun Chamber No. 12 (East or Left) bouched this afternoon.

[1] *Lt. Col. Stephen Elliott Jr., commander of Fort Sumter, reported 1 Nov. 1863: "The fire yesterday proceeded from two monitors, two heavy and two light rifled guns at Gregg, three heavy rifled guns and four 10-inch mortars at the middle battery and four rifled guns at Wagner; 443 rifled shots were fired from the land batteries, of which 61 missed; 86 shots were fired from the monitors, all of which were reported as having struck, and 373 from mortars, of which 120 missed...The fire of the land batteries was directed chiefly at southwest angle, which suffered severely. The flag-staff was shot away twice and replaced...." [OR XXVIII (1), p. 632]*

Extract from diary of Rear Adm. John A. Dahlgren, USN: "October 31 — Went up about noon in the gunboat Ottawa to examine progress on Sumter...The southeast front much cut down...northeast face disfigured, but retains its form; northwest front looks to be breached; southwest front not visible...The flag pole (at southwest angle) shot away twice, once by [U.S. monitor] Lehigh. A man got out on the wall and put it up." [ONR 15, p. 85]

[2] *Abstract log of the U.S. mortar schooner C.P. Williams: "October 31, 1863 — At 8:15 a.m. the Marblehead took us in tow and proceeded [up Folly River] to Secessionville Creek and anchored. Called to quarters and commenced shelling the woods. Discharged 28 rounds from 32-pounder, 27 rounds from Parrott rifle, and 11 rounds from howitzer. At 11:30 were again taken in tow and anchored in our former position." [ONR 15, p. 90]*

Sunday, 1 November 1863.

Firing as usual from the Yankee Batteries on Fort Sumter. After Midday two Monitors moved up and joined in the firing. Battery Simkins & the Brooke Gun Battery replying occasionally.

Sunday Inspections as usual.

No Casualties to report.

(Countersign "Donelson")

Edward Manigault
Major &c.

About 12 O'clock (Midnight) order came by Telegraph for 27 S.C.V. to go to Fort Sumter. This turned out to be a mistake but the 27th were relieved from Picket about 2 A.M. so as to be ready to go in Case the Order was correct.

Legare's [Point], James Island.
Monday, 2 November 1863.

The Enemy firing as usual at Sumter. After Midday, three Monitors moved up and joined in the Bombardment. Battery Simkins replying with her mortars.

Negro force engaged on Battery Tatum & Battery Ryan (Right). Carpenters engaged in putting down Platforms at Ryan (Left). About Midday Capt. Gregorie set hands to work in Modifying Gun Chamber No. 4 (from Right) at Haskell, formerly No. 8, also in throwing up Merlon to Mask the Columbiad from the fire of Gregg & Wagner.

We moved 4.62 in. No. 2 from Battery Haskell to Battery Tatum with Ammunition & Implements.

Lieut Hasell was detached by Col. Gonzales to act as "Asst. Chief of Artillery" and Inspector of Artillery.

Capt. [*S. Porcher*] Smith visited City on business connected with his Caissons which have been a long time at the Charleston Arsenal for repair.

Lieut. Wilson went home on furlough for fifteen days.

No Casualties to report.

(Countersign "Seven Pines")

Edward Manigault
Major, &c.

Legare's [Point], James Island.
Tuesday, 3 November 1863.

The Enemy's fire not quite so heavy as previously. Battery Simkins and the Brooke Gun Battery firing in return. The Monitors as usual taking their position about the time of high water on the Ebb and joining in the Bombardment [*of Fort Sumter*].

A negro force engaged on Gun Chambers Nos. 4 & 12 at Battery Haskell. Large force at Battery Tatum. Thirty five to forty at Ryan (right), and Carpenters laying down platforms at Ryan (left).

No Casualties to report.

(Countersign "Shiloh")

Edward Manigault
[*Rank, etc., omitted*]

Legare's [Point], James Island.
Wednesday, 4 November 1863.

The enemy's fire as usual on Fort Sumter but not quite so fast. About 1 P.M. President Davis, accompanied by Gov. Bonham, Genl. Beauregard, Genl. Hagood, Col. Gonzales and others, arrived at Hd. Qrs. Legare's Point and after receiving the Salute of the 27th S.C.V. & 54th Georgia Vol. drawn up in line of battle (also of Co. "A" Siege Train) passed on to Battery Haskell where they remained a short time in observation, then returned and passed along the Lines towards Stono. Genl. Soule and Bishop Lynch followed in a Barouche.

(In the evening there was some doubt as to whether the 54th Georgia or the 27th S.C. should furnish the detail for Picket duty. The officers of the 27th Supposing that orders had been given for each Regiment to furnish the detail for 4 nights consecutively while those of 54th Georgia supposed that the arrangement was only to last until the 27th had made up to the 54th the 4 nights consecutively that they did Picket duty, occasioned by the Non-Arrival of the 27th at the Post (a delay occasioned by the 27th waiting in Charleston to receive their uniforms). As there were no written orders from Hd. Qrs. on the Subject, and as the 27th had already paid back the four nights consecutive picket duty, it was decided that the usual rule of Alternate nights should be adopted, and accordingly the 27th S.C.V. went on duty, the 54th having gone last night.) (Major Abney used up.)

Adjutant Gardner went into the City on furlough for the day.

Col. Way, 54th Georgia, Arrived from Savannah about 7.30 P.M.

No Casualties to report.

(Countersign "Secessionville")

Edward Manigault
Major, &c.

One Banded 24 Pounder moved from Redoubt No. 1 to Battery Ryan (left) and put in position on platform No. 3 just completed.

Also, at Battery Tatum platform of 1 gun Battery to Right completed, also that of Gun Chamber No. 1 in battery proper.

Thursday, 5 November 1863.

Firing as usual from the Enemy's Batteries on Morris Island. Fort Moultrie occasionally replying with Mortars. Monitors engaged in the afternoon.

Negro force still engaged on Ryan (right) on Tatum and at Battery Haskell.

Genl. Taliaferro and Col. Gonzales visited Battery Haskell about 4 P.M.

Three 12 pounder Howitzers (Bronze) delivered at Battery Ryan (right) about 5 P.M. and ammunition for them about 9 P.M. No implements whatever sent with the Howitzers.

In Consequence of information received the Cannoneers were increased in number at the different Batteries and the pickets or Supporting Infantry force strengthened.

No Casualties to report.

Countersign "Vicksburg."

Edward Manigault
Major Comdg. Arty.

Legare's [Point], James Island.
Friday, 6 November 1863

Enemy firing as usual from Morris Island. Fort Moultrie replying occasionally with her Mortars. About 2 or 2½ P.M. one of the Monitors came into the outer harbor and lay for some time between Gregg and Fort Sumter. Both herself and another Monitor lower down fired on Fort Sumter. Fort Moultrie fired at her and also the Brooke Gun Battery but apparently without effect. She went out again about 3.30 P.M.

General Hagood visited Hd. Qrs. at Legare's Point about 10 A.M.

Captain Webb in accordance with instructions took Command of Battery Haskell with his Company leaving his Drivers under a Sergeant to take charge of the two Guns, Caissons & horses at his former Camp near Hd. Qrs. Legare's House. Capt. [*S. Porcher*] Smith took Command of the Batteries Tatum & Ryan (he had previously had command of Tatum) with his Company, the Detachment of his Company previously at Battery Haskell reporting back to him.

Another 12 pndr. Howitzer was sent to Battery Ryan (right) this morning. Also one to Tatum.

A considerable Negro force engaged at Batteries Haskell, Tatum and Ryan (right)

About 4.30 P.M. one of the Enemy's Steamers appeared in the Creek between Black Island & Long Island. When particularly noticed she appeared to be at the Row of piles driven across the Creek which runs southwards of Long Island and perhaps was engaged in endeavouring to remove some of them. She was an ordinary Ferry Boat similar to those between New York & Brooklyn.

Fired three Shot at her from 30 pounder Parrott Gun in Redoubt No. 1 when She was lying at East end of Long Island. Supposed distance 2½ miles.

1st Shot	3½ lbs Powder	30 lb. Shell	14° Elevation	17″ Fuze (Selma)	Burst very high, probably after 8 or 10 Sec.
2 ″	″ ″ ″ ″	″ ″ ″	15° ″	18″ ″ ″	Did not burst, fell say ⅓ Mile Short, good line.
3 ″	″ ″ ″ ″	″ ″ ″	17° ″	20″ ″ ″	Did not burst, fell probably ¼ Mile Short.

The Steamer then went behind Long Island and was lost to view.

After we had fired two Shots, a Yankee Gunboat in Lt. [*Light*] House Inlet opened fire. The first Shell (percussion) fell about 200 to 250 yds Short of Redoubt No. 1 and the second about 200 yds Short. The third was fired at Secessionville.

Capt. Webb went to City to get pay for his Company.

No Casualties to report.
Countersign "Lodi"

Edward Manigault
Major &c.

Legare's [Point], James Island.
Saturday, 7 November 1863

The enemy firing from Morris Island but more slowly than usual. Force of Negroes engaged on Battery Haskell, Tatum & Ryan (Right) and to Right of Ryan left. Col. Gonzales Came to Ryan (Right) about Midday.

In the afternoon two of the Gunboats in Light House Inlet threw some Shells at Secessionville and at Bridge leading there.[1] No damage done.

No Casualties to report.
Countersign "Murfreesboro"

Edward Manigault
Major &c.

Genls. Taliaferro & Hagood and Col. Gonzales made the Rounds about 12 or 1 O'clock at night.

[1] *This bridge was the shortest route between Manigault's batteries and Fort Lamar at Secessionville. It also enabled the Confederates to reinforce Fort Lamar during the Battle of Secessionville, 16 June 1862. [See Introduction, pp. ix, x. Also, 17 Oct. 1863, note]*

Legare's [Point], James Island.
Sunday, 8 November 1863

Slow fire all day from Morris Island at Fort Sumter.

Genl. Hagood visited Battery Haskell about Midday. Col. Gonzales soon afterwards.

In the afternoon a Steamer passed through the Creek between Black & Long Islands. She was reported to have troops on board. When nearest, She was probably about 2 Miles from Battery Tatum. Fired 3 Shots Solid at her from that Battery with 4.62 in. Rifle. First shot 11° the other two 12°. All fell a little Short but quite near.

Immediately after a second Steamer passed through the same route. Fired 2 Solid Shots at her at 12°. Supposed to fall a little short.

Put out a new Picket Boat with 4 Men in advance of the Right Flank of Haskell. The Boat however leaked so badly that after a time the Picket had to return.

No Casualties to report.
Countersign "Waterloo"

About dark Capt. Beals of 22 Georgia Arty Battalion reported for duty with his Company (53 Aggregate) (Co. "C" 22 Ga. Arty) at Hd. Qrs. Legare's. A detachment of 20 was immediately sent to serve the two

12 Pndr. Howitzers at Ryan (Right) which Capt. [*George W.*] Johnson could not Man and the rest of the Company was moved down to Haskell.

Edward Manigault
Major, &c.

(Attended Brigade Drill by Genl. Hagood.)
Col. Gaillard came to Hd. Qrs. of his Regiment.[1]

---

[1] *Gaillard's 27th Rgmt., S.C. Infantry, which had been organized 30 Sept. 1863, initially had been split between the 5th District, Charleston, and the 7th on James Island. On 29 Oct. 1863 the seven companies in Charleston were ordered to join the two stationed on James Island. The colonel, who had lost a hand in the Morris Island fighting in August, presumably had been in the city recovering from the wound. [OR XXVIII (2), p. 468]*

Legare's [Point]

Monday, 9 November 1863 [*Entry in the Diary erroneously dated 10 Nov.*]

The firing from Morris Island slow during the day. At night the firing was more rapid than it has been for some time, both of Guns and Mortars.

A Negro force engaged at Tatum & Ryan. Platform for 1 gun Battery to left of Tatum was laid down.

Capt. [*S. Porcher*] Smith went to town on private business.

Had the new Picket Boat Caulked and the picket sent out to a point in the Creek in advance of Right Flank of Battery Haskell.

No Casualties to report.

Countersign "Elkhorn"

Edward Manigault
Major

Col. Way made Rounds of Command Shortly before Midnight.

Lt. Willingham, Co. C, Ga. Siege Train, came back from Sick Furlough.

Tuesday, 10 November 1863

The Enemy's Batteries on Morris's Island firing slowly. About 3 P.M. a Monitor came between Battery Wagner & Fort Sumter and fired on the latter. She lay there an hour or two.

Capt. Gregorie's Negro force engaged at Haskell in raising platforms of Nos. 4 & 7 (formerly Nos. 5 & 8). These platforms were relaid. Also platform for gun in Mortar Battery No. 1. Negro force at Tatum engaged on Bomb Proof.

A large Negro force from Capt. Ramsay's division engaged in widen-

ing and improving Road to Battery Haskell.
No Casualties to report
Countersign "Moscow"

Edward Manigault
Major

I made the Rounds from Redoubt No. 1 to Haskell from 12 to 3 A.M. (of 11th)

Wednesday, 11 November 1863

Firing very slowly from the Yankee Batteries. Simkins & the Brooke Gun Battery near Fort Johnson firing slowly in reply.

Captain Gregorie commenced cutting an Embrazure to SW of Gun Chamber No. 4 on left of Battery Tatum to Enfilade the front of Battery. Also putting Merlon on Right flanking Battery of Gun Chamber to traverse from fire of Morris Island. Also commenced Continuation of Rifle pits from where they ended between Tatum & Ryan, on the left Flank of Ryan Left. Some hands still going on with the Bomb Proof at Tatum. At Battery Haskell a Breastwork or Rifle Pit was commenced along the Marsh on North side of the battery. The negro force of Captain Ramsay's division Completed the Road to Battery Haskell about 4.30 P.M.

About 9 P.M. a pretty heavy Musketry fire seen & heard in the direction of Battery Wagner. Whether on the island, or on the water beyond, could not be ascertained. Cause not known.[1]

Near Midnight a fire was observed in Charleston.[2]
Countersign "Lexington"
No Casualties to report.

Edward Manigault
Major, &c.

[1] *Extract from journal, Dept. of S.C., Ga. and Fla., 11 Nov. 1863: "...At 9 p.m. rapid musketry firing was observed at Battery Gregg, while voices were heard to cry out 'Halt!' It is supposed that two parties of the Yankees met on the beach, and, mistaking each other for enemies, commenced firing. The result of the affair has not been discovered. The firing continued for about ten minutes, during which time several hundred of small-arms were discharged...." [OR XXVIII (1), p. 160] No Federal reports have been found.*

[2] *A Charleston newspaper, The Daily Courier, stated on 12 Nov. 1863: "Fire — An alarm of fire was given about a quarter to 12 o'clock last night caused by the burning of a large, unoccupied kitchen [Charleston kitchens, in those days, were separate from houses for this very reason] situated in a lot on Meeting Street, opposite Spring [St.] in Ward 7."*

Legare's [Point]
Thursday, 12 November 1863

Battery Gregg and auxiliary Mortar Battery firing slowly during the greater part of the day. Fort Moultrie & Battery Simkins replying slowly. In the afternoon the firing was brisker. Soon after Nightfall the enemy's fire (principally Mortar fire) became pretty heavy and lasted so through a great part of the night.

Captain Gregorie's force engaged partly on Breastwork on North of Battery Haskell. Another portion on New Embrazure & on Merlon at Battery Tatum, and in sodding the same. Other hands in extending the Rifle pits between Tatum & Ryan (left). A force also Commenced raising the frame of a Bombproof at Battery Ryan (left).

About 100 hands from Captain Ramsay's division commenced constructing Infantry Breastworks on the peninsula between Redoubt No. 1 & Secessionville. Also a Road force improving and widening the Road to Secessionville.

No Casualties to report.

Countersign "Lutzen"

Edward Manigault
Major, &c.

Legare's [Point]
Friday, 13 November 1863

A pretty sharp fire exchanged between the Batteries on Morris Isld. and Fort Moultrie, Battery Bee & Battery Simkins. The Morris Island Batteries fired indiscriminately on the Sullivan's Island batteries, on Fort Sumter and on Battery Simkins.

Hands still employed on Breastwork to North of Haskell. Others still employed at Tatum. The Rifle pits continued to left Flank of Ryan (left). Late in afternoon Commenced 1 gun Battery between Ryan & Tatum. Frame of Bombproof at Ryan (left) erected, and some of the covering timber laid on top.

Capt. Ramsay's hands still engaged on Breastwork across peninsula to South of Redoubt No. 1. Also another gang engaged on the Road to Secessionville.

At 10 P.M. an alarm occurred at Battery Haskell in consequence of a Sentinel mistaking another light for the Blue light of the Eastern Picket Boat. This was soon discovered to be a false alarm.

No Casualties to report.

Countersign "Belmount"

Edward Manigault
Major, &c.

Legare's [Point]
Saturday, 14 November 1863

About 10 A.M. a Steamer and a Sloop passed from behind Long Island into Light House Inlet by the route approaching Black Island. Two Shots were fired at the Steamer and then at the Sloop from 4.62 Guns

Nos. 1 & 2 in Battery Tatum. Distance about 2 Miles. 10° Elev. Solid Conical Shot fired, wgt. 24 lbs. or 19 lbs. Two or three of the shots fell near the vessels but none hit. They passed very rapidly and were soon out of effective range.

Lt. Stiles in charge of the Engineer force, Captain Gregorie having gone off on furlough. Negroes employed at Haskell, Tatum, 1 gun battery between Tatum & Ryan, and in piling earth against the Bomb Proof at Ryan (left).

Captain Webb issuing the Harness he has lately got for his Battery.

No Casualties to report.

Countersign "Yorktown"

Edward Manigault

Major

Legare's [Point]
Sunday, 15 November 1863

Sunday Inspections as usual. About Midday an Enemy's Steamer passed from Creek beyond Long Island to Light House Inlet by the route approaching Black Island at one point. We fired Six Shot at her from the 4.62 in. Rifles at Battery Tatum. Most of these Shots fell Short. In reply to this fire, the Yankee gunboats in Light House Inlet threw six Shell at Batteries Tatum & Ryan, none of which did any damage though a Shrapnel Shot pierced a plank within five feet of two of the Garrison of Battery Ryan.

The Gunboats also threw a good many shell at Secessionville.

Major Mayo, Asst. Chief of Artillery, visited Legare's about 1 P.M. in order to procure reports of Artillery, Ordnance & Ordnance Stores.

No Casualties to report.

Countersign "Springfield"

Edward Manigault

Major, &c.

Note. The 4.62 in. Rifles have been fired in Battery Tatum.

5 Shots fired Nov. 8. All from 5750 Gun (No. 2 of Haskell). 65 Shots brought forward. Total 70 Shots.

5 do. Nov. 14. 3 from No. 1 of Haskell. 2 from No. 2. 261 before bouching + 3 = 264 Shots No. 1. 70 + 2 = 72 Total No. 2.

7 do. Nov. 15. 4 from No. 1, 3 from No. 2. 264 + 4 = 268 Total. 75 Total No. 2.

Legare's [Point]
Monday, 16 November 1863

About 7 A.M. a very heavy fire was Commenced from Fort Moultrie and Batteries Bee, Beauregard &c. on Battery Gregg and one of the Monitors which appeared to be aground near Gregg. This fire was replied to by Gregg and the other Monitors slowly. This fire lasted heavily until 9 or 10 O'clock. The grounded Monitor afterwards got off and was towed away by another one.[1]

The "Ironsides" moved up today, from 12 to 3 O'clock, to a point opposite Battery Wagner, and returned again to her old anchorage below "Graham's Head Quarters." She moved very slowly.

Engineer Force at work as usual on Haskell, Tatum, 1 gun Battery and on Bombproof at Ryan (left).

About 11 A.M. one 42 pndr. Carronade & Slide Carriage was delivered at Battery Haskell. No Pintle or Pintle Block delivered with it. This Carronade is to be put in the extreme left Gun Chamber, but in Consequence of the lowness of the Carriage, much alteration will be necessary to the parapet.[2]

No Casualties to report.

Countersign "Charleston"

Edward Manigault

Major, &c.

[1] *The grounded monitor was the Lehigh. She had anchored close to Morris Island during the previous evening to prevent an anticipated Confederate boat attack on the northern end of the island. The attack didn't materialize. However, when the Lehigh attempted to get under way at daylight, it was discovered that she was aground. Her captain stated that he had anchored in sufficient water, but that the vessel had swung with the tide during the night and "...touched a lump, and there hung." He said that the water was calm and that she grounded so gently that none of the crew had noticed.*

The Lehigh immediately signaled for help and was soon joined by the monitors Nahant, Montauk and, later, the Passaic. The Confederate forts opened fire on the stranded vessel, fire that was reciprocated by the monitors assisted by the Federal batteries on Morris Island. While the battle raged, volunteers from the Lehigh and Nahant attempted to pass a hawser between the ships. Twice it was cut by enemy fire. The third attempt was successful and the Lehigh was dragged off the bank into deep water.

During the three or four hours that she was under fire, the Lehigh received 22 hits and had seven of the men passing the lines wounded. Two days later, she suddenly began taking on water from a serious leak, apparently a delayed result of the battle. Emergency repairs were made and the vessel was kept afloat. The other monitors received only superficial damage.

The Confederates reported that 52 shots were fired by the monitors and 21 by the Federal land batteries. Fort Moultrie, the main Confederate work engaged, fired 189 shot and shell and was hit a number of times by enemy fire. One of her guns, a 32-pounder, was destroyed. One man was killed and three injured. [ONR 15, pp. 117-127]

[2] *The carronade, a relatively light weapon devised for shipboard use, fired a proportionately large, heavy ball with minimum velocity on the theory that this would cause maximum splintering of wooden hulls. The carriage consisted of two parts. The top, which held the weapon, slid along the section below, thus dissipating the shock of recoil. To prevent the entire carriage from sliding backward when the carronade was fired, and also to permit the weapon to be traversed, the bottom part of the carriage pivoted from the front around an iron pintle anchored to a heavy block, in this case probably of wood, buried in the ground. [Ripley, pp. 89, 182, 183, 204]*

Tuesday, 17 November 1863

At 11 A.M. a second 42-Pounder Carronade was delivered at Battery Haskell with its Slide & Carriage. It was placed near New Gun Chamber in Right Mortar Battery.

At 11.20 A.M. the enemy Commenced Shelling the City of Charleston from the Battery to South of Gregg.[1] The gun is lowered by machinery after each discharge, for the convenience of loading. After being loaded, it is again raised by Machinery to the level of the firing Platform at which time several feet of the Chase can be seen above the parapet, from Battery Haskell. After the Elevation and direction are verified, it is fired. It recoils several feet, is run again to Battery, and descends again to be loaded.[2] The Sound of Motion of Shell through the air could be distinctly heard apparently until it had passed far beyond any part of James Island and then the explosion of the Shells in the City would be heard. The firing Continued at the average rate of One Shot every 6 or 8 minutes for two or more hours.

At 1 P.M. a Steamer (supposed the *"Planter"*)[3] passed through the Creek to S.W. of Black Island on route between Little Folly Creek and Light House Inlet. Fired 8 Shots at her from the 4.62 in. guns in Battery Tatum. None of these Shot hit, though several went very near her.

Charge 4 lbs. powder. Shot 19 to 24 lb. Elevation 10°. Distance [*Omitted in diary*] Miles. Total No. Shot No. 1, 272 in all, 11 Since Rebanding & Bouching. No 2, 79 in all.

The Enemy fired several Shell in return but principally at Secessionville.

Engineer force engaged on breastwork to North of Haskell. Another on Bombproof at Tatum. Another portion on 1 gun Battery between Tatum & Ryan.

No Casualties to report.

Countersign "Augusta"

Edward Manigault

Major, &c.

[1] *This was Battery Chatfield, armed with two 100-pounder and one 300-pounder Parrott rifles. The battery was named in an order dated 28 Oct. 1863 for Col. John R. Chatfield, commander of the 6th Rgmt., Conn. Infantry, who was killed in the disastrous Federal assault on Battery Wagner 18 July 1863. [OR XXVIII (1), pp. 15, 16; OR XXXV (2), p. 42; OR LIII (Supplement), pp. 8, 91, 94]*

[2] *Specifications for this carriage have not been found. However, it apparently was an improvised wood carriage and not operated by machinery as Manigault surmised. It was mentioned in an 1879 book by a member of the 3rd R.I. Heavy Artillery as: "...the new carriage...which was kept secret from all visitors...consisted of long elastic timbers of such size and adjustment as allowed the gun to spring down and backward on a parabolic curve...." [Rev. Frederic Denison, Shot and Shell, the Third Rhode Island Heavy Artillery, p. 253]*

[3] *The Planter was a wood, 300-ton, 147-foot inland steamer used as a dispatch boat in the Charleston area. She had twin engines and was considered the fastest boat in the*

harbor. *During the early morning hours of 13 May 1862, while her white officers were asleep ashore, the vessel's slave crew sneaked aboard, fired up the boilers and ran her past Fort Sumter to the blockading fleet. The Planter was used by the Federal Army during the remainder of the war, mainly on South Carolina waters where her speed and shallow draft made her exceptionally valuable for supply duties and military operations along the various tidal creeks. Following the war, the vessel was sold to private owners and was lost in 1876 while trying to save another vessel near Cape Romain, S.C. [ONR 12, pp. 820-826; The News and Courier (Charleston newspaper), 31 March 1876, p. 4]*

Wednesday, 18 November 1863

About 10 O'clock one of Capt. Beals' Men, Co. C, 22 Battalion Georgia Artillery, in violation of Standing Orders, shot at a Crane in the middle of the Camp at Battery Haskell, and killed a horse belonging to Captn. Gregg's Battery, Co. "C" S.C. Siege Train. He was immediately arrested and Charges preferred against him.

Captn. Smith went to City on official business, and Adjutant Gardner on leave for the day.

About Midday a Steamer passed through Creek leading to South of Long Island. Fired three Shots at her from 4.62 No. 1 at Battery Tatum. Charge 4 lbs. Shell about 24 lbs. Elev. 12°. McEvoy Igniter,[1] 15 Sec. fuze. All three shells exploded too soon. (Total No. Shot from 4.62 No. 1, 275. 14 since Rebouche[*d*].

The Enemy immediately fired five or Six Shells at Secessionville from a Battery on Black Island. This is the first time that it was known positively that shells were thrown from Black Island.

No Casualties to report

Countersign "Atlanta"

Edward Manigault
Major, &c.

Reported that several Shots were fired to day from Marsh Battery No. 1.[2]

[1] *See glossary.*

[2] *See note 15 Aug. 1863. After the 8-inch Parrott burst, the Marsh Battery was armed with two 10-inch mortars. They were replaced later by a 30-pounder Parrott. These weapons fired on Fort Sumter, not the city.*

Thursday, 19 November 1863

The enemy firing slowly upon Sumter. Towards Midday the Enemy again commenced shelling the City. It is thought from observation from Battery Haskell that 12 Shells were discharged towards the city.

Engineer force of about 40 or 50 negroes engaged on Bomb Proof at Tatum. Nearly as many more on the Bombproof at Battery Ryan (left).

One horse belonging to Co. "A" Siege Train died this morning and one Mule belonging to Co. "B" Siege Train. Both appeared to die of Cholic

85

superinduced perhaps by the inferior Corn furnished to the Animals and the want of fodder.

A little after dark this evening one shot was reported to be fired from the Marsh Battery No. 1. It is not known in what direction it was fired.

No Casualties to report.

Countersign "Richmond"

Edward Manigault
Major, &c.

Friday, 20 November 1863

An hour or two before day there was some Musketry firing from Fort Sumter, which gave rise to the belief that an Assault was being made. It turned out however that it was simply a Yankee reconnoitering party who advanced too near the Fort & was fired into.

About 10 A.M. the Yankees commenced throwing Shells into the City. This was continued off & on until 4 P.M.

Engaged in Making very carefully a complete Inventory of the contents of the Magazines at Battery Haskell. Introduced there additional supports under beam in the Main Magazine.

Captain Webb went into City to day on private business.

No Casualties to report

Countersign "Nashville"

Edward Manigault
Major, &c.

Saturday, 21 November 1863

The usual firing going on from the Yankee batteries. Nothing to record especially worthy of note.

Proceeding with a careful inventory of All Ordnance Stores, &c.

No Casualties to report

Countersign "Memphis"

Edward Manigault
Major, &c.

Sunday, 22 November 1863

Heavy firing between our Batteries and those of the enemy. Battery Gregg firing heavy Rifle guns at Simkins during the whole day and with great accuracy. Principally Mortars fired on Fort Sumter. Fort Johnson and several of our Batteries practicing Ricochet firing in front of and around Sumter so as to get the range in preparation for a Boat attack on that work.

In the afternoon (about 5 P.M.) a detail of 100 Men from the Companies of the Old Charleston Battalion (now part of 27 S.C.V.) and 6 officers [*Only five listed in diary*] was sent off to Fort Sumter. Capt. Hopkins in Command. Lieuts. Muckenfuss, Hendricks, Kemmerly [*Kemmerlin*] & Trim.

The Left or East Picket Boat at Battery Haskell returned after being out for some time in consequence of the boat making so much water that they found it impossible to remain.

No Casualties to report

Countersign "Wilmington"

Edward Manigault
Major, &c

Monday, 23 November 1863

Battery Gregg still firing upon Simkins with heavy rifle guns. In the afternoon a heavy mortar fire upon Fort Johnson.

About 5 P.M. a Steamer (Supposed the *Planter*) passed through the Route from Long Island to Light House Inlet. Fired three Shells at her from the 30 Pounder Parrott gun in Redoubt No. 1.

1st Shot	12° Elev.	15″ Fuze	Fell to Right and a little Short. Did not burst.
2 "	13° "	15″ "	Fell to Right. Did not burst.
3 "	13° "	14″ "	Did not see where it fell.

Total Shots up to This Time 16.
Also fired 7 Shots from Tatum at the same vessel.

1st Shot	12°	Did not see the result.	
2 "	12°	" " " " "	
3 "	11½°	" " " "	4.62 No. 1, 282 Shots in all or 21
4 "	11°	" " " "	Shots Since rebanding.
5 "	11°	" " " "	
6 "	10½°	" " " "	
7 "	10°	12 Second fuze. Did not see explode	

The evening was dark & Murky and the wind high from the N.E. which explains the fact of scarcely any of the projectiles being seen to fall. The Enemy immediately opened on Secessionville from Black Island and fired some 8 or 10 Shots.

Capt. Beals Moved his Camp from Haskell to Ryan (right) in obedience to orders.

No Casualties to report

Countersign "Macon"

Edward Manigault
Major, &c.

Tuesday, 24 November 1863 [Diary erroneously dated 25 November]

The Enemy's fire was not near so heavy as yesterday. Nothing especially worthy of record.

No Casualties to report
Countersign "Columbia"

Edward Manigault
Major, &c.

Legare's Point, James Island.
Wednesday, 25 November 1863

The enemy's fire comparatively Moderate during the whole day. The Engineer force engaged in Constructing a Banquette for Musketry fire against the inner Slope of Battery Tatum, and in giving the Superior Slope such an inclination as would enable infantry to hit men landing upon the beach. Another portion of the Engineer hands engaged on the Bombproof at Ryan left.

The Second Battery for field Howitzer between Tatum & Ryan was Completed yesterday or the day before.

Sent one of Captn. Webb's wagons to Charleston Arsenal in pursuance of instructions of Col. Gonzales with following Ord. Stores.

(48) 4 in. Blakely Shell. To be sewed up in cloth.
(20) 20 pndr. Parrott Shell.⎫
(20) 10 pndr. Parrott Shell.⎭ To have the Girardey fuze attached.

The wagon was to bring back
1 Box of 6 — 20 pndr. Parrott Polygonal Shell.[1]
& 1 Box of 6 — 3½ in. Blakely   do   do.

These boxes, however, were not sent, as the proper Requisitions were not sent. Col. Gonzales apparently had not made the proper arrangements.

Capt. [S. Porcher] Smith's horses also were sent to the Charleston Arsenal to get two of his Caissons. They were completed & were brought out.

No Casualties to report
Countersign "Branchville"

Edward Manigault
Major, &c.

Lieut. Nesbit on Court Martial.

[1] *Polygonal cavity shells were cast with segmented interiors. This forced the projectile to fracture along segment lines and dispersed a definite number of fragments of a predetermined size and shape. [Ripley, p. 261]*

Thursday, 26 November 1863

A heavy fire from Gregg upon Fort Johnson & Battery Simkins

during a large part of the day. Very heavy Shells fired on Simkins, principally percussion Shells.

Capt. [*S. Porcher*] Smith went to the City with horses & Drivers and brought 2 Austrian Howitzers [1] and two 12 Pounder Howitzers (one Iron and the other Bronze) to Tatum & Ryan (left). These were brought out by Order of Col. Gonzales and are intended to replaced Capt. Smith's four 8 in. Siege Howitzers which are to be withdrawn.

Lieut. Nesbit on Court Martial.

Engineer Hands engaged partly on Banquette at Battery Tatum and in strengthening Breastwork to East of Tatum. Another portion on the Bombproof at Ryan (left).

No Casualties to report

Countersign "Camden"

Edward Manigault

[*Rank, etc. omitted*]

[1] *Gen. Josiah Gorgas, Confederate Chief of Ordnance, stated: "...twenty-seven [his figures total 24] bronze field pieces have been introduced into the C.S. service from Austria. Seven are 24-pounder howitzers cast in Vienna in 1857-59 of caliber 5.87 instead of 5.82 [the American standard for a 24-pounder]. The remaining 17 are 6-pounders cast in Vienna in 1826 and 1859 of caliber 3.74 instead of 3.67. By having the balls enclosed in canvas, the ordinary ammunition issued for the approximate calibers in C.S. service may be used with these guns and howitzers...." [Field Manual, Confederate States of America, Richmond, Va., 1 July 1862, p. 21]*

Friday, 27 November 1863

Gregg and the adjacent batteries firing upon Sumter, Simkins & Fort Johnson. Apparently 1 Mortar & 1 very heavy gun kept employed in firing on Simkins during greater part of the time. Simkins replying slowly, I think, with both Mortar & Gun.

One portion of the Engineer hands (about 40) engaged on Bomb Proof at Battery Ryan (left) and about 35 engaged in throwing a Causeway across the head of Marsh between Ryan (right) & Ryan (left).

The Enemy shelled the City during a part of the Morning. About 3 O'clock some heavy guns were fired from the vicinity of Gadberry Hill and lower down. Not known what they were directed at.

Dr. Winthrop went to the City on leave for the day.

No Casualties to report

Countersign "Pocotaligo"

Edward Manigault

Major, &c.

Saturday, 28 November 1863

Shortly before day three of the Men in the Right Picket Boat at Haskell deserted to the Enemy on Black Island. They left their picket post in the boat Carrying the fourth Man with them by force. On arriving, the fourth man says, within 100 yds. of Black Island, the three jumped out leaving their arms in the boat. The fourth man immediately pushed back and with considerable difficulty got back to Battery Haskell about 7 A.M. All four of the men were Irishmen belonging to the 27th S.C. Vol. (Simons' and Mulvany's Companies).

The usual firing going on between our batteries and those of the Enemy on Morris Island.

The Engineer hands engaged on the Bombproof at Ryan (left) and on Causeway between Ryan, right & left.

In consequence of the desertion of the three men above spoken of, Most of the Men were ordered to Sleep at their guns as usual.

No Casualties to report

Countersign "Savannah"

Edward Manigault
Major, &c.

Col. Way went to City on leave for the day.

Very wet and dark night.

Sunday, 29 November 1863

Very wet day. Nothing to record worthy of note.

No Casualties to report

Countersign "Mount Pleasant"

Edward Manigault
Major

Monday, 30 November 1863

Slow firing from the Enemy. Engineer hands engaged on Bombproof at Battery Ryan, left, and on causeway between Ryan left & right.

The usual inspections which take place on the last day of month.

At 1 P.M. the 12 Pndr. Bronze Howitzer which was brought down to Tatum on 26th Inst. was Carried back to Central Ord. Depot in Charleston by order of Genl. Hagood on request of Major C.K Huger, Asst. Chief of Ordnance.

No Casualties to report

Countersign "Lynchburg"

Edward Manigault
Major, &c.

Tuesday, 1 December 1863

At Midday the Yankees fired a salute from all their Land Batteries which we supposed as in honor of Grant's late success near Chattanooga [25 Nov. 1863]. The "Ironsides" fired a salute about 2½ to 3 O'clock P.M.

At about 5 P.M. a heavy Bombardment of Fort Johnson & Battery

Simkins from Morris Island and a counter Bombardment from Sullivan's Island Batteries.

Genl. Hagood visited Legare's House about 1 P.M.

No Casualties to report

Countersign "Virginia"

Edward Manigault
Major, &c.

Wednesday, 2 December 1863

The enemy firing as usual on Fort Sumter and other points, but slowly. The Engineer Force engaged on Bombproof at Battery Ryan (left). The Causeway between Ryan right & left completed, but Bridge not finished.

No Casualties to report

Countersign "Maryland"

Edward Manigault
Major, &c.

After dark there was a considerable fire directed from our Batteries on Sullivan's Island, &c. upon Morris Island.

Black Island is being gradually cleared more & more. There are two works upon it. The one to the West is a Sunken or half-sunken Battery and is regularly palisaded. It is impossible to See any guns mounted though there are guns there as they have several times fired upon Secessionville.

The Other Battery is an Elevated Battery East of Middle of the Island where the woods were thickest. We cannot as yet see guns mounted, though they may be.

There are probably about 60 Tents on the Island besides some Shanties and one or more framed Houses. Probably there are 300 or 400 men on the Island.

Thursday, 3 December 1863

About 3 or 4 O'clock in the Morning the Enemy commenced Shelling the City pretty heavily from Battery Gregg and adjacent battery. Our batteries fired upon them in return. This shelling lasted until 30 or 40 Shells had been thrown. During the day, the firing continued slowly as usual upon Sumter, Battery Simkins, Fort Johnson, &c.

The Engineer force engaged on Bombproof at Ryan (left) and in putting a new entrance to the Magazine.

Lieut. Legare's Sling Cart carried away two of the 10 in. Mortar Beds (wood) from Battery Haskell.

Capt. Webb visited the City on leave for the day.

No Casualties to report
Countersign "Missouri"

Edward Manigault
Major, &c.

Capt. [*George W.*] Johnson Off on 20 days leave of absence.
Heavy firing heard to the S.W. as if at Port Royal or Savannah.

Friday, 4 December 1863

Slow firing as usual. Adjutant Gardner went to City on leave for the day.

The 32 Pndr. Short Navy Gun on Siege Carriage was sent away from Battery Tatum to be transported to some part of the Lines in St. Andrews Parrish on the Main[*land*].

Bridge between Ryan (Right & Left) completed. Hands still at work on the Bomb Proof and Magazine entrance at Ryan (left).

Capt. Beals went to Savannah on 7 days leave of absence.

No Casualties to report
Countersign "Kentucky"

Edward Manigault
Major, &c.

Some heavy firing again heard to S.W. as if at Port Royal or Savannah.

Saturday, 5 December 1863

About 9 O'clock A.M. received orders to withdraw the Siege Train to the vicinity of Fort Pemberton. About 10 O'clock Major Campbell, whose command [*Palmetto Battalion, Light Artillery*] is to relieve the Siege Train in Manning the Batteries on Section 2 arrived. Major Manigault went round the lines with him and explained as far as possible the Arrangements for the Guards, Posts, Picket Boats, &c. and stated what standing orders there were in reference to these matters.

Afterwards rode to Genl. Hagood's Hd. Qrs. and asked for certain information on one or two points, as to the delivery of the Guns we are ordered to turn over &c. Then Rode to select the ground for Encampment.

The Engineer force on Bomb Proof at Ryan (left). Also a part engaged in thickening earth on Mortar Magazine at Haskell.

No Casualties to report
Countersign "Tennessee"

Edward Manigault
Major, &c.

Note. At the time of the Siege Train's leaving Sect. 2
The 4.62 No. 1.   Total No. of Shots 282   of which 21 Since bouching
                                              & Rebanding.
    do No. 2.   "   "   "   "   79

30 Pndr. Parrott in Redoubt No. 1, 16 Shots.

Edward Manigault

[*Rank, etc. omitted*]

Sunday, 6 December 1863

At 8 A.M. Capt. Webb moved with his Battery from Legare's. In passing the Ordnance Depot at Dill's Bluff he turned over all his Ammunition for the 3½ in. Blakely Guns and also whatever Implements &c. were contained in the Caissons, according to Department Orders. The four (4) 3½ in. Blakely Rifles were then carried to the C. & S. R.R. [*Charleston & Savannah Railroad*] Depot and delivered there according to orders though there was neither Q.M. or Ordnance Officer to received them. The Caissons were carried to the new encampment of the Siege Train at Lebby's [*House*] to S.W. of the Wappoo Bridges, on the Road to Fort Pemberton. Capt. Webb's Company moved from Battery Haskell as soon as it was relieved by Capt. Holtzclaw's Company, viz about Midday, and marched to New Encampment at Lebby's (Webb's pieces go to Capt. Villepigue.

Capt. [*S. Porcher*] Smith marched from Battery Tatum with his Battery & Company as soon as relieved by a portion of Capt. [*S.M.*] Richardson's Company (The whole under Command of Major Campbell) and proceeded to Camp at Lebby's. Capt. Smith was relieved after Midday.

Lieut. Willingham, Commanding Co. "C" Georgia Siege Train moved his train as soon as he could turn over the Ammunition for his 20 pndr. Parrott at Battery Haskell and get the 4 inch Blakely and ammunition from same battery. He left Legare's about 10 A.M. In passing he turned over the Ammunition for 10 pndr. Parrott to the Ordnance Depot at Dill's Bluff then delivered the 10 pndr. Parrott to C. & S. R.R. Depot according to orders (to be carried to Capt. Humphreys [*F.C. Humphreys, Superintendent Columbus, Ga., Arsenal*]. There was neither Ordnance Officer, nor Q.M. to receive the Gun. The 4 inch Blakely, 2 Caissons, Battery Wagon, Forge, &c. carried on to New Encampment of Siege Train at Lebby's.

Lieut. Head with the detachment of Co. "C" Ga. Siege Train garrisoning Redoubt No. 1, moved to Same point as soon as relieved by a part of Capt. Beals' Company about 1 P.M.

No forage could be obtained to day for our horses, so that they were without any thing to eat from 7 A.M. on 6th to about 2 P.M. on 7th and this at a time that they had a good deal of work to do.

Edward Manigault

Major, &c.

Lebby's House, James Island
Monday, 7 December 1863

No forage for horses until after 1 P.M. Had the Battery horses turned out to browse and pick up what they could.

About 1 P.M. one of Capt. Smith's horses was driven up from Camp of the 5th S.C. Cavalry with a bad wound in the Right Side supposed to be Made with an axe, Hatchet, Sabre or knife. Supposed that being hungry he annoyed some cavalry Soldier by endeavouring to get at his forage and was wounded in consequence. Addressed note to Col. Dunnovant on the subject. He was unable to find out the party Committing the act.

The day cold and the men engaged in Pitching their tents building Shanties and Making themselves as comfortable as possible under the circumstances of a deficiency of Tents.

Applied to Genl. Colquitt to know whether I should order Capt. Gregg to report with his Company at Lebby's. Was directed not to move Capt. Gregg.

[Not signed]

Tuesday, 8 December 1863

Large fatigue [*party*] engaged in clearing up ground for Encampment in front of Lebby's House. Capt. Webb officer of the day.

[Not signed]

Wednesday, 9 December 1863

A Fatigue party of 45 men detailed to Clear a Drill ground under Capt. Smith, Officer of the Day.

About Midday received orders to furnish a Guard before 4 P.M. for each of the two Wappoo Bridges and the Commissary Stores at McLeod's [*House*].

Guard at each Bridge	6 privates and 2 N.C. Off = 12 Priv. & 4 N.C. Off =	16
Guard to Com. [*Commissary*] Stores at McLeod's	18 privates & 2 N.C. Off =	20
	Total outguards 1 Com. Officer and	36
	Camp Guards 9 privates and 3 N. Com. Off.	12
	Total Guard	48

At 3 P.M. Lt. Mellichamp marched off with his guard to the Bridges. At same time the guard Marched off to Coms'y Stores at McLeod's.

In the afternoon the Yankees Shelling the City. Again at night very heavily.

[Not signed]

Thursday, 10 December 1863

Fatigue of 30 men still engaged in clearing Drill ground. Lieut. Willingham Officer of the Day.

No forage could be got for horses.

[*Not signed*]

Friday, 11 December 1863

Fatigue of 30 men engaged in clearing up Drill ground. Lt. Chapman Off. of the day.

No Corn Could be got for horses but some fodder.

Three wagons furnished to Capt. [*John G.*] Clark, A.Q.M., to go into Country for forage.

Very heavy firing from the Entrance of the harbor all day.[1]

Note. The "Effective Total" of the three Companies at Lebby's 298 out of which we furnish 36 for Bridge & Commissary Guard, 12 for Camp Guard, and 4 for Battalion Comy [*Commissary*] Store House Guard = Total 52.

Capt. Gregg furnishes Guard for James Island Creek & Newtown Cut Bridges, 2 non. Com. Off. & 3 men on each Bridge = 10 men in all. Effective total 107.

[*Not signed*]

[1] *At 9:30 a.m. the small-arms magazine in Fort Sumter suddenly exploded killing 11 men and injuring 41. The magazine, in the southwest section of the fort, held about 150 pounds of powder in an inner room. An outer compartment, due to the crowded condition of the fort, was used as a commissary. The men were lined up drawing rations when the explosion occurred. The enemy had not fired that day and the cause of the blast was never determined. It may have been due to a tipped over lantern or even static electricity. Damage to Fort Sumter was extensive but did not materially reduce its defensive capability. Smoke billowing above the work brought immediate enemy fire from Morris Island. This, termed the Second Minor Bombardment, lasted only one day. It consisted of 220 rounds fired in an effort to interfere with Confederates fighting fires caused by the explosion. [OR XXVIII (1) pp. 177, 178, 643, 644]*

Saturday, 12 December 1863

Lieut. Hasell with 2 Caissons and 10 Extra Horses sent at 10 A.M. to Redoubt No. 1 to bring the 30 Pndr. Parrott, Implements & Ammunition, assigned to Capt. Webb's Company. The Gun was brought up about 4 P.M. but as it had Commenced to rain heavily no ammunition was brought. in the Caissons.

Heavy Rain all the evening & night.

[*Not signed*]

Sunday, 13 December 1863

Rain off and on. Weather warm & moist.

[*Not signed*]

Lebby's House, James Island
Monday, 14 December 1863

Lieut. Chapman went to Charleston Arsenal with Horses and two Caissons to bring out the 30 pndr. Parrott reported ready, together with its ammunition. At 5 P.M. arrived with the Gun at Lebby's but did not succeed in getting the Ammunition.

Adjutant Gardner went to City on leave for the day.

Fine Clear day, high Westerly or N.W. wind, but not cold.

Major J.G. Barnwell inspected Battalion of Dunovant Cavalry (5th S.C.) encamped near us.

[Not signed]

Tuesday, 15 December 1863

Capt. Webb went to City on leave for the day.

At 10 O'Clock Lieut. Brux Started for Legare's Point with 2 Caissons for the Ammunition for 30 Pndr. Parrott No. 1 which we failed in getting last Saturday.

Fine clear day & mild.

About 4 P.M. Lieut. Brux returned with all the 30 pndr. Parrott Amm. at Redoubt No. 1.

No corn for the horses.

Edward Manigault
Major, Comdg

Wednesday, 16 December 1863

Lieut. Willingham went to City on leave for the day.

Warm day with rain occasionally.

Nothing worthy of note. Got only 15 Sacks of corn of which Capt. Webb's horses had five, Capts. Smith & Gregg four each and Field & Staff 2.

Comp. A	62 Public Horses & 8 Public Mules =		70 + 5 private Horses	Total = 75			
Co. B	42 Public do	35 Public Mules =	77 + 4 do	do	do do 81		
Co. C	43 do do	40 do do =	83 + 3 do	do	do do 86		

Quarter Master Dept. including Med & Staff wagons, N.C. Staff
Horses, 7 Public Horses, 20 Public Mules, 3 private do   30

Total animals   272

272 Animals at 12 lbs. Corn — — 3264 lbs. Corn.

do   10½   — — 2856 lbs. Long forage.

We have had for the last 2 *[Days?]*

Capt. *[George W.]* Johnson, Comdg. Co. C, Ga. Siege Train, who draws separately, has 47 horses and 6 mules. Total 53 Animals.

53 animals at 12 lbs corn, 636 lbs Corn.

"   "   " 10½ fodder, 557 lbs Fodder.

[Not signed]

Thursday, 17 December 1863

Capt. Mordecai reported for duty having returned from his trip in search of forage for the Q.M. Department. Reported at 11 A.M.
Very Rainy day.

[Not signed]

Friday, 18 December 1863

Capt. Webb took 30 pndr. Parrott No. 1 to Fort Pemberton to fire off load which has been in it for some time. Also fired 3 other Shots.

1st Shot	Target 1500 yds.	3½ ° Elev.		Length of fuze not known. Supposed 5 Sec. Little to R. of target. Shell burst just beyond.
2	” ” ” ”	do	4½ Sec Fuze.	Very near Target. Shell burst just beyond.
3	” ” ” ”	do	4 Sec,	Shell burst prob. 1000 yds from gun.
4	” Target 2⅜ Miles	Elev. 12°	14 Sec fuze.	Shell burst beyond Target. Good Shot.

This makes a Total of 20 Shots from 30 Pndr. No. 1.

[Not signed]

Saturday, 19 December 1863

Detail of about 120 men sent to be present at Execution of Deserter at Freer's X Roads [*Presumably at Freer's store. See map*].
Captain Smith went to City on Sick leave. Cold day, wind N.W.
Drew for Battalion Train 60 Sacks Corn ⁵ 18 for each Co., 5 for Field & Staff, 1 for Capt. Mordecai (2 days Rations).

[Not signed]

Sunday, 20 December 1863

Very Cold day wind North & N.E.

[Not signed]

Monday, 21 December 1863

Made large details for building a Guard House, &c.
Lieut. Willingham went with detail [*of*] Drivers, Horses, Caissons, Wagon, &c. to bring up 20 pndr. Parrott, Implements & Ammunition, Blakely Ammunition, &c. from Battery Haskell. He set out about 11.30 A.M. (The order for the 20 pndr. Parrott Came about 11 A.M.). Lt. W. returned with Gun, Caisson, Ammunition &c. about 4 P.M. Some of the Blakely ammunition damaged.

[Not signed]

Tuesday, 22 December 1863

Capt. Mordecai moved up to our Hd Qrs. from Gregg's Camp. Capt. R.V. Gaines, Inspector Field Transportation (from Sav[annah] Ga.) came to inspect our Artillery Horses, &c. Major Burke came with him.

At 2 p.m. Major Glover & Capt. Lloyd, 25 S.C.V., came as a Board and inspected the Transportation of the Siege Train.

About 5 P.M. a Courier arrived from Col. Kemper at the Church Flats directing "Captains Webb & Smith to Come on with their Batteries." As we had received no orders, did not know what to make of it, and sent the Courier on to Genl. Hagood's. About 7 P.M. Lieut McKee, Acting Adjutant for Col. Kemper, arrived with similar instructions, and on being told that we had received no orders, He showed copy of an Extract from order of Genl. Jordan dated 17th Decr. directing Captains Webb & Smith to make all necessary preparations and report to Lt. Col. Kemper at Church Flats. Lieut. McKee was referred to Genl. Hagood, through whom the order should have come. Capt. Webb, Comdg. Co. "A" and Lieut. Nesbit Comdg. Co. "B" (Capt. Smith being Sick) were sent with him to Hd Qrs. About 11 O'Clock they returned with Genl. Hagood's orders to march as soon as possible.[1] The men were awaked, ammunition arranged, One of the 30 pndrs. put into its travelling bed (the other already there), Rammers, Sponges, Worms, &c tied on, horses harnessed, Seven days rations of hard bread & beans got from Major Hay.

At half past two A.M. Capt. Webb's Battery Moved off and soon after Lieut Nesbit's battery. At 3 A.M. the last wagon got off. Night calm, clear & rather cold towards Morning. Brilliant Moon.

Capt. Webb's Battery consisted of [the] following. Two 30 Pndr. Parrotts with 12 horses in each — 2 Caissons containing only 74 Rounds of ammunition (Requisition had been made on 14th — that is the Ammunition was sent for on that date which we were told officially was ready for us). One Caisson 8 Horses — the other 6 horses. 1 Battery wagon — One Wagon containing 7 days Rations and the forage on hand (one feed) — 1 Captain — 2 Lieutenants (Mellichamp & Hasell) 3 Sergeants (Girardeau, Webb & Logan) 5 Corporals (Girardeau, Bland, Nagle [Nagel], Manson, Addy) — 35 Cannoneers — about 25 Drivers — 3 Artificers, making almost exactly 75 Men.

Lieut. Nesbit took Capt. Smith's Battery — (4) four 8 in. Siege Howitzers. 4 Caissons — 1 Forge. 1 ammunition Wagon — 1 do employed to Carry forage and one 2 horse Wagon with 7 days rations for the Company. This company also made an aggregate of about 75 Men.

Lieut. Brux remained in charge of the Camp and few remaining men of Co. "A" while Lieut. Wilson remained in Charge of Camp &c. of Co. "B".

(Lt. Chapman was off on 48 hours leave)

[Not signed]

---

[1] *Hagood queried Gen. Beauregard's headquarters in Charleston for clarification and was informed that Smith's and Webb's batteries were to report for special service to*

Lt. Col. Kemper at Church Flats (John's Island) as soon as possible with a week's rations, forage and a full supply of ammunition [OR XXVIII (2), p. 568]

Wednesday, 23 December 1863

Asst. Surgeon Winthrop made all needful preparations early in the Morning and went off for Church Flats at 11 A.M. with 1 Two Horse Medical Wagon, One 2 Horse Ambulance and a riding horse — (Tindal, Olney & Graham accompanying him).

The Guard duty required of us now with reduced Command is as follows —

Guard at Wappoo Bridges	12 Men &	4 N. Com Off		16
Commissary at McLeod's	21 "	3 "	"	24
Gregg's Guard at Jas. Isld. Ck Bridges	3 "	2 "	"	5
do do New Town Ck [*Cut*] Bridge	3 "	2 "	"	5
do do at his Camp	6 "	2 "	"	8
Capt. Johnson's Camp Guard	6 "	2 "	"	8
Capt. Webb's " "	3 "	- "	"	3
Capt. Smith's " "	6 "	2 "	"	8
			Total	77 men

Our "Effective Total" Decr. 24 [=] 250 — from which must be deducted as follows — [*Capt. George W.*] Johnson's Drivers & Extra duty men 30. Gregg's do about 40. Non. Com. Staff 3. Wagon-Master 1. Non. Com. Off. in Charge Camps 2. Waggoneers for Forage, Rations &c. 3 or 4. Making 80 men not available for Guard duty and leaving only 170 for Guard duty — 77/170 = 2.2 or in other words requiring the men to go on duty every other night.

Major Manigault spent day in town from 11 A.M. Capt. Johnson returned from 20 day furlough and reported this morning.

[Not signed]

Thursday, 24 December 1863

Made Statement of heavy Guard duty and asked to be relieved of a portion of it. Went to see Capt. Behre and Mr. McLeod in relation to an Ornamental Tree said to be cut down by a Squad of Captain Gregg's men. They were both absent — Mr. McLeod not to return til Monday or Tuesday.

Day quite Cold. Lieut. Chapman reported at dark.

[Not signed]

Friday, 25 December 1863

At about 1 or 1½ A.M. the Yankees commenced shelling the City very heavily from Morris Island. Our Batteries on Sullivan's and James

Islands firing on them in return. A Shell set fire to Burke's Stationary store one door from Corner of Church Street in Broad which was burnt. Also four Houses in Church Street just South of St. Michael's Alley and then adjoining the Cotton Press, making 6 buildings burnt in all. One Man lost his leg from a Shell and it is said that there were one or two other casualties, but slight ones. The enemy continued throwing Shells until near Midday. They probably threw 80 to 100 Shells.

At 6 A.M. the Artillery under Col. Kemper (Cos. "A" & "B" "Siege Train;" Capt. Schultz [*Schulz*] Battery; 1 Section of Marion Artillery, Capt. Parker & "Inglis Artillery," Capt. Charles) all of which formed part of an Expedition under Col. Page, commenced firing upon a Gun-

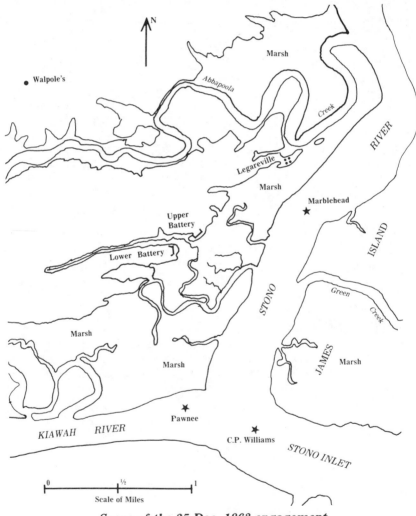

Scene of the 25 Dec. 1863 engagement.

boat (supposed the *Marblehead*) at Legareville on Stono River. To explain this properly, however, it would be well to go back and narrate from the beginning.

It was known from Capt. Walpole's Scout Company on John's Island that the Yankees were pulling down the houses at Legareville and carrying the Materials over to Kiawah Island to erect buildings for sheltering the troops there. The party engaged in pulling down these houses was protected by one, or sometimes two, Gunboats anchored just in front of Legareville.

It was accordingly determined to send an Expedition to endeavour to Capture, sink or cripple the Gunboats, or at least to drive them off, and to capture the party in the village engaged in pulling down the houses. As our Pickets were tolerably near the village so as to prevent the Yankees from roving about, workmen and labourers were sent down, who constructed two sunken Batteries each for two guns, on a Peninsula (and masked by a wood), about ¾ mile below Legareville in direct line. These two Batteries were only 50 or 75 yds. apart, both sunken batteries. Another Battery was constructed 250 to 300 yds. lower down on another peninsula though the distance round by land was probably from 1 to 2 Miles. This battery was a raised battery. Another Platform or Battery was said to be placed on the Road in rear of Legareville from which Legareville might be shelled.

Col. Page of 56th Virginia Regt. Commanded the Expedition composed as follows — 460 Infantry from 56th & 27th Virginia;[1] Artillery, Co. "A" Siege Train with two 30 Pndr. Parrotts, Co. "B" Siege Train with 4 8 in. Howitzers, Capt. Schulz's Light Battery, Captain Charles' Light Battery ("Inglis Light Artillery"), 1 Section of Marion Arty., Lieut. Strohecker Comdg.; Cavalry, "The Rebel Troop," "The Cadet Rangers" and Capt. Walpole's company of Mounted Scouts (20 men).

Through some mistake Cos. A & B of Siege Train received no orders until Tuesday Night 22nd inst. 11½ P.M. They marched before 3 A.M. Wednesday 23.

The whole force assembled at Camp at Walpole's place about 6 miles from Legareville and 7 miles beyond Church Flats) on the afternoon of Wednesday 23. That night and the next day the force rested.

At dark Thursday 24th, the train moved on and everything was got into position so as to be ready to open fire on the enemy at daylight next morning. The following was the disposition of the force: Capt. Webb's 2 30 pndr. Parrotts were put in Right one of the Batteries ¾ mile below Legareville and Two of Lieut Nesbit's 8 in. Howitzers in the Left Battery 50 or 100 yds from it. The third one of Lt. Nesbit's Howitzers was put in the Lower Battery (250 or 300 yds. lower down) with 3 of Capt. Schulz's Field pieces — Lieut. Spivey in charge of Howitzer (Capt. Schulz comdg. the Battery). The fourth 8 in Howitzer was sent (under Sergt. Causey) with Section of Marion Artillery on the road in rear of Legareville in order to Shell the Village at the proper Signal. Captain Charles' Battery was put between Legareville and Capt. Webb's 30 pndr. Howitzers [*should be Parrotts*] in order to fire on either the Gunboats or Legareville.

The Infantry was in the woods nearest to Legareville to charge the village as soon as it had been sufficiently Shelled, and the fire of the Gunboats was kept under or drawn away by our own artillery fire.

There was only one Gunboat (Supposed to be the *Marblehead*) visible. The night was a brilliantly clear Moonlight night. Moon full, pretty cold. At 6 A.M. Webb's two 30 pndr. Parrotts and Nesbit's two 8 in. Howitzers opened fire upon the Gunboat, distance estimated variously at from 600 to 1000 yds. Capt. Charles' Napoleon Guns also opened on Gunboat. It was some minutes before the *Marblehead* replied, but the officers all say that when she did her practice was beautiful. The *Pawnee* which was lying round a point, and before [*she moved*] invisible to our troops, immediately got under way and ran into Kiawah River where She took up a position and enfiladed the different Batteries. A schooner rigged Gunboat [*C.P. Williams*] also immediately made sail from her anchorage near Coles Island and came to the assistance of the *Marblehead*. After about ¾ of an hour the enemy's fire became so hot that Col. Kemper determined to withdraw the guns. Private Ancrum of Co. "A" had his leg shot off by a shell which killed both the horses he was driving (he was next to the lead driver of one of the 30 pndr. Parrott Guns. Capt. Webb who was within a few feet of him (he had gone to the rear by order of Col. Kemper to bring up the horses to carry off the Guns) received a severe concussion from the explosion of the same shell. Corpl. Bland of the same Company was stunned by a concussion. Private Zorn was shot through the hand by [*a*] fragment of shell. One of the other horses of Co. "A" was killed, and a fourth wounded, probably mortally. By great exertions the two 30 pndr. Parrotts were got off.

One of the 8 in. Howitzers under charge of Lieut. Nesbit was got off; but the other had to be abandoned; as two horses belonging to it were Killed & several wounded and the remainder had run off in great alarm so that it was impossible to get together more than 7 horses with which the first howitzer was got off. Private W.F. Johnson of Co. "B" was killed instantly by the same shell which killed his two horses. Several others experienced concussions from bursting of shells near them.

The 8 in. Howitzer at the lower Battery under command of Capt. Schultz [*Schulz*] was also abandoned in consequence of the breaking of the harness and running away of the horses, who were twice hitched in, and broke away both times; after which Capt. Schultz [*Schulz*] ordered the howitzer to be abandoned.

Capt. Charles lost one Man killed and one wounded.

The Infantry is said to have done nothing. In a short time the whole force retreated to Roper's place 2½ or 3 miles in rear of Legareville

One of the 8-inch siege howitzers abandoned by the Confederates. Both weapons today are displayed at the Washington (D.C.) Navy Yard.

where they remained until [*time omitted in manuscript*]. They then went on to Walpole's place where they had encamped the first night. At about 8 O'Clock at Night (Friday) the two Companies of the Siege Train marched from Camp and crossed the bridge over Church Flats and arrived at the Camp about 2 miles on this side from 12 till 2 O'clock. (note that two of the guns had stalled at some bad spot in the road and did not reach the Camp until 2 hours after the others).[2]

[Not signed]

[1] *Col. Page commanded the 26th, not the 56th Va. (see page 321). The Virginia regiments engaged were the 26th and 59th. Manigault was mistaken in listing the 56th and 27th which did not serve in South Carolina.*

[2] *The Marblehead was a 158-foot, two-masted, screw steamer of 507 tons. At the time of the engagement, she mounted four 24-pounders and a 9-inch, all smoothbore, and a 20-pounder (3.67-inch) Parrott rifle. [ONR (II) Vol. 1, p. 134]. Manigault's description of the action is substantially correct. The Confederates later blamed failure of the expedition primarily on poor shooting. However, Federal after-action reports showed the Marblehead was struck by 20 shot and shell in hull and aloft causing considerable damage, killing three men and wounding four. Unfortunately for the Confederates, the shells didn't explode and observers thought they had missed. Poor ammunition was part of the problem. However, the expedition was doomed from the outset. This was not a case of a single vessel, such as the Isaac Smith (See Note 3, Tuesday, 25 Aug. 1863), hemmed in by a narrow river with no room to maneuver and bring her broadside batteries to bear. Once the Marblehead was under way — her port boiler was down for repairs which caused a few minutes delay — she swept the Confederate positions with fire. Similarly, the Pawnee — a 1,289-ton, twin-screw steamer — from the Kiawah River, beyond range of the Southern Guns, enfiladed the positions with her 100-ppounder (6.4-inch) Parrott rifle, a 50-pounder (5.1-inch) Dahlgren rifle and eight 9-inch smoothbores. The mortar schooner C.P. Williams, coming up from Folly River under sail, fired 20 rounds from her 13-inch mortar and 43 from lighter weapons.*

Shortly after the Confederate retreat, a Yankee force landed. The Federals carried off an ammunition chest — left behind when Capt. Webb's 30-pounder Parrotts hurriedly moved out — as well as abandoned shovels and knapsacks. However, they were unable to move the 8-inch howitzers, each weighing more than 2,600 pounds. Instead, the Federals immobilized the pieces by dismounting them and carrying off the carriage wheels.

Afraid to remain after dark, the Yankees fell back to the ships. The Confederates returned that night with horses but were unable to remove the disabled pieces.

Both sides tried to salvage the weapons, the Confederates at night and the Federals during the day. However, Confederate attempts to bring up sling carts met with delays. Meanwhile, the Pawnee's boat crews found a creek which ran to one position and within 100 yards of the other. On Dec. 28, the howitzers were loaded into boats and transported triumphantly to the ships. Both trophies were later deposited at the Washington Navy Yard where they are displayed today. [OR XXVIII (1), 747-750. ONR 15, p. 188-208]

Saturday, 26 December 1863

Early in the Morning Capt. Webb left the Camp with his own and Capt. [*S. Porcher*] Smith's Company (Lieut. Nesbit commdg.) and arrived at Hd. Qrs. Lebby's, James Island, about 3½ P.M.

The losses resulting to Siege Train from the expedition are as follows:

Private W.F. Johnson — Killed — Co. "B".

Private Ancrum, Co. "A" Mortally Wounded (since died).

Private Zorn, Co. "B" Severely wounded through hand.

Capt. Webb, Co, "A", Concussion.

Corpl. Bland do   do   (Several others concussed).

2 Howitzers of Co. "B" Lost.

4 Horses of Co. "B" Killed — and two or three wounded.

3 Horses of Co. "A" Killed. One probably mortally wounded.

3 Sets of Single horse Harness & 1 amm. Chest, Co. "A" lost.

[*blank*] Sets of [*blank*] Co. "B" [*blank*]

Dr. Winthrop left the Camp at Walpole's about 9 A.M. in the Ambulance, crossed John's Island Ferry and arrived at Hd. Qrs. Lebby's at 2½ P.M.

[Not signed]

[*Sunday-Monday, 27-28 December 1863, omitted in diary.*]

Tuesday, 29 December 1863

Lieut. Chapman sent for Ammunition of 30 pndr. Parrott Guns. He got 60 Cartridges and 141 Shell at Dill's Bluff. (The Cartridges proved too large to go into the guns).

[Not signed]

[*Wednesday, 30 December 1863, omitted in diary.*]

Thursday, 31 December 1863

Cloudy day and rainy a part of the time. The Horses harnessed and the Batteries ready for Inspection Muster from 10 A.M. At 4½ P.M. some of the horses were unharnessed (Webb's & [*S. Porcher*] Smith's) and carried to Water. Capt. J.J. Allen, 27th Ga., the Inspecting and Mustering Officer,[1] arrived about 5 P.M. and inspected the three Companies at Lebby's. He is to inspect Capt. Gregg's Company tomorrow. Rain during night and afterwards very high wind from S.W. and West.

Ordered and had Board of Survey to inspect 30 Pndr. Parrott cartridges reported too large to go into the Guns.

[*Not signed*]

[1] *See Appendix 2, pp. 268, 269.*

Camp at Lebby's, James Island
Friday, 1 January 1864

Very high West Wind gradually shifting to North West and getting very Cold.

Captn. Webb went off on 15 days furlough.

[*Not signed*]

Saturday, 2 January 1864

Very Cold. Cloudy.

[*Not signed*]

Sunday, 3 January 1864

Very Cold. Ice about 1 inch thick. Went to Genl. Hagood's Quarters in obedience to summons. He gave me instructions for Artillery Practice once a week.[1] After Midday it commenced raining.

[*Not signed*]

[1] *This order no doubt resulted from the Confederate belief that poor shooting led to failure of the Marblehead expedition. See 26 Dec. 1863, note.*

Monday, 4 January 1864

Sent 30 pndr. Parrott to the Charleston Arsenal to have the vent Cleared which had been effectually stopped up by bad friction Tubes at the Action near Legareville. We had attempted to drill the hole afresh, but our Artificers Could not do it. Got 300 ft. of Boards for Artillery Target.

[*Not signed*]

Tuesday, 5 January 1864

The 30 Pndr. Parrott sent back to Camp, the Vent having been cleared. Genl. A.M.M.[1] visited our Quarters. Dr. Winthrop went to City for day. Also Lt. Nesbit.

[*Not signed*]

[1] *Edward's brother, Brig. Gen. Arthur Middleton Manigault.*

Wednesday, 6 January 1864

Went to select a good range for Artillery Practice near Fort Pemberton. Day very unfit for such purpose being cold, rainy & misty. Ordered details for clearing &c. but as it rained heavily soon after, nothing was done.

Major M. went to town on leave for the day. Very heavy Rain and Execrable Roads.

[*Not signed*]

Thursday, 7 January 1864

Rainy & Cold day. Wind N.E. Made no details of fatigue parties as the day was too inclement.

[*Not signed*]

Friday, 8 January 1864

Cloudy and keen cold wind. Could do little for want of axes. Had 32 logs Cut 14 & 12 ft long for the guard house at Pontoon or lower Bridge [1] and had them hauled to spot.

At dark received orders for Capt. [*George W.*] Johnson, Comdg. Co. "C" Ga. Siege Train to report to Genl. Mercer in Savannah.

One of the Staff Mules very lame in left fore arm. Apparently Shot there.

[*Not signed*]

[1] *Over Wappoo Creek.*

Saturday, 9 January 1864

Cold & Clear. Wind N.W. Water froze wherever it was spilt. Issued 5 axes to Lt. Nesbit.

At 12 M. Capt. [*George W.*] Johnson marched with his Company to C & S. R.R. [*Charleston and Savannah Railroad*] Depot on way to Savannah.

Adjutant Gardner went to City on leave for the day. Commenced building Guard House at Pontoon Bridge.

[*Not signed*]

Sunday, 10 January 1864

Cold, Clear, Calm morning. Heavy white frost giving almost the appearance of Snow. Water froze wherever it was spilt. Cloudy later in the day, and a little sleet after dark.

Made a detail of 1 off & 30 men for Capt. Behre for fatigue duty. This makes with our Bridge Guards, Commissary Guards & Camp Guards upwards of 100 Men detailed as follows —

Wappoo Bridges	4 N.C. off & 12 Men.	Total 16		
Commissary Buildings	3 "	21 "	24	55 at Wappoo & Lebby's 55
Camp & Home Comy.	3 "	12 "	15	
			55	

Capt. Gregg's for Jas. Isld. CK. & Newtown Cut Bridge, 5 N.C. off & Men each	10	18	
Camp Guard	8		
	18		
		73	
Add to which Detail for Capt. Behre.		30	
		103	

There was also a detail for Lt. Cunningham for Ord. fatigue (but not used) 30 Men.

Lt. Chapman got 173, 30 pndr. Parrott Cartridges from Lt. Cunningham & returned the 60 which were too large.

[*Not signed*]

Monday, 11 January 1864

Thin ice. Water froze wherever spilt.

Same detail of 30 men to report to Capt. Behre.

Had an Artillery Target Made. Also Sentry Box for duty at Wappoo Bridge

Lt. Hasell officer Comdg. Guard at the Wappoo Bridges reported that one of the Pontoons at the lower or "Pontoon Bridge" Sunk at 11 O'Clock last night, i.e. became waterlogged and broke away from its fastenings and was carried by the Tide against the Piles of the Upper Bridge (Draw Bridge) — The Irishmen who attended the Bridge say that the *De Kalb*[1] in coming to the landing yesterday Morning struck this pontoon. In consequence the Communication by this Bridge is for the present suspended.

I reported the fact immediately to Gen. Colquitt.

At about 3.30 P.M. Major Bryan, Inspector Genl. on Genl. Beauregard's Staff, came to Hd. Qrs. Siege Train to inquire of and report on Certain Matters embraced under Genl. Orders in connection with Siege Train — viz. as to whether all the Genl. Orders from Richmond & Department Hd. Qrs. were received. 2nd. whether they were read out on Dress Parade. 3rd. Whether the proper drills were gone through with.

Weather becoming warmer, and rain after dark.

Heavy firing on City from Morris Island.[2]

[*Not signed*]

[1] *One of several small steam ships used by the Confederates on the tidal creeks and rivers of the South Carolina Lowcountry.*

² This was the start of a 9-day bombardment of Charleston from Federal guns on Morris Island. During the period, some 1,500 projectiles were fired. Most were relatively light weight shells and a high percentage failed to reach the city. Damage was negligible. [OR XXXV (1) pp. 132-137; Charleston Daily Courier, issues of 12-22 Jan. 1864]

Tuesday, 12 January 1864

The morning so foggy and unpromising that deferred the Artillery Practice (Raining till about 9 A.M.)

The Rain ceased however & then fog cleared off before 11 A.M. and the practice might have taken place, but that the orders had been countermanded and the Target not erected (Ready framed however to erect).

Heavy firing upon the City from Morris Island.

[*Not signed*]

Wednesday, 13 January 1864

Rainy day. Still details were made of fatigue parties to cut poles for stables and for Guard Houses.

In consequence of the want of axes and wagons not much could be done.

Still firing upon the City from Morris Island.

[*Not signed*]

Thursday, 14 January 1864

Heavy fog which did not clear off till near 11 O'Clock. Fatigues employed in Roofing Guard House at Hd. Qrs. and that at Pontoon Bridge and in cutting poles for that at Draw Bridge

At 12.40 P.M. order came to detail 20 men to report to Capt Behre. Lt. Chapman officer of the day.

Enemy still Shelling the City.

[*Not signed*]

Friday, 15 January 1864

Fine clear day. Sent Target on Wagon and had it erected beyond the Road leading from Fort Pemberton to Newtown Cut Bridge. The erection of the Target and Clearing occupied until 2.30 P.M.

The Road between Capt. Gregg's Camp and Lebby's being impassable for heavy Artillery, his guns were not brought up. The two 30 Pndr. Parrotts of Co. "A" and two 8 in. Howitzers of Co. "B" were put in battery just to West of Redoubt between Lebby's & Fort Pemberton, a distance of 700 yards from the Target. 1st Shot fired at 2.30 and last shot at 5 P.M. In the interim it had commenced raining, though not heavily. Wind westerly but not high. Evening damp & Cool.

Table of Fire

No. of Shot	Distance to Target	Kind of Gun or How.	Charge of Powder	Weight of Shell	Elevation	Length of Fuze	Observed Time of Flight.	Results & Remarks Target 40 ft. long x 7 ft. high. Observation of time of Flight by watch ably great. Charges of Powder as invoiced to us. Wgts. of Shells as in the Ordnance Tables.
	Yds.		Lbs.	Lbs.		Seconds	Seconds	
1	700	30 Pnd. Parrott	3½	29	1°45′	2 Sec	Failed in observing	Burst at 640 yds & about 10 ft. high. Apparently Hd. of Shell passed on some distance. 1 Fragment 40 ft. from Center R. 1 do 63 ft. Short, on Line, found. 1 do 58 ft. Short, on Line. 1 do 47 ft. from Center left. 1 do Hit Target 10 ft. left of Center.
2	do	30 Pnd. Parrott	do	do	1°45′	2½″	Failed in observing	First Graze 168 yds. beyond Target = 868 yds. Passed directly over center of Target. Ricochetted long distance. Could not find it. Did not burst.
3	do	8 in. Siege How.	3	45	3°30′	3½″	Failed in observing	Ricochetted & fell 30 yds beyond Target, bursting as it fell. A little left of Center.
4	do	do	3	do	5°	4″	4″	1st Graze 111 yds. beyond Target. Burst after 2nd Graze 126 yds. beyond Target, over center of Target.
5	do	30 Pnd. Parrott	3½	29	1°45′	2¼″	3″	Burst 20 yds. beyond Target about 15 ft. high. The Fragments struck the ground 30 & 40 yds. beyond. Good line Shot.
6	do	do	3½	29	1°37½′	2¼″	3″	Burst about 15 yds. beyond Target.
7	do	8 in. Siege How.	3	45	4°30′	3⅝″	Failed	Burst 40 yds. Short. 1st Graze 103 yds. Short?
8	do	do	3	45	4°15′	3¾″	4″	1st Graze 79 yds. Short. Burst about 30 yds. Short. 1 Fragment struck Target, 12 ft. beyond Center, 1 ft. from bottom. Another Grazed top, 9 ft. from Center R.

The officers in Charge of the pieces were Called on to Estimate the distance before it was measured. Their Estimate was as follows — each one given without the others hearing it.

Lt. Spivey (Junior Officer) 700 yds. Lt. Mellichamp 900 yds. Lt. Nesbit 800 yds. Lt Chapman 650 yds. The distance was measured with a tape line and turned out to be 700 yds.

I sent the duplicates [*of returns*] of Ordnance and Ordnance Stores in Redoubt No. 1 & Batteries Ryan (Right & Left), Tatum & Haskell at the time they were turned over, Dec. 6, 1863, to Major Campbell, he got them and acknowledged the Receipt.

Enemy shelling the City — one shell thrown up to John Street near Corner John & Alexander & Chapel Streets.

Several fires in City, said to be work of Incendiaries.

[*Not signed*]

Saturday, 16 January 1864

Clear & fine day — cool but not cold. Sent Report of Yesterday's Artillery Practice to Genl. Colquitt about 3 P.M. The report was addressed to Capt. J.M. Otey who signed the order No. 287 requiring Practice every week with our guns.

Dr. Winthrop went to City on Official business. Adjt. Gardner do, on leave for the day.

Captain Webb returned from furlough shortly after Sunrise.

Shelling of the City continuing. Shells thrown in George Street.

Guard House at Pontoon Bridge Roofed & completed all to stopping up crevices.

Fatigue party working on Guard House at upper Bridge (Draw Bridge).

Lt. Charles Gregg went on 15 day furlough about Midday today.

[Not signed]

Sunday, 17 January 1864

Undecided day. Sometimes sunny and at other times cloudy. Commenced drizzling shortly after dark.

The Enemy shelling the City very heavily.

[Not signed]

Monday, 18 January 1864

Raining all day. Cleared and very heavy wind from West at Night.

[Not signed]

Tuesday, 19 January 1864

High West wind, cold & clear. Too much wind for Artillery Practice.

Major Manigault went to Genl. Ripley's Quarters at Mount Pleasant under Orders as one of a Board to investigate claims of certain Enlisted Men of 1st S.C. Infantry, 1st S.C. Arty & Lucas Battalion to be discharged at end of 3 years. Col. Simonton and himself spent night at Genl. Ripley's Quarters.

Capt. Webb went to City on Official Business.

[Not signed]

Wednesday, 20 January 1864

Left Mt. Pleasant for City after Breakfasting with Genl. Ripley & Capt. Nance. Major Manigault returned to Camp about 4 P.M.

Capt. Webb, comdg. in Maj. M's absence, had some artillery Practice with his two 30 Pndr. Parrott guns and Capt. [*S. Porcher*] Smith's 2, 8 in. Siege Howitzers. Day fine, clear & calm. Practiced at Same Target and Same distance as on 15th inst.

Table of Fire

No. of Shot	Distance to Target	Kind of Gun or Howitzer	Charge of Powder	Wgt. of Shell	Elevation	Length of Fuze	Observed Time of Flight	Results & Remarks Target 40 ft. x 7 ft. high. Times of flight observed with ordinary Second hand watch. Commenced firing 10.30 A.M. to 11 A.M. Day calm & clear. Light Westerly wind.
	Yds.		Lbs.	Lbs.		Seconds	Seconds	1st Graze (impossible) [*Added later?*]
1	700	30 Pnd. Parrott	3½	29	1°30′	2⅛	Failed	No burst. 600 yds. beyond Target, ricochetted & fell on Edge River.
2	"	" "	do	do	1°—	2⅕	do	No burst. 1st Graze 70 yds. Short. 2nd Graze 88 yds. beyond. Extreme Range 102 yds. beyond Target.
3	"	8 in. Siege How.	3	45	3°—	3	3	1st Graze 40 yds. Short of Target. 2nd 30 yds. Short & burst. Shell went through bank on side of Road 8 ft. thick.
4	"	" "	do	do	3¼°	3	3	1st Graze 114 yds. beyond. 2nd Graze 500 yds. beyond and burst.
5	"	30 Pnd. Parrott	3½	29	1°15′	2	1½	Fuze bad, burst 300 yds. Short.
6	"	" "	do	do	1°15′	2½	failed	40 yds. Short & burst. 1 Fragment in Target 18 in. R. of center and 5 in. from top.
7	"	8 in. Siege How.	3	45	3°30′	3½	failed	Shell burst a little high and 50 yds. short.
8	"	" "	do	do	4°—	3¾	—	1st Graze 115 yds. beyond Target. Good line. Burst 250 yds. beyond.
9	"	30 Pnd. Parrott	3½	29	1°15′	2¾		Burst 50 yds. from Gun. Fragments struck Ground 60 yds and Bank 70 yds. from Gun.
10	"	" "	do	do	1°15′	2⅝		1st Graze 70 yds. Short of Target & burst.
11	"	8 in. Siege How.	3	45	3°45′	3¾		6 or 8 yds. too much to R. 1st Graze 50 yds. Short, then through Bank & burst.
12	"	" "	3	45	3°45′	3¾		1st Graze 47 yds. Short. Passed through Bank 40 yds. Short & Burst.
13	"	30 Pnd. Parrott	3½	29	1°15′	2¾		Burst too high, 120 yds. beyond.
14	"	" "	do	29	1°15′	2⅗		Through Target 11 ft. R of Center, 1 ft. from Top. Burst 22 ft. beyond.
15	"	8 in. Siege How.	3	65	4°45′	4½		Spher. Case. 1st Graze 96 yds. beyond, burst 105 yds beyond. Set grass on fire.
16	"	" "	3	65	4°30′	4—		This could not be determined as the grass had been set on fire by previous Shell, and the flames & Smoke prevented observation.
								Ceased firing between 3 & 4 P.M.

The Roads were still too bad for Capt. Gregg's Howitzers to be moved up to the Practice Ground, hence they took no part in the practice.

[*Not signed*]

Thursday, 21 January 1864

Fine clear day. Wind Westerly. Mild weather.

Selected ground for Artillery Practice at longer Range.

Found one of Battery Horses of Co. A in a well near Redoubt between Lebby's & Fort Pemberton. This horse was periodically blind and in that state fell into well. He had been missing since Friday or Saturday last. Had been searched for without Success. His groans attracted my attention.

Dispatched a Fatigue Party of about 30 men who got him out with great difficulty about 9 O'clock at Night. It was found that his Right Fore leg was broken above the Knee. He was accordingly dispatched.

Dr. Winthrop went off on 15 day furlough at 8 P.M.

J.P. Huger[1] enlisted in Co. "A" Siege Train to day. Wrote to his Father for his consent, Jany. 22. (Written consent given dated Jany. 23.)

[*Not signed*]

[1] *See entry in Appendix 3, p. 313.*

Friday, 22 January 1864

Very fine, clear, Mild day. Busy about some Returns, Journal, &c.

[*Not signed*]

Saturday, 23 January 1864

The roads being sufficiently good Capt. Gregg brought up his two Howitzers and practiced at the Target to West of Road from Fort Pemberton to Newtown Cut.

Table of Fire

No. of Shot	Dist. to Target (Yds.)	Kind of Gun or Howitzer	Charge of Powder (Lbs.)	Wgt. of Shell (Lbs.)	Elevation	Length of Fuze (Seconds)	Observed Time of Flight (Seconds)	Results & Remarks — Target 40 x 7; Day Calm, Clear & Mild. Commenced firing at 12 M. Ceased firing about 3 P.M.
1	700	8 in. Siege How.	4	45	2°55′	3	Failed	Thro' Target 10 ft. left of Center, 1 ft. from Top. 1st Graze 45 yds. beyond. Burst on the Ground 250 yds. beyond Target.
2	do	do	4	"	" "	3		Thro' Center of Target 1 ft. from Top. 1st Graze 46 yds. beyond. Burst on the Ground 300 yds. beyond.
3	do	do	4	"	" "	2.50		Thro' Target 11 ft. left of Center, 3 ft. from Top. 1st Graze 36 yds. beyond, 2nd Graze 200 yds., 3rd Graze 400 yds. Did not burst.
4	do	do	4	"	" "	2.45		1st Graze 145 yds. beyond, 2nd Graze 200 yds. & Burst. Good line Shot.
5	do	do	4	"	" "	2.40	Officer had no Watch.	Burst just over Center of Target. Several pieces struck into the ground 8 to 10 yds. beyond.
6	do	do	4	"	" "	2.40		Burst about 65 yds. Short of Target.
7	do	do	4	"	" "	2.50		Thro' Target bottom Board 12 ft. from Center Right. 1st Graze 15 yds beyond, 2nd Graze 25 yds. beyond and burst.
8	do	do	4	"	" "	2.50		Thro' Target 12 ft. from Center Right, 3 ft. from Top. 1st Graze 24 yds. beyond, 2nd Graze 28 yds. beyond, 3rd Graze 30 yds. beyond. Extr. Range 200 yds. beyond, did not burst.
9	do	do	4	"	" "	2.50		Burst 44 yds. Short.
10	do	do	4	"	" "	2.50		Burst about 100 yds. Short.

Major Manigault went to the City to see Col. Waddy about Ordnance Quarterly Returns. Did not see Col. Waddy but saw Major Huger who is an assistant in Col. Waddy's office. Returned to Camp about 5 P.M.

["# Remember" *is inserted in the diary above the following paragraph*]

Major Lucas complained that some of the men of the Command (Co. "A") had broken down some of the buildings at Mr. Heyward's place (next to Lebby's) and had taken off the windows, doors, sashes &c. from the Dwelling house. Capt. Webb was immediately called upon to replace the Articles taken away.

[*Not signed*]

Sunday, 24 January 1864

Very fine day — clear, mild & calm. Capt. Webb went to City on leave for the day.

Lt. Chapman had the doors, windows, &c. of Heyward's House replaced but did not have the Weather Boarding replaced where it had been torn down.

[*Not signed*]

Monday, 25 January 1864

Garrison Court Martial of which Capt. Gregg was President, commenced its sessions to day.

Capt. S. Porcher Smith reported for duty to day. Adjt. Gardner went to town in Afternoon.

Some frost in the morning, but quite warm at Midday. Clear fine weather. Detailed men to work at Guard House.

Wrote to Capt. [*George W.*] Johnson Comdg. Co. "C" Georgia Siege Train in Savannah for his Quarterly Return of Dec. 31.

No corn or Fodder for the horses.

[*Not signed*]

Tuesday, 26 January 1864

The Company Commanders A & B busy in making out Quarterly Returns and Capt. Gregg absent as witness on Genl. Court Martial, hence there was no Artillery practice to day as was intended. Nor any sitting of Garrison Court Martial.

Very fine Clear day with moderate wind from the West and Spring like.

Company Commanders busy preparing their Quarterly Returns of Ordnance hence no practice to day — Note, Bridge over Elliott's Cut has 25 ft. Span and three Sleepers perhaps 12 x 14 laid flatways. As there are one or two Mortices in Sleepers perhaps they are equivalent to 12 x 12. This is a weak Bridge to transport 30 pndr. Parrotts, tho I think Sufficient.

[Not signed]

Wednesday, 27 January 1864

Mild, warm day, Southerly wind. Bright Sun but atmosphere Hazy.
Called to see Capt Behre about Cedar Tree at McLeod's cut down by Capt. Gregg's men. Capt. B. was absent but Mr. McLeod showed me the Stump of Tree. It was about 285 yds. from the house but evidently on an ornamental avenue and within what used to be the Enclosure.
Garrison Court Martial Sitting.

[Not signed]

Thursday, 28 January 1864

Spring like day. Wind Southerly. Atmosphere Hazy.
Companies "A" & "B" practiced with their Guns at Target to West of Road from Fort Pemberton to New Town Cut but from a new Position.

Table of Fire

No. of Shot	Dist. to Target	Kind of Artillery	Charge Powder	Wgt. Shell	Elevation	Length Fuze	Observed Time of Flight	Results & Remarks — Target 40 ft. x 7 ft. Day calm & warm & Hazy. Light South Wind. Commenced firing at 12.30 P.M. Ceased firing 4.55 P.M. Time of flight observed by ordinary Second hand Watch, hence great accuracy cannot be expected.
	Yds.		Lbs.	Lbs.		Seconds	Seconds	
1	1158	30 Pnd. Parrott	3½	29	2°15′	3½″	3½″	Did not see burst. Could not find 1st Graze, but from observation suppose 200 yds. beyond Target. Ricochetted & went into River. Good line Shot.
2	do	do	do	do	2°00′	3¾″	3¾″	Struck ground to R. & burst as it Struck 45 yds. Short. Could not find the fragments.
3	do	8 in. Siege How.	3	45	6°00′	7″	—	Did not burst. Struck to R. 102 yds. Short. 2nd Graze 83 yds. Short. Went in Bank at Side of Road.
4	do	do	do	do	6°15′	6″	6″	1st Graze 138 yds. Short. 2nd Graze & burst 87 yds. Short. Good Line Shot.
5	do	30 Pnd. Parrott	3½	29	2°00′	3½″	—	Shell wobbled or made apparently a succession of zig-zags. Probably lost the Sabot immediately. 1st Graze 130 yds. beyond Target. 2nd = 152 yds. 3rd 190 yds. Shell picked up 260 beyond Target. Deviation to R. 30 ft.
6	do	do	do	do	2°20′	3⅝″	4″	Did not burst. Wobbled. Could not find 1st Graze. Ricochetted immensely. No doubt 1st Graze far beyond the Target.
7	do	8 in. Siege How.	3	45	6°30′	6″	7″	Burst high & to R. about 350 yds. beyond the Target.
8	do	do	do	do	6°30′	6″	6″	Struck ground 193 yds. Short. Ricochetted & burst 90 yds. Short.
9	do	30 Pnd. Parrott	3½	29	1°45′	3¼″	3½″	Wobbled. Burst near ground 150 yds. Short. 1 Fragment thro' Target 5 ft. from Center left, 4 ft. from Bottom. Good line Shot.
10	do	do	do	do	2°00′	3½″	4″	Did not burst. 1st Graze 75 yds. beyond. Ricochetted to River.
11	do	8 in. Siege How.	3	45	6°15′	6″	7″	Did not burst. 1st Graze 86 yds. beyond, 10 yds. to Right. Ricochetted over into the Marsh.
12	do	do	do	do	6°40′	6″	6″	40 ft. to R. 1st Graze 2 yds. beyond. 2nd Graze 88 yds. beyond & burst.

Before measuring the distance the officers each made his Estimate of what it was. Capt. Smith's estimate was 1,000 yds., Lieut. Nesbit's 850 yds., Lieut Hasell's estimate 1,000 yds. These Estimates were of course made separately and without each others priority.

[Not signed]

Friday, 29 January 1864

Warm, Hazy day. Wind Southerly. Very busy arranging, correcting & classifying the Quarterly returns of the different companies.

Adjutant Gardner went into town on leave in the afternoon.

[Not signed]

Saturday, 30 January 1864

Warm, hazy and about 11 looked like rain.

Sent J.A. Simmons of 11th S.C.V., who was arrested yesterday at Wappoo Bridge attempting to pass on forged Ticket, to Col. Gantt under guard. Also two Men of Co. "F" 2nd S.C. Artillery who were arrested in attempting to pass on a permit of which the date had been altered, down to Col. Frederick.

Post-Courier Photo by Thomas Spain

Battery Pringle today consists of tree-covered, weathered mounds.

At 11 A.M. went with Major Lucas to Battery Pringle in order to see as to the enlistments of the Men of that Post whether enlisted for "Three Years" or "Three years or the war" and if necessary to examine the N. Com. Officers as to their understanding and that of the Men of the terms. Found that they were all enlisted for 3 years.[1]

While at Battery Pringle saw some practice at long Range and some Ricochet firing. Also with grape over the land, &c. Rode home by Battery Tynes and made the same inquiries there concerning the enlistments of the Men. Some of them were enlisted "for 3 years," some for "3 years or the War" and some "for the War."

115

Captain Gregg moved his Howitzers up and fired 10 Shots. Distance 1158 yds.

Table of Fire

No. of Shot	Dist. to Target	Kind of Artillery	Charge Powder	Wgt. Shell	Elevation	Length Fuze	Observed Time of Flight	Results & Remarks Target 40 ft. x 7 ft. Day warm. Wind light from South. Commenced firing about 11 A.M. Ceased firing about 1½ P.M.
	Yds.		Lbs.	Lbs.	Deg. M	Seconds	Seconds	
1	1158	8 in. Siege How.	4	29	4° 55'	5″		1st Graze 76 yds. Short, 10 ft. to left. Picked up Shell 150 yds beyond Target, did not burst.
2	do	do	″	″	5° 10'	5″		Burst 50 yds. Short, good height.
3	do	do	″	″	5° 10'	6″		Burst 150 yds. Short, rather high.
4	″	do	″	″	5° 00'	8″		1st Graze 32 yds. beyond Target. 2nd Graze do 102 yds. 3rd 142 yds beyond and burst. About 40 ft. R.
5	″	do	″	″	5° 00'	8″	Officer had no Watch.	1st Graze 159 yds beyond. Burst in the Ground 160 yds. — good line Shot.
6	″	do	″	″	5° 00'	10″		1st Graze 165 yds. beyond. Burst about 350 yds. beyond.
7	″	do	″	″	5° 00'	10″		Burst about 100 yds. short.
8	″	do	″	″	4° 56'	8″		1st Graze 42 yds. short. Ricochetted thro' the Target 9 ft. from Center L, 2 ft. from bottom. 2nd Graze 8 yds. beyond Target, picked up Shell 29 yds. beyond Target, did not burst.
9	″	do	″	″	5° 00'	7″		1st Graze 160 yds. beyond Target. Ricochetted over into Marsh. Did not burst.
10	″	do	″	″	5° 00'	7″		1st Graze 165 yds. beyond Target. Ricochetted into Marsh. Did not burst.

Captain Gregg Estimated the distance at 1075 yds. Lieut. Edwards at 1200 yds.

[*Not signed*]

[1] *This survey seems to have been the outgrowth of a dispute between Col. John S. Preston, superintendent of the Bureau of Conscription at Richmond and Gen. P.G.T. Beauregard of the Dept. of S.C., Ga. and Fla. Preston charged that conscripts from South Carolina were swelling the ranks of relatively inactive Palmetto State units to the detriment of combat regiments in Virginia. On 29 Jan. 1864 Beauregard published an order requiring all members of S.C. reserve regiments in Confederate service to select a preferred unit "for the war." Those who failed to do so prior to expiration of their term of enlistment would be reassigned to one of the units already in service from their congressional district.*

Sunday, 31 January 1864

Warm & bright day. Had careful Inspections at Lebby's and Capt. Gregg's Camp at James Island Creek Bridge.

Heavy fire in the woods to South, either to South of New Lines or on extreme South line of James Island or perhaps on Long or Folly Islands.[1]

[Not signed]

[1] No explanation of this firing has been found.

Monday, 1 February 1864

Went into City to Attend Meeting of Board to investigate Matter of Enlistments of Soldiers "for 3 years or the war."[1] Met at 11 A.M. at Mr. [Edward Leonard] Trenholm's house corner of Rutledge & Montague Streets. Board broke up about half past 2 P.M. and I return to Camp.

Day windy & Marchlike. Wind Westerly.

[Not signed]

[1] See entry of 30 Jan. 1864

Tuesday, 2 February 1864

Captain Bridges came with Capt. [1st. Lt.] Toutant to make arrangements about the organization of Co. "D" Siege Train. Gave him list of the Men to be detailed for his Company.[1]

No Corn or fodder for Horses to day.

[Not signed]

[1] Co. D of the Siege Train was formed per order of 12 Feb. 1864 of men serving in Cos. A and B.

Wednesday, 3 February 1864

Major Manigault went to town to See Col. Waddy about Ordnance Returns. Also the Hospital Steward for medicines for the Month (which were obtained). Returned at 3 P.M.

Windy, Clear & Cold day. Wind West & North West.

[Not signed]

Thursday, 4 February 1864

Clear, bright & rather cold day. Wind Westerly.

Went to Fort Pemberton to see Maj. Lucas & procure certain Acts of Congress in reference to Enlistments.

Examined Platform at Fort Pemberton for Artillery Practice.

Rather too much wind for practice to day.

[Not signed]

Friday, 5 February 1864

Drove down to Col. Simonton's about business of investigating Claims to discharge of "3 years and for the war" men. Then to Genl. Taliaferro's about my appointment on Genl. Court Martial to which cannot attend being on Board above referred to.

Day windy & cool. Some Rain about 11 O'clock. Wind S.E., S. & S.W.

Called Battalion Court Martial again together to review their proceedings.

Dr. Winthrop's furlough extended for 10 days on acct. of illness of his Father

[*Not signed*]

Saturday, 6 February 1864

Busy about opinion in Case of Enlistments of 3 years Men. Most of the day writing.

Lieut. Nesbit went off to day at 1 P.M. on N.E. R.Rd. [*North Eastern Rail Road*] on 15 days furlough.

[*Not signed*]

Sunday, 7 February 1864

Cold, clear day. Wrote out opinion in matter above referred to. Also made up Quarterly accounts of Ordnance — i.e. examined and supplied defects &c. wrote letter of transmittal.

Distance from intersection of Fort Pemberton Road with "West Lines' (Lebby's) to turn in Lines to Southwards 1320 Steps. Note. At 30 in. to Step = 3300 ft. or 1100 yds, or from Lebby's House 1200 yds. It is full this, perhaps more.

[*Not signed*]

Monday, 8 February 1864

Cool, clear day. Went to City at 10 A.M. and attended meeting of Board on Enlistment question at 11 at Corner Rutledge & Montague Streets. [*Edward Leonard Trenholm's house*]

Carried Ordnance Returns (Quarterly) to Col. Waddy's Office myself about 1 P.M.

Returned about 3 P.M. to Camp.

Genl. Beauregard Reviewed troops on [*James*] Island. Capt. Webb commanded the Siege Train as I was absent.

[*Not signed*]

Tuesday, 9 February 1864

The Yankees drove in our pickets on John's Island.[1]

Went down to Col. Simonton's about business of Board &c. Capt. Mordecai rode towards Wiltown [*Willtown on South Edisto River about 30 miles southwest of Charleston*] with Col. White but returned on hearing of attack on Black [*Manigault must have meant John's*] Island.

Colquitt's Brigade moving towards Savannah. At dress Parade read out Sentences of 8 Prisoners.

[*Not signed*]

[1] *This demonstration, by troops under command of U.S. Brig. Gen. Alexander Schimmelfennig, was a diversion to distract the Confederate's attention from a Federal expedition to the Jacksonville, Fla., area. Schimmelfennig's force landed on John's Island on the 9th and drove in the Confederate pickets. They consolidated their position on the 10th, then pushed forward about three miles on the 11th. That night, in accordance with orders, they fell back, abandoned John's Island and returned to their original camps on nearby islands. Casualties were light on both sides. [OR XXXV (1), pp. 30, 31, 144-151]*

Wednesday, 10 February 1864

Went to City to attend Meeting of Board. Owing to a mistake as to Col. Simonton's instructions, I did not go in until after the hour. But met the Board and transacted our final business (Supposed final).

Called on Genl. Jordan about the Accountability for Ord. Stores.

Early in morning wind N.E. and Cold. About & after Midday wind S.E. and South and searching.

Capt. Mordecai appointed Acting Brigade Commissary of Western Division by Col. Simonton's order dated yesterday.

[*Not signed*]

Thursday, 11 February 1864

Cold, clear day. Wind N.E. Building Stable for Staff Mules.

Made exploration of Woods & Shore near Newtown Cut. About 3 P.M. a heavy cannonading commenced on John's Island. This was an artillery duel between the Marion Artillery and the Enemy in which the Enemy's guns were silenced.[1]

Capt. Bridges (Co. "D") reported to Camp about 4 P.M.

[*Not signed*]

[1] *See Tuesday, 9 Feb. 1864, note.*

Friday, 12 February 1864

Cold Morning, Wind N.E. Steamer *Chesterfield* passed through Wappoo Creek for transportation of troops &c from Fort Pemberton to John's Island.

Drew 76 Austrian Rifles and accoutrements &c from Ord. Depot at McLeod's.

At 4 P.M. received Orders to hold the Siege Train in readiness to go to John's Island. Made immediate arrangements for moving. At about 9 P.M. heard that the enemy had evacuated John's Island.

At 12 or 1 O'clock at night received orders that the Siege Train would not be required to move.

[*Not signed*]

Saturday, 13 February 1864

Mild Hazy day. Heavy details made on Siege Train.

	Guard Duty	72 men
	Telegraph duty	25
	Fort Pemberton	25 (Mounting Guns)
		122 Men
	N.C. Off	12
		134 Enlisted Men
		3 Officers
		137 Aggregate

This was besides 20 men for Policing Camp & 2 building
Staff Mule Stables — 22
Also Building Stables for Capt. Webb's Battery Horses — 4

163 Total detail
Also include 9 Prisoners — 9

172

Received no Corn to day but had a large amount of Fodder furnished.
Louisianians turned over to Capt. Bridges' Company [*Company D, Siege Train*]. He had his first Roll Call at Retreat.[1]
Dr. Winthrop returned from Furlough.

[*Not signed*]

[1] *See Appendix I, Co. D, Manigault's Bn.*

Sunday, 14 February 1864

Hazy, Spring like day with fresh wind from West. Steamer *Chesterfield* passed back to City through Wappoo Creek about 1 P.M.

At Dress Parade Read Order appointing N.C. Officers of Capt. Bridges' Co. "D". Also order for election of one 1st & two 2nd Lieutenants of same company to take place tomorrow. Also order removing Mackey as Chief Bugler and appointing Peleun [*Pellerin*] in his place. Also order prohibiting Shouting in Camp.

Capt. Mordecai got a supply of 60 Boxes of Corn to day.

[*Not signed*]

Monday, 15 February 1864

High March wind from S & S.W. Clouds of dust.

Had an Election of 1st Lieut & two 2nd Lieutenants in Co. "D" (Nomination & Election unanimous.) Vienne elected 1st Lieut. Painparé elected Senior 2nd Lieut. Damarin [*elected*] Jr. 2nd Lieut.

Brought a load of Ammunition from St. Andrews Depot for Co. "A" and sent it to Fort Pemberton. 7 large Boxes carried.

Clouds of dust. Rain about 5.30 P.M. which did not last long. Wind S.W. With the Rain the wind went down.

[*Not signed*]

Tuesday, 16 February 1864

Cloudy morning wind N.W. and cool. About 10 O'clock Cleared off. From about 12, high N.W. wind and clouds of dust. Not cold.

Walked to Commissary Station (McLeod's) [*house*] and inspected our posts.

Capt. Frost's 2 Commissary Store Houses	1 post	1 corp.	3 privates
Capt. Behre's 2 do	1 post, No. 1	1 sergt.	3 privates
" " Sentinel at Officers quarters at night	1 " " 2		3 privates
" " Meal House	1 " " 3		3 privates
" " House nearest Bridge	1 " " 4		3 privates
" " Butcher Pen	1 " " 5	1 corp.	3 privates
Ordnance Stores	1 post		3
Total Required		1 sergt. 2 corp.	21 Men
Total demanded		1 " 2 "	24
Being 3 too Many.			

On further enquiry, I find that these three are employed as lanced or acting Corporals.

Wagon brought rest of Ammunition for Co. "A" from St. Andrew's Depot and carried to Fort Pemberton except a few shell put in Caissons. 16 Boxes Shells (15 of 6 each, 90 & 1 of 3) 93 Shells & 1 Box of 500 Fuzes.

About 4 P.M. a heavy fire broke out on the fields to South of Fort Pemberton where the Broom grass was very thick. The dry condition of every thing and the high wind caused it to spread very rapidly. It extended quite down to New Town Cut and burnt a good deal of felled timber in front of the Western lines.

Visited the line or North Boundary of fire, returned home at 8½ P.M.

[*Not signed*]

Wednesday, 17 February 1864

Ice ⅛ inch thick in Sheltered piazza. Water spilt in small quantities soon Froze.

Wind N.W. Clear day.

Inspection of Siege Train ordered for 11 A.M., did not, however, receive order until near half past 10, hence inspection did not take place until 12 M. Lieut. Meade of Genl. Taliaferro's staff inspecting officer. Inspected Capt. Gregg's Company at his Camp. Got through inspection about 3½ P.M. Rode to see what damage the fire of last night had done. Got home about 4½ P.M.

Order from Genl. Taliaferro to go to his Hd Qrs about Matters connected with the Siege Train. Got back at 8½ P.M. Cold afternoon & night.

Capt. Whilden, formerly of [*Thomas*] Pinckney's Company, now of 5th S.C.C. [*South Carolina Cavalry*] came to my quarters to see about the order for the organization of his Company 1st May 1864. Referred him to order book turned over to Major Byrd.

Note. The U.S. Steam Sloop *"Housatonic"* was sunk to night by a Torpedo Boat.[1]

[*Not signed*]

[1] *Although called a torpedo boat by Manigault and others in contemporary records, the vessel was a true submarine. She has been known through the years as the C.S. Hunley, in honor of her inventor, Horace L. Hunley. However, the craft seems to have been nameless when she earned her niche in history by being the first submarine to sink an enemy warship. She was an estimated 35 to 40 feet long and made of boiler plate. She had two fins, controlled from inside the vessel. These enabled her to dive and, with luck, to surface. The only air was that in the boat at the time she submerged. She carried a crew of nine — eight to man the cranks that turned her propeller and the ninth to steer. She was designed to approach a target on the surface, then dive beneath it while towing a torpedo on a line astern. Theoretically, the torpedo would be dragged into the target and the Hunley would be protected from the resulting explosion by the bulk of the target ship. Unfortunately, the Hunley was so slow that she had difficulty keeping ahead of the torpedo. This danger, coupled with two or more accidental sinkings during trials, convinced Gen. Beauregard that diving was too hazardous. He ordered her fitted with a spar torpedo of the type used by the semi-submersible torpedo boats known as Davids and with which the Hunley often is confused. The boat went hunting during the evening of 17 Feb. 1864 and managed to ram her torpedo against the U.S. Housatonic, a 207-foot screw steamer of 1,240 tons mounting 12 guns of various types. The Housatonic settled in 27 feet of water while her crew escaped by climbing into the rigging. The Hunley apparently was swamped by the explosion. After the war, the hulk of Housatonic was removed, but the tiny submarine was not recovered. [Burton, pp. 227-241; OR XXVIII (2), OR XXXV (2), ONR XV, passim]*

Thursday, 18 February 1864

Cloudy day, Wind N.E. Ice ⅛ in. thick in South piazza at Lebby's. Very cold all day.

At 12½ P.M. had drill of Batteries of Cos. A & B. At 2¾ sent 30 Pndr. Parrott No. 1 to Charleston Arsenal to have Sights adjusted (by order Genl. Taliaferro).

This morning made Requisition by order of Genl. Taliaferro for Rope Traces, Halters, &c. &c. for Cos. A & B Siege Train.

Afternoon bitter cold. Wind a little East of North.

At 5.30 P.M. Snow commenced falling in beautiful Star Crystals (6 rayed). After dark a slight fall of snow sufficient merely to make the surface of ground quite white. Severe night on our horses which have no Shelter from the North wind which is high.

[*Not signed*]

Friday, 19 February 1864

Wind N. East and very cold & Keen. Ice about 1/16 [*inch*] thick in Lebby South piazza; day not bright but not entirely clouded. Wherever water fell it froze in a few minutes.

Detail of 1 Officer and 30 Men to report to Capt. Behre at 8 A.M.

Ice in ditches ½ inch thick; remained all day in Sheltered places.

Made Shelter for Staff Mules against the North wind.
Bitter Cold.
Sent horses for Gun No. 1 but it was not ready.

[*Not Signed*]

Saturday, 20 February 1864

Ice ¾ inch thick in South piazza of Lebby's. Wind N. and little East but not much of it. Fine clear Sunny Day but ice continued throughout the day in some places exposed to direct rays of Sun. Ice in our Bucket all day in the Sun. Ice in ditches & ponds about ¾ in. thick.

Received three Boxes of Harness for Co. "A" from Capt. Ingraham.

Got cartridges from Fort Pemberton to try whether they fitted the Guns.

Capt. Mordecai commenced slaughtering Beef and issuing Stores from Heyward's House (Guard of 3 Men & 1 Corporal from Siege Train)

A part of afternoon Wind S.E. and very piercing.

About 10 A.M. sent Parrott Gun No. 2 to Charleston Arsenal. After dark Gun No. 1 arrived from Arsenal with Sights adjusted.

Weather moderated at night. Much Ice about Well all day where Water was spilt & frozen.

Young men belonging to Signal Corps, Legare, Clark & Lawrence, putting up Salt Works on Point to N.W. of Lebby's.

Capt. Bridges went to town on leave for day.

[*Not signed*]

Sunday, 21 February 1864

Heavy fog at Sunrise. Wind Southerly. Much more Moderate. Ice 1/16 [*inch*] thick in Lebby's South piazza.

Lieut. Chapman fitting harness received yesterday, to the Battery Horses.

Co. "A" has in Caissons 228 Cartridges & 192 Shells. With Centre Box of one of Limbers Supplied could take 228 Cart. & 216 Shells.

Returned rest of Cartridges (187 in No.) back to Fort Pemberton.

[*Not signed*]

Monday, 22 February 1864

Some fog and a little White Frost. No ice. Wind South.

Had Drill of 3 companies of Siege Train on foot & in Ranks according to Form laid down for Lt. [*Light*] Artillery p. 69 No. 8, "Instruction for Field Artillery."

Lieut. Nesbitt returned from furlough after night.

[*Not signed*]

Tuesday, 23 February 1864

Very mild morning. Wind South West.

At 10 A.M. Sent for Parrott Gun No. 2 to Charleston Arsenal. Also 5 horses to be shod.

Gun Arrived after dark.

[*Not signed*]

Wednesday, 24 February 1864

Warm & Smoky & Murky; looked like rain.

Had Drill of 2 Sections in Morning, from 10½ to 12 M.

Had Drill of 3 Companies on foot & in Ranks in evening.

[*Not signed*]

Thursday, 25 February 1864

Morning cool — Wind northerly.

Went into City on private business and spent the day. Returned into Camp about 6 P.M. Very fine day. Cool in evening.

Found order for Board to Examine into competency of Sergt. Richardson, elected 2nd Lieutenant in Co. K, Palm. [*Palmetto*] Battn. [*Battalion*] Light Artillery.

[*Not signed*]

Friday, 26 February 1864

North Wind and quite cool.

Sergt. Richardson, the Officer Elected to be examined arrived at 10 A.M. but Capt. Humbert did not arrive until after 12 M. and Capt. Hayne not at all. Sent notice for meeting of Board at 10 A.M. tomorrow.

At 2 P.M. received Order for Co. "A" Siege Train to report as soon as possible to the Officer Comdg. Confederate forces at "Lake City" Florida. Telegraphed Maj. Pringle, Q.M., that the Company would be ready at 8 P.M. to start for Florida. At 8 P.M. the Company was at the C & S R.R. Depot, but had to wait until Morning before getting on the Cars. Night quite cool.

[*Not signed*]

Saturday, 27 February 1864

Commenced loading on Cars about 7.30 A.M. One 30 pndr. Parrott broke through platform. Cold & Frosty morning but no ice. The Train with Co. "A" did not leave the Depot until 11.30 A.M. The following was the force &c. carried.

(5)	Five Officers		
(83)	Eighty three Men		
(78)	Seventy Eight Horses & Mules		
(2)	Two 30 pndr. Parrott Guns		
(4)	Four Caissons containing	232 Cartridges &	224 Shells
(1)	One Travelling Forge		
(1)	One Battery Wagon		
(1)	One Ordnance Wagon containing	71 Cartridges &	59 Shells
		303	283
(2)	Two Baggage & Forage Wagons		

The day was clear & bright. The wind East & cool if not cold.

Examined Sergt. Richardson. The Examination lasting from 10½ to 3 P.M. The Board consisting of Major Manigault, Captain Humbert & Captain Hayne.

About 9 P.M. received Orders for Co. "D" Capt. Bridges to be at Depot C & S R. Rd. at 6½ A.M. tomorrow to go to Ashepoo [*River, about 35 miles west of Charleston*] & report to Brig. Genl. Robertson. Capt. Bridges turned in his Austrian Rifles & Accoutrements.

[*Not signed*]

Sunday, 28 February 1864

Capt. Bridges left in 7½ A.M. Train for Ashepoo with 51 "present." Aggregate Pres't & Absent 73.

Day clear & bright. A little frost in Morning but no ice. Wind S.W.

[*Not signed*]

Monday, 29 February 1864

Day Warm, Wind S.W. High Wind & very dusty.

At 10 A.M. went to Fort Pemberton & Inspected & Mustered Field, Staff & Band, Steward & Hospital attendants, and Capt. S.M. Richardson's Co. "K" P.B.L.A. [*Palmetto Battalion Light Artillery*]

Then went to "Battery Tynes"[1] and inspected & Mustered Capt. Guignard Richardson's Co. "B" Lucas Battalion of Heavy Artillery.

Then went to Battery Pringle and inspected and Mustered Capt. T.B. Hayne's Co. "C" Lucas Batt. Heavy Artillery.

Went to Col. Simonton's to get instructions about Reports. Home at 4½ P.M.

[*Not signed*]

[1] *Battery Tynes, an earthwork on the Stono River, is one of the few American fortifications named for an enlisted man. Samuel A. Tynes, listed erroneously in the Official*

Records as T.H. Tynes, was 1st Sgt. of Co. A, Lucas' Bn., S.C. Heavy Artillery. He died 24 July 1863 of wounds received at Battery Wagner 20 July. The battery was named in his honor 18 Oct. 1863. Batteries Pringle and Tynes survive today in good condition. [Personnel records, Samuel A. Tynes; OR XXVIII (2), p. 424]

Tuesday, 1 March 1864

Windy, Gusty, March day. Clouds of dust. Wind S.W.

Meeting of Board of Examination to verify proceedings in case of Sergt. Richardson and to record their opinion of his Competency. Met at 10 A.M. Adjourned at 1.15 P.M. Capt. Humbert & Self rode to Fort Pemberton to give Sergt. Richardson a practical drill, but he was off on furlough. His going off was premature and should not have been permitted. The Board of Examination had not dismissed him nor in any way intimated that he was at liberty to be absent.

Clouds of dust & very high S.W. Wind. Wind subsided about 8 P.M. and there was a little rain during night.

Dr. Winthrop went to City. Also Lieut. Edwards.

[Not signed]

Wednesday, 2 March 1864

Wind North and a little East and quite fresh. Morning and day quite cool.

Sent off Muster Rolls to Office A & I Genl. [Adjutant and Inspector General] Richmond.

Adjt. Gardner went to City on leave.

[Not signed]

Thursday, 3 March 1864

Wind N. East and fresh. Quite cool. Clear day.

Yankees shelling City heavily all day.

Dr. Winthrop went to City to see his Brother.[1]

[Not signed]

[1] Probably Dr. Henry Winthrop. The brothers practiced medicine at a Tradd Street address prior to the war. [Charleston City Directory, 1859]

Friday, 4 March 1864

In morning Wind N.E. & cool & cloudy. Afterwards day warmer & Sun came out.

Yankees Shelling the City heavily all night and during day. Often 1 Shot every 5 Minutes.

Adjt. Gardner went to Savannah on 7½ A.M. Train on 15 days furlough.

Note that Adjutant Gardner continued absent until June 29th when he reported for duty at Artillery X Roads. His physician (a Confederate

Surgeon) having decided that an operation was necessary of a very serious nature and his recovery was very slow.[1]

[*Not signed*]

[1] *Manigault apparently anticipated a change in the length of Gardner's leave and left sufficient room at the end of the 4 March entry to insert the note, which obviously was appended later.*

Saturday, 5 March 1864

Wind Westerly; looked like rain but did not. Morning tolerably cool, day rather warm in sun.

Major M. [*Manigault*] spent day in town to See his brother G.M. [*Gabriel Manigault*]. Returned at 7 P.M.

Yankees did not appear to be shelling much.

[*Not signed*]

Sunday, 6 March 1864

Wind West, perhaps a little north of West. Morning Cool.

Dr. Winthrop went to City.

Fine day.

[*Not signed*]

Monday, 7 March 1864

Calm Morning. Very light Frost. Wind North East, what little there was of it.

A Torpedo Boat passed back from Stono towards the City.

Went with brother [*not identified but probably Gabriel*] to visit Fort Pemberton & "Battery Pringle." Also rode along the "New Lines."[1] Stopped by Col. Simonton's. He was drilling his Regiment at Genl. Hagood's Hd. Qrs.

[*Not signed*]

[1] *See Thursday, 22 Oct. 1863, note.*

Tuesday, 8 March 1864

Wind S.W. Cloudy & looking like Rain.

Major M. Went to City at 9½ A.M.

A walk round the most exposed parts of City shows that the visible damage is really much less than Could have been expected. Walking down King Street, the first damage visible is on building opposite Enston's Store, corner of King & Cumberland Streets [*now King and Horlbeck Alley*]. A Shell had gone through this and struck in the Street, its fragments have struck Enston's. 2 Shells through back of Mills House [*115 Meeting Street*]. 1 Shell through back Pediment of Hibernian Hall [*105 Meeting Street*]. Along Broad [*Street*] from King to

1865 view of Meeting and Broad Streets. St. Michael's Church, center. City Hall is at left and the County Court House, right.

Modern view of Nathaniel Russell House, 51 Meeting St.

Meeting, Many glasses broken. State House or Court House [*northwest corner, Meeting and Broad*] struck by one Shell. Guard House [*southwest corner, Meeting and Broad. Destroyed by earthquake in 1886. Now site of U.S. Post Office*] struck by 3 Shells. Down Meeting, 1 Shell through Church yard Wall of St. Michael's [*Protestant Episcopal Church, southeast corner, Meeting and Broad*]. 1 shell through S.C. Hall [*South Carolina Society Hall, 72 Meeting*]. 1 Shell through Mr. Mordecai's House [*69 Meeting*]. 1 Shell in alley below S.C. Hall [*Ropemaker's Lane*]. 1 Shell in house N.E. Corner Meeting & Tradd [*60 Meeting*]. 1 Shell struck Stable of Barbot House [*59 Meeting*]. 1 Shell through Old Russell House [*Nathaniel Russell House, 51 Meeting*]. Several Shells in Water Street. Mr. Danl. [*Daniel*] Heyward's house on [*The*]

East Battery in 1865. Daniel Heyward's house (1); Charles Alston's (2); James G. Holmes' (3) and William Ravenel's (4).

Battery [*25 East Battery*] struck by Fragment. Kitchen or Stable back of Mr. Holmes' [*House, 19 East Battery*] Tiles [*of roof*] all loosened. DeSaussure's House [*45 East Bay (prolongation north of East Battery)*] opposite Southern Wharf, Piazza Much injured by Shell. Vanderhorst's buildings, [*76-80 East Bay*] two or three Shells through them. Boyce's South Wharf [*approximately 100 East Bay*] where Ironclad [*the Columbia*] is building, Struck 5 times by Shells & Fragments, several others in Wharf & Street. Two Shells in 4 Story Brick building N.W. corner

Elliott Street & [*East*] Bay. Bank of State [*southwest corner, Broad and East Bay*] Struck. Broad Street from Bay to Meeting Street not one building in 15 appeared to be Struck. Near Charleston Hotel [*200 Meeting. Hotel was demolished 1959-60 to make way for a motel*] two or three Stores struck. 3 Shells struck City Hall [*northeast corner, Broad and Meeting*].

The longest range of any shell was up to corner of John & Chappel [*Chapel*] Streets = 4⅞ miles [*from Morris Island*]. Some Shells fell a little to South & S.E. of the Charleston College dist. [*district*] say 4⅝ miles.

As seen from Top of Orphan House, [*the building, northeast corner Calhoun and St. Philip, was demolished in 1952*] the flash of a gun at Battery Gregg preceded the Report by average of 18 Seconds (1100 x 18 = 19800 ft. = 3 Miles, 3960 [*feet*] = 3¾ Miles). This cannot be accurate tho' made by Prof. Gibbes. The explosion of the Shell is generally heard at least 28 seconds after the flash of gun. Some however are as late as 38 seconds after flash of Gun.

Bishop Lynch estimates damage at $200 per each Shell thrown. (This includes fires).

Returned to Camp at 7 P.M.

[*Not signed*]

Wednesday, 9 March 1864

Wind East & Fresh, not cold.

By direction of Genl. Hagood rode to his Hd. Quarters at 10 A.M. Afterwards stopped at Gregg's Camp. Relieved him from arrest.[1]

Heavy firing in direction of Fort Sumter. Also a light Battery practising with Shells near Genl. Hagood's Quarters.

Rain during night. Wind South. Light Showers about 9 & 10 O'clock, but heavy rain & high Wind towards Morning.

[*Not signed*]

[1] *No report has been found regarding the circumstances of his arrest.*

Thursday, 10 March 1864

High S.W. Wind and cloudy with light rains.

Busy writing all Morning. Co. "B" Wanted Beef to day and many of them came to me to procure it for them. Dismissed them summarily with the information that the Government was doing its best to supply them.

They have been without Meat Tuesday, Wednesday & Thursday but Commutation has been given them in Meal one day, Wheat flour another day & Molasses the third day which is the best our Commissary can do and in accordance with Orders from Hd. Qrs. which says that when there is no Meat, a ration of one of the following articles will be supplied, viz. Rice, Corn Meal, Wheat flour, Lard, Sugar or Molasses, according as the individual Commissary can best spare it.

Some Lightning (distant) in evening.

[*Not signed*]

Friday, 11 March 1864

South West wind. Rain early in Morning. Then heavy Rain and much lightning at 9 A.M., again at 10 A.M.

Lieut. Philips Came to Camp. Told him to Report to Genl. Hagood as on 30th July he had been assigned as Ordnance Officer at Legare's Point and that Assignment had never been revoked. Sent Notice to Capt. Bridges that Examination of Vienne, Painparé & Damarin should be ordered by Genl. Robertson. Also notice that Election Returns had been forwarded to Hd. Qrs. Dept. of S.C., G. [*Georgia*] & Fla.

[*Not signed*]

Saturday, 12 March 1864

Beautifully clear day. Wind S.W. Pleasant all day. Very Calm and Clear evening & night, rather Cool.

Detail of 1 Off. & 20 Men at Work all day at Capt. Behre's Moving, loading and unloading Stores.

Sent a Monthly Return of Siege Train to Office of A & I Genl., Richmond, with letter explaining the cause of delay.

Wrote to Capt. Webb telling him to send his Monthly Return direct to Richmond and Duplicate to me. Also informing him that Dr. Wm. Alston had applied for a place in his Company.

Extensive policing of Camp in Afternoon.

Beautifully calm & clear evening & night.

[*Not signed*]

Sunday, 13 March 1864

Fine Morning. Wind a little North of West. Pleasant & fresh but not cold.

Sergeant Major Gaillard went to City on leave for the day.

[*Not signed*]

Monday, 14 March 1864

Fine Morning. Wind directly North and quite cool.

Had Section Drill in Morning, Squad Drills in afternoon.

Afternoon & night cloudy.

[*Not signed*]

Tuesday, 15 March 1864

Wind N.W. fresh and quite cool if not cold.

Had Section Drill in afternoon as several of the Drivers had just come off guard in the Morning.

Dr. Winthrop went to town.

Issued Austrian Rifles to Capt. Gregg.

Yankees firing on Fort Sumter.[1]

[Not signed]

[1] *This was termed the Fourth Minor Bombardment of Fort Sumter. It was short, a single day, and was brought on by Federal discovery of Confederate efforts to build protection for the Three Gun Battery in Fort Sumter. At the end of the day, and some 140 rounds, the work was splintered and partially demolished but the battery was uninjured. Casualties were light, six wounded. [OR XXXV (2) p. 361; Johnson, pp. 202, 205]*

Wednesday, 16 March 1864

Wind North and a little West, quite cold. Cold all day.

Drill of officers at Manual.

In afternoon Drill in Section.

Dr. Winthrop went to City again to day.

Gregg's men came on Guard with Austrian Rifles for the first time.

[Not signed]

Thursday, 17 March 1864

Wind Northerly. Quite cold. Water froze when spilt in South Piazza of Lebby's house, also Ice in Bucket. About Midday Wind shifted to South and was very Keen, presenting one of the instances of Southerly wind being very cold after several days prevalence of cold North Winds.

Had Morning Drill of officers in Manual.

Evening Drill of Sections of Artillery.

Some firing down on Stono this evening. Supposed practice at Battery Pringle.

[Not signed]

Friday, 18 March 1864

Considerable White Frost and a very little ice in buckets exposed. Calm in Morning, afterwards high S.W. Wind, quite cool.

There was no drill to day as the drivers were busy completing Stable, &c.

Capt. Mordecai went off in the 7.30 A.M. Train for Hardeeville [*About 80 miles southwest of Charleston*] to see Capt. [*John G.*] Clark in order to settle up some accounts with him. He has leave of absence for 4 days.

[Not signed]

Saturday, 19 March 1864.

Morning cool but not cold. Wind S.W.

Made Exploration of Shore of St. Andrews [*Parish*] up to Ravenel's[1] noting landings, &c.

[*Not signed*]

[1] *This was Farm Field Plantation, owned by William Ravenel (see Appendix 3, p. 332). The plantation house, a few miles east of Charleston, survives today.*

Sunday, 20 March 1864

Wind Westerly, Cloudy, a little rain in Morning. About Midday wind got N.W. and cooler. Warm again towards night.

Showers of Rain at Night.

[*Not signed*]

Monday, 21 March 1864

Wind North. Cool & damp. About 2.30 P.M. a cold N.E. Rain set in which lasted all night (with occasional short intermissions) and accompanied most of the time with high wind.

Dunovant's Regiment, 5th S.C. Cav. (encamped near us) ordered to Virginia.

[*Not signed*]

Tuesday, 22 March 1864

Equinox. High N.E. Wind with cold rain. Rain ceased after 2 P.M. Wind went round to N.W. and became very keen. A bitter night for our horses which have in a measure shed their hair.

Capt. Mordecai returned from Savannah at 4½ P.M.[1]

Drill of N.C. Officers in afternoon.

[*Not signed*]

[1] *Mordecai had left Friday, 18 March, for Hardeeville on 4-day leave and presumably had continued to Savannah, Ga., about 15 miles farther south.*

Wednesday, 23 March 1864

Lead Coloured Morning. Ice in Bucket thick as a dollar. Water spilt soon froze. Wind North a little West. Sun came out about 7 O'clock. The rest of the day beautiful and quite cool & Bracing.

Dr. Winthrop went to City to send off furniture.[1]

Drill of officers in Morning. Section Drill in afternoon.

Visited picket at New Town Cut Bridge after Sunset.

[*Not signed*]

[1] *Winthrop's office, and probably his residence, were on Tradd Street in the lower part of the city and thus subject to Federal artillery fire from Morris Island. He no doubt moved his furniture farther uptown or out of the city.*

Thursday, 24 March 1864

Frost but no ice. Wind N.E. in Morning. East & very keen after Midday.

Lt. Nesbit, acting Inspr. Genl. Reviewed & Inspected Co. "B".

Explored the woods down near New Town Cut.

Dr. Winthrop went to town on same business as yesterday.

Drilled N.C. Officers in afternoon.

Capt. Mordecai went to Fort Sumter at Night.

Night cloudy. Commenced raining during night.

[*Not signed*]

Friday, 25 March 1864

Rain, Wind N. East. About Midday wind went round to South & So. West and it became quite warm.

Capt. Mordecai returned about 3½ P.M.

Drilled Officers at 2 P.M. & N.C. Officers at 3½ P.M. in Manual.

Some Rain again at Night but cleared off beautifully before Morning.

[*Not signed*]

Saturday, 26 March 1864

Beautiful day, wind West, a little North.

Sent 9 Couriers to Col. Simonton's & Genl. Taliaferro's Hd. Quarters. This was to supply the place of Couriers from Dunovant's Cavalry Regiment which it was supposed would be ordered off immediately.[1] Most of the Couriers were sent back.

No Drill to day, but extensive policing, and ditching about the Stables.

[*Not signed*]

[1] *To Virginia. See Monday, 21 March 1864.*

Sunday, 27 March 1864

Fine day, wind N.W. but not cold.

Nine Couriers again sent to Col. Simonton's & Genl. Taliaferro's Hd. Quarters. They were sent back with notice that they would not be wanted till further orders.

Wind changed to South, a little before Sunset.

[*Not signed*]

Monday, 28 March 1864

Cloudy Morning. Light air from N.E.

Drill of N.C. Off. at 2 P.M. Section Drill at 4 P.M.

East wind and cool in afternoon. Rain at night.

[*Not signed*]

Tuesday, 29 March 1864

Rainy or rather Showery Morning. Wind South and S.E.
Capt. [*S. Porcher*] Smith reported for duty.
Lieut. Spivey off on Furlough — 10 A.M. — for 15 days.
Cleared up at Midday.
Drill of N.C. Officers in Manual at 3½ P.M.
Wind Westerly in afternoon.

[*Not signed*]

Wednesday, 30 March 1864

Clear Morning. Wind West & high. Quite cool and fresh.
Adjt. Gardner's Servant Frank sent to Savannah by his direction.
Orders received at 8½ A.M. to prepare for inspection by Col. Roman.
Horses harnessed from 11 A.M. til 6 P.M. Col. Roman did not come.
At 10 A.M. Went down to Col. Simonton's & Genl. Taliaferro's. Neither was at home. Came back about 12½.
At 8 P.M. received orders again to be ready again tomorrow for Inspection by Col. Roman.
At 3½ P.M. as Col. Roman did not come, had a Section Drill. 7 hours in harness.
Cold all day and also with high west wind till Night. Fine Calm starlight Night.
Dr. Winthrop went into town on business.
Capt. [*S. Porcher*] Smith went into County on 24 hours leave of absence to get a horse.

[*Not signed*]

Thursday, 31 March 1864

Clear Morning. Quite Cool. Wind Westerly.
Had horses harnessed immediately after Guard Mounting.
Dr. Winthrop went again into Town on business.
At 4 P.M. Col. Roman not coming, I had a Section Drill.
Horses not unharnessed until 6.20 P.M. (Sunset) = 9 hours in Harness.
Capt. [*S. Porcher*] Smith, Co. B, returned late at night.
Day pleasant & Mild.

[*Not signed*]

Friday, 1 April 1864

Day Cloudy & Showery.
No drill to day. Very busy about Monthly & Quarterly Returns.
Capt. [*S. Porcher*] Smith in command of his Company.
High west wind all night & occasionally rain from 8 to 10 P.M.
Nine Couriers furnished from Siege Train to Genl. Taliaferro's and Col. Simonton's Hd. Qrs. and to Advanced Pickets in place of Couriers from Dunovant's Regt. ordered off [*to Virginia*].

[*Not signed*]

Saturday, 2 April 1864

High West wind. Cloudy & cold.

Private Bellinger of Co. "A" sent off to join his Company in Florida having Capt. Webb's "Company Box" in Charge.

Wind West & N.W. all day and quite cold for the season.

No Drill to day, but extensive policing.

Col. Dunovant's 5th Regt. S.C. Cavalry marched to day for Virginia.

[Not signed]

Sunday, 3 April 1864

Wind North, clear & cool. Before Sunset Wind South & Milder.

Yankees commenced bombarding the City from Morris Island in the evening and continued almost all night.

[Not signed]

Monday, 4 April 1864

Wind N.E. damp & Cloudy.

Furnished to day the following details.

Bridge, Comy. [Commissary] & Camp Guards	1 Off.	& 66 Men
Fatigue party to Capt. Behre	1 "	20 "
Fatigue party Engineers at B. [Battery] Pringle	1 "	20 "
Couriers		9 "
	3 Off.	115 Men

Showery all day. Wind southerly in afternoon. Exceedingly high tides, 6½ P.M. or 7 P.M. The Steamboat with Subsistence Stores was not discharged to day. The detail of 1 off & 20 Men ordered back in the morning.

[Not signed]

Tuesday, 5 April 1864

High West, a little North, Wind. Fresh & Cool morning & day. Clear.

Furnished same detail as yesterday.

1 Officer & 66 Men		Guard
1 " 20 "		Fatigue Party to Battery Pringle
1 " 20 "		do do to Capt. Behre
9		Couriers
3 115		

The fatigue party at Battery Pringle is employed in constructing the Rampart to enclose the work. Battery Pringle has hitherto been a simple Battery towards the River and open in rear, but now it is intended to make an enclosed work of it. There are 100 men from 25 S.C.V., 50 men from 2nd S.C. Arty, 30 from Lucas' Battalion & 20 from the Siege Train. Total 200 men at work on the Rear or Gorge portion.

Lieut. Hasell, Co. "A" Siege Train, came to Lebby's to get the Men, Tents, Harness &c. left behind when the Company went to Florida.

[*Not signed*]

Wednesday, 6 April 1864

Beautiful Morning. Wind North and quite Cool. Sun bright and middle of day rather warm for Exercise.

Lieut. Hasell carried most of the property of Co. "A" to Charleston to take out what is wanted to go to Florida and to put the rest in Depot in the City.

Busy in making out Quarterly Returns.

[*Not signed*]

Thursday, 7 April 1864

Morning calm & rather cloudy. (Anniversary of [*ironclad*] attack on Fort Sumter).[1] Wind came out [*of*] N.E. Cloudy day.

Lt. Hasell took off the remainder of the property of Co. "A". Also the 8 men who had been left behind when the Company went to Florida — viz. — Chrietzberg, Brown, Reeder, Roumillat, Knott, Moise, Posten & Taylor. Knoblock, the Mail Carrier, will remain as before.

In the afternoon found the boat belonging to Mr. Gardner which had been lost; it had been sold for $15 to Dougherty of Legare & Clark's Salt Works. Dougherty had the receipt, signed by one of the Palmetto Guard Co. "A", but I think the name was forged, ie, one member of the Company had forged the name of another member of the Company.

Wrote to Capt. Johnson, Baldwin, Fla., requesting him to sign and return the Ordnance Rec[ts]. accompanying.

Wrote to Capt. Bridges, Green Pond, [*about 40 miles west of Charleston*] specifying mistakes in his Monthly Return.

[*Not signed*]

[1] *See Introduction, pp. viii, x.*

Friday, 8 April 1864

Morning Calm & cloudy. A little Rain fell. Wind afterwards came out of N. East and the day was rather cool.

Rode down to Hd. Qrs. and got Lt. Cunningham to give [*me*] duplicate of the Invoice of Austrian Rifles &c. which he had neglected to do.

Handed my quarterly Ordnance Return to March 31, 1864, to Lt. Moffett, A.A.A. Genl. for Lieut. Barton, Ord. Off. of West Lines.

Rode to Dougherty to get the Receipt given him in order to hold it for conviction of the parties. He had burnt it.[1]

At night it rained. At 8½ P.M. received orders from Genl. Taliaferro's Hd. Qrs. to move the Siege Train down to such point of the New Lines as Col. Simonton Might designate.

[*Not signed*]

¹*See Thursday, 7 April 1864.*

Saturday, 9 April 1864

Rain. Wind S.E. Afterwards due South and then S.W. All day more or less rain. Commenced clearing off about 9 or 10 O'clock at Night.

[*Not signed*]

Sunday, 10 April 1864

Beautiful day.

Rode down to Col. Simonton's and obtained permission not to move until tomorrow.

Went down and selected Camp Ground at Artillery X Roads.

Detail sent off to Battery Pringle to day but sent back again as no Work to be done to day.

[*Not signed*]

Monday, 11 April 1864

Fine Clear day.

Capt. [*S. Porcher*] Smith's Company moved from Lebby's at 11 A.M.

Capt. Gregg's Company got down to Artillery X Roads about half past Eleven. At 12 P.M. I got down & designated the Camp Ground in Angle to N.E. of Intersection of Cross Roads.

Front of Camp faces S. 22½ [*degrees*] E.

No detail for Battery Pringle to day, it being excused on account of our being employed in moving.

[*Not signed*]

Tuesday, 12 April 1864

Fine day.

Rode to Col. Simonton to report that I had got into the Camp at Artillery X Roads. Then to Lebby's to see after things to be brought down — Shanties & lumber.

In afternoon visited the advanced Pickets in Company with Col. Simonton.

On East End of Dickson's [*Dixon's*] Island there is a battery of 3 guns not more than ¼ mile from Legare's West House (Sol. [*Solomon*] Legare's). The Pickets here are within 250 yds. of each other in the day and much nearer by night.

The 3 gun battery spoken of commands the Creek called Dickson's [*Dixon's*] Creek up to that point and beyond. Called by Some little Folly River. It is not certain however whether the guns are real or "Dumbies" "Dummies." [*Sic*]

The Yankees have another work on Long Island about ⅓ miles further off which is a Tete de pont.

Further back still there is a third Battery which has considerable relief and is altogether a Considerable work.

Returned home at 6.30 P.M. High West & S.W. Wind.

No detail to day for Battery Pringle.

A little Rain about 10 O'clock.

Lieut Barton handed me my Quarterly Ordnance Return for slight correction.

[Not signed]

Wednesday, 13 April 1864

Fine day. Wind N.W. & cool, but the Sun quite Hot.

Furnished our Full Guard & 18 men to Capt. Behre & 15 men to Batty. Pringle.

Handed in person my Quarterly Return back to Lieut Barton with Corrections.

[Not signed]

Thursday, 14 April 1864

Was Field Officer of the Day (for Pickets) (Countersign "Charleston"). Reported to Lt. Col. Pressley at 8½ A.M. Relieved Capt. Lloyd.

Capt. Humbert, Comdg. Guard & Reserve. Lieut Mosely, comdg. Guard of 30 men first night at Legare's overseer's House and Reserve 2nd Night. Lt. Russell, Comdg. Stono [River] Pickets. Lt. Bush with Capt. Humbert at Legare's Overseer's House. Lt. [A.A. or J.B.] Connor, Comdg. Guard of 20 at Legare's burnt House.

All of the above of Frederick's Regt, 2 Arty, S.C.V. (150 men).

Capt. Owens & 2 Lieutenants with 52 and 55 men put on Night Posts from Sol Legare's burnt house to Easternmost point — from Graham's 21st Regt. S.C.V.

Stono Picket Posts Nos. 1, 2, 3, 4, 5 & 6 on River. 7, 8, 9 & 10 on Edge of the Marsh trending back from River (50 men). Reserve of 50 men at Hd. of Grimball's Causeway.

8 posts at Legare's Overseer's House — (30 men).

3 posts at Legare's burnt House — (20 men).

6 posts from Legare's Burnt House to East Point — (37 men).

6 Posts from River Road to Marsh to Fort Lamar, Secessionville — (18 men).

Night drizzly & rain and very dark. Posts visited at 10 P.M. by Lt. Bush.

Posts visited by me from 12 til 4 A.M. and Stono Post at Daybreak.

[Not signed]

Friday, 15 April 1864

Relieved by Capt. China, 25th S.C.V. at 10.45 A.M.

Made written Report to Lt. Col. Pressley, comdg. Pickets.

At about 5 P.M. a Yankee Gunboat came up the Stono and Commenced Shelling our advanced Pickets about Legare's Overseer's House. At the same time a number of Hale's War Rockets[1] were thrown from Dickson's [Dixon's] Island at the Stations occupied by the pickets and a force of probably 200 men was thrown forward from "Horse-Shoe Island" on to Bottany Island. Our Pickets, however, maintained their ground and the enemy soon retired.

Some of the Rockets thrown were picked up. The entire Case including head was 23 inches long, 3¼ in. diameter with 5 spiral orifices in a recess on the side for the escape of gas generated by the Burning Composition, also an opening at the rear end for escape of Gas. These Rocket cases empty, I judged to weigh about 18 pounds.

The cases were entirely of cast iron, the head rivetted on to the body post.

By 6.45 Col. Simonton rode into our Camp to say that the enemy had retired and We would not be wanted. The horses were accordingly unharnessed.

[Not signed]

[1] The rocket was invented by William Hale of England in the 1840s and licensed for production in this country. It consisted of a central rear orifice for escape of the propellant gasses and a number of small vents, set at a tangent, to impart a rotary motion for stability and control. Several types, differing mainly in the number and location of the vents, were used during the Civil War in the Charleston area. Manigault gives insufficient information to determine which type was used in this case. [Ripley, pp. 345-347]

Saturday, 16 April 1864

Very fine day. At 9 A.M. had a drill of the Officers in the Manual.

Note that at this time (yesterday) we commenced putting on one guard at Wappoo Bridge & Commissary Depot for 48 hours instead of 24. This was for the purpose of saving the long walk each day [about five miles].

At 3½ P.M. took out the Sections of Cos. "B" & "C" and put the Howitzers in succession in the Supplemental Batteries along the New Lines between Nos. 3 & 2, Nos. 2 & 1, & No. 1 and Battery Pringle.[1]

Fresh wind from West & quite cool.

[Not signed]

[1] It was a common Confederate practice along the South Carolina coast to build gun positions at strategic locations. Normally, they were unoccupied. However, field or siege pieces could be rolled into position quickly if the need occurred. In this case, Manigault was simply drilling his gun sections.

Sunday, 17 April 1864

Very fine day but quite Cool. Fresh wind from N.W.

Private Gory of Capt. Mazyck's Co. 25 S.C.V. was arrested at Wappoo Bridge with forged pass. He broke his arrest. I went to see Col. Pressley about him.

Col. Gaillard & Capt. [R. Press] Smith at our Camp.

[Not signed]

Monday, 18 April 1864

Some Rain in the Morning and a heavy, cold rain with high Southerly wind during day & afternoon.

There was a total suspension of Drill in consequence of Rain. But we furnished men on duty as follows —

Guard. 1 Officer & 66 men	1 Off	& 66 Men
Fatigues at Battery Pringle	1 off	& 20
Fatigues at James Island Creek Bridge	1 "	& 20
Mounted Couriers	—	11
	3 off	117 Men

(from about 213 men)

[*Not signed*]

Tuesday, 19 April 1864

Keen N.W. wind all day. Quite Cold. A little rain from half past 5 to 7 P.M.

Busy all day in hauling logs for Stable for our horses.

Capt. [*S. Porcher*] Smith & Lieut. Gregg went to City to day on leave for the day.

Men still very busy in hauling & building their houses.

[*Not signed*]

Wednesday, 20 April 1864

(Note, Stable built for our horses to day, 20th)

Countersign "Missouri"

Cool Northerly wind. Fine day. About 3 or 4 P.M. wind shifted to S.E. Still Cool.

At 8½ A.M. reported to Lt. Col. Pressley as Field Officer of the day.

Relieved Capt. Sellers. Rode all round the lines and got to Camp at 2 P.M. for dinner. At 3½ P.M. Started for Pickets. At sunset met Detail for Secessionville (Graham's Regt.) at Rivers Causeway and posted them after Dark, say commenced at 7.15 P.M. After posting got back to Legare's Overseer's house at 8.45. Some noise from Yankee pickets at the bridge from Dickson's [*Dixon's*] Island. I went there to see about it, returned at 9.25 P.M.

At 12 Midnight commenced my Rounds with Lt. Bethea. Visited the 8 Advanced posts which occupied till 1.20 A.M. (Beautiful moonlight night or it would have taken much longer).

Occupied otherwise for a short time then the discharge of a Rifle towards Dickson's [*Dixon's*] Island Caused me to go and inquire about it. Apparently a Yankee sentinel accidentally discharged his piece.

At 2 A.M. Commenced Rounds towards Sol Legare [*Island*] & Secessionville. Men all vigilent. Got back to Legare's overseer's house at 3.20. Rode immediately to make the Rounds of the Stono Pickets. Got through there at Daybreak, 4.45. Returned to Legare's overseer's House (Hd. Qrs. Pickets Line) at 5.20 A.M.

Thursday, 21 April 1864

Couriers relieved about 9 O'clock. The Pickets (from 25th Regt. S.C.V.) relieved by Picket from 2nd Artillery at 9.45. I was relieved by Capt. Carson at 10 A.M.

Immediately after I was relieved a Gunboat was reported coming up Stono River. She fired one or two shots, apparently without any very definite mark. I rode with Capt. Carson and showed him the Eastern Posts, Then back with him to see what the Gunboat would do. After firing 4 or 5 Shots, she went again down the River and apparently came to anchor near Legareville. I got back to Camp at 1 P.M. Sent written Report to Col. Pressley about 3 P.M.

Note, there was heavy firing from the Batteries at the mouth of the harbor commencing at Midnight and continuing for an hour or more.

Lt. Kemmerly [*Kennerly*] was the ranking Lt. and in charge of advanced Posts. Lt. Bethea assisted him. Lt. [*F.B.*] Brown in charge of the Stono Pickets. Lt. Lesesne[1] in charge of Picket at Sol Legare's burnt House. Lt. Taft commanded the Reserve.

Capt. Stallins [*Stallings*] & Lt. Mosely relieved Kemmerly [*Kennerly*] & Bethea.

[1] *Either Charles or Edward R. Lesesne. At this date both were lieutenants in Co. K, 25th Rgmt., S.C. Infantry.*

Friday, 22 April 1864

Fine day, rather warm.

Saturday, 23 April 1864

Rather warm day. Wind Southerly.

Rode to Genl. Taliaferro's Hd. Qrs. to get permission to move a Building from Dunnovant's [*Dunovant's*] Camp. Afterwards [*went*] to said Camp and selected the Building.

The 26th Virginia Volunteers, Col. Page's Regt., just returned from Florida, encamped in the Skirt of woods to the East of us.

Sunday, 24 April 1864

Cloudy morning. Wind S. 20 [*degrees*] East. Afterwards South Wind and rain almost all day.

In afternoon walked to Col. Simonton's.

Monday, 25 April 1864

Beautiful day. Wind N.W. early in the Morning, afterwards S.W. and fresh.

Officer Drill at 10 A.M. at 3½ P.M. Men Drilled, some at the pieces and some in Manual of the Rifle.

[Not signed]

Tuesday, 26 April 1864

(Countersign "Virginia")

Reported to Col. Pressley at 8.30 A.M. as Field Officer of the day and immediately relieved Capt. Sellers of 25th S.C.V. The Pickets composed of men & officers from 25 S.C.V.

Lieut. McCoy [*McKay*] ranking Lieutenant at Main Picket Station at Legare's Overseer's House. With him Lieut. Smith. Lieut. Montgomery in charge of Legare's Burnt House. Lieut. Lalane in charge of the Reserve at head of Grimball's Causeway. Lieut. [*Name omitted in diary*] in charge of the 12 Stono Pickets Posts.

The Yankees relieved their Guard and Pickets on Dickson [*Dixon's*] & Horse Shoe Islands at 10 A.M. The Relief appeared to me to consist of about 150 Men.

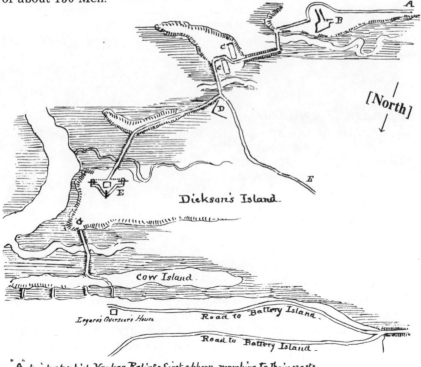

"A" point at which Yankee Reliefs first appear marching to their posts.
"B" large unfinished Earthwork.
"CC." Tete de Ponts. Earthworks.
"D" Stockaded work.
"DE" Road by which the Pickets proceed to Dickson's Island.
"E" 3 gun Battery.
"G." Advanced Picket Station.

Manigault's sketch of U.S. defenses on Dixon's and Horse Shoe Islands.

Did not leave the Lookout until about 11 O'clock. Rode Battery Island Causeway and to Yankee graves of officers & men killed June 16, 1862. [*Battle of Secessionville. See Introduction pp. ix, x.*] Then visited the posts at Eastern End of the line. Then explored the Chain of islands running from Grimball's Causeway to the Stono. Then rode home to dinner, reached Camp at 2 P.M. Day very hot, wind S.W.

At 4.30 Started out and passed the Picket posts to Legare's Overseer's House. At 6.35 met the Guard from Secessionville for Eastern Pickets and posted them after dark. Unfortunately the Lieut. comdg. Pickets next to Secessionville had the wrong Countersign.

(Capt. Dubose of Graham's Regt. [*21st South Carolina Volunteers*] in charge of the Pickets (Eastern) from that Regiment) [*Parenthetical material apparently inserted later*]

Evening close & calm. Moschetoes [*mosquitoes*] & Sand flies terrible, and continued so all night. Our Pickets suffered intolerably.

Got back to Picket Hd. Qrs. at 8.20 P.M. passed most of the time in Lookout. At 11.20 the Moon rose. At 12 Midnight commenced Rounds, and got through at 4 A.M. Got back to Picket Hd. Qrs. at 4.20, thus having visited each post on the Line 3 times in the 24 hours, once before dinner, once after dinner, and once at night. The whole picket line, exclusive of the separate portion next Secessionville, is at least 4 Miles long, perhaps 5 Miles and including the part near Secessionville, at least 6 Miles. So that to visit the posts on the line first named 3 times would require walking & riding, and going and returning to the central point at least 24 Miles.

[*Not signed*]

Wednesday, 27 April 1864

At 9 A.M. the old guard was relieved by Capt. China with 150 men of 25 S.C.V. (same Regiment as that of old guard) and at 9.30 I was relieved by Capt. Carson as Officer of the day.

Reached Camp at 10.15 A.M.

Capt. Gregg in City on leave for the day.

Fine day but hot.

Made Report in writing to Lt. Col. Pressley.

[*Not signed*]

Thursday, 28 April 1864

Wind Westerly, day warm. At about 3 P.M. a sudden change of wind to North East and temperature lowered very much.

Hagood's Brigade ordered off to North Carolina, viz. 21st (Graham's), 25th (Simonton's), 27th (Gaillard's) & Nelson's Battalion [*7th Bn., S.C. Inf.*] constitute the Infantry.

Graham's Regt. moved off to day, 6 Companies of Simonton's at night and part of the 27th also at night. Col. Simonton remains in command

of the West Lines. Lt. Col. Pressley Commands the Regiment.
Made a rough Copy of Map of part of James Island.

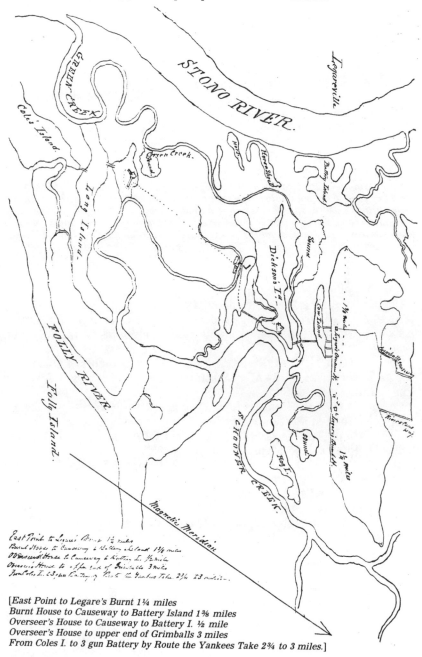

[East Point to Legare's Burnt 1¼ miles
Burnt House to Causeway to Battery Island 1⅜ miles
Overseer's House to Causeway to Battery I. ½ mile
Overseer's House to upper end of Grimballs 3 miles
From Coles I. to 3 gun Battery by Route the Yankees Take 2¾ to 3 miles.]

Manigault's map entitled: "South Front of James Island, April 28, 1864."

Capt. Gregg went to town as witness in case of Private Martin of his Company charged with Sleeping on Post.

[*Not signed*]

Friday, 29 April 1864

Wind East & cool.

Sent two wagons to Col. Pressley to assist him to move.

Rode down to Legare's Point. The 27th S.C.V. had all gone. The 27th Georgia just moving to take their place at Legare's Point.

Yankees Shelling Sumter with Mortars.[1]

Ordered by Special Orders No. 60, Hd. Qrs. West Lines to inspect Col. Frederick's Command tomorrow.

[*Not signed*]

---

[1] *The Fifth Minor Bombardment of Fort Sumter began 28 April and lasted through 4 May. Designed to disrupt Confederate repair efforts, the bombardment was marked by volley firing of the 10- and 13-inch mortars on Morris Island. The Confederates, accustomed to ducking a single mortar round, now found seven or so descending at the same time. The seven-day bombardment cost the Confederates one casualty and the Yankees 510 rounds. [OR XXXV (1) pp. 205-207; Johnson, pp. 205, 206, appendix xvi]*

Saturday, 30 April 1864

Cloudy day and a little rain about 10 A.M.

At 10 A.M. reported to Col. Frederick's Head Quarters, 2nd Arty, to inspect his Command. Inspected his four Companies in the following order.

Co. "G", Capt. G.W. Stallings, Comdg. (1 Capt. 3 Lieuts) 4 Officers, 5 Sergts. 4 Corporals & 134 Men. Stationed at Batteries Nos. 1 & 2, New Lines, James Island, S.C.

Co. "I", Capt. J.B. Humbert [*Jr.*], Comdg. 1 capt, 4 Lieuts. 4 Sergts. 4 Corps. & 120 Men. Station Batty No. 3.

Co. "F" Capt. T.K. Legare (J.B. Connor, Lt. Comdg.) 1 Capt, 4 Lieuts, 5 Sergts, 4 Corp. & 96 Men. Station Batty. No. 4.

Co. "H" Capt. W.H. Kennedy [*Kennady*]. 1 Capt. 3 Lieuts, 4 Sergts, 4 Corp & 109 Men. Sta. Batty No. 5.

Also Inspected Field Staff & Band and Hospital Attendants.

Inspected also Batteries 1, 2, 3, 4 & 5.

Inspected about as thoroughly as I could. Commenced inspection say at 10.30 A.M. and completed it at 5.30 P.M.

Battery No. 1 One 12 Pndr. Siege Smooth Bore (on Right)
One 24 Pndr. Siege " "
One 24 Pndr. " " "
One 12 Pndr. Siege Rifled. 70 Shot & plugged Shell. 12 Shell.
One 12 Pndr. Siege Smooth (on Left)

30 24 pndr. Cartridges (6 lbs) damaged. 2 12 pndr. Rifle Cartridges (2 lbs) do. Otherwise good supply of ammunition. Magazine in good order. But Ammunition chests in bad order. Tops loose & hinges broke off. Bomb Proof unfinished.

Battery No. 2   One 24 Pndr. Siege Smooth bore (on Right)
One 8 in. Sea Coast Howitzer on Siege Carriage.
One 32 Pndr. Barbette
One 32 Pndr. Barbette
One 8 inch Navy Shell gun (56 cwt) Barbette (on Left)

Supply of ammunition ample. Magazine wet, water under the flooring. In fact the floor of the Magazine is but little above the level of the water in the surrounding Borrow Pits. Besides which the Entrance to the Magazine slopes downwards, so that Rain water runs in. The Entrance should be covered.

47 24 Pndr. Cartridges (6 lbs) damaged.
43 32 Pndr. 8 in. Howitzer Cartridges (8 lbs) damaged.

Some of the Ammunition chests have very bad covers.

Battery No. 3   One 18 Pndr. Siege Smooth Bore (on Right)
One 24 Pndr. Siege   "   "
One 18 Pndr.   "   "
One 24 Pndr.   "   "
One 18 Pndr.   "   "   (on Left)

No Magazine proper. No Bomb Proof. Every thing in excellent order, except the Ammunition chests which have the covers loose. These guns say average 60 Rounds solid Shot; 25 Rounds grape; 25 do. Canister, Besides what is in the Expense Magazine.

Battery No. 4   One 24 Pounder Siege Smooth Bore (on Right)
One 8 in. Sea Coast Howitzer, Siege Carriage.
One 32 Pndr. Regulation (about 7500 lbs.) Barbette [*Carriage*]
One 32 Pndr. Navy Gun 41 cwt.
One 24 Pndr. Siege.

Supply Ammunition Ample.
No Magazine proper, but Open expense Magazine. No Bomb Proof.
Ammunition Chests have bad covers.

Battery No. 5   One 24 Pndr. Austrian Howitzer (Bronze). On Right.
One 24 Pndr. Siege
One 24 Pndr. Siege
One 12 Pndr. Siege

Supply Ammunition Sufficient.
No Magazine proper but open Expense ones under Traverses. No Bomb Proof.
Ammunition Chests have bad covers.

Co. "G" Capt. Stallings   Only Moderately well disciplined & instructed and moderatedly good "Military Appearance."
Arms much Mixed.
Virginia Muskets, flint & steel altered — 1816-1817.
So. Carolina Muskets   "   "   "   1820 & 1822, 3 &c.
"Palmetto Works Muskets Percussion 1853 &c.
U.S. Musket Model 1822, altered to Percussion.
U.S. Muskets Model 1842.
These Muskets are almost all in bad condition.
Accoutrements tolerably good.
Clothing is indifferent.

This Company is from Barnwell [*S.C.*].

Co. "I" Capt. J.B. Humbert.	This Company is in all respects in fine condition — well disciplined, well instructed, presenting good Military Appearance. Well Clothed.
	Arms, "Cadet Muskets" in excellent condition.
	Accoutrements good.
	The Cabins good & clean. The Camp well policed. The Battery in admirable order.
	(This Company is from Orangeburg [*S.C.*])
Co. "F" Capt. Legare	This company is in good condition. The Discipline, Instruction and military appearance all pretty good — Clothing pretty good.
	Arms mixed but serviceable. U.S. Muskets Model 1822 altered to Percussion, also Model 1842 Perc.
	These arms are only in tolerable condition.
	Accoutrements pretty good.
	(This Company is from Orangeburg).
Co. "H" Capt. Kennedy[1]	This Company is not in very good condition. The Discipline, Instruction & Military appearance did not seem to be very good. The Clothing bad, many of the men without shoes.
	The arms are very much mixed and not in good condition. Old Virginia Muskets 1816, U.S. Model 1822, Palmetto Factory Muskets 1853 &c. Some few U.S. Model 1842.
	22 Bayonets wanting & 15 sets of accoutrements as men stood in Ranks.
	(This Company is from Barnwell).

Co. "A" Siege Train, Capt Webb, arrived from Florida to day and was inspected & mustered near McLeod's [*house*] by Lieut. Warley, adjt. of Lucas' Battalion.

[*Not signed*]

[1] *Kennady.*

Sunday, 1 May 1864

Countersign "Mountain"

Was Field Officer of the Day. At 9 A.M. went down to the "Reserve" at Grimball's Causeway and relieved the Major [*not identified*] of the 26th Virginia. At about 10 A.M. Capt. Humbert with 100 of 2nd Arty and 50 of the 26th Virginia relieved the old officer of the Pickets. Remained for some time in our Lookout to see if the Yankees would relieve Pickets. They did not. Went to the Extreme Eastern End of the Island to East of "Cow Island" and spied at their Battery. I think two at least of their guns are dummies or Quakers.

Then visited the pickets at Battery Island Causeway, then to extreme East Point of South picket Line, then home to dinner.

After dinner Rode all round the picket Line and met the night picket of the 6th Georgia from Secessionville at Post No. 1 of their line. Rain came up suddenly at this time with vivid lightning & Sharp Thunder. Established 7 posts, then rode towards Secessionville to visit the Pickets on that side. It suddenly becoming very dark, and the ground there being very broken, I soon gave it up and tried to get back on the South Line. My horse was lost three times and I was obliged to dismount and feel my way. With great difficulty I got across the low ground beyond Rivers Causeway.

Lieut. [*T.H.*] Jones of Co. H, 2nd Arty, had relieved Capt. Humbert who goes on as Field Officer of the day tomorrow. Eastern Pickets from the 6th Regt. Georgia Vol. (from Secessionville).

At 12 O'clock (Midnight) I commenced my Rounds and got through at day-break (4 A.M.)

I was relieved by Capt. Humbert at 10 A.M.

[Not signed]

Monday, 2 May 1864

Got to Camp near 11 A.M. got breakfast and then went to Sleep.

[Not signed]

Tuesday, 3 May 1864

Beautiful day. Dr. Winthrop went to city. Capt. Mordecai returned from Columbia yesterday and paid a visit to Camp at Arty X Roads.

Very busy in comparing and verifying the Muster Rolls. In afternoon got order to move with Companies B & C to Legare's Point and relieve Major Campbell. Col. Simonton advised me to see Major Campbell in the Morning and learn when he would be ready to move.

At 11 P.M. got orders to furnish 50 men to relieve like number of the 26th Virginia on Picket (Said Regiment being ordered to Virginia). Also to send 30 men to Battery Pringle to relieve a like Number of the same Regiment there. At the same time the order to move to Legare's Point was suspended. Sent the 50 men & 2 officers on Picket but had no arms to furnish 30 men for Battery Pringle, hence did not send them.

[Not signed]

Wednesday, 4 May 1864

Beautiful day.

The 26th Virginia went off [*to Virginia*] this morning.

I rode to Col. Simonton's & then to Genl. Taliaferro's Hd. Qrs. to get information &c. and back to Camp where commenced writing.

The [*James Island*] Presbyterian Church near Battery No. 2 was burnt down to day about 3 O'clock. The 26th Virg. Regt. had left the woods on fire; a spark fell on the Roof and as there was neither ladder nor Sky-light it was impossible to save it.

Capt. S.P. Smith went off to day to attend his brother's wedding.

After dark went to Col. Simonton's with a statement of the heavy

Guard duty required of us. He relieved us of 21 Men at Capt. Behre's & the Wappoo Bridges.

[*Not signed*]

Thursday, 5 May 1864

Fine day.

Made written Report to Col. Simonton of Inspection & muster of troops of Saturday 30 April, after which was busy in other ways. (Also wrote up Journal).

In afternoon returned Pay Rolls signed to Cos. F, H & I of 2nd Arty. Had returned Capt. Stallings (Co. "G") on Tuesday.

Lieut. Gregg & Lieut Mellichamp went on Picket to day with 50 men for 48 hours.

[*Not signed*]

Friday, 6 May 1864

Fine day.

Dr. Winthrop attended first meeting of Medical Examining Board of which he has been appointed a Member.

Mailed Muster Rolls of Companies &c of Col. Frederick's Command to A & I Genl. Office, Richmond, also note to Capt. Bridges.

Capt. Webb was Field Officer of the day for Picket Lines.

[*Not signed*]

Saturday, 7 May 1864

Fine day.

Countersign "Country" [*Appended in margin of page*]

Got two houses from the Deserted camp of the Eutaw Regiment.

At 9 A.M. relieved Capt. Webb as Field Officer of the day.[1] At 10 A.M. a Two-Masted side wheel steamer Came up Stono to a point near Legareville and threw 3 Shells into it. We could not see whether any landing was made in boats. Probably there was none, as the steamer backed down the River shortly after her last shot.

The Steamer had booms or spars, something like studding sail booms, extended out on each side of her, say 5 or 6 on each side. At the ends of these booms there was a sort of network of ropes for the purpose of keeping off Torpedo Boats.[2] At the Bow & Stern there were similar projecting spars. When the Steamer was under steam, all of these Booms are lifted out of water, but when at anchor they are lowered so as to be at the water edge.

At about 5 P.M. several Yankee officers came down to Picket Station at East End of Dickson's Island and scrutinized the Causeway & Bridge leading over to James Island. One was a very big man whom I took to be a Field Officer. They had their swords on as if on duty, so I thought some forward movement might be contemplated.

When it was near sunset, finding no Picket reported at Rivers Causeway I rode on to Secessionville and learned from Col. Brown that he had orders not to furnish any. Accordingly I threw out two additional posts from the "Burnt House" at Nos. 5 & 7. Got back to Picket Hd. Qrs. at 9 P.M.

At Midnight commenced Rounds and got back to Hd. Qrs. at 4.20 A.M.

[*Not signed*]

¹ *See Appendix 2, p. 269.*

² *Such nets probably were designed to protect the ships from floating torpedoes rather than torpedo boats.*

Sunday, 8 May 1864

A little before 9 A.M. four or five Yankees landed on the long narrow island S.W. of Secessionville and about 500 or 600 yds from our Post No. 7. Fort Lamar commenced Shelling them. They had not left the Island, however, when I came off [*duty*]. I was relieved by Capt. Gregg at 9 A.M.

The Picket was composed of 4 Non Com Officers & 50 men of Siege Train and N. Comm. Offices & 100 men of 2nd Arty. Lieut. Shuler of Co. F. (Legare's) 2nd Arty was ranking Lieut and commander at Picket Hd. Qrs. Lt. Russell of Capt. Humbert's Company commanded the Stono Pickets, Lieut Chapman the Battery Island pickets & Lieut Spivey those at the "Burnt House".

Intensely hot day.

[*Not signed*]

Monday, 9 May 1864

Fine Morning.

Reveille punctually at 5 A.M. Had the new Pickets formed immediately after to relieve, if Possible, at 6 A.M. This in accordance with orders received last night.

Total Details. Bridge & Commissary Guards, Camp Guards, Picket.

				Total
Wappoo Bridge Guard	2 Non. Com. Officers		3 Men	5
Capt. Behre's Commissary Guard	2 " " "		9 "	11
Capt. Mordecai's Camp Guard	1 " " "		3 "	4
Capt. Smith's old Camp Guard	2 " " "		4 "	6
Capt. Gregg's Garden Guard	0 " " "		3 "	3
James Island Creek Bridge Guard	1 " " "		3 "	4
Camp Guards Artillery X Roads	2 " " "		18 "	20
	10 N. Com. Off.		43 Men	53
Pickets, 1 Field Off of Day, 2 Officers	4 " " "		50 "	54
(Capt Smith & Lieuts Brux & Phillips)	14 Non. Com. Off.		93 Men	107
Couriers			11 "	11
	14 Non. Com. Off.		104 Privates	118
1 Field Off of Day, 2 Officers		Aggr. [*Aggregate*]		121

Double the above and you get the total number "on duty" or requiring rest after duty.

Capt. Webb on duty to verify the Return of transferred men to their Companies by order of Genl. Taliaferro.

Dr. Winthrop attended meeting of Medical Examining Board.

Lieut. Cunningham received 400 Muskets this evening.

[Not signed]

Tuesday, 10 May 1864

Fine day, fresh S.W. wind during whole day after 10 A.M.

(Capt. Humbert Field Officer of the Day)

Went to Col. Simonton's after breakfast to inquire about Small Arms. Then to Genl. Taliaferro's to see Lt. Cunningham, Ord. Officer.

Dr. Winthrop went to City on leave for the day. Capt. [S. Porcher] Smith also.

Sent in Monthly Report to Adjutant General's Office, this being the last day. Also Sent Monthly Artillery Return to Hd. Quarters.

About 6 P.M. received from Lt. H.C. Cunningham:

100 Muskets, Cal. 69 no Bayonets.

76 Cartridge Boxes

75 Cap Pouches

76 Shoulder Belts

76 Waist Belts

Capt. Webb went to Walterboro to attend the Funeral of his Father.

Pretty Sharp firing between Secessionville & [Omitted in Diary] about 11 to 12 O'Clock to day.[1]

[Not signed]

Note to Manigault found with his Diary.

[1] *Brig. Gen. W.B. Taliaferro reported at 9:25 p.m. 10 May 1864: "...The enemy opened*

to-day on Secessionville from a small island lying to southeast of Long Island, in the same creek, with two Parrott guns, apparently 20-pounders." Taliaferro probably was referring to the southern fork at the eastern end of Lawton's Long Island which is a peninsula, not an island. [OR XXXV (2) p. 479]

Wednesday, 11 May 1864

Cloudy and like rain, Wind Southerly.

Was Field Officer of the day. Relieved Capt. Humbert at 9 A.M. Lt. Charles E. Gregg, ranking Lieutenant, was at Legare's Overseer's House. Lieut Mellichamp at Battery Island Causeway. Lt. [*A.A. or J.B.*] Connor at Burnt House & Lieut Bolivar in command of the Stono Pickets. The Pickets were composed of 50 men from Cos. A & B Siege Train and 100 men from 2nd Arty.

Countersign "Village".

The Yankees relieved their Guard & Pickets at 10 A.M. Three (3) Officers and 75 men apparently formed the Relief. I watched them from the time they first became visible on the road from Coles Island. No men were left in the most distant work visible. Five (5) men were left in the Earthwork beyond the Bridge & 10 men in the Stockade on this side the same Bridge. 30 Men appeared to be employed as Pickets on Dickson & Horse Island[s], 15 Men in the 3 Gun Battery opposite Legare's Overseer's House and 15 Men from the Picket at the Causeway leading to James Island at same point. A Drummer and a Bugler accompanied the Relief. A like number left after being relieved.

Rode and examined all the Southern posts and explored certain portions of the ground in areas with which I was not thoroughly acquainted. Home to dinner at 2 P.M. Set out again at 4 P.M. Dr. Winthrop rode with me down to Battery Island.

Got from Lebby's 24 Cart. Boxes, 23 cap Pouches, 24 Shoulder Belts, 24 Waist Belts. These issued to Co. "A"

	Corp	Privates
Posts At Legare's Overseer's House		
No. 1 on left, 4 men. At Bridge 1 corp & 6 men. On Cow Island, 3 posts of 3 each = 9 =	1	19
Reserve at House last night	1	15
	2	34
Battery Island Posts		
No. 1 left, 3 Privates. No. 2, 3 Privates. No. 3 at Reserve, 3 Privates.		
Battery Island Causeway, 3 Men. Relief for same, 3 men. Post to Right, 3 men.	1 sergt	18
N.C. Off.	3	52 Men
Stono Pickets 1 Officer, 2 N.C. Off, 50 Men.	2	50
At Burnt House three posts, 3 each 9		
Reserve 3		
Posts Nos. 1, 2 & 3, three each 9 men		
Nos. 4, 5, 6 & 7, 4 each 16 25		
2 Non. Com. Officers & 37 Men	2	37
Reserve — at Hd. of Grimball's Causeway	1	15
	8	154 Men

Night dark, heavy thunder storm threatened at 11 to 12 but blew away. Still we had some rain. Commenced rounds by guess at Midnight but it must have been later. Could not see my watch as we had no fire. All quiet. Daylight before I got through my Rounds.

[*Not signed*]

Thursday, 12 May 1864

Relieved by Capt. [*S. Porcher*] Smith at 7½ A.M. Got to Camp at 8.30. Cool, damp cloudy morning.

Slept for near 4 hours.

At 5 P.M. received orders for Gregg's Company [*Co. C, S.C. Siege Train*] to go to Virginia. A visit from Col. Frederick.

Went to see Col. Simonton about Gregg's Company.

Capt. Gregg went to City to day.

Some Rain at night.

[*Not signed*]

Friday, 13 May 1864

Cloudy day and quite cool.

Capt. Gregg Field Officer of the Day.

Rode into the City and saw Genl. Jones in relation to Gregg's Co. being ordered to Virginia. He said that he was very sorry for it, but could not prevent it. Dined in the City and returned to Camp after seeing Col. Simonton at 8 P.M.

Five of our men on Picket at Post No. 5 (Yankee Battery from which Secessionville was Shelled in 1862) were Captured this Morning about 1 hour after Sunrise. This must have been the result of gross carelessness, they were probably all asleep. Corporal Moorer was in charge.

[*Not signed*]

Saturday, 14 May 1864

Fine day, still cool.

Busy at Camp. Capt Gregg went to City.

In afternoon went to Col. Simonton about our Details. He was not at home. Some Showers of rain at night.

[*Not signed*]

Sunday, 15 May 1864

Fine day, S.W. & Westerly wind.

We furnished no picket. It was furnished by Capt. Walter's detachment of 27 S.C.V.

Went to see Col. Simonton about detail. Then rode to Capt. Mordecai about business.

In the afternoon Capt. Gregg turned over his ordnance & ordnance stores to Lt. Barton and his horses & mules &c. to Capt. Mordecai.

[Not signed]

Monday, 16 May 1864

Capt. Gregg's Company went off. They have 4 days furlough and are to meet at Marion C.H. on Friday to go off by the Wilmington & Manchester R.R. and report to Gen. Robert E. Lee in Virginia.

At 7½ A.M. received orders to serve as Field Officer of the Day. At 9 O'clock arrived at Legare's Overseer's House to relieve Capt. Kennedy [*Kennady*] but he had gone at 7½ A.M. having to attend as witness at Court Martial in Charleston.

Observed from the Lookout. No relief of the Yankee Pickets to day. Rode round the Battery Island Posts, also scouted all the back ground. Rode to East Point of Picket Line. Then explored the Chain of Islands to North of Battery Island and selected post for Picket &c. Rode home to dinner at 2.35 P.M.

At 4½ P.M. went again round the posts and gave Countersign "Sea" and instructions. Rode with Lieut Rush of Stallings' Company and showed him the advanced Post on chain of Western Islands.

Lieut Huguenin, 27th S.C.V., Commanded at Overseer's House with detachment of that Regt.

Lieut Axson with some of the same Regt at the Causeway at Battery Island.

Lieut Bush at Burnt House.

Lieut Rush in command of the Stono Pickets.

Force disposed thus:

Lt. Bush. 10 Posts from Burnt House to East Point.	40 Men	2 N. Com. Off.
Lieut. Huguenin. Cow Island. 6 posts, 3 & 3 & 6 & 3 & 3 & 3.	21 "	2 " " "
Lieut Axson. Battery Island. 5 Posts & Reserve. 3 each.	18 "	2 " " "
Lieut Rush. 12 Stono posts, 50 men.	50 "	4 " " "
Advanced Post 4. Patrol 4.	8 "	– " " "
Reserve.	4 "	1 " " "
	141 "	11 " " "

At 4½ P.M. Rain for about ¾ hour. After posting the Eastern Pickets got back to Overseer's House at 9 P.M. By that time clear & the Moon shining brightly. Alarms & guns discharged at Post No. 1 East Pickets & at Battery Island Causeway. On being questioned however the Sentinels admitted that they had fired on a false alarm.

Commenced Rounds at 11 O'Clock in consequence of said alarms.

Moon bright but a heavy Mist or Fog. The dawn showed itself before I got through.

[Not signed]

Tuesday, 17 May 1864

Was relieved by Capt. Humbert at 9 A.M. Immediately after breakfast sent in my Reports and took a sleep of 3 hours.

About 3½ or 4 P.M. some firing from Yankee Gunboat on Stono.

Rain at 12 or 1 O'clock.

Sent down 2 Officers, 4 non com off & 50 men at Midday to the Picket lines.

[Not signed]

Wednesday, 18 May 1864

Day somewhat Cloudy.

Capt. S.P. Smith Field Off. of the Day.

Was appointed by Col. Simonton Superintendent in Command of the Pickets. As the order arrived late I did not assume command that night.

[Not signed]

Thursday, 19 May 1864

Capt. Stallings reported to me as Field Officer of the day. Countersign "Italy".

Rode with Col. Simonton & Col. Frederick to the Front. A Flag of Truce was sent by Lieut Axson to the Enemy at Bridge to Dickson's Island. The object was sending some clothing and money to men of the Picket which was captured on the 13th inst.

During the Flag of truce, two of the Enemy's Pickets deserted & crossed the Marsh from Dickson's Island to James Island. One was an Irishman probably 35 years of age who not being able to swim was nearly drowned in the creek, and the other a young German I think (though Col. Simonton said he was an Irishman) who said he was a Substitute. They wish to communicate with "the General" as they had important information to Communicate. The information was that the Enemy had an expedition on foot for cutting off our Pickets. A large force was to be thrown upon the island at various points at the same time and completely surround and cut off the Pickets. They were sent up to Hd. Quarters.

Rode with Capt. Stallings and fixed upon the points for 5 new Posts. And made arrangements for keeping up the posts with the reduced number of 100 men. Returned to dinner. After dinner to Col. Simonton's. Met him on the way.

At Dusk, 100 additional men & 2 Lieuts, all from the 2nd Artillery, reported to me at the head of Grimball's Causeway.

156

Disposition of Force.

Lieut [*T.H.*] Jones, Co. "H" (Capt. Kennedy) [*Kennady*] in Command of Stono Pickets now reduced to following posts, Nos. 7, 9, 10, 11 & 12, 4 men each.

	N.C.O.	Men
Lieut [*T.H.*] Jones... 4 men each.	2 N.C.O.	20 Men
Also in Command Stono Islands 3 posts of 4 men each	No N.C.O.	12 "
Lt. Kitchens in command 3 Cow Island posts = 9, Dixon's Isl. Bridge 6 and two more toward East = 6	2 N.C.O.	21 "
Sergeant in Command Batty. Id. Causeway 3, that to Right 3, next 3, next 3, next 3, Reserve 3	2 N.C.O.	18 "
Sergeant in Comd. Stone House posts & post to East Point	2 N.C.O.	40 "
	8	111 Men
Lieuts. J.B. Connor & Bolivar in Command of Reserve		89 "
Total on South & West Fronts	2 N.C.O.	200 Men

Capt. Blake had a Section of Napoleon Guns at Hd. Rivers Causeway, Say 20 men.
Lt. Phillips in Command 40 men of Co. B. Siege Train as Support

60		60 "
		260 Men

Very high tide in evening, sands to Stono Islands all covered, hence only put out two posts early at Dusk as we had not men for the 3rd until the Reserve arrived. Did not put out 3rd post until 10 or 11 O'clock when I visited the posts with Lieut [*T.H.*] Jones and put out the third post.

I myself put out the two Secret posts to the N.W. of Overseer's House.

Rode round to Head of Rivers Causeway and saw that Lieut Phillips had reported with his 40 men. Was continuously in saddle until after 12.

The night was beautifully clear moonlight. At ten minutes to 2 O'clock a cool North wind spring [*sic*] up and brought a thick mist or fog which at times entirely obscured the moon. At 3½ A.M. the fog cleared off and it became again beautifully bright.

[Not signed]

Friday, 20 May 1864

The Reserve and Blake's Section with its support retired at day Break. As all was quiet, I left Lines for Camp shortly after Sunrise.

Spent most of the Morning sleeping.

Capt. Kennedy [*Kennady*] Officer of the Day. Countersign "China" [*The word "Japan" is crossed out and "China" appended*].

In afternoon went down on Picket Lines and spent the night on them. Same officer in command of Picket Lines as Last night.

Lieut Shuler (with Lt. Russell) in Command 100 men from 2nd Arty as Reserve.

The early part of the night quiet still & sultry. Moschetoes & Sandflies very troublesome. About 1 O'clock a cool northerly wind, with a heavy mist which lasted until 7 or 8 O'clock in the Morning.

Did not leave the Lookout until twenty minutes after 6 O'clock as in consequence of Mist could not see anything on the enemy's Side.

[Not signed]

Saturday, 21 May 1864

Rode home to breakfast a little after 7 O'clock.

Spent most of the Morning sleeping.

In afternoon went down on Picket Lines and spent the night there.

100 Men of 2nd Arty served as pickets. <u>100 men from 2nd Cav.</u> served <u>as Reserve</u> (except such as we were forced to take to Complete pickets) viz — 20 to Stone House with 1 N.C.O., 1 N.C.O. & 10 men to Overseer's House & 2 pickets.

Captain Humbert Field Officer of the day (Countersign "Burmah") Lieut Bush of Stalling's Co. in Command of Pickets at Overseer's House. Lieut [*A.A. or J.B.*] Connor in command of Stono Pickets.

Disposition of forces.

Pickets on Bank of Stono. 3 of 3 each.			9 men
Do. from there to Reserve. 4 of 4 each.	1 Lieut.	1 N.C.O.	16 "
Stono Islands Pickets. 3 of 4 each.			12 "
Overseer's House Pickets. 5 of 3 each & 1 of 6.		1 N.C.O.	21 "
Battery Isd. Pickets. 5 of 3 each & Reserve of 3.		1 N.C.O.	18 "
Secret Posts on North or Back line. 3 men each.			
(of 2nd Cavalry)	1 Lieut.		6 "
Reserve at Overseer's House.		2 N.C.O.	10 "
Stone House. 3 Posts of 3 and 7 Posts of 4. Reserve			
of 3 men.		2 "	40 "
		7 "	132 "
Reserve at Head of Grimball's Causeway.	2 Lieuts.	5 "	68 "

The night was Clear, Moon full, and a pleasant S.W. Breeze kept off the Moschetoes & Sandflies.

Captain Humbert commenced his rounds about 11 O'clock and got through about 3½ A.M.

[Not signed]

Sunday, 22 May 1864

After daylight, I went up into the Lookout and as soon as it was light enough I perceived that the Enemy had more men than usual at the head of the Causeway leading from Dixon's to James Island. I first counted 25 or 30 and as they exposed themselves a little more incautiously I made out upwards of 60 near the head of the Causeway, besides those in 3 gun Battery, &c. I immediately suspected something. Just at this time the Courier from the Stone House galloped [*sic*] up with a message from the Sergeant in command at that point that 150 or 200 Yankees had [*"had" is penned heavily over "were"*] crossing [*"crossing" not corrected to past tense*] from Long Island over to James Island. I immediately wrote a dispatch to Col. Simonton stating that

150 of the Enemy were crossing over from Long Island to a point beyond the Stone House. That a considerable number of men was accumulated at East End of Dixon's Island and that a Gunboat was lying off Battery Island. Asked for reinforcements and begged that the Artillery (which had withdrawn at daybreak) might be sent back to Head of Rivers' Causeway.

Immediately after I had sent off this dispatch the Enemy commenced throwing Hale's Rockets from East End of Dixon's Island at the Overseer's House. I gallopped towards the Stone House and on approaching it say [*Manigault obviously meant "saw"*] a body of 75 or 100 Yankees drawn up about 200 yds. beyond the House. Our Pickets had retired. This body of Yankees was Evidently a Skirmishers "Reserve." I gallopped back to Overseer's House and ordered Capt. Humbert to ride rapidly to Battery Island and bring up our Pickets stationed there. As soon as they came in sight I made Lt. Bush withdraw the Picket at foot of Causeway opposite Dixon's Island. When all were assembled, we withdrew at a walk — 3 officers, 4 N.C.O. & about 55 men & 2 couriers. A Rocket thrown very accurately passed just over the heads of this retreating force. At the first turn of the Road a second Rocket struck the ground and ricochetted passing between the men and falling just beyond the angle of the Road just as one of the Couriers was passing. It exploded and a fragment shattered the left hind leg of his horse which fell after a moment. We continued marching at a walk until beyond the turn of the road leading to the Causeway. I should have stated that before we left the house, our Reserve at the Battery at head of Grimball's Causeway ¾ mile in our rear was engaged with the enemy's skirmishers. As this Causeway and a narrow strip of Sand to the West of it was our only route by which we could retreat, and as it was evident that the Enemy's skirmishers had already approached it, the passage of that point was plainly a very ticklish affair.

After passing the turn of the Road leading directly to the Causeway, I made the men deploy as skirmishers and we advanced at a double quick towards the head of the Causeway. On reaching it, I made the men get behind it and commence firing on the line of the Enemy's Skirmishers distant about 115 yds. The men, however, were unused to skirmishing, and I could not get more than 12 or 15 men to advance beyond the fringe of Woods which was to the East of the Causeway while the rest hung back behind the woods and the left of our line of skirmishers hung back in the Hammock to west of causeway from which Capt. Humbert could not get them to advance. They fired from that Hammock at long Range and did not see the actual necessity of securing the Causeway. I accordingly rode there and forced them to go forward obliquely towards the Causeway. In trying to follow them my horse shyed and would not cross a strip of marsh. As he turned round he was shot through the Jaws by a Musket Ball and either immediately before or immediately after was struck in the right hind leg by another shot. As he staggered and became unmanageable, I dismounted and on examining his wounds thought one of them was mortal. I was very

159

loath to lose my saddle & cloak, and cast a wistful glance on them before I decided upon abandoning them. But the saddle was a very heavy one and I doubted much my ability to carry it off under the Circumstances. Besides, it was evident that my utmost attention and effort was needed to encourage & instruct the men how to return the enemy's fire, yet to fall back along the Causeway towards their support. I accordingly showed several of the men how, after firing, they should pass on several yards and then stop and fire again. At this time one of the Enemy was distinctly seen to fall, and I myself saw several running to the rear. Our fire had evidently checked them. [*Following note penned in margin:* Dead body of Yankee found afterwards 115 yds. from Causeway. Other skirmishers were, I think, nearer.]

Just at this time the force I had seen on Dixon's Island, who had laid down Planks on the bridge as soon as our Picket had retired, Came up in our Rear and fired several volleys at us. Getting to a part of the Causeway which was somewhat covered from the enemy's view by a skirt of low bushes, We double quicked from thence to our Reserve thus escaping exceedingly narrowly being cut off. Three of our Men were wounded. One (of 2nd Arty) had his thigh Broken by a musket ball. He was carried safely to the rear. [*Margin note states:* The man who had his thigh broken (Kennedy's [*Kennady's*] Co. 2nd Arty) died three days afterwards.] A second (Wm. Johnson, Co. "B" Siege Train) was shot through the ancle (he crawled some distance on his hands & Knees and was afterwards brought in by Two of our men. [*Margin note states:* Johnson's foot was amputated.] The third received a superficial wound in the hip or groin. He was within a few feet of me and instinctively dropped his Musket when hit, but was able to keep up with us and reach the reserve. (This last man died also, but it is said from over-feeding in Hospital. His Father came from Country & gave him too many good things).

One of our horses was killed, a second said to be killed (but we could never find the body) and my own horse wounded, but he turned up again after two days, saddle, bridle & all safe.

The enemy's skirmishers had pressed up on the left flank of the Battery in which our Reserve was posted at Head of Grimball's Causeway. Our Reserve promptly seized the Bank & Ditch to East of the Battery and held them in Check. As soon as I reached the Battery with the advanced pickets the enemy Commenced retiring. A detachment of the 2nd S.C. Cavalry constituted our Reserve and behaved well. They had moved off after daylight as was usual, but my courier overtaking them had turned them back. If they had not got back in time, the Overseer's House and Battery Island Picquets must have infallibly been cut off.

The Stone House Pickets (40 men) under charge of Sergt. Riley, Legare's Company, 2nd Regt. Arty, retired early and were in no danger of being cut off. They did good service, however, on our line of ultimate defence. The Stono Pickets were by my order drawn in to the Reserve and did good service also. Lieut [*A.A. or J.B.*] Connor in command of them. The Overseer's House & Battery Island picquets, whose retreat I have described, were very much exposed from the nature and direction of the attack and because I thought it proper to hold on to our post and preserve a firm attitude to the very last moment. Hence we were very near being cut off. Upon the whole I now think that I was somewhat imprudent in remaining so long knowing as I did that there was but one route for our retreat. If the enemy had been a little more daring and had promptly seized the Causeway, instead of deploying his skirmishers within tolerably close Range so as to fire at us as we passed, we must have been cut off. As it was his fire was pretty Sharp.

If Capt. Blake's Section with its Support of 40 men had been in position at head of Rivers' Causeway (it was withdrawn at DayBreak) it would have made it a very different affair. By shelling the Enemy's Skirmishers it probably would have nipped the whole matter in the bud, especially as his position there must have been entirely unknown to the enemy.

We had in all about 200 men engaged. It would puzzle one to say what the enemy's force was. I should suppose at least 500 or 600 men.[1] A deserter who gave himself up during the fight said that there were details from (7) seven Regiments present and that the whole was equivalent to about Two full Regiments. Our pickets at the Stone House, when re-established in the afternoon, report that they saw "2 Regiments or Battalions" cross the Bridge from James Island to Dixon's Island and that the planks were then taken up. (Our pickets captured on the 13th inst. when exchanged said there were 3 or 4 Regiments).

We remained in position on the line between Grimball's & Rivers' Causeway (Blake's Section and 40 men of Co. B Siege Train & 20 men of [unit omitted in diary] under Lt. Ford (the whole support under Capt. [S. Porcher] Smith) were [unintelligible word, perhaps repetition of "were"] replaced at Hd. of Rivers' Causeway) during almost the whole day. Extra Rations of Hard Bread & Raw bacon were served out to the men.

At about 11 or 12 O'clock Capt. Smith, under orders from Col. Simonton, threw pickets across from the Hd. of Rivers' Causeway to the post 200 or 300 yds. to East of Stone House and scouted all the ground to East of said line of picquets. At 12 or 1 O'clock the enemy sounded his recall. At 3 or 4 O'clock P.M. Genl. Taliaferro and Col. Simonton ordered the West End of Island to be scouted. This was done by Lieut. [P.C.] Johnson of the Engineers & 4 Men on foot, then by Messrs. Theodore Stoney and Frank Porcher on horseback, then by Major Screven and Lieut. Kemper on horseback. The enemy was reported as having left the island.

[Margin note states: Countersign "Japan"]

At about 5 P.M. by order of Col. Simonton, Capt. S.P. Smith (who had relieved Capt. Humbert as Officer of the day) moved over his picquets while I with the Detachment of the 2nd Cavalry scoured the woods on North Side as far down as Battery Island. Shortly before sunset the pickets were all re-established and the Reserve moved back to Battery near head of Grimball's Causeway. I then returned to Camp for some rest and refreshment. I found no difficulty in sleeping that night.

Capt. Smith reported that the night passed off quietly except some shelling from the 10 or 20 pndr. Parrotts on Long Island.

Note. That Keitt's Regiment & the Charleston Fire Brigade and a Detachment of 32 Georgia were massed in the afternoon of 22nd behind Battery No. 2. It was a lively scene when I passed there in coming home about Sunset.

[*The following note apparently was inserted at a later date:*] Note. That the men of the Picket who were captured on 13th May and who were exchanged about 15th June said upon their return to us that they heard the Yankees admit to loss of 20 men in this expedition. I give this report for what it is worth, but I doubt its correctness. They also say there were two or three thousand of the enemy tho' all did not cross over to this Island.

[*Not signed*]

[1] *Brig. Gen. Alexander Schimmelfennig, commander of U.S. troops in the Charleston area stated 23 May 1864: "...On Long Island, Major [Joseph] Morrison, of the One hundred and third New York Volunteers, with 150 men of his regiment...and 250 men of the Fifty-fifth Massachusetts Colored Regiment,...waded through the marsh of James Island and attacked the enemy early yesterday morning (the 22nd). They drove the enemy's pickets, about 120 men, far to the north of Battery Wright [Federal battery at the time of the Battle of Secessionville in June 1862].*

"During this time a detachment of the Seventy-fourth Pennsylvania Volunteers and Forty-first New York Volunteers repaired the bridges from Cole's Island to James Island and crossed over, the Rocket Battery on Cole's Island and the guns of the fort at Long Island supporting the movement. At Battery Wright Major Morrison halted his command, gave nine cheers for the Union, and awaited my further orders....

"The enemy showed in the first part of the engagement about 400 to 500 infantry and was re-enforced about noon by 200 more infantry and a light battery of four pieces.

"During the afternoon columns of dust on the road showed plainly that the enemy was advancing with considerable force against our troops on James Island, and, my objective being accomplished, I gave orders to retire....

"My loss on the 22d was, wounded, 11." [OR XXXV (1) pp. 58, 59]

Schimmelfennig amplified his report on 28 May 1864: "...from the detailed reports sent in by the different commanders relative to the demonstration on the 22d and 23d instant, it is known that the enemy left 2 dead on the ground when they retired; also that his ambulances were in motion during the forenoon of the 22d and the afternoon of the 23d. The Seventy-fourth Regiment Pennsylvania Volunteers captured 1 horse, slightly wounded, and brought him over from James Island to Cole's Island."

Monday, 23 May 1864

Major Screven, Field Officer of the Day, reported to me at 8½ A.M. Countersign "Canary". Very hot day.

About 4 P.M. two Gunboats came up Stono River and commenced a furious shelling of our Pickets, at the same time Hale's Rockets were thrown from Dixon's Island and also a 12 Pndr. Boat Howitzer (probably) discharged from thence. The 10 Pndr. Parrotts on Long Island shelled the Stone House.

When I got to Grimball's Causeway, I found that Maj. Screven had withdrawn all the Pickets to that point. The Reserve of the 2nd Cavalry had been withdrawn about 3 O'clock. I met them between my camp and the Presbyterian Church Site.

I rode cautiously over to the middle of the advanced Island or Peninsula, to a point whence I could see to the East beyond the Stone House & to the West down to Battery Island. Could see no signs of the enemy.

After 6 P.M. (about) the Gunboats ceased shelling. The Parrott Guns from Long Island continued shelling almost all night. Also there were repeated discharges of Canister from Boat Howitzers in the Creeks where they approached nearest the shore of James Island.

About 6½ P.M. the Enemy commenced a sharp Fusilade all along the front of Dickson's Island and probably Battery Island; we could hear the balls strike the Overseer's House at times. What was the object of this fusilading, except to show that they had a considerable force and wished to intimidate us, I cannot conceive. About dark it ceased.

Just before dark I got Lieut Mosley, who was in Command of the Stono Picquets, to scout the "Stono Islands" as far as one advanced post, and to re-establish his Pickets. When just about to move forward to re-establish our Battery Island, Overseer's House & Stone House picquets, I received a message from Col. Simonton informing me that Capt. Colhoun reported from battery Pringle that 3 Sidewheel Steamers had been seen apparently landing troops on the Peninsula which I have Called "Stono Islands," from the fact that there are a number of Elevations above the level of the Sands, which at Spring Tide form so many islands — I accordingly deferred our forward movement until we could have the whole of these islands scouted.

I should have mentioned that about 8 O'clock P.M. Major White of the Citadel Academy, reported to me with 45 Citadel Cadets and Capt. [*S.M.*] Richardson's Co. K, P.B.L.A. of about 50 men. Total 95 Muskets. Deciding after receiving the Message from Col. Simonton, upon not moving forward immediately, I threw out a good line of skirmishers from the head of Grimball's Causeway to meet Capt. [*S. Porcher*] Smith's thrown out to Right from head of Rivers' Causeway. This line was composed of Detachment of 2nd Artillery and Capt. Richardson's Company. The Cadets were posted in the Battery at Head of Grimball's Causeway. I put Major Screven in charge of the skirmishers while Major White took charge of the Cadets, and of course, during my absence, would take charge of the Stono Pickets also.

Lieut Rush of Stallings Company, with 4 men was sent to Scout the entire island in front from the East Point to Battery Island and Lieut. Mosley, with 4 men, was directed to Scout the Peninsula called "Stono Islands," to its furthest point. Lt. Rush returned about 2½ A.M. saying that he had scouted from the East End to the Overseer's House and had seen no signs of the enemy, but that he had not scouted towards Battery Island, the men being rather afraid of involving themselves in the woods where the Enemy might be concealed.

Lt. Mosley reported about 3½ A.M. that he had scouted the entire

"Stono Islands" and found no enemy.

At about 4 O'clock We moved forward simultaneously to re-establish our Pickets. Major Screven with 2 Cadet officers, 2 N.C.O. & 36 men moved forward as a line of skirmishers, guide in the Centre, directing himself on the Centre of the Outline of Woods on Goat Island, as seen against the Sky (which would bring him nearly to the Stone House). He was directed to Scout the whole eastern part of the island and re-establish the pickets if the enemy was not encountered.

At the same time, I moved over Grimball's Causeway (throwing forward an advanced Guard) with about 40 men under Lt. Rush, and about the same number under Capt. [S.M.] Richardson. Upon passing the other end of the Causeway, each of the detachments was deployed as Skirmishers, Lt. Rush proceeding in advance was directed to swing his right round at the turn of the Road, and advancing cautiously on the Overseer's House, to examine the Battery behind it, and if he saw nothing of the Enemy to re-establish his day posts. After he had advanced about ¼ mile, I moved forward Capt. Richardson's Company in the same open order and scouted the whole North Side of the Peninsula including the woods. The enemy was not upon the Island; the Posts were re-established, also a new day Post for the observation of the Stono Marshes to North of Battery Island. It was broad day light when we completed our scouting.

While the Pickets were being re-established, three rockets were thrown at us, and upon my going up into the Lookout, a boat howitzer with canister was fired at me, from behind some bushes on the Edge of Dixon's Island, near the Causeway. The Shot all fell below me. The distance was some 400 to 500 yds. I gave them an opportunity of taking a second shot at me, and waited quietly some 10 minutes after their gun was loaded, but they did not try it again.

Capt. Stoney came down with a message from Col. Simonton. I thought it best to see Col. Simonton myself and leaving Major Screven in Command, I saw Col. Simonton at Battery No. 2 and then went to Camp to Breakfast & Rest.

Note that Dr. Rivers reported to me as Surgeon at Grimball's Causeway last night and Dr. Winthrop was with Capt. [S. Porcher] Smith at Rivers' Causeway.

[Not signed]

Tuesday, 24 May 1864

Slept from 10½ or 11 till 3 P.M.

Capt. Colhoun Field Officer of the Day. Countersign "Orkney"

The Charleston Fire Brigade was marched back for Charleston this afternoon.

At 6 P.M. I met Detachment of 32 Georgia at Battery No. 2. They were ordered to report to me as Reserve for tonight. I conducted them to Grimball's Causeway and relieved the Citadel Cadets (then under Command of Capt. [Hugh Smith] Thompson.

Made the requisite details and carried them over. Went with Capt. Colhoun and established the two night Posts on back or North line.

At 9.5 P.M. got a note from Col. Simonton that some torpedo boats were going down Stono to night. Gave this information as soon as possible to Lt. Mosley in charge of the Stono Posts.

Returned to Camp at 10½ P.M. and had good night's sleep.

[*Not signed*]

Wednesday, 25 May 1864

Rather Cloudy Day. Capt. Stallings Field Officer of the Day. Reported to me at 8½ A.M. Countersign "Corsica"

Busy all day in writing. At 6 P.M. rode over to Camp of 2nd Cavalry from which a detail of 100 men was ordered to report to me. Directed them to follow me to Battery at head of Grimball's Causeway. Hurried on and instructed the Stono Posts that Sergeant White would go down river to plant Torpedoes. (The boat did go down and stopped at some of the posts.)

Capt. Westfield in Command of Reserve of 2 Lieutenants (Stack & Tolbot [*Tolbert*]) N.C.O. & 100 privates of 2nd Cavalry.

Lieut. J.B. Connor in Command of the Stono Posts (about 40 men)	40
Lieut Bolivar in Command of Overseer's House. 21 men & Reserve of 5	26
Lt. Tolbot [*Tolbert*] in reserve at Overseer's House with 29 Men.	29
I posted the pickets on North side of Peninsula.	6
At Battery Island 18 Men	18
At Stone House of 2nd Arty.	20
	139 Men
In reserve at Grimball's Causeway	61
	200 Men

Also (20) men of 2nd Cavalry whom we had intended to relieve but the Relief came too late.

Night rather dark. I returned to Camp at 12.30 "A.M."

The Enemy building to day a Lookout on Horse Island.

[*Not signed*]

Thursday, 26 May 1864

Col. Simonton relieved from Command of West Lines and ordered to Virginia; he left about 9 A.M. Col. Frederick assumed Command of the West Lines.

Dined with Col. Frederick. Heavy Rain Storm at 5 P.M.

Detachn.ent of 32 Ga. Vol. (Col. Harrison's) ordered away. (Two Companies to Sullivans Island and one to Adams' Run [*S.C.*]) They went off same evening.

At 6 P.M. rode down to the Front.

Capt. Kennedy [*Kennady*], 2nd Arty, [*Field*] Officer of the day. Countersign "Denmark"

The Detachment of 2nd Cav. under Capt. Westfield relieved by 100 men of 2nd Artillery under Lieutenants Rush and Russell. Rush arrived at dark with 29 men of Stallings Co., say 7½ P.M. Lieut. Russell with the rest did not arrive until 8 P.M. being a full hour behind the time.

Lieut. J.B. Connor, Stono Pickets & Stono Islands		39 to 40 Men
Lt. Bolivar, Overseer's House	3 N.C.O.	21
Reserve of Same		10
Sergt. at Battery Island	1 N.C.O.	18
Back Posts on Grimball's Marsh		6
Stone House & East Point Pickets, Lt. Rush	3 N.C.O.	40
		134
Reserve at Head of Grimball's Causeway		60
		200

Capt. Blake's Section at Rivers' Causeway 2 guns, say 20 men		
Support of men from Siege Train under Lt. Phillips,	40	
	60	60
		260

Night rather dark. Got to Camp at 10 P.M.

Note that to day about 8 O'clock the Yankees attempted to ascend the Ashepoo River with 5 Gunboats & Transports. They were driven back by Earle's Battery. We heard the firing distinctly.[1]

[*Not signed*]

[1] *The firing resulted in destruction of the unarmed Federal transport Boston by a small Confederate earthwork known as Chapman's Fort.*

Loaded with about 300 troops and some 80 cavalry horses, the Boston was part of an expedition designed to march up the peninsula between the South Edisto and Ashepoo Rivers and cut the Charleston and Savannah Railroad.

The Boston missed a turnoff at the assembly point during the night of 25 May 1864 and blundered far up the Ashepoo where she grounded on a mudbank about 1,000 yards from the fort.

At dawn of the 26th the Confederates opened fire from a field battery of two 6-pounders, commanded by Capt. William E. Earle, which had been rolled into position during the night.

The Boston, unable to reply or escape, was struck 70 or 80 times while crew and troops abandoned ship. They made their way to the safety of nearby marsh or drifted downriver clinging to wreckage that floated away from the ship. Other vessels eventually came to their aid. Heavy guns soon silenced Earle's 6-pounders, and the men were rescued from the river. The Boston, however, was considered beyond salvage. She was set afire by the Federals and burned to the waterline destroying those horses not already killed by the bombardment.

Northern casualties were surprisingly light — about 13 dead. The Confederates escaped without a single injury. One of the guns of Co. D, S.C. Siege Train, was parked near Chapman's Fort in support of Earle's Battery but took no part in the engagement. [Ripley, Battle of Chapman's Fort, pp. 37-61; OR XXXV (1) pp. 7-11, 400, 401; ONR XV, pp. 461, 462]

Friday, 27 May 1864

Captain Humbert, Field Officer of the day, reported to me at 8½

A.M. (Countersign "Scotland")

Details on West Lines.

1. Two Commissioned Officers, complement of N.C.O. & 100 men to report at 6 A.M. on the Front for 48 hours Picket Duty. This is generally furnished by 2nd Arty.

2. Three Commissioned Officers, a complement of N. Com. Off. & 100 men to report at Grimball's Causeway at Dusk for 24 hours duty. This is furnished by 2nd Cav. or 32nd Georgia, or Citadel Cadets & [*S.M.*] Richardson's Company P.B.L.A., or in case no other corps is available, by 2nd Artillery.

3. Blake's Section of Artillery at Dusk at Hd. of Rivers Causeway, relieves itself at 7 A.M.

4. Support for Same, 40 men from Siege Train, relieves itself at 7 A.M.

5. Picket established nightly between Batteries Pringle & Tynes, relieves itself at Daylight.

6. Eight Couriers from Siege Train, 5 for Picket front, 2 to Hd. Qrs. & 1 to Fort Pemberton, report every morning at 8 A.M. for 24 hours duty.

At 5 P.M. reported to Col. Frederick by Order, then to Genl. Taliaferro about disposition of Gregg's horses. [*Gregg's company had been sent to Virginia, see Thursday, 12 May 1864*] Rode down to Reserve at Head of Grimball's Causeway by 7 P.M.

Reserve Composed of 43 Cadets under Lieut Coffin & 34 men of Capt. [*S.M.*] Richardson's Co. P.B.L.A. The Cadets were left in position at Hd. of Grimball's Causeway. Lt. Richardson with 20 men of Co. "K" sent to Stone House. 14 men to Overseer's House of which 6 went to the two Secret posts on Back Line.

Lt. Shuler, Co. F, 2nd Arty, in Command at Overseer's House. Lt. Richardson, Co. K, P.B.L.A. in command Stone House pickets.

Lt. Bush in Command of the Stono Pickets. Lt. Coffin in Command of Reserve (Cadets).

I rode round a part of the Picket Lines with Major White, Superintendent of Citadel Academy, who wished to see them. Got to Camp at 11 P.M.

Fine Starlight night.

[*S. Porcher*] Smith's Company did not furnish detail for Support of Artillery at Rivers' Causeway.

[*Not signed*]

Saturday, 28 May 1864

Capt. S.P. Smith, Field Officer of the Day. Countersign "France"

At 4 P.M. drilled Co. "B" in Skirmish Drill.[1] At 6 went down to Picket Lines. Co. "B" furnished 40 men in support of Blake's Section at Rivers' Causeway.

Same Officers in command of Pickets as last night. Reserve of 100 men furnished by 2nd Artillery.

Lieuts. Kitchens & [*T.H.*] Jones of Kennedy's [*Kennady's*] Co. in charge of it. Sent Lieut. Jones to Stone House.

Posted back pickets. Got to Camp at 11.30 P.M. A heavy Rain Storm came up immediately after. I thought our Tents would be blown down. The Rain continued more or less for several hours but the wind subsided after 1 or 2 hours.

Co. "B" Siege Train furnished 40 men as Support to Blake's Section at Hd. of Rivers' Causeway.

[*Not signed*]

[1] *The drill apparently was to correct deficiencies Manigault had noted during the engagement of 22 May 1864.*

Sunday, 29 May 1864

Major Screven, Field Officer of the Day. Countersign "Malta"

Wind N.E. day clear & cool after 10 A.M. Before that it had been cloudy & quite cold.

The Horses of the 2nd Cavalry arrived about 9 A.M. They made a sorry procession. ⅓ or upwards was new horses and of fair size and in fair Condition, the remainder were old horses, small, emaciated & broke down, drawn up, hide-bound, flea-bitten.

At 5 P.M. rode down on Picket lines.

The Picket force was furnished from the 2nd Cavalry, Capt. [*Tillman H.*] Clark in Command at Overseer's House. Lt. Winter in Command Stono Pickets.

Capt. [*S.M.*] Richardson with 36 men of Co. "K" P.B.L.A. and Lieut Coffin in command 41 Cadets formed the Reserve, of these, Capt. Richardson's whole company was taken to fill out the Pickets, 20 men under Lt. Stevens to the "Stone House," 16 men under [*a*] Sergeant to Overseer's House, of these last, 6 men put on secret Posts on Grimball's Marsh. 9 Cadets reported to Lt. Winter for Stono Posts.

In consequence of the [*Field*] Officer of the Day's being new to his position I had to post the Secret Posts on Grimball's Marsh and also all the Eastern Posts, hence I did not get home until half past 12 O'clock A.M. Fine clear night.

Co. "B" Siege Train furnished 40 men as Support to Section of Blake's Battery at head of Rivers' Causeway.

[*Not signed*]

Monday, 30 May 1864

Morning somewhat misty. Day clear & bright and much warmer than yesterday; still pleasant for the season.

Capt. Colhoun Field Officer of the day. Countersign "Borneo"

Col. Lipscomb, 2nd Cav., Capt. Felder & Capt. Legare met at my Camp to appraise our private horses. As I had received the notice only 5 minutes before and as three of the horses were at Legare's Point (horses of the officers of Co. "A") I requested them to postpone the Meeting of the Board until tomorrow. This suited all parties better and was readily agreed to.

Col. Lipscomb mentioned that in the Spring of 1862 he carried out to Virginia 600 horses & upwards. That during the time the Regiment was there, there were 825 horses added by purchase. That they took 150 to 175 horses in Pennsylvania and that he only had 48 horses for duty when he left Virginia to return.

He mentioned that the Government furnished an average of only 3 lbs of Grain per day per horse and that he had only 4 bales of Fodder from 1st Oct. to 1st July last. By great exertions he was able to procure in addition an average of 3 lbs grain which made 6 lbs per day per horse.[1]

At 4 P.M. drilled Co. "B" as Skirmishers. Then went to Col. Frederick's on business, then to the Observatory near Secessionville to get a full view of the Enemy's Camps on Folly & Coles Islands. Did not go down on Picket Lines this night.

[*Not signed*]

[1] *The normal daily ration for a horse was approximately 14 lbs. of hay and 12 lbs. of oats, barley or corn. [Gibbon, Artillerist's Manual, p. 397]*

Tuesday, 31 May 1864

Capt. Stallings, Field Officer of the day. Countersign "Iceland"

At 8 A.M. Capt. John Chesnut reported at Grimball's Causeway with 2 N.C.O. & 30 men of 2nd Cav.

It should be stated that about 7 A.M. Redoubt No. 1 & Battery Ryan opened fire suddenly upon the "Mud Fort"[1] in the Marsh near Black Island which is now used by the Yankees as a picket station. The Morning was foggy. This was followed by a general shelling all round. Secessionville and the Eastern portion of New Lines were shelled from Black Island & Long Island. This Shelling lasted about one hour. Shortly after 8 O'clock Capt. Stallings moved over with Lt. Lee & 14 men towards Stone House and I led Capt. Chesnut with 16 men to Overseer's House. The Enemy immediately commenced shelling us with his 20 pndr. Parrotts from Long Island; some of his shells fell quite near us, but without doing any harm.

The day posts on the point were arranged as follows:

Dixon's Island Causeway		1 N.C.O.	4 Privates
Near Battery Island, South Side		1	3
Back Line, towards Battery Island			3
Overseer's House	1 Captain		6
		2	16
Stone House Reserve	1 Lt.	1	8
" " Picket			3
Day Post, Yankee Battery		1	3
		14	14
		4 N.C.O.	30 Privates

Returned and informed Col. Frederick that I should want 1 N.C.O. & 10 men to report at Grimball's Causeway at Dusk, and that 40 men had better hereafter be detailed from the Cavalry.

Lieuts. [A.A. or J.B.] Connor & Rush in command of 75 men from 2nd Artillery took the Stono Posts and the Reserve Station. There was no change made in these posts.

At 4 P.M. inspected Co. "B" Siege Train. At 5 P.M. a salute fired by the Yankees west End of Folly Island, or in mouth of Stono.[2] At 5.30 set out to ride with Col. Frederick & Capt. Humbert down to Front. I waited for the detail of 1 N.C.O. & 10 men from 2nd Cavalry and set out to ride back to camp. Met them on the way, at a loss as to the true route. Accordingly guided them to Capt. Chesnut at Overseer's House.

Got to Camp at 10.20 P.M.

Note. Our Private Horses were appraised to day by Col. Lipscomb, Capt. Felder and Capt. T.K. Legare.

[Not signed]

[1] *Manigault probably means Marsh Battery No. 2 (see journal entry 25 Aug. 1863) rather than the Swamp Angel site (see journal 15 Aug. 1863).*

[2] *The salute presumably was fired in honor of Maj. Gen. John G. Foster. He had assumed command of the Department of the South 26 May 1864 and visited various areas of the command, including Morris and Folly Islands, between 28 May and 6 June. [OR XXXV (1) pp. 2, 8]*

Wednesday, 1 June 1864

Day bright & hot. Capt. Kennedy *[Kennady]* Field Officer of the Day. Countersign "Savannah"

Lieut Stack with 40 men of the 2nd Cavalry relieved Capt. Chesnut about 9 A.M.

The position of the Night Pickets intended to be as follows.

Dixon's Island Causeway		1 N.C.O.	6 Privates	
Battery Island Causeway including the Reserve		1	6	
Back Picket on Grimball's Marsh			3	
Picket opposite West End of Cow Island			3	
Picket East End of Cow Island			3	
Patrol from Overseer's House towards Battery Island			3	
	1 Com. Officer	2 N.C.O.	24 Privates	24
Pickets at Stone House	1 do. do.	1 "	3	
" No. 1			3	
" No. 4			3	
" No. 5		1 "	3	
" No. 7			3	
		2	15	15
				39 Privates

The Stono & Stono Island Pickets are same as before so also the Reserve.

Rode down on Picket Line at about 5½ P.M. Capt. Kennedy [*Kennady*], F. Off. [*Field Officer*] of Day, Sick. Found him lying down in Officers Tent of Stono Pickets. Advised him if he continued sick to go home.

Lt. [*A.A. or J.B.*] Connor in Command Reserve. Lt. Rush in command Stono Picket, 75 Men of 2nd Arty.

Lt. Stack in Command at Overseer's House. Lt. Tolbot [*Tolbert*] in command at "Stone House."

I went round and posted all the Pickets to East of Stone House, also verified the others and gave full instructions. Got a dispatch from Col. Frederick to F.O.D. [*Field Officer of the Day*] who being sick, I went to Col. F's Hd. Quarters and reported in person the Condition of Line &c. Got to Camp at 11 P.M. To bed shortly after.

Section of Blake's Arty, I believe, and 40 men from Cavalry as Support at Rivers' Causeway.

[*Not signed*]

Thursday, 2 June 1864

Capt. Humbert, F.O.D., reported at 8 A.M. Countersign "Shetland." Day Sultry & cloudy. A little Rain in afternoon.

At 3 P.M. Lieut [*John B. W.*] Phillips with 40 men of Co. "B" set off to relieve the Citadel Cadets acting as Reserve at Grimball's Causeway.

Rode down at 5½ P.M. to Picket Lines. Found Lt. Richardson, Co. "K" P.B.L.A. sending off his men to the Stono Island posts, under a Sergeant who acknowledged that he did not know the posts exactly. I stopped them and made the Lieut go with me and we posted them ourselves. I told the Lieut that this was the duty of the <u>Lieutenant himself</u> and should not be entrusted to any one else. The tide covered much of the Sands.

Rode on and met Capt. Humbert and Moved one of his posts viz from No. 3 to No. 7 at extreme Eastern End of Peninsula.

Lt. Thompson, 2nd Cav. in Command at Overseer's House. Lt. [*Jeremiah*] Phillips, 2nd Cav. in command at Stone House but much incapacitated by "rising on his leg."

Night dark & Cloudy. Got back to Camp at five Minutes to 12 Midnight. Commenced raining immediately after.

Note. That for the first time to day we have had negro soldiers opposite to us on Dixon's Island.

[*Not signed*]

Friday, 3 June 1864

Capt. S.P. Smith F.O.D. Countersign "Baltimore"

Day Cloudy & Sultry.

Co. "A" 2nd Cavalry, Capt. John Chesnut commanding, Marched for Adams' Run [*About 25 miles west of Charleston*] this Morning.

At 5½ P.M. rode down to Picket lines. Lt. Richardson was posting his pickets on Stono Islands. I gave instructions to all the pickets as I pleased. Found Capt. Smith at Overseer's House with Lieut Hunt of 2nd Cavalry. Went up into Lookout. Undeniably Negro Sentinels in our front. No change whatever visible.

Left Capt. Smith at Dark about to post his pickets to East of Stone House, Lt. Roach Comdg. Rode over to Rivers' Causeway. The Cavalry Support arrived there about 5 minutes after 8 P.M. Lieut. Thompson Comdg. 42 Men & 2 N.C.O. Lieut. LaBorde with Section of Blake's Artillery arrived at Site of Rivers' House at 8.15, only the Pieces, no Caissons. Rode back to Rivers' Causeway with Lt. Laborde and gave instructions, also detailed 1 corp. & 9 Men to form a picket at foot of Rivers' Marsh Road.

Got to Camp at 9h. 10m. At about 10 or 15 Min. after, two Rockets were thrown up by the Enemy, one said to be from Mortar Schooner, and the other from Long Island. At the same time Red & Blue lights were said to have been displayed at the Observatory on Dixon's Island.

During the night our Pickets at East End, post No. 7, fired twice into a small boat which immediately retired.

Our Pickets at No. 4 near East End, report that they heard Sentinels challenging three times on the little Sandy Island in the Marsh about 150 yds. from the Shore at that point.

Commenced raining about 10 O'clock and rained off & on during night.

Note. On Tuesday 31st May, A Board of Officers consisting of Col. T.J. Lipscombe, 2nd Regt. S.C. Cavalry, Capt. E.J. Felder, 2nd Arty & Capt. T.K. Legare, 2nd Arty, met & made an appraisal of the value of the private horses belonging to the Officers of the Siege Train in pursuance of Special Order No. 4 dated Hd. Quarters West Lines May 29, 1864. The following is a copy of their Report.

"The Board met pursuant to the above Order and hearby set the following valuation on the horses belonging to the following named Officers"

Officers of S.C. Siege Train		Horses	Valuation
Major E. Manigault		1 Bay Horse	$1830
Lt. W.H. Chapman,	Co. A	1 Grey Mare	2500
Capt. B.C. Webb,	" "	1 Sorrel Horse	2066
Lt. T.M. Hasell,	" "	1 Bay Mare	1430
Lt. I.A. Brux,	" "	1 Sorrel Mare	1783
Lt. R.E. Mellichamp,	" "	1 Sorrel Mare	1966
Lt. R. Nesbit,	Co. B	1 Sorrel Horse	2666

(Signed) T.J. Lipscombe, Col. 2nd Regt. S.C. Cavalry
(Signed) E.J. Felder, Capt. & A.Q.M. 2nd Arty
(Signed) T.K. Legare, Capt. Co. F, 2nd Arty

[*Not signed*]

Saturday, 4 June 1864

Major Screven 2nd Cavalry, Field Officer of the day. Countersign "Ocean"

Capt. Deane [*Dean*], 2nd Cavalry, in Command at Overseer's House. Lt. Tolbot [*Tolbert*] in Command at Stone House.

Capt. Deane [*Dean*] had 23 Mounted Men, 2nd Cav. Lieut. Tolbot [*Tolbert*] 17 <u>dismounted.</u>

Lt. Bush in Command of the Stono Pickets. Lieut. Kitchens in Command of the Reserve.

At 5½ P.M. rode down towards Picket Lines. Stopped at Capt. Humberts and got some percussion Caps as I heard that some of the pickets were without them (300 Caps.)

As Co. "C" of 2nd Cavalry was ordered off [*To Adams Run, S.C.*] tomorrow, Seven Men from other Companies went down to relieve that number of men of Co. "C". As they moved incautiously together over Grimball's Causeway they were fired at by Yankee Battery on Long Island. No damage done.

Distributed percussion Caps to such men as needed them. Accompanied Maj. Screven & Lieut. Tolbot [*Tolbert*] in posting their pickets. Night quite dark and threats of a Thunder Storm. Rode to Rivers' Causeway, Lieut. [*T.H.*] Jones of Company H in Command of 40 men of that Regiment [*2nd Artillery, S.C.V.*] as a Support to Section of the "Chatham Artillery" held in readiness at Site of Rivers' House. Posted 1 sergt & 8 men at End of Rivers' Marsh Road.

Got to Camp at 10h. 10m. Rain off & on during night.

Note, that a second Company ("B" or "D") of 2nd Cav. marched to day for Adams Run.

[*Not signed*]

Sunday, 5 June 1864

Capt. Kennedy [*Kennady*], Co. H, 2nd Arty, F.O.D. Countersign <u>"Macon".</u> Day cloudy. Wind S.W.

Co. "C" 2nd Cavalry, Marched this Morning for Adams Run.

At 5½ P.M. rode down to Picket Lines.

Lt. Bush in Comd. Stono Pickets. Lt. Kitchens in Comd. Reserve.

Capt. Deane [*Dean*] in Comd. Overseer's House. Lt. Hunt in Comd. Stone House.

Guided Lt. Stephens in Command of Co. "K" P.B.L.A. to Rivers' Causeway, placed him with 2 N.C.O. & 24 men there, and 1 N.C.O. & 8 men at End of Rivers' Marsh Road.

Lieut. DeLArme [*DeLorme*] in command of 1 section of Blake's Artillery at Site of Rivers' House.

Got to Camp at 9.15 P.M.

[*Not signed*]

Monday, 6 June 1864

Pleasant Morning, Wind S.W. Capt. Westfield, 2nd Cav., F.O.D. Countersign <u>"Selma"</u>

Rode down to Overseer's House on Picket Lines and fixed up the ladder to Lookout, which had been pulled down. Rode with Capt. West-

173

field over the whole Line. Got back to Camp at 1.30 P.M.

Capt. Westfield sick and did not return to the Picket Lines.

At 5 P.M. Rode down to Lines. Fort Lamar [at Secessionville] firing upon Long Island Battery and Pine Island. Long Island Battery & Light House Inlet replying.

Lieut. Moseley in Command Stono Pickets. Lt. [A.A. or J.B.] Connor in Command of Reserve. Total 75 men 2nd Arty.

Lieut. Thompson (Deane's [Dean's] Co. 2 Cav.) in Command Overseer's House. Lt. Hunt (Westfield's Co. 2nd Cav.) in Command Stone House Pickets.

I posted all the Eastern pickets myself, after having ridden round the whole Lines and given instructions.

More lights than usual seen on Folly Island to night.

Rode to Rivers' Causeway &c. Lt. [A.A. or J.B.] Connor (the larger) in Command 40 Men 2nd Arty at Rivers' Causeway.

Lieut. Henry [Hendry] in Command Section of Chatham Artillery at Rivers' House Site.

Got to Camp at 10.20 P.M.

About an hour before day the picket at Post No. 7 towards Secessionville fired 14 or 15 shots at what they took to be two Barges which advanced to within 30 or 40 yds. of them. The Barges did not return their fire and shortly afterwards retired. Doubtfull if they were not firing at Porpoises.

[Not signed]

Tuesday, 7 June 1864

Capt. Humbert F.O.D. Countersign "Richmond"

Long Island Battery firing upon New Lines James Island from 9 O'clock.

Heavy firing in the harbor from and early hour (after daylight), ascertained afterwards to be Battery Gregg firing upon the Steamer Etiwan which got aground on Reef near Fort Johnson. She was entirely destroyed by the fire.

About 10 A.M. went to Col. Frederick's Hd. Qrs. about business.

At 5.45 P.M. Rode down to Picket Lines.

Lt. Moseley in Comd. Stono Posts. Lt. [A.A. or J.B.] Connor in Comd. Reserve.

Capt. Deane [Dean] in Comd. Overseer's House (2nd Cav.) Lt. [Jeremiah] Phillips 2nd Cav in Comd. Stone House.

Capt. Humbert by my direction, took 3 men of the Cavalry before dark and passed to rear of Peninsula (from Rivers' Causeway) and posted them at Post No. 7 immediately after dark. This picket was doubled by the addition of 3 men of Siege Train from the Support at Rivers' Causeway.

I posted myself the other pickets to East of Stone House (accompanied however by Lieut [Jeremiah] Phillips who was suffering severely from boils on his leg).

Lt. Spivey in Command of Support of Rivers' Causeway (19 men & 6 at Rivers' Road, 3 at Picquet No. 7 and 3 or 4 N.C.O.)

Lieut LaBorde in Command Section of Blake's Artillery at Rivers' House.

Got back to Camp at 10.15 P.M.

At 10.20 a rocket thrown up from the East (probably Morris' Island) this Signal was answered by another Rocket thrown up at Mortar Schooner. No demonstration whatever, however, followed these Signals.

Saw Steam Derrick apparently making her way from Light House Inlet into Folly River a little before dark.

Hot Sultry Evening, Moschetoes very bad.

[*Not signed*]

Wednesday, 8 June 1864

Capt. S.P. Smith F.O.D. Countersign "Greenville"

At 9 A.M. rode down to Picket Lines, examined Stono Islands more carefully, also Crossing to west of Grimball's Causeway. More practicable for horses. Examined also Island to N.W. of our day Post near graves of Lt. Upson, Co. F, 7th Conn. Vol. & Lt. Hooton same Regiment. [*Killed at Battle of Secessionville, 16 June 1862*] Also Course of Creek to north of same which goes close up to Battery Island.

At 1 P.M. went up into Lookout. Saw Steam Derrick, accompanied by a Propeller Tug boat near Campbell's House [*on Folly Island*] in Folly River. They afterwards went on to Stono [*River*]. Also a large Schooner passed through Folly River on towards Light House Inlet.

Got to Camp at 2.15 P.M.

At about 3 P.M. the Long Island & Light House Inlet Batteries commenced shelling Secessionville which replied slowly.

At 6 P.M. rode down to Picket Lines. Met Capt. Smith and assisted in establishing Night Posts.

Lieut Bolivar, 2nd Arty, in command Stono Pickets. Lt. [*T.H.*] Jones, 2nd Arty, in Command Reserve.

Lieut Thompson (Deane's [*Dean's*] Co. 2nd Cav.) in Command Overseer's House.

Lieut Hunt (Westfield's Co. 2nd Cav.) in command of Stone House.

Lieut Richardson in Command 32 men Co. "K" P.B.L.A. at Rivers' Causeway.

Lieut Palmer in Command Section Chatham Artillery, Rivers' Burnt House.

Doubled the Picket at No. 7 towards Secessionville.

Got back to Camp at 11 P.M.

Lieut. D.W. Edwards of Co. "C" came down to Camp to get extension of his Sick furlough.

[*Not signed*]

Thursday, 9 June 1864

Capt. Guignard Richardson, Lucas Battalion Arty, F.O.D. Countersign "Baldwin"

Col. Frederick went to City in the morning.

Capt. S.P. Smith went to City on leave for the day.

Employed all morning in Camp. Dined with Capt. Mordecai. Genl. Taliaferro, Col. Frederick, Capt. Page, Major Burke, Dr. Lebby Sen[ior] & [Dr.] Lebby Jun[r]. present.

Did not get back to Camp till Sunset, did not go down to the Front.

[Not signed]

Friday, 10 June 1864

Capt. Colhoun F.O.D. Countersign "Leeds"

Lt. Edwards went off to day. (Lt. Edwards went off this morning on his return home) [*Parenthetical entry apparently added later*]

At 10 A.M. I rode down to the Front. Very hot day, wind N.W. Returned to Camp at 2 P.M. Heavy rain from 3½ P.M. to 4½ P.M.

Capt. Colhoun reported Sick in afternoon and Capt. Kennedy [*Kennady*] reported to me as F.O.D. at 6 P.M.

At 6½ P.M. Orders Came for Co. "B" to relieve Co. "A" at Secessionville and one 8 in. Siege Howitzer to go to "Battery Ryan Left" to be put in place of Rifled & Banded 24 Pounder moved from thence to Secessionville.

As the Co. ("B") was very much broken up by Guard details, I rode to Genl. Taliaferro at Col. Frederick's request to explain how matters stood.

Co. "B" is thus divided by details.

Permanent Guards or Details

Capt. Mordecai's Commissary Stores	1 N.C.O.	3 Privates
" " Pasturing Cattle		2 "
McLeod's Commissary Stores	1 "	3 "
James Island Bridge	1 "	3 "
Capt. Smith's Garden		3 "
Horses of Co. "C"	2 "	10 "
	5 "	24 "

Daily Detail (i.e. "on" and "off" 24 or 48h.

Wappoo Bridge	2 N.C.O.	3 Privates	
Camp Guard	2 "	9 "	
Couriers		9 "	
	4	21 "	
As above	5	24 "	
	9 N.C.O.	45 Privates	54 Total

Genl. Taliaferro directed me to send such men as I could immediately and said he would get Lt. Cunningham to transport the Howitzer. Went to Col. Frederick and stated substance of order.

At 9½ P.M. Lieut Spivey with 3 N.C.O. & 29 Privates armed as Infantry, marched for Secessionville.

Col. Frederick and myself having concluded that it was safe to send the howitzer to Battery Ryan at night, Lieut Barton came to Camp at about 10 P.M. with orders to move the Howitzer. At 12 (Midnight) One 8 in. Howitzer & 1 Caisson started for Battery Ryan, Capt. [*S. Porcher*] Smith Commanding & Lieut. Barton in Company. Reached Battery Ryan without difficulty and Howitzer & Caisson turned over to a Lieut. of Capt. Bowden's Company.

Company "A" with horses & harness (no guns) ordered to some point in Genl. Robertson's District (Adams Run or Ashepoo) as a Raid is expected there.

Note. Dr. Lebby [*Jr.*] went off on Furlough & Dr. Winthrop took Charge of Hospital.

[*Not signed*]

Saturday, 11 June 1864

Countersign "York"

Four Caissons of Co. "A" turned over to our Camp at Arty X Roads at 7 A.M. to keep — Two with [*Ammunition*] Chests & two without. No Ammunition. 5 Sponge & Tar Buckets.

Capt. S.M. Richardson reported as F.O.D. at 8 A.M. (His first tour of duty). Capt. [*S. Porcher*] Smith furnished a horse & I the Adjutant's Saddle.

At 1.30 P.M. went to Observatory near Secessionville and remained in observation until 3½ P.M. Very few vessels in Lt. House Inlet. Steam Derrick behind Coles Island.

At 6 P.M. rode down to Picket Line. Lt. Rush in Command of Stono Pickets, Lt. Shuler in Comd of Reserve, Lt. [*Jeremiah*] Phillips, 2nd Cav., in Comd at Overseer's House, Sergt Davis in Comd Stone House, Lt. Stevens in Comd 36 men Co. K., P.B.L.A. at Rivers' Causeway, Lt. LaBorde Comdg Blake's Section of Arty at Rivers' House site.

Got to Camp at 10 P.M.

[*Not signed*]

Sunday, 12 June 1864

Capt. Humbert F.O.D. Countersign "Barnet"

About 2½ P.M. Cold N.E. Rain commenced and lasted off & on during this afternoon & night.

[*Not signed*]

Monday, 13 June 1864

Cold N.E. Wind and rain almost all day. With my winter Clothing and overcoat on I sat in my Tent cold all day.

Capt. Guignard Richardson, Lucas' Battalion, F.O.D. Countersign "Georgia"

At 5 P.M. rode down on the Line.

Lt. [*A.A. or J.B.*] Connor, Co. "F" (the larger) in Comd. Stono Pickets, Lt. Kitchens Comd. Reserve, Lt. Thompson in Comd Overseer's House, Sergt Johnson[1] at Stone House, Sergt Hendricks at Day Post.

Lt. [*A.A. or J.B.*] Connor, Co. "F" (the smaller) in Comd. Supporting party at Rivers' Causeway, Lt. DeLorme in Comd. Blake's Section.

Rode round with Capt. [*Guignard*] Richardson posting Pickets.

Got to Camp at 10 P.M. a little wet through India Rubber Coat, overcoat & thick uniform coat.

[*Not signed*]

[1] *No positive identification. Either Sgt. J.E. Johnson, Co. B, 2nd Rgmt., S.C. Arty, or Sgt. G.T. Johnson, Co. F, 2nd Rgmt., S.C. Cav. Men of both units were on picket duty.*

Tuesday, 14 June 1864

Capt. S.P. Smith F.O.D. Countersign "Rhodes"

At 7.45 A.M. got notice that Capt. Warwick of Maj. Genl. Jones' Staff would arrive at District Hd. Qrs. at 8 A.M. to bear a Flag of Truce to the Enemy at Dixon's Island. Breakfasted and hastened up to Genl. Taliaferro's Hd. Qrs.

Started with Capt. Warwick & Lieut Meade and got escort of Lieut Perry & 2 Sergeants from 2nd Cavalry. Rode down to Overseer's House and Capt. Warwick carried his Flag of Truce about 11 A.M.

As two Negro infantry soldiers with their muskets formed part of the Escort of the Yankee Officer, Capt. Warwick refused to deliver his letter on the express ground that he could not do so to officers commanding negro troops; and requested that as he was a Staff Officer that a Staff Officer might be sent for the other side to receive the message.

The Yankee Officers (a Captain & a Lieut) accordingly said that they would send Capt. Warwick's request to Hd. Quarters that a Staff Officer should be sent to receive an important Communication.

About 3½ P.M. three Officers appeared on the Yankee side (they appeared to be Staff Officers) and received the Communication. There was considerable difficulty in crossing the Bridge as the tide was high and the Timbers slippery with rain. They said that an answer would be returned to-morrow, or the day after.

Got back to Camp at 4½ P.M. The whole day wet & Cold. Wind N. East and continual showers. In spite of overcoats it was unpleasantly Cool.

No corn brought to day for our horses.

Capt., Bridges with Co. "D" reported to Genl. Taliaferro to day and was sent to Secessionville.

[*Not signed*]

Wednesday, 15 June 1864

Wind N.E. but day clear. Sun came out. Delightful day, somewhat overcast.

Capt. Kennedy [*Kennady*] F.O.D. Countersign "Lisbon"

The Yankees have been firing all night into the City, the result probably of [a] Message under the Flag of Truce that 5 Generals, 9 Colonels, 25 Lt. Colonels & 11 Majors have been put in Charleston under the fire of their Guns at Morris Island.[1]

Walked up to Gen. Taliaferro's to see him on Business. Late in the day to Col. Fredericks about the same business, viz. the reduction of the details from Co. "B".

Capt. Webb Came to my Camp about 11 A.M. to see about his Caissons which were left with me. He has received for his Company two 20 Pndr. Parrotts, with the promise of two more or 2 Napoleon Guns.

About 5 P.M. went up into Secessionville Observatory to make Observations upon Folly Island. Could not notice any increase of troops upon Folly Island tho' there are a large number of tents, which have been there however for some weeks. It is reported by the lookout men that troops were landed on Monday or Tuesday, and also this morning.

While in the observatory there was a sharp Cannonade between Fort Lamar, the Long Island Batteries (there are now two) and the Batteries at Light House Inlet. As the Observatory is in the line of fire of the Long Island Batteries, it is a position of some risk. Only one fragment of a shell however hit the Observatory.

Afterwards rode down to Picket Lines. The Non. Com. Officer in charge of the Picket and Dixon's Island Bridge reported that when Battery Pringle was firing this afternoon, say 4 or 5 P.M., "Four squadrons of Yankees doublequicked" up to the Picket on opposite side. He said that probably there were about 50 in each squadron. This probably is a great exaggeration. No Commissioned Officers saw the Yankees. They remained about an hour the N.C.O. said.

Lt. [T.H.] Jones of Co. "H" ["K" is overstruck "H"] in Comd. Stono Pickets. Lt. Bolivar Co. "g" [Co. I] in Comd. Reserve at Grimball's Causeway.

Lt. Hunt, 2nd Cav., in Command Overseeer's House. Sergt. Pearson[2] in Comd. Stone House.

Lt. Rush in Comd. Reserve at Rivers' Causeway. Lt. LaBorde in Comd. one Section Blake's Arty.

Night still. Moschetoes & gnats troublesome. Got to Camp at 10.15 P.M.

[Not signed]

[1] The flag of truce (see Journal entry 14 June 1864), as Manigault said, notified the Federals that 50 high-ranking officers would be placed in a section of town subject to fire from Morris Island. They were imprisoned in a residence which today is 180 Broad St.

The North promptly sent a similar number of Confederate officers to be placed under fire on Morris Island. However, all of these officers were exchanged (see 3 Aug. 1864). Treatment of the prisoners by both sides seems to have been excellent considering the circumstances.

The South, in the hope of further exchanges, soon sent 600 more prisoners, mainly officers, to Charleston where they were imprisoned at various locations in the city.

However, the Federals, realizing the advantages of prisoner exchanges to the personnel-starved South, soon put a halt to the custom. They also shipped 600 officers and men from Fort Delaware to Morris Island. These prisoners, soon dubbed by the

South "The Immortal 600," were penned in a hastily-built stockade near former Confederate Battery Wagner where they were endangered by Confederate artillery fire.

Living conditions on the island were bad, to say the least. Drinking water was the brackish output of holes dug in the sand and subject to pollution from nearby latrines. Food was limited and reportedly wormy. Guards were Negro troops who had little love for the Confederates.

Finally, both sides compromised. The Federal prisoners were sent off to a prisoner-of-war camp, where conditions probably were worse than in Charleston. "The Immortal 600" were jammed into two casemates at Fort Pulaski, near Savannah, Ga., where conditions were little better. [O.R. XXXV (1), pp. 24, 25; ibid. (2), numerous pages, especially 147, 163, 210, 254, 275, 285, 312-315]

[2] No positive identification. Probably James P. Pearson, 1st Sgt. of Co. E, 2nd Rgmt., S.C. Cav., or 1st Sgt. John A. Pearson of Co. K, same regiment.

Thursday, 16 June 1864

Capt. Humbert F.O.D. Countersign "Dunbar"

At 5½ P.M. our Batteries from Battery Tynes clear round to Eastern End of Sullivan's Island opened for practice, and perhaps a "show". The firing from the New Lines on James Island very slow & undecided, which was said to be owing to inferior quality of the friction tubes.

Capt. [S. Porcher] Smith went to City to day. Lt. [John B. W.] Phillips went down to Secessionville yesterday, relieving Lt. Spivey.

The Garrison of 3 gun Battery on Dixon's Island and the accompanying picket was composed of negroes. The Pickets along and at West End of Dixon's Island were White Men.

Saw for the first time a horse evidently ridden from Coles Island to Bridge over Creek beyond Stockade & Tete Du pont seen from Overseer's House in direction of Coles Island.

This horse was ridden by an Officer. Also horses at Campbell's House on Folly Island.

Our firing produced no stir in the Yankee Camps, tho' there was signalling from Dixon's Island Lookout & from Campbell's house.

Some four or five Shell were thrown towards Secessionville to day. The pickets near Battery Island say they were from the Lower Battery on Horse Island.

Returned to Camp at 9 P.M. Visit from Col. Frederick.

The Number of our Couriers reduced to day to 5. Also only 1 Cattle Guard.

[Not signed]

Friday, 17 June 1864

Capt. Colhoun F.O.D. Countersign "York"

Heavy Shelling from Long Island this Morning at about 5 A.M. 35 Shells thrown at Secessionville in a few minutes. One of the Gun Carriages disabled (No. 6 Rifle).

Details of Co. "B" (5 Sergt, 5 Corp, 51 Privates. 8 on Extra duty. 3 in Arrest. Effective 72.)

Capt. Mordecai's Commissary Guard	1 N.C.O.	3
Cattle Guard		1
McLeod's Comsy. Guard	1	3
James Island Creek Bridge	1	3
Garden of Co. "B"		3
Guard for horses of Co. C	2	10
	5	23
Couriers on duty		5
	5	28
Camp Guard	2	9
	7	37 = 44 Total on Duty
Couriers off duty & resting		5
	7	42 = 49 not available for drilling.

At Secessionville   1 Lieut   3 N.C.O.   30 Privates

At 5.55 P.M. Started for Picket Lines. At about 6.10 P.M. the Enemy threw four Rockets at Overseer's House. One burst in the Oak Tree; two passed through the house & one went over. No harm done.

On arriving there I went up into the Lookout to observe if this might be the precursor of any advance but saw nothing unusual. They prepared their rocket stand apparently intending to give me a Volley. At this time I observed a boat (4 oars) rounding the point from Folly River about Campbell's House which on its nearer approach I saw carried a white flag. After a time the boat landed at the Battery and two Officers came forward with a Flag of Truce. Capt. Colhoun met them on the Bridge. One announced himself as a Staff Officer of Genl. Foster and the other as Staff Officer of Genl. Schimmelfingar [*Schimmelfennig*] and they delivered the answer to our flag of Truce of Tuesday last.

The two Communications addressed to Genl. Jones were delivered at 7.35 P.M. when it was getting pretty dark. As Capt. Colhoun was rather short of men and could not well spare a Cavalry Soldier as Courier, I carried the Dispatches (Sealed) to Col. Frederick's and then to Genl. Taliaferro's into whose hands I delivered them at 8.45 P.M. Genl. Taliaferro forwarded them soon after to Genl. Jones' Hd. Qrs.

Two Hundred (200) Men of Bonaud's Battalion arrived this afternoon and were directed to encamp near Battery No. 5.

The Remaining Cos. of Black's Regt. Cav. also arrived this afternoon.

The Pee Dee Artillery, Capt. Zimmerman, arrived [*from Virginia*] to night, 77 strong.[1] They were ordered to Secessionville.

Went to bed at 10.30 P.M.

Lt. Bush in Comd. Stono Pickets. Lt. Mosley in Comd Reserve at Rivers' Causeway.

Lt. [*John B.W.*] Phillips in Comd Overseer's House. Sergt [*James P. or John A.*] Pearson in Comd. Stone House.

Lieut Spivey in Comd Reserve at Rivers' Causeway. 2 N.C.O. & 9

Privates of Co. "B" S.C. Siege Train, the rest from 2nd Arty.
Lt. DeLorme in Comd of Section of Blake's Artillery.

[*Not signed*]

¹ *This unit replaced Gregg's outfit as Co. C of the Siege Train.*

Saturday, 18 June 1864

The Most Western Long Island Battery Shelled our Reserve at Rivers' Causeway this morning at 5½ to 6 A.M. Many of their shells were thrown with great accuracy, one striking the Parapet of Battery at Rivers' Causeway. No harm done.

At 7½ A.M. Capt. Zimmerman made a requisition on me for Wagon to transport his Baggage & Cooking utensils &c. from Hatch's Wharf to Secessionville. I lent him our Staff wagon for the day and gave notice to Capt. Mordecai of the arrival of the Company.

Capt. Guignard Richardson F.O.D. Countersign "Barnet"

At 5.45 P.M. rode down to Picket Lines. All quiet.

Lieut A.A. Connor Comdg. Stono Pickets. Lt. Rush Comdg Reserve at Grimball's Causeway.

Lt. Hunt Comdg Overseer's House. S'g^t Caldwell Comdg Stone House.

Returned early to meet wagon with barrels for wells,¹ but did not meet it so went to Camp at 9.15 P.M.

A Brigantine or Hermaphrodite Brig lying along side of Mortar Schooner near Campbell's. Also two schooners in upper part of Folly River, where they have been some days.

[*Not signed*]

¹ *A barrel was a convenient method of forming a frame, or curb, around the upper part of a well to prevent the earth from caving in. See 29 July 1864.*

Sunday, 19 June 1864

Capt. Stallings F.O.D. Countersign "Hudson"

The last Squadron of Lipscomb's Regt 2nd Cav. (Captns. Westfield's & Dean's Companies) was relieved to day by Col. Black's Command of whom 45 were put on picket duty. Capt. Dean's Company was ordered and left for John's Island to relieve the "Rebel Troop" and Capt. Westfield was ordered to Adams Run.

Lieut Dargan of the Pee Dee Artillery came to my Tent about 10 A.M. and applied for Tents & horses to be turned over to his Company. Rode with him to Genl. Taliaferro's and afterwards to Col. Fredericks. Got order for Capt. Mordecai to turn over tents & horses.

Rode to Capt. Mordecai's and made the arrangements. Dined with Capt. M.

Returned to Camp at 5.50 P.M.

Rode down to Front at 6.45. All quiet, very high tide.

Lt. Rush in Comd Stono Pickets. Lt. A.A. Connor in Comd Reserve at Grimball's Causeway.

Capt. Trezevant in Comd Overseer's House. Lieut Roberts in Comd Stone House.

Lieut [*John B. W.*] Phillips in Comd Reserve at Rivers' Causeway. Lt. DeLorme in Comd Section of Blake's Battery.

Returned to Camp at 10.20 P.M.

[*Not signed*]

Monday, 20 June 1864

Capt. S.P. Smith F.O.D. Countersign "Hastings"

In the morning Early [*7 A.M. inserted later*] two Steamers, one a two Masted, side-wheel steamer gun boat with heavy gun (probably Rifle) at Bows and probably one astern. The other a Northern Ferry Boat, *McDonough*, mounting a heavy Rifle gun in Bows and (I think) one astern (the same vessel which used to shell us from Light House inlet) Came up the Stono and anchored a little below Legareville. What they immediately did I do not know, as only their Masts could be seen over Battery Island and no one had energy enough to climb a tree. As soon as I got through my battalion business, I went down [*To the picket line*]. Did not reach there till 12.30. Getting into the top of a tree which enabled me to have a good view of them I saw 8 boats lying against the Steamer, principally, at the smaller one, i.e. the Ferry Boat. A landing had evidently been made at Legareville as I saw one or two men on end of the lower footbridge and two or three boats returned from the landing to the Steamers.

About 1.30 or 1.45 I noticed suddenly a dense smoke in the direction of the Batteries which were constructed last December below Legareville (and which were used in the attack on a Gunboat on Christmas day) [*See Diary 25 December 1863*]. As soon as this smoke became visible, the boats put off from the Steamers and went to the landing. Only six boats were used tho' there were Eight around the Steamers. Four of these boats appeared to be skiffs with head & stern rising well out of the water. I judged that they were near 30 ft. in length, but that they were light boats drawing little water and intended for the special purpose of landing troops. Each when empty was rowed with two oars & steered by an oar. The two other boats were probably ships "long boats" or perhaps "launches". When empty they were rowed with 4 oars double-banked.

About 2 P.M. I saw a party of about 50 commence filing down on the foot Bridge leading from the village to the landing. Shortly after a party of about 75. Then about 25 some what scattered and afterwards about 50 others. The branches of the Oak in which I was were swaying a good deal backwards and forwards (the wind being high) so that I could not keep My telescope always upon them, and consequently could not count with perfect accuracy; still I think that 200 is a pretty close approximation to their entire number.

They commenced re-embarking about 2.30 P.M. and finished about 3 P.M. The Gun boat weighed anchor & Stood down the river about 3.30

P.M. and the Ferry Boat after manoeuvering about for some time in a manner I did not understand, also Stood down the river about 4 P.M. with 6 boats in tow. I got to Camp at 5.30 P.M. I am not aware that the men from the Steamers made any landing on the James Island side of the River. A party of Signal men were at the Yankee battery on Horse Shoe Island and as soon as the expedition returned they telegraphed to Folly Island. Apparently they withdrew when the Steamers did.

The Stono Posts and the Reserve at Grimball's Causeway was furnished to day from Major Bonaud's Battalion of Infantry for the first time on this duty. Capt. Goodson [*Godwin*] Commanded the Stono Posts and Lieut Lawrence the Reserve, 75 men & about 5 N.C.O.

Capt. [*L.J.*] Johnson of Black's Cavalry Commanded the Overseer's House and Lt. Ratchford at the Stone House.

I did not go down on the Picket line at night.

Capt. [*S. Porcher*] Smith reports that a third Steamer (small) came up to Battery Island at 11 A.M. she had gone away before I got down at 12.30 P.M.

[*Not signed*]

Tuesday, 21 June 1864

Capt. Kennedy [*Kennady*] F.O.D. Countersign "Wise"

Received a visit from Capt. Zimmerman of the Pee Dee Artillery who desired to draw clothing for his men, also Tents, Wagon, &c.

Drilled Co. "B" in skirmish firing for about 1½ hours from 10 till 11.30.

At 5 O'clock Capt. Zimmerman came to receive the horses & Mules turned over by Capt. Gregg to the Qr. Master Department.

At 5½ P.M. rode down to the Front. All quiet and no signs of increased numbers on Folly Island. The Yankees have erected (not yet completed) a new Signal Station or Lookout about 200 or 300 yds. to East of Campbell's House on Folly Island.

Negro Pickets opposite to us on Dixon's Island.

Capt. Goodson [*Godwin*] (Bonaud's Battalion) in Comd. Reserve at Grimball's Causeway.

Lieut. Lawrence (same Battalion) in Comd Stono Pickets.

Detail from Bonaud's Battn.

Capt. Wilson (Black's Regt. Cavalry) in Comd. Overseer's House. (He is Capt. of the Chester Co.)

Lieut. Blasinghame [*Blassinghame*] in Comd Stone House.

Lt. Bolivar in Comd Reserve at Rivers' Causeway.

Lt. Kemper in Comd. Section of Blake's Battery.

Returned to Camp at 9.20 P.M.

[*Not signed*]

Wednesday, 22 June 1864

Capt. Humbert F.O.D. Countersign "Sumter"

Drilled Co. "B" in skirmish Drill from 10 to 11.45 A.M.

A Transport lying in Folly River near Campbell's House this morning. (Steam Tug supply boat probably)

Capt. Humbert reports that at about 1½ P.M. a Steamer came up Stono to Battery Island and that 7 men landed & Scouted the Island. Then that there was considerable passing & repassing to & from the Steamer to Horse Island in boats. (Suppose landing Commissary & Ordnance Supplies)

At about 5 P.M. the Horse Island Battery commenced shelling our Pickets near Battery Island. Threw about 7 Shells. At about 6 P.M. the Enemy Commenced throwing rockets at Overseer's House from two Stands, one in position near the two Palmetto trees and the other from the 3 gun Battery. They threw 9 at the House and about 3 to the Right & 3 to the left, making about 15 in all. They did no harm.

Capt. Humbert sunk a well near the Overseer's House with two Rice Barrels. The Rice barrels which were sent to Reserve were burnt last night by the men of Bonaud's Battalion.

Lieut. Kitchens in Comd. Stono Pickets. Lieut Shuler in Comd. Reserve at Grimball's Causeway.

Capt. Clayton in Comd. Overseer's House. Lieut Glover in Comd. Stone House.

Lt. Spivey in Comd. Reserve at Rivers' Causeway. Lt. Askew in Comd. Section of Artillery.

I supervised the posting of some of the pickets. Evening pleasant with fresh Easterly wind.

Got to Camp at 10 P.M.

[*Not signed*]

Thursday, 23 June 1864

Capt. Stallings F.O.D. (Capt. Colhoun being off on Sick leave). Countersign "Dover"

After transaction of morning business set off for City at 9 A.M. All quiet in City.

Got back to Camp at about 7½ P.M.

All quiet on the Front.

Major Bonaud's Battalion having been shelled at their first Camp Ground, moved over to open field just on our left.

[*Not signed*]

Friday, 24 June 1864

Capt. [*S. Porcher*] Smith F.O.D. (Capt. Guignard Richardson being Sick). Countersign "London"

Busy all morning in writing letters. Comp. "B" was inspected by Lt. Nesbit A. I. Genl. at 4 P.M.

At 6 P.M. I rode down to the front.

Lieut Bush in Comd. Stono pickets. Lt. Bolivar in Comd. Reserve at Grimball's Causeway.

Capt. Watley or Watleigh [*Whatley*] in Comd. Overseer's House. Lt. White in Comd. Stone House pickets.

Capt. Trezevant who came off duty this morning about 11 A.M. reported that men were seen to go from Horse Island to Battery Island over the foot Bridge with loads upon their shoulders. Could not see what.

Lt. Rush in Comd. Reserve at Rivers' Causeway.

Lt. Palmer in Comd. of Section of Chatham Artillery.

Wind S.W. Day has been hot. Moschetoes bad on the Front. Got back to Camp at 9 P.M.

[Not signed]

Saturday, 25 June 1864

Capt. Kennedy[*Kennady*] F.O.D. Countersign "Macon"

About 10 O'Clock A.M. rode down to the Front. Got up into an Oak Tree to observe any Movements of the enemy which might take place. About 11.30 a large Yawl or Ship's boat with 6 Men in it came sailing up the Stono and landed on Horse Island to S.W. of the Battery.

About 12 M. She Commenced towing a floating object about 100 yds. long towards the piles which are driven below Battery Island. At the end of this object was a barrel and the intermediate points were supported by floats. A large Skiff, probably 30 ft. long, Came to their assistance (Containing 8 men). Apparently they made their Tow fast to the piles and then hauled back a Cable to Horse Island near the Battery.

I could not of course tell the object or purpose of their movements, but thought it possible that they might be attaching Torpedoes to the Row of piles, for the purpose of destroying our "Davids" should they venture down. I got back to Camp at 3 P.M. quite fatigued, as remaining for 3 or 3½ hours in a Constrained position in a Tree top is very trying.

At 7½ P.M. started for the front. Took 12 men of Co. "B" under Lieut [*John B.W.*] Phillips, and 20 men of 2nd Arty from the Reserve, under Lt. Bush, and went over on Battery Island. We crossed over on Island about 10.30 and crossed back again at 12.45 A.M. We avoided the roads & Paths being apprehensive of Torpedoes. We saw no evidence whatever of any present occupation by the Yankees. Got back to Camp at 2.20 A.M.

Lieut. Bolivar in Comd. Stono Pickets. Lt. Bush in Comd. Reserve at Grimball's Causeway.

Capt. [*later Maj.*] Nesbitt in Comd. Overseer's House. Lt. Hankerson [*Hankinson*] in Comd. Stone House.

Lt. Spivey in Comd 30 men Co. B at Rivers' Causeway. Seg^t. Whaley in Comd Section of Blake's Arty.

[Not signed]

Sunday, 26 June 1864

Capt. Humbert F.O.D. Countersign "Oxford"
Did not go down on Front to day.

[*Not signed*]

Monday, 27 June 1864

Capt. Stallings F.O.D. Countersign "Berlin"
Capt. [*S. Porcher*] Smith & Dr. Winthrop went to City to day on leave.
I rode up to Capt. Mordecai's to procure some clothing.
Between 4 & 5 O'Clock P.M. a small Yankee Sail Boat approached Legareville and was fired on by our Pickets at that point. She immediately made off. Soon after she had got out of the line of fire several shell were thrown from the Batteries on Horse Island and lower down, at Legareville. Nothing further occurred.
The soldiers & Sentinels on Eastern end of Dixon's Island were negroes. The Pickets on West End of same and on Horse Island were white men.

Lieut Walton, of Bonaud's Battalion	in Comd.	Stono Pickets
Lieut Stroud, do do	in Comd.	Reserve at Grimball's Causeway
Capt. Wilson, 1st S.C. Cavalry	in Comd.	Overseer's House.
Lieut Horsey, do do	in Comd.	Stone House Pickets.
Lieut Shuler, Co. F, 2nd Arty	in Comd.	Reserve at Rivers' Causeway.
Lt. Laborde, Blake's Battery	in Comd.	Section of Artillery at Rivers'

[*Causeway*] but the Section did not arrive at its post until 9 P.M. and Lt. Laborde was not then with it.

For the first time I noticed this evening that Campbell's House on Folly Island has either been burnt or pulled down.
Got to Camp at 9.30 P.M.

[*Not signed*]

Tuesday, 28 June 1864

Capt. S.P. Smith F.O.D. Countersign "Russia"
Morning close & hot. Wind Northerly. About Midday wind shifted East and became cool. A little rain about 4 P.M. Evening and night Cool.
Did not go down to front this Evening.

[*Not signed*]

Wednesday, 29 June 1864

Capt. Guignard Richardson F.O.D. Countersign "Cork"
At 9 A.M. rode to Freer's house to see its condition. Then to Secessionville observatory and continued some time in observation. Then down on the Front.
The Yankees very busy clearing Horse Island; could not see whether they were erecting a battery or not.

Returned Home at 2½ P.M.

Capt. Trezevant in Comd Overseer's House. Lt. Lusk in Comd Stone House.

Lt. Mosley in Comd Reserve at Grimball's Causeway.

Lt. A.A. Connor in Comd Stono Pickets.

At 5 P.M. drilled Co. "B" in skirmish Drill. Did not go down on Front.

Lt. Gardner reported for duty today, just returned from Savannah where he has been since March 3rd.

[Not signed]

Thursday, 30 June 1864

Capt. Kennedy [*Kennady*] F.O.D. Countersign "Perth"

At 9.30 A.M. started to Inspect & Muster Major Lucas Battalion Arty. The following were the Inspecting officers appointed by Genl. Order No. 6, Hd. Qrs. West Lines June 29:

Maj. J.J. Lucas will Muster & Inspect	2nd Arty New Lines
Capt. T.K. Legare " " "	Bonaud's Battalion
Maj. Manigault " " "	Lucas Battn. Arty
Major Bonaud " " "	S.C. Siege Train

FORT PEMBERTON

Felix Warley, Adjt. in temporary Comd. Dr. W.R. Caldwell, Asst. Surgeon. 24 Men of Capt. Guignard Richardson's Co. "B" formed Garrison of which 18 inspected in ranks, 5 on Guard and one Sick.

Discipline	Good.
Instruction	Good.
Mil. App.	Good.
Arms.	Mixed. Muskets 1842 & Flint[*locks*] altered to Percussion in good condition.
Accoutrements	Good.
Clothing	Good (issued about 6 weeks) but 9 men in 23 barefooted and rest of shoes bad.
Guard House	dilapidated but Clean.
Quarters	Good, Airy & Clean.
Hospital	Well arranged & Clean. Hospital Attendants Comely & Clean.
Sinks	Good.

Battery

1 32 Pndr. Rifled & Banded, to Right. Garrison
   or S.C. [*Sea Coast*] Gun   Barbette

1 32 pndr. Navy Smooth Bore, 61 cwt.   "

1 32 do " " " do   "

1 32 do Rifled & Banded, to Left. Garrison
   or S.C. [*Sea Coast*] Gun   "

Guns Good. Carriages somewhat split but in good serviceable order.

Main Magazine.	Brick & well arched. Very damp. All the Cartridges felt damp. Should recommend that all Ammunition not needed should be removed. The other Magazines I did not examine as there was nothing in them.
Transportation.	1 horse, 4 Mules, 1 ambulance, 1 Cart, 1 Wagon. 2 Wagons & 8 mules with Major Burke or District Q.M.

BATTERY TYNES

Capt. Guignard Richardson's Co. "B" formed Garrison. Capt. Richardson, Lt. Moses, Lt. Heyward. Lt. [*J. Drayton*] Ford on duty at Fort Pemberton as Commissary or Q.M.

28 Men in Ranks, of which 7 without Shoes. 8 guard, 5 Prisoners, 8 on duty as Wappoo Bridge, or Ord. Stores at McLeod's Guard. 1 Sergt & 24 Privates on Duty at Ft. Pemberton, 2 on Detached Service at Fort Pemberton, 2 Detached in Engr. Department, 3 sergts in Ranks, 1 Sergt Sick, 1 absent Sick, 2 Absent without leave & in Confinement, 2 musicians, 2 present Sick. Total 89.

Actual Total 89.

Muster Roll. 4 Officers & 89 enlisted men.

Discipline	Good.
Instruction	Good.
Mil. Appearance	Good.
Arms	Mixed. Musket Model 1842 and [*flintlock*] altered to percussion. In good condition.
Accoutrements	Good.
Clothing	Good (issued about 6 weeks). Many Shoes wanting, probably ¼, and rest bad.
Quarters	New, Airy & Clean. Parade Clean & well swept. Guard House clean and well kept.

Battery
1 Rifle 32, Banded, on Barbette Carriage
1   do   do   do
1 Rifled 42,   on Columbiad carriage.
1 Rifled 32,   do   do   do
1 8 in. Columbiad do   do   do   Circle broken.
Abundance of Shot & Shell. Implements in good order.

Magazine	In excellent condition, dry & well ventilated. But both it and the Bomb Proof not sufficiently covered with Earth or sodded.
No Hospital	The Sick are sent to Fort Pemberton.

1 Post Horse

The following Books are kept: (1) Morning Report Book, (2) Guard Report Book, (3) "Remark Book" showing daily duty, (4) Descriptive Book, (5) Clothing Acct. Book, (6) Post Order Book, (7) Company Order Book, (8) Property Return.

These Books are kept with great care & accuracy.

189

BATTERY PRINGLE

Colhoun's Co. "A" garrison. E.B. Colhoun, Capt., Wm. G. Ogier 1st Lt., W.D. Martin 1st Lt., Thos. E. Lucas 2nd Lt., 84 Enlisted Men, Total.

46 Men in Ranks (of which 32 bare footed) & 2 Sergeants, 2 N.C.O. & 6 men on Camp Guard, 9 men on Guard elsewhere, 3 absent Sick, 4 on detached Service, 2 Absent with leave, 2 cooks, 1 Waggoner, 1 Ord. Corp^l. Total 78 Acc^d. for.

Discipline	Good
Instruction	Good
Mil. App.	Good, except Clothing not uniform & 32 bare feet
Arms	Mixed, Musket 1842 & old [*flintlock*] altered to percussion, Good order.
Accoutrements	Good, but 8 Cart. Boxes & some Cap pouches wanting.
Clothing	Good, but want of Uniformity. 32 without Shoes. Some Blankets wanting and a few Knapsacks.

Parade & Grounds clean & well swept. Quarters Clean.

Surgeon Girardeau has no hospital. The sick are carried to Fort Pemberton.

2 Mules & wagon. Harness worn out & Mules in bad Condition.

1 Horse & Ambulance. Horse worn out, Ambulance broken & no harness.

1 Post Horse.

The following books are kept: 1. Morning Report Book, 2. Guard Report Book, 3. Company Order Book, 4. Letter Book, 5. Descriptive Book, 6. Clothing acct. Book.

Battery
1   32 pndr. Rifled & Banded. Barbette Carriage.
1   42   "   do   do   Barbette Carriage.
1   10 inch   Columbiad Carriage.
1   32 pnd. Rifled & Banded
1   42   "   "   & double banded, Columbiad Carriage, no elevation, i.e. only 7 degrees.
1   8 in. Columbiad
1   8 in. Navy Shell gun, 56 cwt. (*Isaac Smith*)[1]
1   do   do   do   do   do

Plenty of Ammunition. Every thing in good order. One or two handspikes wanting.

Magazines
The Right Magazine is damp (rather), the Left is better.
Shell Room is in the Bomb Proof and is very bad & wet.
Bomb Proof is full of water in wet weather and is not sufficiently covered and not Sodded.

Finished Inspection & got to Camp at 4 P.M.

At 10 o'clock got note from Col. Frederick stating that the force on Long Island had been increased and requiring great watchfulness. Ordered Co. "B" to lie on their arms and started down on the front myself at 11 P.M. Adjt. Gardner accompanied me. Staid all night on front. All quiet. The Yankees still Clearing Horse Island.

Lt. [*T.H.*] Jones in Comd. Stono Pickets. Lt. J.B. Connor in Comd. Reserve at G[*rimball*]'s Causeway.

Capt. Whatley in Comd. Overseer's House, 1st S.C. Cav.

Lt. [*Name omitted*] in command Stone House.

Lt. Palmer in Comd. Section Chatham Artillery.

Lt. Bush in Comd. of his Support at Rivers' Causeway.

Got back to Camp at 7.30 A.M. 1st July.

[*Not Signed*]

¹ *See 25 Aug. 1863, note 3. No 8-inch shellguns of 56 cwt. were made. These probably would have been the Model 1845 of 55 or 63 cwt. [Ripley, pp. 103, 370]*

Friday, 1 July 1864

Capt. Stallings F.O.D.

Various interruptions & occupations. About 11 A.M. threw myself on bed and slept till 3.30 P.M. Busy all evening in writing up Journal &c. Did not go down to Front. Went to bed about 10 P.M.

Lt. J.B. Connor in Comd Stono Pickets. Lt. Jones in Comd Reserve (All 2nd Arty)

Capt. Nesbitt in Comd Overseer's House. Lt. [*later Capt.*] Leak in Comd Stone House.

Lt. Spivey in Comd. Reserve Rivers' Causeway (20 men). Lt. DeLorme in Comd Section of Blake's Batty. at Rivers.

[*Not Signed*]

Saturday, 2 July 1864

At Daylight the Yankees appeared suddenly at East End of James Island. Lieut DeLorme, who had his horses all hitched in, gallopped down to Rivers' Causeway. The Enemy advanced at first in Column (or probably by a flank 4 deep) along the back beach of James Island from the East. Lieut DeLorme immediately opened fire upon them at first with Shell & Case Shot and afterwards with Canister. Two advances he repulsed. The troops, a large number of whom were negroes, broke, in spite of the exertions of a mounted officer who led them, and who is said to have acted with great gallantry. They then advanced the third time somewhat in the manner of a line of skirmishers and flanking the Section on both sides, Lt. DeLorme gave orders to cease firing and retire. Lt. DeLorme says that as soon as he gave the Command "Cease Firing" his Cannoneers left him. The infantry Support (from Siege Train under Lt. Spivey) was too small to render effectual resistance. Lieut D. then attempted to limber up his pieces with his drivers, but one of the wheel drivers running off caused such delay that he was finally obliged to abandon his pieces, saving his horses and limbers and all of his men, except one who went and hid himself in a ditch evidently to be taken. Lieut. DeLorme's own horse was killed being (as was afterwards seen when we recovered the position) pierced by 8 bullets. Lt D. then had a foot race across the fields to save himself. 2 men of Co. "A" S.C.C. [*South Carolina Cavalry*] were cut off; also 6 horses.

Two of the Siege Train were wounded, Private Roberts in the left breast and Private Wiggins in the hip. Lt. Delorme fired 54 Rounds (he had 64 rounds in his Limber Chests before the action and there were only 10 remaining after it was over). The losses of the Enemy were severe. 12 dead bodies (8 negro & 4 white) were found nearly in one place, and about 10 in another. Altogether from 25 to 30 were said to be found unburied when we got possession of the place next day. A prisoner who was taken when we were putting out the Secessionville picket at night said that about 90 were killed. He probably meant killed and wounded. The loss of the two excellent Napoleon Guns 12 pndr. was a serious one to us.

As soon as I dressed I rode down, passing by Battery No. 2, to Grimball's and saw the armed Steam Ferry Boat, *The McDonough*, which used to lie at Light House Inlet, taking up a position in Stono River to enfilade our line of pickets. Riding on I met our Line of Pickets deployed as Skirmishers in full retreat. I came to them just as they were approaching a Bank and Ditch running East & West nearly, and extending from Grimball's Causeway Road to a point about half a mile Eastwards. I ordered a halt immediately and made the men shelter themselves in the ditch, Extending the line as well as I could to the West.* To some Staff Officer from Col. Frederick, I think it was Lt. Nesbit, I reported our position and requested that Battery Pringle should be immediately ordered to fire upon this Steamer in Stono River which I expected every moment would enfilade our position and perhaps render it untenable.

Battery Pringle shortly afterwards commenced firing upon the Steamer, *The McDonough*, which replied and did not fire upon us. The Shooting from Battery Pringle was very bad, but the Steamer was finally driven off. Distance [*Omitted in diary. Probably about 1½*] miles.

About this time Major Bonaud's Battalion reported to me. I took 25 or 30 men of it (Co. "B" S.C. Siege Train, 50 or 60 men, joined me first) and completed my Skirmish Line up to Grimball's Road, filling up the Gap between the 2nd Artillery & Capt. Nesbitt with his 40 Cavalry who held the hedge to west of Grimball's Road up to the Spring near the Bridge. Fifty more of Bonaud's Battalion I ordered to report to Capt. Stallings who would fill up his line Eastwardly. The remainder of Bonaud's Battalion only 75 or so in number, I held as a Reserve about

---

I first sent Adjutant Gardner to report our position, to ask for reinforcements, and to request that Battery Pringle might open. Lt. Nesbit came afterwards.

200 to 250 yds, or 300 yds, in rear of the Centre of our line as then posted and near the Road from Battery No. 2 to Grimball's Causeway.

Shortly after 104 men of Black's Cavalry reported to me (dismounted) under Lieut Beckham. I took 20 of these and ordered them to Capt. Nesbitt on the Right to strengthen his force.

I then sent for Lieut [*T.H*] Jones, of Co. H, 2nd Arty, who knew the ground well and told him to take charge of 20 more Cavalrymen which I furnished him and proceed along the Cross Road running East from Grimball's and through the wood, and scout towards the South Edge of said woods, and see if the enemy approached on that flank.

I also sent for Capt. S.P. Smith and put the remaining 64 dismounted Cavalry under his Command and told him to take them and dispose of them as he best could, occupying the hedges, as near as possible on the same line with our line already established, as far as the Road from Batty. No. 4 to Horace Rivers' Place. I thought that the fire of Secessionville would suffice to prevent the Yankees from advancing on the East side of Said road. I afterwards sent 20 Mounted Cavalry men to reinforce Capt. Smith.

The Yankees appeared as skirmishers in the wood to N.W. of Battery at head of Grimball's Causeway. Of course it was impossible to decide upon their numbers in so thick a wood. I immediately sent word to Col. Frederick requesting that a section of Artillery should be sent down to shell the wood. Shortly after a line of Skirmishers extending from said wood to near Stono River advanced over the open field with their reserves in the rear. I do not think that the skirmishers visible in the field were more than two Companies, each Company with its reserve. I was told that a line of Battle was formed in rear of the Line of Skirmishers, and just north of Grimball's Causeway. This I could not see from my position.

Shortly afterwards the Yankees commenced throwing Hale's Rockets from the wood, and then skirmishers disposed along a hedge 250 to 300 yds. off commenced firing upon us. As our men were completely protected by the bank, I did not allow them to return the fire. After firing about 15 or 20 minutes, and finding that we did not reply, they ceased their Musketry fire, but occasionally threw their Rockets. Blake's Section arrived just before they commenced their musketry fire and he reported to me for orders. I told him to fire over our heads and Shell the woods and also their skirmish line., He was talking to me about 30 to 50 paces in rear of our line, when the Enemy's skirmishers opened on us. As he was mounted & of course ran great risk, we ceased our conversation immediately and he returned to his Section posted about 300 to 400 yds. in rear of our line.

Blake's Section soon Silenced the Rocket Battery, and the Skirmishers soon after (probably having exhausted their Cartridge boxes) ceased firing and fell back some 300 or 400 yds. We had not a single man wounded (except one who shot off his finger by accident) nor did we fire a shot in return, that is of small arms. I am satisfied that the enemy could have got no idea of our actual numbers.

Our force was as follows. Picket Reserve, 2nd Arty, 75. Capt. Nesbitt's Cavalry Pickets, 40. Bonaud's Battalion, 150. Co. B. Siege Train, 60. 1st Cavalry, 124. Total 449 men.

The above was nominally the force, but there were many stragglers and men who reported sick, and especially was this the case as the day progressed, the intense heat prostrating many of the men and occasioning something very like <u>Sun Stroke</u> but in moderate degree. In some of the Commands nearly one fourth were reported incapacitated.

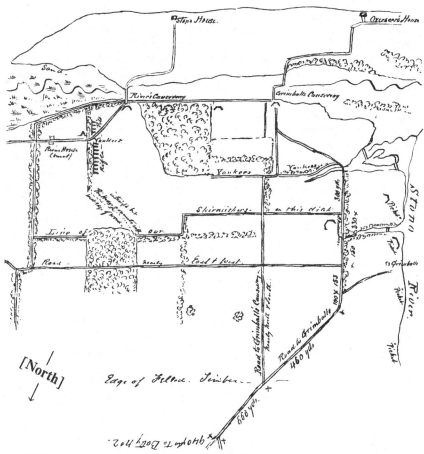

This sketch accompanied Manigault's description of the action.

Capt. Blake's Section continued to fire occasionally upon the line of Yankee Skirmishers and we were informed by a prisoner did a good deal of damage. He was afterwards relieved by a Section of Wheaton's Battery under Lieut. Askew. The Artillery was withdrawn after dark.

After every thing became quiet on the Right of the line I rode over to the left and saw the Yankees Collected apparently in force at the point where the Road runs through the hedge to west of Horace Rivers'

House. They had erected a small battery and Rifle pits at that point (Marked "A" in Map) and opened on us first with Shell and then with Canister. No damage was done. In the afternoon on being Sent for by Genl. Taliaferro, I went to Battery No. 2 where I saw himself, Col. Harrison & Col. Frederick probably 4 P.M. I remember my intense Thirst. Major Echols "Bureau Battalion" reported at this time. About 70 men. Also Battalion of 7 Companies, 1st Arty & 1st Infantry from Sullivans Isl[d]. Say 450 men.

At dark, hearing that the enemy manifested a disposition to land near Grimball's, I went with Capt. Nesbitt and posted a picket (Mounted) at the Battery on Grimball's place on Bank of River with orders to report immediately any atempt at landing. We saw two Steamers just below, and though we could not see them we could hear boats plying to and from the shore, or rather about to ply. I ordered Capt. Nesbitt to withdraw the Right of his Skirmish line a little so as not to be cut off by a party landing above. I then reported to head quarters that Steamers were at the point indicated and apparently about to land troops, and requested that Battery Pringle should open on that part of the River.

I then rode back to Road from No. 2 to Grimball's Causeway and found Lieut J.B. Connor moving off with his Command of the 2nd Arty which had been relieved, he had not more than 25 or 30 men with him. I took these and went to Grimball's and established another Picket higher up. I then dismissed Connor & his men and rode back to the front.

During the whole night the enemy was reported landing troops just below our line on the Extreme Right. I fully expected that a large force would be concentrated there and at day-break a rush made, and an attempt to cut us off from the Lines. I gave full notice of this to Head Quarters through Lieut Nesbit, whom at my request Col. Frederick sent to me as bearer of dispatches. I then waited anxiously for daylight.[1]

[Not signed]

---

[1] *The James Island engagement was part of a large Federal demonstration against Charleston and the railroad to Savannah ordered by Maj. Gen. John G. Foster. The James Island attack was carried out by the 55th Massachusetts, the 33rd U.S. Colored Troops and the 103rd N.Y. Volunteers. The most detailed Federal report was by Maj. Joseph Morrison, commander of the 103rd. He complained that due to conflicting orders, his men spent the 24 hours or so preceding the assault rowing in small boats between various islands and wading ashore through deep mud. Although badly fatigued and somewhat disorganized, the regiment was ordered to advance. At this juncture, Morrison discovered that his skirmishers had disappeared in the wrong direction and could not be recalled in time to lead the attack. He pressed other men into service as skirmishers, but they were untrained and virtually useless. His attack rolled forward until the men were fired upon by Confederate infantry and then by Lt. DeLorme's Napoleons. As Morrison described it: "... The first fire of the enemy killed 7 of my men and wounded many others, and, as my regiment was taken completely by surprise and in no position to charge the battery, I was compelled to fall back a few rods and reform behind a strong rifle-pit running in front of the enemy's works. At the time the enemy opened upon my regiment with canister, the Thirty-third U.S. Colored Troops on my left commenced firing. After forming my regiment behind the rifle-pits, I received orders to advance by the left flank on the rebel works, which I did, but did not arrive*

until [after] the Fifty-fifth Massachusetts Volunteers had possession." [OR XXXV (1) pp. 14, 15, 78, 79]

Sunday, 3 July 1864

I had all the Skirmishers waked about an hour before day and waited anxiously for the expected attack, fearing however that all the advantages of our position in front would be of no avail in consequence of the supposed heavy force upon our Right flank.

Just at day break we heard firing in the direction of Fort Johnson which proved to indicate an attack on that post in barges. This attack was repulsed.[1]

After broad day light we perceived that the enemy was not in our immediate front at all, but had been drawn off during the night. The supposed Landing of troops on our Right must rather have been the <u>Embarkation</u>. Whatever the operation was, the fire of Battery Pringle appeared to be highly annoying to them.

I went up to Head Quarters (probably about 6½ or 7 A.M.) at an intimation to that effect from the Brig. Genl. Comdg [*Taliaferro*]. Communicated with Gen. Taliaferro & Col. Frederick and soon returned to the front.

About 9 O'Clock Col. Harrison came down with 5 Companies of his Regt. (32 Georgia) and nominally 100 dismounted Cavalry of 1st S.C.C. under Capt. Trezevant (they were only 62 in fact). With this force we proceeded to our left and then advanced to the intersection of Rivers' Road and the Secessionville Road (Near Horace Rivers' Burnt House). Two Companies under Major Bacon were thrown forward as skirmishers and the other Companies and the Cavalry followed as a Reserve. We then pushed forward to Rivers' Causeway and occupied the line from Rivers to Grimball's Causeway, having sent out scouts and ascertained that no heavy body of the enemy was immediately in our front.

The enemy's Pickets extended from near the Stone House to beyond Grimball's Causeway. We could not see any large force near the Overseer's House, but heavy clouds of dust betokened the presence of considerable forces.

The enemy commenced shelling our line, as soon as it was established, from the Gunboats in Stono, and occasionally from light pieces near South End of Grimball's Causeway. Our line must have been established about 10 O'clock. The Sun was intensely hot and many of the men were incapacitated by heat.

The enemy appeared to have abandoned their position in great haste. Muskets, accoutrements, Spades, Canteens, Blankets, India Rubber Coats were gathered by our soldiers in large numbers.

About 4 or 5 P.M. Long Island Battery commenced firing upon the Yankee Battery & Rifle Pits at which our Reserve was stationed (See "A") [*Sketch by Maj. Manigault, Page 194*]. It was very lucky for us that this fire was not commenced sooner.

At about 6½ P.M. I was relieved by the arrival of Col. Harrison, Major Blanding and Capt. Humbert. I left the front about 7 P.M. and was glad to get some Supper and a good night's rest. Major Blanding with about 120 of the 1st Arty picketted the Right from Grimball's landing to Grimball's Causeway while Col. Harrison with his 5 Companies and 62 Cavalry picketted the Left to some distance beyond the Rivers' Road. The night passed off quietly except [*for*] some shelling — and also our own men firing upon the Officer of the day and Major Blanding, on which the Yankees also fired.

Note. At this time we had on New Lines James Island 2 Cos. 1st S.C. Arty; 5 Cos. 1st S.C. Infantry; 5th Ga.; 7th Ga.;[2] 32 Ga.; 47th Georgia; Bonaud's Battn. Ga. Vols.; 4 Cos. 2nd Arty, Capt. Legare; 2 Cos. do, Capt. Dickson; Co. B Siege Train; and part of Black's 1st S.C. Cavalry, also Echols "Bureau Battalion." Afterwards we also had the 10th N.C. Battn. Heavy Arty.

[Not signed]

[1] *The attack on Fort Johnson was another facet of the demonstration against Charleston (see 2 July 1864, note). The Federals attacked in boats from Morris Island. Conflicting orders, delays and poor leadership led to confusion. Some of the boats grounded, others retreated prematurely, and a few made it to shore. The men who landed overran two Confederate batteries but, with no hope of support, were captured trying to take Fort Johnson. Federal casualties in the retreating boats were not recorded. Seven of the men who landed were killed and five officers and 135 enlisted men, some of them wounded, were captured. Confederate casualties were light. [OR XXXV (1) 15, 40, 41, 86-103, 159, 160, 260]*

[2] *Manigault's reference to the 7th Ga. is puzzling since the unit was in Virginia at this date. He may have meant to write 47th. Then, having added that unit in numerical sequence later in the sentence, he neglected to delete the erroneous 7th. See 15 July 1864 (page 206) where Manigault again listed the 7th when he obviously meant the 47th.*

Monday, 4 July 1864

Rested all day. A tremendous Rain at 2 or 3 O'clock P.M. Two or three times to day I am told the Yankees made demonstrations of attack with negro troops, but fell back on a show of resistance.

At about 5½ P.M. went to Hd. Quarters. Relief for tonight as follows.

Capt. Rivers in Comd his own & Capt. Witherspoon's Co., 1st [*S.C.*] Infantry	126
Capt. R. Press Smith [*Jr*] in Comd his own, Capt. Burnett's & Capt. Calhoun's Cos. Same Regt.	181
	307
Lieut. Hancock in Comd Men of 1st S.C.C.	34
Total	341
Besides this, however, Capt. Trezevant was retained with his Comd to support	40
Blake's Section, Say 20 Artillerists &	381 Infantry & Cavalry

Rode down to front and found a party of Capt. Lewis' Co. 32 Georgia firing upon a few men to Right of Battery at head of Grimball's Causeway. Lewis' Men were behind the hedge to East of said Battery and Lieut. [*Eldred J.*] Simkins of 1st Arty had taken a few of his men to edge of Marsh to West to try and entrap the Yankee Pickets. Lieut. Simkins having moved from his proper place which was the Battery, and his men being dressed in dark blue jackets and Lewis' Men not having observed the movement, they opened fire upon them and broke one man's collar bone. The mistake was not perceived until an unarmed man was sent to inform Lewis that he was firing upon our own men.

I, accompanied by the Sergeant Major [*Gaillard*], arrived just at this time and was fired upon by the Yankee Battery on South Side of this Causeway. 1st a Shell, then Canister, then another Shell. The Canister passed quite over us.

Then went and saw Major Blanding at foot of Grimball's Road. At early dark Simkins men foolishly firing upon the Enemy with Smooth Bore guns at 600 yds, I hastened Capt. Rivers Comd down to the Battery. Took 40 men under Command of Lieut Martin and put them in Charge of the Battery. Then posted 1 N.C.O. & 4 Men at each of the following posts. No. 12, No. 11½, No. 11, No. 10, No. 9½, No. 9, No. 8, No. 7, No. 6, No. 5, No. 4, No. 3, No. 2, No. 1 = 14 Posts x 5 = 70 men + 11 men additional in Battery at Grimball's = 121. Capt. Rivers I put in charge of the Right with his own Co. under Martin & Capt. Witherspoon's Co. with Capt. Witherspoon & Lt. Claiborne.

By the fire of the Enemy's Battery just at dark a Corp[l]. of Co. D. 1st Arty was killed near the Battery at Grimball's Causeway. Sent [*A.T.*] Gaillard for Ambulance to convey away the dead body.

Rode over with Lieut [*Iredell*] Jones, Col. Rhett's Special Adjutant or Aid) to Left Flank and saw Capt. Blake and moved his Section to intersection of Road from Grimball's to Secessionville & Rivers' Road. This was in obedience to orders from Genl. Taliaferro. Capt. Trezevant acting as Support to Blake's Section with 40 men. Lt. Hancock Picketting to Secessionville.

Rode and saw Capt. Smith and then along the front to Grimball's Causeway. The Enemy's Mortar Shells fell very beautifully on the Rivers' Causeway.

Hitched my horse in the rear & went to Battery expecting an attack at Day break. No attack however was made, and withdrew 28 men leaving 12 men in the Battery. The 28 men were disposed behind the hedge.

[*Not signed*]

Tuesday, 5 July 1864

Saw Enemy drilling about 7 A.M.

Nothing occurred until about 10 or 12 O'clock when a formidable line of Yankees made its appearance on the further side of Grimball's Causeway. A line of Infantry extending from the Overseer's House to the South End of Grimball's Causeway (as well as I could see) and in some places this line was doubled. As well as I could judge, the entire line must have been 1 Mile long which would give from 3000 to 5000 men according to the greater or less degree of precision with which they were drawn up.

They then drew up in two lines near the Causeway & commenced firing on our Battery by Battalion, by Wing, by Division, by Company & by platoon. Everything betokened an immediate advance (Distance 750 yds, yet their balls went among us & over us).

I sent for Capt. Rivers to bring his Command behind the hedge where I was stationed and had Capt. Burnett to move his Company forward until pretty nearly on a line with the Battery. They lay down on the field deployed as Skirmishers without any shelter whatever.

The enemy remained in position for one & half or nearly two hours, Marching & Countermarching portions of their lines. At the expiration of that time they withdrew leaving only their pickets & small portions of their forces in position. Blake's Section tried to Shell them from Rivers' Causeway but few of the shells reached. Secesionville also fired upon them & also Battery Pringle but with scarcely any effect, the distance being too great. The Yankees brought up on their side a Section of Light Arty and Shelled Blake's Section which was also Shelled from Long Island.

In the Mean time, two Monitors (*Lehigh* & *Montauk*)[1] 1 Steamer (the *McDonough*)[2] (our old friend of Light House Inlet) and one Mortar Boat (Schooner *Racer*)[3] opened fire upon our position. This fire must have commenced about 12 M. [*Midday*] and continued without intermission. The hedge gave some slight protection to the 28 men of Martin's Command which had been withdrawn from the Battery, also to Witherspoon's Company, but Burnett's men were entirely exposed. Lieut Martin with 12 Men was slightly protected under the Right Epaulement of the Battery, but this protection was slight. A Monitor Shell cut through the Parapet of the Battery behind which they were lying (as it did with the opposite Epaulement) and might have killed many of them.

At about 4 P.M. the Enemy again showed signs of advancing but appeared to intend to try and flank our Right by advancing over the Creek to West of Grimball's Causeway. They set vigorously to work to make a bridge or causeway over said Creek. About this time I received instructions from Gen. Taliaferro not to sacrifice too many of my men in an attempt to hold the position.

At 5.15 P.M. I pretty much made up my mind that if the enemy advanced and we deployed to meet him, with the Gunboats enfilading our lines, that while thus retreating before an overwhelming force and thus enfiladed, our loss would be very severe. I accordingly consulted with Captains Rivers, Burnett & Witherspoon and finding that they fully coincided with me in opinion, I determined to fall back to our 2nd line extending from Grimball's place over to Rivers' Road.

I accordingly drew in our pickets of 4 men to the Right and filing along the hedge in good order we took up our position on the Ditch referred to. Lieut Martin was withdrawn from the Battery last. The Enemy did not attempt to follow, apprehending perhaps an ambuscade for he shelled the intervening woods vigorously for some time.

The Gunboats threw a few shell at us in our new position but not to any great extent. I fully expected to be attacked at Dark and provided for it as far as possible. None was made, however. Later in the evening,

I went up to Head Quarters at Battery No. 2 on an intimation to that effect from Genl. Taliaferro. While Genl. T. was speaking to me I dozed. I returned to the front about 12 or 1 O'clock and being completely worn out, threw my Cloak upon the ground, wet as it was with dew & the rain of Monday and went to sleep in spite of the Moschetoes. This is the first time I have lain down to sleep since I had anything to do with the Picket lines. I got up again at 3 A.M. and had the men waked so as to be ready for an attack at day break. None was made.

[*Not signed*]

¹ *The monitors differed in armament. The Lehigh had a 15-inch Dahlgren smoothbore and an 8-inch Parrott rifle. The Montauk carried two Dahlgren smoothbores, 15 and 11 inch, and two 12-pounder Dahlgren smoothbore boat howitzers.*

² *Armament of the McDonough, a former ferry boat, has not been found in available records.*

³ *The schooner Racer was armed with two 32-pounders and a 13-inch mortar.*

Wednesday, 6 July 1864

At 3½ P.M. I was relieved by Lieut Col. Bacon, 32nd Georgia Vols. & Capt. [*R. Press, Jr*] Smith was relieved by Capt. G. Richardson. As our horses had all broken loose in consequence of a shell bursting near where they were hitched, we were obliged to walk over the whole line in order that I might point out to him everything of importance. Having dined al fresco, I then walked to Battery No. 2 which I reached about dark. While I was there, news came that a large number of Boats & Men were assembling at Swamp Angel Battery and men were sent to Fort Johnson & Legare's Point. I walked to Camp and to bed Completely worn out.

140 men 2nd Arty, 58 men Co. "B" Siege Train & about 102 men of Cavalry formed the Picket to night = 300.

Note. Only one man (Rivers' Co.) wounded through foot by Shrapnel to day about 2 P.M. (Half of his foot Amputated).

[*Not signed*]

Thursday, 7 July 1864

I wrote & rested during morning & went to Hd. Qrs. at Batty No. 2 about Midday.

The 32nd Georgia, 47th Ga. & Bonaud's Battalion ordered to Fort Pemberton to Embark for John's Island. They Marched in the afternoon.

Capt. Humbert appointed as Supt. Pickets for the night & tomorrow. Capt. Dixon [*Dickson*] F.O.D. I got Genl. Taliaferro to order Lt. Col. Brown to furnish 21 men as Pickets from Secessionville to connect with our Left at Rivers' Road.

Picket force, 116 Men 3rd S.C.C. (Colcock's) under Capt. Peeples & 84 men of 2nd Arty under Capt. Rickenbaker & Lt. [*T.H.*] Jones. Total 200.

I agreed with Capt. Humbert that I would Superintend the left while he superintended the Right in posting the pickets.

I rode down to Secessionville and saw Col. Brown about his pickets. Found that there was some mistake, as Lieut Damarin did not connect his pickets with the left of our line. Our pickets mistook Lt. Damarin for one of the enemy, and forming the arc of a circle the[y] caught him. In consequence of this mistake and our 21 men being already posted, I did not alter the arrangement and had to keep Capt. Humbert's Co. on duty.

Col. Bacon was relieved late. I returned to Camp about 10½ to 11 P.M.

[Not signed]

Friday, 8 July 1864

The Gunboats commenced firing heavily upon Battery Pringle this morning. The *Pawnee* firing her bow and stern Pivot Guns, probably 100 pndr. Rifles.[1] The Steam ferry Boat (The *McDonough*) [fired] her heavy Bow Gun. The Monitors [*Lehigh and Montauk*] their 15 inch Guns and two Mortar Schooners [*Para and Racer*] their 13 inch Shells.[2] A good deal of damage was done to Battery Pringle.

Col. Frederick was to day relieved from the charge of the West Lines and Col. Rhett put in Command.

The Yankees have evidently landed a large force on John's Island, and it is supposed are erecting Batteries at Gervais' plantation with which to attack Batteries Pringle & Tynes and enfilade our lines. Their base is at "Legare's Point House" where there appear Many tents and Much Army material.

My Tour of duty to-night as Supt. Pickets and Capt. Kennedy [*Kennady*] F.O.D. Countersign "Olivia." 200 men 1st S.C. Arty.[3] made the Guard. Capt. Rivers in Command. Captains Burnett, Witherspoon and [*J. Hamilton*] Warley in Comd of their Companies.

Col. Brown furnished 1 Officer & 21 Men to picket from Left of our line to Secessionville.

I went & posted the Pickets & Skirmishers on our Right Flank. Relieved Dr. Goethe at request of Senior Surgeon Lebby. Dr. Turner Surgeon in Centre. Dr. Rivers Surgeon on Left. Night passed quietly. Mortar Boats kept up fire on Pringle every 15 Minutes throughout the night.

One man of Witherspoon's Company wounded in hip by his Comrade on picket line. He had stepped to the rear for a Moment & in returning was fired on.

One or more Steamers plying all night between Battery Island and Legare's Point House on John's Island. Probably conveying troops over to John's Island.

[Not signed]

---

[1] At this date, the Pawnee was armed with a 100-pounder Parrott rifle, a 50-pounder

Dahlgren rifle, and ten 9-inch Dahlgren smoothbores, two more than she had during the engagement at Legareville (see 25 Dec. 1863, note). [ONR II (1) Ship Statistics]

[2] The Racer was armed with two 32-pounder smoothbores and a 13-inch mortar. The Para, although she later carried a 13-inch mortar, at this date was armed with two 32-pounder smoothbores, one 12-pounder rifle, probably a Dahlgren, and two 20-pounder Parrott rifles. [ONR II (1) Ship Statistics]

[3] Manigault was mistaken. The men were in the 1st Rgt. S.C. Infantry (Regulars), also known as 3rd Rgmt., S.C. Arty.]

Saturday, 9 July 1864

At 3 A.M. had the men waked & ready to repel attack if made.

At 4.45 A.M. by my watch, heard heavy roll of musketry on John's Island near Gervais' House. This musketry continued sharp & heavy until 4.52½ = 27½ Minutes, only 3 or 4 discharges of Cannon. The Musketry ceased altogether.

At 5.48 the Sound of Musketry was again heard accompanied by a good deal of Artillery firing. This action appeared to extend over a much larger space than the first. The firing lasted about half an hour.[1]

At Day break the *Pawnee* Commenced firing on Pringle with her Rifle Guns, also the Steam Ferry Boat [*McDonough*], also the two Monitors [*Lehigh and Montauk*], also two Wiard Guns on the decks of the Monitors.[2] The mortar boats also continued their firing.

The day intensely hot. The Yankees did not fire a single shot upon us until in the afternoon when they shelled the Battery at Grimball's.

Rode down to Secessionville in the afternoon and recommended modification of line of pickets. Then rode to Camp. Found order for my Relief.

Capt. Dickson to act as Supt. Pickets to night. Capt. Stallings F.O.D. Picket force 92 of 1st Arty, 108 of 2nd Arty = 200 men.

Rode down with Capt. Dickson & Supervised posting of Right Wing of Pickets. Returned to Camp 10 or 11 P.M. Yankees had large fires on West bank Stono River below Gervais.

Should have stated that saw some Yankees still remained on James Island (near further end of Grimball's Causeway) but not numerous.

Yankees sent fire Rafts against the Bridge between Pringle & Tynes but our men contrived to keep them off.[3]

[*Not signed*]

[1] The fighting on John's Island was part of the overall demonstration against Charleston (see 2 July 1864, note). The Federals landed on the island 2 July and withdrew on the 9th after beating off Confederate assaults in the morning. Northern casualties during the entire period amounted to 11 dead, 71 wounded and an unspecified number missing. The Confederates lost more than 100 in killed and wounded on the 9th. Their previous casualties, if any, were not reported. [OR XXXV (1) pp. 85, 86, 123]

[2] Dahlgrens, not Wiards. See 5 July 1864, note 1, armament of the monitors.

[3] The bridge was across the Stono River between James and John's Islands. The James Island end was between Batteries Pringle and Tynes.

Sunday, 10 July 1864

Slept rather late. During morning writing and reading papers &c.

Note. A Small body of Cavalry about 30 in number seen on Dixon's Island afternoon of the 10th. [*This note was inserted, apparently later, above the date of this diary entry*]

In evening relieved Capt. Dickson as Supt. of Pickets & Capt. Guignard Richardson relieved Capt. Stallings as F.O.D.

All the Gunboats withdrew from their position in Stono River to the Reach below towards Legareville, except one Monitor which maintained her position just below Grimball's until dark when she also withdrew.

Yankee forces appear to have all withdrawn from John's Island; large numbers were seen to Cross the lower part of James Island going towards Folly Island. The lookout Man in the Secessionville Observatory reports (5) five Regiments seen to Cross.

Troops forming Picket Relief.

72 Men form Capt. Dickson's Command, 2nd Arty, posted on Right.

54 Men Co. "B" S.C. Siege Train, Lieuts [*John B.W.*] Phillips & Spivey, posted   on Left.

50 Men Capt. Peeples' Comd., 3rd S.C. Cavalry, Left Centre.

24 Men Lt. Bush, 2nd Arty, whom we could not relieve and hence   they were retained (48h[*ours*])

—————

200

21 from Secessionville formed the Secessionville Picket on our left.

Yankees burnt down the "Overseer's House" and made large fires on the same line after dark. A Steamer in Schooner Creek soon after Commenced throwing Mortar Shells in vicinity of North End of Grimball's Causeway. This was continued all night & until after day light next morning.

The *Pawnee* also fired regularly & steadily every 10 or 15 Minutes on John's Island.

[Not signed]

Monday, 11 July 1864

Early in Morning sent out a Scouting party on Peninsula. They saw no Yankees from the Stone House. My glass could discover no Yankees in any direction.

About 8 or 8½ A.M. the two Monitors [*Lehigh and Montauk*], the *Pawnee*, the Armed Ferry Boat [*McDonough*], two (2) transport Steamers all left their anchorages and went down the River.

Rode with Genl. Taliaferro & Col. Rhett to Grimball's Causeway, saw no signs of the Yankees. Sent out 5 Scouts of Trezevant's Co. 1st S.C.C. to scout as far as Battery Island. They reported that they saw no Yankees.

At 1 P.M. I left Capt. G. Richardson, F.O.D. in Charge of the Line and went to see Adjt. Boylston about the detail for the night.

Returned to Camp at 1.30 and immediately threw myself on bed and slept til 3 P.M. Dined.

At 6 P.M. met troops at Battery No. 2. <u>Capt. Humbert F.O.D.</u>

100 Men 5th Georgia Vols. went down to day about 4 P.M. to relieve Dickson's Men & Bush's men.

80 Men 5 Ga. Vols.	Sent down to Left flank with
20 Men Peeple's Comd. 3 S.C.C.	Capt. Humbert.
200	

21 Men from Secessionville.

I rode down and posted the first hundred men above referred to on Right Flank. Note that we re-established the line on front between Grimball's & Rivers' Causeway. [*This note is repeated on the margin of the diary as:* Line between Rivers and Grimballs Causeways reestablished to night]. Reserve of 50 Men in Battery at Grimball's and 12 Posts to Right — 4 Men each = 48. Two Captains & Two Lieuts at the Reserve. Two Lieuts & 4 N.C.O. at the Right posts.

Returned to Camp at 10 P.M.

Note. The Detachment of 5 Companies of 1st Infantry returned to Sullivan's Island this evening.[1]

[*Not signed*]

[1] *The unit had arrived on James Island 2 July 1864.*

Tuesday, 12 July 1864

Intensely hot in the Morning. Did not go out.

In afternoon at 6 P.M. went to [*Headquarters at*] Battery No. 2. Capt. Kennedy [*Kennady*] F.O.D. reported for duty. Also 100 men of 47th Georgia Vols. Also 20 men of 1st S.C. Cav. were ordered to report.

Put 50 men under charge of Capt. Kennedy [*Kennady*] to post on the left, and posted the Right Pickets myself, with reserve of 15 at Battery at Grimball's Causeway.

About 9 P.M. 20 soldiers of 1st S.C. Cav. reported under Lieut. Blassinghame.

As the Capt. of 5th Georgia, who was relieved, reported firing from the [?] Island this afternoon, I did not think proper to advance the videttes beyond our infantry Line, during the night, but directed Capt. Kennedy [*Kennady*] to have it done soon after day break.

I returned to Camp, i.e. left the line, about 11 O'clock.

[*Not signed*]

Wednesday, 13 July 1864

Batteries Gregg & Wagner fired 161 Shots on Sumter from 8 A.M. to 6 P.M.[1]

About 10 A.M. rode down to the Front. Overtaken by Col. Rhett and his A.D.C. Iredell Jones. Rode over to Peninsula which has been picketted by our Cavalry since day break. The Yankees have done a good deal of work and have thrown up a double line of intrenchments across the Western portion of Peninsula.

They have raised & strengthened the Bank and ditch to East of the Overseer's House in some places planting Sharpened Stakes & Abattis in front of it. They have a second line of Entrenchments about ¼ mile to West of the first. Both of these are extended down to the marsh on either flank.

They have also thrown up rough intrenchments on the Edge of the Marsh through which flows Grimball's Creek and where there was already a high Dam they have established an abbatis about 50 to 75 yds. in front.

They have also Commenced a Causeway leading from the Peninsula over towards Post No. 1 Stono Islands in order that they might be able to turn our Right Flank. This Causeway is not more than one quarter completed.

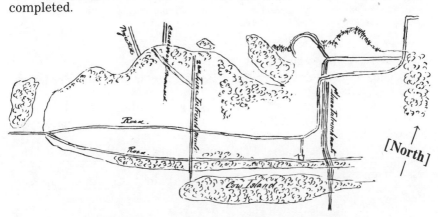

Manigault's sketch of the Federal defenses.

In short, the whole of the Peninsula from Grimball's Causeway Westwards was being converted into a strong intrenched Camp which could not be taken without great sacrifice of life. This portion of the Peninsula was to form their base of operations. The other portions were not altered or fortified in any respect.

Rode with Capt. Kennedy [*Kennady*] inspecting Eastern & Middle portions of peninsula, then returned to Camp at 1½ P.M. Day intensely hot.

Saw 8 bodies of negro Soldiers killed in the attack on Blake's Section July 2.

Note. That there was a Sling Cart at Battery on Dickson's Island and also a Garrison Gin used in Mounting a Gun. I have no doubt but that the "Dummies" have been removed and real guns substituted in their places. The one looking towards "Overseer's House" seemed to me to be a 30 pndr. Parrott.

At 6 P.M. went to Battery No 2. 100 Men of 10th N.C. Battalion of Heavy Artillery formed the Picket force to night together with 20 of 1st S.C. Cav.

Gave 50 Men of 10th N.C. Batt. to Capt. Stallings F.O.D. to post on the Left and took 50 men myself and posted them on Stono Posts & reserve Station on Grimball's Causeway.

All quiet on the Front. Returned to Camp at 9.45 P.M.

Some rain at night, or rather towards Morning.

[*Not signed*]

[1] *This was part of the Third Major Bombardment of Fort Sumter. Maj. Gen. John G. Foster, who had recently assumed command of the Department of the South, decided that Fort Sumter had never been properly demolished. He ordered the bombardment to correct this oversight. It began 7 July 1864, although not mentioned by Maj. Manigault on that date, and lasted until 4 Sept. Some 14,600 shot and shell were fired at the fort and cost the garrison 16 dead and 65 wounded. Foster also planned to shake down the walls by floating rafts loaded with explosives against the base of the fort. However, these "torpedo rafts," as they were called, exploded harmlessly a short distance away. Damage to the bastion, as in previous bombardments, was repaired at night and when the guns fell silent, the fort was as strong as ever.*

Thursday, 14 July 1864

Busy in Camp all day in writing a Report required by Col. Frederick. Very heavy fire on Fort Sumter.

About 5 or 5½ P.M. the Battery on Dickson's Island opened on Some Cavalry Videttes we had on the peninsula and crippled one of the horses.

The Detachment of the 1st Artillery returned to Sullivan's Island this Evening at 6 P.M.

Col. Rhett having left, Col. Frederick again in Command of West Line.

77 men of 10th Battalion N.C. Heavy Arty. |
23 men of 47th Regt. Georgia Vols. | formed picket force.

Also 20 Men 1st S.C. Cav. under Lieut Miller. Cavalry Videttes on the Front.

Capt. Humbert F.O.D.

I posted the Right Pickets. Capt. Humbert the left.

Returned to Camp at 11.15 P.M.

From 8 A.M. to 6 P.M. Batteries Gregg & Wagner fired 254 Shots on Fort Sumter.

[*Not signed*]

Friday, 15 July 1864

Sent in my Report to Col. Frederick about 11 A.M.

Adjutant Gardner went into City on leave for the day. Very heavy firing on Fort Sumter.

One Hundred Men (100) from 2nd S.C. Arty went on Picket at 6 P.M. relieving the 10th N.C. Battalion & 7th Ga. Vols.[1]

Capt. Fulton of 5th Ga. Vol. F.O.D. Lieut Bolivar Commanded Right from Grimball's landing to Grimball's Causeway. Lieut. J.B. Connor Commanded Left from Grimball's Causeway to Rivers' Road.

Lieut in Command (Ratchford) of 20 Men of 1st S.C. Cav. posted his men on the front. About Midnight Several Shots were fired by the Cavalry and they immediately afterwards dashed in, saying that they had fired upon a party of Yankees. Capt. Fulton rode forward and could see nothing, and the videttes were posted again.

I returned to Camp at 10.15 P.M.

[*Not signed*]

¹*Manigault obviously meant 47th Ga. Vols. See picket force 14 July 1864.*

Saturday, 16 July 1864

Very heavy firing upon Sumter.

At 9.15 A.M. started for a complete examination of the Front & returned to Camp at 2.45 P.M. = 5½ hours.

The enemy is very busy improving and repairing the 3-gun Battery on Dixon's Island, also in cutting down all the the trees immediately surrounding. I think also a Glacis is being constructed towards the water. All the working parties were Composed of Negroes and so indeed were all whom I saw. The Camp at that point appears sufficient for about 2 Companies.

None of the Enemy are to be seen on James Island nor on Battery Island.

Note. The direct distance from End to End of Grimball's Causeway is about 750 yds. by my Stepping. Making allowance for my having Stepped short, say 700 yds.

Note. From papers picked up on lower end of James Island it would appear that some of the troops on the Island on 6, 7 & 9th July were "103rd N.Y. Vol. with 2 field & Staff, 9 line Officers, 251 Enlisted men" for duty.

21st U.S.C.F. (Coloured Forces?) 228 Enlisted men, A.G. Bennett, Lt. Col. Comdg.

Also the 54th Massachusetts Vol. appears to have been present.

"Brig Genl. Schimmelfennig" appears to have been in Command. W.B. Dean, Lieut & a.a.a. Genl.

In evening there was some delay in consequence of a horse wanting for Capt. Kiddoo, 5th Ga. Vols. F.O.D.

The 5th Ga. Vol. furnished the picket of 100 men, under Capt. Burroughs [*Burrus*] (Columbus [*Ga.*]), Lieut Barrett (Augusta [*Ga.*]), Lieut [*later Capt. John*] Thompson and Lieut, Name not Known.

After inspecting the whole picket, I returned to Camp at 10 P.M.

Wind North and East and very high tides.

[*Not signed*]

Sunday, 17 July 1864

Remained in Camp all day.

At 6 P.M. went to Battery No. 2. 100 men from Bonaud's Battalion reported for Picket duty. Lieut Lawrence Comdg, Lieut Walton assisting.

Also 20 Men from 1st S.C.C. for picket service on Extreme Front reported 4½ P.M.

Capt. Hurt, 5th Ga. Vols. F.O.D.

Posted in person all the Right Pickets and verified those on the Left.

Heavy Rain about 9 P.M. and lighter rain all night. Wind East. Very high tides.

Returned to Camp at 10.45 P.M. Pretty wet.

[Not signed]

Monday, 18 July 1864

Busy in Camp all day. Heavy firing on Fort Sumter.

At 6 P.M. went to Battery No. 2. 100 Men from 47th Ga. Vols. for Picket duty, Capt. Sheffield Comdg, Lieut[s]. Patterson, Potter & [*Omitted in diary.*]

Also 20 Men from 1st S.C.Cav. under Lieut. White on Extreme front as Videttes.

The Battery on Dixon's Island commenced firing on the Pickets about 6 O'clock and continued until dark. No damage done.

Capt. Guignard Richardson, F.O.D.

I posted all the Pickets on the Right and then verified those on the Left. Some confusion about the Cavalry Pickets, which however I left the F.O.D. to rectify.

Returned to Camp at 9.15 P.M.

Made Report to Col. Frederick immediately after my return.

Some rain during the night. Very high tides. The Moon in Perigee & full tomorrow morning.

[Not signed]

Tuesday, 19 July 1864

Heavy firing on Fort Sumter,   356 Shots in day.

<u>199 shots at night.</u>

555 Total.

Busy all day in verifying & signing Muster & Pay Rolls of Lucas' Battalion for June 1864, the late attack on Battery Pringle [*9 July 1864*] having prevented their being made up before.

In afternoon returned Muster & Pay Rolls to Lieuts. Moses & Martin of Cos. "A" and "B" [*should be "B" and "A"*] of Lucas' Battalion.

100 Men from 5th Ga. Vols, Capt. King, for Picket duty to night and 20 men of 1st S.C. Cav. for advanced Picket. As the Yankees have been shelling us from Dixon's Island, I did not move the Relief down until dark.

Capt. Kennedy [*Kennady*], 2nd Arty, F.O.D. Posted all the right pickets myself and verified the others. Rode and saw some of the Videttes and altered their position somewhat.

Lt. Barton, who is both a physician and an Ordnance Officer, was out on a tour in search of Skeletons & 15-inch Shells.

Returned to Camp at 12.20 A.M.

[Not signed]

Wednesday, 20 July 1864

Heavy firing on Fort Sumter. 425 Shots in all.

Busy about Monthly Returns. Rain during Morning.

Capt. Humbert F.O.D. 100 Men (nominally but only 90 in fact) of the 10th N.C. Battalion of Heavy Arty formed Picket. 20 men from 1st S.C.C. formed videttes.

Firing during afternoon from Long Island Battery and also three or four shots fired from Dixon's Island.

Posted myself the Right Pickets, and verified the others. Only 2 Pickets to left Rivers' Causeway.

Returned to Camp at 11 P.M.

Capt. John C. Mitchell [*Mitchel*][1] was mortally wounded about 1 P.M. at Fort Sumter to day. He died about 5 P.M.

[*Not signed*]

[1] *See biography, Appendix 3, pp. 286, 287.*

Thursday, 21 July 1864

Heavy firing on Fort Sumter. Batty. Gregg [*fired*] 288 Shots.

At 9 A.M. Set off for City. Busy till 2½ P.M. Intensely hot. Rain at 5½ or 6 P.M. Left City shortly after 7 P.M. Became very dark & heavy Rain. Wind N.E.

Got back to Camp about 9 P.M. Heavy Rain.

Some difficulty about the Picket Relief. Order had not been extended. My adjutant was at Battery No. 2 by my direction at the proper time and waited there but no Relief reported. The Reliefs were not posted till 11 or 12 O'clock.

Bonaud's Battalion furnished 100 men. The 1st S.C.C. 20 men.

Capt. Sheffield F.O.D. Rain all night.

"Kirk's Squadron"[1] I met near S.C.R.R. Depot (in Spring St.) The 10th N.C. Battn. Heavy Arty went off to day [*to N.C. where this unit had been stationed previously*].

[*Not signed*]

[1] *Kirk's Squadron, S.C. Partisan Rangers, Capt. Manning J. Kirk, commander.*

Friday, 22 July 1864

(From 8 A.M. to 6 P.M. Battery Gregg fired 252 Shots upon Sumter)

Cool, Foggy or Misty day, with occasional light Showers. Wind N.E.

Capt. S.P. Smith went off to Pon Pon [*south of Charleston near Parker's Ferry*] on 48 hours' furlough.

Very busy all day in Making up My Quarterly account of Ordnance. Went in afternoon with it to Lieut Barton.

The 5th Ga. Vol. furnished 100 men for picket duty. Capt. O'Connor Comdg & 3 Lieutenants.

The 1st S.C.C. furnished 20 men for vidette duty on the front.

Capt. Jos. Dedge (47th Ga. Vol.)

At 7 P.M. went with picket and posted those on Right, then verified those on left. The officers appeared intelligent & efficient. Night very dark at first but after the Moon rose (though dim & obscured) there was light enough. Very high tide.

Returned to Camp at 10.45 P.M.

[Not signed]

Saturday, 23 July 1864

Cool, cloudy day. Heavy firing on Fort Sumter. 155 Shots from Batt. Gregg. None from Wagner.

Busy at my Quarterly Return of Ordnance. Handed it to Lieut. Barton's Office at 2.30 P.M.

Dark evening. Capt. Lawrence 47th Ga. Vol. F.O.D. Lieut A.A. Connor with 70 Men 2nd Arty & Lieut [*John B.W.*] Phillips with 30 Men Co. "B" S.C. Siege Tr. formed the Infantry Picket. Lieut Horsey with 20 men 1st S.C.C. the Cavalry Picket. Posted the Right pickets in person by which time the night became intensely dark. Tried to pass along the line from Grimball's to Rivers' Causeway. My horse totally unable to keep the path. Therefore, as Lieut. Phillips & his men were thoroughly instructed and thoroughly acquainted with the ground, I did not persevere, but returned to Camp at 10.45 P.M.

It Commenced raining before I got to Camp and rained more or less during the night, i.e. "a Scotch Mist" or light winter rain. Night quite cool, fire would have been pleasant.

Received this afternoon news of great battle fought by Hood against Sherman [*Peachtree Creek, 20 July 1864, or Atlanta on the 22nd*].

[Not signed]

Sunday, 24 July 1864

Cold, rainy day, wind N.E., like a rainy day in April. Fire would have been pleasant.

Firing on Fort Sumter. 71 Shots from Gregg. None from Wagner.

Disposition to clear up about 2 P.M. The sun came out. Rained again afterwards.

100 men from 47th Ga. Vol. formed infantry Picket, Lieut Bourquine Comdg. Lieut Potter on the Right. Lieut Chesser on the Left. 20 men 1st S.C.C. acted as videttes.

Capt. Colhoun F.O.D. All quiet on Front.

Posted the Right Pickets myself and verified the others.

Returned to Camp at 10.15 P.M. Clear Starlight night. Wind N.W. Night quite cold. My sleeping was prevented by the cold.

Two of the videttes fired about 1 or 2 A.M. and ran in. They say their fire was returned, but it is supposed that they were simply scared.

[Not signed]

Monday, 25 July 1864

(Water in Bucket very cold in the morning) Not a clear day, but still there was some sun. Very little wind, atmosphere Hazy.

Busy all morning in making out number of Shots fired by 30 Pndr. Parrott guns for Lieut. H.C. Cunningham, Ord. Officer. Sent it in about 4 P.M.

Capt. Fulton 47th Georgia[1] F.O.D. Bonaud's Battn. furnished 100 men for pickets, Lieut. Irvine or Irving [Irwin] Comdg. Lieut Kendrick assisting. 1st S.C.C. furnished 20 men under Lieut Hancock for Vidette duty.

Posted the right Pickets myself and verified the others. Night star light but not clear.

Returned to Camp at 10.40 P.M.

An alarm at [Battery] Haskell at 2 A.M. It turned out to be nothing but the Yankee Picket Boats.

[Not signed]

[1] No Capt. Fulton has been found in personnel records of the 47th. This probably was Capt. John A. Fulton, Co. E, 5th Rgmt., Ga. Inf.

Tuesday, 26 July 1864

Cloudy Morning but clear day. Wind East. Sun hot, but day cool for season.

Went to see Col. Frederick on business & he examined my Map of James Island. [Not found]

Afterwards went to Genl. Taliaferro's on an intimation from him about the horses of the Siege Train and other Matters.

In afternoon some shell thrown at our Pickets from Dixon's Island & Long Island.

The 5th Georgia furnished 100 men for picket duty. Capt. Duffie [Duffey] Comdg. Lieut Neely Commanded the Right Pickets, Capt. Duffie [Duffey] the Battery at Grimball's Causeway, Lieut Snipes the Left Centre pickets & Lieut Jennings the left Pickets. The 1st S.C.C. furnished 20 men under Lieut Blassinghame for picket duty. Posted the Right pickets in person and verified the Left.

Returned to Camp at 10.50 P.M.

Capt. Guignard Richardson F.O.D.

At a little after Moonrise, say 12½ to 1 A.M. some of the videttes fired off their pieces and ran in over Rivers' Causeway. They say that they were first fired on by a party of Yankees and then they returned the fire and went in. Six men in all came in, the Coolest and Steadiest of them after 20 minutes delay. The two Videttes on extreme left did not come in but continued out all night. One of these latter said that perhaps he saw 1 Man, but that he was too distant to fire on. None of them could vouch for having Seen more than 4 men, but some said that they heard a considerable party in the bushes. Five of the Videttes were sent out again but on foot to the further end of the Causeway (Rivers).

They said they saw a considerable number of Men and fired on them. They dodged back in the bushes and were not again seen.

At daylight the Cavalry again took their horses and were posted in the day Posts. I rode to several of the posts and spied on the Dixon's Island Battery from the Stone House. Gun to East Mounted En barbette. Gun to North on Siege Carriage, probably 30 pndr. Parrott. The third gun I could not see. I am doubtful if the first mentioned gun is a real one or not. There is a Berm Constructed around the Battery and either on that berm or in a ditch inside of it, there is a complete row of Sharpened Stakes driven into the Ground. Also all the trees round the Battery have been cut down and disposed as abbatis. The work in its present condition is pretty strong against assault.

I counted about 12 Wall Tents & about 25 Army tents back of the Battery; also about 15 Shanties or Flies at the Picket Station near the Causeway. I think that one or two Companies could be accom[m]odated. The Stringers & plank of the Bridge are taken up.

Returned to Camp at about 6½ A.M.

[*Not signed*]

Wednesday, 27 July 1864

Busy writing &c. Took about 1 hour's nap. Went out at 1 P.M. with a fatigue force and dug a well for videttes & their horses at the Stone House. Also another well to north of Rivers Causeway.

The Enemy still busy in improving their defences on Dixon's Island. In some places in front of their battery they have a double row of Stakes.

Saw two boats towing from Folly Island up toward the Dixon's Island Battery two singular Structures, the nature of which I could not make out. They looked like exaggerations of Indian boats or canoes or proas with high heads & sterns.

Manigault's drawing of boats towing two "singular structures."

These non-descripts towed badly and sometimes turned cross ways to the direction in which the men were trying to tow them. I then could see that the heads & sterns did not apparently come to a point but seemed to be as wide as the Midship Section and also that the whole seemed to be built of plank.

Perhaps these are flat Arches built of plank, to support the Roadway of one of their foot Bridges. They were carried into the Creek which makes up into the Marsh back of Dixon's Island Battery.

About 5½ P.M. I went to see what was the disposition of the Secessionville Pickets. I found 1 Lieut, 1 Sergeant & 21 Men of the 1st Georgia Regulars at the reserve station. The Lieutenant told me that he had received orders to post one picket at the End of the Bank and ditch leading Southwards down to the Marsh, two pickets to left at 50 yds. apart and 4 Pickets to Right at 50 yds. apart. I cannot tell where this absurd arrangement originated, but it is totally at variance with the directions I gave July 9th which was to post the pickets at uniform intervals from Fort Lamar to the left of our line at Rivers's Marsh Road.

This arrangement pickets heavily where the Marsh is wide & deep & cannot well be crossed and leaves an interval of about 600 yds. between our left flank and their right flank...and leaves totally without observation the portion where the Creek Comes up to the high land. I did not alter the directions as the orders given to the officer may have Come from higher authority (L^t. Col. Brown) but I determined to represent this error immediately to Genl. Taliaferro.

Rode to Battery No. 2 and gave instructions to F.O.D. & the other Officers of the Pickets and then went to Camp about 7.45 P.M. as I had been on duty for 24 hours. Night very hot & sultry and moschetoes bad.

Capt. Kiddoo F.O.D. 2nd Arty, 70 men, Lieut[s] Mosley & A.A. Connor. Co. "B" Siege Train, 20 men, Lieut Spivey Comdg. As we had only 90 men I had to leave out two Posts on the Stono Line.

1st S.C.C. 20 men, under a lieutenant.

Night was quiet.

[*Not signed*]

Thursday, 28 July 1864

Busy all morning in Tent.

At 5½ P.M. went down to the Secessionville pickets and made a new arrangement in posting of the pickets, placing the Right Picket where the Creek makes up to the high land and the others at nearly uniform distances between it and the left flank about 125 yds. apart.

Rode to Battery No. 2 and gave instructions to F.O.D. Capt. Hurt, 5th Ga. Vol. and to the Officers of Pickets.

100 Men furnished by 47th. Ga. for Pickets, 1 Capt. and 2 Lieutenants.

20 men furnished by 1st S.C.C. as Videttes. 1 Lieut (Henkerson) [*Hankinson*].

Rode to Col. Frederick and made arrangements about sending down barrels for wells on the Front.

To Camp about 8 P.M. or 8½. Hot night. Moschetoes very bad.

There was some alarm among our Videttes. One, an old soldier, says he distinctly saw four men stooping and running along in an open place apparently making for the nearest cover to his left & rear. He was stationed where the straight road from the Stone House to rear intersects the high bank & ditch. He fired at them and fell back 40 or 50 yds and reloaded, his companion accompanying him. Two or three of the Videttes came in to the line of infantry pickets. Probably there were Yankee scouting parties out.

[*Not signed*]

Friday, 29 July 1864

About 9 O'clock or perhaps as early as 8 A.M. The Battery on Dixon's Island commenced shelling our picket lines. One 10 inch Columbiad shell was thrown into Rampart of Breastwork at Grimball's Causeway and taken out unexploded.

As soon as I had got through the Morning's work, I rode down on the front. Went to Extreme end of the Stono Islands and made all possible observation on the enemy's front. No Yankees whatever on the "Peninsula" or on Battery Island. Some 26 Tents visible in rear of Battery on Horse Island (nearest to Battery Island) but it is probable that there are others between those seen, a clump of woods serving as a screen. I estimate accommodation for 100 to 150 men. Not many men, however, visible. I saw 8 vessels in Stono. Probably there were more.

I then rode along the front expecting a shot every moment, but none was fired. Rode with Lieut. Henkerson [*Hankinson*] to visit his posts and gave him fresh instructions. At the "Stone House" and the Post beyond, I stopped some time and observed Dixon's Island as exactly as I could with my glass. There appears to be one 10 inch Columbiad or 9 in Dahlgren, I could not tell which at the distance, mounted on [*the*] East flank, one 30 pndr. Parrott on Siege Carriage in Centre and another gun on the West flank (this last, however, I could not see, but I told the videttes to watch closely when they fired and report to me the number & position of the Guns; and it is from this information that I report the third gun on the left flank of the work.) Some 50 tents visible behind the battery but not many men visible. Accommodation for 200 to 250 men.

I then went to the reserve Station of the Secessionville pickets and gave the Lieut. in charge precise instructions as to posts &c. While here witnessed an Artillery duel between Fort Lamar & the Long Island Battery in which the latter appeared to get the worst of it. Fort Lamar exploded five or six shells with the utmost precision in and about the Long Island Battery and the latter ceased firing. The firing commenced from the Long Island battery at about 2½ P.M. and it was apparently silenced in about half an hour. Fort Lamar, however, continued firing some time longer.

I returned to Camp about 3½ P.M. having been on front about 6 hours.

Had a well dug at Reserve Station near Grimball's Causeway and a Tierce carried down after dark to be used as a Curb or Kerb.[1]

The 5th Ga. Vol. furnished 100 men under Capt. Rowlin [*Rowland*] with 3 Lieutenants.

The 1st S.C.C. furnished 20 men, 1 Lieutenant (Young).

Capt. Dedge, 47th Ga. F.O.D.

Rode down to Grimball's Causeway and remained till nearly all the pickets were posted.

Got back to Camp at 9.45 P.M.

I should have stated that about 5 O'clock in the evening the "Dixon's Island Battery" Shelled our Picket lines for some time, but without doing any damage. Evidently one or more heavy guns were used.

Repeated Showers during the day. Weather Sultry. Moschetoes & gnats troublesome.

A great many tents on Folly Island, but I cannot see many men.

Our Cavalry Videttes had an alarm early in the night. They say that the enemy fired two shots on one of the posts which they returned with three. All the Cavalry came in, but they were sent out again and remained until morning.

[Not signed]

¹ See 18 June 1864, note.

Saturday, 30 July 1864

Busy all morning in Camp. About 5 P.M. heavy rain.

The 2nd Arty furnished 100 men. Capt. Humbert commanded at Grimball's Causeway. Lieut J.B. Connor Commanded Stono Pickets. Lieut Bush Commanded at Rivers' Causeway.

The 1st S.C. Cav. furnished 20 men & 1 Lieut (Livingston.)

Capt. S.R. Lawrence, 47th. Ga. Vol. F.O.D.

Went down with the Picket. Returned to Camp at 10.15 P.M. The night had cleared off and was good Starlight. Moschetoes very bad.

No firing whatever by the Yankees on our Picket Front to day.

Lt. Spivey went off on 10 day furlough to day. Capt. [S. Porcher] Smith & Lieut Nesbit went to City on leave for the day.

[Not signed]

Sunday, 31 July 1864

(During Saturday & Sunday Batty. Gregg fired 468 shots on Sumter. Sunday the Sullivan's Island Batteries fired 111 shots on Battery Gregg. Gregg returned 31.) [Parenthetical material is appended above the 31 July 1864 date]

Writing all morning. Very heavy & continuous firing in direction of the Harbor.

Capt. Humbert relieved as Comdg. Off. Pickets because he ranked Capt. Lawrence of 47th Ga. F.O.D. Lieut [T.H.] Jones, Co. "H" [2nd Artillery] went on to make up the complement of officers.

Capt. S.P. Smith F.O.D. 47th Ga. furnished 100 men. Lieut Bourquine Comdg with 2 other Lieuts.

1st S.C.C. 20 men as videttes under Lt. Crews.

Rode down with relief and passed along the lines. The Enemy have been perfectly quiet to day. Not a gun fired on the front.

Returned to Camp at 10.20 P.M. Very heavy thunder Shower about 11 P.M.

All quiet at night.

No Corn for horses.

[Not signed]

Monday, 1 August 1864

Battery Gregg fired 162 shots on Sumter. Sullivan's Island 61 Shots at Gregg. Battery Gregg 45 Shots at Sull. Isld.

At 10½ A.M. Rode down to Picket front. Gave fresh instructions to the Lieutenant in Command of the Secessionville pickets. Visited all the Left pickets on the Peninsula. Observed closely with my glass from the Stone House the Dixon's Island Battery, and also the tents on Folly Island. Could see no change.

Went down to Extremity of Stono Islands. No sign of Yankees on Peninsula or Battery Island. Same number of tents on Horse Island as there were on Friday last, viz. 26 to 30.

Returned to Camp about 3½ P.M.

Measured to day the Shell thrown by Left Gun on Dixon's Island Battery. It was a 10 inch Columbiad Shell. [See Friday, 29 July 1864]

Went down with Relief at 7 P.M.

Capt. Guignard Richardson F.O.D. 5th Regt. Ga. Vol. 100 men, Lt. [Name omitted in Diary] Comdg. at Grimball's Causeway. Lieut. Hightower Commanded Right at Grimball's Causeway. Lt. [Name omitted in Diary] the left.

1st S.C. Cav. 20 men under Lt. Roberts.

Enemy have been perfectly quiet to day.

Returned to Camp about 9 or 9½ P.M.

Note. The 1st Georgia Regulars were withdrawn from Secessionville to day and sent to Savannah. The 47th Georgia Vols. put in their place.

No Corn for horses.

[Not signed]

Tuesday, 2 August 1864

100 Shots fired by Batty. Gregg at Fort Sumter. 39 Shells thrown into Charleston.

Enemy fired several shots on our pickets about 9 A.M.

Busy all morning in Camp. In afternoon at 7 P.M. Rode down to Picket Front.

Capt. Colhoun F.O.D. 75 men from 2nd Arty, Lt. Kitchens Comdg. and 25 men from Co. "B" S.C. Siege Train Lieut [John B.W.] Phillips Comdg, formed the Picket.

1st S.C. Cav. 20 men as Videttes. Lieut White.

Lieut Phillips with Co. "B" on Stono Posts. Lieut Kitchens at Grimball's Causeway. Lieut Bolivar at Rivers' Causeway.

Got to Camp late, probably 11 P.M. Had no light and could not see the hour by my watch.

No Corn for horses.

[Not signed]

Wednesday, 3 August 1864

Tuesday night Gregg fired 169 Shots at Sumter & 4 at City. Wednesday 29 at Sumter & 14 at Sull. Isld. Sull. I. fired 20 Shots back. Small number owning to Flag of Truce.

Adjutant Gardner went to Savannah on Sick furlough (20 days).

At 9½ A.M. Rode to front. Visited the post (reserve) of the Secessionville picket and gave fresh instructions (or rather renewed the same instructions) to the Lieut of pickets. The 47th Ga. Vol. were on picket there. Visited all the Vidette Stations and gave instructions to the Lieut. No change whatever visible in Dixon's Island or Folly Island.

Went to Extreme End of Stono Islands. No signs of Yankees on Peninsula or Battery Isld.

I counted 9 vessels of all kinds in mouth of Stono River. There may be more which I could not see. Returned to Camp at 2.45 P.M.

Wind Northerly and abundant and rather pleasant, but the Sun hot.

Note. There was an Exchange to day of Yankee General & Field officers 50 in number brought to Charleston to be put under fire and a like number of our own officers brought to Morris Island for a like purpose.[1]

At 7 P.M. went to Battery No. 2. Capt. Fulton, 5th Ga. Vol. F.O.D.

5th Geo. Vol. furnished 100 men, Lieut Thompson Comdg. Lt. Neely Comdg Stono Posts.

1st S.C.C. 20 men as videttes under Lieut Hill.

Did not go down to Front myself as I had been there for several hours to day & as the F.O.D. & Officers & Men of the pickets were thoroughly instructed in their duties.

Night close & sultry, but clear. Moschetoes bad. All quiet.

Major Warley[2] Exchanged to day. Visited Col. Frederick's Hd. Qrs. to night.

No Corn for Horses.

[Not signed]

[1] See 15 June 1864, note.

[2] 2nd Rgmt., S.C. Arty. See biography, Appendix 3, p. 293.

Thursday, 4 August 1864

Sun very hot.

293 Shots fired on Sumter from 6 P.M. Wednesday to 6 P.M. Thursday, & 65 Shells at City.

Busy in Camp all day.

Capt. S.P. Smith F.O.D. 100 men from 2nd Arty, Lt. Mosley Comdg, formed picket. Lieut Shuler Commanded Right pickets. Lt. Mosley Centre & Lt. A.A. Connor the Left.

1st S.C. Cav. 20 men as Videttes, Lieut. Beckham Comdg.

Rode round picket Lines. All quiet. Returned to Camp about 9½ P.M.

Fodder to day but no Corn.

[Not signed]

Friday, 5 August 1864

Thursday Night 211 Shots at Fort Sumter. Friday up to 6 P.M. 125 Shots, at City 57.

Very hot morning, little or no air.

At 10 A.M. Rode out and examined river front from Battery Pringle down to Grimball's with a view to placing pickets there in Case of need. At this time (neap tides & hot suns) one can ride along the edge of the Marsh the whole way. I think it possible that an enemy might land any where on the Marsh, which although wide is not very soft. The actual high ground is covered with a dense growth of weeds intermingled with timber which has been cut down and would be hard to picket or penetrate.

I then went and observed the enemy's front from Extreme end of Stono Islands, also from the vidette Stations 1, 2, 3 & 4 (4 being the Stone House). I could see no signs of Yankees on the Peninsula or Battery Island. Every thing remains unchanged.

I saw to day that there were one 10 inch Columbiad & two Parrott Guns on Siege Carriages in the Battery on Dixon's Island. There may have been a fourth gun.

Last night all the Cavalry videttes came in on a false alarm but were sent out again.

Early this morning Private J.F. Higgs, Co. "I" [2nd Artillery] strayed carelessly from the Battery at Grimball's Causeway and going down towards Stono Islands attempted to cross the Creek. Not being able to do so, he came higher up and Crossed over to Peninsula. He then got permission from the Cavalry Videttes to go and see the Yankee intrenchments. He accordingly went off and did not return. He either deserted or was cut off by the Yankees. He was quite young (his Mother resides in Augusta) and rather a strange boy. It is supposed that he deserted as he had made some remarks about "going to the Yankees to get some Coffee" and others of a similar character, which at the time were supposed to be merely in jest. One of the Cavalry videttes, however, says that about half an hour after he went several shots were fired from the direction of Battery Island and He thinks he may have been shot or captured.

Adjutant Frederick having gone to the City to day, there was some bungling about the appointment of the Officer of the Day. I went down with the relief and finding that the Officer of the Day did not come, I relieved Capt. [S. Porcher] Smith, old Of. of the Day, and remained in his place.

Capt. Hurt, 5th Ga. Vol. relieved me at Midnight and I returned to Camp.

The 5th Ga. Vol. furnished 100 men Lieut Calhoun, Comdg. Lieut Ward Commanded the Stono posts, Lieutenant Calhoun the Reserve at Grimball's Causeway and Lieut Seely [Sealy] the Left.

1st S.C.C. furnished 20 Men mounted under Lieut Henkerson [Hankinson].

Note. I to day counted near Mouth of the Stono, 2 Hermaphrodite

Brigs, 3 Schooners, [*and*] as well as I could judge about 2 Steam Gunboats and 1 River Steamer.

At night a good many Meteoric or "Shooting Stars."

[*Not signed*]

Saturday, 6 August 1864

Remained in Camp all day. Capt. [*S. Porcher*] Smith went to City to day.

Considerable firing between Fort Lamar & the Long Island Battery from 12 to 2 P.M. Long Island Battery was firing part of the time on the Working Party at Battery No. 4.

All quiet on our Picket Line to day.

The 2nd S.C. Arty furnished 100 Men, Lieut J.B. Connor Comdg. Lieut Bush took the Stono Posts, Lieut Connor the Centre, Lieut [*T.H.*] Jones the Left.

1st S.C. Cav. furnished 20 men as Videttes under Lieut. [*Name omitted in Diary*]

Waited on Front a long time for F.O.D. to report, Capt. G. Richardson. As he did not report, I relieved Capt. Hurt and rode to Hd. Qrs. to report the fact. Was told that Capt. Richardson had sent in a Surgeon's Certificate that he was not fit for duty and that Capt. Colhoun had been ordered to report to the front.

Returned to Camp a little after 10 P.M.

[*Not signed*]

Sunday, 7 August 1864

Remained in Camp all day reading. Lt. [*John B.W.*] Phillips went to City to day.

Towards evening giddiness, weakness, chilliness & symptoms of an approaching fever. Did not go down on Picket front but only gave instructions at Battery No. 2. Went to Col. Frederick's Hd. Qrs. and stated that I was too unwell to go down on picket line.

The 5th Ga. furnished 100 Men for Picket, Lieut Bourquine Comdg.

The 1st S.C. Cav. 20 men under Lieut [*Name omitted in Diary*].

Capt. Colhoun F.O.D. He will be relieved at 8 A.M. tomorrow.

A night of fever.

From Friday 6 P.M. to Sunday 6 P.M. 568 Shots thrown at Fort Sumter.

[*Not signed*]

Monday, 8 August 1864

Capt. Burrus reported as F.O.D. at 8 A.M.

Went into City on leave for the day. Met my Brother, P.M. [*Peter Manigault*]

Returned to Camp at 7½ P.M.

2nd Reg. Arty furnished 2 off & 79 men & Suitable No. of Non. Com. Off. Co. "B" S.C. Siege Train furnished 1 off. & 21 men & N.C. Officers. 1st S.C.C. 20 men & 1 Lieut for Vidette duty.

Night all quiet.

[Not signed]

Tuesday, 9 August 1864

Heavy firing in morning on Fort Sumter (This was at Stranded Blockade Runner *Prince Albert*). 126 Shots at Sumter.

Capt. Hurt reported as F.O.D. at 8 A.M.

Major Jenkins reports from John's Island Augt. 8 to Col. Frederick. "Three (3) Brigs, 1 Gunboat, four (4) Supply Schooners, Two (2) Mortar Schooners & 1 small Tug Boat in the Stono & Folly Rivers.

"One of the Brigs is at the Kiawah [*Island*] Wharf. A large number of tents are visible on Coles & Folly Islands and (2) two on Kiawah Island. One Gunboat in North Edisto River." (Dispatch sent to me at 2½ P.M. 9th. Aug^t.)

At 7 P.M. went down to Batt. No. 2. 5th Ga. furnished 100 men under Lieut. Adams. 2 other Lieuts with him, Lieut Calhoun one.

1st S.C.C. furnished 20 men under Lieut [*W.D.*] Connor (A cousin of A.A. Connor & J. B. Connor, 2nd Arty).

Did not go down on the line myself.

After night a suspicious character reported on the Picket Line. I sent order to have him arrested.

[Not signed]

Wednesday, 10 August 1864

Light rain before day, also Showers from 8 to 10½ A.M.

Dr. Winthrop went to City on leave for the day. 142 Shots fired on Sumter to day. 14 into City.

"Three (3) Schooners, four (4) Brigs, one (1) gunboat and two (2) Steamers came down Folly River & went out."

Received by me from Col. Frederick's Hd. Qrs. 1 P.M. Augt. 10, 1864. Signed Maj. Jenkins, "John's Island" Augt. 9th.

At 6.45 P.M. went to Battery No. 2. 2nd Arty furnished 100 men, 3 off. & 6 n.c. off. for Picket. Lieut Mosley Commanded Centre, Lt. Bush Commanded the Right & Lt. A.A. Connor the left.

Lieut Horsey with 20 Men 1st S.C.C. did vidette duty.

Night cool and pleasant. Wind S.W.

Returned to Camp at 9.15 P.M.

[Not signed]

Thursday, 11 August 1864

201 Shots at Sumter. [*Appended above 11 August 1864*]

Capt. G. Richardson reported as F.O.D. at 7 A.M. (Day cloudy & pleasant. Wind S.W.)

Telegram. "Johns Island, Augt. 10 via Fort Pemberton Augt. 11, 1864" "Two (2) Briggs, One Iron Clad, One (1) Gunboat, Two Supply & 2 Mortar Schooners in Stono & Folly Rivers. At 11 O'clock a large Steamer went out. One Gunboat in North Edisto River."

Rec^d. by Genl. Taliaferro about 12 m. 11th. inst. Signed Major Jenkins.

"Secessionville, Augt. 11, 1864" Telegram.

"Very large Transport just came in from South, now lying off Coles Island. No troops to be seen on board. Transport & Gunboat came from Fleet off Bar and are now lying at same point."

Rec^d. at Genl. Taliaferro's at 12 m. 11th. (Signed) Welsman Brown, Lt. Col.

5th Ga. furnished 2 off, 3 n.c.o. & 50 men, 2nd S.C. Arty 3 n.c.o. & 50 men, Co. "B" S.C. S. Train 1 off. Lt. Snipes Comd Right Pickets, Lt. Brooks, Centre, Lt. Spivey left.

Lieut Blassinghame Comd 20 men 1st S.C. Cav.

Returned to Camp at 10 P.M. Night quiet.

[*Not signed*]

Friday, 12 August 1864

(201 Shots on Sumter) [*Appended above 12 August 1864*]

Capt. Colhoun reported by letter as F.O.D. (reason given the lateness of hour when horse came).

Visited Battery No. 0 (Zero). 1   8 inch Columbiad Rifled & double banded.

1 Cannon Mortar, viz, 32 Pounder with about 2 ft 2 inches of Chase cut off, Rifled with 13 grooves and banded. Mounted on Ship Carriage.

1 State of So. Ca. 10 inch Mortar (Used to be in Citadel in Charleston) [1]

Capt. S.P. Smith went to Richmond to bring his Sick Father home (10 days).

2nd Regt. S.C. Arty furnished 50 men under Lieut. J.B. Connor. 5th Ga. Vol. furnished 50 men, 3 n.c.o. & 2 Lieutenants. Lieut [*Name omitted in Diary*] Comdg. Right, Lt. Connor Centre, & Lt. Seely [*Sealy*] left.

1st S.C.C. 20 men as Videttes under Lieut [*Name omitted in Diary*].

I returned home at 8 P.M. Night clear, calm & quiet.

[*Not signed*]

[1] *This weapon undoubtedly had been cast in the North prior to the war for the State of South Carolina. Customarily, it would have been marked with an S.C. and, probably, the palmetto tree insignia of the state.*

Saturday, 13 August 1864

(Gregg fired 95 Shots at Sumter) [*Appended above 13 August 1864 date*]

Capt. Humbert reported as F.O.D. at 7½ A.M.

At 9 A.M. set out with Lieut Hall of the Engineers to examine the Picket line with a view to strengthening it with Rifle pits &c. Returned to Camp at 11 A.M.

2nd Artillery furnished 50 men, 5th Ga. 2 Officers & 30 men & 3 n.c.o. Co. "B" S.C. S. Train 1 officer & 18 men.

1st S.C. Cav. 20 men under Lieut Henkerson [*Hankinson*].

Lieut Hightower 5th Ga. Commanded Stono Pickets, Lieut King,[1] same Regt, the Centre, Lieut [*John B.W.*] Phillips the left.

Shortly after dark moved the pickets forward to hither edge of Peninsula, ie, South End of Grimball's Causeway, big dam running N.E. & S.W. with left resting beyond Rivers' Causeway. Dismounted the Cavalry.

We then set 100 negroes to work and commenced demolishing certain dams in the low ground between the higher land and the Peninsula, which might serve as cover for the Yankees in making their approaches. Dug away 270 yds of one bank Continuously, and about 30 yds. of the same further on making about 300 yds. Also Commenced on the two parallel dams running from wood in centre of picket line to Grimball's Causeway. Shortly after the Moon went down (2 A.M. by Lopez watch) Knocked off and sent the negroes home. John Lopez had charge of the negroes assisted by Private[s] Padgett 2nd Arty & Willis.

I got to Camp about 3 or 3½ A.M. Orion had risen Completely for some time.

The Pickets were withdrawn at day break to their usual position.

[*Not signed*]

[1] *No Lt. King is listed in personnel records of the 5th Georgia. This man probably was Capt. Jacob S. King, commander of Co. K.*

Sunday, 14 August 1864

(42 Shots fired on Sumter) [*Appended above 14 August 1864*]

Capt. Burrus reported as F.O.D. at 7 A.M. (5th Ga. Vol)

5th Regt furnished 50 men, 3 n.c.o. & 2 officers. 2nd Arty 1 officer, 3 n.c.o. & 50 men.

1st S.C.C. Lieut Young & 20 men.

Note. At 4 P.M. a company of Yankees (about 60 or 70 in number) crossed over from Dixon's Island to the Peninsula and set some brush on fire which burnt all the evening & night. I think they have discovered that our picket line has been changed, and apprehensive of an attack, are making counter demonstrations intended to serve as a check to us.

At dark moved down and posted pickets. Lieut Driver 5th Ga. Comd Right or Stono Posts, Lieut [*Name omitted in Diary*] Commanded Centre & Lieut Kitchens Commanded Left.

About 160 negroes commenced work about 8 P.M. in removing dams running from Centre wood to Grimball's Causeway. They worked until 3 A.M. having levelled about 200 yds of larger Bank (to South) and 240 yds of smaller bank. The moon went down a little before 3 A.M. Negroes safely sent to rear by 3½ A.M.

Pickets drawn in from 4 to 4½ A.M. — 7* nearly overhead.[1]

I reached Camp at 5½ A.M.

Note. The old dams are of very hard material and should be worked by the Pick, but the Engineer Department has no picks. The clink of the Spades heard a long distance, but wind S.W. hence not audible to the Yankees.

The Yankees threw 8 or 9 Hale's Rockets over on Peninsula at 11 or 12 at night but not towards our Lines. They appeared to suspect that we were lurking about the site of the Overseer's House and threw them in that direction.

[*Not signed*]

[1] *This comment, with its asterisk-type symbol, probably was Maj. Manigault's way of indicating the Pleiades, also known as the Seven Sisters. The cluster of stars would have been directly overhead at this date.*

Monday, 15 August 1864

(166 shots fired by Gregg at Sumter. A Parrott Gun burst at Gregg [1]) (120 Shots fired during Monday night) [*Parenthetical material appended above 15 August 1864*]

Capt. Fulton, 5th Ga. Vol, reported as F.O.D. at 7 A.M.

5th Ga. Regt furnished 2 Lieuts, 3 n.c.o. & 50 men, and 2nd S.C. Arty 1 off. 3 n.c.o. & 50 privates.

1st S.C.C. furnished 20 men under Lieut White for Vidette duty.

Lieut Seely [*Sealy*] 5th Ga. Commanded the Stono Pickets, Lieut. [*John*] Thompson 5th Ga. the Centre, Lt. [*T.H.*] Jones 2nd Arty the left.

27 men, 2 n.c.o. & Lt. Seely [*Sealy*] on the 9 Stono posts (two least important left out.)

1 n.c.o. & 6 men in Grimball's Causeway Battery — 3 men on first line of Causeway, 3 men at 2nd Angle.

4 Infty & 4 Cav. at End Grimball's Causeway — 3   100 yds. to left, 3 at Turn of Bank, 3   100 yds. on left.

2 Cav. at intersection of 1st Road with hedge — 3 inf. at point 100 yds left, 2 cav. 100 yds left, 3 infty 100 yds left, 3 inf & 2 Cav at intersection of Stone House Road with hedge, 3 inf. 100 yds left.

2 Cav. & 3 inf at intersection of 2nd Stone House Road with hedge, 3 inf at big ditch 150 yds N.W.

2 Cav. near wood S.W. of Rivers' Causeway. 2 Cav in wood S.E. of Rivers' Causeway. 3 infty on Edge of Sands S.E. of Rivers' Causeway & 3 with working party. (Total 27 + 49 + 18 = 94). + 6 n.c.o. = 100.

6 at Rivers' Causeway, 12 in three posts beyond. Total 18.

Mr. Lopez with 140 negroes went in and Commenced work at 8 P.M. in levelling the dams running from Centre Wood to Grimball's Causeway. Having a better supply of Picks, the work proceeded more rapidly and satisfactorily. 250 yds of the bigger (South) dam were levelled and 100 yds of the smaller one, leaving 320 yds of big dam still to be done and 430 of the smaller one.

Negroes worked until 3 A.M. when they were mustered and sent to Camp.

Our Pickets were drawn in from 4 to 4.30 A.M. I left the line at 4.35 A.M. and got to Camp at 5.15 A.M.

Yankees were perfectly quiet all night.

[Not signed]

¹ *The Parrott, although an excellent rifle, had a tendency to burst. Quite a number were destroyed on Morris Island where they were fired with heavy charges and often under adverse conditions.*

Tuesday, 16 August 1864

(Battery Gregg, 47 Shots at Fort Sumter. Swamp Angel 47 do.) [*Appended above 16 August 1864*]

Capt. Guignard Richardson reported at 7½ A.M. as F.O.D.

5th Ga furnished Capt Rowland, Lt Hightower,	3 n.c.o. &	50 men	
2nd S.C. Arty " Lieut Bolivar,	3 n.c.o. &	50 men	
Co. "B" Siege Train " Lieut Spivey,	1 " &	16 men	Picket duty
1st S.C. Cav. " Lieut Glover,	1 " &	20 men	
1 Capt.4 Lieutenants	8 n.c.o. &	136 men	

Lieut Hightower Commanded Stono Pickets, 9 posts,	2 n.c.o. &	27 Men	
N.C. Officer [*Commanded*] Battery at Grimball's Causeway,	1 " &	6 "	
Lieut Spivey Guard to Working Party on Grimball's Causeway,	1 "	16 "	
1st Picket at 2nd Turn of Causeway,	—	3 "	
2nd at S. End of Grimball's Causeway,	—	8 "	(4 Cav. & 4 inf.)
3rd in rear of Wood to Left Grimball's Causeway,	—	3 "	infantry
4th At Turn of Bank & ditch	—	3 "	do.
5 100 yds to left,	—	3 "	do.
6 At intersection of 1st Road with Hedge,	—	2 "	Cavalry
7 100 yds to left,	—	3 "	Infantry
8 100 " " left,	—	2 "	Cav.
9 100 yds to left,	1 "	3 "	infantry
10 at intersection of Stone House Road & Hedge,	—	5 "	2 Cav. & 3 inftry
11 100 yds to left,	—	3 "	Infantry
12 at intersection 2nd Road to Stone House & Hedge,	—	5 "	2 Cav. & 3 inftry
13 On big ditch,	—	3 "	Inftry
14 In front of Wood South of Rivers' Causeway,	—	2 "	Cavalry
15 100 yds to left,	—	3 "	Inftry
16 Left Vidette Station,	—	2 "	Cav.
17 Extreme left advanced picket,	—	3 "	Inftry
Lieut Bolivar at Rivers' Causeway,	1 "	9 "	Inftry
4 left posts to North of Marsh,	1 "	12 "	do
	7 "	126 Men	
4 Cav. guarding horses at Rivers' Causeway		4	
Riding with Lieut of Vidette	1		
	8 n.c.o.	130 Men	

2 were not furnished from 2nd Arty (only 48, not 50 men) 4 others lost, straggled, sick or scattered.   6

139 Negroes Commenced work at 8 P.M. under Charge of Mr. Lopez. Levelled 270 yds of big or South Bank leaving only 100 yds still to be done. Levelled 290 yds smaller or North Bank leaving 140 still to be done. Negroes worked well and the work progressed well.

At 3 A.M. Knocked off and sent negroes to the rear.

Our advanced Infantry pickets relieved from 4 to 4.30 A.M.

Sun rose & Moon set at 5.10 A.M. by my watch.

I left Picket Line at 4.50 A.M. and arrived at Camp at 5.30 A.M. Slept till 8.30.

[*Not signed*]

Wednesday, 17 August 1864

Battery Gregg 121 Shots at Sumter. 38 at Sullivan's Island. Sullivan's Island 35 at Gregg. [*Appended above 17 August 1864*]

Capt. Colhoun F.O.D.

At 6.30 P.M. went to Battery No. 2.

5th Ga Vol furnished	2 Off.	3 n.c.o. &	50 men	Capt. Duffey[1] in Comd.
2nd S.C. Arty "	1	3	50 "	Lieut Mosley
Lieut Calhoun Commanded Stono Posts				
Co. "B" S.C. Siege Train	1	2	20	Lieut Spivey
1st S.C.C.	1		20	Lieut Crews
		5	140	

Lieut Calhoun Commanded Stono Posts 27 men. [*Note unexplained duplication of a portion of this entry above.*] 1 Sergt. Comd. Battery at Grimball's Causeway, 6 men.

Capt. Duffey Commanded Centre, Lt. Crews [*Commanded*] Right Picket of 10 at S. End of Grimball's Causeway.

Lieut Mosley Commanded 4 Pickets & 9 men at Rivers' Causeway.

Posted all the Pickets myself. The Yankees fired 2 Shots from Long Island to the Peninsula and there were a number of signals made.

Mr. Lopez with 152 negroes Commenced work at 8 P.M. 37 on Rifle Pits in wood between Rivers & Grimball's Causeways. The rest engaged in levelling dams as before. Finished levelling dams at 12 O'clock (Midnight). 100 yds of Bigger dam & 140 yds smaller dam. Total length of each dam about 770 yds. Note. West End of Big dam 360 yds from Battery at Grimball's Causeway.

Negroes then were all engaged on Rifle Pits. At 3 A.M. Knocked off and 3.30 sent safely to rear.

Infantry pickets retired from 4 to 4.30 A.M.

I left picket line at 4.50 A.M. Arrived at Camp at 5.30 A.M.

[*Not signed*]

Thursday, 18 August 1864

(Gregg fired 33 Shots at Sumter & Swamp Angel 12 Shots at do.)
[*Appended above 18 August 1864*]

Capt. Kennedy [*Kennady*] reported as F.O.D. at 7¼ A.M.

All quiet. One 20 pndr. Parrott Shell thrown from Dixon's Island to Battery at Grimball's Causeway.

5th Ga. Vol. furnished	2 off	3 n.c.o.		Capt. O'Connor, Comdg.
		&	50 men	Lt. Barrett assistg.
2nd S.C. Arty. "	1 "	3 "	50 "	Lt. Bush, Comdg.
1st S.C.C. "	1 "		20 "	Lt. Hill, Comdg.

The work in advance of the usual picket line having been gotten through with, the infantry pickets were retired to that line. The Cavalry Vidette left as usual in advance.

Lieut. Barrett Commanded the 9 Stono Posts	2 n.c.o. &	27 men	
Capt. O'Connor " Batty at Grimball's			
Causeway	1 "	17 "	} 35 men
Also, say 6 posts to Left	1 "	18 "	
Lt. Bush [*Commanded*] Rivers' Causeway			
& posts to Left	2 "	18 "	} 33
Also, say 5 posts to Right		15 "	
	6 n.c.o.	95 men	

Five Men wanting.

The full picket line is as follows.	n.c.o.	Privates
11 Stono Posts (of which 5 are actually on the River and 6 retired from same.)	2	33
12 Post between Grimball's & Rivers' Causeways (7 in field & 5 on Edge of wood.)	1	36
4 Posts to Left or East of Rivers' Causeway.	1	12
	4	81
Total detail.	6	100

| This leaves 1 n.c.o. & 11 men to Grimball's Causeway. | | |
| 1 do 8 men to Rivers' Causeway. | 2 | 19 |

The advanced Picket Line is as follows when fully manned:

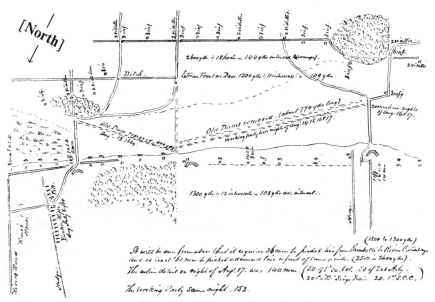

Manigault's sketch of the picket line. The legend is repeated below.

(1200 to 1300 yds)
[*It will be seen from above that it requires 36 men to picket from Grimball's to Rivers Causeway. and at least 61 men to picket advanced line in front of some points. (2500 to 2600 yds). The entire detail on night of Aug. 17 was 140 men.* (50 of 5th Ga. Vol, 50 of 2nd Arty.)
(20 Co. "B" Siege Train, 20 1st st S.C.C.)

The working Party same night, 152.]

Lopez with 93 negroes Continued work on Rifle Pits. Beautiful moon-light night with fresh S.W. Wind.

I returned to Camp at 10.20 P.M. having been up 5 entire nights.

Note. Distance from Reserve Sta. of Secessionville Pickets to end of Rivers' Marsh Road — 800 to 880 yds. As there are 4 Posts or 5 intervals, the average interval is 160 to 176 yds.

[*Not signed*]

Friday, 19 August 1864

Thursday night Gregg 23 Shots & Swamp Angel 8 Shots at Sumter. Friday Gregg 45 & Swamp Angel 15 at Sumter. [*Appended above 19 August 1864*]

Capt. Humbert reported as F.O.D. at 7 A.M.

Busy in Camp writing up Journal, arranging Picket Line, &c.

At 4½ P.M. Lieut Hall came to see me about Rifle Pits on Picket Line.

At 6½ P.M. went to Battery No. 2 and accompanied picket force to their Stations.

5th Ga. Vol. furnished	2 off	3 n.c.o. &	50 men	Lieut Burr Comdg. Lt. Glen [*Glenn*] assisting.
2nd S.C. Arty. "	1 "	3 "	50 "	Lieut Kitchens, Comdg.
1st S.C.C. "	1 "		20 "	Lt. Roberts, Comdg.

Lt. Glen [*Glenn*] Comdg. Stono Posts, 2 n.c.o. & 27 men. Lieut Burr, Grimball's Causeway, 1 n.c.o. & 14 men.

Lt. Kitchens Comdg left with 1 n.c.o. and 6 men at Rivers' Causeway.

4 men as moveable Guard to Working Party, who were besides immediately on the Picket Line.

Lieut Hall & Lopez with 88 negro Hands and 3 overseers Commenced work at 8 P.M. Four (4) Rifle pits were nearly Completed when I left at 1.30 A.M. and the 5th Commenced. The Rifle pits were not Continuous but the work was laid out with faces of 60 yds & flanks of 20 yds — Cremaillere Line — but for the present only 40 ft Constructed on the faces and 15 ft on the flanks, so that there may be some immediate shelter for the pickets, and the intervening portions may be dug when we have more time and labour.

The cremaillere line as drawn in the Diary by Manigault.

(Note that these Rifle pits are improperly placed. They follow the path — They should have followed the brow of the hill)

(½ Sum of Sides : ½ Diff. of Sides :: Tangt. ½ Sum Ang. to Tangt. ½ Diff. Or, 120 ft : 60 ft :: Tangt 45° : Tangt 26°34′ [*Or*] Sin 71°34′ : Sin 90° :: 180 ft : 189¾ ft)

Returned to Camp 2.20 A.M.

[*Not signed*]

Saturday, 20 August 1864

Capt. Burrus 5th Ga. Vol. Reported as F.O.D. at 7 A.M.

1642 lbs. of Corn in the Shuck furnished to Cos. "B" & "C" and myself to last for some time.

5th Ga. Vol. furnished	2 off	3 n.c.o. and	50 men	
2nd S.C. Arty. "	1 "	3 "	50 "	
1st S.C.C. "	1 "		20 "	Lt. J.B. Connor.

Lt. J.B. Connor Commanded the Left.

I went and inspected the line before dark and found that I was correct as to the false position of the Rifle pits.

Genl. Taliaferro visited the line at Grimball's Causeway about 8 P.M. Lieut Hall & Mr. Lopez brought 87 negroes as a working party. While I was there, the negroes were engaged on each flank of Battery at Grimball's Causeway in shifting the bank of the Rifle pits made by the Yankees July 2, 1864 to the South side of the Pits.

The Village of Legareville[1] was burnt between the hours of 9 & 11 P.M.

I returned to Camp at 11 P.M. Some hard showers of Rain during night.

[Not signed]

[1] *U.S. Brig. Gen. Alexander Schimmelfennig, commanding the Northern District of the Department of the South, stated 24 aug. 1864: "...nothing of special interest has occurred since my last report except the burning of Legareville by the enemy on the night of the 20th instant. This was evidently done to prevent our obtaining lumber from there, as we have done lately...."*

Confederate Maj. John Jenkins, commanding on John's Island, reported 21 August: "...Last night at 9 o'clock I burnt Legareville. The buildings were at almost the same instant set on fire and were in a few minutes a sheet of flames...When the determination to destroy the village was announced, the Stono Scouts, owners of property on the place, volunteered to aid the detachment from Captain [Tillman H.] Clark's company ordered for the purpose, 16 such members applying the torches to their own dwellings. Today, after sixteen months duty on this outpost, I turn over the command...and report to my regiment with regret that my last official act on the island should have been, under an imperative sense of duty, to recommend the destruction of the property of our own people (most of them my relatives and friends), and assisting with my own hands in applying the torch to their dwellings. I am only reconciled by reflection that the property had served useful ends to the enemy, who were removing it for their accommodation to the islands in their possession, and it would have been in any event lost to the owners...." [OR XXXV (1) pp. 73, 74, 268, 269]

Sunday, 21 August 1864

Capt. Fulton 5th Ga. Vol. reported as F.O.D. at 7 A.M.

Rainy Day.

<u>Lieut Nesbit sick.</u>

5th Ga. Vol. [*Furnished*]	2 Lieuts.	3 n.c.o. &	50 men.	Lieut Adams Comdg.
2nd Arty.	1	3	50	Lieut. [*T.H.*] Jones Comdg.
1st S.C.C.	1		20	Lieut. [*Name omitted*]

Lieut Avery [*Averett*] Commanded Stono Pickets, Lt. Adams Grimball's Causeway, Lieut Jones Rivers' Causeway.

Early part of night quite dark and some rain. Moon Rise 9.25 P.M. but completely overclouded. Still some light from reflection of Western Clouds. More or less clear latter part of night.

I returned to Camp at 9 P.M.

No working Party on Picket line to night.

[Not signed]

Monday, 22 August 1864

(Battery Gregg 58 Shots & Swamp Angel 21 at Fort Sumter.) [*Appended above 22 August 1864*]

Capt. Kennedy [*Kennady*] reported at 7½ A.M. as F.O.D.

Slight Rain at 7 A.M.

At 9.45 A.M. Started out and visited the whole Picket Line. Went to End of Stono Islands and Scanned the Yankee front. No evidence of the Enemy on Battery Island. Saw about 8 vessels in Stono River opposite Coles Island & lower down 2 Gunboats, 1 Brig & 5 Schooners. Can only see two Houses standing in Legareville. The Church is burnt.

From Stone House observed Dixon's Island; perhaps there are from 6 to 10 fewer Tents near the 3-gun Battery. All the men I saw were negroes.

Visited the Reserve Station of Secessionville Picket and renewed the Same instructions. The Picket duty is done by 47th Ga. Vol.

Distance from Rivers' Marsh Road to Bank & Ditch at which the Secessionville Reserve is posted is exactly 800 yds. The distance of Picket line along Marsh may be about 825 yds.

Returned to Camp at 2.45 P.M.

5th Ga. Vol. furnished	2 n.c.o. &	32 men.	Capt. Duffey Comdg.
2 S.C. Arty.	2 "	50 "	Lieut. Shuler Comdg.
Co. "B" S.C. Siege Train	1	18 "	Lieut. Phillips Comdg.
1st S.C.C.		20 "	Lieut. [*Name omitted*]
	5 n.c.o	120 men	

Lieut [*John B.W.*] Phillips Commanded Stono Posts. Capt. Duffey, Grimball's Causeway. Lt. Shuler, Rivers' Causeway.

Did not go down further than fork of Roads. Returned to Camp at 8 P.M.

No Working party on Picket Line to night.

[Not signed]

Tuesday, 23 August 1864

(Battery Gregg 50 Shots at Sumter, 18 at Sull. Isld. Swamp Angel 23 Shots at Sumter. Wagner 23 Shots at Sull. Ild. 11 Shells thrown at City) [*Appended above 23 August 1864*]

Capt. Rowland reported at 7 A.M. as F.O.D.

About 10 A.M. rode to Battery Glover to see Lieut Hall about Rifle Pits on the picket line. He was not at home, having gone to John's Island near Fripp's to lay out some work.

Hinson's house to East of Battery Glover is occupied by Capt. Prioleau Ravenel as a Commissary Station. The Camp of 1st S.C. Cav. is on Ground occupied last summer by Transportion of 54th Ga. Vol.

230

Returned to Camp about 12 M.

The 5th Ga. Vol. furnished	2 off.	3 n.c.o. &	50 men.	Lieut Codie [Cody] Comdg.
The 2 S.C. Arty.	"	1 "	3 "	50 "	Lieut. Mosley Comdg.
The 1st S.C.C.	"	1 "	—	20 "	Lieut. Jackson "

Lieut Codie [Cody] Commanded Stono Posts. Lieut Driver, Grimball's Causeway. Lt. Mosley, Rivers' Causeway.

Returned to Camp at 8.45 P.M. No working party to night.

Note that for several nights during this past week a dog has been constantly barking on that part of the Peninsula at and near the Overseer's House. The dog apparently a small one, say a Terrier or Fice, barks in the way such dogs do in hunting Rabbits. The Conclusion is that the Yankees have a picket on the Peninsula, about the Overseer's House every night.

[*Not signed*]

Wednesday, 24 August 1864

(152 Shots at Fort Sumter, 54 at City) [*Appended above 24 August 1864*]

Capt. Burrus, 5th Ga. Vol. reported at F.O.D. at 7 A.M.

At 8 A.M. rode down on Picket line. No change visible on Dixon's Island. All the Soldiers visible there are negroes. To day for the first time I noticed a Mound of Earth or Battery on Long Island, probably a half mile S.W. of what we know as the "Long Island Battery." This mound or Battery has evidently been there for considerable time as it has weeds growing upon it. It can only be seen from the Clump of Trees to S.W. of Stone House as Goat Island and the nearer portion of Long Island shut off the view of it from any other point.

Dixon's Island Battery fired two shots on Picket lines this morning at about 7½ A.M. and another shot about 1 P.M.

No sign of the Enemy on the Peninsula nor on Battery Island. On Horse Island there are more tents than there were, 19 to S.E. of Battery & 10 or 12 to S.W. All the men seen were negroes. Several boats fishing, full of them. The Enemy have the bank of the river picketted for some distance to S.W. of Horse Island Battery.

Returned to Camp at about 1¼ P.M.

In afternoon Mr. Robert B. Lester, missionary from "Georgia Conference" to Jackson's Brigade (5th & 47th Ga. &c.) visited me to endeavour to procure a horse to assist him in his clerical duties. His application was endorsed by Col. Daniel. I sent a note to Capt. Zimmerman on the subject.

5th Ga. Vol. furnished	2 off.	3 n.c.o. &	50 men.	Capt. O'Connor, Comdg.
2nd Arty	1 "	3	50 "	Lieut. Bush Comdg.
1st S.C.C.	1 "	—	20 "	Lieut. Lusk, Comdg.

Lieut Seely [*Sealy*] Comd. Stono Posts. Capt. O'Connor, Grimball's Causeway. Lt. Bush, Rivers' Causeway.

I returned to Camp at 8.45 P.M.

The left Picket fired during the night at what they took to be a boat in the Marsh, but as the tide was low at the time they were probably in error.

[*Not signed*]

Thursday, 25 August 1864

(Morris Id. Batteries at Ft. Sumter 191 Shots. Sull. Id. at Morris Id, 109 Shots. Batt. Wagner at Sull. Id, 75 Shots. Batt. Wagner at [*Batteries*] Simkins & Cheves, 42 Shots. Simkins & Cheves at Gregg, 34 Shots. Total 451 Shots.) [*Appended above 25 August 1864*]

Very heavy firing in the harbor at 2 or 3 O'clock in the Morning. (This was said to be the firing of our Batteries on a Working Party at Battery Gregg.)

Capt. Fulton, 5th Ga. Vol. reported as F.O.D. at 7 A.M. The early part of day very close & hot. The Dixon's Island Battery fired 3 Shots at the Grimball's Causeway Battery but did no harm.

About 2 P.M. I arrested and sent to Col. Frederick's Hd. Qrs. (Col. Daniel being now in command as Col. Frederick is on leave of absence) one John Jacobs, a Pedlar, a German Jew who is said to have deserted from the Yankee Army in Kentucky. Col. Daniel sent him to the Hd. Qrs. of Genl. Taliaferro. One of Genl. T's Staff told me that the man was considered Safe.

5th Ga. Vol. furnished	1 off.	3 n.c.o. &	50 men.	Lieut. McNeal [*McNeil*] Comdg.
2 S.C. Arty "	1 "	3 "	50 "	Lt. Kitchens, Comdg.

Sergeant Commanded the Stono Posts with 21 men from 5th Ga. Lt. McNeal [*McNeil*], the Battery at Grimball's Causeway. Lt. Kitchens at Rivers' Causeway.

The Cavalry Detail did not report in time and I saw nothing of it.

I returned to Camp at 8.40 P.M.

Mr. Lester got a horse from Capt. Zimmerman this afternoon.

[*Not signed*]

Friday, 26 August 1864

(Gregg fired 59 Shots and Swamp Angel 36 Shots at Sumter. 32 time fuze Shells from Gregg to City) [*Appended above 26 August 1864*]

Capt. Kennedy [*Kennady*] reported as F.O.D. at 8 A.M.

About 9.15 A.M. rode to Bridge across the Stono between [*Batteries*] "Tynes" & "Pringle." This Bridge is (by my Stepping) about 1080 ft. from end to end. Tho' perhaps only 800 ft long from low water mark to Low water mark. There are 3 piles in each Bent and the Bents 20 to 24 feet apart (very irregular). The Roadway is 18 ft wide. The Causeway beyond is of mud thrown up from the sides. 18 ft roadway. Not sufficient Berm is left for such loose mud.

Then rode to Lebby's and saw Capt. Mordecai about some business. Much sickness at our Station at James Island Creek Bridge.

5th Ga. furnished	1 Off.	2 n.c.o. &	33 men	Lt. [*Name omitted, probably Snipes*] Comdg.
The 2nd Arty	1	3 "	50 "	Lt. Shuler Comdg.
Co. "B" S.C. Siege Train	1	2	17	Lt. Spivey, Comdg.

Lt. Spivey Comd Stono Posts. Lt. Snipes, Grimball's Causeway. Lt. Shuler, Rivers' Causeway.

I returned to Camp about 9 P.M.

Had a visit from Capt. Bridges this afternoon.

[Not signed]

Saturday, 27 August 1864

Capt. Rowland reported as F.O.D. at 7 A.M.

Rain about 8 A.M. Lt. Shuler was relieved from Picket in the Morning to attend to "Examining Board."

After attending to some business about Camp, &c. rode down to Picket line about 12 M. Continual showers of Rain which prevented my seeing very well, but there was no perceptible change visible from either Stone House or End of Stono Islands, except that there appeared to be fewer vessels in Stono. I could not see more than three or four.

Returned to Camp at 3½ P.M.

A very heavy Gust from N.W. and heavy Rain about 5 P.M. by which the roofs of some of our Cabins were blown off.

5th Ga. Vol. Furnished	2 off.	3 n.c. off. &	50 men.	(Lieut Adams & Lieut Averett.
2 S.C. Arty	1 "	3 "	50	Lieut Mosley Comdg.
1 S.C. Cav	1 "	—	20	Lieut Blassinghame Comdg.

Lt. Averett Comdg Stono Pickets, Lt. Adams Grimball's Causeway, Lt. Mosley River's Causeway.

Returned to Camp about 9 P.M.

[Not signed]

Sunday, 28 August 1864

Saturday and Sunday Batty Gregg 87 Shots & Swamp Angel 23 at Fort Sumter. Sull Id. & Batt Wagner 5 Shots each at other. Batty Simpkins [*Simkins*] 36 at Swp. Angel. Batty Wagner 52 at Batt. Simkins. [*Appended above 28 August 1864*]

Capt. Burrus reported as F.O.D. at 8 A.M.

Enemy throwing time Shells into City this Morning.

5th Ga. furnished	2 Off.	3 n.c.o. &	50 men.	Lt. [*Name omitted*] Comdg.
				Lt. Barrett Asst.
2 S.C. Arty	1	3 "	50 "	Lieut Bush Comdg.
1st S.C. Cav.	1		20 "	Lieut Ratchford Comdg.

Lieut Barrett Comd. Stono Posts, Lt. [*Name omitted*] Grimball's Causeway, Lt. Bush Rivers' do.

One of 1st S.C.C. taken very ill (Cholera Morbus). I requested Dr. Goodwyn of 2nd Arty to go down for him with Ambulance.

Returned to Camp at about 9 P.M. Just after I reached Camp heard a very heavy Explosion in the direction of Fort Sumter. This turned out to be the explosion of a Yankee "Monster Torpedo" against the S.W. Angle of the Berm of Fort Sumter.[1] It must have Contained several hundred pounds of gunpowder. No harm was done.

Heard Rice Birds [*bobolink*] for first time to night.

[Not signed]

[1] *See 13 July 1864, note.*

Monday, 29 August 1864

Capt. Fulton reported as F.O.D. at 7 A.M.

At 8.45 A.M. Started in Ambulance for City having leave of Absence for the day. On my arrival in town say 10.30 a fine fire broke out in Hayne Street.[1]

For Curiosity and future reference it is worth while preserving a record of the prices of several articles in Confederate Currency.

Ordinary Foolscap Paper $8 per Quire. Ordinary letter paper $7 per Quire.

Ordinary Blank Book 8" x 12" about 3 quires of paper & bound in board $30.00

Ordinary English, grey, Felt Hat "Wide-Awake" usual price say $4, now $80.00

High laced double Sole Shoes, usual price say $6.00 now $120.00

Saddle Girth, of doubled Homespun Cloth with leather Straps & Buckles at ends $7.00

After getting through my more immediate business, I walked through the lower part of the City. From the "Bend" of King Street, fennel, weeds & grass growing in gutters. Broad Street has the pavement Clear for the breadth of a single Carriage way; all the rest grown up in Grass with Weeds & Fennel in the Gutters, some of the fennel more than 6 ft high. The Cows are actually grazing in the lower part of Meeting & Church Streets.

Col. Ashe's House on South Bay [*Modern 32 South Battery Street*] has been struck by two Shells (I only saw one however). I saw no marks of Shells on the neighbouring houses. Mr. John Ravenel's [*5 East Battery*]

Stable has been struck by a shell. The Roper house [*9 East Battery*] has had the Architectural projection of the porch blown away by a shell. Mr. Wm. Ravenel's house [*13 East Battery*] has been struck by one Shell. A small portion of the parapet of Mr. Charles Alston's house [*21 East Battery*] has been demolished by a shell which also apparently

Modern view of 21 East Battery.

penetrated Mr. Dan Heyward's Stable [*25 East Battery*] in rear. The front Steps & Entrance of Mr. D. Heyward's house have been demolished by a Shell.

Along East Bay I noticed but little damage in addition to what I noticed in December or Jany. last [*8 March 1864*]. The old (Colonial) post Office & Custom House [*Old Exchange Building, East Bay at Broad*] appears to have been struck by two shells.

In passing along Broad Street I noticed that just where I used to sit making out Estimates, Returns, Monthly do, Requisitions, &c in the then office of C&S [*Charleston & Savannah*] R.Rd. [*34 Broad St.*] a shell had knocked away the wall. If I had been sitting there at the time I would have had no further trouble in this life. This was in 3rd Story over Edgerton & Richard's Store [*merchant tailors, 32-34 Broad St.*].

St Philip's Church [*150 Church St.*] has been struck by three Shells, one of which has done Considerable damage. On way back passed the scene of fire at Force & Mitchell's. The fire subdued and Engines returning. Interior of Store Completely ruined.

Returned to my Brother H's [*Henry Middleton Manigault*] house at 2.45 P.M. My cousin L.I.G. [*Louisa Izard Gibbes*] on a visit. Returned to Camp about 8 P.M.

1 negro woman was killed by Shell in City to day.

[*Not signed*]

¹ The fire, according to a local newspaper, burned the third and fourth stories of Force and Mitchell's wholesale boot and shoe store at 21 Hayne St. The first two floors suffered extensive water damage. The blaze, attributed to an incendiary by the newspaper, broke out again at 8 o'clock that night but was quickly extinguished. [*Charleston Daily Courier, 30 Aug. 1864*]

Tuesday, 30 August 1864

Capt. Duffey reported as F.O.D. at 7 A.M.

During morning went to Lookout at Col. Frederick's and observed but could see nothing.

5th Ga. furnished	1 off.	2 n.c.o. &	30 men.	Lieut Snipes Comdg.
2 S.C. Arty	1 ”	3 n.c.o.	50 men.	Lieut [*T.H.*] Jones Comdg.
Co. "B" Siege Train	1 ”	3 ”	19 men.	Lieut [*John B.W.*] Phillips Comdg.

Lieut Phillips Comd Stono Post, Lt. Snipes Grimball's Causeway, Lt. Jones Rivers' Causeway.

I returned to Camp at 9½ P.M.

Col. Yates telegraphed that a small steamer landed troops on Folly Island from Morris Island this afternoon. This notice was given to me about 9½ P.M.

[*Not signed*]

Wednesday, 31 August 1864

Capt. O'Connor, 5th Ga., reported as F.O.D. at 7 A.M.

At 9 A.M. Started out and reported to Col. Frederick's Hd. Qrs. As the Non. Com. Staff & Band were not ready for inspection & muster I proceeded to inspect the Companies & Batteries.

BATTERY ZERO

Sergt. [*Cpl.*] Wolfe & 15 privates, Co. "I" formed the Garrison. (Lieut. Bolivar being off on Furlough and Lt. Mosley Sick.)

Armament: 1 old Style 10 in. Mortar on Extreme Right, bad order inside. 12 Bar. [*Barrels*] Powder in Mag. [*Magazine*] & 200 10 in. Shell (112 & 87 [*pounds*])

1 Rifled & Banded 32 (1829) [*Date of manufacture*] 26 in. of Chase cut off. Used as long range Mortar. Mounted on Ship Carriage. 50 Shell & Sufficient

Cartridges in Magazine.

1 8 in. Rifle double banded, 10 grooves Saw fashion.[1] Full Circle Carriage [*Barbette, center pintle carriage*] new & good. Chamber traversed & Sodded. Cartridges in Magazine. 25 Square headed Bolts, 14 frusto-Conoidal Bolts, 1 nondescript ("Hardin")[2] 29 8 in. Rifle Shell in Magazine. 21 8 in. Canister.

1 8 in. Navy Shell gun, not mounted.

The Scarp of work is not revetted or sodded. The Right traverse is revetted including Gun Chamber of 8 in Rifle, but nothing else. Magazine also is Sodded.

The Magazine is dry & well constructed but the entrance slopes inwards and if there are heavy rains, the Magazine will infallibly be flooded.

Quarters Comfortable (Tents). Matter of sinks attended to. Grounds clean except where there is rubbish in consequence of unfinished State of Work.

BATTERY NO. 1

1 8 in. Siege Howitzer to Rt.
1 12 pndr. Siege Smooth[*bore*].
1 24 Pndr. Siege Smooth.
1 do 24 Pndr. (Cartridge Bags worm Eaten).
1 12 pndr. Siege Rifled. Elev. Screw handle broken.
1 12 pndr. (light) Smooth, Elev. Screw bad.
1 8 in. Siege Howitzer.
(Bores of Guns all want oil.)
Total 7 Guns.

3 Austrian Caissons in bad Condition with ammunition for 8 in. Howitzers. The rest of the Cartridges principally in Amm[*unition*] Chests in Gun Chambers. Am[*munition*] Chests have bad Tops, but cartridges generally good. Guns appear to have, many of them, near 150 to 200 rounds apiece, as for instance, 12 pndr. Smooth, 51 Rounds Shot, 51 Canister [— *102*]. 24 pndr. 96 Shot, 30 grape, 62 Canister — 188. 12-pounder Rifle, 70 Bolts, 12 Shells, 44 Canister — 126. 24-pounder, 61 Shot, 30 Grape, 67 Canister — 158.

Magazine is dry, but not floored. The entrance is bad and some water flows in. Bomb Proof incomplete. Traverses Sodded except on top surface. About ½ (or say 4/7) of Scarp is sodded. The Superior Slope of Parapet not turfed.

The Garrison of No. 1 is detailed from Co. "G" (Stallings).

BATTERY NO. 2

1 24 Pndr. Siege.
1 8 in. S.C. Howr.
1 32 pndr. Barbette [*Carriage*].

1 32 pr. barbette.
1 8 in Navy Shell gun, barbette.

The Supply of Ammunition is ample and in good condition, except in a few cases where the Cartridges are damaged, the Am. Chests having defective tops. Implements & Equipments good.

Only South face of Scarp Sodded, say ⅓ of total. Superior Slope not sodded. The Traverses are sodded entirely. Some of the Sodding is shrunk & cracked, recommend that the cracks be filled up at once before rain sets in.

Magazine not sodded on outside. Interior dry at present. Floor should be raised 1 ft, though it will involve stooping. The whole is floored (Sodding just commenced).

The Quarters Comfortable & clean. Sinks provided.

Co. "G" 56 men in Ranks, 15 men on Picket, 8 on guard "on" & "off", 11 detailed in Ord, Q.M., Comy. & Medical & Engr Departments and Band, 17 Sick & Hospital, 7 on Furlough, 4 Sick Furlough, 6 absent without leave, on leave for day 1, Absent in Arrest 1, Discharged 1, Lieut Elect 1, Ord. Sergt 1, Sergts in front 3, 1 discharged. Total 133 Accounted for. Total of Roll, 5 Sergts, 4 corp. 128 Privates — 137.

Discipline Fair. Instruction fair. Mil. Appearance fair. Arms mixed, but in good condition. (U.S. Musket 1821, U.S. Musket 1842, Virginia Muskets, "Palmetto Armory" Muskets.) Accoutrements good. Clothing good but not uniform. All well-shod.

BATTERY NO. 3. New Lines, James Island.

1 18 pnd^r. Siege (Smooth).
1 24 pnd^r. Siege, Smooth, Wheels bad (Condemned) (60 Shot, 56 grape, 44 Canister — 160 rounds.)
1 18 pnd^r. Siege, Smooth (56 Shot, 26 grape, 15 Canister — 97 Rds.)
1 24 pnd^r. Siege (Smooth). Wheels bad (Condemned).
1 18 pnd^r. Siege, Smooth. (59 Shot, 39 grape, 55 canister — 153 rounds.)
Bore of Guns want oil.

Interior Slope of Parapet Sodded and the Traverses to height of same. Traverses above that not sodded. Scarp not sodded, nor Superior Slope and both very much washed.

Expense Magazines in rear of Traverses want new Skids to rest the Amm. Chests on.

The Main Magazine unfinished, raised only to level of top of Timber roof.

Co. "I"   Capt. Humbert. 38 in Ranks, 3 Sergts in front, 16 at
            Battery Zero, 11 on Picket, 21 detailed in Ordnance,
            Engr, Qr. Master & Commissary Departments and
            as Mechanics, 1 Company Commissary, 26 Pres. &
            Abs. Sick, 5 on Furlough, 1 Absent without leave, 6
            on Guard, 2 gardeners, 1 Ordnance Sergt, 1 Com-
            pany Courier, 1 to City.
                        Total 130 Accounted for. [*Actually 133
            — Manigault overstruck 4 making it 5 on furlough
            and 4 to 6 on guard without correcting the total to
            133 from 130*].
            Muster Roll, 5 Off, 4 Sergts, 4 Corpls & 124 Privates.
            Total 132 Enlisted men. Capt. Humbert on duty.
            W.S. Barton, Sr. 1st Lt., acting Ord. Officer. J.W.
            Mosley, Jr. 1st Lt. Sick. Geo. Bolivar, Sr. 2nd Lt. on
            leave [*of*] absence. S.D. Russell, Jr. 2[*nd Lt.*] Acting
            Adjutant.
            Discipline Good. Instruction Good. Mil. Appearance
            Good, except Clothing not uniform. Arms, Cadet
            Muskets in excellent condition. Accoutrements
            Good. Clothing good but not uniform. Men well sup-
            plied with Shoes but many their own property or
            private supply.
            Quarters good & Clean. Sinks attended to. Excellent
            Garden. Books well kept.

"FIELD STAFF & BAND"

            Col. A.D. Frederick. Lt. Col. J.W. Brown. F.F. Warley,
            Major.
            E.J. Frederick, Adjutant. E.J. Felder, Regt. Qr. M.
            R. Lebby, Surgeon. T.J. Goodwyn, Asst. Surgeon.
            P. Hawkins, Chaplain awaiting appointment.
            J. Millar, Sergt. Maj. J.C. Pike, Q.M. Sergt. J.R. Jor-
            dan, Ord. Sergt.
            J.K. Hane, Color Sergt.
            14 Men Constituting the Band.
            5 Men as Hospital Stewards, 3 Nurses-Ambulance Dri-
            vers = 8.

BATTERY NO. 4

            1 24 Pnd^r. Siege, Smooth.
            1 8 in. S.C. How, Barbette (was previously on Siege
            Carriage.)
            1 32 Pnd^r. Barbette, Land Regulation, say 7200 lbs.

1 32 pnd^r. Navy Shell [*Gun*] barbette.

1 24 Pnd^r. Siege, Smooth.

A good supply of ammunition and in good order.

Magazine just Completed. Not Sodded. Not floored except inner Chamber. Floor on level of surrounding ground. Dry. I found some Cartridges on the floor.

No Sodding on the Work except inner revetment of parapet & traverses to the same height.

Co. "F" Capt. Legare. 54 men in ranks, 12 on Guard, 13 on Picket, 11 Detached in Ord. Engr. & Comy. Departments. 1 Mail Carrier, 1 Company Commissary, 10 Present Sick, 5 Absent Sick, 1 Guard Telegraph Office, 1 Company Ord. Serg^t, 2 Regt. Q.M. Dept, 1 before Med Board, 9 furloughed, 4 on 12 hour permits, 2 without leave, 1 in Medical Department.

Total 128 accounted for.

Muster Roll 5 Off, 5 Serg^{ts}, 4 Corporals & 123 Privates. Capt. T.K. Legare, Actg. Comd^t New Lines, [*Sr.?*] 1st Lt. W.W. Legare, Actg. Ord. Off, Dill's Bluff, Jr. 1st Lt. B.M. Shuler Commanded Company at Muster. J.B. Connor, Sr. 2nd Lieut. on furlough. A.A. Connor Jr. 2[*nd Lt.*] Sick pres^t.

Discipline Good, Instruction Good, Mil. App. Good but not uniform. Arms Mixed 10 Bayonets wanting, in pretty good condition. Accoutrements good. Clothing good, but not uniform. Men supplied with Shoes, but many have supplied themselves.

Quarters good & Clean. Parade Clean. Attention to Sinks, &c.

BATTERY NO. 5

1 24 Pnd^r. Austrian How, Bronze on Field Carriage.

1 24 Pnd. Siege Gun, Iron, Wheels Condemned.

1 24 Pnd. do do Wheels Condemned.

1 12 Pnd^r. Siege.

A good Supply of Ammunition but Am. Chests have bad Covers.

Magazine just Commenced, and I am sorry to see the floor will be beneath the level of the ground.

The Battery is only Sodded on inner [*Interior*] Slope of parapet and traverses as high.

Co. "H" Capt. Kennedy [*Kennady*]. 58 men in Ranks, 4 on Guard, 13 on Picket, 15 Detailed in the Engr, Ordnance, Qr. M., Comy, Government Farm & Medical Departments. 1 Regl. [*Regimental*] Teamster, 1

Company Commissary, 1 present Sick, 6 Absent Sick, 4 Abs. without leave, 5 absent with leave, 1 before Examining Board, 1 discharged, 1 died in Hospital, 1 on Retired List, 1 on 12 hour leave, 1 Recruit.

Total 114 Accounted for.

Muster Roll 3 Off, 5 Sergts, 4 Corporals, 107 Privates.

Capt. W.H. Kennedy [*Kennady*], 1st Lt. J.B. Kitchens absent with leave, T.H. Jones on Picket, R.C. Ashley Prest. Qrs. [*Present, Quarters*] Cashiered July 13, 1864.

Discipline not very good. Instruction tolerable. Mil. Appearance Tolerable. Arms Mixed, 18 Bayonets wanting. Arms not in good Condition. Accoutrements good except some scabbards wanting. Clothing good but not uniform. Shoes Supplied but many I believe by the Men themselves.

Capt. E.J. Felder, A.Q.M., 2nd S.C. Arty, Reports as follows and I verified the same as far as I could at the Wagon Yard.

	Horses	Mules	4 Horse Wagons	2 Horse Wagons	2 horse Ambulance	1 horse Field Amb.	Cart	Setts Harness	Wagon Saddles	Riding Saddles	Riding Bridles
At Wagon Yard	6	16	4	1	1	2	1	18	6	2	3
At Major Burke['s]	—	12	3	—	—	—	—	12			

Got back to Camp at 6 P.M. having been 9 hours on duty in inspecting & Mustering 2nd Arty and the 6 Batteries they garrison.

Sent Sergeant Major Gaillard to Battery No. 2 to say that I would not be down there and to tell the Officers to proceed to the picket line. Lt. Bush was there and left with the detail from 2nd Arty at proper time, but the Detail from 5th Ga. did not relieve the picket until 10.30 P.M.

A little Rain about 7 or 8 O'clock. Afterwards the wind later at night Came round to N.E. and it became much cooler.

Note. My Report sent in to Lieut. Frederick a.a.a.g. is in following order:

1. Field, Staff & Band
   Col. & Maj. on Furlough.
   Lt. Col. Comdg Secessionville.

Dr. Lebby detached as Senior Surg. 7th Mil. District.
Rest of officers present & also N.C. Staff.
Band present and Instruction, Clothing & Mil. Appearance Satisfactory.

2. Hospital Attendants.
3. Co. F.
4. Co. G.
5. Co. H.
6. Co. I.
7. Battery Zero.
8. Battery No. 1.
9.   do No. 2.
10. do No. 3.
11. do No. 4.
12. do No. 5.
13. Regimental Transportation

[1] *This type rifling was invented by John Mercer Brooke (1820-1906) and generally known as Brooke rifling. [Ripley, pp. 127, 128]*

[2] *Developed by Capt. James Harding of the Charleston Arsenal. [OR XXXV (1) p. 514; Ripley, pp. 328, 362]*

At this point, Major Manigault's Diary comes to an abrupt end. He had used every available page in the book, including the inside of the front and rear covers. Presumably, since there was no apparent reason to end the journal here, it was continued. However, no additional volumes have been found. Information on the major's early, and later, career will be found in the Introduction and Appendices.

Appendix 1

The following report of the Battle of Grimball's Causeway, James Island, S.C., 10 Feb. 1865, was printed in The Sunday News (Sunday edition of The News and Courier) 30 Nov. 1902, p. 6. To it, in an effort to settle arguments regarding the "last fight for Charleston," the newspaper appended a short account of the "Affair at Battery Simkins."

BATTLE OF GRIMBALL'S

GRAPHIC ACCOUNT OF THE LAST FIGHT FOR CHARLESTON

Personal Narrative of the Late Major Edward Manigault of the South Carolina Siege Train, 18th Battalion of Artillery, C.S.A. The Confederates Fight Against Heavy Odds, but the Federal Casualties were "Three and a Half to One of Ours."

The following narrative, written by the late Major Manigault, with no view to publication, is of interest to all students of the wonderful defense of Charleston:

February (Friday) 10th, 1865.

(A bitter cold day, wind N.W.)

About sunrise the Yankees commenced shelling our picket line, or line of Rifle pits, between Grimball's and Rivers' Causeways, from four gunboats and a mortar schooner lying in Legare's Creek or Little Folly River. As soon as I could have my horse saddled, I rode down to the picket line. Found the vessels as above described, shelling briskly; also three other gunboats in Stono River, which last, however, were shelling only occasionally. When I arrived, a considerable force of Yankees had landed and were drawn up near Legare's overseer's house. Our force at that time consisted of 100 infantry, and a cavalry picket of 20. Total 120, being the regular picket on the line. Capt. [*W.H.*] Kennedy [*Kennady*], 2nd S.C. Arty., as officer of the day, relieved the

243

preceding officer, almost immediately after I arrived. I directed him to take charge of the left of the line, while I would remain at Grimball's Causeway, where the attack was threatened. I told him to assist me as well as he was able with the left Picket force, if the attack should be made on Grimball's Causeway. I drew in the pickets on the bank of the Stono River on the extreme right and concentrated them as well as I could from the long entrenchment facing peninsula extending toward the Stono in the direction of Legareville, along the rifle pits to Grimball's Causeway. I sent dispatches to Col. [*J. Welsman*] Brown, giving information and asking reinforcements, as soon as could be done.

Col. Brown sent me the "Palmetto Guard," Capt. [*Benjamin C.*] Webb — "[*Co. A, Cobb*] Guard[*s*]," Capt. Cullen [*Cullens*] — the [*Co. B,*] "Cobb Guard[*s*]," Capt. Turnipseed; also 29 dismounted Cavalry under Lieut. [*William G.*] Roberts, 1st S.C. Cav. He ordered me through Lieut. [*Thomas Morritt*] Hasell "to hold the picket line to the last extremity." Our force then stood thus:

Regular Infantry picket, 2nd S.C. Arty.	100	
Reg. Cav., do	20	120 men

REINFORCEMENTS

Palmetto Guard, Infantry, Capt. Webb	52	
Capt. Cullen's [*Cullens'*] Co.	50	
Capt. Turnipseed's Co.	57	159 men
Also Lieut. Roberts' dismounted Cav. of 1st S.C.		29 men
Making in all		308 men

This force occupied a line one mile long. Forty-eight of them occupied the Left posts, and I could not withdraw them as an attack might be made by Rivers' Causeway. Also, the mounted Cavalry and dismounted Cavalry were kept at Rivers' Causeway for the same reason.

ONLY 161 MEN ACTUALLY ENGAGED

This left me 211 men; of this 211 Capt. Cullen's [*Cullens'*] Co., 50, were left in reserve, so that I had only 161 men on this part of the line actually attacked.

The shelling continued for several hours with no effect whatever. Average distance 1 mile; 8 and, I think, 11 inch guns, besides rifles of different calibres and one 13 inch mortar. After much marching and countermarching, the Yankees advanced their skirmishers about 3 P.M., supported by a pretty heavy line in rear. A strong line of skirmishers advanced to within 300 or 330 yds., the main body being drawn up beyond the sands, in the road leading to Legare's "overseer's house," distance 700 yards. A pretty sharp fire was exchanged between their skirmishers and our line, when after some time their skirmishers were recalled.

Previous to this I had estimated their force at from 1500 to 2000 men. They evidently had 5 regiments, one of which appeared to be a very large regiment, judging by the front it occupied, say even as much as

800 men; the four other regiments, estimated at 250 apiece, would give 1000; say 1800 men.

After some time had elapsed, a section of Artillery advanced to near south end of Grimball's Causeway, distance 700 yds., and commenced shelling us; no damage was done by this fire.

GENERAL ADVANCE OF THE FEDERALS

At about 5 P.M., a general advance of their line took place. Their skirmishers on their left, composed of 54th New York (white) and one company of the 144th New York (white) made a most beautiful charge at a run, extending interval as soon as they disengaged themselves from the marsh and approaching our line obliquely, so that it was very hard to hit them. Seeing the danger of the extreme right of our line, I immediately ran to the next rifle pit on the right of Grimball's Causeway and ordered Lieut. [*C.C. Rush*] of Co. G, 2nd S.C. Arty, to take 20 or 25 men with him and reinforce the extreme right rifle pits. I then turned to go back to the little earthwork at Grimball's Causeway, where the attack in line or column would evidently be made, when on being called to by Lieut. [*name omitted*] I turned, and saw that our men on the extreme right were giving way.

I returned to Grimball's Causeway; the Yankee line was then 60 to 70 yards distant, as well as I could judge; they seemed to me to be wavering and if the right of our line had not given way and I could have got at Cullen's [*Cullens'*] Company, immediately, I think the main attacking force would have been driven back.

CORPL. MANSON'S GALLANTRY

But turning and seeing the men of our right rifle pits in full retreat and the enemy pressing on them, I gave the order to retreat, and I followed as soon as the line had passed me. Handling skirmishers in retreat when 6 or 8 times their number are firing upon them, is rather an impracticable affair. Corporal [*George H.*] Manson behaved very bravely during the retreat, halting, facing about and firing at the enemy.

MAJOR MANIGAULT WOUNDED

Immediately afterwards I fell, struck by a minie ball in the back, within an eighth of an inch of the base of the spine. Corporal [*Alexander*] Macbeth passed me immediately afterwards. I told him to hurry on, that I was mortally wounded. He gave me a mouthful of water from his canteen and hurried on. Bowie [*either James A, or Alexander*], of the "Palmetto Guard," came up and said he could go no further. I urged him to hurry on, that a stand would be made at the next hedge, and ditch, etc., but he appeared to be broken down (though young and robust, having been much weakened by chill and fever). Immediately after, 6 men of 54th N.Y. (with unmistakable brogue) came up and took him prisoner, and then took me. I was in a moment despoiled of my watch, sword, pistol and field glass and, shortly after, taken on a blanket to Grimball's Causeway where Capt. [*Gustav*] Blau, 54th New York, was in command of our men's rifle pits, or earthwork, which we had just abandoned.

SEACOAST OPERATIONS AGAINST CHARLESTON—BRILLIANT DASH AND CAPTURE OF REBEL RIFLE-PITS AND PRISONERS BY THE U. S. TROOPS ON JAMES ISLAND, S. C., FEB. 9.—FROM A SKETCH BY OUR SPECIAL ARTIST. W. T. CRANE.

Exaggerated view of the engagement on James Island published 4 Mar. 1865 in Frank Leslie's Illustrated Newspaper. The battle is erroneously dated 9, instead of 10, Feb. 1865.

IN THE HANDS OF THE ENEMY

I fell, I suppose 300 yards in rear of our lines, believing that the wound was mortal. I was utterly powerless from the shock, though not exactly paralyzed. I fainted immediately after being taken up in a blanket, though I think that my unconsciousness lasted but a moment. Capt Blau, who was very polite, ordered four men to take me on a stretcher to the Yankee Hospital on Dixon's Island, where I arrived considerably after dark. In going to the rear, I passed two Regiments in reserve, one behind the other, the first perhaps 350 yards from our line and the other perhaps 500 yds. from it. I also passed the Yankee commander and his staff (whether [Brig.] Gen. [Alexander] Schimmel-fennig or Col. [Augustus G.] Bennett, I cannot say). They were mounted and stationary on the sands a little to the right, or West, of Grimball's Causeway, about 300 yds. from our lines. The Yankees had engaged the 54th New York (white); 144th New York (white); 32nd United States colored troops; 33rd United States colored troops; 55th United States colored troops [55th Massachusetts Volunteers], and one section of artillery; probably from 1250 to 1500 men (one of their officers ad-mitted to me that they had 1200 men).

Capt. Blau, 54th N.Y., commanded the skirmishers who attacked the right of our line, composed of the 54th N.Y. and 1 company of the 144th N.Y. The other Companies of the 144th N.Y. and one colored regiment (the 144th on right) made the attack in line on main position at Grim-ball's Causeway. Two negro regiments held in reserve in rear of this last named attacking party. Gen. Schimmelfennig was said to be in command, but Col. Bennett in immediate command of the attacking force. I was told that after the first demonstration, it was intended to retire, but [Maj.] Gen. [Quincy A.] Gillmore [commander, Department of the South] himself ordered the last attack.

CASUALTIES ON BOTH SIDES

The casualties among the Yankees amounted to 88. I heard this from undoubted authority. Our casualties were as follows: Corp. [William P.] Nagel and Private [C.H.] Kerr, Palmetto Guard, killed; also four or five others wounded but not prisoners.

Myself and Lieut Wells, Co. B, "Cobb Guard," Privates [W.L.] Camp-bell, [A.R.] Haig, [W.W.] Houston, [W.R.] Mouzon of Palmetto Guard; Privates [Erasmus D.] Swan, [not identified] Wood, Mills, Johnson of Cobb Guard were all wounded and taken prisoners. Total 10.

Two Bowies [James A. and Alexander], [John T.] Humphreys, Pri-vates, "Palmetto Gd." and Privates Jackson and three others [not iden-tified] of "Cobb Gd." were taken prisoners, unwounded. Total, 7.

The total casualties on our side, then — 17 taken prisoners, and 7 or 8 either killed or wounded, not taken prisoners. Total, 25.

The Yankees, therefore, did not gain much by their attack, as their casualties were 3½ to 1 of ours.

Mills and Johnson of the "Cobb Guard" died, the rest recovered.

"YANKEES RETIRED THAT NIGHT"

The Yankees retired that night from our picket line, which was reoccupied the next day by our troops. As soon as I arrived at the temporary Hospital at Dixon's Island, the bullet was cut out of my hip. The next evening, about sunset, we were moved in a steam boat to Folly Island. Remained there till the 13th (Monday) evening, when we were put on board the steamer *Canonicas*. Tuesday about midday, started for Hilton Head. Arrived there about sunset. Landed Yankee wounded and proceeded to Beaufort; carried to Port [*Post?*] Hospital in charge of Dr. Shue about 9 A.M. February 15.

May 9, discharged from Hospital and sent to Hilton Head as prisoner of war, accompanied by Campbell, Haig, Houston and Mouzon. Paroled May 10. Left Hilton Head 11.30 P.M. May 11, 1865.

Arrived at Charleston 7 A.M. May 12. I write this February 9, 1866. Tomorrow will be one year since I was wounded. I am still on my crutches.

THE AFFAIR AT BATTERY SIMKINS

Some question having arisen as to whether the fight at Grimball's was the last engagement in the defence of Charleston, one of the veterans who fought under Major Manigault recently addressed letters to Mr. John Harleston, of the 1st South Carolina regular artillery, and Dr. Robert Lebby Jr. of Gen. Taliaferro's staff. The attention of these gentlemen was called to the alleged barge repulse at Battery Simkins on February 11, 1865, mentioned in report of Gen. Hardee to Adjt. Gen. Cooper, page 1,070, Serial No. 98, "War of the Rebellion," official records [*OR 47 (1) pp. 1070, 1071*]. The replies seem to indicate that the affair at Battery Simkins was of little moment to the Confederates. Mr. John Harleston thinks it was not "serious."

Dr. Lebby in a letter, which, like Major Manigault's narrative, was not intended for publication, says:

My recollection of the attack on Battery Simkins, to which you refer, was not an attack properly speaking on Simkins, but was an affair of their own, as the Federals mistook their picket boats for ours and opened fire on them (four I think) and we, thinking it was to be an attack on us, opened fire also as soon as our boats reported at the battery. The Federal boats (two of them, I think) were seen the next morning on the inner beach at Cummings' Point, apparently much injured. The Federal long roll was beat and so was ours, and the infantry camped at Mikell's field were ordered to the point at a double quick and the hospital bombproof lighted up for work. The whole affair occurred at 1 o'clock A.M. and was a false alarm. This is my recollection of the affair, which I think is about correct.

Maj. John Johnson in his THE DEFENSE OF CHARLESTON, 1863-1865, pp. 248-249, described the battle as follows:

The scene of the action on James Island was nearly the same as that of the previous summer, being the southern point of the island, where the Stono and the Folly Rivers approach each other. The Confederate lines and batteries were all as before, with heavy artillery and ammunition, but the light batteries and infantry troops had been moving to the rear for some days, leaving but a scant force of pickets to man the rifle pits. These extended almost from one river to the other, were nearly two miles in advance of the fortifications and were accessible to the enemy on the side of Stono by Grimball's Causeway; on the other side by River's Causeway. Lieutenant-Colonel James Welsman Brown at Secessionville, with Major Edward Manigault of the South Carolina Siege Train in advance, second in command, had been left to defend the ground.

While matters were in this condition, the attack was begun early on the morning of February 10th by a heavy shelling from two gunboats in Folly River and two others in Stono, the latter being soon joined by the monitor Lehigh. From the Union forces on Morris and Folly Islands, under Brigadier-General Schimmelfennig, two regiments with field-guns and two companies of skirmishers, commanded by Colonel A.S. Hartwell, moved on the Confederate outposts by the way of Grimball's Causeway, on the right of the line, skirmishing and advancing twice to the attack. Here, Major Manigault, receiving orders to hold on to the last extremity, made a stubborn defense. He had, all told, but 131 men, only 80 being in front at the rifle-pits with no light artillery at all; and he held those rifle-pits for four hours, until over one-third of his little force was either killed, wounded, or captured, he himself being severely wounded and made a prisoner.

The pits were carried by a front and flanking charge about 3.30 p.m., though not without a loss to the enemy of upward of 90 men. The position, however, was not held, for the troops fell back to the cover of their gunboats the same evening and did not again advance. But the naval fire was continued all night and for several days and nights.

James Harvey McKee in his book, BACK IN WAR TIMES, History of the 144th Regiment, New York Volunteers, published in 1903, stated on page 215:

Among the prisoners was Maj. Merrigault [sic], who commanded the forces of the enemy ... After Major Merrigault's wounds had been dressed and he had been made comfortable by Surgeon [William M.] Bryce, he evinced a desire to fight out the battle in words and the doctor, nothing loth, in friendly converse as he could find time from other cases, kept the Major company late into the night; but the matter was not settled. As so often, on this question "the man convinced against his will was of the same opinion still."

O.R. XLVII (2), p. 1142, has several reports of the Feb. 10 action including:

Battery No. 2, *February 10, 1865 - 6.35 p.m.*

General Hardee

The enemy have driven in my picket line, who have fallen back to the line of rifle-pits. Enemy slowly advancing. Major Manigault reported killed. Only 430 reinforcements have arrived.

S. Elliott
Brigadier-General

(Same to General Taliaferro)

Appendix 2

Following are miscellaneous documents pertaining to Major Edward Manigault or to his Diary. Many are reports, or extracts, published in the Official Records of the Union and Confederate Armies. Some of these were copied from the Diary, either verbatim or with minor changes. Others are from journals of higher authorities, correspondence or reports. References to the applicable dates in the Manigault Diary are bracketed in bold italic type. Sources are bracketed in light italic type.

[*See Introduction, p. vii*]

Office Charleston and Savannah Railroad
Charleston, November 19, 1860

To.
   His Excellency
    W.H. Gist
     Sir.
       I have the honor to request You to bear in mind that my services are at all times ready at the Call of the State. Even if I do not get a position in the Line, I hope that my experience as a Civil Engineer together with what little military service I have seen in a Foreign Country [*Mexico*] in time of war, may make me to be useful in making reconnoissances, examinations of topographical features, settling upon plans of defence, laying out the positions of Batteries, &c. and indeed in attending to all such operations as in a regularly organized service are superintended by Military Engineers.

Allow me to call Your Excellency's attention to the fact that the Siege Gun Carriages in the Citadel [*at Charleston, S.C.*] all require to be overhauled. I was Lieut of Ordnance in 1851-52 when these carriages were constructed. The timber was of good quality, but inasmuch as there was no time to have it thoroughly seasoned, it has <u>Shrunk</u>; and the Iron work is consequently all loose. To render the carriages efficient (for to use them in their present condition would knock them to pieces immediately) it will be necessary to have the Tires cut and again "shrunk on". The same with the Bands or Rings to the Hubs of the wheels. The Boxes should be wedged tightly; and the iron work generally screwed up, and if necessary cut and rewelded in order to fit tightly upon the wood. I estimate that all that is necessary to make the Carriages perfectly efficient may be done at an expense of from $20 to $40 per Carriage, that is, at from 5 per cent to 10 per cent of the original cost.

If Your Excellency will authorize me to have these repairs made, I will devote my personal attention to them, and see that they are properly executed.

Very Respectfully
Your Most Obed^t Servant
Edward Manigault

P.S. I presume that Your Excellency would have at least half of these guns immediately mounted.

[*Personnel records, Edward Manigault*]

[*See Introduction, p. vii*]

Charleston, Sept. 21st 1861

The Honble J.H. Means

Dear Sir:

I suppose you are aware that the Board of Ordnance is not quite dead altho it has been long asleep.

It will be necessary to have a meeting shortly as my Brother, for sundry good reasons, will not retain the post of Col. of Ordnance longer than he can help. The transactions and accounts of the department will be brought up to the 1st of October, to be laid before the Board for examination.

Being the only member of the Board whom it suited to be much in Charleston, I have for nine months given much of my time to the business of the ordnance department, but shall do so no longer. We have not the means of doing what is necessary. We are doing many things for the ordnance department of the Confederate States which pass for their work, and not ours, and it is high time that the Confederate ordnance office should supply what is wanted. But these are smaller considerations.

Writing to you with the utmost frankness I will say that the reason why I do not choose to be longer active in these matters and desire that my Brother should get rid of his [*the word "office" is struck out*] post as Col. of Ordnance is this — The duties of the Ordnance department are in many people's minds confounded with the military measures for the defence of the sea coast and in my opinion those measures are under the control of military and engineering incapacity. I will not here give you my reasons for holding this opinion.

I have, however, great faith in the incapacity and want of enterprise of our Yankee foes, and believe that the works of our engineers and the [*the word "dispositions" is struck out*] military dispositions of our generals will prove effectual against the enemy should they fail to attack us.

Hoping that when summoned, you will attend the meeting of the Board, and lend your aid to the ordnance officer in closing [*the word "up" is struck out*] his connection with the department, I remain

Truly and Respectfully Yours

G. [*Gabriel*] Manigault

[*Unpublished letter in possession of the Manigault family*]

[*See Introduction, pp. vii, viii*]

Charleston, S.C. May 18, 1863

The Hon.
    James A. Seddon
       Secretary of War
       Richmond, Va.
Sir.

    I have the honor to apply for the command of the Battalion of Siege Artillery now in this City, rendered vacant by the resignation of Major Alston; and for a Commission of suitable grade for the exercise of said command.

    In support of this application and for information as to the amount of service I have experienced, I would respectfully state that during the War between the United States and Mexico, I was for seven months Major in Command of the 13th Infantry U.S.A. and continued in command of that Regiment until its disbandment at the conclusion of the War. That, for one year after the Secession of South Carolina from the Federal Union, I held the position of Chief of Ordnance for that State; which post I left in order to take command of a Mixed Battalion of Infantry, Cavalry and Artillery, raised by Special permission of the War Department for "Local Coast Defence". This Battalion was broken up and myself ejected by the operation of the Conscription Act.

    Hoping that the experience in Military Command above referred to may be a sufficient warrant for the present application, I have the honor to subscribe myself Very Respectfully

Your Obed^t Sv^t.
Edward Manigault

[*Personnel records, Edward Manigault*]

[*See Introduction, p. i; Diary, 14 July 1863*]

SPECIAL ORDERS   Hdqrs. Dept. of S.C., Ga. and Fla.
No. 141   *Charleston, S.C., July 15, 1863*
    *   *   *   *   *   *   *

    X. The commanding officers of posts and batteries actively engaged against the enemy will keep a daily journal of operations, forwarding a copy of the same to these headquarters through district commanders. Engineer officers will report likewise through the chief engineer.

    By command of General Beauregard:

JNO. M. OTEY
Assistant Adjutant-General

[*OR XXVIII (2) p. 202*]

[*See Diary, 26-27 July 1863*]

Headquarters Legare's Point,
James Island, July 26, 1863

    CAPTAIN: I beg leave to call the attention of the proper authorities to the character and condition of the work constructed at Legare's Point.

    These fortifications were commenced with the sole view of defense against an attack in barges from the direction of Black Island, or against batteries which might be erected on that island. They consist of short sections or portions of a parapet, each one long enough to cover a gun from fire in front, thick enough to resist cannon shot, and of a height such that guns mounted on siege-carriages might fire *en barbette* over them. These short parapets were disposed, at invervals of 35 to 40 yards, on a slightly curved line corresponding with the indention of the shore. Behind each of these short parapets, a platform was laid for a gun. A simple breastwork for riflemen connected these paparets together.

The platforms were laid, against my advice, with an inclination toward Black Island equal to that which is usually adopted with siege platforms, where the guns are intended to fire in one direction only. The result of this mode of construction is that, from the lowness of the parapet, the absence of epaulements or flank defenses, the stringing out of the guns on a line approximating a straight one, the absence of merlons and traverses, and the inclination of the platforms, the work is totally unfit for either bringing a fire to bear on, or sustaining a fire from, any other point but one nearly in the direction of Black Island. I do not hesitate to pronounce it, in its present condition, totally unfit to fire on, or sustain a fire from, Morris Island.

It is true that in the last two days traverses have been constructed, not between each two guns, but in the rear of the space between two guns. These traverses would afford no protection whatever to the guns unless they were withdrawn entirely from the platforms and placed behind the traverses, in which position they would be of no manner of use. If the battery is to be of any use against Morris Island, those guns which have sufficient range should be fired through embrasures of splay suffcient to give a field of fire corresponding to the distance from the advanced Yankee batteries on Morris Island (or if desired from Craig's Hill) to Battery Wagner, and such guns as have not range sufficient had better be shut in entirely in that direction by merlons or traverses.

As none of our siege-carriages are constructed to admit of sufficient elevation to reach Morris Island (distance 2½ miles), when the wheels and trail are upon the same level, it would be well to dispense with platforms altogether for those guns intended to fire on that island; and after leveling, packing, and ramming the platform space well, to leave it to the artillerists to lay planks for the wheels to rest on, while the trail will rest upon planks in the bottom of a trench dug for the express purpose of sinking or lowering the trail. This plan should only adopted with those guns intended for very long range; the platforms for the other guns might remain as they are.

Again, if the battery should be called on to sustain a fire from Black Island from a superior number and caliber of guns, the small height over which it is possible to fire with guns mounted on siege-carriages would indicate the propriety of the use of embrasures in that direction. also.

With the exception of the two or three guns which might be put in position at the extreme point facing Morris Island, there should be no obstruction to each guns's firing to the right over the parapet. With most of the guns, this would be in the direction of the creeks and marshes toward Secessionville.

I beg that this report may meet with immediate attention.

Very respectfully, your obedient servant,

EDWARD MANIGAULT

Major, Commanding Post

Capt. J.M. Carson,

Assistant Adjutant-General, Royal's, James Island.

Headquarters First Military District
Charleston, July 27, 1863.
Respectfully forwarded and recommended to the attention of the general commanding the department.

R.S. RIPLEY,
Brigadier-General, Commanding.

Hdqrs. Department of South Carolina, &c.,
Charleston, S.C., August 4, 1863
Respectfully referred to Lieutenant-Colonel Harris to know if the objections referred to by Major Manigault have been remedied where practicable.

G.T. BEAUREGARD
General, Commanding.

Office of Chief Engineer
Charleston, August 6, 1863.
Respectfully returned.

Battery Haskell has been prepared for two guns on columbiad carriages and six siege guns in embrasures, to fire on Morris Island from Graham's house and Battery Wagner inclusive. One gun has been arranged to fire on Morris Island and the approaches to Secessionville which is the only one that is necessary or practicable to be made to bear in that direction. Orders have been given and are now being executed for a similar arrangement in Battery Haskell for eight field pieces.

The traverses to which Major Manigault refers were constructed by my order for the purpose of protecting the pieces when not in position, which I considered important in the exposed condition of the battery, as at first constructed *en barbette.*

Battery Ryan and battery at the Point of Pines, when completed, will command Black Island and all the approaches to Secessionville, in conjunction with the eastern redoubt of the lines and the guns at Secessionville.

D.B. HARRIS
Lieutenant-Colonel, and Chief Engineer.

[*OR XXVIII (1), pp. 552-554*]

Hdqrs. Dept. of South Carolina, Georgia and Florida
Charleston, S.C. August 6, 1863.
Maj. E. Manigault.
Comdg. Legare's Point, James Island, S.C.:
MAJOR: Your letter of the 26th ultimo, addressed to Capt. J.M. Carson, calling attention to the proper authorities to the works constructed at Legare's Point, has been received and referred to Lieutenant-Colonel Harris, chief engineer, whose remarks upon the same I am instructed to communicate to you, as follows: [*See preceeding letter of Lt. Col. D.B. Harris, quoted here verbatim*]
Very respectfully, your obedient servant,

CLIFTON H. SMITH
Assistant Adjutant-General

[*OR XXVIII (2), p. 260*]

Extracts from diary of Maj. Edward Manigault, C.S. Artillery, commanding Artillery at Legare's Point, August 19—September 7.*

*These extracts were forwarded from day to day, those for August 19 and September 1-7 to Capt. P.K. Molony, assistant adjutant-general, the others to Lieut. E.K. Bryan, acting assistant adjutant general, on duty at Brig. Gen. Johnson Hagood's Headquarters; from there they were transmitted to department [*South Carolina, Georgia and Florida, Charleston, S.C.*] headquarters.

August 19. — Opened fired at 5.30 a.m. with 8-inch columbiad and 30-pounder Parrott gun; also, shortly after, with 10-inch sea-coast mortar. At the thirteenth round, the 30-pounder Parrott gun burst; 1 man badly stunned and 1 slightly so; no other damage done; this took place at 7.45 a.m. After 4 shots with mortar, suspended firing it until I could communicate with Captain Mitchel at Battery Simkins and make arrangements for signaling to me the range of our mortar shells.

The fuses, as before, proved very defective, very few of the shells bursting. At 11.30 a.m. commenced firing with the 4-inch Blakely gun. The shells failed to reach Morris Island, and after 9 shots we ceased firing.

At about 12 m. commenced firing 10-inch sea-coast mortar, Captain Mitchel having sent one of the signal corps to signal to us whether our shells fell short, went over, or proved correct.

Moved a rifle 24-pounder from Battery Ryan to Battery Haskell and put it in battery. Four 3½-inch Blakely guns for Company A, South Carolina Siege Train, arrived about 12 o'clock last night from the Charleston Arsenal. Ceased firing at 6.45 p.m.

Mortar platform for No. 2 unserviceable, and needs being relaid.

The 8-inch columbiad fired 54 shells; the 30-pounder Parrott, 13 shells; the 4-inch Blakely, 9 shells; the 10-inch mortar, 18 shells.

I respectfully call your attention to the above note of the unserviceable condition of mortar platform No. 2. I hope that a requisition will be made immediately upon the engineers for its repair.

[Indorsements]

Headquarters East Lines,
August 19, 1863.

Respectfully forwarded, and attention asked to remarks upon fuses and mortar platform.

JOHNSON HAGOOD
Brigadier-General, Commanding.

Headquarters James Island
August 20, 1863.

Respectfully forwarded. Have called attention before to the condition of the mortar beds, and respectfully ask that evil be remedied.

WM. B. TALIAFERRO
Brigadier-General

August 23. — At 3 a.m. heavy firing was heard in the direction of Fort Sumter. As there was a very heavy fog, nothing could be seen, but, from the peculiar sound of the shells, we concluded that two or more monitors were firing, at short range, on Fort Sumter. The fire appeared to be returned from the fort. The fire continued heavily for half an hour, when it slackened off. The monitors appeared to have gone off before the fog lifted. The Ironsides was seen to go off after it cleared off, about 8 o'clock.

After the fog lifted, commenced firing 8-inch columbiad, first at the Marsh Battery and afterward at the heavy rifle battery to the south of Graham's headquarters. Later in the day, fired upon one of the advanced batteries of the enemy. Did not fire the other guns, as they were kept in reserve for the battery in the marsh.

Sent Capt. S.P. Smith to the city about 12 m., on special ordnance duty.

Lieutenant [Felix] Lake, of Company K, Second Regiment, South Carolina Artillery, who has been in command of the detachment working the columbiad and mortars, was relieved at 4 p.m. by Lieutenant [T.A.] Pitts, of the same regiment. This change was made by special request and arrangement of Lieutenant-Colonel Brown.

At 5 p.m. commenced firing 8-inch sea-coast howitzers and 4-inch Blakely gun on the Marsh Battery, in order to ascertain the direction and range for night firing. A considerable number of men seen at the Marsh Battery a little before sunset.

August 25. — During the night the enemy has thrown up another battery in the marsh, about 400 yards to the east of the eastern extremity of Black Island. This battery is about the same distance from Battery Haskell as Black Island is, viz, about 1¼ miles. (The conclusion which I draw from the erection of this battery is that the enemy is about to attack this point, and it would be folly to suppose that he will confine himself to building batteries in the marsh when the firm ground of Black Island, not more distant, offers so many superior advantages. I have no doubt, therefore, but that there either are or soon will be strong batteries on Black Island.) Only the base of the battery is as yet thrown up (probably to a height of 4 feet). It is likely that the remaining height will be given by sandbags. *It should be noted that there are only two platforms at Battery Haskell from which guns can be brought to bear upon this battery in the marsh (No. 2).*

In consequence of the heavy showers of last night, five of the platforms of Battery Haskell were under water this morning, and the planks in some of them were floating. One or two of these platforms we were unable to drain, as the level of the platforms was below the surface of the water in the borrow pits. The engineers have been called on by me (in pursuance of oral instructions to me from General Beauregard) to take measures to drain the borrow pits, but nothing has been done; on the contrary, a road has been made which backs up an additional quantity of water.

A considerable engineer force employed in finishing magazine at Battery Ryan (central battery or section). *The magazine, which is in two compartments, is, however, small, and the water was dripping through it at 2 p.m. to-day.*

At 2 p.m. the 8-inch navy shell gun (one of the guns from the Isaac P. Smith) was mounted in southeast angle of Redoubt No. 1. *It is mounted on a columbiad carriage of pine wood, 1½ inches too wide between the cheeks. The maximum elevation possible, 10°. The elevating screw is out of order.*

At 2 p.m. Captain Smith arrived with one section of 8-inch siege howitzers, Company B, Siege Train, at Point of Pines, in accordance with orders previously given.

At about 4 p.m. Colonel Gonzales, chief of artillery, visited Battery Haskell, to inspect the condition of the same. (This inspection was in consequence of the unfavorable report of them which I sent to headquarters to-day.)

At 7 p.m. received orders to fire with all available guns on Morris Island to south of Battery Wagner, as the enemy was reported advancing in heavy force. Opened immediately from the 8-inch columbiad, and from 4.62-inch rifle and 24-pounder rifle (5.82-inch caliber), as soon as the skids upon which the wheels rested (for elevation) could be turned in the new direction. (They had been trained on Marsh Battery No. 1, preparatory to night firing.) Fired 33 shells from the 8-inch columbiad, 22 from 4.62-inch Rifle, and 15 from 5.82-inch rifle. As the firing of small-arms ceased in front of Battery Wagner, the fire of our guns was slackened and finally ceased also. It did not appear to us that an actual assault was made on Battery Wagner, as our men did not seem to be driven in from the rifle-pits in front of that work.

The enemy made many signals from Light-House Inlet during the engagement, by means of rockets, and red, blue, green, and white lights.

The infantry supports at Battery Haskell and point of Pines were strongly re-enforced by Major Glover.

Heavy showers fell about this time, say 8.30 to 9 o'clock, and lighter ones off and on until early in the morning.

At 1 a.m. two ordnance wagons arrived from Fort Johnson with ammunition, &c, viz, fuses, gunners' pouches, 4-inch Blakely shells, 8-inch canister and grape, rammer and sponge, &c.

[Indorsements]
Hdqrs. 1st Mil. Dist., Dept. of S.C., Ga., and Fla.,
Charleston, August 28, 1863.
Respectfully forwarded. Wants noted [in italics] and ordered to be supplied at once.

R.S. RIPLEY
Brigadier-General, Commanding.

Hdqrs. Dept. South Carolina, Georgia, and Florida
Charleston, August 29, 1863.
Respectfully referred to Lieutenant-Colonel Harris, chief engineer, who will please attend at once to the wants of the battery at Legare's Point and return this paper to these headquarters.

By command of General Beauregard:

CLIFTON H. SMITH
Assistant Adjutant-General

August 26. — Captain [T.B.] Lee, of the engineers, engaged in opening the embrasures at Battery Haskell, so as to extend the field of fire to the southward.

While his hands were so employed, we were prevented from firing upon Morris Island or the Marsh Battery No. 1. In the afternoon, fired several shots at the Marsh Battery No. 1.

Nothing more has been done by the enemy on Marsh Battery No. 2. It is possible that this battery may be only a sham to attract our notice and draw our fire, while the true batteries are being erected on Black Island. Battery Haskell has not yet fired on this battery, and will not do so until there are further evidences of its being a real work. It has, however, been fired on from either Battery Cheves or one of the batteries at Fort Johnson.

At 6.40 p.m. the enemy made an attack upon the rifle-pits in front of Battery Wagner. All of the James Island batteries opened a rapid fire upon the portion of Morris Island to the south of said rifle-pits. The 8-inch columbiad, 5.82-inch rifle, and 4.62-inch rifle were used for this purpose at Battery Haskell. As the evidences of musketry fire at Battery Wagner ceased, our fire was suspended. Later we received orders from General Taliaferro to continue the fire at intervals as nearly as possible upon the rifle-pits, which were reported to be in the hands of the enemy. Accordingly, fire was kept up all night from the 8-inch columbiad and 4.62-inch rifle, at intervals of ten to fifteen minutes.

The detachment from the Siege Train (20 men) which has been on duty at Battery Wagner, was relieved at 1 o'clock this morning (27th), and returned to James Island. Night stormy and rainy. Wind at first southeast, then permanently northeast.

August 27. — The enemy very busy in intrenching himself in the sand-hill about 200 or 250 yards in front of Battery Wagner (of which he got possession last night). The 8-inch columbiad in Battery Haskell was brought to bear upon the working parties, and continued firing slowly until the ammunition was so nearly exhausted as to render it prudent to reserve what remained (the difficulty is to procure 8-inch shells). The 24-pounder rifle and 4.62-inch rifle were then brought to bear, and continued firing steadily (with some interval from 4 to 5 p.m) during the remainder of the day. Some very good shots were made with the 4.62-inch rifle; but the failure of the shells to explode rendered the fire comparatively ineffective. Battery Simkins was also firing slowly at the same point. Battery Cheves did not fire.

At 8 p.m. received orders to be prepared for firing on Morris Island to south of Battery Wagner, in case of a further attack on that post. The guns were accordingly prepared, but as no attack was made, we did not fire.

August 28. — Some object resembling a gun is visible this morning in Marsh Battery No. 2. It is impossible, however, to decide if it be a real gun or not. The battery has not been built higher since it was first observed on the morning of 25th instant.

About 11 o'clock Major Mallett, of the Confederate Ordnance Department, came to Legare's Point for the purpose of inspecting, and if possible, remedying the defects of the fuses and other ordnance stores. He remained, witnessing the firing, &c., for two hours, and had full evidence of the worthlessness of the fuses.

About 3 p.m. Colonel [John F.] Lay, inspector of artillery, visited Battery Haskell, and remained until 4.30 p.m.

Fired, by order, at the old rifle-pits in front of Battery Wagner, with the columbiad, 4 solid shot; with the 24-pounder rifle, 8 shells; with 4.62-inch rifle, 18 shells. Some of the shots were very good, the round shot and shells being several times thrown into the enemy's works, but the failure of the shells to explode prevented the fire from being effective.

Capt. Lee's engineer hands engaged in widening the embrasures more to the southward. The borrow pits have been in a great measure drained; but this has been done by cutting through the roads and interior communications of the battery, so as to interfere with the moving of the guns, &c., from one part of the battery to another. It is probable, however, that this interruption of the communications is only temporary. Heavy rain about 6 p.m. lasting about an hour.

August 31. — J.H. Lopez, artificer, of Company A., South Carolina Siege Train, was sent to the city to endeavor to procure seasoned oak for repairing mortar beds.

Lieutenant [Ralph] Nesbit sick. This is particularly unfortunate, as he was the only officer available for the special service of the rifle guns firing upon Morris Island. Application has been made to headquarters for a detail — of one, at least — of Captain [B.C.] Webb's (Company A, Siege Train) lieutenants, but no notice has been taken of it.

The companies and detachments (artillery) at Legare's Point inspected and mustered about 12 m. to-day.

In consequence of the high wind, Lieutenant Nesbit's sickness, and the occupation of other officers in inspection and muster and other duties usual on last day of month, there was no firing from Battery Haskell to-day. These latter reasons would not be sufficient, and would not be given if it were not that it is seriously doubted whether, at 2⅜ miles' range, and with a high wind blowing, we can effect anything with our shells, which do not explode.

Ninety-eight 8-inch columbiad shells and 200 sabots received at Battery Haskell to-day.

At 2.30 p.m. four monitors moved up and engaged Fort Moultrie, Battery Bee, Battery Beauregard, and Battery Gregg; all at long range excepting Battery Gregg. After about one and a half to two hours they retired, one, it is thought, precipitately.

Generals Taliaferro and Hagood, Colonels Roman, Lay, and others, visited Battery Haskell about 5 p.m.

The engineers engage today in strengthening the parapet of Battery Tatom (Point of Pines).

September 1. — All the officers very busy making up monthly returns — ordnance returns, weekly returns, artillery, &c. Made report to chief of artillery of bursting of 4.62-inch gun, August 22, at Battery Haskell; also report of Captain Smith's trials in shelling Black Island from Point of Pines (Battery Tatom) [*See Diary entry, Saturday, 29 Aug. 1863*].

At 12.30 p.m. Generals Ripley and Taliaferro visited Battery Haskell.

At 1 p.m. engineer hands commenced repair of magazine at Battery Ryan.

At the same time, another party commenced a more thorough drainage of the interior of Battery Haskell. I visited Battery Cheves to see the 8-inch navy shell guns of 55 and 56 cwt., one of which is promised to Battery Haskell under certain contingencies. Took measurement of same in order to adapt a carriage to them. Rode to Fort Johnson and saw Lieutenant-Colonel Yates, who said we might have one of the guns; and also one columbiad pattern carriage and chassis, provided there were two of them. As there turned out to be only one, of course we could not get it.

At 6 p.m. the Second Battalion, Twenty-fifth Regiment South Carolina Volunteers, Major Glover commanding, was relieved by the Fifty-fourth Georgia, Lieutenant-Colonel Rawls commanding. The battalion of the Twenty-fifth (Eutaw) marched immediately to Fort Johnson, preparatory to going to Morris Island.

At 11 p.m. a heavy cannonade commenced between Fort Moultrie and Batteries Bee, Beauregard and Gregg, and the Yankee ironclads. This firing lasted almost all night.

September. 2 — At early dawn, four monitors were seen to go off from the neighborhood of Fort Sumter. Some persons assert that there were six of them;

but this is far from certain. Their fire appears to have been principally directed against Fort Sumter. During the morning, and again in the afternoon, we fired with the 8-inch columbiad upon Marsh Battery No. 1 whenever any person was seen about it. Generals Beauregard, Taliaferro, and Hagood visited Battery Haskell about 12.30 p.m.

Sent wagon into town to carry the wrought-iron work of two mortar beds to the Charleston Arsenal, to be used with the new iron mortar beds which are being cast for Battery Haskell.

About 8 p.m. a wooden mortar bed was brought to Battery Haskell.

Very quiet during the night; scarcely any firing at all, except occasionally from Battery Wagner.

September 3. — At about 10 a.m. sent carriage and limber of the 30-pounder Parrott which burst at Battery Haskell, August 19, to central ordnance depot in Charleston, together with the chase portion of the exploded gun. Lieutenant-Colonel Waddy, chief of ordnance, had directed the carriage and limber only to be carried to the city, but, in pursuance of a verbal order given by General Beauregard yesterday, such portion of the gun as could be gotten on the carriage was sent also. Lieutenant [W.W.] Legare, ordnance officer, furnished the mules and drivers by order.

Moved the 4-inch Blakely gun from Platform No. 7 in Battery Haskell to Platform No. 9. Moved the 4.62-inch rifle siege gun, received August 30, to Platform No. 7, but accidently it was dismounted while being shifted from the traveling bed to trunnion beds. As we were not provided with the proper blocks, levers, ropes, &c., sent immediately to Lieutenant Legare, ordnance officer, requesting that a garrison gin should be sent down with hands to mount the gun. The gin arrived at Battery Haskell about 7 p.m. but without block and tackle. The labor of shifting guns at Battery Haskell is very great, as the road communication in rear of the platforms is cut through by open drains between each two platforms, in order to drain the borrow pits; hence heavy skids have to be moved from drain to drain to pass the guns over.

In the forenoon, fired 10 shots from the 8-inch columbiad at Marsh Battery No. 1, about which some of the enemy were seen. Only 1 shot struck the battery though several went near it. The enemy went off or concealed themselves closely in the battery.

Lieutenant Nesbit went to the city on surgeon's certificate; as he was much prostrated by sickness, four hours' leave of absence was granted to Captain Smith to accompany him to hospital, and make proper arrangements for him, &c. In consequence, however, of several hours delay at the Ashley River Bridge (which is undergoing repair), Captain Smith did not report again to headquarters at Legare's Point until 8 p.m.

As a good many of the enemy were visible in the hills to the south of Fort Wagner, about 5 p.m. commenced firing on them with 8-inch columbiad and 4.62-inch rifle No. 1. Fourteen shots were fired from the 4.62-inch rifle and 10 from the columbiad. Only 1 of the shells from each gun burst, and in both cases they were short. Four of the shells from the 4.62-inch fell in the very midst of the enemy, but as they did not burst, it is not likely that much, if any, damage was done. They did not interrupt the enemy's operations. The practice with the 8-inch columbiad was rather wild, and none of its shells appeared to fall in immediate contiguity with the enemy (distance 2⅝ miles). At dark ceased firing, as no reliance could be had in our shells by night.

At 5 p.m. Lieutenants [J.A.] Brux and [R.E.] Mellichamp, of Company A, Siege Train, reported for duty at Battery Haskell.

At 5 p.m. the enemy fired 3 shots from east end of Black Island toward Battery Haskell. The shots appeared to come from a rifled piece of small caliber, say 30-pounder at most; but as all the shell broke or burst prematurely, none reached Battery Haskell, and it was impossible to judge what was the caliber of the piece used. After 3 shots the enemy ceased firing. No reply was made from Battery Haskell, as their fire was not at all annoying, and it was not deemed worth while to reply.

P.S. Unusually quiet to-day. Very little firing on either side.

[Indorsement]

Headquarters James Island
September 4, 1863.
Respectfully forwarded. Attention particularly called to the fact, so often reported, of the worthlessness of the fuses furnished, which it is hoped will be improved. Also to the firing of the enemy from Black Island, and particularly to their opening with what I conceive to be boat howitzers. No works can be seen.

WM. B. TALIAFERRO
Brigadier-General

September 4. — One of the 10-inch mortars remounted, but on an old pine mortar bed which will not probably stand many shots. The 4.62-inch rifle, which was accidentally dismounted yesterday, was also remounted.

As the enemy was seen working very assiduously on a battery or breastwork in front of Battery Wagner, which is constructed on a line open to direct enfilading fire from Battery Haskell, at 1 p.m. we opened fire on him with the 4.62-inch gun No. 1. Fired 18 shells, of which 3 burst short, and 2 broke to pieces or burst prematurely. No others burst at all. Three or 4 shots were very good, and scattered the workmen, but they appear to be practiced hands, and returned instantly to work as soon as the danger was past, without one moment's delay or loss of time. About 3 p.m. ceased firing, to allow the gun to cool and the men to get their dinner. At 5 p.m. commenced firing from the same gun (which is by far the most accurate and reliable one we have) at the same point. Fired 18 shells, of which 3 burst short, and 3 of them exceedingly near the working parties. We could not at the distance (2⅜ miles) see if any one was injured, though observing with two glasses. The workmen scattered as usual whenever a shell went near them, but instantly returned to work as soon as the danger was past. At 6.15 p.m. the enemy's reliefs moved up from the neighborhood of Graham's headquarters. They appeared so numerous that it was supposed that an assault was intended, and fire was opened from the 8-inch columbiad on them. Six shells were thrown at them, but did not burst. By this time it became evident, from the number of men returning toward Graham's from the different batteries, that the body of men first seen was simply the relief. Ceased firing at dark.

The Marsh Battery No. 1, of which the parapet to the north was considerably damaged and displaced by the concussion of the gun, has been repaired. The muzzle of the gun which showed over the parapet no longer appears. From the indications noticed, it is likely that the damaged gun will soon be replaced by a new one.

Very little firing during the night. An occasional shot from Battery Cheves toward Marsh Battery No. 1, and rifle battery to south of Graham's headquarters.

September 5. — The Ironsides and two or three monitors bombarded Battery Wagner from early dawn, the land batteries aiding slightly. This was continued until about midday. The bombardment was very heavy. Battery Wagner returned the fire slowly until about 10 a.m.

In the afternoon the bombardment was continued by the heavy rifle batteries near Graham's headquarters (the iron-clads having retired). The bombardment of the afternoon was also very severe.

About 5.30 p.m. we received notice from General Hagood that an attack on Cumming's Point was probable. All the available guns in Battery Haskell were immediately prepared for firing upon Morris Island in case of assault. While preparing the 4.62-inch gun, No. 2, for firing, the gun was accidentally spiked by a gunner's gimlet breaking off in the vent. For the time the gun was rendered unserviceable.

In the afternoon, 7 shots were fired from the 4.62-inch rifle, No. 1, upon Morris Island. Some of the shots were good, but only 1 shell burst. Six shots were also fired from the smooth-bore 24-pounder at second battery to north of Graham's headquarters. One of the shots struck very near the battery and made some of the gunners scatter (distance 2½ miles).

After nightfall, a monitor took up a position to northeast of Battery Gregg, occasionally firing, and being fired at from Battery Gregg. The Yankee land batteries at the same time shelled Wagner and the hills between Wagner and Gregg. Captain [John H.] Mickler came to Legare's Point to-day about 2.30 p.m. preparing for some scouting expedition.

September 6. — At 1 a.m. precisely, being about one hour after the moon had risen, the Yankees attacked Cumming's Point in barges. A heavy fire from the enemy's boat howitzers and from two of our 12-pounder howitzers, together with a sharp musketry fire, opened the attack. Battery Gregg does not appear to have fired her heavy guns at all. The Yankee land batteries immediately commenced to shell Wagner heavily, and also that portion of the island between Gregg and Wagner. The James Island batteries immediately directed their fire against different points of the enemy's batteries on Morris Island. The fire of the 8-inch columbiad, one 24-pounder rifle, one 24-pounder smoothbore, and one 4.62-inch rifle, in Battery Haskell, was directed at a calcium light visible on one of the mortar batteries, between one-fourth and one-half mile south of Battery Wagner. One 10-inch mortar was fired toward a battery still farther to the south. The 8-inch columbiad was fired fourteen times; the 10-inch mortar, thirteen times; the 24-pounder rifle, seven times; the 24-pounder smooth-bore, thirteen times; the 4.62-inch rifle, seven times. As it was night, we did not ascertain if any damage was done by our fire. After twenty or thirty minutes, the attack on Cumming's Point ceased, and the attacking party was repulsed. The fire on both sides gradually subsided. The enemy fired slowly and steadily after this, and only occasional shots were fired from our batteries in return. At 3.30 a.m. dismissed the men from their guns. At day dawn the Ironsides and two or three monitors commenced a heavy bombardment of Battery Wagner. This was continued by the land batteries in the afternoon.

I sent to headquarters the following papers: (1) Weekly return of ordnance at Battery Haskell, (for Colonel Waddy). (2) Weekly return of ordnance at Redoubt No. 1, for same officer. (3) Return of small-arms, accouterments, and ammunition, to Lieut. H.C. Cunningham, ordnance officer. (4) Requisition for mechanic to drill vent of 4.62-inch rifle; for friction tubes (1,000), and for nails to strap shells. (5) Captain Webb's return of light artillery to Colonel Gonzales. (6) Note to Captain Taliaferro about an objectionable part of my diary of 31st August.

About 12 m. a barbette carriage and chassis arrived at Battery Haskell for a double-banded 24-pounder rifle. This description of carriage does not give a field of fire sufficient for the position in which it is proposed to place the gun. It would have been infinitely better if the gun could be traversed on a full circle.

At 3.30 p.m. a double-banded 24-pounder was brought to Battery Haskell. Inner band, 31 inches by 1⅝ inches thick. Outer band, 25¾ inches by 1¾ inches. Also, about dark, 54 immensely heavy solid conical shot for same gun. I think they will necessarily strain the gun. At 7 p.m. received notice that Morris Island will be evacuated to-night, with orders to have every available gun ready to check the advance of the Yankees on our retreating troops. The guns were accordingly prepared and the detachments at their posts. Up to 12 o'clock there was nothing to indicate that such a movement was intended.

September 7. — About 2 a.m. the Yankees appeared to have become aware that some unusual movement was going on, for they ceased firing into Fort Wagner, and commenced shelling the ground between Wagner and Gregg tolerably vigorously.

At 3 a.m. 3 rockets were thrown up from the direction of Shell Point, which was the signal previously arranged for opening fire upon the sites of Batteries Wagner and Gregg (it had been intended to blow up those works). As the expected destruction of the works had not taken place, and as Colonel Yates, at Fort Johnson, so much nearer the scene of operations, had not opened fire, I hesitated to fire for some minutes. Under General Taliaferro's direction (who passed the night from about 10 p.m. to 3.30 a.m. at Battery Haskell), I dispatched a courier to Colonel Yates to inquire if any change had been made in the signals previously decided on. In the meantime commenced firing slowly upon Morris Island to south of Battery Wagner, and gradually (as Colonel Yates' reply did not arrive) upon Battery Wagner itself. Fired till daylight, and then ceased. The Second Battalion, Twenty-fifth Regiment South Carolina Volunteers from Battery Wagner, arrived at their camp at Legare's shortly before day. They left this point to go to Morris Island on Tuesday evening, September 1. Some of the companies went over that night, and the rest the next night. Battery Simkins and Cheves firing upon Gregg and Wagner and the intervening space during the day. The enemy did not return the fire. Battery Haskell did not fire until about 5 p.m., and then only a few shots.

The engineer hands engaged in constructing a covered way and causeway from the mortar battery on right flank of Battery Haskell to the covered way already constructed on north side of the road to the point.

At 6.15 p.m. the Ironsides and five monitors entered the harbor (above Battery Gregg) and had an engagement, lasting from forty-five to sixty minutes, with Fort Moultrie and Batteries Bee and Beauregard. The firing was at long range. Shortly after 7 p.m. the iron-clads retired. General Hagood visited Battery Haskell at nightfall and gave certain directions for increased vigilance. He afterward visited Battery Ryan and gave similar directions. The shots fired from Battery Haskell on Morris Island from 3.30 a.m. to daybreak were as follows: 10-inch mortar, 8 shots; 8-inch columbiad, 4 shots; 24-pounder smooth-bore, 7 shots; 24-pounder rifle, 4 shots; 4.62-inch rifle, 4 shots. Total, 27.

[*OR XXVIII (1) pp. 554-563*]

[*See Diary, 24 Sept. 1863*]

Charleston, *September 25, 1863*

Lieut. Col. J.R. Waddy,
    Chief of Ordnance Department:
    COLONEL: On the 24th instant I inspected the ordnance and ordnance stores at the following batteries: Haskell, Tatom, Ryan, and Redoubt No. 1, eastern lines, all under the command of Maj. Edward Manigault, and have the honor to submit the following report:
    These works, with the Batteries Simkins and Cheves, constitute the defensive lines on the eastern shore of James Island, facing Morris Island, Simkins, and Redoubt No. 1, the right and left flanks, respectively. The armament of Battery Haskell consists of the following pieces: One sea-coast howitzer, 8-inch siege-carriage, one 4-inch Blakely, one of the James bronzed field pieces, captured at Shiloh, one 20-pounder Parrott, one smooth 24-pounder, two 4.62-inch, one 24-pounder double-banded rifle, and two mortars, 10-inch; in all, ten pieces.
    The Blakely projectiles are reported by Maj. Manigault inefficient, having neither the range nor accuracy required, and it is respectfully recommended that other shot be cast for these guns of the pattern now in general use for rifled pieces, with flexible metallic sabots.
    One of the 4.62 banded rifles has been fired in this battery 261 rounds only, and now exhibits evidence of weakness, the rear or breech band having started from its original seat. The two mortars are on cast-iron beds, with wooden transoms of pine timber. These transoms are severely shaken, and cannot sustain many more discharges from long range.
    The armament of Batteries Ryan and Tatom are from the guns belonging to the siege train, all of which are in order.
    Redoubt No. 1 will be noticed in this report on the eastern lines, to which it properly belongs.
    In my last report, on the 23d instant, I expressed my reason for reporting on the construction of magazines and which I need not again repeat.
    The magazines of Haskell, Tatom, and Ryan, are all defective in construction, cramped in accommodation, and unfit for the storage of powder. The struts of the door have sprung from pressure. The revetment is of round timber, which will roll out of place when the struts fail, and to the entrance of one the sod revetment is perpendicular. The earth on this has cracked open on the right of the doorway, and will certainly fall in when shaken by the first shell that may lodge in or near the magazine. It is considered so unsafe that the commandant of the post deems it prudent to keep his ammunition outside, in chests.
    I beg leave to entail upon you the trouble of reading the following remarks in reference to the alteration of guns from smooth to rifled, the banding of guns, weight of projectiles, the wear and tear of carriages, which is deemed important to the economy of ordnance, and of your consideration. The conclu-

sions arrived at are based on the evidence of facts and experience in the field, and will be placed before you as concisely as a clear expression will admit.

First. Some manufacturers of ordnance deny the fact that a gun is weakened by rifling and attribute their frequent bursting to the heavier projectiles used. While there is some truth as regards weight of projectiles, it is a fact that the fractures in rifled guns follow the edge of the groove exactly as ice and granite fracture in lines cut upon the surface. It is known that acute re-entering angles upon the surface of guns are the usual lines of rupture, hence the present external form of guns without moldings. From these facts, no rifled guns should have acute or sharp-edged grooves, but a flattened curve thus ⌒ as the Parrott, which, though it does not remedy the injury from rifling, has been proved to be the least injurious form.

Second. Banded guns, facts and experience prove, to be weaker at the breech than at the re-enforce, as of four which I have examined on the front of our defenses, all have fractured square at the vent, throwing the breech to the rear. If the breech is strengthened, explosions would not be so frequent. It would be economical, therefore, to use the wrought-iron shackles of Captain Brooke, although the expense of banding would be double. Some suppose this arrangement weakens the trunnion, but it is a mistake. A trunnion that is not previously fractured is never torn off by the recoil, which shock it is only subjected to, and to which the additional weight of the shackle would add but little momentum. An improvement on this plan would be to cast or turn off a hemispherical breech, over which fit a wrought iron band accurately adjusted, and over this the trunnion shackle, or any other method that would secure the breech in a wrought-iron shell in close or firm contact with the cast iron.

Third. We are certainly in error as regards weight of elongated projectiles, which requires immediate correction for effective service, as well as on the score of economy. We must have some safe, fixed limit determined for the weight of shot, beyond which weight it should be made penal to serve, for we cannot afford experiments in the field, excepting at the cost of dismantling our works, and this it would be more judicious, as well as economical, to leave to the prowess of the enemy.

In Battery Haskell we have 60-pound shells and 80-pound shots for 24-pounder rifled guns. The initial velocity of 1,600 feet per second has been fixed upon by the experience of the past as a maximum for economy and efficiency for a 24-pounder and some other calibers. To double this velocity, if possible, would be straining the gun beyond a safe limit, yet it is a common practice here to use projectiles of twice the weight, which is equivalent to velocity x 2. To meet this additional strain, guns are banded, and the economy of the service demands that the banding should increase the strength of the piece to twice the resistance of the casting. This is not the case, however. Banded guns, fired with elongated shot, are not safe for over 300 rounds, when with round shot, guns not banded are equal to 1,500 rounds. A 24-pounder, fired with a bolt of 80 pounds, is equivalent to firing 426 pounds from a 10-inch. A safe limit for banded guns should be double the weight due the caliber for either shot or shell, and this, with an initial velocity of 1,000 feet, gives 10,600 pounds impact over round shot at 40 feet from the gun, and a much greater impact and [at?] extreme ranges.

Fourth. Experience as regards columbiad barbette carriages shows that they are too weak in design and plan to sustain long-continued firing at high angles. In one of our batteries out of five pieces all are without eccentric wheels. It is respectfully suggested that the use of rear eccentric wheels be abandoned; that strong lunettes be placed on the rear and bottom of the carriage, to be worked with rolling handspikes.

Fifth. In mortar beds wooden transoms will not answer. There are four mortars in our batteries which are unserviceable from this cause.

The foregoing remarks were suggested by the present condition of our batteries now playing on the enemy's works.

I have the pleasure of reporting Major Manigault's batteries in good keeping and well preserved.

Respectfully submitted.

JOHN G. BARNWELL,
Major, Corps of Artillery, C.S. Army, Insp. Ord. Dept.

[Indorsements]

HEADQUARTERS ORDNANCE DEPARTMENT,
Charleston, October 14, 1863.

Respectfully forwarded to the department headquarters.

The defects referred to in the Blakely projectiles have been before reported upon, and I am informed by the commanding officer of the arsenal that they are the same projectiles sent from England with the guns. Some of this officer's ideas on rifling guns are good. Other suggestions are approved.

J.R. WADDY,
Chief of Ordnance

October 16, 1863.

Send extract relating to rifling of guns, &c. to Colonel Rains, of Augusta Arsenal, for his views and such instructions as he thinks ought to be given on the subject.

G.T.B. [BEAUREGARD].
General, Commanding.

[*OR XXVIII (2) pp. 377-379*]

[*See Diary, 21 Oct. 1863*]

SPECIAL ORDERS   Hdqrs. Dept. of S.C., Ga. and Fla.
No. 216   Charleston, S.C., October 21, 1863

I. The armament of the batteries along the eastern margin of James Island, from Secessionville to Fort Johnson, and also of the harbor batteries on the same island, will be rearranged as follows:

Redoubt No. 1: One 8-inch shell gun; one 32-pounder smooth-bore; one 30-pounder Parrott.

Secessionville (rear): One 24-pounder, rifled; two 32-pounders, smooth-bore, to be mounted on barbette carriage; one 30-pounder Parrott, whenever received from Macon.

Battery Ryan (right): Two 12-pounder James guns, reamed to 18-pounder or 24-pounder howitzers, one to be taken from Battery Tatom, and the other from Battery Haskell; two 24-pounder Austrian howitzers.

Battery Ryan (left): Two 24-pounders, rifled and banded; two 8-inch siege howitzers; one of the 24-pounders to be taken from Redoubt No. 1, and the other from those on "old lines," not already otherwise assigned.

Battery Tatom: Two 8-inch siege howitzers; two 4.62 rifled guns, one to be taken from Battery Haskell, the other to be put in position whenever received; two shell

267

guns, to be designated by the chief of artillery.

Battery Haskell: One 4-inch Blakely; one 8-inch sea-coast howitzer; one 20-pounder Parrott; one 24-pounder, rifled and double banded; one 24-pounder smooth-bore; two 10-inch sea-coast mortars; one 8-inch columbiad, to be taken from Battery Cheves, and to be used only as a shell gun; two 42-pounder carronades (already ordered), which will be placed in position as soon as available.

Battery Cheves: Three 8-inch columbiads, to be used only as shell guns.

Brooke Gun Battery: One 8-inch shell gun, to be taken from Battery Simkins (the one most worn).

Battery Simkins: One 8-inch navy shell gun; three 10-inch sea-coast mortars; one 8-inch columbiad, to be taken from Battery Cheves and used only as a shell gun.

Bay batteries: Three 10-inch columbiads.

Fort Johnson: One 8-inch rifled and banded.

Tower Battery: Three 10-inch columbiads; one 42-pounder, rifled and double banded; one 7-inch Brooke; one 6.40-inch Brooke, to be taken from Simkins.

Battery Wampler: Two 10-inch columbiads (one already ordered from city).

Battery Glover: Three 32-pounders, rifled.

Battery No. 5 (new lines): Two 24-pounders, smooth-bore, to be taken from Battery Reid; two 24-pounder howitzers, to be taken from old lines.

II. Battery commanders will report the armament of their respective batteries to these headquarters, one week after the receipt of this order.

By command of General Beauregard:

JNO. M. OTEY,
Assistant Adjutant General

[*OR XXVIII (2) pp. 438, 439*]

[*See Diary, 31 Dec. 1863*]

Camp of Twenty-Seventh Georgia Volunteers,
James Island, S.C., December 31, 1863

CAPTAIN: In pursuance of an order from headquarters, dated December 31, I have the honor to report of an inspection and muster of the artillery of the west lines, James Island.

*   *   *   *   *

Siege Train, Major Manigault commanding:

Company A, Capt. B.C. Webb commanding: Two 30-pounder Parrotts; no breech sights, otherwise good. Eighty-two cartridges and 192 shells, for same. Condition of camp and garrison equipage is good, and, with officers' baggage, is two wagon-loads. Two four-horse wagons and teams serviceable; 8 mules, 56 horses (public), ordinary condition. Harness new. One forge, one battery wagon, complete appurtenances. Military appearance and discipline good. Present, 5 officers, 13 non-commissioned, 100 privates. Rations, beef and corn-meal. Police fair. Beach used for sinks. Rules and Articles of War read and orders from headquarters published.

Company B, Siege Train, Captain Smith commanding: Two 8-inch howitzers with 120 rounds. Condition of camp and garrison equipage is good, and with baggage, officers' clothing &c., two wagon-loads. Thirty-eight horses, 35 mules (public), fair condition; two four-horse wagons and teams, serviceable; one ordnance wagon and team, serviceable; one ambulance, no horse. Harness in good order. Military appearance and discipline good. Present, 3 officers, 9 non-commissioned, 96 privates. Absent, Captain Smith, sick; Senior Second Lieut. J.B.W. Phillips, sick. Ration, beef and corn-meal. Police fair. Beach used for sinks. Rules and Articles of War not read recently, nor orders published.

Company C, Georgia Siege Train, Capt. G.W. Johnson commanding: One 20-pounder Parrott, and 90 rounds and 139 shell; one 4-inch Blakely, and 135 rounds, 159 shell. Camp and garrison equipage good, which, with baggage same as usual, two wagon-loads. One two-horse wagon, one four-horse wagon, and teams serviceable. Forty-six horses and harness in fine condition. One forge and battery wagon complete. Military appearance, drill and discipline very good. Present, 3 officers, 5 non-commissioned, 61 privates. Rations beef and corn meal. Police good. For sinks, use the beach. Rules and Articles of War are read; orders not published.

Siege Train, Company C, Capt. Gregg commanding: Two 8-inch siege howitzers (good), 134 cartridges for same, and 138 shell and canister. Camp equipage, &c., is good, and with baggage, officers' clothing, forms two wagon-loads. One forge and battery wagon (complete), two ordnance wagons and teams, one forage wagon and team, one ambulance and team, good condition. Forty-one horses and 39 mules in fine condition and 6 horses unserviceable. Military appearance and discipline good. Present, 3 officers, 11 non-commissioned, 102 privates. Ration, beef and corn-meal. Beach used for sinks. Police good. Rules and Articles of War read and orders published.

JOHN J. ALLEN,
Captain, and Actg. Asst. Insp. Gen., Colquitt's Brigade.

[*O.R. XXVIII (2) pp. 598-600*]

[*See Diary, 7 May 1864*]

Hd Qrs. West Lines
James Island, May 6th 1864

Special Orders
No 70

III   Major E. Manigault, SC Siege Train will be Field Officer of the Day tomorrow 7 inst, and will relieve the present officer in charge of the picket on the front at 9 oclk AM

By Command of
Col Simonton
Wm D. Martin
A Adjt

To
Major Manigault
SC Siege Train

[*Order found with Manigault's Diary*]

Appendix 3

INDEX TO UNITS

The following information on units and individuals was obtained primarily from *The War of the Rebellion: A Compilation of the Official Records of the Union and Confederate Armies, Washington, 1880-1901, 128 Vols.* (especially Vols. 1, 6, 14, 28, 35, 42, 47 and 53) and *Compiled Service Records of Confederate Soldiers Who Served in Organizations in South Carolina* (and other states). The latter records are on microfilm, published by The National Archives, Washington, D.C.

Unfortunately, many Confederate units were known by more than one name. Manigault's Battalion, for instance, also was called the 18th Battalion, South Carolina Artillery, or the South Carolina Siege Train. The name may also refer to an entirely different unit, the 6th Battalion, South Carolina Infantry. To avoid confusion, the following index of alternate names mentioned in the Diary precedes the main list of organizations. The name under which the unit will be found is printed in italics.

3rd Bn., S.C. Light Arty. — *Palmetto Bn., Light Arty. (S.C.)*
3rd Rgmt., S.C. Arty. — *1st Rgmt., S.C. Inf. (Regulars)*
15th Bn., S.C. Arty. — *Lucas' Bn., S.C. Heavy Arty.*
18th Bn., S.C. Arty. — *Manigault's Bn., S.C. Arty.*
Arsenal Cadets — *Bn. of State Cadets (S.C. Inf.)*
Axson's Co. — *Co. A, 27th Rgmt., S.C. Inf.*
Beal's Co. — *Co. C, 22nd Bn., Ga. Heavy Arty.*
Black's Rgmt. — *1st Rgmt., S.C. Cav.*
Blake's Co. — *Co. A, 1st Rgmt., S.C. Arty.*
Bonaud's Bn. — *28th Bn., Ga. Siege Arty.*
Bowden's Co. — *Co. I, Palmetto Bn., Light Arty. (S.C)*
Bridges' Co. — *Co. D, Manigault's Bn., S.C. Arty.*
Buist's Co. — *Co. G, 27th Rgmt., S.C. Inf.*
Burnett's Co. — *Co. F, 1st Rgmt., S.C. Inf. (Regulars)*
Burrus' Co. — *Co. I, 5th Rgmt., Ga. Inf.*
Butler's Rgmt. — *1st Rgmt., S.C. Inf. (Regulars)*
Calhoun's Co. — *Co. D, 1st Rgmt., S.C. Inf. (Regulars)*
Carson's Co. — *Co. A, 25th Rgmt., S.C. Inf.*

Charles' Co. — *Co. D, 2nd Rgmt., S.C. Arty.*
Charleston Battalion — *27th Rgmt., S.C. Inf.*
Chesnut's Co. — *Co. A, 2nd Rgmt., S.C. Cav.*
China's Co. — *Co. C, 25th Rgmt., S.C. Inf.*
Citadel Cadets — *Bn. of State Cadets (S.C. Inf.)*
Clark's Co. — *Co. I, 2nd Rgmt., S.C. Cav.*
Clayton's Co. — *Co. F, 1st Rgmt., S.C. Cav.*
Colcock's Rgmt. — *3rd Rgmt., S.C. Cav.*
Colhoun's Co. — *Lucas' Bn., S.C. Heavy Arty.*
Daniel's Rgmt. — *5th Rgmt., Ga. Inf.*
Dean's Co. — *Co. E, 2nd Rgmt., S.C. Cav.*
Dedge's Co. — *Co. F, 47th Rgmt., Ga. Inf.*
Dickson's Co. — *Co. E, 2nd Rgmt., S.C. Arty.*
Duffey's Co. — *Co. B, 5th Rgmt., Ga. Inf.*
Dunovant's Rgmt. — *5th Rgmt., S.C. Cav.*
Earle's Co. — *Co. A, Palmetto Bn. Light Arty. (S.C.)*
Edward's Co. — *Co. A, 5th Rgmt., S.C. Cav.*
Eutaw Regiment — *25th Rgmt., S.C. Inf.*
Frederick's Rgmt. — *2nd Rgmt., S.C. Arty.*
Fulton's Co. — *Co. E, 5th Rgmt., Ga. Inf.*
Gaillard's Rgmt. — *27th Rgmt., S.C. Inf.*
Gantt's Rgmt. — *11th Rgmt., S.C. Inf.*
Georgia Siege Train — *Co. C, 12th Bn., Ga. Light Arty.*
Graham's Rgmt. — *21st Rgmt., S.C. Inf.*
Gregg's Co. — *Co. C, Manigault's Bn., S.C. Arty.*
Harrison's Rgmt. — *32nd Rgmt., Ga. Inf.*
Hayne's Co. — *Co. C, Lucas' Bn., S.C. Heavy Arty.*
Holtzclaw's Co. — *Co. H, Palmetto Bn., Light Arty. (S.C.)*
Hopkins' Co. — *Co. D, 27th Rgmt., S.C. Inf.*
Huguenin's Co. — *Co. F, 27th Rgmt., S.C. Inf.*
Humbert's Co. — *Co. I, 2nd Rgmt., S.C. Arty.*
Hurt's Co. — *Co. G, 5th Rgmt., Ga. Inf.*
Inglis Light Arty. — *Co. D, 2nd Rgmt., S.C. Arty.*
George W. Johnson's Co. — *Co. C, 12th Bn., Ga. Light Arty.*
L.J. Johnson's Co. — *Co. G, 1st Rgmt., S.C. Cav.*
Kanapaux's Co. — *Co. D, Palmetto Bn., Light Arty. (S.C.)*
Keitt's Rgmt. — *20th Rgmt., S.C. Inf.*
Kennady's Co. — *Co. H, 2nd Rgmt., S.C. Arty.*
Kiddoo's Co. — *Co. F, 5th Rgmt., Ga. Inf.*
King's Co. — *Co. K, 5th Rgmt., Ga. Inf.*
Lawrence's Co. — *Co. B, 47th Rgmt., Ga. Inf.*
Leak's Co. — *Co. B, 1st Rgmt., S.C. Cav.*
Legare's Co. — *Co. F, 2nd Rgmt., S.C. Arty.*
Lesesne's Co. — *Co. K, 25th Rgmt., S.C. Inf.*
Lewis's Co. — *Co. I, 32nd Rgmt., Ga. Inf.*
Lipscomb's Rgmt. — *2nd Rgmt., S.C. Cav.*
Lloyd's Co. — *Co. B, 25th Rgmt., S.C. Inf.*
Manigault's Bn. — *6th Bn., S.C. Inf. (See also, Manigault's Bn., S.C. Arty.)*
Mazyck's Co. — *Co. E, 25th Rgmt., S.C. Inf.*
Mickler's Co. — *Co. E, 11th Bn., S.C. Inf.*
Mitchel's Co. — *Co. I, 1st Rgmt., S.C. Arty.*
Nelson's Bn. — *7th Bn., S.C. Inf.*

O'Connor's Co. — *Co. C, 5th Rgmt., Ga. Inf.*
Owen's Co. — *Co. K, 21st Rgmt., S.C. Inf.*
Page's Rgmt. — *26th Rgmt., Va. Inf.*
Palmetto Guard Arty. — *Co. A, Manigault's Bn., S.C. Arty.*
Parker's Co. — *Marion Light Arty., S.C. Volunteers.*
Pee Dee Arty. — *Co. C, Manigault's Bn., S.C. Arty. (Zimmerman's Co.)*
Peeple's Co. — *Co. K, 3rd Rgmt., S.C. Cav.*
Pinckney's Co. — *Co. E, 5th Rgmt., S.C. Cav.*
Rhett's Rgmt. — *1st Rgmt., S.C. Arty.*
Guignard Richardson's Co. — *Co. B, Lucas' Bn., S.C. Heavy Arty.*
Samuel M. Richardson's Co. — *Co. K, Palmetto Bn. Light Arty. (S.C.)*
Rickenbaker's Co. — *Co. C, 2nd Rgmt., S.C. Arty.*
Rivers' Co. — *Co. K, 1st Rgmt., S.C. Inf. (Regulars)*
Rowland's Co. — *Co. A, 5th Rgmt., Ga. Inf.*
Schulz's Co. — *Co. F, Palmetto Bn. Light Arty. (S.C.)*
Seller's Co. — *Co. F, 25th Rgmt., S.C. Inf.*
Sheffield's Co. — *Co. K, 47th Rgmt., Ga. Inf.*
Simonton's Rgmt. — *25th Rgmt., S.C. Inf.*
R. Press Smith Jr.'s Co. — *Co. E, 1st Rgmt., S.C. Inf. (Regulars)*
S. Porcher Smith's Co. — *Co. B, Manigault's Bn., S.C. Arty.*
S.C. Siege Train — *Manigault's Bn., S.C. Arty.*
Stallings' Co. — *Co. G, 2nd Rgmt., S.C. Arty.*
Thompson's Co. — *Co. D, 5th Rgmt., Ga. Inf.*
Trezevant's Co. — *Co. E, 1st Rgmt., S.C. Cav.*
Villepigue's Co. — *Kilcrease Light Arty. (Fla.)*
Walpole's Co. (or Scouts) — *Stono Scouts (S.C. Cav.)*
Walter's Co. — *Co. I, 27th Rgmt., S.C. Inf.*
Warley's Co. — *Co. B, 1st Rgmt., S.C. Inf. (Regulars)*
Webb's Co. — *Co. A, Manigault's Bn., S.C. Arty.*
Westfield's Co. — *Co. F, 2nd Rgmt., S.C. Cav.*
Whatley's Co. — *Co. C, 1st Rgmt., S.C. Cav.*
Wheaton's Co. — *Chatham (Light) Arty. (Ga)*
Whilden's Co. — *Co. E, 5th Rgmt., S.C. Cav.*
Edward B. White's Bn. — *Palmetto Bn. Light Arty. (S.C.)*
John B. White's Bn. — *Bn. of State Cadets (S.C. Inf.)*
Wilson's Co. — *Co. D, 1st Rgmt., S.C. Cav.*
Witherspoon's Co. — *Co. C, 1st Rgmt., S.C. Inf. (Regulars)*
Zimmerman's Co. — *Co. C, Manigault's Bn., S.C. Arty.*

FLORIDA UNITS

KILCREASE (FLORIDA) LIGHT ARTILLERY COMPANY
This unit was organized 25 May 1863 by dividing Capt. R.H. Gamble's Co., Florida Light Artillery, into two units. Capt. F.L. Villepigue was named commander of the new company. He resigned in November 1864 and 1st Lt. Patrick Houstoun took command although Villepigue continued to be designated as commander in official records until about March 1865 when Houstoun was promoted Capt. The unit served in the Carolinas and Florida, winding up in the latter state at the end of the war. The company initially was armed with four 3.5-inch Blakely (British) Rifles and later with two 6-pounder bronze guns and two 12-pounder howitzers.

VILLEPIGUE, F.L. Capt. Commander, Kilcrease Light Artillery. Apparently entered service 3 Mar. 1862 as 1st Lt. of Capt. Gamble's Co. Promoted Capt. and transferred to command of the Kilcrease Co. 26 Mar. 1863. Resigned commission 24 Nov. 1864 to serve as a secretary of the Florida State Senate.

GEORGIA UNITS

5TH REGIMENT, GEORGIA INFANTRY
The regiment was organized about May 1861 and served throughout the war. It was first stationed at Pensacola, Fla., then joined the Army of Tennessee, participating in the major battles of Murfreesboro, 31 Dec. 1862, and Chickamauga, 19-20 Sept. 1863. It later served on James Island and in other parts of South Carolina and, finally, in North Carolina where it surrendered at the end of April 1865. Also known as Col. Charles P. Daniel's Rgmt., Ga. Inf.

DANIEL, Charles P. Col. Commander, 5th Rgmt. Enlisted 10 May 1861 at Macon, Ga. as 1st Sgt. of Co. B. Elected Capt. Co. B on 20 Feb. 1862. Promoted Maj. and transferred to regimental staff 8 May 1862. Promoted Col. and regimental commander 31 Dec. 1862. Paroled 1 May 1865 at Greensboro, N.C.

Co. A, 5th Rgmt, Ga. Inf.
This unit also was known as Capt. Samuel H. Rowland's Co.

ADAMS, George. 1st Lt. Enlisted at Macon, Ga., 11 May 1861 as a Sgt. in Co. A. Promoted 2nd Lt. 19 May 1862 and 1st Lt. 31 Dec. 1862. He is listed on final records in his personnel file, Nov.-Dec. 1864, as absent, sick.
NEELY, John Jr. 2nd Lt. Enlisted 11 May 1861 at Macon, Ga., as a Pvt. in Co. A. Promoted 1st Sgt. in July or Aug. 1862 and 2nd Lt. 1 Aug. 1863. Listed on the final company muster roll, Nov.-Dec. 1864, as absent, sick.
ROWLAND, Samuel H. Capt. Commander, Co. A. Enlisted 11 May 1861 at Macon, Ga., as 1st Sgt. of Co. A. Elected 1st Lt. at the reorganization of the unit 8 May 1862 and promoted Capt. 31 Dec. 1862. Paroled 1 May 1865 at Greensboro, N.C.

Co. B, 5th Rgmt, Ga. Inf.
This unit also was known as the Griffin Light Guard and as Capt. William J. Duffey's Co.

BURR, George W. 1st Lt. Enlisted at Macon, Ga., 10 May 1861 as a Pvt. in Co. B. Promoted 1st Sgt. 8 May 1862. Appointed 1st Lt. 30 June 1864. He was paroled 1 May 1865 at Greensboro, N.C.

DRIVER, Robert P. 2nd Lt. Enlisted 10 May 1861 at Macon, Ga., as a Pvt. in Co. B. Promoted 2nd Lt. 30 June 1864. Listed as absent, sick in hospital, on the final company muster roll, Nov.-Dec. 1864.

DUFFEY, William J. Capt. Commander, Co. B. Enlisted 10 May 1861 at Macon, Ga., as a Sgt. in Co. B. Promoted 2nd Lt. 4 Oct. 1861, 1st Lt. 19 May 1862 and Capt. 9 June 1862. He reverted to the rank of 1st Lt. 29 Aug. 1862 and was again promoted Capt. 24 June 1863. Listed as present on the final company muster roll, Nov.-Dec. 1864.

Co. C, 5th Rgmt, Ga. Inf.
This unit also was known as Capt. Michael J. O'Connor's Co.

BARRETT, James. 2nd Lt. Enlisted at Tyner, Tenn. 18 Aug. 1862 as a Pvt. in Co. A. Transferred to Co. C and promoted 2nd Lt. 23 May 1863. Listed on the final records in his personnel file, Nov.-Dec. 1864, as absent, inspector of military prisons at Florence, S.C.

O'CONNOR, Michael J. Capt. Commander, Co. C. Entered service 11 May 1861 at Macon, Ga., as a 2nd Lt. in Co. C. Promoted 1st Lt. in May 1862 and Capt. 24 Jan. 1863. Paroled 1 May 1865 at Greensboro, N.C.

Co. D, 5th Rgmt, Ga. Inf.
This unit also was known as Capt. John Thompson's Co.

CODY, Eleazar E. 2nd Lt. Enlisted at Macon, Ga., 11 May 1861 as a Pvt. in Co. D. Promoted Cpl. and then Sgt. during the first six months of 1862. Promoted 2nd Lt. during the early part of 1864. He was wounded sightly in the fighting around Pensacola, Fla., in Oct. 1861 and severely at Murfreesboro, Tenn., 31 Dec. 1862. Listed as present on the final company muster roll, Nov.-Dec. 1864.

THOMPSON, John. Capt. Commander, Co. D. Enlisted 11 May 1861 at Macon, Ga., as 1st Sgt. of Co. D. Elected 2nd Lt. at the reorganization of the unit 8 May 1862. Promoted 1st Lt. 19 Jan. 1864 and Capt. 1 Sept. 1864. Listed as absent, sick, on the final company muster roll, Nov.-Dec. 1864.

Co. E, 5th Rgmt, Ga. Inf.
This unit also was known as Capt. John A. Fulton's Co.

FULTON, John A. Capt. Commander, Co. E. Enlisted 11 May 1861 at Macon, Ga., as a Pvt. in Co. E. Promoted 1st Lt. 19 May 1862 and Capt. 29 Aug. 1862. Paroled 1 May 1865 at Greensboro, N.C.

GLENN, John W. 2nd Lt. Enlisted 26 Aug. 1862 at Pensacola, Fla., as a Pvt. in Co. E. He later was promoted to 1st Sgt. and then, 13 Aug. 1864, to 2nd Lt. He was paroled 1 May 1865 at Greensboro, N.C.

Co. F, 5th Rgmt, Ga. Inf.
This unit also was known as the Cuthbert Rifles and as Capt. John F. Kiddoo's Co.

KIDDOO, John F. Capt. Commander, Co. F. Enlisted 10 May 1861 at Macon, Ga., as a Pvt. in Co. F. Elected Capt. in the reorganization of the unit 8 May

1862. Listed as present on the final company muster roll, Nov.-Dec. 1864. Wounded at Battle of Murfreesboro, Tenn., 31 Dec. 1862.

MCNEIL, Samuel A. 1st Lt. Enlisted 10 May 1861 at Macon, Ga., as a Pvt. in Co. F. Promoted 2nd Lt. 20 Feb. 1863 and 1st Lt. 2 Apr. 1863. Listed as present, sick, on the final company muster roll, Nov.-Dec. 1864.

SEALY, James F. 2nd Lt. Enlisted 10 May 1861 at Macon, Ga., as a Pvt. in Co. F. Severely wounded and captured at the Battle of Murfreesboro, Tenn., 31 Dec. 1862. Imprisoned in Indiana and later exchanged. Promoted 2nd Lt. during the latter part of 1863 or early 1864. Paroled 1 May 1865 at Greensboro, N.C.

WARD, William D. 2nd Lt. Enlisted 10 May 1861 at Macon, Ga., as a Pvt. in Co. F. Promoted 1st Sgt. about May 1862 and 2nd Lt. 8 April 1863. Listed on final company muster roll, Nov.-Dec. 1864, as absent without leave. Apparently, he later returned to the regiment, was reduced in rank and transferred to Co. H. for a William Ward was paroled in that company as a Pvt. 10 May 1865. Ward was slightly wounded in the Battle of Murfreesboro, Tenn., 31 Dec. 1862.

Co. G, 5th Rgmt, Ga. Inf.
This unit also was known as Capt. John T. Hurt's Co.

HURT, John T. Capt. Commander, Co. G. Enlisted 11 May 1861 at Macon, Ga., as a Pvt. in Co. G. Elected Capt. and company commander in the reorganization of the unit 8 May 1862. Paroled 1 May 1865 at Greensboro, N.C.

SNIPES, James Jr. 2nd Lt. Enlisted 11 May 1861 at Macon, Ga., as a Cpl. in Co G. Appointed 2nd Lt. and transferred to Co. K on 4 June 1862, but returned to Co. G. and reduced in rank to Sgt. on 29 Aug. 1862. Promoted 2nd Lt. 20 Feb. 1863. Paroled 1 May 1865 at Greensboro, N.C. Wounded at the Battle of Murfreesboro, Tenn., 31 Dec. 1862.

Co. H, 5th Rgmt, Ga. Inf.
At the end of the war, this unit was known as Capt. Homer C. Brooks' Co.

BROOKS, Homer C. 2nd Lt. Enlisted at Pensacola, Fla., 2 July 1861 as a Pvt. in Co. H. Promoted 2nd Lt. 8 May 1862. He signed the final company muster roll, Nov.-Dec. 1864, as a 2nd Lt. However, he was paroled 28 April 1865 as Capt., commanding Co. H. He was at this time a patient in a Greensboro, N.C., hospital.

Co. I, 5th Rgmt, Ga. Inf.
This unit also was known as Capt. Lawrence M. Burrus' Co.

AVERETT, Eli M. 2nd Lt. Enlisted 20 June 1861 at Pensacola, Fla. as a Pvt. in Co. I. Promoted 1st Sgt. during the summer of 1862. Listed as 2nd Lt. in Feb. 1864. Paroled 1 May 1865 at Jamestown, N.C.

BURRUS, Lawrence M. Capt. Commander, Co. I. Entered service at Macon, Ga., 11 May 1861 as a 2nd Lt. in Co. I. Promoted 1st Lt. 25 Aug. 1861 and Capt. 9 Sept. 1862. Listed as absent, sick, on the final records in his personnel file, Nov.-Dec. 1864.

CALHOUN, Alpha T. 2nd Lt. Enlisted at Macon, Ga., 11 May 1861 as a Sgt. in Co. I. Promoted 2nd Lt. 19 May 1862. Paroled 1 May 1865 at Greensboro, N.C.

Co. K, 5th Rgmt, Ga. Inf.

This unit also was known as the Schley Guards and as Capt. Jacob S. King's Co.

HIGHTOWER, Andrew H. 1st Lt. Enlisted 11 May 1861 at Macon, Ga., as a Pvt. in Co. K. Promoted 2nd Lt. 23 July 1862 and 1st Lt. 21 Dec. 1863. The final records in his personnel file state that he was on sick leave as of 5 Sept. 1864.

JENNINGS, Henry T. 2nd Lt. Enlisted 11 May 1861 at Macon, Ga., as a Pvt. in Co. K. Promoted Cpl. during the summer of 1862 and by 15 Apr. 1864 was serving as a 2nd Lt. Listed as absent without leave on the final records in his personnel file 31 Aug. 1864.

KING, Jacob S. Capt. Commander, Co. K. Entered service 11 May 1862 at Macon, Ga., as 1st Lt. of Co. K. Promoted Capt. 16 Jan. 1864. The final records in his personnel file show that he was on leave as of 5 Sept. 1864.

Co C, 12th Bn., Ga. Light Arty.

This company was organized at Stone Mountain, Ga., 1 April 1862 as Co. C. It was redesignated Co. E about Nov. 1862 and again Co. C in Jan. or Feb. 1863. Later that year it was attached to the Ga. Siege Train and served on James Island, returning to the Savannah, Ga., area in March or April 1864. It later was transferred to Va. Also known as Capt. George W. Johnson's Co. and often referred to, erroneously, as Co. C, Ga. Siege Train.

HEAD, W.G. 1st Lt. Enlisted 24 Apr. 1862 at Stone Mountain, Ga., as a Sgt. in Co. C. Promoted 2nd Lt. 26 Aug. 1862 and 1st Lt. in Jan. or Feb. 1863. Killed in action at Cedar Creek, Va., 19 Oct. 1864.

JOHNSON, George W. Capt. Commander, Co. C. Entered service in Oct. 1861, but rank and unit have not been found. Organized and became commander of Co. C on 1 Apr. 1862, which dated his rank as Capt. Listed as the unit's commander on the last available muster roll, 31 Dec. 1864. At that time, Co. C was near New Market, Va.

WILLINGHAM, J.T. 1st Lt. Enlisted at Stone Mountain, Ga., 1 May 1862 as the company 1st Sgt. Appointed 1st Lt. 26 Aug. 1862. Reported sick 25 Sept. 1864 in Va. and, after transferring to various hospitals, was listed 30 Dec. 1864 at his Stone Mountain residence. His name was dropped from the rolls 31 Mar. 1865.

Co C, 22nd. Bn., Ga. Heavy Arty.

This company was organized initially as Co. A, Oglethorpe Siege Arty., under the Ga. state establishment and was taken into Confederate service 16 April 1862. It was combined with other independent companies 26 Nov. 1862 and became Co. C, 22nd. Bn., Ga. Heavy Arty. It also was known as Capt. Joseph A. Beals' Co.

BEALS, Joseph A. Capt. Commander, Co. C. Entered service 14 May 1862 as a 2nd Lt. in the company. Promoted 1st Lt. 19 June 1862 and Capt. 14 Sept. 1863. He was paroled 28 April 1865 while sick in a hospital at Greensboro, N.C.

27TH REGIMENT, GEORGIA INFANTRY

ALLEN, John J. Capt. Acting Assistant Inspector General of Gen. Alfred H. Colquitt's Brigade.

28TH BATTALION, GEORGIA SIEGE ARTILLERY

This battalion was organized and mustered into Confederate service 6 Aug. 1863. Although organized as siege artillery, from January 1864 until the end of the war it served as infantry. It generally was known as Maj. A. Bonaud's Bn., Ga. Siege Arty., or later, Ga. Inf.

BONAUD, A. Maj. Commander, 28th Bn. Entered service at Savannah, Ga., 6 Feb. 1862 as commander of an independent company known as the Emmett Rifles. In Nov. 1862 this and other separate units were reorganized and combined into the 22nd Bn., Ga. Heavy Arty., the Emmett Rifles becoming Co. F. However, in an election of company officers, Bonaud was ousted as commander and returned to the ranks. In a letter to superiors seeking reinstatement to command, he blamed his changed circumstances on the exercise of too much zeal as company commander. His appeal apparently was turned down. However, on 6 Aug. 1863 he was promoted Maj. and given command of the newly organized 28th Bn., Ga. Siege Arty. which he led throughout the remainder of the war.

Co B, 28th Bn., Ga. Siege Arty.
This company was formed at the organization of the battalion 6 Aug. 1863. It also was known as Co. B, Bonaud's Bn., Ga. Siege Arty.

STROUD, A.B. 1st Lt. Elected 2nd Lt. of Co. B on 1 Aug. 1863. Promoted 1st Lt. 17 May 1864. Died of dysentery in a James Island hospital 6 Nov. 1864.

Co C, 28th Bn., Ga. Siege Arty.
This company was organized at the same time as the battalion, 6 Aug. 1863. It also was known as Co. C, Bonaud's Bn., Ga. Siege Arty.

KENDRICK, Burrell Jr. 2nd Lt. Entered service at Smithville, Ga., 5 Aug. 1863 as a 3rd Lt. of Co. C. Promoted 2nd Lt. in Sept. or Oct. 1863. Final entry in his personnel records states that he was serving with the company as late as Nov.-Dec. 1864.

Co G, 28th Bn., Ga. Siege Arty.
This company was formed at the organization of the battalion 6 Aug. 1863. It also was known as Co. G, Bonaud's Bn., Ga. Siege Arty., and as Capt. John D. Godwin's Co., Bonaud's Bn.

GODWIN, John D. Capt. Commander, Co. G. Enlisted 20 April 1861 at Columbus, Ga., as a Pvt. in Co. A, 2nd Bn., Ga. Inf. He was serving in the Army of Northern Virginia when on 14 Aug. 1863 he was elected Capt. and commander of Co. G in the 28th Bn. Notification of this was forwarded immediately to Richmond. However, processing of orders was delayed and it was several months before he finally joined the company. Records in his personnel file show that he was still serving in Bonaud's Bn. on James Island as late as 7 Feb. 1865.

LAWRENCE, James W. 2nd Lt. Entered service 14 Aug. 1863 at Columbus, Ga., as a 3rd Lt. in Co. G. Elected 2nd Lt. 14 Sept. 1863. He received a 60-day medical furlough from 24 Oct. to 24 Dec. 1864 and was listed as absent without leave after the latter date. His name was dropped from the company rolls 9 Feb. 1865.

Co I, 28th Bn., Ga. Siege Arty.
Unit was attached to the battalion 28 Jan. 1864. It also was known as Co. I, Bonaud's Bn., Ga. Siege Arty., and as Co. I, Bonaud's Bn., Ga. Volunteers.

IRWIN, R.C. 2nd Lt. Elected a 2nd Lt. in Co. I on 16 April 1863. Retired, apparently for medical reasons, 17 Feb. 1865.

WALTON, J.T. 2nd Lt. Elected 2nd Lt. of Co. I on 6 Nov. 1863. Despite a request for promotion and command of Co. I, due to absence without leave of the other company officers, Walton was still a 2nd Lt. when captured in a Raleigh, N.C., hospital 13 April 1865. He was recuperating from amputation of his left arm after being wounded in combat 16 Mar. 1865.

32ND REGIMENT, GEORGIA INFANTRY

This unit apparently was formed under the Georgia state establishment in 1861 and was reorganized for Confederate service 15 May 1862. It served in Georgia and the Carolinas, surrendering at Greensboro, N.C., at the end of the war. Also known as Col. George P. Harrison's Rgmt., Ga. Inf.

BACON, E.H. Jr. Lt. Col. Appointed a 2nd Lt. in the state establishment about July 1861. Elected Maj. in the regimental reorganization of May 1862 and promoted Lt. Col. 20 Oct. 1863. Commanded the regiment much of the time from about July 1864 until the end of the war in the absence of Col. Harrison who was serving as commandant of the Florence military prison or as a brigade commander. Bacon was paroled 1 May 1865 at Greensboro, N.C.

HARRISON, George P. Jr. Col. Commander, 32nd Rgmt. Commissioned Col. 25 Oct. 1861 and re-elected regimental commander in the reorganization 15 May 1862. Commanded troops on Morris Island during much of the bitter siege of Battery Wagner in 1863. He served on James Island and then became commandant of the Confederate military prison at Florence, S.C. The end of the war found him commanding a brigade although, technically, still commander of the 32nd. He was paroled 1 May 1865 at Greensboro, N.C.

Co. I, 32nd Rgmt., Ga. Inf.

This company apparently was organized during 1861 and was mustered into Confederate service 1 Apr. 1862. Also known as Capt. John F. Lewis' Co.

LEWIS, John F. Capt. Commander, Co. I. Appointed Capt., Co. I, on 18 Apr. 1862. Previous service, if any, not available. Final records in his personnel file state that he was on detached service as of 25 Sept. 1864.

47TH REGIMENT, GEORGIA INFANTRY

The companies of this unit, with exception of Co. K, initially were organized 22 Mar. 1862 as the 11th Bn., Ga. Inf. The battalion was reorganized as a regiment 18 May 1862.

Co. B, 47th Rgmt., Ga. Inf.

This unit initially was Co. B, 11th Bn., Ga. Inf. It also was known as Capt. Seaborn R. Lawrence's Co. and as the Randolph (county) Light Guards.

LAWRENCE, Seaborn R. Capt. Commander, Co. B. Served in the 5th Rgmt., Ga. Inf. from 10 May 1861 to 26 Jan. 1862, rank not available. Enlisted 4 Mar. 1862 as a Sgt. in Co. B. Elected 2nd Lt. 24 July 1862. Promoted 1st Lt. 15 Apr. 1863 and Capt., commanding officer, 6 May 1864. Personnel records state that he was still serving with the company in Mar. 1865.

Co. D, 47th Rgmt., Ga. Inf.

This unit originally was Co. D, 11th Bn., Ga. Inf. It also was known as the Screven Guards.

POTTER, M.M. 1st Lt. Enlistment date and rank not available. Elected 2nd Lt. in Sept. or Oct. to replace a company officer killed at the Battle of Chickamauga 19-20 Sept. 1863. Promoted 1st Lt. 19 Jan. 1864 when another officer died. Personnel records show that he was still serving in the company in Mar. 1865. However, other records indicate that he was paroled as a Capt., commander of Co. G, 1st Rgmt., Ga. Regulars.

Co. F, 47th Rgmt., Ga. Inf.

This unit initially was Co. F, 11th Bn., Ga. Inf. It also was known as Capt. Joseph G. Dedge's Co. and as the Appling (county) Rangers.

DEDGE, Joseph G. Capt. Commander, Co. F. Entered service 4 Mar. 1862 at Hinesville, Ga., as 1st Lt. of the company. Promoted Capt. and commanding officer 26 Oct. 1863. Personnel records show that he was still with the company in Mar. 1865.

PATTERSON, James S. 2nd Lt. Entered service at Hinesville, Ga., 4 Mar. 1862 as a 2nd Lt. in the company and, waiving his right to promotion, remained in this rank throughout the war. Personnel records state that he was still in the company in Mar. 1865.

Co. H, 47th Rgmt., Ga. Inf.

This unit originally was Co. H of the 11th Bn., Ga. Inf. It also was known as the Liberty (county) Rangers.

CHESSER, J.M. 2nd Lt. Enlisted 4 Mar. 1862 at Hinesville, Ga., as a Pvt. Elected 2nd Lt. 22 Dec. 1862. Personnel records show that he was still with the company in Mar. 1865.

Co. I, 47th Rgmt., Ga. Inf.

This unit, formerly Co. I of the 11th Bn., Ga. Inf., also was known as the Empire State Guards.

BOURQUINE, R.T. 2nd Lt. Enlisted 4 Mar. 1862 as a Pvt. in the company but soon was promoted to 1st. Sgt. Elected 2nd Lt. 18 Feb. 1863. Personnel records show that he was still in the company in Mar. 1865.

Co. K, 47th Rgmt., Ga. Inf.

This unit was the only company in the regiment not previously in the 11th Bn., Ga. Inf. It also was known as Capt. Peter C. Sheffield's Co.

SHEFFIELD, Peter C. Capt. Commander, Co. K. Enlisted 6 May 1862 as a Pvt. in the company. Elected 2nd Lt. 2 June 1862. Promoted 1st Lt. 24 May 1863 and Capt. 28 June 1864. Personnel records show that he was still commanding the company in Mar. 1865.

54TH REGIMENT, GEORGIA INFANTRY

This unit apparently was organized in May 1862. It served near Savannah,

Ga., in the Charleston area, the defense of Atlanta and in North Carolina. By 31 Mar. 1865, combat losses had reduced it to a lieutenant's command. Shortly before it surrendered in North Carolina at the end of April 1865, it was combined with the 37th Rgmt., Ga. Inf. and the 4th Bn., Ga. Sharp Shooters into the 54th Rgmt., Ga. Inf. (Consolidated). It was also known as Col. Charlton H. Way's Rgmt., Ga. Inf.

CLARK, John G. Capt. Assistant Quartermaster. Served at Savannah as early as Mar. 1862, but rank and unit not available. Appointed Capt. and A.Q.M. of the 54th 1 Aug. 1863. Stationed at James Island 29 Aug. 1863. Relieved of duty with the 54th on 24 Sept. 1864 and ordered to Macon, Ga., as inspector of field transportation. Still serving in that capacity as late as 30 Mar. 1865.

RAWLS, Morgan. Lt. Col. Served as Capt., commander of a company of Georgia Rangers in the 1st (Volunteer) Rgmt., Ga. Inf. during 1861. Appointed Lt. Col. of the 54th Rgmt. 16 May 1862. Wounded in the fighting near Atlanta 22 July 1864, and was on medical leave as late as Sept. 1864. Rawls was cited for distinguished service on Morris Island during the siege of Battery Wagner in 1863. He also went on leave 30 Oct. 1863 to attend a session of the Georgia Legislature as a representative of Effingham County.

WAY, Charlton H. Col. Regimental commander. Served as Capt., commander of the Forest City Rangers, 1st (Volunteer) Rgmt., Ga. Inf. during 1861. Appointed Col., commander of the 54th, on 13 May 1862. He was listed as commander of the regiment as late as 20 Sept. 1864.

Chatham (Ga.) Artillery

This unit was organized 1 Aug. 1861 as a 12-months company known as the Chatham Arty. Co. of the 1st Volunteer Rgmt. Ga. Inf., or as Capt. Joseph S. Claghorn's Co. After Claghorn resigned when the company was reorganized for the war, 12 Dec. 1862, it became known as Capt. John F. Wheaton's Co. A light artillery company armed with four Napoleons, it served in the Carolinas, Georgia and Florida.

ASKEW, Thomas A. 1st Lt. Enlisted at Savannah, Ga., 1 Aug. 1861 as a Sgt. in Claghorn's Co. Promoted 2nd Lt. in late 1861 or early 1862. Elected 1st Lt. 12 Dec. 1862 in the company reorganization. Final records in his personnel file show that he was serving with the company as late as Jan.-Feb. 1865.

HENDRY, George N. 2nd Lt. Enlisted 1 Mar. 1862 as a Pvt. and by Sept. 1862 had been promoted Sgt. Elected 2nd Lt. in the reorganization of 12 Dec. 1862. Final records in his personnel file show that he was serving with the company as late as Jan.-Feb. 1865.

PALMER, Samuel B. 1st Lt. Enlisted 29 Nov. 1861 as a Pvt. in Claghorn's Co. Elected 2nd Lt. 17 May 1862 and 1st Lt. in the reorganization of 12 Dec. 1862. Final records in his personnel file state that he was serving with the company as late as Jan.-Feb. 1865.

WHEATON, John F. Capt. Commander, Chatham Artillery. Enlisted 7 Mar. 1861 in the Orleans Guard and transferred to the Chatham Arty. as a Sgt. when the unit was organized 1 Aug. 1861. By June 1862 he was serving as 1st Lt. Promoted Capt. and company commander in the reorganization of 12 Dec. 1862. Final records in his personnel file state that he was serving with the company as late as Jan.-Feb. 1865.

Co. A, Cobb Guards, Ga. Inf.

This unit on 19 Sept. 1863 was attached to the 22nd Bn., Ga. Heavy Arty. Personnel often are listed under both units.

CULLENS, Francis T. Capt. Commander Co. A, Cobb Guards. Also listed as commander, Co. G, 22nd Bn., Ga. Heavy Arty.

SWANN, Erasmus D. Pvt. Co. A, Cobb Guards. Also listed in Co. G, 22nd Bn., Ga. Heavy Arty.

Co. B, Cobb Guards, Ga. Inf.

This unit on 19 Sept. 1863 was attached to the 22nd Bn., Ga. Heavy Arty. Personnel often are listed under both units.

TURNIPSEED, Richard A. Capt. Commander Co. B, Cobb Guards. Also listed as commander, Co. H, 22nd Bn. Ga. Heavy Arty.

WELLS, John C. 1st Lt. Co. B, Cobb Guards. Also listed in Co. H, 22nd Bn. Ga. Heavy Arty.

Cobb Guards, Ga. Inf. (Miscellaneous)

JACKSON, Pvt. Not identified
JOHNSON, Pvt. Not Identified.
MILLS, Pvt. Not Identified.
WOOD, Pvt. Not Identified.

SOUTH CAROLINA UNITS

1ST REGIMENT, S.C. ARTILLERY

This unit was organized before formation of the Confederacy as the 1st Bn., S.C. Arty, with five companies — A through E. It was mustered into Confederate service in May 1861. Co. F was added in Oct. 1861 and Co. G in Nov. 1861. Cos. H and I were added in Feb. 1862. The unit was reorganized as the 1st Rgmt., S.C. Arty., 25 Mar. 1862. Co. K was added 12 Apr. 1862. It also was known as Col. Alfred Rhett's Rgmt., S.C. Arty.

BLANDING, Ormsby. Maj. Entered service 24 May 1861 at Ft. Moultrie as 1st Lt. of Co. E. Promoted Capt. 6 Aug. 1861 and transferred to command Co. C. Promoted Maj. 5 Sept. 1862 and transferred to the regimental staff. Served at Fort Sumter Nov.-Dec. 1862 and May-June 1863. On detached service, James Island, Sept.-Oct. 1863. Admitted to hospital at Greensboro, N.C., 19 Mar. 1865 and furloughed 12 April 1865.

JONES, Iredell. 1st Lt. Entered service in March or April 1862 as 2nd Lt. of Co. D. Transferred in Jan. or Feb. 1863 to Co. B. Promoted 1st Lt. 22 June 1863. Paroled near Greensboro, N.C., 28 April 1865. Went on detached service 28 Oct. 1863 to regimental staff as aide-de-camp to the commanding officer, Col. Alfred Rhett.

RHETT, Alfred. Col. Commander, 1st Rgmt, S.C. Arty. Entered service 16 Mar. 1861 as 1st Lt. Co. B, 1st Bn., S.C. Arty. Promoted Capt. 24 May 1861; Maj. 1st Rgmt., S.C. Arty., 25 Mar. 1862; Lt. Col. 17 July 1862; and Col. 5 Sept. 1862. Rhett was in command of Fort Sumter during the celebrated Ironclad Attack of 7 April 1863. Captured at Averasborough, N.C., 15 Mar. 1865, he was taken to New York then imprisoned at Fort Delaware. He was released 24 July 1865 after signing an oath of allegiance.

YATES, Joseph A. Lt. Col. Entered service 19 Mar. 1861 as 1st Lt. of Co. D. Promoted Capt. 24 May 1861 and transferred to Co. E. Promoted Maj. 17 July 1862 and transferred to regimental staff. Promoted Lt. Col. 5 Sept. 1862. Paroled at Greensboro, N.C., 28 April 1865. Yates was in command of the artillery when Federal troops captured the south end of Morris Island 10 July 1863. He also was the inventor of a traversing device for heavy artillery, called a "traverser" which official reports say contributed to the successful defense of Fort Sumter against the Ironclad Attack of 7 April 1863.

Co. A, 1st Rgmt. S.C. Arty.

One of the original companies of the 1st Bn., S.C. Arty., it became Co. A of the 1st Rgmt., S.C. Arty 25 Mar. 1862. Also known as Capt. Francis D. Blake's Co.

BLAKE, Francis D. Capt. Commander, Co. A. Listed on muster roll of May-June 1861 as 2nd Lt. Co. B. Promoted 1st Lt. 6 July 1861. Promoted Capt. 2 Apr. 1863 and transferred to Co. A as commanding officer. Captured at Bentonville, N.C., 22 Mar. 1865. Taken to New York, then transferred to Fort Delaware, near Delaware City, Dela., 15 Apr. 1865. Released 17 June 1865 after signing oath of allegiance.

DELORME, Thomas M. 2nd Lt. Apparently entered service 17 Aug. 1863 as 2nd Lt. of Co. A. Admitted to hospital at Greensboro, N.C., 19 Mar. 1865.

KEMPER, William H. 1st Lt. Listed as a member of Co. A on the rolls of Jan.-Feb. 1864. On detached service as adjutant of Light Arty. on James Island Mar.-July 1864. Transferred to 2nd Military District, S.C., 27 July 1864.

LABORDE, Oscar W. 1st Lt. Appointed 2nd Lt. of Blake's Co. 28 Mar. 1862. Promoted 1st Lt. 18 July 1863. Listed as present on final Co. A muster roll, Nov.-Dec. 1864.

RIVERS, Mallory C. Lt. and Asst. Surgeon. Entered service 25 Oct. 1862 but his contract was cancelled 16 Dec. 1862. He was reappointed and on 5 Feb. 1863 was assigned as Asst. Surgeon of the 2nd Rgmt., S.C. Arty. However, by June 1863 he had been transferred to the 1st Rgmt. and assigned as Asst. Surgeon of Co. A where he continued to serve, at least through the middle of 1864.

WHALEY, John R. Sgt. Maj. Enlisted at Charleston 28 Mar. 1861 as 1st Sgt. Co. A. Transferred 1 Feb. 1862 to Co. E, then on 1 Sept. 1862 back to Co. A. Promoted Sgt. Maj. 1 Nov. 1862, but continued to be carried as 1st Sgt. of Co. A on muster rolls through Aug. 1864. Paroled 28 April 1865 at Greensboro, N.C., as Sgt. Maj. of the regiment. Prior to the war, Whaley had served six years as a non-commissioned officer in the U.S. Army.

Co. D, 1st Rgmt. S.C. Arty.

One of the original companies of the 1st Bn., S.C. Arty. mustered into Confederate service in May 1861. Became Co. D, 1st Rgmt., S.C. Arty, in the reorganization of 25 Mar. 1862.

SIMKINS, William Stewart. 1st Lt. Entered service in July or Aug. 1861 as 2nd Lt. of Co. D. Promoted 1st Lt. 25 Mar. 1862. Paroled at Greensboro, N.C., about 28 April 1865. On detached service on the staff of the light artillery on James Island Sept.-Oct. 1863. Absent, sick, May-June 1864, and present, sick in quarters, July-Aug. 1864.

Co. H, 1st Rgmt. S.C. Arty.

This unit was added to the 1st Bn., S.C. Arty. in Feb. 1862. It became Co. H, 1st Rgmt., S.C. Arty., in the reorganization of 25 Mar. 1862.

SIMKINS, Eldred Jr. 1st Lt. Entered service 5 Aug. 1862 as 2nd Lt. Co. H. Promoted 1st Lt. 24 Nov. 1863. Co. H muster rolls carry Simkins as present for duty from May until 22 Aug. 1864 when he went on unspecified detached service.

Co. I, 1st Rgmt. S.C. Arty.

Co. I was added to the 1st. Bn., S.C. Arty, in Feb. 1862. The battalion was reorganized 25 Mar. 1862 and this unit became Co. I, 1st. Rgmt., S.C. Arty. It also was known as Capt. John C. Mitchel's Co.

MITCHEL, John C. Capt. Commander, Co. I. Entered service March or April 1861 as 2nd Lt. of Co. B. Promoted 1st Lt. in May or June 1861 and transferred to Co. C. Promoted Capt. 25 Mar. 1862 and transferred to assume command of Co. I. Assigned 15 July 1863 as commander of Shell Point Battery (later named Battery Simkins) and the artillery in nearby Fort Johnson. Ordered to command of Fort Sumter 4 May 1864. Fatally wounded at Fort Sumter 20 July 1864.

1ST REGIMENT, S.C. CAVALRY

This unit was organized in the latter part of 1861 as the 1st Bn., S.C. Cav., with six companies, A through F. Three other companies were added during the early part of 1862. About 25 June 1862 another company was added and the battalion was redesignated as the 1st Rgmt., S.C. Cav. It also was known as Col. John L. Black's Cav. Rgmt.

BLACK, John L. Col. Commander, 1st Rgmt., S.C. Cav. Entered service 31 Oct. 1861 as Lt. Col., presumably the same date as organization of the 1st Bn., S.C. Cav., which he commanded. Promoted Col. 25 June 1862, date of reorganization of the unit as a regiment. Detached as commander of the East Lines, James Island, from May through Dec. 1864, and probably until the evacuation of Charleston in Feb. 1865. Serving at the head of his regiment in N.C. as late as 10 April 1865.

NESBITT, Niles. Maj. Entered service in Laurens County, S.C., 22 Aug. 1861 as Capt. and commander of the Ferguson Rangers. Promoted Maj. 15 Sept. 1864. Relieved as Co. B commander by Capt. W.J. Leak and transferred to regimental staff. Listed as present on final field and staff muster roll, Nov.-Dec. 1864. Participated in engagement at Brandy Station, Va., 9 June 1863.

Co. A, 1st Rgmt., S.C. Cav.

Organized during the latter part of 1861 as Co. A, 1st Bn., S.C. Cav. Redesignated about 25 June 1862 as Co. A, 1st Rgmt., S.C. Cav. Also known as Capt. M.T. Owen's Cav. Co., S.C. Volunteers.

CREWS, Thomas B. 1st Lt. Enlisted at Abbeville, S.C., 23 Aug. 1861 as 1st Sgt. of Capt. Owen's Co. Apparently promoted 2nd Lt. Mar. or Apr. 1863 and 1st Lt. Sept. or Oct. 1863. Listed as present on final muster roll in his personnel file, Nov.-Dec. 1864.

ROBERTS, William G. 2nd Lt. Enlisted at Abbeville, S.C., 3 Jan. 1862 as a Cpl. in Capt. Owen's Co. Promoted 2nd Lt. during the summer of 1863. Paroled at Augusta, Ga., 19 May 1865.

Co. B, 1st Rgmt., S.C. Cav.

Organized during the latter part of 1861 as Co. B, 1st Bn., S.C. Cav. Redesignated about 25 June 1862 as Co. B, 1st Rgmt., S.C. Cav. Also known as Capt. N. Nesbitt's Cav. Co., S.C. Volunteers; as the Ferguson Rangers; and, after 12 Sept. 1864, as Capt. W.J. Leak's Cav. Co.

LEAK, W.J. Capt. Commander, Co. B. Entered service 25 May 1861 in Laurens County as 1st Lt. of Capt. Nesbitt's Co. Promoted Capt. and assumed command Co. B. 12 Sept. 1864. Listed on muster roll as absent, on picket, as of 1 July 1864. Listed as present on final company muster roll, Nov.-Dec. 1864.

NESBITT, Niles. See listing under Regimental Staff.

YOUNG, B.N. 1st Lt. Enlisted at age 25 in Laurens County, S.C., 22 Aug. 1861 as a Cpl. in Capt. Nesbitt's Co. Promoted 2nd Lt. 18 June 1862 and 1st Lt. 15 Sept. 1864. Listed as present on final Co. B muster roll in his personnel file, Nov.-Dec. 1864.

Co. C, 1st Rgmt., S.C. Cav.
Organized during the latter part of 1861 as Co. C, 1st Bn., S.C. Cav. Redesignated about 25 June 1862 as Co. C, 1st Rgmt., S.C. Cav. Also known as Capt. J.D. Twiggs' Cav. Co., S.C. Volunteers; the Edgefield Rangers; and, after May 1862, as Capt. Thomas W. Whatley's Co.

HANCOCK, D.O. 2nd Lt. Enlisted at age 24 at Hamburg, opposite Augusta, Ga., 27 Aug. 1861 as a Pvt. in Capt. Twiggs' Co. Promoted 2nd Lt. 7 July 1862. Last entry in his personnel file states that he was on detached service at Pocotaligo, S.C., as of 10 Dec. 1864.

HANKINSON, John N. 2nd Lt. Enlisted at age 21 at Hamburg, opposite Augusta, Ga., 18 Sept. 1861 as a Pvt. in Capt. Twigg's Co. Appointed 2nd Lt. 7 July 1862. Paroled at Augusta, Ga., 20 May 1865.

MILLER, Thomas S. 1st Lt. Entered service at Hamburg, opposite Augusta, Ga., 27 Aug. 1861 as 2nd Lt. of Capt. Twiggs' Co. Promoted 1st Lt. 26 June 1862. Listed as present on final company muster roll, Nov.-Dec. 1864.

WHATLEY, Thomas W. Capt. Commander, Co. C. Entered service at age 34 at Hamburg, opposite Augusta, Ga., 18 Sept. 1861 as 1st Lt. Promoted Capt. 26 May 1862 and became commander of the company. Paroled at Augusta, Ga., 20 May 1865.

Co. D, 1st Rgmt., S.C. Cav.
Organized during the latter part of 1861 as Co. D, 1st Bn., S.C. Cav. Redesignated about 25 June 1862 as Co. D, 1st Rgmt., S.C. Cav. Also known as Capt. W.A. Walker's Cav. Co., S.C. Volunteers; after June 1863 as Capt. J.S. Wilson's Cav. Co.; and also as the Chester Troop, S.C. Volunteers.

WILSON, J.S. Capt. Commander, Co. D. Entered service at age 40 at Chester, S.C., 10 Sept. 1861 as 1st Lt. of Capt. Walker's Co. Promoted Capt. May or June 1863 and became company commander. Final records in his personnel file state that he was on leave as of 20 Dec. 1864.

Co. E, 1st Rgmt., S.C. Cav.
Organized during the latter part of 1861 as Co. E, 1st Bn., S.C. Cav. Redesignated about 25 June 1862 as Co. E, 1st Rgmt., S.C. Cav. Also known as Capt. James Davis Trezevant's Cav. Co., S.C. Volunteers.

CONNOR, W.D. 3rd Lt. Enlisted at age 20 at Ft. Motte, S.C., 26 Oct. 1861 as a Pvt. in Trezevant's Co. Promoted Sgt. in Nov. or Dec. 1861, but reduced to Pvt. 13 Aug. 1862 for reasons unspecified in his personnel records. Promoted 3rd Lt. Mar. or Apr. 1863. Listed as present on final muster roll in his files, Nov.-Dec. 1864.

GLOVER, Florence. 2nd Lt. Enlisted at Coosawhatchie, S.C., 14 Nov. 1861 as a Pvt. in Co. E. Promoted Sgt. during March or April 1862 and 2nd Lt. 28 Nov. 1862. Final entry in his personnel file states that he was in charge of the guard at Wappoo Bridge, James Island, as of 20 Dec. 1864.

HILL, J.R. 1st Lt. Enlisted at Adams Run, S.C. 19 Mar. 1862 as a Pvt. in Co. E. Promoted 1st Lt. 28 Nov. 1862. Listed as present on final company muster roll, Nov.-Dec. 1864.

TREZEVANT, James Davis. Capt. Commander, Co. E. Entered service at Fort Motte, S.C., 26 Oct. 1861 as company commander. Final reports in his personnel file state that he was serving in the Branchville, S.C., area as late as Feb. 1865.

Co. F, 1st Rgmt., S.C. Cav.

Organized during the latter part of 1861 as Co. F, 1st Bn., S.C. Cav. Redesignated about 25 June 1862 as Co. F, 1st Rgmt., S.C. Cav. Also known as Capt. Elam Sharpe's Cav. Co., S.C. Volunteers, and, after 1 Nov. 1863, as Capt. A.J. Clayton's Cav. Co.

BLASSINGHAME, B.F. 1st Lt. Enlisted 4 Dec. 1861, age 37, at Pickens S.C., as a Pvt. in Capt. Sharpe's Co. Elected 2nd Lt. 12 July 1862 and promoted 1st Lt. 1 Nov. 1863. Final record in his personnel file states that he was on leave as of 3 Jan. 1865.

CLAYTON, A.J. Capt. Commander Co. F. Entered service at age 32 at Pickens, S.C., 4 Dec. 1861 as 1st Lt. of Capt. Sharpe's Co. Promoted Capt. 1 Nov. 1863 and became company commander. Final entry in his personnel records states that he was on leave as of 27 Dec. 1864.

LUSK, L.W. 2nd Lt. Enlisted at age 25 at Pickens, S.C., 4 Dec. 1861 as a Pvt. in Capt. Sharpe's Co. Promoted Cpl. in Sept. or Oct. 1862 and 2nd Lt. 1 Nov. 1862. Listed as present on final Co. F muster roll, Nov.-Dec. 1864. However, OR XLVII (2) p. 1070 places Lusk, perhaps erroneously, in Co. E as of 31 Jan. 1865.

Co. G, 1st Rgmt., S.C. Cav.

Organized during the latter part of 1861 as Co. G, 1st Bn., S.C. Cav. Redesignated about 25 June 1862 as Co. G, 1st Rgmt., S.C. Cav. Also known as Capt. L.J. Johnson's Cav. Co., S.C. Volunteers.

JACKSON, G.T. 2nd Lt. Entered service 8 Jan. 1862 at Abbeville, S.C., as 2nd Lt. of Co. G. He was still serving with the unit as late as Aug. 1864.

JOHNSON, L.J. Capt. Commander, Co. G. Entered service at Abbeville, S.C., 8 Jan. 1862 as Capt. and company commander. Listed as present on final company muster roll, Nov.-Dec. 1864.

LIVINGSTON, J.F. 1st Lt. Entered service at Abbeville, S.C., 8 Jan. 1862 as 1st Lt. of Co. G. Listed as present on final company muster roll, Nov.-Dec. 1864.

Co. H, 1st Rgmt., S.C. Cav.

Organized during the latter part of 1861 as Co. H, 1st Bn., S.C. Cav. Redesignated about 25 June 1862 as Co. H, 1st Rgmt., S.C. Cav. Also known as Capt. Robin ApC. Jones' Cav. Co., S.C. Volunteers.

BECKHAM, William H. 2nd Lt. Enlisted 9 Jan. 1861 at Rock Hill, S.C., at age 27 as a Pvt. in Capt. Jones' Co. Promoted Sgt. during March or April 1862 and 2nd Lt. 15 June 1863. Listed as present on final company muster roll, Nov.-Dec. 1864.

RATCHFORD, James A. 2nd Lt. Enlisted at age 37 at Rock Hill, S.C., 15 Jan. 1861 as a Pvt. in Capt. Jones' Co. Promoted 3rd Lt. in Nov. or Dec. 1862 and 2nd Lt. in Sept. or Oct. 1863. Paroled near Greensboro, N.C., at the end of April 1865.

WHITE, James W. 1st Lt. Entered service at age 21 at Rock Hill, S.C., 9 Jan. 1862 as 2nd Lt. of Capt. Jones' Co. Promoted 1st Lt. 10 June 1863. Final records in his personnel file state that he was on detached service at Pocotaligo, S.C., as of 10 Dec. 1864.

Co. I, 1st Rgmt., S.C. Cav.

Organized during the latter part of 1861 as Co. I, 1st Bn., S.C. Cav. Redesignated about 25 June 1862 as Co. I, 1st Rgmt., S.C. Cav. Also known as Capt. J.R.P. Fox's Cav. Co., S.C. Volunteers.

HORSEY, Fred. 1st Lt. Entered service at Parker's Ferry, S.C., 3 April 1862 as 2nd Lt. of Capt. Fox's Co. Promoted 1st Lt. in Nov. or Dec. 1862. Listed as present on final company muster roll, Nov.-Dec. 1864.

1ST REGIMENT, S.C. INFANTRY, (REGULARS)
(Also known as 3rd. Rgmt., S.C. Arty.)

This unit first served in the Army of the State of South Carolina with 10 companies, but was accepted into Confederate service in May 1861 with 8 — A through H. Cos. I and K were added early in 1862. Although called infantry, the regiment served as heavy artillery and in May 1863 was designated the 3rd. Rgmt., S.C. Arty., by the Adjutant and Inspector General's Office in Richmond. However, the designation was not confirmed even though the regiment continued service as artillery. It also was known until 7 Nov. 1862 as Col. John Dunovant's Rgmt. and, thereafter, as Col. William Butler's Rgmt.

Co. B, 1st Rgmt., S.C. Inf. (Regulars)

This unit was organized 4 Mar. 1861 under the state establishment as Co. E. When the regiment was accepted into Confederate service, 17 May 1861, it became Co. B. Also known as Capt. John C. Simkins' Co. (Simkins later was promoted Maj. and then Lt. Col. He was killed at Battery Wagner, Morris Island, S.C., during the Federal attack of 18 July 1863.) After 1 Feb. 1863, the unit also was known as Capt. J. Hamilton Warley's Co.

WARLEY, J. Hamilton. Capt. Commander, Co. B. Entered service 31 Mar. 1861 as a 2nd Lt. in Co. C, 1st Rgmt., S.C. Inf., under the state establishment. Transferred 17 May 1861 to Co. A. Promoted 1st Lt. 22 July 1861. Promoted Capt. 19 Jan. 1863 and transferred to Co. B as commander 1 Feb. 1863. Final records in his personnel file state that he was admitted to a hospital at Greensboro, N.C., 19 Mar. 1865.

Co. C, 1st Rgmt., S.C. Inf. (Regulars)

This company was organized under the state establishment, probably in Mar. 1861. It became Co. C when the regiment was accepted into Confederate service 17 May 1861. The unit also was known as Capt. Robert De Treville's Co. After his promotion to Maj. 18 July 1863, the company became known as Capt. Bartlett J. Witherspoon's Co. in honor of its new commander.

WITHERSPOON, Bartlett J. Capt. Commander, Co. C. Entered service in March or April 1861 as a 2nd Lt. in Co. B under the state establishment. Transferred to Co. H when the regiment was accepted into Confederate service 17 May 1861. Promoted 1st Lt. 8 Oct. 1861. Transferred to Co. F in Nov. or Dec. 1861. Promoted Capt. 18 July 1863 and assumed command of Co. C, succeeding Capt. Robert De Treville who was promoted Maj. Paroled at Greensboro, N.C., 3 May 1865.

Co. D, 1st Rgmt., S.C. Inf. (Regulars)

This company probably was mustered into state service in Mar. 1861. When the regiment was accepted into Confederate service 17 May 1861, it became Co. D. It also was known as Capt. Charles T. Haskell Jr.'s Co. (See 15 July 1863, note). After May or June 1864, Co. D also was known as Lt. (later Capt.) Duff G. Calhoun's Co.

CALHOUN, Duff G. Capt. Commander, Co. D. Entered service 24 May 1861 as a 2nd Lt. in Capt. Warren Adams' Co., later Co. H. Transferred 5 June 1861 to Capt. Robert Martin's Co., subsequently Co. G. Promoted 1st Lt. 19 Oct. 1861. Transferred to Co. E in June 1862. Transferred to Co. D as commanding officer in May or June 1864. Promoted Capt. 19 Oct. 1864. Admitted to a hospital at Greensboro, N.C., 19 Mar. 1865.

Co. E, 1st Rgmt., S.C. Inf. (Regulars)

This unit was organized 4 Mar. 1861 under the state establishment and was accepted into Confederate service 17 May 1861 as Co. E. It also was known as Capt. John L. Black's Co. Black was promoted Maj. and Capt. R. Press Smith Jr. assumed command 23 Oct. 1861. In Jan. 1862 the company seems to have been divided. Smith retained Co. E, and the remaining men were organized as Co. K under command of Capt. Constant H. Rivers.

SMITH, R. Press Jr. Capt. Commander, Co. E. Entered service 4 Mar. 1861 as 1st Lt., probably of Capt. John L. Black's Co. Transferred 17 May 1861 to Co. C, 1st Rgmt., S.C. Inf. and in July or Aug. 1861 to Co. B. Promoted Capt. 23 Oct. 1861 and transferred to Co. E where he replaced Black (promoted Maj.) as commanding officer. When the unit was divided in Jan. 1862, Smith retained Co. E. Final records in his personnel file state that he was admitted to a hospital at Greensboro, N.C., 19 Mar. 1865. (*Note, see also R. Press Smith, Quartermaster, 27th Rgmt., S.C. Inf.*)

Co. F, 1st Rgmt., S.C. Inf. (Regulars)

This unit, although probably organized earlier, first appears in available records 17 May 1861 as Co. F. It also was known as Capt. Thomas M. Baker's Co. After Baker was promoted Maj., about 18 Nov. 1862, it also was known as Capt. B.S. Burnett's Co. in honor of its new commander.

BURNETT, B.S. Capt. Commander, Co. F. Entered service at Sullivan's Island, S.C., 19 Mar. 1861 as a 2nd Lt. in Capt. John L. Black's Co. Promoted 1st Lt. about May 1861 and transferred to Co. H. Transferred Nov. or Dec. 1861 to Co. C. Promoted Capt. 18 Nov. 1862 and appointed commander, Co. F. Admitted to hospital at High Point, N.C., 19 Mar. 1865 with undisclosed wounds. Died there 29 Mar. 1865.

Co. K, 1st Rgmt., S.C. Inf. (Regulars)

This unit was organized 4 Mar. 1861 under the state establishment and was accepted into Confederate service 17 May 1861 as Co. E. It also was known as Capt. John L. Black's Co. Black was promoted Maj. and Capt. R. Press Smith Jr. assumed command 23 Oct. 1861. The company seems to have been divided in Jan. 1862. Smith retained Co. E, and the remaining men were organized as Co. K. which also was known as Capt. Constant H. Rivers' Co. in honor of its new commander.

CLAIBORNE, Charles H. 2nd Lt. Enlisted, age 19, on 3 Mar. 1861 as a Sgt. in Capt. Robert Martin's Co., subsequently Co. G, 1st Rgmt., S.C. Inf. He was discharged 3 Mar. 1862 at expiration of his enlistment. Reenlisted 1 Dec. 1862 as a Pvt. in the same company. Promoted 2nd Lt. 18 Nov. 1863 and transferred to Co. K on 7 Dec. 1863. He was still with Co. K as late as Nov.-Dec. 1864.

RIVERS, Constant H. Capt. Commander, Co. K. Entered service 11 April 1861 as 1st Lt. of Co. F. Transferred in May or June 1861 to Co. E. Went on detached service 24 Aug. 1861 as aide-de-camp to Brig. (later Lt.) Gen. Richard H. Anderson. Promoted Capt. 1 Jan. 1862 and appointed commander of Co. K. Paroled 28 April 1865 while in a hospital at Greensboro, N.C.

2ND REGIMENT, SOUTH CAROLINA ARTILLERY:

This regiment was formed about April 1862 by addition of six companies to the 2nd Bn., S.C. Arty., also known as Thomas G. Lamar's Bn., S.C. Arty. The regiment initially was called the 1st, but the designation subsequently was changed to the 2nd. Lamar's Bn. had been organized in the latter part of 1861 with four companies, including then Capt., Lamar's, which, after various changes, became Co. B of the 2nd Rgmt. Lamar commanded Fort (also called Battery) Lamar during the Battle of Secessionville, 16 June 1862 (See Introduction, pp. ix and x). He was wounded and died 17 Oct. 1862. The unit also was known as Col. A.D. Frederick's Rgmt., S.C. Arty.

BROWN, J. Welsman. Lt. Col. Entered service as 1st Lt. 4 Oct. 1861. Promoted Capt., commander Co. C, Lamar's Bn. (subsequently Co. K, 2nd Rgmt., S.C. Arty.) 1 Jan. 1862; Maj., Nov. or Dec. 1862; and then Lt. Col in Mar. or Apr. 1863. He later commanded the 2nd Rgmt. and, at the surrender of Gen. Joseph E. Johnston's army, 26 April 1865, in N. C., was serving as a brigade commander. Brown participated in the capture of the U.S.S. Isaac Smith *(see 25 Aug. 1863, note 3)* and commanded the artillery during the fighting on Morris Island for a few days in Aug. 1863.

FELDER, E.J. Capt. Regimental Quartermaster. Entered service at Ft. Johnson (James Island, S.C.) 1 Feb. 1862, as quartermaster of the Rgmt. Detailed as brigade quartermaster, West Lines, 10 Feb. 1864. Paroled at Greensboro, N.C., as brigade quartermaster 28 April 1865.

FREDERICK, A.D. Col. Commander 2nd Rgmt. Entered service at age 43 at Orangeburg, S.C., 19 Nov. 1861, as Capt., commander of Co. A, Lamar's Bn. Later served as Lt. Col. of the 1st Rgmt. and then Col., commanding, the 2nd Rgmt. Was in command of the East Lines, James Island, during part of 1863. On 26 May 1864 relieved Col. Charles H. Simonton, 25th S.C. Inf., as commander of the West Lines. Mentioned in the Official Records as late as 25 Jan. 1865 as commander of the 2nd Rgmt. on James Island.

FREDERICK, E.J. Adjutant. Entered service as a Lt. and regimental adjutant 15 Feb. 1862 on James Island, S.C. On detached service as acting assistant adjutant general of the West Lines, James Island, 25 May 1864. Paroled as adjutant of the 2nd Rgmt. at Greensboro, N.C., 28 April 1865.

GOODWYN, T.J. Assistant Surgeon. The field and staff muster roll of July-Aug. 1864 lists Goodwyn as assistant surgeon, in charge of the regimental hospital.

HANE, J.K. Color Sgt. Enlisted 17 March 1862 at Ft. Johnson (James Island, S.C.) in Co. I. Appointed Color Sgt. 17 Jan. 1863. Served in this capacity until paroled at Greensboro, N.C. in April 1865.

HAWKINS, Perry. Chaplain. The field and staff muster roll of July-Aug. 1864 lists Hawkins as chaplain, awaiting appointment. However, later personnel records show the date of his commission as 1 Aug. 1864. Paroled at Greensboro, N.C, 28 April 1865.

JORDAN, James R. Ordnance Sgt. Enlisted at Ft. Johnson (James Island, S.C.) 19 March 1862 as a Sgt. in Co. E. Carried on field and staff muster roll of Nov.-Dec. 1862 as regimental Ordnance Sgt. Personnel records show him serving in that capacity as late as 23 March 1865.

LEBBY, Robert Jr. Surgeon. Entered service on James Island as chief surgeon of 2nd Rgmt. 17 Oct. 1862. However, he apparently was soon detached for service as surgeon in charge of the brigade hospital on James Island.

MILLAR, John. Sgt. Maj. Enlisted 9 May 1861 at Richmond, Va. Transferred 11 Sept. 1862 from 2nd Rgmt., S.C. Volunteers, Army of Northern Virginia, to 2nd Rgmt, S.C. Arty, as Sgt. Maj. Final field and staff muster roll, Nov.-Dec. 1864, shows Millar serving as Sgt. Maj.

PIKE, J.C. Quartermaster Sgt. Enlisted at Coles Island, S.C., 9 April 1862 as a Pvt. in Co. F. Detached to Quartermaster Dept. 1 May 1862. Promoted Quartermaster Sgt. 2 May 1863. Paroled at Greensboro, N.C., 28 April 1865.

WARLEY, Frederick F. Maj. Entered service, age 31, at Darlington, S.C., 20 Mar. 1862 as Capt. and commander of the unit which subsequently became Co. D. Promoted Maj. 17 Oct. 1862 and transferred to the regimental staff. He was serving as chief of artillery at Battery Wagner, Morris Island, when he was wounded in the left leg by a shell fragment and was captured 4 Sept. 1863 while being conveyed by small boat to Charleston. He was taken aboard the U.S. hospital ship *Cosmopolitan* and then to a hospital at Beaufort, S.C., where he remained until 4 Dec. 1863 when he was transferred to the Federal base on Hilton Head Island. He was sent to Ft. Columbus, N.Y. Harbor, where he arrived 18 Jan. 1864; then to Ft. McHenry, Baltimore, Md. (12 Feb.) and to Ft. Delaware, near New Castle, Dela. (16 June). He was returned to Morris Island as a member of "The Immortal 600" *(see 15 June 1864, note)*. Following exchange, 3 Aug. 1864, Warley returned to his staff duties and was paroled at Greensboro, N.C., 28 April 1865.

Co. B, 2nd Rgmt., S.C. Arty.

Successively designated Capt. Thomas G. Lamar's Co., S.C. Arty.; Capt. Lamar's Co., Lamar's Bn., S.C. Arty.; Co. D, Lamar's Bn., S.C. Arty.; Co. D, 1st Rgmt., S.C. Arty.; Co. B, 1st Rgmt., S.C. Arty.; and Co. B, 2nd Rgmt., S.C. Arty.

JOHNSON, J.E. Sgt. Enlisted, age 22, on 10 Oct. 1861 as a Pvt. in the company. Promoted Cpl. 1 Jan. 1862 and Sgt. 3 May 1863. He is listed as present on the final company muster roll, Nov.-Dec. 1864.

Co. C, 2nd Rgmt., S.C. Arty.

Initially designated Co. C, 1st Rgmt., S.C. Arty., it subsequently became Co. C, 2nd Rgmt., S.C. Arty. It also was known as Capt. Medicus Rickenbaker's Co., S.C. Arty.

RICKENBAKER, Medicus. Capt. Entered service at Orangeburg, S.C., 19 Nov. 1862 as 1st Lt. and was promoted Capt. 10 Sept. 1862. Served as commanding officer, Co. C, through final muster roll, Nov.-Dec. 1864.

Co. D, 2nd Rgmt., S.C. Arty.

This unit was successively designated Capt. Frederick F. Warley's Co., Thomas G. Lamar's Bn, S.C. Arty.; Co. D, 1st Rgmt., S.C. Arty.; and Co. D, 2nd Rgmt., S.C. Arty. It also was known as the Inglis Light Arty. and as Capt. William E. Charles' Co., S.C. Arty.

CHARLES, William E. Capt. Commander, Co. D. Entered service at Darlington, S.C., 20 Mar. 1862 at age 25 as 1st Lt. of Capt. Warley's Co. Promoted Capt. 17 Oct. 1862. Paroled 1 May 1865 at Greensboro, N.C. Although his unit techinically was Co. D, 2nd Rgmt., S.C. Arty., it is generally listed in various records as Capt. Charles' Co., Inglis Light Arty.

Co. E, 2nd Rgmt., S.C. Arty.

Initially designated Co. E, 1st Rgmt., S.C. Arty., and then Co. E, 2nd Rgmt. S.C. Arty. It also was known as Capt. B.E. Dickson's Co., S.C. Arty.

DICKSON, B.E. Capt. Entered service 10 Aug. 1861 as 2nd Lt. of Co. E, 25th Rgmt., Miss. Inf. Assumed command of Co. E, 2nd Rgmt., S.C. Arty. at Ft. Johnson (James Island, S.C.) 19 March 1862 and was promoted Capt. three days later. Paroled at Greensboro, N.C., 28 April 1865.

Co. F, 2nd Rgmt., S.C. Arty.

Organized initially as the 2nd Co, 1st Rgmt., S.C. Inf., this company in March 1862 joined Thomas G. Lamar's Bn., S.C. Arty. In April 1862, it became Co. F, 1st Rgmt., S.C. Arty. and, subsequently, Co. F, 2nd Rgmt., S.C. Arty. It also was known as Capt. T.K. Legare's Co., S.C. Arty.

CONNOR, A.A. 2nd Lt. Enlisted at Coles Island, S.C., 9 April 1862 as 1st Sgt. Elected 2nd Lt. 24 Jan. 1863. Paroled at Greensboro, N.C., 28 April 1865.

CONNOR, J.B. 2nd Lt. Entered service at Coles Island, S.C., 9 April 1862 as 2nd Lt. When A.A. Connor was elected 2nd Lt. 24 Jan. 1863, J.B. Connor automatically became senior 2nd Lt. of the company and was so listed on the final muster roll, Nov.-Dec. 1864.

LEGARE, T.K. Capt. Elected commander of Co. F. 23 Mar. 1862 at Coles Island, S.C. Listed in that capacity on final muster roll of Nov.-Dec. 1864.

LEGARE, W.W. 1st Lt. Elected 1st Lt. of Co. F. 23 Mar. 1862. Listed on the Nov.-Dec. 1862 muster roll as acting ordnance officer for East James Island. Later rolls carry him as acting ordnance officer for the entire island. He was still serving in that capacity at the time of the final company roll, Nov.-Dec. 1864.

MOORER, W.J.D. Cpl. Enlisted at Coles Island, S.C. 9 April 1862 as a Cpl. in Co. F. Captured on James Island 13 May 1864. Exchanged at Port Royal Ferry, S.C., 16 Aug. 1864, and rejoined his unit. Paroled near Greensboro, N.C., 28 April 1865.

RILEY, M.N. Sgt. Enlisted at Coles Island, S.C., 9 April 1862 as a Cpl. Promoted Sgt. during the summer of 1862. Paroled at Greensboro, N.C., 28 April 1865.

SHULER, B.M. 1st Lt. Entered service at Coles Island, S.C., 9 April 1862 as 2nd Lt. Promoted 1st Lt. 24 Jan. 1863. Paroled at Greensboro, N.C., 28 April 1865.

Co. G, 2nd Rgmt., S.C. Arty.

Organized initially as the 6th Co, 1st Rgmt., S.C. Inf., this company in March 1862 joined Thomas G. Lamar's Bn., S.C. Arty. In April 1862 it became Co. G, 1st Rgmt., S.C. Arty. and subsequently Co. G, 2nd Rgmt., S.C. Arty. It also was known as Capt. G.W. Stallings' Co., S.C. Arty.

BUSH, George P. 1st Lt. Entered service at Coles Island, S.C., 9 April 1862 as 3rd Lt. of Co. G. Promoted 2nd Lt. 13 Oct. 1862 and 1st Lt. 1 Aug. 1864. Paroled at Greensboro, N.C., 1 May 1865.

RUSH, C.C. 1st Lt. Enlisted at Coles Island, S.C., 9 April 1862 as a Sgt. Elected 2nd Lt. 12 Jan. 1863. Promoted 1st Lt. 1 Aug. 1864. Was in charge of a 6.4-inch Brooke Rifle which burst at Battery Simkins 26 July 1864 while firing on Federal batteries on Morris Island. One man was killed and three wounded. Rush was uninjured. He is listed as present on the final company muster roll, Nov.-Dec. 1864.

STALLINGS, G.W. Capt. Commander Co. G. Stallings was 1st Lt. of the 6th Inf. Co. and became commanding officer after the unit transferred to artillery. He was promoted Capt. 17 April 1862 and was still serving as Co. G. commander when paroled at Greensboro, N.C., 2 May 1865.

Co. H, 2nd Rgmt., S.C. Arty.

Initially designated Co. H, 1st Rgmt., S.C. Arty., this unit subsequently became Co. H, 2nd Rgmt., S.C. Arty. It also was known as Capt. William H. Kennady's Co., S.C. Arty.

ASHLEY, R.C. 2nd Lt. Enlisted at Barnwell, S.C., 25 March 1862 as a Cpl. Promoted 2nd Lt. 22 Sept. 1862. Carried on muster rolls from March through June 1864 as present, in arrest. Cashiered 13 July 1864 following a court martial. No charges recorded in his personnel records.

JONES, T.H. 2nd Lt. Enlisted at Barnwell, S.C., 25 March 1862 as a Pvt. Elected 2nd Lt.. 31 Dec. 1862. Listed as wounded (contusion) during the fighting on Morris Island Aug. 20-Sept. 6, 1863. Carried on final company muster roll,

Nov.-Dec. 1864 as absent, sick since 15 Oct. 1864.

KENNADY, William H. Capt. Commander, Co. H. Entered service 25 Mar. 1862 at Barnwell, S.C., as Capt. and company commander. Admitted to CSA General Hospital, Charlotte, N.C., 25 March 1865. Furloughed 12 April 1865.

KITCHENS, J.B. 1st Lt. Entered service at Barnwell, S.C., 25 March 1862 as a 2nd Lt. in Co. H. Promoted 1st Lt. 22 Sept. 1862. Paroled at Greensboro, N.C., 3 May 1865.

WILLIS, E.R. Pvt. Enlisted at Ft. Johnson (James Island, S.C.) 16 Jan. 1862 in Co. D. Transferred 4 Apr. 1862 to Co. H. where muster rolls for Jan. 1863 through Dec. 1864 carry him as absent, serving as regimental teamster.

Co. I, 2nd Rgmt., S.C. Arty.

Successively designated Capt. A.D. Frederick's Co., Thomas G. Lamar's Bn., S.C. Arty.; Co. A, Lamar's Bn., S.C. Arty.; Co. I, 1st Rgmt., S.C. Arty.; and Co. I, 2nd Rgmt., S.C. Arty. It also was known as Capt. J.B. Humbert's Co., S.C. Arty.

BARTON, W.S. 1st Lt. Entered service at Orangeburg, S.C., 19 Nov. 1861, age 24, as a 2nd Lt. Promoted 1st Lt. 9 Sept. 1862. Paroled near Greensboro, N.C., 28 April 1865 as 1st Lt. of Co. I. Went on detached service 11 Aug. 1864 as Ordnance Officer of the West Lines.

BOLIVAR, George. 2nd Lt. Enlisted at Orangeburg, S.C., 11 Nov. 1861, as a Cpl. Promoted 2nd Lt. 9 Jan. 1863. Severely wounded in the Battle of Secessionville, 16 June 1862 (*See pp. vii and viii*). Recovered and returned to duty.

HIGGS, John F. Pvt. Enlisted on James Island, S.C., 1 March 1864. Listed on company rolls as deserted 5 Aug. 1864. Federal records state that Higgs, 17, arrived at Coles Island the same date.

HUMBERT, J.B. Jr. Capt. Commander, Co. I. Entered service, age 24, at Orangeburg, S.C., 19 Nov. 1861 as 1st Lt. of Capt. Frederick's Co. He succeeded to command and was promoted Capt. 9 Sept. 1862. He participated in the Battle of Averasborough, N.C., 15 March 1865.

MOSLEY, J.W. 1st Lt. Enlisted, age 25, at Orangeburg, S.C., 19 Nov. 1861 as a Sgt. in Capt. Frederick's Co. Elected 2nd Lt. 27 May 1862 and promoted 1st Lt. 9 Jan. 1863. Paroled at Greensboro, N.C., 28 April 1865.

RUSSELL, S.D. 2nd Lt. Enlisted, age 28, at Orangeburg, S.C., 19 Nov. 1861 as a Sgt. Appointed 1st Sgt. 4 April 1862. Elected 2nd Lt. 24 Jan. 1863. Served as regimental adjutant from 29 May until Sept. or Oct. 1864. Paroled at Greensboro, N.C., 28 April 1865.

WOLFE, J.R.D. Cpl. Enlisted 11 Jan. 1862 at Fort Johnson as a Pvt. in Co. I. Promoted Cpl. 15 Jan. 1863. Paroled near Greensboro, N.C., 28 April 1865.

Co. K, 2nd Rgmt., S.C. Arty.

Successively designated as Capt. J. Welsman Brown's Co., Thomas G. Lamar's Bn, S.C. Arty.; Co. C, Lamar's Bn., S.C. Arty.; Co. K, 1st Rgmt., S.C. Arty.; and Co. K, 2nd Rgmt., S.C. Arty.

BERRY. J. Oliver. Pvt. Enlisted, age 17, at Edgefield, S.C., 4 Oct. 1861. On detached service at Battery Haskell when wounded 18 Sept. 1863. Returned to duty and was listed with the company as late as Feb. 1864.

LAKE, Felix. 2nd Lt. Enlisted, age 18, at Edgefield, S.C., as a Pvt. Promoted Sgt. 1 Jan. 1862 and later became 1st Sgt. of the company. Elected 2nd Lt. 13

Dec. 1862. Listed as present on final company muster roll, Nov.-Dec. 1864.

MILLS, Wade. Pvt. Enlisted 16 Mar. 1862 at Ft. Johnson (James Island, S.C.). Listed on the company muster roll of Sept.-Oct. 1863 as killed in action at Battery Haskell 18 Sept. 1863.

PADGETT, D.W. Pvt. Enlisted at Fort Lamar (James Island, S.C.) 31 Jan. 1863 in Co. K. Detached to the Engineer Dept. 29 July 1863. Receipt roll of May 1864 lists the nature of his service as overseer at the Holmes House. Paroled at Augusta, Ga., 2 June 1865.

PITTS, T.A. 2nd Lt. Enlisted at Edgefield, S.C., 10 Oct. 1861 as a Pvt. Promoted Cpl. 1 Jan. 1862 and Sgt. in Nov. Elected 2nd Lt. 1 Dec. 1862. Company muster roll of July-Aug. 1863 lists him on detached service at Battery Haskell. Surrendered and paroled 25 May 1865 at Augusta, Ga.

SECOND REGIMENT, S.C. CAVALRY

The regiment was formed 22 Aug. 1862 by consolidation of the cavalry battalion known as Hampton's Legion; the 4th Bn., S.C. Cav.; Capt. A.H. Boykin's Co., S.C. Cav.; and Capt. Thomas J. Lipscomb's Co., S.C. Cav. The unit also was known as Col. Matthew C. Butler's Rgmt. and, later, as Col. Thomas J. Lipscomb's Rgmt.

LIPSCOMB, Thomas J. Col. Commander, 2nd Rgmt., S.C. Cav. Entered service at the beginning of the war, age 28, as a Lt. of the 3rd S.C. Volunteers and saw action in Va. On 10 Apr. 1862 he was promoted Capt. and named commander of Lipscomb's Cav. Co., subsequently Co. G of the 2nd Rgmt. He was promoted Maj. and transferred to the regimental staff in the consolidation of 22 Aug. 1862. Promoted Lt. Col. 10 June 1863 and Col. 1 Sept. 1863. He succeeded Col. Matthew C. Butler (promoted to Brig. Gen.) as regimental commander. Lipscomb was captured near Goldsboro, N.C., 25 Mar. 1865.

SCREVEN, Thomas E. Maj. Entered service 22 June 1861 as Capt., commander of the Beaufort (S.C.) Detachment, Hampton Legion. He became commander of Co. B, 2nd Rgmt., S.C. Cav., in the consolidation of 22 Aug. 1862. Promoted Maj. and transferred to regimental staff 10 June 1863. Final entry in his personnel file lists him as absent, sick furlough, as of 28 June 1864.

Co. A, 2nd Rgmt., S.C. Cav.

Organized initially as Capt. A.H. Boykin's Co., S.C. Cav., it became Co. A, 2nd Rgmt., S.C. Cav., in the consolidation of 22 Aug. 1862. The unit also was known as the Mounted Rangers; Capt. Boykin's Co., S.C. Cav.; and, after Nov. 1862, as Capt. John Chesnut's Co., S.C. Cav.

CHESNUT, John. Capt. Commander, Co. A. Entered service 26 June 1861 as 1st Lt. of Capt. Boykin's Co. Promoted Capt. and assumed command of the company between Sept. and Nov. 1862. Was serving in North Carolina as late as 10 Mar. 1865.

LEE, Thomas C. 1st Lt. Entered service 26 June 1861 as a 2nd Lt. in Capt. Boykin's Co. Promoted 1st Lt. Nov. or Dec. 1862. Listed as serving in the Wilmington, N.C. area 14 Dec. 1864.

Co. C, 2nd Rgmt., S.C. Cav.

Organized originally as Capt. F. Hampton's Cav. Co., S.C. Volunteers, this unit subsequently became Co. B, 4th Bn., S.C. Cav., which also was known as the 3rd Bn., S.C. Cav., its designation at first muster. It became Co. C, 2nd Rgmt., S.C. Cav., in the consolidation of cavalry units 22 Aug. 1862.

ROACH, Charles A. 2nd Lt. Enlisted, probably in late 1861, as a Pvt. in Capt. Hampton's Co. Promoted Sgt., Co. B, 12 June 1862. Appointed 2nd Lt., Co. C, 24 Oct. 1862. Paroled at Greensboro, N.C., 1 May 1865.

STACK, William H. 1st Lt. Entered service, probably in late 1861, as 3rd Lt. of Capt. Hampton's Co. Appointed 1st Lt. 1 Feb. 1862. Final records in his personnel file state that he was absent, sick at home, as of Oct. 1864.

Co. D, 2nd Rgmt., S.C. Cav.

Organized 7 Feb. 1862 as Capt. J.C. McKewn's Co., S.C. Cav., this unit subsequently became Co. D, 4th Bn., S.C. Cav., although it also was known as Co. D, 3rd Bn., S.C. Cav., its designation at first muster. It was consolidated with other cavalry units 22 Aug. 1862 and became Co. D, 2nd Rgmt., S.C. Cav.

WINTER, Thomas H. 1st Lt. Entered service 7 Feb. 1862, age 33, at Charleston as 2nd Lt. of Capt. McKewn's Co. Promoted 1st Lt. 23 May 1863. Final entry in his personnel records shows that he was still in Co. D as of Nov. 1864.

Co. E, 2nd Rgmt., S.C. Cav.

Organized about 29 Jan. 1862 as Capt. A.H. Dean's Co., S.C. Cav. This unit subsequently became Co. C, 4th Bn., S.C. Cav., which also was known as the 3rd Bn., S.C. Cav., its designation at first muster. It became Co. E, 2nd Rgmt., S.C. Cav., in the consolidation of 22 Aug. 1862. After 23 Feb. 1863, it also was known as Capt. George B. Dean's Co., S.C. Cav.

DAVIS, M.T. Sgt. Enlisted 29 Jan. 1862 at Columbia, S.C., as a Sgt. in Dean's Co. He is listed as present on the final available company muster roll, Sept.-Oct. 1864.

DEAN, George B. Capt. Commander, Co. E. Enlisted 18 Mar. 1862 at Mt. Pleasant, S.C., as a Pvt. Elected 1st Lt. 17 May 1862. Promoted Capt. 23 Feb. 1863 and assumed command of the company. He was serving in the Charleston area as late as 31 Oct. 1864. When G.B. Dean enlisted, the company was under command of Capt. A.H. Dean who had been appointed 29 Jan. 1862. A.H. Dean resigned 23 Feb. 1863 due to the necessity of taking care of his ill wife and two small children. However, he returned to Co. E. in Sept. or Oct. 1864 as a 2nd Lt. and apparently served in that rank throughout the remainder of the war. The relationship, if any, between the two men has not been found in available records.

PEARSON, James P. 1st Sgt. Enlisted at Charleston 12 June 1862 as a Sgt. in Dean's Co. Promoted 1st Sgt. 1 July 1864. He is listed as present on the final available company muster roll, Sept.-Oct. 1864.

THOMPSON, C.S. 1st Lt. Entered service 29 Jan. 1862 as a 2nd Lt. in Capt. A.H. Dean's Co. Promoted 1st Lt. in July or Aug. 1863. Final records in his personnel file, Sept.-Oct. 1864, state that he was on duty at Adams Run, S.C., as of 15 Sept. 1864.

Co. F, 2nd Rgmt., S.C. Cav.

This unit was organized about Dec. 1861 as Capt. W.K. Easley's Co., S.C. Cav. It subsequently became Co. A, 4th Bn., S.C. Cav., which also was known as the 3rd Bn., S.C. Cav., its designation at first muster. It was consolidated with other cavalry units 22 Aug. 1862 and became Co. F, 2nd Rgmt., S.C. Cav. It also was known as Capt. John Westfield's Co., S.C. Cav.

HUNT, William P. 1st Lt. Entered service 28 Dec. 1861, age 33, as 3rd Lt. of Capt. Easley's Co. Promoted 2nd Lt., Co. A, 21 Feb. 1862, and 1st Lt., Co. F, in Nov. or Dec. 1863. Admitted to hospital at Greensboro, N.C., 8 Mar. 1865.

JOHNSON, G.T. Sgt. Enlisted at Greenville, S.C., 27 May 1862 as a Sgt. in the company. The last item in his personnel file, a receipt for clothing, indicates that he was present with the company on 5 Sept. 1864.

PHILLIPS, Jeremiah. 2nd Lt. Enlisted 28 Dec. 1861, age 34, at Pickens, S.C., as a Cpl. in Capt. Easley's Co. Promoted 1st Sgt., Co. A, 26 May 1862. Elected 2nd Lt., Co. F, 24 Oct. 1862. Final entry in his personnel file is a payroll voucher which he signed 17 Jan. 1865.

WESTFIELD, John. Capt. Commander, Co. F. Appointed Capt. and company commander 19 Feb. 1862. Detached 5 Aug. 1864 for three months to manufacture saddles which were badly needed by the regiment. Final record in his personnel file is a payroll voucher which he signed 20 Jan. 1865.

Co. I, 2nd Rgmt., S.C. Cav.

Organized about June 1861 as Capt. Matthew C. Butler's Cav. Co, this unit subsequently became Co. A, Cav. Bn., Hampton Legion. After Butler's promotion to Maj., it was commanded by Capt. Jeremiah J. Bunch. The unit was designated Co. I, 2nd Rgmt., S.C. Cav., in the consolidation of various units 22 Aug. 1862. At this time, or shortly thereafter, it became known as Capt. Tillman H. Clark's Co. for its new commander.

CLARK, Tillman H. Capt. Commander, Co. I. Enlisted, age 32, at Edgefield, S.C., 6 June 1861 as a Pvt. in Capt. Butler's Co. Promoted 1st Sgt. 24 June 1861 and 2nd Lt. 30 Aug. 1861. Promoted Capt. prior to Nov. 1862 (probably in August). Listed as present on final company muster roll, Nov.-Dec. 1864.

TOLBERT, John R. 2nd Lt. Entered service 1 Nov. 1861 at Edgefield, S.C., as a 2nd Lt. Paroled at Augusta, Ga., 24 May 1865.

Co. K, 2nd Rgmt., S.C. Cav.

Organized about 1 June 1861 as Capt. John F. Lanneau's Cav. Co., this unit on 12 June 1861 became Co. B, Cav. Bn., Hampton Legion, S.C. Volunteers. It was consolidated with other cavalry units 22 Aug. 1862 and was designated Co. K, 2nd Rgmt., S.C. Cav.

PEARSON, John A. 1st Sgt. Enlisted at Greenville, S.C., 6 June 1861 as a Sgt. in Capt. Lanneau's Co. Promoted 1st Sgt. during the summer or fall of 1863. He is listed as present on the final company muster roll, Nov.-Dec. 1864.

PERRY, William H. 1st Lt. Enlisted at Greenville, S.C., about 1 June 1861 as a Sgt. in Capt. Lanneau's Co. and apparently was elected 1st Lt. 12 June 1861 when the unit became Co. B, Hampton Legion. Final entry in his personnel file is a payroll voucher he signed 21 Jan. 1865.

3RD REGIMENT, S.C. CAVALRY

This unit was organized as the 3rd Bn., S.C. Cav., in May 1862 from seven independent companies. It also was known as the 2nd Bn., S.C. Cav. In Aug. 1862 three companies were added and designation changed to 3rd Rgmt., S.C. Cav. It also was known as the 2nd Rgmt., S.C. Cav., and as Col. Charles J. Colcock's Rgmt., S.C. Cav.

COLCOCK, Charles J. Col. Commander, 3rd Rgmt., S.C. Cav. Entered service 28 Feb. 1862 as commander of Colcock's Co., S.C. Cav., also known as the Ashley Dragoons. Promoted Lt. Col. (apparently in May 1862 when the 3rd Bn., S.C. Cav., was organized) and Col. 21 Aug. 1862 when the unit became a regiment. During the summer of 1864 he served as commander of the 3rd Military District with headquarters at Pocotaligo, S.C., and as late as 4 April 1865 he was serving with his regiment near Charlotte, N.C.

JENKINS, John. Maj. Entered service, age 36, at Charleston 27 Feb. 1862 as Capt. and commander of a cavalry company known as the Rebel Troop. Promoted Maj. 19 Aug. 1862 and transferred to staff of the 3rd Rgmt. when it was formed two days later. However, he did not join the main body but spent the remainder of the war on detached service, first on John's Island, then at Pocotaligo and, finally, at Orangeburg, S.C., where he was in command of troops at the end of the war in April 1865.

Co. H, 3rd Rgmt., S.C. Cav.

Organized during the early part of the war as the Ashley Dragoons, this unit generally was known as Capt. C.J. Colcock's Co., S.C. Volunteers. It subsequently became Co. G, 2nd Rgmt., S.C. Cav.; Co. G, 3rd Rgmt., S.C. Cav.; and, finally, Co. H, 3rd Rgmt., S.C. Cav.

MANIGAULT, Peter. Pvt. Although old for field service — he was born in 1805 — Manigault enlisted as a Pvt. 28 Feb. 1862 in Capt. Colcock's Co. and served with the unit until he was killed in action 23 Nov. 1864 at Ball's Ferry, near Oconee Bridge, a few miles east of Madison, Ga. He was a brother of Edward Manigault. Peter is erroneously listed as Stephen in an account of the battle on page 37, OR 53. His twin, Charles Drayton Manigault, died in 1838.

Co. K, 3rd Rgmt., S.C. Cav.

This unit was organized as the Savannah River Guards under Capt. Thomas H. Johnson. In May 1862 it became Co. F, 3rd (also known as the 2nd) Bn., S.C. Cav., and 21 Aug. 1862 was designated Co. K, 3rd (also known as the 2nd) Rgmt., S.C. Cav., under command of Capt. A.B. Estes. It also was known, after 12 Nov. 1862, as Capt. William B. Peeples's Co., S.C. Cav.

PEEPLES, William B. Capt. Commander, Co. K. Entered service 27 Jan. 1862, age 30, as a 2nd Lt. in Capt. Thomas H. Johnson's Co. Promoted 1st Lt. in May or June 1862 and Capt. 12 Nov. 1862. He was serving as commander of Co. K as late as 24 Jan. 1865.

Co. D, 4th Rgmt., S.C. Cav.

This company was formerly Co. A, or Capt. Thomas Pinckney's Co., 6th Bn., S.C. Inf., better known as Maj. Edward Manigault's Bn. The company was divided 1 May 1862 into Cos. A and B, Pinckney retaining Co. A. When the 6th Bn. was disbanded during the latter part of May 1862, Co. A became Co. D, 4th Rgmt., S.C. Cav. Co. B, commanded by Capt. Louis A. Whilden, became an independent company and later Co. E, 5th Rgmt., S.C. Cav.

PINCKNEY, Thomas. Capt. Commander of Co. D. Entered service 15 April 1861 as commander of Capt. Thomas Pinckney's Independent Mounted Riflemen, S.C. Volunteers, which in Dec. 1861 became Co. A, Manigault's Bn. Subsequently, he became commander of Co. D, 4th Rgmt., S.C. Cav. Pinckney was captured in Va. 28 May 1864. He was sent to Point Lookout, Md., and then to Fort Delaware. On 20 Aug. 1864 he was transferred to Hilton Head, S.C., and on 20 Oct. to Fort Pulaski, Ga., where he spent the remainder of the war.

5TH REGIMENT, S.C. CAVALRY
Formed 18 Jan. 1863 by consolidation of the 14th and 17th Bns., S.C. Cav.,and Capts. Harlan's and Whilden's Independent Cos., S.C. Cav. The regiment was sent from S.C. to Va. in Mar. 1864 where it served in Brig. Gen. Matthew C. Butler's Cavalry Division. Also known as Col. Samuel W. Ferguson's Rgmt., S.C. Cav., and, after July 1863, as Col. John Dunovant's Rgmt., S.C. Cav.

DUNOVANT, John. Brig. Gen. Commander (as Col.) 5th Rgmt., S.C. Cav. Served as a Maj. of Inf. at Fort Moultrie during bombardment of Fort Sumter 12-13 April 1861. Promoted Col. 22 July 1861 and assumed command of 1st Rgmt. S.C. Inf. (Regulars), also called 3rd Rgmt., S.C. Arty. Dismissed from service 7 Nov. 1862 for drunkeness. Regained his commission in July 1863 and was appointed commander 5th Rgmt., S.C. Cav., succeeding Col. Samuel W. Ferguson who was promoted Brig. Gen. Dunovant was promoted Brig. Gen. 22 Aug. 1864 and was killed leading his brigade in Va. 1 Oct. 1864.

Co. A, 5th Rgmt., S.C. Cav.
This unit was organized as Capt. J.C. Edwards' Co., 1st Bn. Cav., S.C. Volunteers, in Dec. 1861 or Jan. 1862. It probably was Co. B. Although the battalion was mustered in the field and generally was known as the 1st, the official designation was 2nd Bn., S.C. Cav. In May 1862 the official designation was changed to Co. B, 14th Bn., S.C. Cav. Orders of 18 Jan. 1863 consolidated the 14th with the 17th Bn., S.C. Cav., and two independent cavalry companies to form the 5th Rgmt., S.C. Cav., and this unit became Co. A.

EDWARDS, J.C. Capt. Commander, Co. A. Entered service 24 Dec. 1861 at Orangeburg, S.C., as Capt. and company commander. Final records of his service show that as of 29 Nov. 1864 he was in Col. H.K. Aiken's Brigade in Va.

Co. E, 5th Rgmt., S.C. Cav.
This unit was organized about April 1861 as Capt. Thomas Pinckney's Independent Mounted Riflemen, S.C. Volunteers. In Dec. 1861 it became Co. A, 6th Bn., S.C. Inf., better known as Maj. (generally called Col. in deference to his previous state rank) Edward Manigault's Bn. This battalion, a mixed unit of infantry, cavalry and artillery, had been raised for service along the coast between North Santee River and Charleston. On 1 May 1862, Co. A was divided into Cos. A and B. Pinckney retained A and when Manigault's Bn. was disbanded later that month, it became Co. D, 4th Rgmt., S.C. Cav. Capt. Louis A. Whilden became commander of Co. B. At the breakup of the battalion, it became an independent cavalry company, known as Capt. Whilden's Co., S.C.

301

Cav., or the St. James, Santee, Mounted Riflemen. It became Co. E of the 5th when that regiment was organized 18 Jan. 1863.

WHILDEN, Louis A. Capt. Commander, Co. E. Entered service 15 April 1861, age 28, as a 2nd Lt. in Capt. Pinckney's Co. Promoted Capt. about 1 May 1862. Entered hospital at Richmond, Va., 23 May 1864 and died there 4 Aug. 1864.

6TH BATTALION, S.C. INFANTRY
This unit was better known as Maj., or often as Col. in deference to his former rank, Edward Manigault's Bn. It was a mixed unit of infantry, cavalry and artillery raised for service along the coast between North Santee River and Charleston. The battalion was disbanded during the latter part of May 1862.

7TH BATTALION, S.C. INFANTRY
The battalion was organized 22 Feb. 1862 with five companies — A through E. Companies F and G were formed 27 May 1862 of men transferred from the other companies. An independent company of partisan rangers, organized 14 July 1862, was assigned 16 Oct. 1862 as Co. H. The organization also was known as the Enfield Rifles and as Lt. Col. Patrick H. Nelson's Bn., S.C. Inf.

NELSON, Patrick H. Lt. Col. Commander, 7th Bn. Entered service 22 Feb. 1862 as Maj. and Bn. Commander. Promoted Lt. Col. 10 July 1862. Killed in action at Petersburg, Va., 24 June 1864.

11TH REGIMENT, S.C. INFANTRY
Organized in 1861 as the 9th Rgmt., S.C. Inf., this unit was composed of companies raised at various times during the year under the state's call for volunteers. It was reorganized 3 May 1862 and mustered into Confederate service as the 11th Rgmt., S.C. Inf. At this time, some of the original companies appear to have retained their 9th Rgmt. letters, others received new designations, and the remainder were disbanded and the personnel organized into new companies.

GANTT, F. Hay. Col. Commander, 11th Rgmt. Entered service 2 Sept. 1861 near Beaufort, S.C., as 1st Lt. of Co. K, 9th Rgmt. Promoted Lt. Col. in the reorganization of 3 May 1862 and Col. 27 Nov. 1862. Paroled at Augusta, Ga., 18 May 1865.

IZARD, Allen C. Lt. Col. Entered service 28 Aug. 1861 at Walterboro, S.C., as a 2nd Lt. in Capt. E.S.P. Bellinger's Co., 9th Rgmt. This company declined to enter Confederate service and was disbanded near the end of 1861. Izard, on 5 Jan. 1862, age 27, was elected Capt. and appointed commander of Co. I. This company retained its designation in the reorganization of 3 May 1862 and became Co. I, 11th Rgmt. It also was called Capt. Izard's Co. He was promoted Maj. 22 Oct. 1862 and Lt. Col. 27 Nov. 1862. Izard was relieved from active field service in Oct. 1864 due to illness and resigned his commission 6 Feb. 1865.

Co. B, 11th Rgmt., S.C. Inf.
No prior history of this unit has been found.

SIMMONS, John. Pvt. Enlisted at Adams Run, S.C., 18 June 1862 as a Sgt.

in Co. B. He is listed on the company muster roll of Jan.-Feb. 1864 as Sgt. and absent without leave as of 28 Feb. 1864. The following roll carries him as a Pvt. and states that he deserted 26 June 1864.

Co. E, 11th Rgmt., S.C. Inf.

Organized, probably about June 1861, as Capt. Middleton Stuart's Co. of the 9th Rgmt. The unit became Co. E of the 11th Rgmt. in the reorganization of 3 May 1862 and also was known as Capt. John H. Mickler's Co.

MICKLER, John H. Capt. Commander, Co. E. Enlisted 24 June 1861 as 1st Sgt. of Capt. Stuart's Co. of the 9th Rgmt. Stuart apparently declined to enter Confederate service in the reorganization of 3 May 1862 and Mickler was elected Capt. and company commander. Final records in Mickler's personnel file indicate that he was still serving in this capacity as late as Oct. 1864.

18TH REGIMENT, S.C. INFANTRY

This unit was organized 2 Jan. 1862 and mustered into Confederate service for 12 months. It was reorganized 5 May 1862 for three year's service.

POPE, D.T. Assistant Surgeon. Appointed Asst. Surgeon of the 18th Rgmt. 25 April 1862 and was still serving in this capacity as late as Jan. 1864.

20TH REGIMENT, S.C. INFANTRY

The regiment was formed 11 Jan. 1862 with 10 companies, A through K, which had been organized for 12 months' service at various dates during Dec. 1861 and early Jan. 1862. Co. L was added in April 1862 and the regiment was reorganized for the duration of the war about 29 April 1862. Other companies were formed at various times until the unit consisted of 10 infantry companies, four cavalry and one light artillery. However, the cavalry and artillery outfits later were transferred to other organizations and the regiment reverted to 10 companies of infantry. On 8 April 1865 the 20th was consolidated with the 2nd (Palmetto) Rgmt., S.C. Inf., and part of a South Carolina reserve outfit to form the (New) 2nd Rgmt., S.C. Inf. which was paroled at Greensboro, N.C., 2 May 1865.

KEITT, Lawrence M. Col. Commander, 20th Rgmt. Appointed Col. and commander of the regiment at its organization 11 Jan. 1862. Commanded the Morris Island, S.C., garrison during the heavy fighting of Aug.-Sept. 1863 and the skillful evacuation of the island during the evening and early morning of 6-7 Sept. He was mortally wounded 1 June 1864 in the Battle of Cold Harbor, Va.

21ST REGIMENT, S.C. INFANTRY

This unit was organized 12 Nov. 1861 and mustered into Confederate service 1 Jan. 1862. It also was known as Col. Robert F. Graham's Rgmt., S.C. Inf. The regiment provided the infantry defense of the southern end of Morris Island during the Federal landing 10 July 1863 and sustained 183 casualties out of approximately 400 men engaged.

GRAHAM, Robert F. Col. Commander, 21st Rgmt. Entered service 12 Nov. 1861 as Col., commander of the regiment. Paroled 1 May 1865 at Greensboro, N.C. Graham commanded the troops on Morris Island during the Federal landing 10 July 1863 and also during the successful defense of Battery Wagner the following day. He later served on James Island and in the Petersburg, Va., campaign.

Co. H, 21st Rgmt. S.C. Infantry
No specific information has been found on this company.

DUBOSE, D.G. Capt. Commander, Co. H. Enlisted at Georgetown, S.C., 1 May 1862 as 1st Sgt. of Co. H. Elected 2nd Lt. 20 Feb. 1863. Promoted Capt. 12 Aug. 1863. Captured at Fort Fisher 15 Jan. 1865. He was taken to Fort Columbus, N.Y., then transferred to City Point, Va., 25 Feb. 1865 for exchange.

Co. K, 21st Rgmt., S.C. Inf.
Organized 28 Dec. 1861 as Capt. James W. Owens' Co., this unit was mustered into Confederate service 1 Jan. 1862 as Co. K, 21st Rgmt., S.C. Inf.

OWENS, James W. Capt. Commander, Co. K. Entered service, age 42, as Capt. and company commander. Died 18 May 1864 in a Richmond, Va., hospital of wounds received 14 May.

25TH REGIMENT, S.C. INFANTRY
The regiment was formed 22 July 1862 by addition of five companies to the 11th Bn., S.C. Inf. Maj. C.H. Simonton, battalion commander, was promoted colonel and became regimental commander. A number of men formerly served in the 1st. Rgmt., S.C. Inf. The 25th, also known as the Eutaw Regiment and as Col. C.H. Simonton's Rgmt., S.C. Inf., served in the Carolinas and Virginia.

GLOVER, John V. Maj. Entered service in Jan. 1861 as Capt., commander of Co. A (later the 11th Co) 1st Rgmt., S.C. Volunteers. Transferred and promoted Maj. of the 25th Rgmt. at its organization 22 July 1862. Died 20 June 1864 in a Richmond, Va., hospital of wounds received at Cold Harbor 4 June.

MOFFETT, George H. 1st Lt. Enlisted 24 Feb. 1862, age 32, as a Pvt. in Co. A. Commissioned 1st Lt. 30 July 1862 and appointed Acting Assistant Adjutant General of the regiment. Detached 23 July 1864 to serve as Acting Adjutant and Inspector General of Hagood's Brigade, a post he still held as late as 1 Mar. 1865.

PRESSLEY, John G. Lt. Col. Entered service 4 Jan. 1861 as Capt. Co. C, 1st Rgmt., S.C. Volunteers. This unit became the 10th Co. when the regiment reorganized in March 1862. He apparently was promoted Maj. of the 1st Rgmt. 30 Apr. 1862 and became Lt. Col. of the 25th Rgmt. at its organization 22 July 1862. Pressley was disabled by wounds 7 May 1864 during the fighting in Virginia. He was a lawyer and 31 years old at the time he was wounded.

SIMONTON, Charles H. Col. Commander, 25th Rgmt. Entered service 20 Nov. 1860, age 30, as Capt. and company commander. Promoted Maj., commander 11th Bn., date not avaliable. Promoted Lt. Col. 30 Apr. 1862 and Col., commander 25th Rgmt., 22 July 1862. Detailed as commander of advance forces on James Island 10 July 1863. Released for duty with the regiment (which had gone to Virginia) 4 June 1864. Detached to Wilmington, N.C., 4 Sept. 1864. Captured at Town Creek, N.C., 20 Feb. 1865. Imprisoned at Fort Delaware and released 26 July 1865.

Co. A, 25th Rgmt., S.C. Inf.

Organized as Capt. C.H. Simonton's Co., this unit became Co. A, 11th Bn., S.C. Inf., then Co. A, 25th Rgmt. It also was known as Co. A, Washington Light Inf., and, later, as Capt. James M. Carson's Co.

CARSON, James M. Capt. Commander, Co. A. Entered service 24 Feb. 1862, age 29, as 1st Lt. of Capt. Simonton's Co. Promoted Capt. and company commander 30 April 1862. Wounded and captured 15 Jan. 1865 at Fort Fisher, N.C. Paroled 17 June 1865.

Co. B, 25th Rgmt., S.C. Inf.

This unit initially was Co. B of the 11th Bn. It also was known as Co. B, Washington Light Inf., and as Capt. Edward W. Lloyd's Co. After his retirement 22 Aug. 1864, it was known as Capt. John S. Hannahan's Co.

CALDWELL, J.S. Sgt. Enlisted 24 Feb. 1862 as a Pvt. in Capt. Simonton's Co., later Co. A. Transferred in Oct. 1862 to Co. B and began extra duty in the regimental Commissary Dept. Appointed Commissary Sgt. 1 July 1863 as extra duty, but carried on the Co. B rolls as a Pvt. Captured 15 Jan. 1865 at Fort Fisher, N.C. Paroled 11 June 1865.

LLOYD, Edward W. Capt. Commander, Co. B. Elected Capt. and company commander 24 Feb. 1862. Listed 25 June 1864 as sick, on furlough. Retired to the Invalid Corps 22 Aug. 1864.

TAFT, Robert M. 2nd Lt. Enlisted 24 Feb. 1862, age 26, as a Sgt. in Capt. Lloyd's Co. Elected 2nd Lt. 20 June 1862. Wounded in action 16 June 1864 and died the following day in a Richmond, Va., hospital. Taft commanded a detachment of the rear guard in the evacuation of Battery Wagner, 6-7 Sept. 1863.

Co. C, 25th Rgmt., S.C. Inf.

Initially, this was Co. C of the 11th. Bn., although called Co. F in some records. The unit also was known as the Wee Nee Volunteers and as Capt. Thomas J. China's Co. After his death, 18 May 1864, it was known as Capt. Calhoun Logan's Co.

CHINA, Thomas J. Capt. Commander, Co. C. Entered service early in 1861 as 1st Lt. of the 10th Co., 1st Rgmt., S.C. Volunteers. Promoted Capt. and company commander 30 Apr. 1862. Transferred to Co. C at the organization of the 25th Rgmt., 22 July 1862. Died 18 May 1864 at Richmond, Va., of wounds received 14 May at Drewry's Bluff.

MONTGOMERY, S. Isaac. 1st Lt. Enlisted 12 Apr. 1862 near Charleston as a Sgt. in Capt. China's Co. Promoted 3rd Lt. 19 Sept. 1863, 2nd Lt. in Jan. or Feb. 1864 and 1st Lt. 18 May 1864. Final records in his personnel file show that he was still with Co. C in Oct. 1864.

Co. D, 25th Rgmt., S.C. Inf.

Co. D also was known as the Marion Light Inf. and as Capt. William J. McKerall's Co.

BETHEA, Pickett P. 2nd Lt. Entered service 15 April 1862 at Marion, S.C., as a 3rd Lt. in Capt. McKerall's Co. Promoted 2nd Lt. 15 Sept. 1863. Killed in action 21 Aug. 1864 near Petersburg, Va.

MCKAY, Daniel J. 1st Lt. Entered service 15 Apr. 1862 as 2nd Lt. of Co. D. Promoted 1st Lt. 19 Sept. 1863. Wounded 2 Oct. 1864 near Chaffin's Farm, Va.

On medical furlough as of 31 Dec. 1864, the final report in his personnel file.

SMITH, Marcus L. 2nd Lt. Enlisted 30 Apr. 1862 at Marion, S.C., as Ordnance Sgt. of Capt. McKerall's Co. Promoted 1st Sgt. in Nov. or Dec. 1862. Elected 2nd Lt. 5 Oct. 1863. Wounded 16 May 1864 at Drewry's Bluff, Va. Final records in his personnel file state that he was on furlough, due to his wounds, as of 26 Nov. 1864.

Co. E, 25th Rgmt., S.C. Inf.

This company, also called Co. D in some records, was one of the original units of the 11th Bn. It also was known as the Beauregard Light Inf. and, until his resignation 3 Sept. 1862, as Capt. Robert D. White's Co. Thereafter it was known as Capt. N.B. Mazyck's Co.

GORY, Patrick. Pvt. Enlisted 21 Feb. 1862, age 30, as a Cpl. in Capt. White's Co. Promoted Sgt. 13 Sept. 1862. Reduced to Pvt. 24 Dec. 1862. Promoted Cpl. 12 Sept. 1863. Reduced to Pvt. 1 Nov. 1863. Listed on final records in his personnel file, dated Oct. 1864, as present with the company but serving extra duty with the regimental Ordnance Dept.

LALANE, George M. 2nd Lt. Elected 2nd Lt. Co. D on 17 Feb. 1863 although at that time he was serving in Virginia with the 2nd Rgmt, S.C. Inf. He joined the company 10 Mar. 1863 and transferred to Co. E. in Sept. or Oct. 1963. Died 31 May 1864 of wounds received 16 May at Drewry's Bluff, Va.

MAZYCK, N.B. Capt. Commander, Co. E. Entered service at Charleston 21 Feb. 1862 as 1st Lt. of Capt. White's Co. Promoted Capt. and company commander 3 Sept. 1862 after White resigned. Captured 20 Feb. 1865 near Town Creek, N.C.Paroled 17 June 1865.

Co. F, 25th Rgmt., S.C. Inf.

This unit, also called Co. C in some records, was one of the original companies of the 11th Bn. It also was known as the St. Matthews Rifles and for its commanders: Capt. M.H. Sellers, killed in action 21 Aug. 1864, and Capt. L.A. Harper who succeeded to command.

SELLERS, M.H. Capt. Commander, Co. F. Entered service in October 1861 as a 2nd Lt. Elected Capt. and company commander 11 Apr. 1862. Killed in action 21 Aug. 1864 near Petersburg, Va.

Co. G, 25th Rgmt., S.C. Inf.

This company was composed of men who initially served in Co. A (later the 11th Co.) 1st Rgmt., S.C. Volunteers. It also was called the Edisto Rifles and Capt. James F. Islar's Co.

KENNERLY, Samuel N. 1st Lt. Entered service 12 Apr. 1861 as 3rd Lt. of Co. A, 1st Rgmt. and was promoted 2nd Lt. 21 Aug. 1861. Elected 1st Lt. of Co. G, 25th Rgmt., 22 July 1862. Killed in action 21 Aug. 1864 near Petersburg, Va.

Co. I, 25th Rgmt., S.C. Inf.

Organized as Capt. Y.N. Butler's Co., this unit subsequently became Co. C, 21st S.C. Inf., then was transferred to the 25th Rgmt. as Co. I. It also was known as the Clarendon Guards.

BROWN, F.B. 1st Lt. Entered service 1 Jan. 1862 as a 3rd Lt. in Capt. Butler's Co. Promoted 2nd Lt. 11 June 1863 and 1st Lt. 29 Aug. 1864. He was serving with Co. I as late as Jan. 1865.

Co. K, 25th Rgmt., S.C. Inf.
Called Co. B in some records, this unit also was known as the Ripley Guards and as Capt. W.B. Gordon's Co. until his death 4 Aug. 1864. Thereafter, it was called Capt. Edward R. Lesesne's Co.

LESESNE, Charles. 1st Lt. Enlisted 29 Dec. 1861 as 1st. Sgt. of Capt. Gordon's Co. Promoted 2nd Lt. 14 Sept. 1863 and 1st Lt. 21 Aug. 1864. Wounded and captured 15 Jan. 1865 at Fort Fisher, N.C. Paroled 17 June 1865.

LESESNE, Edward R. Capt. Commander, Co. K. Enlisted 29 Dec. 1861 as a Sgt. in Capt. Gordon's Co. Promoted 2nd Lt. in Oct. 1862 and Capt. 21 Aug. 1864. Paroled 1 May 1865 at Greensboro, N.C.

27TH REGIMENT, S.C. INFANTRY
The regiment was formed 30 Sept. 1863 by consolidation of the 1st, or Charleston, Bn., S.C. Inf. and the 1st Bn., S.C. Sharp Shooters. The Charleston Bn. had been accepted into the state establishment 17 Feb. 1862 and the following month was mustered into Confederate service with Lt. Col. P.C. Gaillard as commander and David Ramsay as Maj. When Ramsay died of wounds 5 Aug. 1863, the senior Capt., J.A. Blake, became Maj. The 1st Sharp Shooters was organized in Confederate service in June 1862 under the command of Maj. Joseph Abney. After consolidation, Gaillard was named Col. of the new Rgmt., Blake became Lt. Col. and Abney, Maj. It also was known as Col. P.C. Gaillard's Rgmt., S.C. Inf.

ABNEY, Joseph. Lt. Col. Commissioned Maj. and commander 1st Bn., S.C. Sharp Shooters 21 June 1862. Became Maj. of the 27th Rgmt. 30 Sept. 1863. Wounded at Drewry's Bluff in May 1864 and carried on the regimental rolls as absent, sick, until 24 Feb. 1865. He retired to the Invalid Corps 6 Mar. 1865.

GAILLARD, Peter C. Col. Commander, 27th Rgmt. In Feb. 1862, Gaillard was appointed Maj., commander of the 1st, or Charleston, Bn., S.C. Inf. Promoted Lt. Col. in Mar. 1862 and Col. 2 Oct. 1863. He lost a hand in the fighting on Morris Island during Aug. 1863 and retired to the Invalid Corps 6 Mar. 1865.

SMITH, R. Press. Capt. Regimental Quartermaster. Entered service 17 Feb. 1862 as Quartermaster of the 1st Bn. Became regimental QM 30 Sept. 1863 in the reorganization. Resigned his commission 8 Sept. 1864 due to an undisclosed illness, possibly resulting from serious wounds he sustained at the Battle of Secessionville, 16 June 1862. (*Note, see also R. Press Smith Jr., Co. E, 1st Rgmt., S.C. Inf., probably his son although no relationship is established in available records.*)

Co. A, 27th Rgmt., S.C. Inf.
This unit originally was Co. E of the 1st, or Charleston, Bn. S.C. Inf.

AXSON, J. Waring. Capt. Commander, Co. A. Entered service 17 Feb. 1862 as a 2nd Lt. in the company. Promoted 1st Lt. 18 Apr. 1864 and Capt. 16 June 1864. Killed in action 24 June 1864 near Petersburg, Va.

Co. B, 27th Rgmt., S.C. Inf.
Originally Co. B of the 1st, or Charleston, Bn., S.C. Inf., this unit also was called Capt. Thomas Y. Simons' Co.

MUCKENFUSS, A.W. 2nd. Lt. Entered service 24 Mar. 1862 as a 2nd Lt. in the company. Captured 21 Aug. 1864 near Petersburg, Va., and sent to Fort Delaware. Exchanged 11 Oct. 1864. Paroled 1 May 1865 at Greensboro, N.C.

SIMONS, Thomas Y. Capt. Commander, Co. B. Elected 17 Feb. 1862 as Capt., commander of Co. B, 1st Bn., S.C. Inf. Although Simons was present with his company when mentioned by Manigault 28 Nov. 1863, he spent much of his military career serving as Judge Advocate of a permanent military court martial in Charleston. He was paroled with the unit 1 May 1865 at Greensboro, N.C.

Co. C, 27th Rgmt., S.C. Inf.
Originally Co. F, 1st, or Charleston, Bn., S.C. Inf.

HENDRICKS, H.W. 2nd Lt. Entered service 4 July 1862 as a 2nd Lt. in the company. Captured 21 Aug. 1864 near Petersburg, Va. He was taken to Fort Delaware and exchanged 11 Oct. 1864. Recaptured 20 Feb. 1865 near Town Creek, N.C., and returned to Fort Delaware. Released in May 1865.

Co. D, 27th Rgmt., S.C. Inf.
This unit initially was Co. D, 1st, or Charleston, Bn., S.C. Inf. It also was known as the Sumter Guards and as Capt. J. Ward Hopkins' Co.

HOPKINS, J. Ward. Capt. Commander, Co. D. Entered service 17 Feb. 1862 as 1st Lt. of the company. Promoted Capt. and company commander 16 June 1862. Killed in action exactly two years later near Petersburg, Va.

Co. E, 27th Rgmt., S.C. Inf.
This unit originally was Co. A, 1st Bn., S.C. Sharp Shooters.

KEMMERLIN, Samuel N. 2nd Lt. Held a commission as Capt. under the state establishment in the 1st (Johnson Hagood's) Rgmt., S.C. Volunteers. He later became an Orderly Sgt. in the 1st Bn., S.C. Sharp Shooters, then on 17 Feb. 1862 was appointed a 2nd Lt. in Co. A. He was wounded 7 May 1864 and sent home on furlough. Resigned his commission 11 Mar. 1865 due to his wounds.

Co. F, 27th Rgmt., S.C. Inf.
This unit originally was Co. B, 1st Bn., S.C. Sharp Shooters.

HUGUENIN, Julius D. Capt. Commander, Co. F. Entered service 17 Feb. 1862 as 1st Lt. of the company. He was captured 20 Feb. 1865 near Town Creek, N.C. Imprisoned at Fort Delaware, he was released 17 June 1865. Although a prisoner of war, Huguenin was promoted Capt. 25 Mar. 1865 for "skill and valor," presumably at Town Creek.

Co. G, 27th Rgmt., S.C. Inf.
Originally, this was Co. C., 1st Bn., S.C. Sharp Shooters. It also was known as Capt. Henry Buist's Co.

BUIST, Henry. Capt. Commander, Co. G. Entered into Confederate service 16 June 1862 as Capt. and commander of the company. Captured 24 June 1864 near Petersburg, Va. He was taken to Fort Monroe, Va.; Point Lookout, Md.; and then to Fort Delaware. He was exchanged in Charleston Harbor, 3 Oct. 1864. He resigned 4 Feb. 1865, probably due to ill health.

Co. H, 27th Rgmt., S.C. Inf.

This unit initially was Co. C, 1st, or Charleston, Bn., S.C. Inf. It became Co. H of the 27th when the Rgmt. was organized 30 Sept. 1863. It also was known as Capt. James M. Mulvaney's Co.

MULVANEY, James M. Capt. Commander, Co. H. Entered service 17 Feb. 1862 as a 2nd Lt. in Co. C, 1st Bn. Promoted 1st Lt. in April 1862 and Capt., company commander, 18 July 1863. Captured 24 June 1864 near Petersburg, Va. He was sent, as a prisoner of war, to Point Lookout, Md., then to Fort Delaware. He was transferred to Hilton Head, S.C., 20 Aug. 1864 and to Fort Pulaski, near Savannah, Ga., on 20 Oct. where, apparently, he spent the remainder of the war.

Co. I, 27th Rgmt., S.C. Inf.

This unit originally was Co. A, 1st, or Charleston, Bn., S.C. Inf. It also was known as Capt. W.D. Walter's Co.

TRIM, W.J. 2nd Lt. Entered service 14 Aug. 1863 as a 2nd Lt. in the company. Retired to the Invalid Corps 17 Feb. 1865, apparently due to wounds.

WALTER, W.D. Capt. Commander, Co. I. Elected 1st Lt. of the company 17 Feb. 1862. Promoted Capt. and company commander in Aug. 1863. Retired to the Invalid Corps on 23 Dec. 1864 because of illness.

LUCAS' BATTALION, SOUTH CAROLINA HEAVY ARTILLERY

The battalion was mustered into Confederate service as infantry with two companies (A and B) 6 June 1861 on James Island, S.C. On 9 July 1861 the unit was ordered to man the fortifications along the James Island shore of the Stono River and subsequently was known as heavy artillery. Capt. Frederick L. Childs' company of light artillery was added to the battalion 15 Nov. 1862 as Co. C. It also was known as the 15th Bn., S.C. Heavy Arty. The batalion served on James Island until the evacuation of Charleston 17-18 Feb. 1865 and then in N.C. under Gen. Joseph E. Johnston. It participated in capture of the U.S. gunboat Isaac Smith 30 Jan. 1863 (See Diary entry of Tuesday, 25 Aug. 1863, note 3) and took its turn in the defense of Battery Wagner, Morris Island, during Aug. 1863 and later of Fort Sumter.

CALDWELL, William R. Assistant Surgeon. Appointed 22 Sept. 1863. Paroled near Greensboro, N.C., 28 April 1865. Caldwell was captured on Morris Island 10 July 1863 and taken to Hilton Head, S.C., aboard the U.S. hospital steamer *Cosmopolitan*. Exchanged later, he was appointed Assistant Surgeon of Lucas' Bn. and placed in charge of the battalion hospital at Fort Pemberton.

GIRARDEAU, T.C. Assistant Surgeon. Entered service 14 June 1862 and within a few months was stationed at Battery Pringle, James Island, S.C. Medically discharged 13 Dec. 1864.

LUCAS, Jonathan J. Maj. Commander, 15th Bn., S.C. Heavy Arty., generally known as Lucas' Bn., S.C. Heavy Arty. He organized the unit 6 June 1861 and commanded it throughout the war. At the end of 1864 he was serving as commander of the James Island West Lines and in Jan. 1865 as commander, Stono Fortifications. Lucas and Manigault were both recommended for the rank of lieutenant colonel by Gen. Beauregard, but neither received the well-merited promotion.

WARLEY, Felix. Adjutant. Appointed 1st Lt. and Adjutant of Lucas' Bn. 6 Feb. 1863. Paroled near Greensboro, N.C., 28 April 1865.

Co. A, Lucas' Bn., S.C. Heavy Arty.

One of the original two companies of the battalion, organized 6 June 1861. Surrendered near Greensboro, N.C. in April 1865. Also known as Capt. E.B. Colhoun's Co., S.C. Heavy Arty.

COLHOUN, E.B. Capt. Commander, Co. A. Entered service 6 June 1861 as 2nd Lt. of Co. A. Promoted 1st Lt. 15 Aug. 1861 and transferred to Co. B. Promoted Capt. 17 Aug. 1863 and transferred back to Co. A to assume command, vice Capt. John H. Gary, fatally injured 13 Aug. 1863 during the defense of Battery Wagner on Morris Island. Listed as present on the final company muster roll, Nov.-Dec. 1865.

LUCAS, Thomas E. 2nd Lt. Entered service 5 Dec. 1863 as a 2nd Lt. Resigned 3 Nov. 1864 to take his seat as a member of the South Carolina Legislature.

MARTIN, William D. 1st Lt. Enlisted in Jan. 1861 as a Pvt. in the Marion Arty. Applied for a commission in the Engineers and when that was not available, accepted appointment 15 Nov. 1863 as a 2nd Lt. in Co. A. Promoted 1st Lt. 31 Jan. 1864. Transferred to Co. B, Cobb Guard, Ga. Arty., 13 Feb. 1865.

OGIER, William G. 1st Lt. Entered service 14 Oct. 1861 as 2nd Lt. of Co. B. Promoted 1st Lt. 3 Jan. 1862. Transferred to Co. A about July 1862. Final entry in his file notes that he was granted leave 5 Jan. 1865.

Co. B, Lucas' Bn., S.C. Heavy Arty.

One of the original two companies of the battalion, organized 6 June 1861. Surrendered near Greensboro, N.C. in April 1865. It also was known as Capt. Guignard Richardson's Co., S.C. Heavy Arty.

FORD, J. Drayton. 1st Lt. Appointed 2nd Lt. 8 June 1861, but resigned within a few days. Reappointed 2nd Lt. 31 Dec. 1861. Promoted 1st Lt. 17 Aug. 1863. He was on detached service at Fort Pemberton as battalion quartermaster from 20 Oct. 1863. Personnel records show him still in that capacity as late as Sept. 1864.

HEYWARD, Thomas Josiah. 2nd Lt. Entered service 12 Nov. 1863. Paroled near Greensboro, N.C., 28 April 1865.

MOSES, H. Claremont. 1st Lt. Appointed 2nd Lt. 3 Sept. 1861. Promoted 1st Lt. 20 Dec. 1861. He was listed as serving in that capacity on final muster roll, Nov.-Dec. 1864.

RICHARDSON, Guignard. Capt. Commander, Co. B. Entered service 2 Aug. 1861 as 2nd Lt. of Co. A. Promoted 1st Lt. 20 Dec. 1861. Promoted Capt. and transferred to Co. B as commanding officer 21 Aug. 1863. He succeeded Capt. Robert Pringle who was killed that day at Battery Wagner, Morris Island.

Co. C, Lucas' Bn., S.C. Heavy Arty.

Organized about May 1861 as Capt. Charles S. Winder's Co. of Light Arty. By Aug. 1861, it was known as Capt. Frederick L. Childs' Co. of Light Arty. Became Co. C of Lucas' Bn. 15 Nov. 1862, and also was known as Capt. Theodore B. Hayne's Co. Surrendered near Greensboro, N.C., at the end of April 1865.

HAYNE, Theodore B. Capt. Commander, Co. C. Entered service 7 Nov. 1862 as captain and became company commander on the 23rd. During Jan.-Feb. 1864 he was on unspecified detached service at battalion headquarters, Fort Pemberton. Hayne was paroled near Greensboro, N.C., 28 April 1865.

MANIGAULT'S BATTALION, SOUTH CAROLINA ARTILLERY

This organization traces its beginning to May or June 1862 when three light artillery companies, that had been serving as independent units, were organized as Companies A, B and C of Maj. Charles Alston's Bn., Light Arty., S.C. Volunteers. Within a few months it was reorganized as the S.C. Siege Train and company designations (as described below under individual units) were rearranged. Alston resigned 27 May 1863, and after Manigault assumed command, 22 June 1863, the unit generally was referred to as Manigault's Bn., S.C. Arty. It also was known as the 18th Bn., S.C. Arty., and as the S.C. Siege Train. Elements of the outfit still were called Manigault's Bn. at the end of the war, several weeks after the major had been captured on James Island 10 Feb. 1865. By the first of 1865, the S.C. Siege Train, as an organization, was being phased out. Some parts of it became independent batteries of field artillery. Others were converted to infantry.

GAILLARD, Augustus T. Sgt. Major. Enlisted at Pocotaligo, S.C., 28 Feb. 1862 as a Pvt. in Buist's Co. Appointed Sgt. Major 1 July 1863 by Maj. Manigault. Listed on final muster roll, Nov.-Dec. 1864, as on 60-day furlough from 2 Dec. 1864.

GARDNER, John H. Adjutant. A native of Savannah, Ga., Gardner was appointed 2nd Lt. in the 2nd Bn., S.C. Sharpshooters, 5 July 1862. The organization was disbanded and he was ordered to the Camp of Instruction at Washington Race Course (now Hampton Park) in Charleston. He was assigned to the Siege Train as adjutant 21 Jan. 1863 and is so listed on the final field and staff muster roll, Nov.-Dec. 1864.

MACKEY, Samuel. Chief Bugler. Initially a member of Co. B, Mackey was transferred to the battalion staff as chief bugler by Maj. Charles Alston on 6 Feb. 1863. He was sent to a local hospital 17 Aug. 1863 then relieved as chief bugler by Maj. Manigault 14 Feb. 1864 due to ill health and long absence from his duties. Mackey was detached to the hospital as a nurse 31 May 1864 and 4 Sept. 1864 received a medical discharge. He was replaced as chief bugler by Victor C. Pellerin (q.v.)

MANIGAULT, Edward. Maj. Commander, Manigault's Bn, S.C. Arty. Entered service 8 Mar. 1847 as a Capt. in the 12th Rgmt., U.S. Inf. Promoted Maj. 16 July 1847 and transferred to the 13th Rgmt., U.S. Inf. Following the War with Mexico, Manigault was a Lt. of Ordnance 1851-52. Served from the end of 1860 until he resigned, 1 Oct. 1861, as Col., Chief of Ordnance for the State of South Carolina. Appointed Maj. 31 Oct. 1861 and assumed command of the 6th Bn., S.C. Inf. 22 Dec. 1861. Served in this capacity until the battalion was disbanded in May 1862. Appointed Maj., C.S.A., 23 May 1863. Assumed command of the S.C. Siege Train 22 Jun. 1863. Wounded and captured on James Island 10 Feb. 1865. Paroled 10 May 1865. (*See Introduction, pp. i-xiii*)

MORDECAI, J. Randolph. Capt. Quartermaster, Manigault's Bn. Reported for duty with the battalion 23 June 1863. Later served as quartermaster of the James Island West Lines and at the evacuation of Charleston, 17-18 Feb. 1865, was quartermaster of Brig. Gen. Stephen Elliott's brigade.

PELLERIN, Victor C. Chief Bugler. Enlisted at Pocotaligo, S.C., 28 Feb. 1862 as a Pvt. in Buist's Co. Served as bugler of Co. A from Jan. 1863 until he was promoted Chief Bugler of the battalion 16 Feb. 1864. Paroled at Greensboro, N.C., 28 April 1865.

WINTHROP, Joseph. Assistant Surgeon. Commissioned Assistant Surgeon at Charleston 14 June 1862. Field and Staff muster rolls of Sept.-Oct. 1864 and later list Winthrop on detached service as commander of the brigade (and later military district) hospital at McLeod's House on James Island, S.C. Paroled 29 April 1865 while a patient in a Greensboro, N.C., hospital.

Co. A, Manigault's Bn., S.C. Arty. *(Webb's Co.)*

This unit is first mentioned in contemporary records 28 Feb. 1862 when it apparently was organized with Capt. George L. Buist as commander. It was known initially as Buist's Company, or, more formally, as the Palmetto Guard Arty. It was incorporated into Maj. Charles Alston's Bn., Light Arty., S.C.V., as Co. C and then redesignated Co. A when the battalion became the S.C. Siege Train. It later became Co. A of Manigault's Bn, S.C. Arty. Buist was promoted Maj. and left the battalion 15 Jan. 1863. His place was taken by Capt. Benjamin C. Webb and the unit became known as Webb's Co., although Webb, and others, often signed official documents in the dual designation of Palmetto Guard Arty. and Co. A, S.C. Siege Train. During the last days of the war, it was redesignated and surrendered in North Carolina as Co. B, Manigault's Bn., S.C. Arty.

ADDY, Thomas R. Cpl. Enlisted at Pocotaligo, S.C., 28 Feb. 1862 in Buist's Co. Listed on company muster rolls through Jan.-Feb. 1865.

ANCRUM, William Heyward. Pvt. Enlisted 2 Mar. 1863 at Charleston. Fatally injured (leg shot off) during engagement with U.S. warships near Legareville, S.C., (Stono River) 25 Dec. 1863.

BELLINGER, Joseph. Pvt. Enlisted at Pocotaligo, S.C., 28 Feb. 1862 in Buist's Co. Transferred to Co. F, 2nd Engr. Rgmt. 17 Sept. 1864 and promoted Master Sgt.

BLAND, M. Alberto. Cpl. Enlisted at Pocotaligo, S.C., 28 Feb. 1862 in Buist's Co. Promoted Cpl. in Nov. or Dec. 1862. Slightly stunned by shell during engagement with U.S. warships near Legareville, S.C. (Stono River) 25 Dec. 1863. Listed on company muster rolls through Jan.-Feb. 1865.

BOWIE, Alexander. Pvt. Enlisted at Charleston 8 Dec., 1862 as a Pvt. in Co. A. Transferred to Co. B, 2nd Rgmt. S.C. Cavalry 4 Feb. 1863 but returned to Co. A 21 May 1863. Captured on James Island 10 Feb. 1865. Listed as a POW at Charleston as of 27 April 1865.

BOWIE, James A. Pvt. Enlisted at Charleston 3 Mar. 1863 as a Pvt. in Co. A. Captured 10 Feb. 1865 on James Island. Listed as a POW at Charleston 27 Apr. 1865.

BROWN, W.K. Pvt. Enlisted at Charleston 18 Mar. 1862 in the Lafayette Arty. Transferred 22 Mar. 1863 to Co. A. Paroled at the end of April 1865 while sick in a hospital at Greensboro, N.C.

BRUX, James Augustus. 1st Lt. Enlisted, age 28, at Pocotaligo, S.C., 28 Feb. 1862 apparently as a Sgt. in Buist's Co. Appointed 2nd Lt. 11 Nov. 1862 and promoted 1st Lt. 24 Feb. 1863. Wounded on James Island during the action of 10 Feb. 1865.

CAMPBELL, William L. Pvt. Enlisted at Pocotaligo, S.C., 28 Feb. 1862 as a Pvt. in Capt. George L. Buist's Co. Captured 10 Feb. 1865 on James Island. Under treatment in Feb. 1865 as a POW at a Beaufort, S.C., Hospital for a gunshot wound of the right thigh.

CHAPMAN, William H. 1st Lt. A native of Georgetown, S.C., Chapman entered service at age 30 at Pocotaligo, S.C., as a 2nd Lt. in Buist's Co. Promoted 1st Lt. 29 Dec. 1862. Paroled at Greensboro, N.C. 28 April 1865.

CHRIETZBERG, A.A. Pvt. Enlisted at Charleston 7 Mar. 1863 as a Pvt. in Co. A. Final muster roll in his file, Jan.-Feb. 1865, states he was sent on unspecified detached service 19 Jan. 1865.

GIRARDEAU, G. Morris. Cpl. Enlisted at Charleston 3 Sept. 1862 as a Pvt. and by the Nov.-Dec. 1862 muster roll had been promoted Cpl. Final return in his file states that he was on a 60-day medical furlough as of 9 Aug. 1864.

GIRARDEAU, Isaac W. 1st. Sgt. Enlisted, age 22, at Pocotaligo, S.C., 28 Feb. 1862 as a Sgt. in Buist's Co. Promoted 1st Sgt. 21 Jan. 1863. The final muster roll, Jan.-Feb. 1865, carries him as absent, sent to hospital in Charleston 16 Feb. 1865.

HAIG, Alexander R. Pvt. Enlisted near Charleston 9 April 1863 as a Pvt. in Co. A. Captured 10 Feb. 1865 on James Island. Under treatment in Feb. 1865 as a POW at a Beaufort, S.C., Hospital for a gunshot wound in the back.

HASELL, Thomas Morritt. 2nd Lt. A native of Summerville, S.C., Hasell enlisted 28 Feb. 1862, age 25, at Pocotaligo, S.C., as a Sgt. in Buist's Co. Elected 2nd Lt. 25 Feb. 1863. Final Co. A muster roll, Jan.-Feb. 1865, carries him as acting battalion adjutant.

HOUSTON, W.W. Pvt. Enlisted at Charleston 20 Feb. 1863 as a Pvt. in Co. A. Captured on James Island 10 Feb. 1865. Under treatment in Feb. 1865 as a POW at a Beaufort, S.C. Hospital for a gunshot wound of the right shoulder.

HUGER, Joseph Proctor. Pvt. Enlisted 21 Jan. 1864 at the age of 17 thus necessitating parental consent. Two days later, at his request, he was transferred from Co. A to the Signal Corps and soon was stationed at Fort Sumter. On 13 April 1864, while standing on a conspicuous part of the fort to watch the firing between Confederate batteries on James Island and the Federal guns on Morris Island, he began waving his cap when the Confederate gunners made a hit. The action drew fire from Morris Island and young Huger was killed instantly by explosion of a 30-pounder Parrott shell. The Huger and Manigault families were close friends and Huger's sister, Mary Proctor, was married to Edward Manigault's brother, Brig. Gen. Arthur Middleton Manigault. Consequently, although he did not mention it in his journal, Huger's death no doubt was a personal loss to the major. (Tower, *A Carolinian Goes to War*, pp. 161, 162, 162n; Johnson, *The Defense of Charleston Harbor*, p. 206n)

HUMPHREYS, John T. Pvt. Enlisted at Pocotaligo, S.C., 5 Mar. 1862 as a Pvt. in Capt. George L. Buist's Co. Captured on James Island 10 Feb. 1865. Listed as a POW at Charleston as of 27 Apr. 1865.

KERR, Charles H. Pvt. Enlisted at Pocotaligo, S.C., 28 Feb. 1862, as a Pvt. in Capt. George L. Buist's Co. Killed in action of James Island 10 Feb. 1865.

KNOBLOCK, William Jr. Enlisted, age 19, at Pocotaligo, S.C., 28 Feb. 1862 in Buist's Co. He was on detached service as a courier to the military district headquarters from 1 May 1864.

KNOTT, Kingston E. Pvt. Enlisted, age 33, at Pocotaligo, S.C., 28 Feb. 1862 in Buist's Co. Paroled while sick in a hospital at Greensboro, N.C., 28 April 1865.

LOGAN, William T. Sgt. Enlisted, age 22, at Pocotaligo, S.C., 28 Feb. 1862 as a Cpl. in Buist's Co. The final Co. A. muster roll, Jan.-Feb. 1865, states that he was sent to a hospital at Cheraw, S.C., 27 Feb. 1865.

LOPEZ, John H. Pvt. A native of Columbus, Ga., Lopez enlisted, age 30, at Charleston 18 Mar. 1863. He is listed in personnel records as a carpenter. He was placed on detached service by higher headquarters 4 June 1864, probably to utilize his skills in construction of the various James Island batteries. Transferred to Co. F, 2nd Engr. Rgmt. 17 Sept. 1864.

MACBETH, Alexander. Cpl. Enlisted at Pocotaligo, S.C., 28 Feb. 1865 as a Pvt. in Capt. George L. Buist's Co. Promoted Cpl. in Sept. or Oct. 1864. He was still serving in Co. A in Feb. 1865.

MANSON, George H. Cpl. Enlisted, age 19, at Pocotaligo, S.C., 28 Feb. 1862 as a Cpl. in Buist's Co. Paroled at Charlotte, N.C., 3 May 1865.

MELLICHAMP, Robert E. 2nd Lt. A native of Beaufort, S.C., Mellichamp enlisted, age 25, at Pocotaligo, S.C., 28 Feb. 1862 as a Sgt. in Buist's Co. Promoted 1st Sgt. 16 Nov. 1862 and elected 2nd Lt. 21 Jan. 1863. Paroled at Greensboro, N.C., 28 April 1865.

MOISE, Edwin H. Pvt. Enlisted at Pocotaligo, S.C., 28 Feb. 1862 in Buist's Co. He is listed on Co. A muster rolls through Jan.-Feb. 1865.

MORDECAI, Isaac W. Pvt. Enlisted 1 May 1863 in St. Andrew's Parish near Charleston. The Army later discovered he had a double hernia and declared him unfit to perform company duty. In October 1863, while on leave at Columbia, S.C., he was attached as a clerk to the Columbia Provost Marshal's office.

MOUZON, William R. Pvt. Enlisted at Pocotaligo, S.C., 28 Feb. 1862 as a Pvt. in Capt. George L. Buist's Co. Captured on James Island 10 Feb. 1865. Under treatment in Feb. 1865 as a POW at a Beaufort, S.C., Hospital for a gunshot wound of the left thigh.

NAGEL, William P. Cpl. Enlisted at Pocotaligo, S.C., 28 Feb. 1862 as a Pvt. in Buist's Co. He is carried on the muster roll of Nov.-Dec. 1862 and thereafter as a Cpl. Nagel was killed in action on James Island 10 Feb. 1865.

OLNEY, Clarence C. Pvt. Enlisted at Pocotaligo, S.C., 28 Feb. 1862 in Buist's Co. He went on detached service 7 May 1864 with the Commissary Dept. at Adams Run, S.C. Paroled at Greensboro, N.C., 1 May 1865.

POSTON, R. Pvt. Enlisted at Columbia, S.C., 8 Feb. 1864. He is listed as present on the final Co. A muster roll, Jan.-Feb. 1865.

REEDER, William. Pvt. Enlisted, age 18, at Pocotaligo, S.C., 28 Feb. 1862 in Buist's Co. He is listed on muster rolls through Jan.-Feb. 1865 where he is carried as absent, sent to hospital in Cheraw, S.C., 27 Feb. 1865.

ROUMILLAT, Jacques E. Pvt. Enlisted, age 18, at Pocotaligo, S.C., 28 Feb. 1862 in Buist's Co. He is listed on the final muster roll, Jan.-Feb. 1865, as absent without leave.

SULLIVAN, D.A.J. Ord. Sgt. Enlisted 17 July 1862 as a Pvt. in Buist's Co. However, he was restricted to light duty by a medical board and on 22 Aug. 1862 was detached to the Ord. Dept. By the end of 1863 he was serving as acting Ord. Sgt. at Dill's Bluff. Final records in his personnel file, Jan.-Feb. 1865, show that he still was carried as a Pvt. in Co. A but on detached service as acting Ord. Sgt.

TAYLOR, Charles G. Pvt. Enlisted, age 20, at Pocotaligo, S.C., 28 Feb. 1862 in Buist's Co. Although Taylor was sent with other Co. A men to rejoin the unit in Florida, personnel records state that he was suffering from "chronic dyspepsia" and considered unfit for general duty. Within a week he was detached for duty with the C.S. Clothing Depot, Quartermaster Dept., Augusta. Ga.

TINDALL, S.H. Pvt. Enlisted at Charleston 21 March 1863 in Co. A. Detached by order of Maj. Manigault 10 Nov. 1863 to serve as battalion hospital steward. Paroled near Greensboro, N.C., 28 April 1865.

WEBB, Benjamin C. Capt. Commander, Co. A. A native of Walterboro, S.C., Webb entered service, age 23, at Pocotaligo, S.C., 28 Feb. 1862 as 2nd Lt. of Buist's Co. Promoted Capt. 20 Jan. 1863, he served as company commander throughout the war. Paroled near Greensboro, N.C., 28 April 1865. Personnel records state that Webb was slightly stunned by the concussion of a bursting shell during the engagement with U.S. warships near Legareville, S.C., 25 Dec. 1863. He also signed a requisition 19 Feb. 1864 for six artillery horses to replace three killed in the Legareville fighting and three others declared unserviceable.

WEBB, Charles. Sgt. Enlisted, age 25, at Pocotaligo, S.C., 28 Feb. 1862 as a Cpl. in Buist's Co. He is listed on the company muster roll of Mar.-Apr. 1863 as a Sgt. On the final muster roll, Jan.-Feb. 1865, Sgt. Webb is carried as absent, sick, sent to hospital 22 Jan. 1865.

ZORN, James W. Pvt. Enlisted at Columbia, S.C., 1 Sept. 1863. Sent to hospital in Charleston 27 Dec. 1863 after being wounded in the wrist by explosion of a shell during the engagement with U.S. warships near Legareville, S.C., 25 Dec. 1863. He was wounded again during the fighting on James Island 10 Feb. 1865 and was sent to a hospital in Charleston the following day.

Co. B, Manigault's Bn., S.C. Arty. (Smith's Co.)

This company is first listed in contemporary records 14 April 1862. It probably was organized about that date as (then Capt.) Charles Alston's Light Arty. Co., S.C. Volunteers. It subsequently became Co. A, Alston's Bn., Light Arty., S.C.V., and then Co. B, S.C. Siege Train. It later was known as Co. B, Manigault's Bn., S.C. Arty. During the waning days of the war it was redesignated Co. D of Manigault's Battalion. It also was known as Capt. S. Porcher Smith's Co.

CAUSEY, Z.J. Sgt. Enlisted, age 24, in Horry County, S.C., 14 April 1862 as a Sgt. in Alston's Co. He is listed on the final Co. B muster roll, Jan.-Feb. 1865, as having been sent to a hospital in Charleston 16 Feb. 1865.

GRAHAM, J.B. Pvt. Enlisted at Columbia, S.C., 14 April 1862 as a Pvt. in Alston's Co. In July or Aug. 1863 he went on detached service as a teamster, driver of the battalion medical wagon. He is listed in this capacity on the final company muster roll, Jan.-Feb. 1865.

JOHNSON, W.F. Pvt. Enlisted in Horry County, S.C., 14 April 1862. Killed 25 Dec. 1863 in the engagement with U.S. warships near Legareville, S.C.

JOHNSON, William. Pvt. Enlisted, age 41, in Horry County, S.C., 14 April 1862. in Alston's Co. Wounded during the action on James Island 22 May 1864. Listed as absent in hospital at Charleston on subsequent muster rolls through Jan.-Feb. 1865.

NESBIT, Ralph. 1st Lt. A native of Georgetown, S.C., Nesbit enlisted as a Pvt. and was elected 2nd Lt. 23 April 1863. He was promoted 1st Lt. 19 May 1863. He was on detached duty as acting Inspector General of the James Island West Lines Feb.-Dec. 1864. Paroled at Greensboro, N.C., 28 April 1865.

PHILLIPS, John B.W. 2nd Lt. Enlisted at Pocotaligo, S.C. 28 Feb. 1862 as a Pvt. in Buist's Co. but by June was acting battalion Ordnance Sgt. Promoted

Ordnance Sgt. 31 Jan. 1863. Elected 2nd Lt. Co. B, 6 June 1863. Detached as Ordnance Officer at Legare's Point 30 July 1863 to 11 March 1864. Paroled at Greensboro, N.C., 28 April 1865.

ROBERTS, J.T. Pvt. Enlisted at Charleston 27 Feb. 1863 in Co. B. Wounded during the fighting on James Island 2 July 1864. Granted 60-day furlough, due to his wounds, by a medical examining board 26 July 1864. On several occasions he was sent to other sections of the state to arrest deserters. Listed as present on final Co. B muster roll, Jan.-Feb. 1865.

SMITH, S. Porcher. Capt. Commander, Co. B. Enlisted at Charleston 10 May 1862 as a Pvt. in Co. A, Alston's Bn. but almost immediately was promoted to battalion Sgt. Major. Appointed 2nd Lt. 13 Sept. 1862 and promoted Capt. 19 May 1863. Admitted to hospital at Greensboro, N.C., 19 March 1865 and recommended for leave by a medical examining board 7 April 1865.

SPIVEY, W.A. 2nd Lt. Enlisted, age 29, in Horry County, S.C., 14 April 1862 as a Sgt. in Alston's Co. Listed on Co. B muster roll of Jan.-Feb. 1863 as Quartermaster Sgt. Elected 2nd Lt. 6 July 1863. Listed as present on the final company muster roll, Jan.-Feb. 1865.

WIGGINS, James. Pvt. Enlisted at Marion, S.C., 6 Oct. 1862 in Co. B. Deserted 19 Jan. 1863 but returned to camp 3 July 1863 and served until 10 Nov. 1864 when he was sent to a general hospital. The following Co. B muster roll carries him as deserted, dropped from the rolls. His file fails to mention that he was wounded in fighting on James Island 2 July 1864. However, an entry in the personal papers of Surgeon Robert Lebby, 2nd Rgmt., S.C. Arty., states that Wiggins was "slightly wounded, July 1864."

WILSON, Samuel J. 1st Lt. Enlisted, age 31, at Columbia, S.C., 15 April 1862 as 1st Sgt. of Alston's Co. Elected 2nd Lt. 6 June 1863 due to the resignation of another company officer. Promoted 1st Lt. 29 June 1863. Served on Morris Island, S.C., during the latter part of Aug. and first few days of Sept. 1863 where he received a slight wound of the hand. The final Co. B muster roll, Jan.-Feb. 1865, lists Wilson as absent on 30-day leave per surgeon's certificate.

Co. C, Manigault's Bn., S.C. Arty. (Gregg's Co.)

This company is first listed in contemporary records 14 April 1862 and probably was organized about that date as Capt. M.B. Stanly's Co., S.C. Arty. At this period it also was known as the McQueen Light Arty. The company subsequently became Co. B of Maj. Charles Alston's Bn., Light Arty., S.C.V.; then Co. C, S.C. Siege Train; and later Co. C, Manigault's Bn., S.C. Arty. Stanly served until 14 May 1863 when he resigned and Capt. Thomas E. Gregg became commanding officer. In May 1864 it became an independent field artillery company, known as Gregg's Co., S.C. Arty., and as such was sent to Virginia where it served the remainder of the war in Lt. Col. William J. Pegram's artillery, Army of Northern Virginia. It was replaced as Co. C by Zimmerman's Co. (q.v.)

EDWARDS, David W. 1st Lt. Entered service at Marion, S.C., 15 April 1862 as 2nd Lt. of Stanly's Co. He failed to pass the qualification examination and was suspended from duty 20 Feb. 1863. He was reexamined by order of the Secretary of War and presumably passed for the muster roll of June-July 1863 carries him as promoted 1st Lt. Served with Co. C. until 23 Sept. 1864 when he tendered his resignation due to ill health.

GREGG, Charles E. 1st Lt. Enlisted at Marion, S.C., 15 April 1862 as a Pvt. in Stanly's Co. and by 1 July had been promoted 1st Sgt. Capt. Stanly and two other company officers, in May 1863, refused to undergo certain required examinations to hold their commissions and resigned. Gregg passed the tests and 14 May 1863 became 1st Lt. of the company, succeeding Thomas E. Gregg who became company commander. The relationship, if any, between the two Greggs has not been found in the records.

GREGG, Thomas E. Capt. Commander, Co. C. Entered service at Marion, S.C., 15 April 1862 as 1st Lt. of Stanly's Co. In May 1863 Stanly refused to submit to certain required examinations and resigned his commission. Gregg assumed command of the company, passed the tests and was promoted Capt. 14 May 1863. On 5 May 1864, Gregg's Co., as an independent field artillery unit, was sent north where it spent the remainder of the war in the Army of Northern Virginia.

MARTIN, Edward B. Pvt. Enlisted 15 Apr. 1862, age 25, at Marion, S.C., in Capt. Stanly's Co. He is listed on the muster roll of Mar.-Apr. 1864 as "present, under arrest." He was tried by court martial 19 Apr. 1864 but no disposition of the case has been found in his personnel records.

Co. C, Manigault's Bn., S.C. Arty. *(Zimmerman's Co.)*

Organized as Co. D, 1st Rgmt., S.C. Inf. (Provisional Army), the unit about March 1862 was converted to a light artillery battery, known as the Pee Dee Arty. It also was known as Capt. D.G. McIntosh's Light Arty. Co.; Capt. E.B. Brunson's Light Arty. Co.; Capt. William E. Zimmerman's Light Arty. Co.; and Co. C, Manigault's Bn., S.C. Arty. The battery served with Lt. Col. William J. Pegram's artillery, Army of Northern Virginia, where it participated in various engagements including Spottsylvania, Hanover Junction and Cold Harbor. Returning to South Carolina in June 1864, the unit became Co. C of Manigault's Bn., replacing Capt. Thomas E. Gregg's Co. (q.v.) which had been sent to Virginia the previous month. The company manned Battery Ryan (left) and Battery Tatom. Following the fall of Charleston, 17-18 Feb. 1865, it served in North Carolina as part of Maj. Basil C. Manly's Bn. of Arty., a field organization composed of independent batteries from various states.

DARGAN, Edwin K. 1st Lt. Enlisted at Darlington, S.C., 2 Sept. 1861 as 1st Sgt. of McIntosh's Co. Elected 2nd Lt. 20 April 1863. Promoted 1st Lt., probably about June 1864. He went on detached service as Acting Assistant Adjutant General of the East Lines, James Island, 21 Aug. 1864 and apparently was still serving in this capacity as late as 14 Jan. 1865.

ZIMMERMAN, William E. Capt. Commander, Co. C. Entered service in May or June 1862 as a 2nd Lt. in McIntosh's Co. Promoted 1st Lt. 2 March 1863 and Capt. in March or April 1864.

Co. D, Manigault's Bn., S.C. Arty. *(Bridges' Co.)*

Organized per Special Order No. 12, Hq. S.C. Siege Train, 12 Feb. 1864, this company was composed of Louisiana men who were serving in Cos. A and B of the battalion. It also was known as Capt. William M. Bridges' Co., Manigault's Bn., S.C. Arty. Shortly after organization, Co. D was sent for duty in the 2nd Military District at Ashepoo, S.C., where it remained until June 1864 when it returned to James Island and manned Battery Ryan (right). During the waning days of the war, it served in North Carolina as an independent field artillery unit, known as Bridges' Louisiana Battery. It was attached to Maj. Basil C. Manly's battalion of independent artillery companies.

BRIDGES, William M. Capt. Commander, Co. D. Appointed Capt. 13 Dec. 1863. Organized and assumed command Co. D 13 Feb. 1864. Previously, as a 1st Lt. in the 1st Rgmt., Louisiana Arty., he participated in the evacuation of Confederate troops from Ship Island, off Gulfport, Miss., 14-16 Sept. 1861; the defense of Fort Jackson, below New Orleans, 16-24 April 1862; the Stones River (or Murfreesboro, Tenn.) campaign, 26 Dec. 1862 to 5 Jan. 1863; and in the defense of Vicksburg, Miss., 19 May-4 July 1863. One of Bridges' guns was in support but took no part in the sinking of the U.S. transport *Boston* in the Ashepoo River, S.C., 22 May 1864. (*See 26 May 1864, note*)

DAMARIN, Alfred. 2nd Lt. Enlisted 9 June 1863 as a Pvt. in Co. A. Transferred to Co. D and elected 2nd Lt. 15 Feb. 1864. Paroled at Greensboro, N.C. 28 April 1865.

PAINPARE', Raphael. 2nd Lt. Enlisted at Pocotaligo, S.C., 28 Feb. 1862 as a Pvt. in Buist's Co. Transferred to Co. D and elected 2nd Lt. 15 Feb. 1864. Paroled at Greensboro, N.C., about the end of April 1865.

VIENNE, Julius G. 1st Lt. Enlisted at Charleston 7 July 1863 as a Pvt. in Co. A. Transferred to Co. D and elected 1st Lt. 15 Feb. 1864. Paroled near Greensboro, N.C., 28 April 1865.

MARION LIGHT ARTILLERY, S.C. VOLUNTEERS

This unit was mustered into service Sept. 1861 as the Marion Arty., 1st Rgmt., S.C. Militia, with Capt. J. Gadsden King as commanding officer. It became an independent light artillery unit 6 June 1862 under Capt. Edward L. Parker and thereafter was designated the Marion Light Arty., S.C.V., although generally referred to as Capt. Parker's Co. From Dec. 1863 through Dec. 1864, and probably until the evacuation of Charleston in Feb. 1865, the company sections generally operated separately on picket duty on Johns and James Islands. During the bombardment of Fort Sumter, 12-13 April 1861, the unit, under Capt. King, manned mortar and channel batteries on Morris Island. Later, as light artillery, it was armed with four 12-pounder Napoleons.

PARKER, Edward L. Capt. Commander, Marion Light Arty. Entered service 1 Sept. 1861 as 1st Lt. of the Marion Arty. and commanded mortars in the Trapier Battery on Morris Island during the Confederate bombardment of Fort Sumter 12-13 April 1861. Promoted Capt. 28 April 1862 and named commanding officer of the company. Retained command when the unit became an independent company 6 June 1862. At the end of Jan. 1865 he was commanding his own company and the Orleans Guard Arty. in the Charleston area.

STROHECKER, John P. 1st Lt. Entered service 9 Sept. 1961 as a Lt. of the Marion Arty and commanded a section of guns on Morris Island guarding the main channel entrance to the harbor during the Confederate bombardment of Fort Sumter 12-13 April 1861. Listed as 1st Lt. Marion Light Arty. as of 6 June 1862 and was still serving in that capacity through Nov.-Dec. 1864.

PALMETTO BATTALION LIGHT ARTILLERY

The battalion was formed about Aug. 1861 with three companies, A, B, and C. Seven others were added at various times up to 21 June 1863. However, the last three, H, I and K, were illegally organized and were disbanded 1 April 1864. Technically designated the 3rd Bn., S.C. Light Arty., it generally was called the Palmetto Bn., Light Arty., or by the initials, P.B.L.A. It was known initially as Col. Edward B. White's Bn., S.C. Light Arty.

CAMPBELL, W.H. Entered service at Greenville, S.C., 15 Aug. 1861 as Capt., commander of the unit that subsequently became Co. A, Palmetto Bn. Promoted Maj. 9 Aug. 1862. Final item in his personnel file states that he was commanding the Ashepoo River lines as of 19 Jan. 1865.

WHITE, Edward B. Col. Commander, Palmetto Bn. Apparently entered service as a Maj. in Nov. 1861. Promoted Lt. Col. 15 Apr. 1862 and Col. 18 Jan. 1864. During Jan.-Feb 1864 he served as chief of heavy artillery in the 6th District, a short distance south of Charleston. He returned to command of the battalion 1 Mar. 1864 and was serving in that capacity as late as 19 Jan. 1865.

Co. A, Palmetto Bn., Light Arty. *(Earle's Co.)*

Organized about 15 Aug. 1861 as Capt. W.H. Campbell's Co., the unit was attached to the 1st Rgmt., S.C. Volunteers, commanded by Col. Maxcy Gregg. It was transferred to Col. E.B. White's Bn., Light Arty., 13 Oct. 1861 and soon became Co. A, Palmetto Bn., Light Arty. On 29 May 1862 it was divided, part becoming Co. H of the Palmetto Bn. and the remainder retaining the Co. A designation. Campbell was transferred to the battalion staff and later promoted Maj. The company was taken over by 1st Lt., later Capt., William E. Earle and became known as Earle's Co. The unit — also known as the Furman Artillery — sank the U.S. steamer Boston in Ashepoo River (See Diary 26 May 1864, note).

EARLE, William E. Capt. Commander, Co. A. Entered service at Greenville, S.C., 15 Aug. 1861 as 1st Lt. of Capt. Campbell's Co. When the company was divided 29 May 1862, Earle became commander and in Sept. or Oct. 1862 was promoted Capt. He was paroled at High Point, N.C., 2 May 1865. *(See Diary 26 May 1864, note).*

Co. D, Palmetto Bn., Light Arty. *(Kanapaux's Co.)*

This unit was organized about 14 Nov. 1861 as Capt. Charles E. Kanapaux's Co. of White's Bn., S.C. Light Arty., or Co. D, Palmetto Bn., Light Arty. It also was known as the Wagner Light Arty.

KANAPAUX, Charles E. Capt. Commander, Co. D. Entered service 14 Nov. 1861, age 35, at Charleston as a Capt., commanding officer of the company. He served in this capacity throughout the war and was paroled at Greensboro, N.C., 1 May 1865.

KENYON, Joseph A. 2nd Lt. Enlisted at Charleston 10 July 1862 as a Pvt. in Co. D. Promoted Sgt. 24 Aug. 1862 and 2nd Lt. 20 June 1863. Paroled at Greensboro, N.C., 1 May 1865.

Co. F, Palmetto Bn., Light Arty. *(Schulz' Co.)*

The company seems to have been organized about the middle of April 1862 of men transferred from Co. D. It also was known as the Chesnut Light Arty., and as Capt. Frederick C. Schulz' Co.

MCKEE, William B. 2nd Lt. Elected 2nd Lt. 21 June 1862. Detached about Nov. 1863 to serve as adjutant for Lt. Col. Del Kemper who at that time was in command of light artillery in Gen. Hagood's Brigade. McKee apparently rejoined his unit a few months later and was listed in Co. F. as late as 14 Jan. 1865.

SCHULZ, Frederick C. Commander, Co. F. Either transferred from Co. D or entered service 15 April 1862, age 38, as 1st Lt. (and probably commanding officer) of Co. F. Promoted Capt. 7 June 1862. Paroled near Bloomington, N.C., 1 May 1865.

Co. H, Palmetto Bn., Light Arty. *(Holtzclaw's Co.)*

Organized 29 May 1862 by division of Co. A, Palmetto Bn. However, it was considered illegally formed and was disbanded 1 April 1864. It also was known as Capt. Thomas A. Holtzclaw's Co.

HOLTZCLAW, Thomas A. Capt. Commander, Co. H. Entered service at Greenville, S.C., 15 Aug. 1861 as 1st Lt. of Campbell's Co., subsequently Co. A, Palmetto Bn. When this company was divided, 29 May 1862, Holtzclaw was promoted Capt. and made commanding officer of Co. H. However, Co. H was considered illegally formed and was disbanded 1 April 1864.

Co. I, Palmetto Bn., Light Arty. *(Bowden's Co.)*

Organized about June 1863 of men from Co. H. It was considered illegally formed and disbanded 1 April 1864. However, it apparently was still functioning as late as 10 June 1864. It also was known as Capt. J.R. Bowden's Co.

BOWDEN, J.R. Capt. Commander, Co. I. Enlisted at Greenville, S.C., 15 Aug. 1861 as Orderly Sgt. of Co. A. Elected 2nd Lt. 25 Dec. 1861. Promoted 1st Lt. 27 May 1862 and transferred to Co. H. Promoted Capt. and transferred to Co. I as commanding officer in June 1863. As of June 1864 he was on leave and no record has been found of his subsequent career.

Co. K, Palmetto Bn., Light Arty. *(Richardson's Co.)*

This company was formed 21 June 1863, apparently of men from Co. G, Palmetto Bn. It was disbanded 1 April 1864 due to illegal organization. However, records indicate the company, or at least part of it, was still in operation on James Island as late as June 1864. It also was known as Capt. Samuel M. Richardson's Co.

RICHARDSON, Samuel M. Capt. Commander, Co. K. Apparently entered service, age 23, on James Island 24 May 1862 as 2nd Lt. of Co. G, Palmetto Bn. Promoted Capt. and named commanding officer of Co. K 21 June 1863. When this unit was disbanded 1 April 1864, he was transferred back to Co. G as a 2nd Lt. and served with the unit at least through 13 Dec. 1864.

RICHARDSON, William S. 2nd Lt. Enlisted 1 May 1862 as a Pvt. in Co. G, Palmetto Bn. Transferred to Co. K 21 June 1863. Carried as absent without leave from 10 May 1862 through 30 June 1863. Promoted Sgt. 10 Oct. 1863 and 2nd Lt. 2 Mar. 1864. The final record in his personnel file is a pay voucher he signed 12 June 1864 as 2nd Lt. Co. K, although the unit had been disbanded officially 1 April 1864.

STEVENS, D.A. 1st Lt. Appointed 1st Lt. of Co. K 21 June 1863 and was still serving in that capacity 29 May 1864 although the company had been disbanded officially 1 April 1864.

BATTALION OF STATE CADETS

This organization was composed of cadets from The Citadel, the South

Carolina Military College at Charleston, serving as Co. A, and the Arsenal Cadets of Columbia, who were younger and officered by Citadel upperclassmen, as Co. B. Members of The Citadel staff served as battalion officers. The cadets fought in the Battle of Tullifinny Creek (near Pocotaligo, S.C.), 7 Dec. 1864. Before organization of the battalion, Citadel cadets fired on the "Star of the West" 9 Jan. 1861 and prevented the U.S. steamer from supplying and reinforcing Fort Sumter

COFFIN, Amory. 2nd Lt. Graduated from The Citadel in 1862, age 20, and joined the faculty as a 2nd Lt. He was assigned to Co. A, but served as adjutant of the Bn. He was wounded in the Battle of Tullifinny Creek, 7 Dec. 1864. Paroled 18 May 1865 at Augusta, Ga. Following the war, Coffin became a civil engineer.

THOMPSON, Hugh Smith. Capt. Commander of Co. A and a member of the Bn. staff. He served as governor of South Carolina from 1882 until 1886 when he resigned to accept the post of assistant secretary of the U.S. treasury.

WHITE, John B. Maj. Graduated from The Citadel in 1849 and served as superintendent from 1861 until the end of the war when the school was occupied by Federal troops. He commanded the cadets during the firing on the "Star of the West," 9 Jan. 1861, and in the Battle of Tullifinny Creek, 7 Dec. 1864.

STONO SCOUTS, S.C. MILITIA

This unit was called into service 10 Nov. 1861 as Capt. John B.L. Walpole's Co., S.C. Cav., to serve as pickets and videttes for the S.C. coast between the North Edisto and Stono Rivers. The unit was disbanded 7 Jan. 1862 and reorganized the following day as the Stono Scouts, S.C. Militia. It also was known as Capt. Walpole's Co. or Capt. Walpole's Scouts.

WALPOLE, John B.L. Capt. Commander, Stono Scouts, S.C. Militia. Entered service 10 Nov. 1861. Paroled at Greensboro, N.C., 1 May 1865.

VIRGINIA UNITS

26TH REGIMENT, VIRGINIA INFANTRY

This unit apparently was formed during the early part of 1862 and was reorganized for Confederate service in May 1862. It left Virginia for South Carolina 14 Sept. 1863 and served on James Island from 31 Dec. 1863 to 30 Apr. 1864. It returned to Virginia in May 1864 and served near Petersburg. It also was known as Col. Powhatan R. Page's Regiment.

PAGE, Powhatan R. Col. Commander, 26th Rgmt. Entered service 20 Apr. 1861 as Capt., commander Co. F, 21st Va. Infantry. Promoted Maj. about 29 Apr. 1861. Assumed command of the post at Gloucester Point, Va., 30 May 1861 as a Lt. Col. Promoted Col. and commander 26th Rgmt. 13 May 1862. Killed in action 17 June 1864 near Petersburg, Va.

UNITED STATES TROOPS

BENNETT, Augustus G. Lt. Col. Commander, 21st U.S. Colored Troops. He was placed in command of Charleston after the city surrendered 18 Feb. 1865.

DEAN, William B. 1st(?) Lt. 127th N.Y. Volunteer Inf. Dean served as Acting Assistant Adjutant General, first for Brig. Gen. Alexander Schimmelfennig, commander of U.S. troops in the Charleston area, then under Brig. Gen. Rufus Saxton. He later was A.A.A.G. for Maj. Gen. John G. Foster, commander, Dept. of the South.

FOSTER, John G. Maj. Gen. Graduated from the U.S. Military Academy at West Point in 1846. Served in the Corps of Engineers during the Mexican War and was a member of the Fort Sumter garrison during the initial bombardment 12-13 April 1861. Served in various capacities during the war, including commander of the Department of the South with headquarters at Hilton Head, S.C., from 26 May 1864 to 11 Feb. 1865. Following the war, he remained with the Corps of Engineers until his death in 1874 at the age of 51.

GILLMORE, Quincy A. Maj. Gen. Commander, Dept. of the South. Graduated U.S. Military Academy 1849 as 2nd Lt. of Engineers. Promoted 1st Lt. 1 July 1856; Capt. 6 Aug. 1861; Lt. Col. 11 Apr. 1862 for services in connection with the capture of Fort Pulaski, near Savannah, Ga.; Brig. Gen. of Volunteers 28 Apr. 1862, and Maj. Gen. of Volunteers 10 July 1863. Commander, Dept. of the South 12 June 1863 to Apr. 1864 and from 9 Feb. to 17 Nov. 1865. Served in various engineering capacities following the war. Died 7 Apr. 1888 at Brooklyn, N.Y., age 63.

HOOTON, Thomas. 2nd(?) Lt. Co. D, 7th Conn. Volunteer Inf. Fatally injured by grapeshot during the Battle of Secessionville 16 June 1862. Buried on James Island.

SCHIMMELFENNIG, Alexander. Brig. Gen. A native of Germany, Schimmelfennig served in the Prussian Army and soon after 1848 migrated to the U.S. At the start of the Civil War, he was elected Col. of a Pa. regiment and was appointed Brig. Gen. in Nov. 1862. He fought at Second Bull Run, Chancellorsville and Gettysburg and served for a time as commander of troops in the Charleston area. He went north on medical leave 8 April 1865 and died at Minersville, Pa., 7 Sept. 1865.

UPSON, Hiram Jr. 2nd Lt. Co. F, 7th Conn. Volunteer Inf. Killed 16 June 1862 in the Battle of Secessionville. Buried on James Island.

SHUE, (Not Identified) Dr. In charge of POW hospital at Beaufort, S.C. in 1865.

MISCELLANEOUS

ALSTON, Charles. His residence, 21 East Battery, was built about 1828 and today is operated as a museum by Historic Charleston Foundation.

ALSTON, William. Assistant Surgeon. Alston apparently applied for a post with the Army about March 1864. However, he was not formally appointed assistant surgeon until 22 Nov. 1864, although he seems to have been serving in that capacity at a much earlier date. On 3 Dec. 1864 he was ordered to report to Augusta, Ga., for service with the reserve forces in that area.

ASHE, John. Col. His house, probably built between 1730 and 1740, is today numbered 32 South Battery.

BARBOT, Louis J. Architect. His residence, now 59 Meeting St., was built c.1750 and bought by his family in 1853.

BARNWELL, John G. Maj. Inspector General, Dept. of S.C., Ga. and Fla. Appointed Maj., Corps of Artillery, 16 Mar. 1861 and joined Gen. Beauregard's staff at Charleston in May. Served in various capacities including artillery, ordnance and as Inspector of Batteries. On 28 Sept. 1864 he was ordered to report to the Augusta, Ga., Arsenal and served there until the end of the war. Paroled 8 May 1865 at Athens, Ga.

BEAUREGARD, A.N. Toutant. Capt. Entered service 1 May 1862 as a 1st Lt. and was appointed aide-de-camp on the staff of his brother, Gen. P.G.T. Beauregard. Apparently promoted Capt. shortly before he resigned his commission 1 Dec. 1863. He was a clerk in the Bank of Louisiana prior to the war and following his resignation sought a government post in Texas dealing with the sale and shipment of cotton.

BEAUREGARD, Pierre Gustave Toutant. General. Commander, Dept. of S.C., Ga. and Fla. A native of New Orleans, Beauregard graduated from the U.S. Military Academy in July 1838 and spent the next few years as a military engineer, mainly in Louisiana. He served with distinction during the Mexican War and was breveted Maj. He returned to engineer duty in 1848, again mainly in Louisiana, and resigned his commission 20 Feb. 1861. He was commissioned a Brigadier General in the Confederate Army 1 Mar. 1861 and promoted General 21 July 1861 following his successful organization of the Charleston defenses which resulted in the capture of Fort Sumter in April, and the victory at First Manassas in July. He succeeded to command at the Battle of Shiloh in April 1862 following the death of Gen. A.S. Johnston. Beauregard later returned to Charleston and 29 Aug. 1862 became commander of the Dept. of S.C., Ga. and Fla., a post he held until 23 Apr. 1864 when he was named commander of the Dept. of N.C. and Southern Va. During the remainder of the war, he held various positions including command of troops at Petersburg and the Military Division of the West. At the end of the war, he was second in command of the Army of Tennessee. He was paroled at Greensboro, N.C., 1 May 1865 and returned to New Orleans where he died 20 Feb. 1893.

BEHRE, Frederick G. Capt. Commissary Dept. Held a commission and served as quartermaster of the 1st Rgmt., S.C. Mounted Militia until the regiment was disbanded about the end of March 1862 and his commission was vacated. Enlisted 17 June 1862 at Adams Run, S.C., as a Pvt. in Co. C (also called Co. B) 2nd Rgmt., S.C. Cavalry and served, mainly on survey duty, until discharged 13 Jan. 1863. Appointed Capt. in the Commissary Dept. 14 Jan. 1863 and assigned to duty at Dills Bluff, James Island. He was still serving in the Commissary Dept. as late as 25 April 1865.

BOGGS, William R. Brig. Gen. Graduated from the U.S. Military Academy in July 1853 as a 2nd Lt. of Topographical Engineers. He was transferred to the Ordnance Corps in June 1854 and remained on ordnance duty until he resigned his commission 1 Feb. 1861. He was appointed a Capt. of Engineers 16 Mar. 1861, although he apparently also served as an artillery officer, and then as Chief Engineer of Georgia. He was promoted Col. 14 July 1862 and Brig. Gen. 4 Nov. 1862. Boggs was Chief of Staff, Dept. of Trans-Mississippi from 23 May 1863 until 24 Apr. 1865 when, at his request, he was transferred to the District of Ark. and West La. He was paroled 9 June 1865 at Shreveport, La.

BONHAM, Milledge Luke. S.C. Gov. and Brig. Gen. Born in the Edgefield District of S.C. in 1815, Bonham graduated from the South Carolina College in 1834 and soon became a lawyer. He served in the Seminole Indian War of 1836 and as a regimental commander in the Mexican War. He was elected to congress in 1856, resigning following secession of his state in December 1860. Appointed a Maj. Gen. of South Carolina troops in March 1861 and Brig. Gen. in the Confederate Army 23 April 1861. He commanded a brigade at First Bull Run then resigned his commission a few months later in a dispute with the government over rank. He was elected to the Confederate Congress in the fall of 1862 and became governor of South Carolina in December. Shortly after his term expired at the end of 1864, he was reappointed a Brig. Gen. and led a cavalry brigade through the remainder of the war. He later served in the State Legislature, was a delegate to the National Democratic Convention of 1868 and then became a railroad commissioner, an office he held at the time of his death in Aug. 1890.

BOYLSTON, S. Cordes. 1st Lt. Acting Assistant Adjutant General on the staff of Col. Alfred Rhett, commander of the 1st Rgmt., S.C. Artillery, later of the 5th Military District and, finally, of a brigade. Initial records in Boylston's personnel file show that he was serving as a 2nd Lt. in Co. B, 1st Artillery, as early as 31 Aug. 1861. He was promoted 1st Lt. 25 Mar. 1862 and appointed regimental adjutant 31 Dec., 1862. Paroled as Acting Assistant Adjutant General of Rhett's Brigade at Greensboro, N.C. about 2 May 1865. Boylston was severely wounded at Fort Sumter 23 Aug. 1863 when a shell knocked down the ceiling in a room where a number of officers were dining.

BRYAN, Henry. Maj. Assistant Adjutant General, Dept. of S.C., Ga. and Fla. Appointed 2nd Lt. of Infantry in Va. 4 Sept. 1861. Promoted Capt. 14 Jan. 1862 and Maj. 1 July 1862. Wounded and transferred to Charleston as Assistant Inspector General on Gen. Beauregard's staff about Nov. 1862. Serving in same capacity when paroled at the end of April 1865 at Greensboro, N.C. Bryan served as a volunteer on Morris Island during the evacuation of Sept. 1863.

BURKE, Thomas A. Maj. Quartermaster, 7th Military District. Appointed Capt. in the Quartermaster Dept. 30 Apr. 1862 and ordered to the 54th Rgmt., Ga. Infantry. Promoted Maj. and appointed brigade quartermaster on Gen. Taliaferro's staff 1 Aug. 1863. Applied 10 Oct. 1863 for transfer to Quitman, Ga., due to ill health and inability to continue service in the field. However, correspondence shows that he was serving in the Quartermaster Dept. at Charleston as late as 12 Jan. 1865.

BYRD, Stephen D.M. Maj. 26th Rgmt., S.C. Infantry. Byrd entered service 13 Jan. 1862 as Capt., commander of Co. E, Manigault's Bn., S.C. Volunteers (6th Inf. Bn.). When the battalion was disbanded in May 1862, Byrd was promoted Maj. and became commander of a newly organized 6th Bn., S.C. Inf., generally known as Byrd's Bn. This unit was consolidated with others 9 Sept. 1862 into the 26th Rgmt., S.C. Inf. Byrd resigned his commission in April 1863 in a dispute over the post of Lt. Col. of the Rgmt. In addition, he had been found deficient by an examining board. Byrd was a member of the State Legislature and was a physician. At this time, he was listed in several records as Lt. Col. although others still carried him as Maj. Byrd's subsequent career is conjectural. However, at least one record, 8 Sept. 1864, states that he was a Capt., commander of Co. I, 26th Rgmt., S.C. Inf. This indicates that he was elected commander of the unit following his resignation. Manigault, in referring to him on 17 Feb. 1864 as Maj., no doubt did so out of politeness.

CLARK, (Not Identified). Pvt. (?). In Signal Corps.

COLQUITT, Alfred H. Brig. Gen. Commander, Western Division, 7th Military District, James Island. Colquitt was serving as Col., commander of the 6th Rgmt., Ga. Infantry, as early as Jan. 1861. Promoted Brig. Gen. 1 Sept. 1862. Paroled 1 May 1865 at Greensboro, N.C. In Oct. 1863 he became commander of the Western Division of James Island. He later served as a brigade commander in the fighting in Virginia.

CUNNINGHAM, H.C. 1st Lt. Ordnance Officer, 7th Military District. Appointed 2nd Lt. and Ordnance Officer on Gen. Taliaferro's staff 14 Apr. 1863. Promoted 1st Lt. 2 May 1863. Paroled 28 Apr. 1865 at Greensboro, N.C.

DAVIS, Jefferson. President, Confederate States. Graduated from the U.S. Military Academy in 1828 and served in the West as a 2nd Lt. of Infantry. Promoted 1st Lt. of Dragoons in 1833. Resigned 1835. Member of the U.S. Congress from Miss. 1845-46. Served in the Mexican War as a Col. of Miss. Infantry 1846-47. Member U.S. Senate from Miss. 1847-51 and 1857-61. Secretary of War 1853-57. President, Confederate States, 1861-65. Following release from prison after the war, he headed an insurance firm for a time then devoted his remaining years to literary pursuits. He died at New Orleans in 1889, age 82.

DeSAUSSURE, Wilmot Gibbes. Charleston lawyer. He entered service at the beginning of the war and served as Lt. Col. commanding the artillery on Morris Island during the bombardment of Fort Sumter 12-13 April 1861. He later became a Brig. Gen. and commanded the 4th Brigade, S.C. Militia. DeSaussure bought the property at 45 East Bay in 1850 and constructed the residence about 1852.

DOUGHERTY (Not identified)

DU BARRY, Franklin B. Capt. Ordnance Officer. Offered his services to the state of S.C. as early as Jan. 1861 and resigned from the U.S. Coastal Survey Service 1 Apr. 1861. Commissioned 2nd Lt. of Artillery 27 Apr. 1861 and reported for ordnance duty at Pensacola, Fla. Appointed Capt. and Chief of Artillery for the Dept. of Ala. and West Fla. 17 Apr. 1862. Ordered to Charleston 31 Oct. 1862 where he served on ordnance duty with the Dept. of S.C., Ga. and Fla. or its various military districts. He died during the summer of 1864.

ECHOLS, William H. Maj. Chief Engineer for South Carolina with headquarters at Charleston. (*See also: Harris, D.B. Lt. Col. Chief Engineer for the Dept. of S.C., Ga. and Fla.*)

ELMORE, John T. Lt. Engineer. Assistant of Brig. Gen. Gabriel J. Rains, Chief of the Confederate Torpedo Bureau. Earlier in 1863 Elmore had seen combat in W. Va. In 1865 he was serving near Mobile, Ala., and apparently surrendered there at the end of the war.

EVANS, T.A.E. (Also listed in personnel records as A.E.) 1st Lt. Engineer.

FOOTE, (Not identified). Dr.

FORD, Edwin A. 1st Lt. Engineer in Confederate Torpedo Service. Served early in the war as a Sgt. in the Madison Arty. of Miss. Commissioned 2nd Lt., Corps of Engrs., 15 Sept. 1862 and ordered to Petersburg, Va. Joined Torpedo Service at Richmond, Va., under Brig. Gen. Gabriel J. Rains 2 June 1863 for special duty in S.C. and Ga. Ordered to Ala. 27 Feb. 1864 and promoted 1st Lt. 17 Mar. 1864. Captured while serving as an engineer in the Mobile area 8 April 1865. A pay voucher shows that Ford was on duty at Charleston 25 Aug. — 1 Oct. 1863.

FRANK (Not identified)

FROST, E.H. Capt. Assistant Commissary, Subsistence, Hagood's Brigade. Paroled at Greensboro, N.C. 1 May 1865.

GAINES, Richard V. Capt. Quartermaster Dept. Gaines served as an artillery officer during the early part of the war but lost his commission during the reorganization of units during 1862. He became a clerk in the Quartermaster Dept. with the duty of inspecting field transportation. He was appointed Capt. and Assistant Quartermaster 1 Oct. 1863 and soon assigned to the Dept. of S.C., Ga. and Fla. as Inspector of Field Transportation, a position he was still holding as late as 9 Mar. 1865.

GARDNER (Not identified)

GIBBES, Lewis R. Professor of mathematics and natural philosophy at the College of Charleston. Gibbes joined the faculty in 1839 and retired in 1892. He was a physician and made major contributions to science in various fields including astronomy, zoology, botany and chemistry. He was in charge of strong lights set up to illuminate the entrance to Charleston Harbor and discourage sneak reinforcement and resupply of Fort Sumter prior to the initial bombardment 12 April 1861.

GIBBES, Louisa Izard. Cousin of Edward Manigault.

GOETHE, James H. Assistant Surgeon. Entered service as a contract surgeon 18 Sept. 1861 at Beaufort, S.C. Appointed Assistant Surgeon 1 July 1863. He was ordered to Virginia 17 Aug. 1863, but the order apparently later was revoked and he remained in South Carolina. He was paroled 23 May 1865 at Augusta, Ga.

GONZALES, Ambrosio Jose. Col. Chief of Artillery, Dept. of S.C., Ga. and Fla. Gonzales was appointed Lt. Col. 4 June 1862 and was promoted Col. and Chief of Artillery 14 Aug. 1862. He was paroled 30 Apr. 1865 at Greensboro, N.C.

GREGORIE, John W. Capt. Engineer Dept. at Charleston. Served during the early days of the war as a 1st Lt. of S.C. Engineers on duty at Port Royal and Charleston. Entered Confederate service 15 Feb. 1862 as a 1st Lt. Promoted Capt. 4 Apr. 1862. He was the engineer in charge of construction of several James Island batteries, including Haskell and Ryan, in July 1863. He was in charge of defenses at Battery Wagner, Morris Island, during August and at Fort Sumter in early Sept. 1863. In Jan. 1864, Gregorie was on duty in the 3rd Military District and by April 1865 was in North Carolina with Hardee's Corps. He was paroled 1 May 1865 at Greensboro, N.C.

HALL, Francis M. 2nd Lt. Engineer. As late as 11 Feb. 1865 he was serving as an engineer at Adams Run, S.C.

HAGOOD, Johnson. Brig. Gen. Commander, Eastern Division, 7th Military District, James Island. Appointed Col., commander of the 1st. Rgmt., S.C. Infantry, 27 Jan. 1861. Promoted Brig. Gen. 21 July 1862. Hagood was assigned command of the First Sub-Division of the First Military District in S.C. 10 July 1863. Following a rearrangement of districts in Oct., he became commander of the Eastern Division, James Island. He served various tours on Morris Island during the siege. He later commanded a brigade in Virginia. A native of Barnwell, S.C., Hagood was a planter and banker. He was named comptroller of the state during the late 1870s and served as governor 1880-82.

HARRIS, David B. Col. Chief Engineer, Dept. of S.C., Ga. and Fla. on Gen. Beauregard's staff. Graduated from the U.S. Military Academy at West Point 1 July 1833. Served in the Creek Nation as a 2nd Lt. of Arty. 1833-34, and as professor of engineering at West Point, 1834-35. He resigned 30 Aug. 1835 and became assistant engineer of the James River and Kanawha Canal, 1835-37, a tobacco merchant for several years and, then, a planter from 1845 to 15 Feb 1862 when he entered Confederate service as a Capt. Promoted Maj. 3 Oct. 1862, Lt. Col. 5 May 1863 and Col. 8 Oct. 1863. He died of yellow fever at Summerville, S.C., 10 Oct. 1864, age 50, just before announcement of his promotion to Brig. Gen. Harris helped build the defenses of Vicksburg, Miss., before being ordered to Charleston 7 Oct. 1862. He became Chief Engineer of the Dept. of S.C., Ga. and Fla. 5 Nov. 1862.

HAY, R.G. Maj. Commissary Dept., Gen. Hagood's Brigade. Entered service 7 Sept. 1861 as Capt., commander of Hay's Co., 9th. Rgmt., S.C. Inf. The unit subsequently became Co. K, 11th. (also called the 9th.) Rgmt., S.C. Inf. These state units were reorganized under Confederate status 2-3 May 1862, but Hay was not reelected. He was dropped from the rolls 5 May 1862, but on 29 May became assistant provost martial at Charleston, rank not stated. He was appointed a Maj. in the commissary Dept. of Hagood's Brigade 4 Oct. 1862, to rank as of 28 Aug. Hay served for a time at Adams Run, S.C., then rejoined headquarters on James Island 19 Dec. 1863. He remained with the brigade until he was paroled 1 May 1865 at Greensboro, N.C.

HENDRICKS, Sgt. Not identified.

HEYWARD, Daniel. His residence burned late in the war and he sold the lot with the ruins in 1883. The present house, 25 East Battery, was completed about 1885.

HILL, Charles S. Capt. Ordnance Officer, First Military District. Served as 1st Lt. of Co. F, 1st Va. Infantry, until the unit was disbanded in Nov. 1861. Appointed 2nd Lt. of Infantry 12 Dec. 1861. Transferred to Mobile, Ala., in Mar. 1862. Served as brigade and division Ordnance Officer until 31 Jan. 1863 when he was transferred to Charleston. He became Ordnance Officer of the First Military District 15 Apr. 1863. Promoted Capt. 13 July 1863 to rank from 10 Jan. 1863. Appointed Ordnance Officer of Maj. Gen. N.B. Forrest's command 9 Dec. 1864. Paroled in Alabama 12 May 1865. During much of the 1863 fighting on Morris Island, Hill was Ordnance Officer of Battery Wagner.

HOLMES, James G. His residence, 19 East Battery, was extensively damaged by the earthquake of 1886. It was further damaged by the hurricane of 1893 and subsequently demolished. The house on the site today was built about 1919.

HUGER, C.K. Maj. Ordnance Officer, Dept. of S.C., Ga. and Fla. Appointed Maj. 4 June 1862 and ordered to Charleston. On 13 Oct. 1863, he was declared physically unfit for field service and was appointed Assistant Ordnance Officer of the Dept. of S.C., Ga. and Fla. He became the Dept. Chief of Ordnance 8 May 1864 and was paroled about a year later as Chief Ordnance Officer of Lt. Gen. W.J. Hardee's Corps.

HUMPHREYS, F.C. Maj. Superintendent of the Columbus (Ga.) Arsenal. Humphreys served in the U.S. Army 1855-61 as a military storekeeper. Appointed Capt. in the Confederate Army 10 June 1861. Promoted Maj. of Ordnance 1 Nov. 1862. Humphreys served initially as Military Storekeeper of

Ordnance at the Augusta (Ga.) Arsenal but soon transferred to Columbus where he spent the remainder of the war.

INGRAHAM, H. Laurens. Capt. Central Ordnance Depot, Charleston, S.C. Entered service as a 1st Lt. 16 Nov. 1861. Promoted Capt. 1 Oct. 1862. He served in Charleston as assistant to the Chief of Artillery, Dept. of S.C. and Ga., then, apparently, in the field as a brigade ordnance officer. During Jan. and Feb. 1864 he was on duty in Charleston at the Central Ordnance Depot, Dept. of S.C., Ga. and Fla. He later became a brigade ordnance officer in the Army of Northern Virginia and was paroled 1 May 1865 at Greensboro, N.C.

JACKSON, John K. Brig. Gen. Entered service 21 May 1861 as a Col. in command of a brigade at Pensacola, Fla. Promoted Brig. Gen. 14 Jan. 1862 and commanded a brigade of Georgia and Mississippi troops. 28 July 1864 he was assigned command of the District of Florida in the Dept. of S.C., Ga. and Fla. and on 29 Sept. was ordered to the Charleston area where he was still serving as late as 6 Feb. 1865.

JACOBS, John. Civilian peddler who was said to have deserted from the Yankees in Kentucky.

JOHNSON, P.C. 1st Lt. Engineer.

JONES, Charles C. Jr. Lt. Col. Chief of Light Artillery, District of Georgia. Entered service 1 Aug. 1861 as 1st Lt. in the Chatham (Ga.) Light Artillery. Promoted Maj. 22 Aug. 1862 and Lt. Col. 14 Oct. 1862. Chief of Light Artillery, District of Ga., from the end of 1862 until the fall or winter of 1864. On 31 Jan. 1865 he was listed as Inspector of Artillery for the Dept. of S.C., Ga. and Fla. From 30 Aug. until 13 Nov. 1863 he was on temporary duty in the Charleston area.

JONES, Samuel. Maj. Gen. Commander, Dept. of S.C., Ga. and Fla. Jones graduated from West Point in July 1841 and served on frontier and garrison duties until 1858 when he became Assistant Judge Advocate of the Army. He resigned his U.S. commission and was appointed a Maj. in the Virginia Artillery in May 1861. He was promoted Lt. Col. later in the month, Col. in June and Brig. Gen. 21 July. He became a Maj. Gen. 10 May 1862. Jones held various brigade and division commands until 20 Apr. 1864 when he was assigned command of the Dept. of S.C, Ga. and Fla. In Oct. 1864 he became commander of the District of S.C. and from 12 Jan. to 10 May 1865 of the Dept. of Fla. and South Ga. He was paroled 10 May 1865 at Tallahassee, Fla. Following the war, Jones farmed until 1880 when he became a civilian employee of the U.S. Army in Washington, a position he held until his death 31 July 1887 at the age of 68.

JORDAN, Thomas. Brig. Gen. Chief of Staff for Gen. Beauregard. Graduated from West Point 1 July 1840. Promoted 1st Lt. 18 June 1846 and Capt., Quartermaster Dept., 3 March 1847. Served in the Seminole Indian War, 1841-42; in the War with Mexico, 1846-48; and in the West, 1850-60. Resigned his U.S. commission 21 May 1861. Prior to his resignation, 16 March 1861, he became a Capt. of Virginia Infantry. He was promoted Lt. Col. 8 May 1861 and by October was listed in records as Col. and Adjutant for Gen. Beauregard. He then served in various commands until 14 April 1862 when he was promoted Brig. Gen. He became Gen. Beauregard's Chief of Staff 8 May 1862. Jordan was paroled 1 May 1865 at Greensboro, N.C.

KEMPER, Delaware. Lt. Col. Inspector of Light Artillery, Dept. of S.C., Ga. and Fla., and later a District Chief of Artillery. Early records of his service are not available. However, Del Kemper, as he was known, was serving as a Capt. and artillery battery commander in May 1861. Promoted Maj. 25 June 1862 and Lt. Col. in April 1863. Despite serious injury to his right arm 30 Aug.

1862 at First Manassas, Kemper returned to duty and 11 April 1863 was transferred to Charleston and assigned as Inspector of Light Artillery for the Dept. of S.C., Ga. and Fla. He was appointed Chief of Artillery for the 7th District on 23 July 1863 and of the 6th District on 7 Dec. 1863. He commanded the artillery in the attack on the *Marblehead* 25 Dec. 1863. By 30 Jan. 1865 he was commanding a brigade of artillery and was paroled 1 May 1865 at Greensboro, N.C.

KIRK, Manning J. Capt. Kirk entered service at Pocotaligo, S.C. 11 July 1862 as Capt. and commander of Kirk's Partisan Rangers. The unit was divided 24 Feb. 1864 and redesignated Cos. A and B, Kirk's Squadron, S.C. Partisan Rangers. Kirk retained Co. A. When the 19th Bn., S.C. Cavalry, was organized with five companies 20 Dec. 1864, Kirk's Squadron became Cos. A and B of the new battalion. Final item in Kirk's personnel file, dated 15 Jan. 1865, lists him as commander of Co. A, 19th Bn., S.C. Cavalry.

LAWRENCE, (Not Identified). Pvt.(?). In Signal Corps.

LAY, John F. Maj. Assistant Adjutant General and Inspector of Cavalry, Dept. of S.C., Ga. and Fla. Lay was appointed a Capt. in the Adjutant General's Dept. 29 April 1862 and promoted Col. of Cavalry in June. However, in the reorganization of his regiment, he was not reelected and, on 24 Nov. 1862, he reverted to his former rank of Capt. and was assigned to Gen. Beauregard's staff at Charleston. Lay was promoted Maj. 4 Dec. 1863 with the official title of Assistant Adjutant General and Inspector of Cavalry for the Dept. of S.C., Ga. and Fla. However, he also is mentioned in the Official Records as Lt. Col., probably in deference to his former rank, and as Inspector of Artillery. He was paroled 28 April 1865 at Richmond, Va.

LEBBY, Robert. Physician. Father of Dr. Robert Lebby Jr., surgeon of the 2nd Rgmt., S.C. Arty.

LEE, Robert E. General. Commander, Army of Northern Virginia. Graduated from West Point 1 July 1829. Promoted 1st Lt. 21 Sept. 1836, Capt. 7 July 1838, Maj. during the Mexican War, Lt. Col. 3 March 1855 and Col. 16 March 1861. Resigned his U.S. commission in April 1861. Served in various engineering positions 1829-46, Mexican War 1846-48, engineering duties 1848-53, frontier posts and other duties 1853-61. Appointed Maj. Gen. of Virginia state forces 23 April 1861, Brig. Gen. C.S.A. in May, General 14 June 1861 and General-in-Chief 31 Jan. 1865. Served in various positions until June 1862 when he became commander of the Army of Northern Virginia, a post he held until the surrender 9 April 1865. He also, on 6 Feb. 1865, was assigned as commander of all armies in the Confederate States. Following the war, Lee became president of Washington College (Washington and Lee University) at Lexington, Va., until his death, age 64, on 12 Oct. 1870.

LEE, Thomas B. Capt. Engineer. Before being transferred to Charleston, Lee served in Va. During the early part of Sept. 1863 he was the engineer at Battery Wagner being relieved on the 6th, only hours before Morris Island was abandoned. He later was the engineer in charge at Baldwin, Fla.

LEGARE, (Not Identified). Pvt.(?). In Signal Corps.

LEGARE, Solomon. Owner of Sol Legare Island adjacent to the southwestern end of James Island.

LESTER, Robert B. Missionary from Georgia.

LOPEZ, John. (Not identified)

LYNCH, Patrick Niesen (1817-1882). Bishop of the Roman Catholic Diocese of Charleston. In 1864, Bishop Lynch was sent by President Jefferson Davis as an emissary to the Vatican to obtain support for the Confederacy. The mission was a failure, and after the war Lynch returned to Charleston. He spent the remainder of his life in a desperate struggle to rebuild the shattered diocese — the cathedral and his residence had burned in 1861 — and repay personal debts.

MALLET, J.W. Lt. Col. Superintendent of Confederate States Ordnance Laboratories. Mallet entered service 16 Nov. 1861 as a 1st Lt. and aide-de-camp to Brig. Gen. R.E. Rodes. He resigned 31 May 1862 having been appointed Capt. of Artillery on the 21st. Promoted Maj. 18 June 1863 and Lt. Col. 19 Feb. 1864. He spent most of his military career as Superintendent of Laboratories at Macon, Ga., where he was captured near the end of April 1865.

MANIGAULT, Arthur Middleton (1824-1886). Brig. Gen. Brother of Edward Manigault. Served during the Mexican War, 1846-1848 as a 1st Lt. in Co. F, Palmetto (S.C.) Regiment. Participated in the siege of Vera Cruz and the Battles of Contreras, Churubusco, Chapultepec and the Garita Belen at Mexico City. Elected Capt. of the North Santee Mounted Rifles 27 Feb. 1861. Appointed Lt. Col., Special aide-de-camp to Gen. Beauregard 1 May 1861. Elected Col., 10th Rgmt., S.C. Volunteers, 31 May 1861. Promoted Brig. Gen. 26 Apr. 1863. Served as regimental or brigade commander in numerous engagements including Murfreesboro, Chickamauga, Missionary Ridge, the campaign from Dalton to Atlanta, the fighting around Atlanta and the Battle of Franklin, Tenn., 30 Nov. 1864, where he was seriously wounded and invalided out of service.

MANIGAULT, Gabriel (1809-1888) Listed in Charleston City Directories prior to the war as a planter. Served on the South Carolina Ordnance Board (*see Introduction, vii*) during the early part of the war while his brother, Edward, was Chief of Ordnance. In 1869, he moved with his family to Ontario, Canada.

MANIGAULT, Henry Middleton (1811-1883). He was a brother of Edward Manigault.

MAYO, George Upshur. Maj. Assistant Inspector of Artillery, Dept. of S.C., Ga. and Fla. Entered service 19 July 1861 as 1st Lt. of Artillery and served as Ordnance Officer in the Dept. of Middle and East Fla. Appointed Maj. 30 Sept. 1862 and became Chief of Ordnance, Dept. of Miss. and East La. Assigned to Dept. of S.C., Ga. and Fla. and stationed at Charleston as Assistant Inspector of Artillery 20 Oct. 1863. He was relieved of duty with the Dept. 15 Feb. 1865 and paroled 15 May 1865 at Tallahassee, Fla.

McLEOD, William Wallace. Owner of residence on James Island near Wappoo Creek. The house was built by McLeod in 1854 and was used by both sides at various times during the war.

MEADE, Richard K. 1st Lt. Enlisted during the first half of 1861 as a Pvt. in the 2nd Rgmt., Va. Inf. He lost an arm 21 July 1861 at First Manassas and was discharged 4 Dec. He was appointed a 2nd Lt. of Inf. 17 Dec. 1861 and served as Assistant Chief of Ordnance for Gen. T.J. Jackson May-July 1862. Promoted 1st Lt. 28 July 1862 and appointed aide-de-camp to Gen. William B. Taliaferro. He apparently was assigned to unspecified duties at Charlottesville, Va., due to ill health, then in July 1863 rejoined Taliaferro's staff at Charleston. He returned to Richmond, Va., 25 Aug. 1864 and was assigned to the Reserves.

MERCER, Hugh W. Brig. Gen. Graduated from the U.S. Military Academy at West Point 1 July 1828 as a 2nd Lt. of Arty. Promoted 1st Lt. 10 Oct. 1834. Served in various forts along the East Coast from 1828 until he resigned his commission 30 April 1835. Employed as a banker at Savannah, Ga., 1841-1861.

Listed in Confederate records of Aug. 1861 as Col., commander of the 1st Rgmt., Ga. Volunteers. Promoted Brig. Gen. 29 Oct. 1861. Commander of the 1st Military District of Ga. until 26 April 1864 when he was transferred to the Army of Tennessee. On 3 Mar. 1865 he was assigned to the Ga. Reserves and the following month was captured at Macon, Ga. After the war, Mercer returned to banking at Savannah, then in 1869 became a commission merchant at Baltimore, Md. He was in Europe from 1872 until his death in Germany 9 June 1877, age 69.

MORDECAI, Moses Cohen. Commission merchant. Mordecai purchased the house at 69 Meeting St. in 1837. After the war, he moved to Baltimore, Md., where he rebuilt the fortune he had lost supporting the Confederacy.

NANCE, William F. Capt. Assistant Adjutant General, 1st Military District, commanded by Brig. Gen. Roswell S. Ripley. Nance served as Maj. in the Adjutant General Dept. of the state establishment 27 Sept. 1861 until he resigned 4 Dec. On 16 July 1862 he was appointed 1st Lt. and Adjutant of the 1st Rgmt., S.C. Inf., but declined the appointment since he had been named Capt. on the staff of the 1st Military District. He first was assigned quartermaster duties, but was relieved when he refused to sign a bond. He later became Assistant Adjutant General of the district and was serving in that capacity as late as Nov. 1864.

OTEY, John M. Lt. Col. Assistant Adjutant General, Dept. of S.C., Ga. and Fla. Otey apparently entered service about June 1861 and served on the staffs of Gens. Braxton Bragg and Leonidas Polk. Promoted Capt. 1 May 1862. Transferred to Gen. P.G.T. Beauregard's command 22 Oct. 1862. Appointed Assistant Adjutant General, Dept. of S.C., Ga. and Fla on 19 Dec. 1862. Promoted Lt. Col. 4 June 1864 and was paroled in that rank as A.A.G. on Beauregard's staff at the end of April 1865.

PAGE, Peyton N. Capt. Assistant Adjutant General under Maj. Gen. William B. Taliaferro. Entered service from Md. 25 Oct. 1861 as a 1st Lt. Promoted Capt. 14 Oct. 1862. Served as an aide to Brig. Gen. Gabriel J. Rains until Jan. 1863 when he became Assistant Adjutant General of the Bureau of Conscription. Transferred 16 Nov. 1862 to the 7th Military District as A.A.G. for Gen. Taliaferro. On 17 Nov. 1864 the 7th District was abolished and Taliaferro became commander of the 2nd and 3rd Sub-Districts (composed of troops of his division) which succeeded it. Page was paroled 2 May 1865 at Greensboro, N.C.

PINCKNEY, C.C. Capt. Ordnance Officer, 1st Military District. Apparently entered service as a 1st Lt. 2 May 1862. Promoted Capt. 2 May 1863. Served as Ordnance Officer of the 1st District during most of his military career. He first was assigned to the Charleston Ordnance Depot and later to the Charleston Arsenal. On 20 Feb. 1865 he was stationed at Columbus, Ga.

PORCHER, Frank. (Not identified)

PRINGLE, Motte A. Maj. Quartermaster, Dept. of S.C., Ga. and Fla. Entered service 16 Nov. 1861 as a Capt. in the Quartermaster Dept. Promoted Maj. 13 Nov. 1862. Appointed Quartermaster, Dept. of S.C., Ga. and Fla., on 2 May 1863 with headquarters at the Charleston QM Depot. He was relieved of duty at Charleston 14 Feb. 1865 and ordered to report to the QM Depot at Richmond, Va.

PROCTOR, Stephen Richard. Capt. Assistant Quartermaster, Dept. of S.C., Ga. and Fla. Appointed Col. in the state establishment 16 April 1861 and served as an aide to his brother-in-law, Gen. P.G.T. Beauregard. He apparently either resigned or was not reappointed in the Confederate Army and returned to his home in Louisiana. However, after the capture of New Orleans, he came back to Charleston rather than take an oath of allegiance. On 16 Feb. 1863 he was appointed Capt., Assistant Quartermaster, Dept. of S.C., Ga. and Fla. He was transferred to Augusta, Ga. 29 Aug. 1864, first as a Paymaster and then as Assistant QM. He was paroled at the end of April 1865 in N.C. as a member of Beauregard's staff. Capt. Proctor was a cousin of Mary Proctor Huger Manigault, wife of Edward Manigault's brother, Brig. Gen. Arthur Middleton Manigault.

RAINS, Gabriel J. Brig. Gen. Chief of Confederate Torpedo Bureau. Graduated as a 2nd Lt. of Inf. from the U.S. Military Academy at West Point 1 July 1827 and served in the West until 1839; in the Seminole Indian War 1839-40; at various post on the East Coast until 1846; War with Mexico, 1846-48; and in Oregon and Washington 1852-60. He resigned his commission 31 July 1861. Promoted 1st Lt. in 1834, Capt. in 1837, Maj., 1851 and Lt. Col. in 1860. Entered Confederate service 16 Mar. 1861 as a Col. of Inf. Promoted Brig. Gen. 23 Sept. 1861. Rains participated as a brigade or division commander in a number of battles until he was wounded at Seven Pines. He became commander of the Conscription and Torpedo Bureaus in Dec. 1862. Following the war, Rains was a clerk in the QM Dept. at Charleston. He died at Aiken, S.C., in 1881, age 78.

RAMSAY, William M. Capt. Engineer. Began service as a military engineer in S.C. 20 Dec. 1860. Promoted Capt. 1 June 1862. Served a tour of duty during July 1863 at Battery Wagner then was assigned to James Island. Ramsay was tried by court martial in March 1864 on undisclosed charges and was dismissed from the service 15 Apr. 1864 following a review of the findings by Gen. P.G.T. Beauregard.

RAVENEL, John. Built the residence at 5 East Battery about 1849.

RAVENEL, S. Prioleau. Capt. Commissary Dept., 7th Military District, commanded by Maj. Gen. William B. Taliaferro. Apparently entered service as a Capt. in the Commissary Dept. 31 March 1862. Final record in his personnel file is a surgeon's certificate, dated 16 Sept. 1864, supporting his application for 30-days leave. At that time he was on duty in Fort Sumter although still assigned to the Commissary Dept. of the 7th District

RAVENEL, William. Commission merchant and owner of Farm Field Plantation a few miles west of the city (see 19 Mar. 1864, note). He built the residence at 13 East Battery in 1845. When Manigault viewed the house in 1864, it had four imposing columns supporting a Greek portico and rising from arches as high as the first story. The columns were toppled by the 1886 earthquake and only the arches remain today.

RIPLEY, Roswell Sabine. Brig. Gen. Graduated as a 2nd Lt. of Arty. from the U.S. Military Academy at West Point 1 July 1843. Served in various garrisons, arsenals and on survey duty until 1846; War with Mexico, 1846-48; Seminole Indian War 1849-50; and in various coastal garrisons until he resigned 2 March 1853. Promoted 1st Lt. 3 March 1847. Breveted Capt. on 18 April 1847 and Maj. 13 Sept. 1847. Upon leaving service, Ripley settled in Charleston as a businessman. When war appeared imminent, he obtained a commission 2 Jan. 1861 as Lt. Col. of the 1st Rgmt., S.C. Arty. Appointed Brig. Gen. 15 Aug. 1861. He commanded the 2nd Military District for a time then, in June 1862, went to Va. where he participated in a number of engagements as a brigade commander. Returning to Charleston in October 1862, he commanded the 1st Military Distict until 1865 when he went to N.C. Following the war, Ripley resided for a time in France, then returned to Charleston and again engaged in business until his death in 1887.

ROBERTSON, Beverly H. Brig. Gen. Commander, 2nd and 6th Military Districts, Adams Run, S.C. Graduated from the U.S. Military Academy 1 July 1849 as a 2nd Lt. of Dragoons. Served on frontier duty in the West 1850-1861. Dismissed from the service 8 Aug. 1861 "having given proof of his disloyalty." Commissioned under the state establishment 21 Aug. 1861 as a Col., commander of the 4th Rgmt., Va. Cav. Appointed Capt., Confederate Corps of Arty. 14 Sept. 1861 and Brig. Gen. 9 June 1862, commanding a brigade of Virginians. Robertson served in Va. and N.C. until 21 Sept. 1863 when he was transferred to South Carolina and, on 15 Oct. 1863, was assigned command of the 2nd Military District south of Charleston. He later commanded both the 2nd and 6th Military Districts. During the final stages of the war in March 1865 he was commanding a brigade of cavalry in N.C.

ROMAN, Alfred. Lt. Col. Inspector General, Dept. of S.C., Ga. and Fla. Served initially in the state establishment as a Col., commander of the 18th Rgmt., La. Volunteer Inf. On 4 Oct. 1862 he was appointed Lt. Col. in the Confederate Army and assigned to Gen. P.G.T. Beauregard's staff where, with brief interruptions, he spent the remainder of the war as Inspector General. Paroled 1 May 1865 at Greensboro, N.C. In 1884, Roman published a two-volume, definitive work on Beauregard's military operations. [See Bibliography, Roman]

ROPER, Robert William. Built the imposing residence at 9 East Battery between 1838 and 1840. Roper died prior to the war but the house was still known by his name.

RUSSELL, Nathaniel. A wealthy Rhode Island merchant, Russell moved to Charleston and built the residence at 51 Meeting St. in 1809. The building, still known as the Nathaniel Russell House, today is operated as a museum by Historic Charleston Foundation.

SCHOOLER, Samuel. Capt. Entered service 6 June 1862 as a 1st Lt. of Arty. Promoted Capt. 12 Nov. 1862. Served on ordnance duty, first at the Fayetteville, N.C. Arsenal, then under Gen. G.J. Rains who was in charge of the Confederate Torpedo Bureau. Schooler was in the Charleston area from about June 1863 until Feb. 1864 when he was assigned to ordnance duty at Richmond, Va. He resigned his commission 31 March 1865.

SOULE, Pierre. Civilian volunteer aide-de-camp, staff of Gen. P.G.T. Beauregard. Soule was born in France in 1802. He became editor of a liberal newspaper and was arrested for attacks on the king's ministers. He sailed for America and became a lawyer at New Orleans and later a member of the state senate. In 1849 he was appointed to the U.S. Senate to fill a vacancy. Initially, Soule was opposed to secession, but after its accomplishment, tendered his services to the Confederacy. He remained in New Orleans due to failing health and was captured when the city fell. Sent to New York as a political prisoner, he was confined at Fort Lafayette in July 1862. He later was paroled and went to Cuba where in May 1863 he was exchanged. Returning to America, Soule became a civilian aide to Gen. Beauregard. Following the war, he resumed his New Orleans law practice but gave it up in 1868 due to ill health. He died in 1870.

STILES, Robert M. 1st Lt. Engineer. In July 1862, Stiles was on duty at Andersonville, Ga. Approximately a year later he was at Battery Haskell on James Island then in Aug. 1863 he was the engineer in charge at Battery Wagner. At the evacuation of Morris Island, 6 Sept. 1863, Stiles was the engineer in charge at Battery Gregg. Jan. 1864 found him at Savannah, Ga., where he was still assigned, but too ill to perform duty, on 8 Sept. 1864.

STONEY, Theodore D. Secretary and Treasurer of the Southern Torpedo Co., builder of small torpedo boats known as Davids.

STONEY, Theodore G. Capt. Served as a volunteer aide-de-camp to Col. (later Brig. Gen.) Arthur Middleton Manigault in 1862. He then became a Capt. and brigade paymaster and on 18 Sept. 1863 was ordered to Charleston. Stoney apparently lost his captaincy during 1864, for on 17 Aug. 1864 he was elected a 2nd Lt. in Capt. J. Raven Matthewes' Co. of S.C. Heavy Arty. where he was still serving as late as 5 Jan. 1865.

TALIAFERRO, Warner T. Capt. Acting Adjutant General, 7th Military District, commanded by Brig. Gen. William B. Taliaferro (relationship not established). Entered service 14 May 1862 as a 1st Lt. Promoted Capt., 10 Sept. 1862. Served as Acting Adjutant General of the 7th Military District until about Nov. 1863 when he was transferred to Savannah, Ga. He was serving in N.C. as late as 31 March 1865 as an aide-de-camp on the staff of Maj. Gen. Daniel H. Hill.

TALIAFERRO, William Booth. Maj. Gen. Commander, 7th Military District, James Island. Graduated from William and Mary College in 1841 and was commissioned Capt. in the 11th Rgmt., U.S. Inf. 9 April 1847. Promoted Maj. in the 9th Rgmt. 12 Aug. 1847. Mustered out 26 Aug. 1848. Entered service in the Provisional Army of Va. 1 May 1861 as Col., commander of the 23rd Rgmt., Va. Inf. Promoted Brig. Gen. in the Confederate Army 4 March 1862 and Maj. Gen. 1 Jan. 1865. He commanded troops at Gloucester Point, Va., in 1861 and later fought in a number of engagements in Va. until March 1863 when he was transferred to Ga. as commander of the Savannah District. In July 1863 he was commanding troops on Morris Island, S.C. and in Aug. those of the First Sub-Division, First Military District, on James Island. On 22 Oct. 1863 the districts were rearranged and Taliaferro's James Island command was designated the 7th Military District. Within a month, the district was divided into two divisions, the Eastern, commanded by Brig. Gen. Johnson Hagood, and the Western, under Brig. Gen. Alfred H. Colquitt. Taliaferro remained over both as District Commander. He led a division in Fla. from Feb. 1864 until May when he returned to his former command on James Island. Although promoted Maj. Gen. in Jan. 1865, he signed reports as Brig. Gen. as late as April 1865 when he was commanding a division in N.C. He was paroled 2 May 1865 at Greensboro, N.C.

TOUTANT, A.J. 1st Lt. Aide-de-camp to Gen. P.G.T. Beauregard. Entered service 29 Oct. 1861 as aide-de-camp to Maj. Gen. Mansfield Lovell, commander of troops at New Orleans when the city was captured in April 1862. Technically, Toutant remained on Lovell's staff. However, in May 1863 he came to Charleston and served as a volunteer aide-de-camp to Gen. Beauregard. When an opening occurred in Dec. 1863 — through resignation of Lt. A.N. Toutant Beauregard, aide-de-camp and brother of the general — Toutant was appointed to the post. In May 1864 he resigned as aide to Gen. Lovell. He continued on Beauregard's staff until the end of April 1865 when, by now listed as a Maj., he was paroled at Greensboro, N.C. Relationship to the Beauregards not established.

TRENHOLM, Edward Leonard. Commission merchant with the firm of John Fraser & Co. which became a major participant in the blockade-running business during the war. He resided at 91 Rutledge Ave. and was a brother of George Alfred Trenholm, Confederate Secretary of the Treasury 1864-65.

TURNER, T.J. Assistant Surgeon. Commissioned 14 March 1863 and assigned to duty in Fla. Transferred to James Island, S.C., 24 April 1863. Apparently transferred across the harbor to Mt. Pleasant in Oct. 1864.

VANDERHORST, Arnoldus. Gov. of S.C. 1794-96. He built the three adjoining brick dwellings, 76-80 East Bay, in 1800. They are still known as Vanderhorst Row.

WADDY, J.R. Lt. Col. Chief of Ordnance, Dept. of S.C., Ga. and Fla. Served as a 2nd Lt. of Arty in the U.S. Army in 1857. Entered service for the South on 16 March 1861 as a 1st Lt. of Arty. Promoted Capt. 11 Sept. 1861, Maj. 11 April 1862 and Lt. Col. 22 Nov. 1862. Served initially in the field in Va. Transferred to S.C. 23 Dec. 1861 and served as Assistant Adjutant General of the Dept. until 27 May 1863 when he was appointed Chief of Ordnance. He was serving as Chief of Ordnance on Gen. P.G.T. Beauregard's staff when paroled at the end of April 1865 at Greensboro, N.C.

WARWICK, P.C. 1st Lt. Aide-de-camp to Maj. Gen. Sam Jones. Served for a number of months at the beginning of the war as a civilian volunteer aide to Gen. Jones. Commissioned 1st Lt. and aide-de-camp to Jones on 10 Dec. 1862. He was recommended for promotion to Capt. in July 1864 but remained a 1st Lt., at least until 21 Feb. 1865, the final record in his personnel file. However, although he signed official correspondence as 1st Lt., other officers, on the same date, referred to him as Capt.

WHITE, (Not Identified). Sgt. Apparently in Torpedo Corps.

WISE, Henry A. Brig. Gen. Commander, 6th Military District. Appointed Brig. Gen. 5 June 1861 although he apparently was in service several months previously. Served as brigade commander in Va. until about Sept. 1863 when he is listed in the Charleston area. On 22 Oct. 1863 he was assigned command of the newly created 6th Military District. Wise later returned to Va. and was serving in defense of Petersburg in Jan. 1865. He was paroled as a brigade commander at Appomattox 9 April 1865. Wise died at Richmond, Va., 10 Sept. 1876.

Glossary

ARMY TENT: Probably the conical Sibley tent or an A-frame tent.

AUSTRIAN HOWITZER: A few cannon made in Austria were absorbed into Confederate service. The bronze, 24-pounder howitzer had a slightly larger bore than American weapons of this caliber — 5.87-inch compared to 5.82. This minor difference caused little problem in operation. (*See 26 Nov. 1863, note*)

BANQUETTE: Platform of a fortification on which troops stood to fire. Technically, the tread of the banquette. (*See, Fortification, diagram*)

BARBETTE CARRIAGE: (*See, Carriages, Seacoast Carriages*)

BATTERY WAGON: Two-wheeled cart which was linked to a standard field limber to form a four-wheeled vehicle. It was virtually a rolling warehouse carrying about 125 different items, such as tools and supplies, necessary to keep wood, leather and cloth equipment of the battery in operation.

BERM: A narrow shelf between the parapet and ditch of a fortification. It was a recognized defect that gave an attacker a place to stand during assault. However, it threw the weight of the parapet rearwood and prevented cave-in of the ditch. It also gave a place for workmen to stand during construction. The berm ranged in width from 18 inches in firm ground up to six feet in soft. (*See, Fortification, diagram*)

BOAT HOWITZER: Small bronze howitzer designed for use in boats by the navy. However, the piece also could be mounted on a type of field carriage.

BOLSTER: Block of wood bolted to the front of a mortar bed and grooved to permit longitudinal movement of an elevating quoin. Also, wood block on the trail of a siege carriage on which the breech of a gun rested in the travelling position.

BOMBPROOF: Covered enclosure of a fortification impervious to penetration by shot and shell.

CAISSON: Two-wheeled cart carrying two ammunition chests which, when linked to a standard field limber, had a capacity of three chests. The total number of rounds depended on the caliber. A caisson for a 6-pounder, for instance, carried 150 rounds, 50 in each chest.

CANISTER: Close-range, anti-personnel projectile consisting of a number of small iron, or lead, balls arranged in tiers and packed in sawdust to prevent movement. They were enclosed in a thin sheet-metal casing with iron top and bottom plates. Upon firing, the container ruptured and the balls continued in the fashion of shotgun pellets.

CANNON MORTAR: A term, probably coined by Manigault, to describe a 32-pounder gun converted to a mortar.

CARRIAGES: There were three main army types — field, siege and seacoast.

Field carriages: Used with relatively small-caliber cannon and were the familiar two-wheeled variety seen in most battlefield parks. They were highly maneuverable and permitted cannon to be employed with troops in the field.

Siege carriages: Two-wheeled carriages of much sturdier construction than the field variety and designed to carry heavier cannon. They were not expected to maneuver with troops and hence could be moved at leisure. During firing, the piece rested on the trunnion bed, hollowed areas in the cheeks, or side pieces. Due to uneven distribution of weight of the heavy cannon, extensive movement required that the piece be shifted to the travelling position (or bed as Manigault called it). This involved manhandling the heavy tube backwards to a point where the breech rested on a block of wood on the trail known as a bolster. The trunnions were held by the heads of heavy bolts on the cheeks.

Reproduction at Fort Moultrie

Front Pintle, Barbette Seacoast Carriage, Model 1839.

Seacoast carriages: These were divided into casemate carriages and barbette carriages. The former fired through an embrasure, or opening in the parapet or epaulement. Barbette carriages fired over the parapet. Both types consisted of a chassis, or bottom frame which could be turned laterally, and a top carriage which held the gun and slid or rolled back and forth on the chassis and was designed to absorb much of the weapon's recoil. Barbette carriages also were known as front pintle or center pintle. The former rotated around a heavy metal pin holding them at the front and were restricted to a relatively narrow arc. The latter revolved around a center pivot and could traverse 360°. Manigault called this type a "Full Circle Carriage." (*See Columbiad, 8-inch, Double-Banded*)

CARRONADE: English weapon invented in 1774 and cast originally at Carron, Scotland, hence the name. Designed for shipboard use, the piece projected a large ball at low velocity on the theory that this would cause maximum splintering of wooden hulls. Carronades, which also fired shells, saw limited employment during the Civil War, mainly by the Confederates. In all cases, they were old weapons emplaced in fortifications for lack of anything better. (*See 16 Nov. 1863, note 2*)

CASCABLE: Today, the word is spelled cascabel and refers only to the knob at the base of the breech of a cannon. Manigault used the term correctly including both the knob and the adjacent base of the breech. The cascabel knob generally was cast oblong and used to facilitate turning the tube in a lathe. It later was finished in one of a variety of shapes and was useful as a handle for lifing or mounting cannon on carriages. In some case, the appendage was threaded for an elevation screw. It was employed by the Navy in connection with breeching tackle.

CASEMATE CARRIAGES: (*See Carriages, Seacoast Carriages*)

CENTER PINTLE CARRIAGES: (*See Carriages, Seacoast Carriages*)

CHASE: Portion of a cannon barrel, approximately between the trunnions and the muzzle face.

CHASSIS: (*See Carriages, Seacoast Carriages*)

CHEEKS: Side pieces of a carriage.

COLUMBIAD (8-INCH, DOUBLE-BANDED): The columbiad was a form of seacoast cannon developed long before the war as a smoothbore to fire both solid shot and shells. A number were rifled by the Confederates and equipped with single or double wrought-iron bands for additional strength, thereby turning them into formidable weapons. Several models would have been available and it is difficult from Manigault's description to pinpoint the type to which he refers. However, chances are it was the U.S. Model 1858. A number of these were acquired by the Confederates when they occupied the Charleston harbor forts in 1861 and some were later rifled and banded. One of these, a double-banded 8-inch, is displayed today at Fort Moultrie (*above*). However, it is rifled with eight "saw-tooth" grooves, not 10, and hence is not the specific weapon mentioned by Manigault. The carriage is a reproduction Center Pintle, Barbette Seacoast Carriage, called a "Full Circle Carriage" by Manigault. (*See Carriages, Sea Coast Carriages*)

COVERED WAY: Passage in a fortification by which troop movements can be concealed from enemy view. (*See Fortification, diagram*)

CREMAILLERE LINE: Saw-tooth shaped line.

DAHLGREN (9-INCH): Smoothbore cannon of a distinctive streamlined shape invented by Adm. John Adolph Dahlgren (1809-1870) of the U.S. Navy. They were made in various bore diameters, including 9 inches.

EPAULEMENT: A covering mass, or breastwork, designed to protect the troops behind it. It differs from a parapet in that an epaulement has no convenient arrangement, such as a banquette, for firing over it.

EXPENSE MAGAZINE: Protected storage area near the guns to hold a small quantity of ammunition for immediate use. It would be resupplied from the main magazine.

FIELD CARRIAGE: (*See Carriages, Field Carriages*)

FLIES: A piece of cloth, such as a tarpaulin or portion of a tent, suspended to afford protection from the elements.

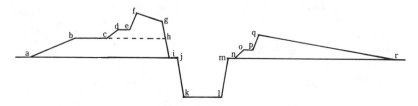

FORTIFICATION PROFILE — Legend:

abhi	—	Rampart or Bulwark
ab	—	Parade Slope
bc	—	Terreplein
cfgh	—	Parapet
cd	—	Banquette Slope
de	—	Tread of the Banquette, or Banquette
ef	—	Interior Slope
fg	—	Superior Slope
gi	—	Exterior Slope (if no Rampart, gh)
ij	—	Berm
jk	—	Scarp Wall
jklm	—	Ditch
kl	—	Bottom of Ditch
lm	—	Counterscarp Wall
mn	—	Covered Way
nqr	—	Glacis
no	—	Glacis Banquette Slope
op	—	Glacis Banquette
pq	—	Glacis Interior Slope
qr	—	Glacis Slope

FRICTION TUBE: Device, also called a friction primer, for firing cannon. It consisted of two small brass, or copper, tubes and a serrated wire. The larger tube **(b)**, about 1¾ inch long and .19-inch diameter, was drilled and the smaller tube **(a)** was soldered into it at a 90° angle. The serrated wire **(c)** was placed in the smaller tube and the tube filled with a friction composition. The larger tube was filled with musket powder. The larger tube was inserted in the vent of the cannon and a lanyard hooked into a loop twisted at the end of the serrated wire. An even, quick pull on the lanyard dragged the serrated wire through the friction compound setting off a spark that ignited the musket powder which flashed down the vent and set off the main charge in the cannon.

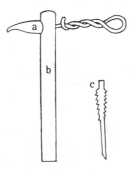

FRONT PINTLE CARRIAGE: (*See Carriages, Seacoast Carriages*)

FULL CIRCLE CARRIAGE: (*See Carriages, Seacoast Carriages*)

GIN: A tripod with blocks, tackle and a windlass for lifting heavy weights and mounting guns.

GLACIS: Gradual slope up to a fortification covered by fire of the defenders. (*See Fortification, diagram*)

GRAPE: Grapeshot, generally shortened to "grape," was a relatively close-range, anti-personnel projectile consisting of a number of iron balls, traditionally nine but often more. They were arranged in three uniform tiers and held between iron top and bottom plates by rings and a heavy bolt. This "stand of grape," as it was called, broke apart on firing and spread with shotgun effect. (*See Canister*)

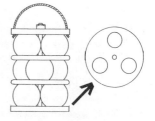

GUNNER'S GIMLET: Heavy wire fashioned into a ring handle at one end and a screw at the other. Used to bore out obstructions in the vent of a cannon.

HALE'S WAR ROCKETS: Rockets used during the Civil War were of two types — signal and war. The former resembled the familiar fireworks types consisting of a paper case attached to a stick for guidance. One type of war rocket, developed by William Hale, consisted of a metal casing containing a propellant and a warhead of shot or shell. (*See 15 Apr. 1864, note*)

HANDSPIKE: Various sized poles of wood (hickory or oak) or iron used in maneuvering cannon. Manigault's men probably used the maneuvering handspike for siege or seacoast artillery. Generally, this type was 66 inches long, tapering from 1.8 to 3 inches in diameter and weighing 8¼ pounds. Round at the smaller end, it was octagonal in the middle and beveled at the larger end to facilitate shoving under objects to be moved.

HOLLOW SHOT: Spherical or elongated projectiles cast around a small sand core to leave a hollow in the center. The sand was either left inside, in which case it was often known as a "blind shell," or knocked out through a hole drilled, or cast, in the shot wall and later plugged. The reason for such projectiles, also known as cored shot, is open to argument. The most plausible theory is that the small hollow detracted little from the strength of the shot, yet reduced the weight which permitted a lighter charge and hence less strain on the cannon.

INTERIOR SLOPE: Part of the parapet extending from the tread of the banquette to the crest of the superior slope. (*See Fortification, diagram*)

LEAD BASE: Lead cast around the base of a rifle projectile. The metal was squeezed into the rifling when fired forcing the projectile to rotate. Also known as lead sabot. (*See Sabot*)

LIMBER: A two-wheeled cart which, when linked to a field carriage, became a highly-maneuverable 4-wheeled vehicle usually drawn by six horses. The limber held a single ammunition chest giving the piece an immediate source of supply. The same limber was used with gun and caisson.

McEVOY FUSE IGNITER: This device consisted of a hollow wood cylinder containing a friction primer encased in lead and hung from a wire at the top of the cylinder. The igniter was attached to the top of a paper fuse. When the gun was fired, the shock flashed the primer which ignited the fuse.

MERLON: The section of parapet between two openings, or embrasures, of a fortification.

MORTAR BEDS: Carriages for mortars normally were called beds. They generally were made of seasoned oak, or iron. Those furnished Manigault, made of pine, did not hold up under the shock of firing.

NAILS: For strapping shells. (*See Sabot*)

NIGHT FIRING: Visual pointing of cannon was difficult, if not impossible, at night. Consequently, cannon were laid during daylight. Those on seacoast carriages (*See Carriages*) could retain the direction by chocking the wheels of the chassis. Siege carriages, which moved with the piece during recoil, required a different system. Strips of wood were nailed to the platform parallel to, but about an inch away from, each wheel. Another stick, of proper width, was laid in the space between the nailed slat and each wheel during adjustment. These sticks were then moved before firing. This permitted the piece to recoil without ripping up the nailed strips. Elevation, also set during daylight, was ratained at night by a stick cut to just fit between the breech and the trail when the piece was properly adjusted. The result was not pinpoint accuracy but permitted fire to be placed on reasonably large targets, such as a fort.

ORDNANCE WAGON: This was a non-regulation vehicle and probably nothing more than a standard commercial wagon adapted to military use.

PARAPET: (*See Epaulement. Also, Fortification, diagram*)

PERCUSSION SHELL: Projectile equipped with a percussion fuse designed to burst the shell on impact. Various types were used, but most depended on the impact of the shell crushing a percussion cap. The resulting flash set off a powder booster which, in turn, ignited the main charge of the shell.

PINTLE (PINTLE BLOCK): (*See Slide Carriages*)

PIVOT GUN: Gun mounted on a pivot carriage. This was a Navy mount consisting of a carriage which held the gun and recoiled along a slide. The slide was anchored by a stout bolt in the front which was dropped into one of several sockets in the deck. Both front and rear of the slide had rollers so the gun could be traversed.

POLYGONAL SHELL: (*See 25 Nov. 1863, note*)

QUAKER GUN: A dummy weapon, generally of wood, emplaced to fool the enemy. So named because of the peaceful nature of the Society of Friends, better known as Quakers.

RICHMOND FUZE: Fuses produced at Richmond, Va., probably at the Richmond Naval Ordnance Works.

RICOCHET FIRE: Employed primarily with solid shot to increase damage from multiple hits on the target.

REDAN: Fortification with two walls set at an angle pointed toward the enemy and open at the rear.

REDOUBT: Small fortification, generally square, enclosed on all sides.

SABOT: Originally a block of wood hollowed to fit the curvature of a round shell. Sabots were attached to the iron shells by means of light metal straps which went over the shell and were nailed to the sabot. This created an elongated projectile and insured that the fuse always faced outward, away from the propelling charge, and prevented it from being driven into and exploding the projectile during firing. With the advent of rifled artillery, the name was applied to the various devices of metal or other material affixed to a projectile to force it to follow the rotation of the rifling.

SCARP: Wall of a fortification ditch facing the enemy. (*See Fortification, diagram*)

SELMA FUSE: Fuses produced at Selma, Ala., presumably at the Confederate Naval Ordnance Works.

SHANTIES: Small shacks thrown up by the troops for living quarters.

SHIP CARRIAGE: This could have been one of several types. However, it likely was the standard 4-truck carriage which had been carrying shipboard cannon for generations.

SHRAPNEL: A form of projectile developed by Gen. Henry Shrapnel (1761-1842) of the British Army. It consisted of lead, sometimes iron, balls in a thin-walled shell with a small bursting charge and a time fuse. At the proper point in the trajectory, the fuse set off the charge which ruptured the case. The balls then proceeded toward the target in the manner of shotgun pellets. In effect, it extended the range of multi-shot projectiles, such as grape or canister, without the dispersion normally associated with long distance. Shrapnel generally was called "case" in this country.

SIEGE CARRIAGE: (*See Carriages, Siege Carriage*)

SLIDE CARRIAGE: Also called boat carriage. A type designed for maritime use but adapted by the Confederates for employment ashore. It consisted of a bed and a slide. The former held the piece and rested on the slide to which it was connected by compressors to create friction and absorb recoil. A pintle held the front of the carriage to deck or platform. This permitted the rear to swing in an arc for traverse.

SLING CART: Two-wheeled vehicle designed to lift and transport heavy cannon.

STRAPPING SHELLS: (*See Sabot*)

SUPERIOR SLOPE: Part of the parapet of a fortification extending from the crest of the interior slope to the crest of the exterior slope. (*See Fortification, diagram*)

TETE-DE-PONT: Bridgehead.

TIME SHELLS: Projectiles with time fuses. These generally consisted of a train of compact powder which burned at a relatively uniform rate and could be set to explode the projectile at a calculated point along its trajectory.

TOP CARRIAGE: (*See Carriages, Seacoast Carriages*)

TORPEDO: (*See 21 Sept. 1863, note*)

TRAVELLING BED: (*See Carriages, Siege Carriages*)

TRAVELLING FORGE: Two-wheeled cart which was linked to a standard field limber to form a four-wheeled vehicle. It contained a forge with bellows, anvil, vise, smith's tools and assorted hardware including 280 horseshoes and sufficient iron to effect field repairs to the metal elements of a battery.

TRAVERSE: A mound of earth, or other substance, between weapons or sections of a fortification to localize the effect of shell bursts and to minimize the effect of enfilading fire.

TRUNNION BED: (*See Carriages, Siege Carriages*)

VENT: Hole drilled near the breech of a cannon from the top of the barrel to the powder chamber to permit ignition of the charge. The vent, about .2-inch diameter, generally was bouched (bushed) with a drilled cylinder of a different metal (often copper) to diminish enlargement by erosion from powder gases.

Bibliography

Appleton's Cyclopedia of American Biography, James Grant Wilson and John Fiske, editors. D. Appleton & Co., New York. 6 Vols. 1894.

Battles and Leaders of the Civil War, Robert Underwood Johnson and Clarence Clough Buel, editors. The Century Co., New York. 4 Vols. 1887.

O.J. Bond, *The Story of The Citadel.* Garrett & Massie, Richmond, Va., 1936.

E. Milby Burton, *The Siege of Charleston 1861-1865.* University of South Carolina Press. 1970

Charleston Daily Courier. Charleston, S.C., newspaper, forerunner of *The News and Courier.*

Compiled Service Records of Confederate Soldiers Who Served in Organizations from Georgia. The National Archives and Records Service, Washington, D.C.

Compiled Service Records of Confederate Soldiers Who Served in Organizations from South Carolina. The National Archives and Records Service, Washington, D.C.

Compiled Service Records of Confederate Soldiers Who Served in Organizations from Virginia. The National Archives and Records Service, Washington, D.C.

Confederate Soldier in the Civil War, Ben LaBree, editor. The Courier-Journal Job Printing Co., Louisville, Ky. 1895.

George W. Cullum, *Biographical Register of the Officers and Graduates of the U.S. Military Academy at West Point, N.Y.* Houghton, Mifflin & Co., New York. 3 Vols. 1891.

Frederic Denison, *Shot and Shell, the Third Rhode Island Heavy Artillery Regiment in the Rebellion 1861-1865.* Published for the Third R.I. Heavy Artillery Veterans Association, Providence, R.I., 1879.

Thomas S. Dickey, and Peter C. George, *Field Artillery Projectiles of the American Civil War.* Arsenal Press, Atlanta, Ga., 1980.

J.H. Easterby, *A History of the College of Charleston, Founded 1770.* Published by the Trustees of the College of Charleston, 1935.

Encyclopedia Americana, A.H. McDannald, editor in chief. Americana Corp., New York. 30 Vols. 1946

John Gibbon, *The Artillerist's Manual.* D. Van Nostrand, New York. 1860. (Also reprint, Benchmark Publishing Co., Glendale, N.Y. 1970).

Q.A. Gillmore, *Engineer and Artillery Operations Against the Defences of Charleston Harbor in 1863.* D. Van Nostrand, New York. 1865.

Q.A. Gillmore, *Supplementary Report to Engineer and Artillery Operations Against the Defences of Charleston Harbor in 1863.* Professional Papers, Corps of Engineers, No. 16. D. Van Nostrand, New York. 1868

Johnson Hagood, *Memoirs of the War of Secession.* The State Co., Columbia, S.C. 1910.

Francis B. Heitman, *Historical Register and Dictionary of the United States Army from Its Organization 29 September 1789 to 2 March 1903.* Government Printing Office, Washington, D.C. 2 Vols. 1903.

Sydney C. Kerksis and Thomas S. Dickey, *Heavy Artillery Projectiles of the Civil War, 1861-1865.* The Phoenix Press, Kennesaw, Ga. 1972.

Charlotte Drayton Manigault, *Diary of.* Unpublished manuscript in possession of the Manigault family.

James Harvey McKee, *Back in War Times, History of the 144th Regiment, N.Y. Volunteer Infantry.* Lt. Horace E. Bailey, publisher. Unadilla, N.Y. 1903.

New Century Cyclopedia of Names. Clarence L. Barnhart, editor. Appleton-Century-Crofts, Inc., New York. 3 Vols. 1954.

(The) News and Courier. Charleston, S.C., newspaper. Successor to the *Charleston Daily Courier.*

Official Records of the Union and Confederate Navies in the War of the Rebellion. Government Printing Office, Washington, D.C. 31 Vols. 1894-1927.

Ordnance Manual for the Use of the Officers of the Confederate States Army. Evans & Cogswell, Charleston, S.C. 1863. (Also, reprint, Morningside Bookshop, Dayton, Ohio. 1976).

Ordnance Manual for the Use of the Officers of the United States Army. J.B. Lippincott & Co., Philadelphia, Pa. 1861. (Also reprint, Ordnance Park Corp., Lyons, Colo. 1970).

Beatrice St. Julien Ravenel, *Architects of Charleston.* Carolina Art Association, Charleston, S.C. 1945.

James D. Richardson, *A Compilation of the Messages and Papers of the Confederacy.* United States Publishing Co., Nashville, Tenn. 2 Vols. 1906.

Warren Ripley, *Artillery and Ammunition of the Civil War.* Van Nostrand, Reinhold Co., New York. 1970. (also, 4th edition, published by the author. 1985).

Warren Ripley, *Battle of Chapman's Fort.* Privately published. 1978.

Alfred Roman, *The Military Operations of General Beauregard.* Harper & Brothers, New York. 2 Vols. 1884.

Alice R. Huger Smith and D.E. Smith, *The Dwelling Houses of Charleston, South Carolina.* J.B. Lippincott Co., Philadelphia, Pa., 1917.

R. Lockwood Tower, editor, *A Carolinian Goes to War, The Civil War Narrative of Arthur Middleton Manigault, Brigadier General, C.S.A.* University of South Carolina Press, Columbia, S.C. 1983

War of the Rebellion, A Compilation of the Official Records of the Union and Confederate Armies. (Generally known as the *Official Records,* or abbreviated, *O.R.*) Government Printing Office, Washington, D.C. 128 Vols. 1880-1901

Index

Asterisks refer to pages with biographical or statistical information.

Boston, USS, 166n, 318, 319
Bourquine, R.T., 2nd Lt., 210, 215, 219, 281*
Bowden, J.R. Capt., 177, 320*
Bowie, Alexander, Pvt., 245, 247, 312*
Bowie, James A., Pvt., 245, 247, 312*
Boyce's Wharf, 129
Boykin, A.H., Capt., 297
Boylston, S. Cordes, 1st Lt., 203, 324*
Bragg, Braxton, Gen., vi, 331
Bridges (general), 63, 63n, 78n, 91-94, 103, 106, 162n, 180, 181, 183, 186, 199, 202, 202n, 212, 232, 233
Bridges, William M., Capt., 117, 119, 120, 125, 131, 137, 150, 178, 233, 317, 318*
Brooke, John Mercer, Capt. (CSN), 237, 242n, 266
Brooks, Homer C., 2nd Lt., 221, 277*
Brown, F.B., 1st Lt., 142, 307*
Brown, J. Welsman, Lt. Col., 17, 45, 150, 200, 201, 213, 221, 239, 244, 249, 257, 292*, 296
Brown, W.K., Pvt., 137, 312*, 313*
Brunson, E.B., Capt. 317
Brux, James Augustus, 1st Lt., 10, 28, 37, 96, 98, 151, 172, 262, 313*
Bryan, E.K. Lt., 256
Bryan, Henry, Maj., 107, 324*
Bryce, William M., Dr., 249
Buist, George L., Capt., 311-315, 318
Buist, Henry, Capt., 71, 308, 309*
Bunch, Jeremiah J., Capt. 299
Bureau Battalion, 195, 197
Bureau of Conscription, 116n
Burke, Thomas A., Maj., 98, 176, 189, 241, 324*
Burke's Stationary Store, 100
Burnett, B.S., Capt., 197, 199, 201, 291*
Burnt House (See, Legare's Burnt House)
Burr, George W., 1st Lt., 228, 276*
Burrus, Lawrence M., Capt., 207, 219, 222, 228, 231, 233, 277*
Bush, George P., 1st Lt., 139, 155, 158, 159, 167, 173, 181, 186, 191, 203, 204, 215, 219, 220, 226, 231, 232, 234, 241, 295*

Butler, Matthew C., Brig. Gen., 297, 299, 301
Butler, William, Col., 290
Butler, Y.N., Capt., 306, 307
Byrd, Stephen D.M., Maj., 121, 324*, 325*

C

Caldwell, J.S., Sgt., 182, 305*
Caldwell, William R., Asst. Surgeon, 188, 309*
Calhoun, Alpha T., 2nd Lt., 218, 220, 225, 277*
Calhoun, Duff G., Capt., 197, 291*
Calhoun fuse, 66
Campbell, W.H., Maj., 71, 92, 93, 109, 149, 319*, 320
Campbell, William L., Pvt., 247, 248, 313*
Campbell's House, 175, 180-182, 184, 185, 187
Canonicas, USS, 248
Cape Romain, S.C., 85n
Carriage, improvised, 84, 84n
Carronade, 70, 83, 83n, 84, 339
Carson, James M., Capt., 142, 144, 254, 255, 305*
Causey, Z.J., Sgt., 102, 315*
Central Ordnance Depot (See, Charleston Central Ordnance Depot)
Chapman, William H., 1st Lt., 4, 64, 70, 95, 96, 98, 99, 104, 107-109, 113, 123, 151, 172, 313*
Charles' Battery (See, Confederate Troops, Inglis Light Arty.)
Charles, William E., Capt., 100-103, 294*
Charleston:
    Arsenal, 9, 10, 14, 27, 36, 37n, 38, 39, 51, 53, 57, 60, 69, 71, 73, 75, 88, 96, 105, 122-124, 242n, 256, 261, 331
    Battalion (See, Confederate Troops, 27th S.C. Inf. Rgmt.)
    Central Ordnance Depot, 27, 61, 90, 261, 328, 331
    (City), i, ii, iv, vi, viii-x, xii, xiii, 17-19, 21n, 27, 28, 36, 40, 41, 57-61, 63, 64, 66, 75-77, 79n, 79,

Ferry Boat, 77, 183, 184, 192
Flag of Truce, 5, 5n, 6n, 16, 36, 178, 179, 179n, 180n, 181, 217
Floating Derrick, 64, 175, 177
Floating Pile Driver, 72, 73
Folly Island, i, xi, xiii, 1, 117, 169, 170, 170n, 174, 175, 179, 184, 187, 203, 212, 215-217, 236, 248, 249
Folly River, 64, 74, 103n, 175, 181, 182, 185, 220, 221, 249
Foote, Dr., 43, 44n, 325*
Force & Mitchell's Store, 235, 236n
Ford, Edwin A., 1st Lt., 46, 47, 52, 326*
Ford, J. Drayton, 1st Lt., 161, 189, 310*
Forrest, N.B., Maj. Gen., 327
Fort:
Chapman, 166n
Delaware, 179n, 293, 301, 304, 308, 309
Johnson, 14n, 15, 20, 26, 32, 41, 45, 48, 50, 55, 56, 60, 61, 66, 68, 71, 86-91, 174, 196, 197n, 200, 258, 260, 264, 267, 268, 292-294, 297
Lamar, ix, x, 66n, 78n, 139, 151, 174, 179, 213, 214, 219, 292, 297
Moultrie, vi, 25, 26, 33-35, 35n, 36, 36n, 55, 56, 59-65, 68, 69, 71, 77, 81, 82, 83n, 260, 264, 301
Pemberton, 66n, 92, 93, 97, 106, 108, 111, 112, 114, 117-121, 123, 125-127, 167, 188-190, 200, 221, 309-311
Pulaski, 180n, 309, 322
Putnam, 32n, 130
Strong, 32n
Sumter, viii-xi, 12, 12n, 13-17, 24n, 27, 35, 54-56, 67, 67n, 68, 68n, 69, 71-74, 74n, 75, 77-79, 81, 85, 85n, 86, 89, 91, 130, 132, 132n, 134, 146, 204, 206, 206n, 207-210, 215-227, 230-234, 256, 257, 260, 261, 285, 301, 309, 313, 318, 321-326, 332
Sumter (Bombardments), 12, 12n, 24n, 54n, 68, 68n, 95n, 132, 132n, 146, 146n, 204, 206n
Sumter (Ironclad Attack), viii, x, 137
Sumter (Magazine Explodes), 95n
Sumter (Small Boat Attack), 35, 36n

Wagner (See Battery Wagner)
Foster, John G., Maj. Gen., 170n, 181, 195n, 206n, 322*
Fox, J.R.P., Capt., 290
Frank (Servant), 135, 326*
Frazer & Co., 24n
Frederick, A.D., Col., 3, 115, 139, 146, 150, 154, 156, 165, 167, 169-171, 174, 176, 179-182, 191, 192, 195, 196, 201, 206, 208, 211, 213, 219, 220, 232, 236, 239, 292*, 296
Frederick, E.J., Adjutant, 218, 239, 241, 293*
Freer's House, 39, 97, 187
Frost, E.H., Capt., 121, 326*
Fulton, John A., Capt., 206, 207, 211, 217, 223, 229, 232, 234, 276*
Furman Artillery (See, Confederate Troops, Palmetto Bn., S.C. Light Arty.)

G

Gadberry Hill, 58, 60, 61, 89
Gaillard, Augustus T., Sgt. Maj., 7, 54, 131, 198, 241, 311*
Gaillard, Peter C., Col., 79, 79n, 140, 144, 307*
Gaines, Richard V., Capt., 98, 326*
Gamble, R.H., Capt., 275
Gantt, F. Hay, Col. 115, 302*
Gardner, 137, 326*
Gardner, John H., Adjutant, 40, 59, 66, 76, 85, 92, 96, 106, 110, 113, 115, 126, 127, 127n, 135, 188, 191, 192, 206, 217, 311*
Gary, John H., Capt., 310
Georgetown, S.C., xiii, 304, 313, 315
Gervais Plantation, 201, 202
Gibbes, Lewis R., Professor, 130, 326*
Gibbes, Louisa Izard (L.I.G.), 236, 326*
Gillmore, Quincy A., Maj. Gen., 247, 322*
Girardeau, G. Morris, Cpl., 98, 313*
Girardeau, Isaac W., 1st Sgt., 98, 313*

Legare, W.W., 1st Lt., 10, 14, 15, 27, 31, 33, 38, 41, 57, 61, 63, 73, 91, 240, 261, 295*

Legare's (See Legare's Point and 3n)

Legare's Burnt House, 139, 142, 143, 151, 153, 155

Legare's Creek, 36

Legare's House (See Legare's Point)

Legare's Overseer's House, 139, 140-144, 153, 155, 157-161, 163-175, 177-187, 191, 196, 198, (burned) 203, 205, 223, 231, 243, 244

Legare's Point, 3-6, 15-17, 23, 45, 55-68, 71-73, 75, 77-82, 88, 91, 93, 96, 131, 146, 149, 168, 200, 253, 255, 256, 258-261, 263, 264, 316

Legare's Point House (John's Island) 201

Legare's West House, 138

Legareville, 100-103, 105, 142, 150, 183, 187, 202n, 203, (burned) 229, 229n, 230, 244, 312, 315

Lehigh, USS, 74n, 83n, 199, 200n, 201-203, 249

Lesesne, Charles, 1st Lt., 142, 142n, 307*

Lesesne, Edward R., Capt., 142, 142n, 307*

Lester, Robert B., 231, 232, 329*

Lewis, John F., Capt., 197, 198, 280*

Light House Inlet, xi, 4, 20, 23, 37, 43, 48, 49, 69, 77, 78, 81, 82, 84, 87, 174, 175, 177, 179, 183, 192, 199, 258

Lipscomb, Thomas J., Col., 168-170, 172, 182, 297*

Little Folly Creek, 84

Little Folly River, 138, 243

Livingston, J.F., 1st Lt., 215, 289*

Lloyd, Edward W., Capt., 98, 139, 305

Logan, Calhoun, Capt., 305

Logan, William T., Sgt., 98, 314*

Long Island, 77, 78, 81, 82, 85, 87, 117, 139, 153n, 158, 159, 162, 162n, 163, 169, 172-175, 179, 180, 182, 191, 196, 199, 209, 211, 214, 219, 225, 231

Lopez, John, 222, 223, 225, 227-229, 329*

Lopez, John H., Pvt., 25, 260, 314*

Lovell, Mansfield, Maj. Gen., 334

Lucas, Jonathan J., Maj., 110, 113, 115, 117, 188, 310*

Lucas, Thomas E., 2nd Lt., 190, 310*

Lusk, L.W., 2nd Lt., 231, 289*

Lynch, Patrick Niesen, Bishop, 76, 130, 329*, 330*

M

Macbeth, Alexander, Pvt., 245, 314*

Mackey, Samuel, Chief Bugler, 120, 311*

Mallet, J.W., Lt. Col., 23, 259, 330*

Manigault, Arthur Middleton, Brig. Gen., iii, iv, xiii, 106, 106n, 313, 330*, 332, 334

Manigault, A.M., Mrs., 313, 332

Manigault, Charles Drayton, 300

Manigault, Charlotte Drayton, iii, viin

Manigault, Edward, Maj., 311*, 312*

(Civilian Life), iv, v, vi, vii

(Death), xiii

(Diary), i, 4, 31, 253, 313

(Engagement, 22 May 1864), 158-162

(Engagement, 2 July 1864), 191-197

(Engagement, 10 Feb. 1865), xii, 243-249, 311, 312

(Infantry Bn.), vii, viii, 253, 311, 312

(Mexican War), vi, vii, 251, 253, 311

(Ordnance Duties), vii, 251-253, 311, 330

(Parole), xiii, 248, 312

(Wounded), 245, 247, 248, 312

Manigault, Gabriel (1704-1781), iii

Manigault, Gabriel (1758-1809), iv

Manigault, Gabriel (1809-1888), vii, 127, 252, 330

Manigault, Henrietta Middleton, iii

Manigault, Henry Middleton, 236, 330*

Manigault, Joseph, iii

Manigault House (See Joseph Manigault House)

Mulvaney, James M. Capt., 90, 309*

361

United States Troops:
  3rd Rgmt., N.H. Inf., 22n
  3rd Rgmt., R.I. Heavy Arty., 84n
  7th Rgmt., Conn. Inf., 175, 322
  12th Rgmt., U.S. Inf., vi, 311
  13th Rgmt., U.S. Inf., vi, 253, 311
  21st Rgmt., U.S. Colored Troops, 207, 322
  24th Rgmt., Mass. Inf., 22n
  32nd Rgmt., U.S. Colored Troops, 247
  33rd Rgmt., U.S. Colored Troops, 195n, 247
  41st Rgmt., N.Y. Inf., 162n
  54th Rgmt., Mass. Inf., 162n, 207
  54th Rgmt., N.Y. Inf., 245, 247
  55th Rgmt., Mass. Inf., 195n, 196n, 247
  74th Rgmt., Penn. Inf., 162n
  103rd Rgmt., N.Y. Inf., 162n, 195n, 207
  127th Rgmt., N.Y. Inf., 322
  144th Rgmt., N.Y. Inf., 245, 247
University of South Carolina, v, vi
Upson, Hiram Jr., 2nd Lt., 175, 322*

V

Vanderhorst, Arnoldus, 129, 335*
Vienne, Julius G., 1st Lt., 120, 131, 318*
Villepigue, F.L., Capt., 93, 275*
Vincent's Creek, 32n
Virginia, CSS, 12n

W

Waddy, J.R., Lt. Col., 27, 31, 113, 117, 118, 261, 264, 265, 267, 335*
Wagner Light Artillery (See, Confederate Troops, Palmetto Bn., Light Arty.)
Walker, W.A., Capt., 288
Walpole, B.L., Capt., 101, 321*
Walpole's Place, 101, 103, 104
Walpole's Scouts (See, Confederate Troops, Stono Scouts)

Walter, W.D., Capt., 145, 309*
Walterboro, 152, 302, 315
Walton, J.T., 2nd Lt., 187, 207, 280*
Wappoo Bridges, 93, 94, 99, 106, 106n, 107, 108, 110, 115, 140, 150, 151, 176, 189, 288
Wappoo Creek, 119, 120, 330
Ward, William D., 2nd Lt., 218, 277*
Warley, Fexix, 1st Lt., 148, 188, 310*
Warley, Frederick F., Maj., 217, 217n, 239, 293*, 294
Warley, J. Hamilton, Capt., 201, 290*
Warwick, P.C., 1st Lt., 178, 335*
Washington, D.C., Navy Yard, 103, 104n
Way, Charlton H., Col., 26, 36, 39, 42, 52, 54, 58, 73, 76, 79, 90, 282*
Webb, Benjamin C., Capt., 14, 15, 17, 31, 44, 51, 53, 60, 61, 66, 67, 73, 77, 82, 85, 88, 91, 93-98, 98n, 101, 102, 104, 104n, 105, 110, 113, 118, 120, 131, 136, 148, 150, 152, 172, 179, 244, 260, 264, 268, 312, 315*
Webb, Charles, Sgt., 98, 315*
Weehawken, USS, 35n
Wells, 182, 182n, 185, 213, 214
Wells, John C., 1st Lt., 247, 283*
Westfield, John, Capt., 165, 166, 173-175, 182, 299*
West Lines, 71, 92, 118, 121, 137, 145, 146, 165, 167, 172, 201, 206, 268, 269, 292, 296, 310, 312, 315
West Point (N.Y.) Foundry, 6n, 44n
Whaley, John R., Sgt. Maj., 186, 286*
Whatley, Thomas W., Capt., 186, 288*
Wheaton, John F., Capt., 194, 282*
Whilden, Louis A., Capt., 121, 300, 301, 302*
White, Sgt., 165, 335*
White, Edward B., Col., 118, 319*
White, James W., 1st Lt., 186, 208, 216, 223, 290*
White, John B., Maj., 163, 167, 321*
White, Robert D., Capt., 306
Wiggins, James, Pvt., 192, 316*
Willingham, J.T., 1st Lt., 79, 93, 95-97, 278*

Willis, E.R., Pvt., 222, 296*
Willtown, 118
Wilson, J.S., Capt., 184, 288*
Wilson, Samuel J., 1st Lt., 15, 29, 75, 98, 187, 316*
Winder, Charles S., Capt., 311
Winter, Thomas H., 1st Lt., 168, 298*
Witherspoon, Bartlett J., Capt., 197-199, 201, 290, 291*
Winthrop, Henry, Dr., 126n
Winthrop, Joseph, Asst. Surgeon, 89, 99, 104, 106, 110, 111, 118, 120, 126, 127, 132, 133, 133n, 134, 135, 149, 150, 152, 153, 164, 177, 187, 220, 312*
Wise, Henry A., Brig. Gen., 48, 335*
Wolfe, J.R.D., Cpl., 236, 296*
Wood, Pvt., 247, 283*

Y

Yates, Joseph A., Lt. Col., 10, 26, 32, 236, 260, 264, 285*
Young, B.N., 1st Lt., 214, 222, 288*

Z

Zimmerman, William E., Capt., 181, 182, 184, 231, 232, 316, 317*
Zorn, James W., Pvt., 102, 104, 315*